WEEKEND GETAWAYS
AROUND
WASHINGTON, D.C.

WEEKEND GETAWAYS
AROUND
WASHINGTON, D.C.

Including Virginia, Maryland, Delaware, Pennsylvania,
New Jersey, West Virginia, and North Carolina

By Robert Shosteck
Edited by Vicki and Ken Heland
Foreword by Willard Scott

PELICAN PUBLISHING COMPANY
GRETNA 2013

1st printing, August 1969
2nd printing, November 1970
3rd printing, July 1971
4th printing (revised), September 1973
5th printing (revised), March 1975
6th printing (revised), June 1977
7th printing (revised), May 1978
8th printing (revised), August 1979
9th printing, November 1980
10th printing, June 1981
11th printing, November 1981
12th printing (revised), October 1982
13th printing, March 1984
14th printing, February 1986
15th printing (revised), September 1988
16th printing, June 1991
17th printing (revised), July 2000
18th printing (revised), October 2004
19th printing (revised), January 2013

Library of Congress Cataloging-in-Publication Data

Shosteck, Robert, 1910-
    Weekend getaways around Washington, D.C. : including
Virginia, Maryland, Delaware, Pennsylvania, New Jersey, West
Virginia, and North Carolina / by Robert Shosteck ; edited by
Victoria J. and Ken Heland ; foreword by Willard Scott.
        p. cm.
    Includes index.
    ISBN 9781455617715 (pbk. : alk. paper)
    1. Washington Region—Guidebooks. 2. Middle Atlantic
States—Guidebooks. I. Heland, Victoria J. II. Heland, Ken. III.
Title.

F192.3.S48 2004
917.4'04—dc22

                                                            2004003454

Printed in the United States of America

Published by Pelican Publishing Company, Inc.
1000 Burmaster Street, Gretna, Louisiana 70053

CONTENTS

FOREWORD

From the desk of
WILLARD H. SCOTT

Hello, fellow weekenders! It's your old friend Willard Scott here, and have I got a forecast for you. After hours of grueling research consulting the finest meteorological equipment in the business (the corn on my big toe), I predict fifty-two weeks of fun and good weather for discovering the best this area has to offer. Flip through the pages of this book and you'll see why I call for a beautiful winter, spring, summer, and fall. With *Weekend Getaways around Washington, D.C.* in hand, you'll know why I love this area so much that no matter where I am on Friday I fly home for the weekend. I learned to swim in Chesapeake Bay and to hike in the Blue Ridge Mountains. I even milked my first cow on a nearby Maryland farm. All in all, I am totally in love with this area. It's got a flavor all its own—for example, did you know that . . .

. . . you can get a state-subsidized massage in West Virginia?

. . . the official sport of Maryland is jousting, and dozens of tournaments are held throughout the state from August to October?

. . . a wall at Virginia's Stratford Plantation that kept livestock off the mansion's lawn is called the Ha-Ha Wall?

. . . the North Carolina state insect is the honey bee?

. . . a popular park in Virginia Beach, built on the site of a former solid waste disposal facility, is called Mt. Trashmore?

Now, that's the kind of history that I like to read! And you'll find more here: where to go skiing, antiquing, join archaeology digs, or catch a polo match . . .

11

You know that ol' Willard would go just about anywhere for a festival. I plan to keep *Weekend Getaways* in my glove compartment (along with my knife and fork and industrial-strength wash 'n dries), so I can keep track of all the crabfests, shoofly pie contests, and bull roasts this area has to offer. In this little book, you will find places to go and things to do that will help you to reap the benefits of this most-beautiful and unique region we call the Mid-Atlantic, and I will always call home (collect, if possible).

Love,

Willard

ACKNOWLEDGMENTS

Robert Shosteck (1910-79), originator of the *Weekender's Guide to the Four Seasons,* on which this book was based, was a gentleman of tireless energy, good humor, and excellent ideas. Mr. Shosteck, a native of Maryland, has left a legacy of pleasure, history, and culture that will continue long into the future.

Editors Victoria J. ("Vicki") and Ken Heland followed the style and format used by Mr. Shosteck to present revised and updated information.

We dedicate this book to all who had a hand in its creation, especially
Colin McAllister and Maureen McAllister, of Salisbury, Maryland, for their love of birding.
Kevin McAllister for providing guidance on hunting and fishing.
Auctioneer Pete Richardson (www.prauctions.com) for sharing his expertise on antiques and auctions.
Tedra Mosley, whose research for the previous edition provided a valuable foundation to this update.
Founder of the International Women's Writing Guild, Hannelore Hahn, who has been a dear friend and a source of inspiration for almost thirty years.
Jim and Marjorie Hrouda, of Richmond, Virginia, who are always ready to "time travel" with us and explore historical sites. Their curiosity and observations enhance our own.
Friends and family (in no particular order): Sigrid and Nils Svensen, Doris and John Curtis, John and Pam Cambardella, Bob Glass, Ruth and Glenn Graves, Kim and Bernard Douglas, Mary Ann Higgins, Peg and John Turano, Sharon and Ken Ball, A. W. Carey, and our dear nieces, nephews, and grands, their spouses, and loved ones.

Wade St. Clair and Bob Niblock, our recently departed friends who, with Mike Richardson, have gone exploring where there is no guidebook.

—Vicki and Ken Heland

HOW TO USE THIS BOOK

Welcome to a world of rolling green hills; long, quiet sandy beaches; country festivals; and American history. This is where you can turn back the clock, watch reenactments of events that shaped our nation, and meet and get the inside story from historical figures portrayed in period dress. This is also where you can find compatible groups of day-trip companions, pick up your cross-country skis, mount your bicycle, and find some of the best antiques in the East. If all this isn't quite what you had in mind, read on, because *Weekend Getaways around Washington, D.C.* is likely to have what you want: steam-engine railroads, hunting and fishing, covered bridges, battlefields, sailing, horse events, dog and flower shows, and the charms, history, and crafts of out-of-the-way places from Cape May to the mountains of West Virginia and the Outer Banks of North Carolina.

But first, a brief word on what this book is not. *Weekend Getaways around Washington, D.C.* is not a guidebook to Washington, D.C., itself. Instead, the city is used as a reference point. This guidebook is for readers who are looking for places of interest outside of Washington, D.C., within a 200-mile or four-hour driving radius of our nation's capitol.

The Structure: Four Major Sections

Weekend Getaways around Washington, D.C. is designed so that the reader can quickly locate places and pastimes of special interest. Important telephone numbers, addresses, and Web sites for obtaining further information are at your fingertips. The material is organized into four major sections. The first, the "Geographic" section, has all or parts of seven states, each a chapter of its own. Under each state, there are subsections that specify particular areas, communities, or major parks. The second, the "Special-Interest" section, lists sports and pastimes in alphabetical order. They vary in length and detail, depending on the nature of the activity and the information available. The "Special-Interest" section, like the "Geographic" section, covers a great variety of places to go and things to do. They do not pretend to be all-inclusive, but offer a wide, representative sampling of ways to enjoy your time. This diversity of choice also describes how entries were selected for the third and fourth sections, the "Calendar of Events" and the "Hot Lines."

Explore and Discover

You will discover a great deal more of everything as you set out into the countryside and wander through the locales described here. You will also discover additional options as you explore the many Web sites offered within this book. Some include virtual tours. Many include links to other sites as well as resources and articles to explore related topics in greater detail.

The calendar of events lists fairs, festivals, and special events by month and then by state. Since these festivities are usually held on different days each year, you will need to verify exact dates. Telephone numbers and Web sites are listed whenever possible. State and local tourist offices and chambers of commerce are also good sources of information about events in their areas. You will find many of them listed in the "Hot Lines" section for easy reference.

The Charms of Off-Season and the Wisdom of Phoning Ahead

You will find that many areas are well worth visiting during the seasons they are not best known for. For example, try cross-country skiing on a snow-covered beach, tennis in summer at a mountain ski resort, or a community festival to shake the cabin fever of a February afternoon.

Some trips, of course, are not for everyone. If you have small children, do not like to walk long distances, or must watch your budget carefully, take note of the entries that interest you and call ahead or visit Web sites to clarify the distances, costs, facilities, and time involved.

Telephoning ahead is appropriate for anything you would like to do. In spite of efforts to make everything in this edition as accurate and up-to-the-minute as possible, some changes cannot be anticipated. Volunteers staff many of the places, activities, and clubs listed in this book, and hours and days of operation may vary. Some telephone numbers are the home phones of volunteers and club members. Because you may sometimes be calling a home number, particularly for organizational activities, don't call at odd hours. Prices continually change too, and so only the fact that there is an admission charge is indicated.

Security Considerations

Since the last edition of *Weekend Getaways* was produced, in the summer of 2000, many of the historic sites listed in the book have become more security-conscious, for obvious reasons. These security precautions have required certain attractions to alter or restrict access, and some—usually those associated with military bases—are no longer open to the public. Even if security requirements have not been specifically mentioned, allow extra time and be prepared to present photo I.D.s or other proof of your identification. Note that some national monuments close without advance notice.

Whenever possible, toll-free numbers are listed. Area codes, phone numbers, e-mail addresses, and Web sites can change as often as prices and hours of operation. Inns and restaurants are not generally listed in this edition unless they have historic significance. There are several fine books on these subjects and not enough space in *Weekend Getaways* to do justice to the many places you will find with 200 miles of Washington, D.C.

The Book as a Starting Point

Enthusiasm or a positive impression may sometimes influence writing style, but no endorsement is implied or intended for any establishment or organization listed in this book. Conversely, the fact that a site, attraction, or club does not appear in these pages is no reflection on its quality. Because of the broad geographic area that is the scope of this book, we continually faced tough choices about what to include. Use this book as a starting point and venture beyond it. Investigate what intrigues you and form your own opinions.

It is best to travel with state or city maps of the areas you intend to visit. Those that show some detail within counties can be especially helpful. You can usually get free maps at the state tourist offices or regional visitor centers listed throughout the book, or request them by calling numbers listed in the "Hot Lines" section. You can also get driving directions to specific locations online.

Everyone who contributed information to *Weekend Getaways around Washington, D.C.* by phone, fax, mail, and e-mail was courteous and helpful. They are eager to have you visit their area and share its delights. You are sure to meet many kind, interesting, and invigorating people as you travel around and join in the activities listed here. Bon voyage and happy trails!

VIRGINIA

For a comprehensive overview of the cities and towns, attractions, and historical sites in Virginia, with links to almost all areas that have their own Web sites, this is a good first stop: www.virginia.org. The Virginia Department of Transportation is now distributing a new map of the 2,600 miles of roads and highways designated as scenic byways, so travelers who prize scenery over predictability and prefer tranquility to traffic can have a better sense of their options. "A Map of Scenic Roads in Virginia" is available at state-highway welcome centers and rest areas. Printed maps can also be ordered online at virginiadot.org/travel/maporder.asp. Online versions are available at virginiadot.org/travel/maps-state.asp.

NORTHERN VIRGINIA

Arlington County

Arlington, one of the smallest counties in the U.S., is immediately west of Washington, D.C., separated from it by the Potomac River and connected to it by four bridges. Arlington falls within the diamond-shaped territory usually thought of as the District of Columbia and was once part of it, but the area was given back to Virginia in 1847. Arlington County has several well-known neighborhoods, but no incorporated cities. Its "close in" location and urban flair make it the favored address of many up-and-coming young professionals who work hard and play hard. It is also a true mixing bowl of cultures, with a rich ethnic diversity and correspondingly rich array of restaurants.

Though almost any Arlington location is close to a major artery, some side streets retain the charm and character of days gone by and seem to exude almost rural ambiance. Outsiders sometimes complain that street names are confusingly similar, but locals orient themselves by major landmarks and take pride in their ability to distinguish streets from roads from avenues of the same name, each of which may have north and south ends that don't necessarily connect. Fortunately, Arlington is well served by the regional subway system, known as Metro, and has ten stations within its borders. Buses are also plentiful. Public transportation is highly recommended, since parking can be scarce.

There is an energy about Arlington that is physical, intellectual, creative, and inspiring. Also inspiring are the notable monuments and sites within its borders. Major attractions include Arlington National Cemetery, the U.S. Marine Corps War Memorial (Iwo Jima), Theodore Roosevelt Island, Lady Bird Johnson Park, Gravelly Point, Ronald Reagan Washington Airport, the Pentagon, the Washington and Old Dominion Trail, and the George Washington Memorial Parkway. The Arlington County Visitors Center, located at 1301 Joyce Street in Pentagon Row Shopping Center at the Pentagon City Metro stop, is open daily 9 A.M. to 5 P.M. Telephone: (800) 296-7996 or (703) 228-0806. Web site: http://www.stayarlington.com.

The entrance to **Arlington National Cemetery** is immediately west of Arlington Memorial Bridge and also has its own Metro stop. Understatement and repetition in the design of the 612-acre cemetery make it poignant and powerful. Gently rolling hills of well-groomed green lawns are dotted with row upon row of stark white headstones that stand like silent sentries. Among the more than 250,000 individuals buried at Arlington are those who fought in every U.S. military conflict, including the American Revolution. Free admission. Fee for parking. Web site: www.arlingtoncemetery.org.

The **Tomb of the Unknowns** (formerly known as the Tomb of the Unknown Soldier) continues to inspire particular reverence. The continuously guarded tomb is a single block of white marble containing remains of unidentified servicemen. Day and night, the Tomb Guard repeats a ritual of 21 paces, followed by a 21-second pause, and then 21 more paces. Guard-changing ceremonies are similarly precise, understated, and powerfully moving. Telephone: (877) 907-8585. Web site: www.arlingtoncemetery.org.

The grounds of Arlington National Cemetery are lands once owned by two notable Virginia families. John Custis, Martha Custis Washington's son, originally purchased the land in 1778. Several generations later it was passed to Mary Anna Randolph Custis, who married U.S. Lieutenant Robert E. Lee in the Greek Revival mansion in 1831. Their seven children were born there. And it was at **Arlington House** (sometimes also called the Custis-Lee Mansion) that Robert E. Lee resigned his U.S. Army commission in 1861 to command Virginia's forces. The mansion has been restored to approximate its appearance when it was the Lee family home. Free admission. Same hours as for cemetery. (See below.) Web site: www.nps.gov/arho.

High upon a hill, the mansion provides a panoramic view of the city across the river (Washington, D.C.) and the seemingly endless rows of graves. **The Tomb of Pierre Charles L'Enfant,** designer of the city, lies on the hillside in front the mansion.

The **Visitors Center** can provide directions to notable graves, including those of former president John F. Kennedy, Jacqueline Kennedy Onassis, their two infant sons, and Robert F. Kennedy. Shuttle tours aboard a Tourmobile are also available. The Visitors Center is open October 1 to March 31, 8 A.M. to 5 P.M.; April 1 to September 30, 8 A.M. to 7 P.M. Free admission. Charge for shuttle tours. Visitors Center telephone: (877) 907-8585. Shuttle-tours telephone: (202) 488-1012.

Web sites: www.arlingtoncemetery.org or www.anctours.com.

Also within Arlington National Cemetery is the **Women in Military Service for America** Memorial, which was dedicated in 1997 to honor the millions of women who have served in national defense and includes an education center. Free admission. Same hours as cemetery. Telephone: 703-892-2606. Web site: www.womensmemorial.org.

The **Netherlands Carillon,** located at the northern border of Arlington Cemetery, is a gift of fifty bells from the Netherlands housed in a 127-foot tower offered in thanks for America's help to the people of Holland during World War II. Concerts are held on Saturdays and national holidays during the summer. Visitors may ascend the tower during concerts. May and September, 2 P.M. to 4 P.M.; June, July, and August, 6 to 8 P.M. Parking is available near the Marine Corps Memorial; enter from Fort Myers Road. Metro stops: Rosslyn, (blue or orange lines) or Arlington Cemetery (blue line), then walk about $^1/_2$ mile. Telephone: (703) 289-2553. Web site: www.nps.gov/gwmp/nethcarillon.htm.

The **U.S. Marine Corps War Memorial,** more commonly known as **Iwo Jima,** is a dramatic, larger-than-life sculpture of Marine planting the U.S. flag during the Battle for the Pacific in 1945. The memorial honors all Marine who have died serving their country since Colonial times. Open 24 hours. Adjacent to the Netherlands Carillon. Parking accessible from Fort Myers Road. Metro stops: Rosslyn (blue or orange lines) or Arlington Cemetery (blue line). Telephone: (703) 289-2500. Web site: www.nps.gov/gwmp/marinecorpswarmemorial.htm.

In the Potomac River southeast of Rosslyn is an eighty-eight-acre island and nature preserve dedicated to the twenty-sixth president of the United States. **Theodore Roosevelt Island and Memorial** provides a habitat for birds and other woodland and wetland creatures, while also providing a convenient oasis for those needing contact with nature. The island, which is connected to Arlington via footbridge, offers 2.5 miles of easy trails through old growth forest and boardwalks over marshes. Memorial fountains at the center of the island provide benches for shaded contemplation. The island is located between the Key and Roosevelt Bridges and also provides a starting point for the ruggedly rewarding Potomac Heritage National Scenic Trail. Parking lots are accessible from the George Washington Memorial Parkway. Look for signs and prepare for a sharp turn off the parkway. Free admission. Telephone: (703) 289-2500. Web sites: www.nps.gov/this/index.htm or (for the Potomac Heritage trail) www.nps.gov/pohe/index.htm.

Just south of Teddy Roosevelt Island along the George Washington Memorial Parkway and the Potomac River is **Lady Bird Johnson Park.** Landscaped with flowering trees, shrubs, bulbs and other plantings, the park is a living testament to the former First Lady's dedication to the beautification of America, including the U.S. capital. Near the south end of the park on the west side (bordered by Boundary Channel) is the 15-acre **Lyndon B. Johnson Memorial Grove,** a serene setting in honor of the 36th U. S. president. At the south end of the park on the Potomac side is the **Navy and Merchant Marine Memorial,** a transcendent sculpture of gulls in flight surrounded by red flowers. The arrangement creates the effect of a fountain and seems to convey the spirit of water, though none is actually used. Lady Bird Johnson Park is accessible from the George Washington Memorial Parkway. Turns into parking areas and the L.B.J. Memorial Grove are abrupt. Open dawn until dark. Telephone (Parkway offices): (703) 289-2500. Web site: www.nps.gov/gwmp.

Gravelly Point is a boat launch park just south of the Merchant Marine Memorial. It also attracts fishermen and, because of its proximity to Reagan National Airport, provides thrilling close-up views of planes coming and going. Earplugs are highly recommended. Heading north on the G. W. Parkway, turn right into the first park/parking area past the airport. Free admission. Extensive renovations to **National Airport** were completed in 1998, and the facility renamed it **Ronald Reagan National Airport** in honor of the fortieth U.S. president. The Metro station is connected to the terminal with covered crosswalks, and shops and restaurants offer diversions for passengers between flights. National is located on the George Washington Parkway, less than 4 miles south of downtown and about 10 miles from Mt. Vernon. Metro stops: National Airport (blue and yellow lines). Telephone: (703) 417-8600. (For information about flights, call the appropriate airline.) Web site: www.metwashairports.com/reagan/reagan.htm.

The **Pentagon** is located between Reagan National Airport and Arlington National Cemetery. The notable five-sided structure has numerous levels below ground and contains 17.5 miles of corridors in a web-like pattern around a central courtyard. It is the world's largest office building, with three times the office space of the Empire State Building. The Pentagon has its own exit off I-395 and also its own Metro stop. This architectural marvel was built in just 16 months during the early stages of U.S. involvement in World War II. The Joint Chiefs of Staff, the Secretary of Defense, and heads of the four branches of the military have their offices here, as do thousands of military and civilian employees making policy decisions that affect members of the Armed Services.

Tours of the Pentagon are available to schools, educational organizations, military units, and other select groups who make advance reservations. Reservations are offered with the understanding that each individual must present valid photo identification and that no tours are given in periods of heightened security awareness. Free admission.

Plans are underway for a two-acre memorial park in the southwest corner of the Pentagon Reservation. The park is designed to honor the 184 individuals who lost their lives during the terrorist attack of September 11, 2001, and it is located less than 200 feet from where the hijacked Boeing 757 struck the Pentagon building. Each memorial unit in the tree-shaded park is to include an illuminated bench inscribed with the name of a victim and a reflecting pool. Victims ranged in age from 3 to 71. A fund-raising campaign headed by a tax-exempt, nonprofit corporation called the Pentagon Memorial Fund,

Inc., hope to raise $20 million to build and maintain the memorial, which will be funded entirely by private donations. It is expected that the memorial will be complete in about two years. Metro stop: Pentagon (blue and yellow lines). Telephone: (703) 697-1776. Web site: http://pentagon.osd.mil/. Memorial Web site: memorial.pentagon.mil/description.htm.

The **Washington & Old Dominion Railroad Regional Trail** is a 45-mile long asphalt-paved route from Shirlington (just west of Alexandria) in Arlington County to Purcellville in Loudoun County farther west. The route crosses numerous restored railroad bridges through a heavily wooded corridor and provides non-stop riding the entire length, though one must watch for cars at road crossings. At the eastern end in Shirlington, there is a link to the Mount Vernon Trail, creating nearly 65 miles of paved bike trails. (For more information, call the trail office or check online.) W. & O. D. Trail office telephone: (703) 729-0596. Web site: www.nvrpa.org. For up-to-the-minute news on portions of the trail that are closed or being repaired, such as the 10-foot hole that resulted from heavy rains in spring 2003, visit the Friends of the W & O. D. Trail's Web site: wodfriends.org.

Stretching southeastward along the Potomac, the magnificently scenic **George Washington Memorial Parkway** is one of four federally maintained parkways in Virginia. From its origin to the north near the American Legion Bridge to Maryland, the Parkway extends for 17 miles. In Arlington the parkway provides splendid cross-river views of Georgetown and the major Washington, D.C., monuments. The views are particularly stunning at night when rush-hour traffic has abated and the monuments are lit. Heading south, en route to Alexandria, you will pass Theodore Roosevelt Island. See the Lincoln and Jefferson memorials, the Washington Monument and the Capitol, pass Lady Bird Johnson Park and the turnoffs to Lyndon Baines Johnson Memorial Grove, the Navy Merchant Marine Memorial, Gravelly Point and National Airport before reaching "Old Town," as Alexandria is often called, where the parkway temporarily becomes Washington Street. A paved multi-use trail with wood bridges over marshland runs parallel to the highway with several points of access and parking, including Theodore Roosevelt Island and Gravelly Point. Below Alexandria the trail wends through **Dyke Marsh,** the largest remaining piece of freshwater tidal wetlands in the area. The trail is of special interest to bird watchers and is also enjoyed used by runners, walkers, in-line skaters, and strollers. Telephone: (parkway offices) (703) 289-2500. Web site: www.nps.gov/gwmp.

"Old Town" Alexandria

Alexandria is one of Virginia's oldest and most historic cities. It probably has more original eighteenth- and early nineteenth-century buildings standing than any city in America, many of which are used as private residences today. Especially fascinating in the Old Town are the unique and varied doorways. Alexandria is named after the Scottish merchant John Alexander, who owned much of the land in this city that was established by an act of the Virginia Assembly in 1749. During the American Revolution, Alexandria was the site of a major colonial port. On the Potomac River just south of Washington, and often compared to Georgetown, Old Town Alexandria really has a flavor and Southern charm of its own. A former warehouse district, this waterfront area on the Virginia shore of the Potomac has been renovated and historic buildings and landscaping have been restored to an earlier splendor. To truly appreciate the history of Old Town, wander along the cobblestone streets of Captain's Row and Gentry Row to view the eighteenth- and nineteenth-century homes of Colonial sea captains and Revolutionary War patriots.

Now the official visitors center, the **Ramsay House** was built circa 1724 by William Ramsay, a Scottish merchant and city founder. The house is believed to have been built downriver and barged to its present location at 221 King Street after Alexandria was established in 1749. Here you can pick up detailed maps, brochures on attractions, and information about seasonal events. Open daily, 9 A.M. to 5 P.M. Closed Thanksgiving, Christmas, and New Year's. Free admission. Telephone: (703) 746-3301. A free forty-page, color brochure may be requested online. Web site: www.funside.com.

The **Stabler-Leadbeater Apothecary Shop,** 105-107 South Fairfax Street, was opened in 1792 and patronized by Washington and Lee. Early prescription books and original collections of pharmaceutical glass and equipment are exhibited. Open Monday through Saturday, 10 A.M. to 4 P.M.; Sunday, 1 to 5 P.M. Admission charge. Telephone: 703.746.3852. Web site: http://alexandriava.gov/Apothecary.

Carlyle House Historic Park is located at 121 North Fairfax Street, between Cameron and King streets. The house was completed in 1752 by John Carlyle, a Scotch merchant and shipowner, also one of the founders of Alexandria. Gen. Edward Braddock used the house as his headquarters prior to the French and Indian Wars. Carlyle House contains many period furnishings and an architectural room documenting the original construction of the house and the techniques used in its restoration. Open Tuesday through Saturday, 10 A.M. to 5 P.M.; Sunday, noon to 5 P.M. Admission charge. Telephone: (703) 549-2997. Web site: www.carlylehouse.org.

Gadsby's Tavern Museum, a national historic landmark, is located at 134 North Royal Street. This famous eighteenth-century hostelry, built in 1770, combines the Coffee House and the larger City Hotel added in 1792. The buildings were named for John Gadsby, the English innkeeper who operated them from 1796 to 1808. The tavern was a center of political, social, and business life in early Alexandria, favored by both locals and travelers for its diverse entertainments. As a young colonial officer, George Washington was among those who enjoyed the tavern's hospitality. In 1798 and 1799, General and Mrs. Washington attended the birthnight balls held in his honor. (These festivities continue today and are held annually on his birth date.) Other notables who have been entertained at the Tavern include John Adams, Thomas Jefferson, James Monroe, and the Marquis de Lafayette. The Tavern Museum is now owned and operated by the City of Alexandria. Visitors can tour the historic rooms and dine in the restaurant, which sometimes features period entertainment. Call for information about special events and classes on such topics as eighteenth-century dances or clothing and deportment. Open April to October, Tuesday through Saturday, 10 A.M. to 5 P.M.; Sunday and Monday, 1 to 5 P.M., last tour 4:15. November to March, Wednesday through Saturday, 11 A.M. to 4 P.M; Sunday, 1 to 4 P.M., last tour 3:15. Closed major holidays. Admission charge. Telephone: (703) 746-4242. Web site: http://alexandriava.gov/GadsbysTavern.

The **Torpedo Factory Art Center**, in a renovated building at 105 North Union Street (corner of King Street), houses a myriad of artist studios. You can watch artists working on ceramics, sculpture, jewelry, paintings, and stained glass. All of their work is for sale. The building, constructed in 1918 as World War I came to an end, manufactured torpedoes on round-the-clock shifts during World War II. Open daily, 10 A.M. to 5 P.M. Closed holidays. Free admission. Telephone: (703) 838-4565. Web site: www.torpedofactory.org.

The Alexandria Black History Resource Center, located at 638 N. Alfred Street, interprets the contributions of African Americans to Alexandria's history and culture. The building was constructed in

1940 as the Robinson Library, the African American community's first public library, after a handful of young black men conducted a sit-in. Located next door to the Alexandria Black History Resource Center is the **Watson Reading Room,** which is a noncirculating research repository focusing on issues of African American history and culture. Ask about sites on a self-guided walking tour. Both the Resource Center and Reading Room are open Tuesday through Saturday, 10 A.M. to 4 P.M. Telephone: (703) 746-4356. Web site: http://alexandriava.gov/BlackHistory.

The Alexandria African American Heritage Park, located off Duke St. on Holland Lane, is an eight-acre memorial park that includes a one-acre, nineteenth-century, African American cemetery. Inside the park is a sculpture group of bronze trees called "Truths that Rise from the Roots Remembered," which is an acknowledgment of the contributions of African Americans to Alexandria. The park is open daily, dawn to dusk. Click on the "Black History Resource" at this Web site: http://alexandriava.gov/BlackHistory.

Gentry's Row and Captain's Row, located in the 100-200 blocks of Prince Street, are imposing blocks of houses of important colonial Alexandrines and sea captains. Legend holds that the cobblestone street was paved by Hessian prisoners during the American Revolution, though more recent research casts doubt on this story.

Atheneum (also spelled Athenaeum), 201 Prince Street, is an important example of Greek Revival architecture. It was built as a bank in 1851 and is now the gallery of the Northern Virginia Fine Arts Association. The building is open when there are art shows and available for rental to hold meetings and parties on weekends (when the activities schedule permits) from the weekend after Easter through October. Telephone: (703) 548-0035. Web site: http://www.nvfaa.org/.

Presbyterian Meeting House, PC (USA), at 321 S. Fairfax Street, was built in 1772. The first Masonic memorial service for Washington was held here. The tomb of the Unknown Soldier of the Revolution is in the churchyard, as are graves of many founding fathers of Alexandria and notables of the Revolutionary period. Courtyard open daily. This historical treasure is also a vital, functioning church; please call for service hours. Telephone: (703) 549-6670. Web site: www.opmh.org.

Friendship Firehouse Museum, 107 S. Alfred Street, was organized as a firehouse, with services available by subscription, in 1774. In a collection of early fire-fighting equipment is the little fire engine donated by George Washington in 1775. Open Friday and Saturday, 10 A.M. to 4 P.M.; Sunday, 1 to 4 P.M. Free admission. Telephone: (703) 746-3891. Web site: http://alexandriava.gov/FriendshipFirehouse.

Boyhood Home of Robert E. Lee is located at 607 Oronoco Street. Gen. Henry "Light-Horse Harry" Lee, of Revolutionary War fame and thrice governor of Virginia, brought his family here in 1812. Robert E. Lee spent his early years here. Now privately owned, the house is not currently open to the public, though it may be viewed from the street, and a virtual tour is available via the Internet. Check with the Ramsey House Visitors Center about possible openings. Web site for virtual tour: leeboyhoodhome.com.

Christ Church, at 118 N. Washington Street, has a fine Georgian interior and an original chandelier. The building was begun in 1767, but its roots in the community date even earlier. Washington was a vestryman here, and later, Lee was a pewholder. Open Monday through Saturday, 9 A.M. to 4 P.M.; Sunday, 2 to 4:00 P.M. Free admission. Telephone: (703) 549-1450. Web site: www.historicchristchurch.org.

Lee-Fendall House, a Victorian mansion at 614 Oronoco Street, was Lee's boyhood home for nine years. The house was built in 1785 and renovated in 1837. Occupied by thirty-seven Lees of Virginia, it has been furnished with period pieces, many of them rare antiques. The garden, the largest walled garden in Old Town, is a charming early American setting, with old brick walls, boxwood, dogwood, and a huge magnolia. Open Tuesday through Saturday, 10 A.M. to 4 P.M.; Sundays, 1 to 4 P.M. Admission charge. Call in advance to ensure the house is not closed for a private function. Telephone: (703) 548-1789. Web site: www.leefendallhouse.org.

The **Lyceum,** 201 S. Washington Street, is housed in a building that was constructed as a lecture hall in 1839 and quickly became Alexandria's cultural center. Since then it was used as a Civil War hospital, a private house, and an office building before its designation as Alexandria's History Museum in 1985. The museum interprets Alexandria's history with special exhibitions and events. There is a museum gift shop. Open Monday through Saturday, 10 A.M. to 5 P.M.; Sundays 1 to 5 P.M. Closed Thanksgiving, Christmas Eve, Christmas, and New Year's. Free admission. Telephone: (703) 838-4994. Web site: http://alexandriava.gov/Lyceum.

George Washington Masonic National Memorial is located at 101

Callahan Drive on Shooter's Hill, a mile west on King Street from the city center. It is a gift of the Freemasons of the nation in honor of George Washington, who was a Mason. Visitors can see the Masonic Museum, Replica Room of the Alexandria-Washington Lodge, the Shrine and Grottoes rooms, and they can view Alexandria from the observation deck of the 333-foot monument. Artifacts include George Washington's family bible, the field trunk he used during the Revolutionary War, and sabers used at his funeral. Open daily, 9 A.M. to 4 P.M. Free admission. Telephone: (703) 683-2007. Web site includes virtual tours: www.gwmemorial.org.

Fort Ward Museum and Historic Site is situated at 4301 West Braddock Road between King Street and Seminary Road, just east of Shirley Highway (I-395). Included within a 45-acre wooded park, Fort Ward is one of the largest of the Civil War forts constructed for the defense of Washington. Its Northwest Bastion has been accurately reconstructed. It now appears exactly as it did over 140 years ago, with guns mounted, ready to fire through the embrasures. It is by far the best restoration of its kind in the region. The Museum has a splendid display of Civil War items. Open Tuesday through Saturday, 9 A.M. to 4 P.M.; Sunday, noon to 5 P.M. Park open daily 9 A.M. to sunset, though both park and museum may limit hours under extreme weather conditions. Free admission. Telephone: (703) 746-4848. Web site: http://alexandriava.gov/FortWard.

Fairfax County, Mount Vernon Area

The George Washington Memorial Parkway ends, appropriately, at **Mount Vernon,** George Washington's home from 1754 until his death 1799. Washington more than doubled the size of the modest house he inherited, which overlooks the Potomac River, and introduced in his home many architectural refinements popular in England at the time. The house is furnished with a combination of period and original Washington pieces. To support the mansion house, he built an extensive village-like group of flanking service buildings, or "dependencies," a dozen of which are open to the public. The gardens remain substantially as they were during Washington's lifetime. The Kitchen Garden is particularly interesting, with its herbs, vegetables, and espaliered fruit and fig trees. You especially don't want to miss the 16-sided (round) barn and wheat treading demonstrations using horses and mules. Open April through August, 8 A.M. to 5 P.M.; March, September, October 9 A.M. to

5 P.M.; November through February 9 A.M. to 4 P.M. Special tours vary by season. Admission charge. Telephone: (703) 780-2000. Web site: www.mountvernon.org.

The **American Horticultural Society,** near Mount Vernon at 7991 E. Boulevard Drive, occupies the eighteenth-century manor house and the 27-acre estate of Tobias Lear, George Washington's secretary and tutor to his children. A new visitors center welcomes guests to what was once Washington's northernmost property, then known as River Farm. The first floor of the manor house is furnished with period furniture and decorations and features rotating art exhibits. Visitors may stroll through the formal rose and dahlia gardens and the large areas devoted to annuals and perennials. A large Osage tree, the second oldest in the nation, is believed to have been given to the Washington family by Thomas Jefferson, who received several seedlings from Lewis and Clark after their Western explorations. Open Monday through Friday, 9 A.M. to 5 P.M. Admission is voluntary contribution. Telephone: (703) 768-5700. Web site: www.ahs.org.

Also nearby is the **George Washington Grist Mill State Park,** on Route 235 three miles west of Mount Vernon. The present building is a reconstruction of the mill George Washington built in 1770 and operated for nearly thirty years, grinding wheat and corn. Guided tours, led by historic interpreters, allow modern visitors to experience the process. Open April through October, seven days a week, 10 A.M. to 5 P.M. Admission charge. Telephone: 703-780-2000. Web site: www.mountvernon.org/visit-his-estate/plan-your-visit/distillery-amp-gristmill.

Near the grist mill, Mount Vernon archaeologists have uncovered the foundation of George Washington's whiskey distillery, which was so successful that, in 1799, it produced 11,000 gallons of whiskey. Washington sold the spirits to farmers in Alexandria and turned a tidy profit.

George Washington presented **Woodlawn Plantation** to his ward, Eleanor Parke Custis, and his nephew, Major Lawrence Lewis, after their marriage in 1799. The gift included 2,000 acres of the Mount Vernon estate, a mill, and a distillery. Dr. William Thornton, first architect of the U.S. Capitol, designed the mansion, which was built circa 1803-1805. Woodlawn is located at the junction of Routes 1 and 235, about a mile beyond the Grist Mill Park. Open daily, March through December, 10 A.M. to 5 P.M. Closed January and February, except

Presidents' Day. Admission charge. Telephone: (703) 780-4000.
Web site: http://woodlawn1805.org/.

In 1964, the **Pope-Leighey House,** designed by Frank Lloyd Wright,
was moved to the grounds of Woodlawn Plantation. The Georgian
mansion and the 1940 Usonian house afford an unusual architectural contrast between early nineteenth-century plantation life and
modest suburban life of the mid-twentieth century. The Pope-
Leighey House is open daily March through December, 10 A.M. to
4:00 P.M. Weekends only during January and February. Admission
charge. Telephone: (703) 780-4000. Web site:
http://popeleighey1940.org/.

The "Parish Church of Mount Vernon," **Pohick Church,** completed
in 1774, is situated on U.S. Route 1 at its juncture with Telegraph
Road. The church's address is 9301 Richmond Highway, ten miles
south of Alexandria. George Washington and George Mason were
both members of the vestry. Open Monday through Saturday, 9 A.M.
to 4:30 P.M.; Sunday, 12:30 P.M. to 4:30 P.M. Free admission, though
donations are welcome. Telephone: (703) 339-6572. Web site:
www.pohick.org.

Further information on the Mount Vernon area and other attractions within the county is available through the Fairfax Convention
and Visitors Bureau, 8180-A Silverbrook Road, Lorton, VA 22079,
(exit 163 off I-95). Telephone: (800) 732-4732. Web site:
www.fxva.com. You may also wish to contact the Fairfax County Park
Authority for more information on county parks. Telephone: (703)
324-8702. Or contact the Northern Virginia Regional Park Authority,
5400 Ox Road, Fairfax Station, VA 22039. Telephone: (703) 352-
5900. Web sites: www.fairfaxcounty.gov/parks/ (or) www.nvrpa.org.

Fairfax County, South to Quantico

Gunston Hall, built 1755-58, was the home of George Mason,
author of the Virginia Declaration of Rights. The elaborate carved
woodwork was executed by William Buckland. The house has been
restored and authentically furnished by the National Society of
Colonial Dames of America. The rustic nature trail that circles
Mason's deer park contrasts interestingly with the formal eighteenth-
century boxwood gardens. The 556-acre estate includes a restored
schoolhouse and kitchen yard. To reach Gunston Hall take Mount
Vernon Memorial Highway (which connects to the George
Washington Parkway at Mt. Vernon) to Route 1 and turn left (south)

and look for signs, or take I-95 south to the Lorton-Gunston Hall exit and follow signs. Open daily, 9:30 A.M. to 5 P.M. Closed Thanksgiving, Christmas, and New Year's Day. Admission charge. Telephone: (703) 550-9220. Web site: www.gunstonhall.org.

The **U.S. Marine Corps Air-Ground Museum,** formerly located at the Marine Corps Base at Quantico, is now closed. A new facility, the National Museum of the Marine Corps, is to be constructed outside the base and is schedule to open in 2005. Public Affairs Office telephone: (703) 784-2606.

The 2,000-acre **Pohick Bay Regional Park** offers boating, camping and picnicking facilities, and an 18-hole golf course, as well as the state's largest swimming pool. "Pohick" is the Algonquin word for the "water place," and water is a key feature in many of the park's activities. Pohick Bay is about seven miles east of I-95 South. Look for signs around Lorton and Mason Neck. Admission charge. For general information, telephone (703) 339-6104; pool: (703) 339-6102; golf course: (703) 339-8585. Web site: www.nvrpa.org/park/pohick_bay/.

Prince William Forest Park is administered by the National Park Service. It is located west of I-95 near Triangle. Reach the park entrance by taking I-95 to exit 150-B (Joplin Road), then state route 619 West to the second right. The 17,000-acre park is the largest remaining natural area in the Washington, D.C., metro region and one of the few remaining Piedmont ecosystems, a sanctuary for native plants and animals. Thirty-five miles of hiking and bicycling trails and fire roads afford access to the wilder regions of the park. Parking areas along park roads provide convenient starting points for many walks. Pine Grove Visitors Center is open daily, 8:30 A.M. to 5 P.M. The Picnic Grounds, near the main park entrance, are open all year, dawn to dusk, and will accommodate about 1,000 people. Tables, fireplaces, garbage receptacles, water, comfort stations, a playfield, and shelter are provided on a first-come, first-served basis. Self-guiding nature trails begin and end at each picnic ground. Camping options include tent and RV sites and cabins. The park is rich in wildlife, including mammals, wild turkey, hawks, and numerous species of songbirds and many kinds of fish, reptiles, and amphibians. Eighty-nine species of trees and shrubs have been identified in the forest. The watersheds of the North and South Branches of Quantico Creek lie almost entirely within the park. Erosion by this creek has exposed the ancient granite, schist, and quartzite of the Piedmont. Before 1920, pyrite, containing iron and sulfur, was mined near the confluence of the North and South

Branches of Quantico Creek. Staff at the Visitors Center can offer tips to help you enjoy and understand the park's forest and wildlife. Guided trips, advice on hike routes, illustrated talks, and other programs are also available. Admission charge. Information: (703) 221-7181; cabin reservations: (703) 221-5843; tent sites: (703) 221-7181. Check the Web site for trail closures and detailed descriptions of camping options, including sites and cabins accommodating groups of 50 to 100. Web site: www.nps.gov/prwi.

Northwest Fairfax County

This area, which forms the western borders of Arlington County and Old Town Alexandria, has several historic points of interest to tourists as well as a number of parks and cultural centers. Among its attractions are Reston, Great Falls Park, and historic buildings in Fairfax and Falls Church. The county also has a network of parks with many recreational facilities. The area is accessible from Washington via several bridges across the Potomac River, the George Washington Parkway, and exits off I-495 (the Capital Beltway).

Additional information is available through the Fairfax Convention and Visitors Bureau, 8180-A Silverbrook Road, Lorton, VA 22079 (exit 163 off I-95). Telephone: (800) 732-4732. Web sites: www.fxva.com or www.co.fairfax.va.us/parks or www.nvrpa.org.

Turkey Run Recreation Area

Located just off George Washington Memorial Parkway, near CIA Headquarters, just seven miles from downtown Washington, D.C., this 700-acre, mostly forested area, under National Park Service jurisdiction, has picnicking facilities and is of special interest to hikers (no bicycling) and those interested in natural history. A well-defined trail follows the bank of the Potomac in both directions. The bottomlands are rich in plant life, and are especially attractive in the springtime. Bird enthusiasts also will find this a rewarding area, as will those interested in a rigorous hike along the steep, rocky hillsides of the Potomac on a sometimes-muddy path that may involve fording streams or stepping rock-to-rock should click on "Potomac Heritage National Scenic Trail" at the Turkey Run Web site. Telephone: (703) 289-2500. Web site: www.nps.gov/gwmp/turkey-run-park.htm.

Approximately a mile below **Turkey Run Recreational Area** is the site of an extensive soapstone quarry, probably abandoned almost a century ago. This quarry is located up a steep and narrow ravine, immediately west of Eagle Rock. An inspection reveals cut stone and rusted machinery.

The **Claude Moore Colonial Farm** is accessible from the George Washington Parkway near Turkey Run via the Route 123 exit. Follow 123 toward McLean for approximately 1 mile, then turn right onto 193 and take the first right onto Colonial Farm Road. Or, from I-495, take Route 193 (Georgetown Pike) toward Langley for 2.3 miles, then turn left onto Colonial Farm Road. The farm is made up of an eighteenth-century colonial cabin with outbuildings, garden, and livestock. A colonial "family" in costume works the farm, using period equipment, tools, and farming methods. Visitors are welcome from Wednesday through Sunday, 10 A.M. to 4:30 P.M. Admission charge. Telephone: (703) 442-7557. Web sites: www.1771.org/ or www.nps.gov/clmo/index.htm.

Ft. Marcy, a noted Civil War fort that served as part of the defenses of Washington, is located 2.5 miles south of the Turkey Run area. Take the George Washington Memorial Parkway to Route 123 south. A path leads to the fort, one-half mile north of the county line, designated by a road sign. Web site: www.nps.gov/gwmp/fort-marcy.htm.

Great Falls Park

Part of the George Washington Memorial Parkway, **Great Falls Park** receives its name from the impressive cataracts of the Potomac which plunge wildly over huge boulders and rocks through the mile-long Stephen Mather Gorge. From I-495, take exit 44 and follow Route 193 West (Georgetown Pike). Turn right on Old Dominion Drive (approximately 4.5 miles), then go straight 1 mile to the park entrance. Great Falls is one of the most important scenic, historic, and recreational areas around Washington. Central features of the park are the falls and the historic locks and trace of the Patowmack Canal. Across the Potomac River is Great Falls, MD, and the C & O Canal National Historic Park. Admission charge. Telephone: (703) 285-2965 or (703) 289-2513. Web site: www.nps.gov/grfa/index.htm.

The Patowmack Company was organized under the leadership of George Washington at Alexandria in May 1785. In the first annual report in 1786, the president outlined plans for a route that would bypass the Great Falls by means of a canal, which included a cut blasted out of the palisades on the Virginia shore. A series of locks would enable boats to descend into the river below the cataracts. In 1793 "Light-Horse Harry" Lee laid out a 43-acre town, named Matildaville. The town had a gristmill, market, sawmill, warehouse, forge, and a stone house for the canal superintendent. Five narrow streets were laid out from the falls to the heights above Difficult Run. Headquarters of the Company and laborers' quarters were located in the town.

The Patowmack Canal scheme was completed in 1802. It was then possible for flat-bottom boats to traverse the Potomac River from Cumberland to Georgetown and Alexandria. Valuable cargoes of flour, corn, whisky, livestock, meats, lumber, and pig iron came into the area from beyond the Allegheny Mountains. On return trips the boats carried manufactured goods for which there was a lively market west of the mountains.

From the very outset the Company had difficulties because of devastating floods and low waters, which interfered with shipping or damaged the canal works. The Company folded and was taken over by the Chesapeake and Ohio Canal Company in 1828. Matildaville was deserted and gradually fell into ruins.

Today one can follow the route of the canal from its beginning, upstream from the falls, a distance of 3,600 feet to the point where it empties into the Potomac River, well below the falls. The locks and canal walls were constructed of Seneca sandstone. These are now weathered to a dark salmon red. Some of these blocks bear low relief signature marks of individual stonecutters.

From Matildaville the path continues through the woods, along the west bank of the canal, and past three locks to the outlet in the Potomac gorge. These locks permitted boats to be lowered over 70 feet into the river. The path goes past Sandy Landing and along the rim of the palisades past Cowhoof Rock promontory. The trail descends precipitously to the mouth of Difficult Run, which is calm and wide, and a rendezvous of local fishermen.

Great Falls Park also has fishing, picnicking, and 15 miles of hiking trails, 5 of which are also used for horseback riding and biking. A slide presentation, ranger talks, and guided walks are available. (See schedule in the Visitors Center or on the Web site.) The park is open daily, except on Christmas, 7 A.M. until dark. The Visitors Center weekday summer hours are 10 A.M. to 5 P.M.; weekends, 10 A.M. to 6 P.M. Winter hours: 10 A.M. to 4 P.M. Admission charge. Telephone: (703) 285-2965 or (703) 289-2513. Web site: www.nps.gov/grfa/index.htm.

At 8700 Potomac Hills Street in Great Falls, **Riverbend Park** includes 400 acres of forest, meadows, ponds, and streams along the Potomac River. Facilities include a boat ramp, picnic tables, and a visitor center with wildlife displays and a naturalist. One can follow the riverside trail upstream a mile or more and fish from the bank, though no swimming is allowed. This area is excellent for nature study. Open: park, 7 A.M. until dusk; visitor center, 9 A.M. to 5 P.M., except Tuesdays; weekends noon to 5 P.M. Special provisions for the handicapped. Free admission. Telephone: (703) 759-9018. Web site: www.fairfaxcounty.gov/parks/riverbend/.

Falls Church and Reston

From colonial times, **Falls Church** has served as the crossroads between North and South, through which trekked the early pioneers, Braddock's British Army during the French and Indian Wars, and the Union Army en route to Manassas. It was here that Ranger Mosby's Confederate raiders often harassed the Union forces. Attractions that remain are the celebrated Falls Church, a building dating from 1768, the earthworks of Fort Taylor, the Lynch House (1797), the Wren House (1770), Hollywood (1750), the Mount (1745), Mount Pleasant (1770), and several other fine old estates.

A noted town landmark is the **Falls Church (Episcopal)** at 115 East Fairfax Street. It was erected in 1768 on the site of a church built in 1734 where George Washington was a vestryman. The church served as a recruiting station in the American Revolution and as both a hospital and stable during the Civil War. Telephone: (703) 241-0003. Web site: http://thefallschurch-episcopal.org/.

Washington & Old Dominion Railroad Regional Park follows the former railway right-of-way through Fairfax County from Shirlington (in Arlington County) to Purcellville (in Loudoun County). It provides a 45-mile hiking and biking trail. Also see the section on Arlington County. Telephone: (703) 729-0596. Web site: www.nvrpa.org/park.

The city of **Fairfax** is noted for its courthouse, dating from 1799. On those courthouse grounds, the scene of some of Confederate Ranger Mosby's exploits, stands a monument to the first Confederate soldier killed in the Civil War. For more information on the city of Fairfax, contact the recently renovated Fairfax Museum and Visitors Bureau, 10209 Main Street, Fairfax, VA 22030. Open daily 9 A.M. to 5 P.M., except major holidays. Online, you can download a self-guided historic walking tour. Telephone: (703) 385-8414. Web site: www.fair-faxva.gov/MuseumVC/MVC.asp.

Bull Run Regional Park, at 7700 Bull Run Drive near Centreville, is part of a 5,000-acre area known as the Bull Run/Occoquan Stream Valley, which extends 25 miles along the stream valley on the Fairfax County side of the Occoquan reservoir. Take I-66 toward Centreville to exit 52 (Route 29). Drive two miles south, turn left onto Bull Run Post Office Road, then follow signs to the park entrance. Characterized chiefly for its series of flat, tree-bordered meadows near the meandering Bull Run, the park is dotted with picnic tables and shelters. The park offers overnight campsites, two nearby bath-houses with showers, washing machines and dryers, and a camp center stocking limited supplies. Other attractions are a skeet/trap-shooting range, a multicircular pool, a playground, the 17-mile Bull Run-Occoquan Trail, an equestrian trail, and an eight-mile history nature trail along Bull Run. Hikes and other activities vary by season. The outdoor pool is open Memorial Day through Labor Day. The main park is closed in winter, but the shooting range is open year-round. Admission charge. Telephone: (703) 631-0550 (main number); (703) 830-2344 (shooting range). Web site: www.nvrpa.org/park/bull_run/.

Farther downstream, southwest of Clifton, on the confluence of Bull Run and the Occoquan, at 12619 Old Yates Ford Road is the 100-acre **Bull Run Marina.** From mid-March to mid-November, boats are available for rent, and fishing and launching of private boats are allowed with a permit from Fountainhead Regional Park. (See next entry.) Fishing supplies are available from the Marina center. Fishermen need a Virginia fishing license. The park has two parking lots, comfort station, playground, and trails along the edge of the Run. Bull Run Marina may be reached from Route 29 or 211 or from Braddock Road. Telephone: (703) 250-9124. Web site: www.nvrpa.org/park/bull_run_marina/.

Fountainhead Regional Park, 10875 Hampton Road, Fairfax Station, can be reached via I-95 south from Alexandria. Take the Ox Road (Route 123) exit and proceed north for approximately 5 miles, then turn left on Hampton Road for three miles to the entrance on the left. Open mid-March to mid-November, the park offers fishing, boat launches, rowboat rental, hiking, mountain-bike trails, miniature golf, a spectacular observation deck over the Occoquan Reservoir, and picnic facilities. Food, tackle, and bait are available.

Telephone: (703) 250-9124. Mountain Bike Trail Hot Line: (703) 250-2473. Web site: www.nvrpa.org/park/fountainhead/.

Vienna's Freeman's Store and Museum, built in 1859, was restored in 1976 as a country general store and museum by Historic Vienna, Inc. Over the years it served as a store, Civil War hospital, train depot, post office, and firehouse. Mementos of its varied history are on display, and it offers bargains on items such as penny candies, baskets, brooms, wood toys, and other goods typical of a nineteenth-century store. The store is at the corner of Church and Mill streets in historic Vienna. Open Saturday, noon to 4 P.M.; Sunday, 1 to 5 P.M. March through October. Free admission. Telephone: (703) 938-5187. Web site: www.viennava.gov/index.aspx?NID=123.

The Web site also gives locations of notable trees in the area, including the magnificent white oak at 802 Marjorie Lane. It began its life around 1680 and is believed to be the oldest tree in Virginia.

Wolftrap Farm Park, run by the National Park Service, is reached via Route 7, three miles west of I-495 to Toulston Road (which becomes Trap Road), then left one mile to the park. At performance times there is also access from the Dulles Airport Road. This 100-acre park includes the Filene Center amphitheater with musical and theatrical performances throughout the summer. The park has picnic facilities and a nature trail. A Theater in the Woods summer program for children, opera camp, and tours of the Center are also offered. Please call for specific information. Telephone: (703) 255-1900. Web site: www.wolftrap.org.

Meadowlark Gardens Regional Park is a 95-acre garden park with 3 lakes surrounded by weeping cherry trees. Located on Beulah Road between Route 7 and Route 123 in Vienna, the gardens are open year-round, though hours vary by season. Admission charge. Telephone: (703) 255-3631. Web sites: www.virginia.org/Listings/OutdoorsAndSports/MeadowlarkGard ensRegionalPark/ or www.nvrpa.org.

Dulles International Airport, whose terminal was designed by Eero Saarinen, is a masterpiece of architecture and engineering. In December 2003 the Smithsonian Institution's National Air and Space Museum opened a new museum on the airport grounds in Chantilly, Virginia, for the display and preservation of its collection of historic aviation and space artifacts. It is called the **Steven F. Udvar-Hazy Center** in honor of its major donor. More than 200 aircraft and 135 spacecraft will be on display when all exhibits are complete, including the *Enola Gay*, the *Space Shuttle Orbiter Enterprise*, and many more. The new museum will serve as a companion to the Air and Space Museum on the National Mall in Washington, D.C. There was simply not enough space in that facility to display many fascinating aircraft in the NASM collection. In fact, 80 percent was in storage. It was opened in time to celebrate the 100th anniversary of the first powered flight of the Wright brothers. Completion of other phases of the museum project will continue through 2005. The center is south of the main terminal, which is approximately 26 miles west of downtown Washington and about 15 miles from the Capital Beltway. Free admission. From I-495, take exit 45A, and follow signs; or, from I-66 West, take exit 67. (There are no tolls for those traveling to the airport.) The Udvar-Hazy Center is at the intersection of routes 28 and 50 in the Dulles corridor. Web site: (for Dulles Airport) www.metwashairports.com/Dulles; (for the NASM Udvar-Hazy Center) www.nasm.si.edu/udvarhazy.

Sully Historic Site is an important landmark restored by the Fairfax County Park Authority. It is on Route 28 (Sully Road) in Chantilly, four miles south of Dulles Airport. From the Dulles Airport Road, take exit 9A and proceed south on Route 28; or from I-495, take the exit for Route 28 North. Completed in 1795, Sully was the home of a brother of Gen. "Light-Horse Harry" Lee and uncle of Gen. Robert E. Lee. Richard Bland Lee served as a delegate to the Virginia General Assembly and to the First Federal Congress in Philadelphia. He was also a founder of Phi Beta Kappa and was influential in bringing the nation's capital to the banks of the Potomac. Sully is completely furnished with antiques of the Federal period. In addition to the home, the plantation includes a kitchen/laundry, smokehouse, and schoolhouse store. Open March through December, 11 A.M. to 4 P.M. Guided tours on the hour, beginning at 11 A.M. Admission charge. Telephone: (703) 437-1794. Web site: www.fairfaxcounty.gov/parks/sully/.

Off Route 657 at 2709 West Ox Road in Herndon, **Frying Pan Park** includes a 1930-era model farm and facilities for fairs and exhibitions, including livestock judging and many horse shows. The site includes facilities for indoor and outdoor horseback riding, as well as an outdoor equestrian trail. Open daily for riding. Call for specific hours and fees. Interpretive tours around the model working farm are offered by appointment. Telephone: (703) 437-9101. Web site: www.fairfaxcounty.gov/parks/fryingpanpark/.

Colvin Run Mill, with its adjacent miller's house at 10017 Colvin Mill Run Road, has been restored by the Fairfax County Park Authority. Off

Route 7, the five-story mill was built by Philip Carper after 1811 on land once owned by George Washington. It was in continuous operation until the mid-1930s. Before the turn of the century, the mill was a business and social center of the nearby farming community.

Today one can visit the mill and learn how grain is ground, and also see the two-story miller's house. It is the only mill powered by twin overshot water wheels in Virginia. Beside the road to the house are the remains of a white oak, well over two centuries old, and nearby is the millrace, which carries the water from the millpond to the water wheels. Visitors can also browse in the general store, see the blacksmith shop, and view the exhibits of arts and crafts in the barn. Open Wednesday through Monday, 11 A.M. to 4 P.M., with tours on the hour. The last starts at 3 P.M. Closed Tuesdays. Admission charge. From I-495, take exit 10B (Route 7 West) to Colvin Mill Run Road, which is approximately 5 miles past Tysons Corner. Call for details and news of scheduled activities. Telephone: (703) 759-2771. Web site: www.fairfaxcounty.gov/parks/crm/.

Lake Fairfax is a 476-acre recreational area, eight miles west of I-495. Take exit 47A off I-495, turn left (west) on Baron Cameron Avenue, and make a second left onto Lake Fairfax Drive, which leads to the park entrance. Lake Fairfax offers picnicking, swimming, fishing, boating, hiking, and family camping facilities. There is also a water park—the Water Mine Family Swimmin' Hole—for children 12 and under, a playground, a carousel, an excursion boat, and a general store. Pedal boats are available for rental. Open 7 A.M. to 8 P.M. all year, though amenities and attractions are seasonal. Charge for camping, water park, carousel, and boat rental. For reservations and seasonal information, contact Lake Fairfax, 1400 Lake Fairfax Drive, Reston, VA 22090. Telephone: (703) 471-5415. Web site: www.fairfaxcounty.gov/parks/lakefairfax/.

The historic farmhouse at **Green Spring Gardens** dates from 1780 and was renovated by Walter Macomber in 1942. Macomber, who spent five years as an architect in Colonial Williamsburg and 30 years as an architect at Mt. Vernon, is responsible for the extensive woodworking in the house and springhouse, excellent examples of high-style Colonial revival. Also in 1942, Beatrix Farrand, niece of Edith Wharton, designer of the gardens at Dumbarton Oaks, and a preeminent female landscape architect, did the garden at Green Spring, which is believed to be her only Virginia garden. This gem of a garden, at 4603 Green Spring Road in Alexandria near the Annandale line, features a horticulture center, a newly expanded greenhouse, demonstration gardens, a children's garden, one of the first native plant gardens in Virginia, and a range of programs for adults and children. A full English tea is served most Sundays, sometimes highlighting a particular era or theme, such as a Jane Austin Tea or a Victorian Tea; on Thursdays, April through October, one can partake of Tea and a Garden Stroll. Reservations required for tea. From I-495, take the exit for Braddock Road East, then turn on to Witch Hazel Road and follow signs leading to the entrance. The horticulture center is open Monday through Saturday, 9 A.M. to 4:30 P.M.; Sunday, noon to 4:30 P.M. Grounds are open daily, dawn to dusk, except Thanksgiving, Christmas, and New Year's. Free admission to the gardens. Charge for tea and special programs. Center telephone: (703) 642-5173. For tea schedule and reservations, telephone: (703) 941-7987. Web site: www.greenspring.org.

Facilities at **Burke Lake Park,** 7315 Ox Road, Fairfax Station, include picnicking, biking, boating, rowboat rental, fishing, camping, an 18-hole par 3 golf course, a carousel, playground equipment, a miniature railroad, and tour-boat rides. From the Capital Beltway, take exit 54A (Braddock Road, west) to a left on Burke Lake Road. Then left on Ox Road to the park entrance. Park open from dawn to dusk. Telephone: (703) 323-6601; picnic reservations: (703) 324-8732. Web site: www.fairfaxcounty.gov/parks/burkelakepark/.

Lake Accotink Park, 7500 Accotink Park Road, Springfield, offers boating, fishing, picnicking, and playground facilities, a carousel, and miniature golf on a 77-acre lake. The park is open daily, dawn to dusk, except Thanksgiving. The refreshment stand, carousel, and miniature golf are opened daily Memorial Day to Labor Day. Check about off-season hours. Reach Lake Accotink from I-95 by taking the Old Keene Mill Road exit west; then turn right on Hanover Ave. and left on Highland Ave. to a right on Accotink Park Road to front entrance on left. Telephone: (703) 569-0285. Web site: www.fairfaxcounty.gov/parks/lake-accotink/.

PIEDMONT REGION

The area, former home to many early American statesmen and presidents, is rich in history and colonial charm. Faithful restorations and frequent historic events provide exciting opportunities to relive the past that is so much a part of Virginia's Piedmont. Charlottesville, the starting place for one tour, may be reached from I-66 west and Route 29 south. Leesburg, the center of a tour closer to Washington, is accessible from Route 7 West, which joins I-495 at exit 10B.

Upper Piedmont

A self-conducted circular auto tour of approximately 150 miles offers a varied view of the Virginia countryside not far from the nation's capital. The suggested tour is from Washington via I-66 to Manassas Battlefield Park and on to Warrenton and the Upper Piedmont Region, which lies at the base of the Blue Ridge Mountains. The return route is via "Hunt Country" and the towns of Upperville, Middleburg, and Leesburg. Depending on the number of sites visited, this circular trip can occupy a full day or a weekend with an overnight stop.

The Manassas area, originally called Tudor Hall, was a sparsely settled region until the Orange and Alexandria Railroad was built in the early 1850s. Because of the importance of the rail junction to the South during the Civil War, two major battles, the First and Second Battles of Manassas (Bull Run), were fought on the rolling farms and woodlands six miles north of the present city. Located at 12521 Lee Highway in Manassas, VA 20109-2005, the **Manassas National Battlefield Park** commemorates these historical events. The park is approximately 25 miles west of Washington. Traveling west on I-66, take Manassas exit 47B and follow signs.

The first important engagement of the war found ill-prepared armies of the North and South struggling for control of this strategic railroad junction. The **First Battle of Manassas** was fought on July 21, 1861, between an impatient Federal army under General McDowell and a Confederate army waiting along Bull Run under generals P. G. T. Beauregard and Joseph E. Johnston. When McDowell's tired and discouraged men began to withdraw late in the afternoon, the retreat at first was orderly. The Warrenton Turnpike (now Routes 29/211) was encumbered with the carriages of congressmen and others who had driven out from Washington to watch the battle. Panic seized many of the soldiers and the retreat back to Washington became a rout. The Confederates were too disorganized to follow up their success. It was at this engagement that Gen. Thomas J. Jackson earned his famous nickname, "Stonewall." An equestrian statue of the famous general can be viewed on the battlefield.

The Second Battle of Manassas, a year later, was fought on August 28-30, 1862. Confederate general Robert E. Lee's Army of Northern

Virginia defeated Gen. John Pope's Union army. This victory provided the incentive for Lee's first invasion of the North.

A stone house and tavern that was pressed into service as a temporary field hospital during both battles has been restored to its 1860s appearance and furnished with pre-Civil War pieces. The Henry Hill Visitor Center on Sudley Road, near the intersection of I-66 and Route 234, contains a museum, a three-dimensional map highlighting the points of interest and the strategies of both battles, a theater, and a sales/gift counter, where books and souvenirs can be purchased. A 45-minute movie, *Manassas, End of Innocence,* is shown on the hour, 9 A.M. to 4 P.M. (Modest extra charge to view the film.) A 1-hour, self-guided walking tour that starts on the terrace of the visitor center covers the fighting of the First Battle of Manassas. A 13-mile, self-guided driving tour of the Second Battle of Manassas is also available. Bird watching, hiking trails, and educational programs are also available. Grounds open daily, dawn to dark. Visitor center open daily in summer, 8:30 A.M. to 6 P.M.; rest of year, 8:30 A.M. to 5 P.M. Visitor center closed Thanksgiving and Christmas. Admission charge. Telephone: (703) 361-1339. Web site: www.nps.gov/mana. For more details about the battles, click on the "In Depth" button on the right side of the Web site.

Warrenton is the county seat of Fauquier (pronounced "Faw-keeer") County, established in 1759 in honor of Lt. Gov. Francis Fauquier on what was then the frontier of English civilization in Virginia. By the time of the Revolution, a settlement had grown up, and in 1790 the Court House was built on its present location, a jail was erected, and an academy named in honor of General Warren was founded. During the Civil War it was the center of the almost unbelievable exploits of the "Gray Ghost" of the Confederacy, Colonel John Mosby and his partisan raiders. Warrenton later became notable for its large horse and cattle farms. In 1888 the Warrenton Hunt was established, and in 1900 the Warrenton Horse Show, now nationally famed as the "Hunter Show of America." The first Virginia Gold Cup Race was run in the spring of 1922. This is a timber race that annually attracts people from all over the United States.

The white-column building, known as the **Old Courthouse,** with its spire and clock, dominates the ancient crossroads where the town began. From its portico the visitor has one of the finest views in the area. The present building (1893) is a replica of its predecessor (1841) adapted from the original eighteenth-century Court House. John Marshall was first licensed to practice law on this historic spot, as were many other notable barristers including Samuel Chilton, U.S. Congressman and defender of John Brown.

A few steps behind the Court House on Main Street is the former county jail, a brick and stone building that serves as a museum with an interesting collection of Fauquier County memorabilia, including Indian artifacts and a Col. John S. Mosby exhibit. The front portion of the **Old Jail Museum** dates from 1808 and is now headquarters for the Fauquier Historical Society. The rear structure (c. 1822) is one of few perfectly preserved old jails with its original cells and exercise yard for prisoners. Open Tuesday through Sunday, 10 A.M. to 4 P.M. Free admission. Other points of interest to the tourist may be found in the brochure *A Walking Tour of Warrenton, Virginia.* Contact the Fauquier Historical Society, P.O. Box 675, Warrenton, VA 22186. Telephone: (540) 347-5525. Web site: www.fauquierhistory.com/. Click on "Old Jail Museum."

The walking-tour brochure and additional information about local events and points of interest are also available from the Warrenton-Fauquier Visitor Center, P.O. Box 127, 183A Keith Street, Warrenton, VA 20186. Telephone: (540) 341-0988. Web site: www.visitfauquier.com.

A drive north on Route 17 will bring visitors to Route 50 where a right turn is made to **Upperville,** a small village surrounded by many magnificent estates and horse breeding farms. A stop may be made at **Trinity Episcopal Church.** It was completed in 1960 after five years of careful study and painstaking work by local craftsmen who were assisted by artists and specialists from many parts of the world. The church contains stained-glass windows made in Europe and fine carvings. It is an example of late Norman architecture, built of sandstone quarried in Virginia. To visit weekdays, stop by the office, 9 A.M. to 4 P.M. Sunday Services, 8 A.M. and 11 A.M. (8 A.M. and 10 A.M. in summer). Telephone: (540) 592-3343. Web site: www.trinityupperville.org.

One of the primary fund-raising events for this special church is the annual Stable Tour, a ticketed event that enables visitors to tour horse farms in the surrounding countryside that are usually closed to the public. Held on Memorial Day weekend. Web site: www.huntcountrystabletour.org/tour.htm.

The Upperville Colt and Horse Show, "the oldest horseshow in America," takes place annually for a week at the beginning of June. Check these Web sites for polo matches in the region and other events involving horses: www.middleburgonline.com and www.visitfauquier.com.

Eight miles east on Route 50 is **Middleburg** in Loudoun County. The unofficial capital of the "Hunt Country," Middleburg was first known as an overnight stagecoach stop, located midway between Alexandria and Winchester. Today, many visitors are attracted to this picturesque community and its many elegant events. Such activities as the Virginia Fall Races, a picturesque annual steeplechase event held at Gleenwood Park, and the Middleburg Wine Festival, combine with Middleburg's unique shops and fine restaurants to make it an interesting place to visit. Check these Web sites for a full range of events: www.middleburgonline.com or www.co.loudoun.va.us.

To continue the circular driving tour, go east on Route 50 to Route 15 and turn left (west) toward Leesburg. In about a mile, you will reach Aldie Mill, 39401 John Mosby Highway. The four-story brick mill built by the Mercer family in 1807 is now restored and open weekends for tours and demonstrations. Admission charge. Open late April through October, Saturday, noon to 5 P.M.; Sunday 1 to 5 P.M. The Mill also hosts an art show in June and a Harvest Festival in October. Telephone: (703) 327-9777. Web site: www.nvrpa.org/park/aldie_mill_historic_park.

Leesburg Area

Oak Hill, President Monroe's home, is visible to the west from Route 15 as you drive to Leesburg, just before the Little River crossing. It is Loudoun County's most prestigious landmark and was designed and built circa 1821 under the direction of Monroe's friend Thomas Jefferson. The home contains many items that were used by President Monroe. Lafayette, in appreciation of Monroe's hospitality in 1825, sent two lovely marble mantels. The famous Monroe Doctrine is said to have been written here. Oak Hill is a private residence, not open to the public. Web site: www.jamesmonroe.net.

Oatlands, 6 miles south of Leesburg on Route 15, (just beyond the bridge over Goose Creek) is a Greek revival mansion built (1803) by George Carter, great-grandson of Robert ("King") Carter. The magnificent gardens contain several sandstone slabs that have the footprints of dinosaurs. The home, gardens, and 261 acres of beautiful countryside have been deeded to the National Trust for Historic Preservation. Oatlands hosts many special events, such as Spring Point-to-Point races and other equestrian events, sheepdog trials, herb and garden shows, and special exhibits of art and handiwork, as well as concerts throughout the season. Open April 1 to December

30, Monday through Saturday, 10 A.M. to 5 P.M.; Sunday, 1 to 5 P.M. Admission charge. Telephone: (703) 777-3174. Web site: www.oatlands.org.

Two miles beyond Oatlands on the left side of Route 15 is a county landmark, **Mountain Gap School,** one of the oldest one-room schools in Loudoun. The tiny school sits alone on a spur of the old road between Leesburg and Oatlands, and serves as a reminder of a way of education as it was before the turn of the century. It was purchased from the County School Board by the late Wilbur C. Hall, who restored the building to the style of 1885. It is now owned by the National Trust for Historic Preservation. Hours vary. Inquire at the Loudoun Museum and Information Center. Telephone: (703) 777-7427. (See listing below.)

Rokeby is located east of Route 15, on Route 650. It is a private residence, not open to the public but visible from the road. Rokeby was built about 1754 and has been extensively remodeled. It is of considerable historic significance because the Declaration of Independence, the Constitution, and other federal papers were kept here secretly in a basement vault in August 1814 when the British sacked Washington.

Originally called Georgetown in honor of King George II, **Leesburg** was chartered by the English Crown in 1757 to have 70 one-half acre lots and six streets. Shortly thereafter a bill was introduced to rename Georgetown to Leesburgh (now Leesburg), in honor of Thomas Lee. Leesburg takes you through two centuries of American history with authentic buildings of diverse architecture. The town has been designated as a Historic District by the Virginia Landmarks Commission. Its brick-lined streets abound with antique shops, specialty stores, and a wide variety of restaurants.

Loudoun County, which was known as "the bread basket of the Revolution," has more historic districts than any other county in Virginia. For additional information, contact or visit the Loudoun Convention and Visitors Association, 222 Catoctin Circle, SE, Suite 100, Leesburg, VA 20175-3732. Open daily, 9 A.M. to 5 P.M. Telephone: (703) 771-2617 or (800) 752-6118. Web site: www.visitloudoun.org.

The **Loudoun Museum and Information Center,** 16 West Loudoun Street, features local artifacts, as well as an orientation video, and walking-tour brochures. Exhibits range from evidence of Native American residents' life in the area 15,000 years ago through the Revolutionary, Civil War, and Victorian eras and include a restored eighteenth-century log cabin. On the third weekend of August, down-town Leesburg serves as the site of August Court Days. This street festival celebrates the opening of the eighteenth-century judicial court with more than 200 Colonial reenactors, mock trials based on historical records, Colonial militia, Royal troops, frontiersmen, as well as crafts, entertainment, and displays. Open Monday through Saturday, 10 A.M. to 5 P.M.; Sunday, 1 to 5 P.M. Telephone: (703) 777-7427. Web site: www.loudounmuseum.org.

The **Court House,** located at the intersection of Routes 7 and 15, was built in 1894-95 on the site of an original brick structure built in 1757. The handsome old elms surrounding the courthouse were witness to many important visitors—George Washington, James Monroe, John Q. Adams, General Lafayette, and Patrick Henry. Many interesting oil portraits hang on the courthouse walls. Open as a working court Monday through Friday, 9 A.M. to 5 P.M.

Fendall House, an office building at 109 Loudoun Street, was formerly Osburn's Tavern, built about 1795. **Laurel Brigade Inn,** 20 West Market Street, is on Route 7, one-half block off Route 15. It was built on an original lot laid out in 1758. Among famous guests at this historic inn were General Lafayette and Pres. John Q. Adams. During the Civil War the inn served as a hospital.

Morven Park, operated by the Westmoreland Davis Memorial Foundation, is located just west of Leesburg off Route 7 on Old Waterford Road. It features a Greek Revival-style mansion on a 1,200-acre estate with magnificent boxwoods. It evolved from a fieldstone farmhouse built in 1781 by Maj. Thomas Swann, father of Gov. Thomas Swann of Maryland, who died here in 1880. During the Civil War, Confederate troops were based at Morven Park. It was purchased in 1903 by Westmoreland Davis, who later became governor of Virginia. In addition to the magnificent mansion, extensive formal gardens and nature trails, there is a carriage museum in which over 100 horse-drawn vehicles are on display, and the Museum of Hounds and Hunting. Throughout the year many equestrian events are held on the grounds and at the International Equestrian Center. Foremost of these activities is the Fall National Hunt Steeplechase races. Open daily, first Saturday in April to early December, Friday through Monday, tours on the hour, noon to 4:00 P.M.; call for Christmas tour dates. Admission charge. Telephone: (703) 777-2414. Web site: www.morvenpark.org.

Even the most seasoned traveler will succumb to the charm of quaint old Waterford, originally settled by Quakers. To reach **Waterford,** go seven miles northwest of Leesburg on Route 698 (old Waterford Road) or three miles north on Routes 7 and 9 and then right two miles on Route 662. A Friend's Meeting was established in the settlement in 1733, and in 1775 a permanent Meeting House was built. In this building originated what George Washington called the "Loudoun Method of five-year crop rotation." In 1780 the small village received its name from Waterford, Ireland.

The Waterford Foundation is a nonprofit organization dedicated to fostering early crafts, restoring the eighteenth-century mill town to its original state, and fending off encroaching development that threatens the character of the historic village. The foundation also sponsors the **Waterford Homes Tour and Crafts Exhibit,** held each October. Waterford homes are open to the public at that time. Artisans and members of craft guilds from Loudoun and adjacent areas offer their products for sale. Demonstrations of handicrafts are staged, and area artists exhibit. Other times of the year, homes may be enjoyed from the streets on a self-guided stroll. Virtual tour available on the Web site. Telephone: (540) 882-3018. Web site: www.waterfordva.org.

The suggested picturesque tour route home to Baltimore or Washington is back through Leesburg with a short visit at Ball's Bluff Cemetery and a crossing of the Potomac River at White's Ferry.

Ball's Bluff National Cemetery, the smallest National Cemetery in the U.S., marks the site of the fourth armed engagement of the Civil War. On October 21, 1861 four Union regiments of Gen. Charles Stone's division, under the command of Colonel Edward D. Baker, U.S. Senator and personal friend of President Lincoln, suffered catastrophic losses at the hands of the Confederate forces. At the top of this steep bluff, Col. Baker was killed and over half his men were either killed, wounded or captured during this short engagement. Another casualty of this battle was a young lieutenant of the 20th Massachusetts, O. W. Holmes, who, upon recovering, later became U.S. Supreme Court Justice Oliver Wendell Holmes. The tragedy that occurred here was the result of what has been referred to as "a classic example on how assault troops should not cross a river." The cemetery is open year-round, with signs for self-guided touring. Booklets describing the battle are available at the Loudoun Museum and Information Center. Free guided tours at Ball's Bluff on weekends, early May through October. Saturday at 11 A.M. and 2 P.M.;

Sunday, 1 P.M. and 3 P.M. For additional information, telephone (703) 737-7800. Web site: www.nvrpa.org/park/ball_s_bluff.
White's Ferry is four miles north of Leesburg off Route 15 on Route 655. The last ferry boat still in operation on the Potomac is named for a famous Confederate general, Jubal Early. Gens. Jeb Stuart and Robert E. Lee crossed the river here with their armies during the Civil War. Beginning around 1833 at what was then known as Conrad's Ferry, passengers and freight were transported across the quarter-mile-wide Potomac River by means of poling a small boat. By 1920 a hay baler engine was used thus allowing two automobiles to cross at the same time. Today the *Gen. Jubal Early* transports up to six cars by a little diesel-powered tug and continues to make its daily crossings. Passengers find quick-and-easy access to and from western Montgomery County, Maryland. Service is offered seven days a week, 5 A.M. to 11 P.M. (except when there are unusually high waters). On the Maryland side there is a store and a scenic picnic area. Bike rental for touring the C & O Canal is also available. The ferry lands at mile marker 35. Toll charge for crossing. Telephone (in Maryland): (301) 349-5200. Web site: www.virginia.org/Listings/OutdoorsAndSports/WhitesFerry/.

Culpeper and Orange Counties

Culpeper, about halfway between Washington and Charlottesville on Route 29, figured prominently in both the Revolutionary and Civil wars. Residents of this charming town were among the first to join the cause at Williamsburg in 1777. Ninety years later, it was a sad example of the many towns split by the Civil War—one moment serving the North, another the South.
The **Culpeper Cavalry Museum** at 803 S. Main Street has exhibits of the largest cavalry battle of the war, the Battle of Brandy Station. Open Monday through Saturday, 11 A.M. to 5 P.M., November through April; Sundays only, 12:30 P.M. to 4 P.M. Closed weekdays May through October. Free admission. Telephone: (540) 829-1749. Web site: www.culpepermuseum.com.
The **Burgandine House,** the oldest in Culpeper (c. 1749), is on S. Main Street next to the library. Contact Culpeper Cavalry Museum for more information and hours. For house history, click on Burgandine on museum Web site: www.culpepermuseum.com.
For addition information about local history and attractions, contact or visit the Culpeper Visitors Center, 109 S. Commerce Street.

Telephone: (888) CULPEPER or (540) 825-8628.
Web site: www.visitculpeperva.com.

The **Roaring Twenties Antique Car Museum,** south of Culpeper on Route 230 near Madison, offers a large collection of antique automobiles. Open by appointment only. Best time to visit is May through October. Admission charge. Telephone: (540) 948-6290. Web site: www.roaring-twenties.com.

Orange County, northeast of Charlottesville, has long enjoyed a national reputation for its outstanding beef and dairy cattle and horse farms. It is also well known for its handsome estates and magnificent gardens. Near Gordonsville, on Route 33 about 15 miles east of Route 29, is **Montebello,** the birthplace of Zachary Taylor. Historians believe the 12th president of the United States was born in a log building which is now a guesthouse on the estate. Montebello is not open to the public, but a roadside marker commemorates the site. Web sites: www.townoforangeva.org or www.visitorangevirginia.com.

James Madison, fourth president of the United States, made his home at **Montpelier,** built in 1760 and located six miles west of Orange, one mile off Route 20, at 11407 Constitution Highway, Montpelier Station, VA 22957. Open daily for house tours April through October, 9:30 A.M. to 5:30 P.M.; November through March, 9:30 to 4:30. Closed New Year's Day, first Saturday in November, Thanksgiving, and Christmas. Admission charge. The Montpelier Hunt Race, held on the grounds on the first Saturday in November, is one of the most respected steeplechase events in the county. Telephone: (540) 672-2728. Web site: www.montpelier.org.

In Orange proper, the **James Madison Museum,** 129 Caroline Street, presents exhibits on Madison's life from his early youth and education to his death, emphasizing his role in securing religious freedom and later in drafting the Constitution. Reflecting Madison's interest in agrarian reform, the museum also features exhibits tracing the development of agriculture during Madison's life, the beginnings of mechanized farming, and the advances that have taken place since his death. Open year-round, Monday through Friday, 9 A.M. to 5 P.M.; March through November, Saturday, 10 A.M. to 5 P.M. and Sunday, 1 to 5 P.M. Closed New Year's, Thanksgiving, and Christmas. Admission charge. Telephone: (540) 672-1776. Web site: www.thejamesmadisonmuseum.org.

Six miles east of Orange on Route 20 is a stone marker and bronze tablet in Leland Memorial Park. It commemorates the site of a meeting between Madison and the Baptist preacher, Leland, which resulted in the religious freedom clause in the Bill of Rights.

Charlottesville Area

Charlottesville is distinguished historically not only by the imprint left upon the city and the surrounding area by Thomas Jefferson, but also as the home of Pres. James Monroe and other illustrious Americans.

One of Charlottesville's principal attractions is the **University of Virginia.** Founded and designed by Thomas Jefferson, the University of Virginia has developed Charlottesville into one of Virginia's major cultural centers. Begin your tour at the "Academical Village," which is crowned by the **Rotunda,** a white-domed building clearly visible to the right off Main Street. This structure, the last designed by Thomas Jefferson who modeled it after Rome's Pantheon, occupies the northern end of the Lawn, the original college rectangle. Tours begin here year-round (except exam time and during school holidays). The Rotunda has some interesting exhibits. Open daily, 9 A.M. to 5 P.M. Free admission. Call or visit Web site for schedule of guided tours of the university.

The **Lawn** is a unique feature of the grounds. White-column professors' quarters line either side, along with lodgings for undergraduates. Paralleling the lawn, and 300 feet to the rear of these buildings, are some lodgings for graduate students. The lovely gardens between these homes are enclosed with serpentine brick walls. The University's **Bayly Museum,** on Rugby Road, can provide additional information. A map of the entire campus is available in the Rotunda. Telephone for historical tour information: (434) 924-7969. Web site (which features a slide show): www.uvaguides.org.

Signs will direct you to The University (for which "the" is typically capitalized by local custom) about two miles west of Charlottesville's Downtown Mall on Main Street. The Downtown Mall has been restored as a pedestrians-only area, complete with restaurants, boutiques, and special events. Additional Web sites: www.virginia.edu/exploring.html or www.cvillechamber.org or www.charlottesville.org.

The **Albemarle County Court House** (1803) is located on Court Square. It is open daily, closed weekends and holidays. Jefferson's will may be seen in the County Office Building. Nearby, in Jackson Park, is the equestrian statue of Stonewall Jackson by Charles Heck.

For more about local history and sites, contact the **Charlottesville Albemarle County Visitors Center** at either of two locations: 200

Second Street, NE, Charlottesville, VA 22902-5245 or on Route 20, just south of the city, off I-64 exit 121, near the road leading to Monticello. Telephones: (toll free) (877)-386-1103; (main office) (434) 293-6789; (434) 295-2176. Web site: www.visitcharlottesville.org.

Monticello, the mountaintop home of Pres. Thomas Jefferson, located 10 minutes from Charlottesville on Route 53, was designed and constructed by him beginning in 1768. In addition to many unique architectural features, the house contains a number of Jefferson's inventions and possessions. He oversaw every aspect of the furnishing of his house. Nearly all the furniture and other objects at Monticello today were owned by Jefferson or his family, reflecting a lifetime of collecting. The house is equipped with a variety of gadgets, suggested by similar devices that Jefferson had seen on his travels. Contrivances such as the seven-day calendar clock in the entrance hall, the single-acting double doors in the parlor, and the dumbwaiters and revolving serving door in the dining room indicate his love of mechanical ingenuity. A revolving reading stand enabled him to have open books on four subjects simultaneously. Jefferson's grave is just below the house. The Thomas Jefferson Memorial Foundation has accurately restored the house, gardens, grounds, and central group of buildings situated on the 658-acre estate. Open March 1 to October 31, 8 A.M. to 5 P.M.; November 1 to February 28, 9 A.M. to 4:30 P.M. Closed Christmas Day. Admission charge. Telephone: (434) 984-9800. Web site: www.monticello.org.

Ash Lawn-Highland, two miles beyond Monticello on Route 795 (1000 James Monroe Parkway), is the charming plantation home of Pres. **James Monroe.** His friend and neighbor, Thomas Jefferson, participated in the planning of the gardens and house, which was originally called Highlands. Its magnificent boxwood garden is among the loveliest in the state and its ancient trees are particularly outstanding. Numerous special events take place throughout the year, including Summer Music Festival, Plantation Days, Christmas festivities, and other cultural events. Admission charge. Open daily April 1 through October, 9 A.M. to 6 P.M.; November 1 through March 31, 10 A.M. to 5 P.M. Telephone: (434) 293-8000. Web site: www.ashlawnhighland.org.

Historic Michie Tavern is a handsomely furnished colonial tavern with an exhibit building offering visitors a striking picture of pre-Revolutionary War life in Virginia. It is located en route to Monticello, one mile southeast, on Route 53. Open daily, 9 A.M. to 5 P.M. Last tour, 4:20 P.M. Admission charge. The **Ordinary,** a converted log slave house used over 200 years ago, serves a Colonial buffet from 11:30 A.M. to 3 P.M. Telephone: (434) 977-1234. Web site: www.michietavern.com.

About 30 minutes west of Charlottesville is Wintergreen Resort, located on 11,000 acres in the heart of Virginia's Blue Ridge Mountains. Wintergreen is a true four-season destination. In addition to year-round golf and tennis, the resort features skiing and snowboarding, an indoor spa and fitness center, 30 miles of hiking trails, conference facilities, nature and family programs, four restaurants, and more than 300 lodging options. Telephone: (434) 325-2200. Web site: www.wintergreenresort.com.

For more information about the Charlottesville area, contact the **Charlottesville-Albemarle County Convention & Visitors Bureau.** Telephones: (toll free) (877)-386-1103; (main office) (434) 293-6789, (434) 295-2176, or (804) 296-1492. Web site: www.visitcharlottesville.org.

Lynchburg Area

About 50 miles southwest of Charlottesville on Route 29 is Lynchburg. Now a city of almost 70,000 people, it dates back to 1757, when John Lynch, a Quaker, built a ferry house here. A town sprung up on his estate, thanks to its proximity to the James River, and Lynch later built the country's first tobacco warehouse. Because Lynchburg served as a supply base for the Confederate army, it suffered a major battle on June 18, 1864. Web site: lynchburgonline.com.

The Lynchburg Museum in the restored Old Court House at 901 Court Street has exhibits of the city's past. Open daily. Closed Thanksgiving, Christmas Eve, Christmas, New Year's, and municipal holidays. Admission charge. Children under 12 free when accompanied by adult. Telephone: (434) 455-6226. Web site: www.lynchburgmuseum.org.

On Cabell Street is the striking Point of Honor, a restored house-museum built in 1815 by Dr. George Cabell, Sr., a friend of Patrick Henry. A remarkably sophisticated example of early nineteenth-century architecture, the house displays an unusual octagon bay façade and finely crafted interior woodwork. Point of Honor combines fine craftsmanship with the Adam-style designs by Owen Biddle of Philadelphia and England's William Paine. With the addition of an authentically re-created plantation kitchen, the Bertha Green Webster Carriage House, and historical landscape sponsored by the

Garden Club of Virginia, Point of Honor provides a unique look back at one of Virginia's most exciting historical eras. Open same hours as the Lynchburg Museum. Admission charge. Telephone: (434) 455-6226 . Web site: www.pointofhonor.org.

At Patrick Henry's last home (1794-99) and burial place, **Red Hill,** the Patrick Henry National Memorial (1250 Red Hill Road in Brookneal) is a restored eighteenth-century plantation honoring this well-known American patriot. The shrine and museum are five miles east of Brookneal, off Route 600, and 35 miles southeast of Lynchburg (follow Route 501). Henry's favorite tree, the oldest Osage orange in the United States, still thrives on the grounds. A 15-minute orientation video will help orient you before touring Red Hill's seven historic buildings. Among the annual special events are a Fourth of July, Revolutionary-era reenactment and a Christmas open house. Open November to March, daily, 9 A.M. to 4 P.M.; April through October, 9 A.M. to 5 P.M. Closed Thanksgiving, Christmas, and New Year's. Admission charge. Telephone: (434) 376-2044. Web site includes a virtual tour: www.redhill.org.

East of Lynchburg about 20 miles on Virginia Route 24 is **Appomattox Court House National Historical Park.** It is a revered shrine of both armies of the Civil War. A total of 27 buildings and sites have been restored or reconstructed to resemble their appearance in 1865. On April 9 of that year, General Lee surrendered the pitiful remnants of the once mighty Confederate Army of Northern Virginia. Gen. Ulysses S. Grant, through his generous terms, won the enduring respect of the South.

At the 1,320-acre park you may visit the reconstructed **McLean House,** where the surrender papers were signed, the **County Jail,** kitchen, guesthouse, and **Clover Hill Tavern.** An interesting event at Appomattox is the living history demonstration where uniformed "soldiers" give first-hand accounts of their impressions and experiences of the final days of the Civil War. The courthouse serves as park museum and headquarters and includes a theater where two, different, 15-minute slide shows are presented on an hourly schedule. Open daily, 8:30 A.M. to 5 P.M. The visitor center is closed Thanksgiving, Christmas, and New Year's. Admission charge. On the edge of the park is the little village of Appomattox, much of which has been restored. Allow at least two hours to tour the village. Telephone: (434) 352-8987, ext. 226. Web site: www.nps.gov/apco.

A number of interesting parks are located in the area surrounding

Appomattox. Fishing requires a valid Virginia fishing license. More information about the following parks can be found on the state Web site, and camping reservations may be made online: www.dcr.virginia.gov/state_parks/state_park.shtml. **Holliday Lake State Park** is approximately 12 miles from the Appomattox Courthouse National Historical Park on Route 24 between Appomattox and Route 60, deep within the **Buckingham-Appomattox State Forest.** It features a 150-acre lake and is a popular place for camping, hiking, swimming, boating, bass and trout fishing, backpacking, and evening campfire programs. The visitors center has exhibits on the history of the park, as well as information on park services and resources. Open Memorial Day to Labor Day, daily, 6 A.M. to 10 P.M.; September 1 through December 1, from dawn to dusk. Charges for some activities such as boating, cabin rental, and parking. Campgrounds reservations: (800) 933-7275; information: (434) 248-6308.

Twin Lakes State Park and the Cedar Crest Conference Center (a day use facility) are located south of Farmville and Rice, about 25 miles east of Appomattox off Route 360 at 788 Twin Lakes Road in Green Bay, Virginia. Seven cabins and one lodge overlook the large lake with its white sand beach surrounded by forest. A modern bathhouse, diving tower, parking area, hiking trails, and picnic ground with tables, barbecue grills and shelter provide comfortable facilities for large and small groups. Reservations: (800) 933-7275; information (434) 392-3435. Five miles away, off Route 460 (about midway between Petersburg and Appomattox Court House, take Route 617 to **Sailor's Creek Battlefield Historic State Park,** where a quarter of Lee's army was captured by Gen. U. S. Grant in the last major battle of the Civil War. The park has reenactments and interpretive programs offered throughout the year. Many hiking trails, no overnight facilities. Telephone: (804) 561-7510.

Another state recreation facility is **Bear Creek Lake State Park,** which is located within Cumberland State Forest, off Route 60. The Park's 326 acres and 40-acre lake have facilities for camping, hiking, biking, boating, fishing, swimming, and evening programs. Concession stands in the summer; 53 tent sites and RV hook-ups. Campground reservations: (800) 933-7275; information: (804) 492-4410.

BLUE RIDGE MOUNTAINS AND SHENANDOAH VALLEY

The two major thoroughfares that traverse the area are I-81 and

Skyline Drive. From Richmond, take I-64 west to Waynesboro, then north or south on Skyline Drive; or continue west on I-64 to Staunton, then north on I-81 to Winchester. From Washington take I-66 west to Front Royal or Route 50 west to Winchester and I-81. From Baltimore, I-95 to Washington and proceed as above.

The Valley of Virginia extends southwestward through the state, nestled between the Blue Ridge and the Shenandoah Mountains. It begins at Harper's Ferry, and ends at the Tennessee line, 360 miles away. **Shenandoah Valley,** its northern and best-known section, is 160 miles long and 10 to 20 miles wide. This picturesque valley is flanked by wooded ridges, 3,000 to 5,000 feet in elevation. The area is devoted to farming with apple orchards predominant in the northern portion. Routes 81 and 11 run the length of the Valley. Good roads penetrate the "gaps" which make easy access at six points between Winchester and Lexington.

The tours described in this section begin at Winchester in the north and proceed southward as far as Natural Bridge and Roanoke. Five or more trips should be planned in order to visit all of the major scenic, historic, and recreational places of interest in the valley. For an overview of area attractions and locations of visitor centers, contact the Shenandoah Valley Travel Association: Telephone: (toll free) (877) VISITSV or (540) 740-3132. Web site: www.visitshenandoah.org. For an on-line overview of historical sites, click on "Attractions," then "History & Heritage" at the following Web site, then search by region in the Blue Ridge Mountains and Shenandoah Valley areas: www.virginia.org.

Winchester Area

Winchester, at the northern end of the Shenandoah Valley, was once Shawnee Indian camping grounds, to which Pennsylvania Quakers and Germans came to settle in 1732. It is the oldest city west of the Blue Ridge Mountains. Thomas Lord Fairfax, proprietor of a 5-million-acre royal grant, employed George Washington in 1749 to survey lands in what is now Frederick County. During Washington's four years in this area, he had his office in a small building at 32 West Cork Street. During the **French and Indian War,** Winchester was a center of defense against Indian raids. In 1755 Washington was a young colonel commanding Virginia troops here, with headquarters in his old survey office. This building is open to the public as a museum, April 1 through October 31, Monday through Saturday, 10

A.M. to 4 P.M.; Sunday, noon to 4 P.M. Admission charge. Telephone: (540) 662-6550. Web site: www.winchesterhistory.org. Winchester was a strategic prize of great importance during the Civil War, and the scene of Stonewall Jackson's military exploits. In Confederate hands, it was a serious threat to the National Capital and to the supply lines of federal armies trying to reach Richmond. In the hands of the Union Army, Winchester made Confederate raids and invasion of the north risky; it opened a protected avenue for Union troop movements, south through the Valley, a threat to Lee's main armies. The area was the scene of six battles during the Civil War, and the city itself changed flags 70 times during the four-year conflict.

In Winchester the visitor today will see many other relics of the area's history. **Abram's Delight,** the oldest home in Winchester, was built by Isaac Hollingsworth in 1754. His father, Abraham Hollingsworth, was an early Quaker settler who declared the spot, with its abundant springs, "a delight to behold." He built a log cabin on the property that is typical of the homes of early settlers. The stone house has been restored and furnished and is open daily, April 1 to October 31, Monday through Saturday, 10 A.M. to 4 P.M.; Sunday, noon to 4 P.M. Admission charge. Located at 1340 S. Pleasant Valley Road. Telephone: (540) 662-6519.

After visiting Abram's Delight, turn right on Pleasant Valley Road, then left at the light onto Cork Street. Continue on Cork to Cameron Street, then, at the light, turn right to 305 E. Boscowen Street, **Mount Hebron Cemetery.** The ruins to the left of the entrance are the **Old Lutheran Church,** built in 1764. Inside the cemetery, near the Lutheran Church ruins, is the grave of the Revolutionary hero, Gen. Daniel Morgan, who earned his fame as the hero of the Battles of Saratoga and Cowpens. There is also the **Stonewall Cemetery,** where more than 1,000 Confederate soldiers, 829 of whom are unknown, are buried under one large mound.

Passing again the Old Lutheran Church ruins and through the front entrance of Mount Hebron Cemetery, turn right and continue to Woodstock Lane. Proceed right on Woodstock Lane and turn left to Lincoln Street. The **National Cemetery,** established in 1866, is located to the right. Here 4,491 Union soldiers are buried, 2,396 of them unknown.

Continue for one block and turn left again to Piccadilly Street. On the right side of Piccadilly Street is the **Old Stone Presbyterian Church.** Built in 1788, the church has been restored by the First Presbyterian

Church of Winchester and is open to the public. Gen. Daniel Morgan was a member of this church. Free admission. Call First Presbyterian Church for hours and access. Telephone: (540) 662-3824.

Proceed to North Avenue, turn left for one block and turn left again to 415 N. Braddock Street. Watch for a sign indicating **Stonewall Jackson's Winter Headquarters.** The building is set back on the right. Jackson and his staff occupied this home from November 1861 to March 1862 prior to his valley campaign. The headquarters is a memorial to Winchester's role during the Civil War. Open April 1 through October 31, Monday through Saturday, 10 A.M. to 4 P.M.; Sunday, noon to 4 P.M. The rest of the year, open Friday and Saturday, 10 A.M. to 4 P.M.; Sunday, noon to 4 P.M. Admission charge. Telephone: (540) 667-3242. Web site: www.winchesterhistory.org.

At 135 North Braddock is the **Logan House,** which now houses Kimberly's, a store featuring baby products and accessories. Note the huge apple, which signifies Virginia's importance in apple production. **Gen. Philip H. Sheridan** used this building as his headquarters in the fall and winter of 1864-65 and from it, on October 19, 1864, made his famous ride to Cedar Creek, where he turned a Confederate victory into a rout. The building is now the home of the local Order of Elks and is not open to the public.

Continue south on Braddock Street and turn right to the **Glen Burnie Historic House and Gardens** at 801 Amherst Street. This 25-acre estate, the homesite of Winchester founder James Wood and six generations of his descendants, is made up of beautiful gardens and a historic house filled with art and antiques. There are 14 unique gardens, numerous fountains, enchanting garden follies, and a historic cemetery. Also on the grounds is the **Museum of the Shenandoah Valley,** a new 55,000-square-foot structure that will interpret three centuries of life in the Shenandoah Valley. An orientation video sets the stage for a tour. Open April 1 through October 31, Tuesday through Saturday, 10 A.M. to 4 P.M.; Sunday, noon to 4 P.M. Call about winter hours. Admission charge. Telephone: (540) 622-1473 or (888) 556-5799. Web site: www.glenburniemuseum.org.

Return to Boscawen Street. In the churchyard of **Christ Episcopal Church** at 114 W. Boscowen lie the remains of **Thomas Lord Fairfax.** Visitors are welcome. Telephone: (540) 662-5843.

Located between Winchester and Strasburg on U.S. 11, with exits to Interstate 81, **Middletown** is nestled in the heart of the historic Shenandoah Valley. Meals and lodging are available at the elegantly restored **Wayside Inn,** 7783 Main Street. Built in 1797, Wayside is the "oldest continuously operating inn in America." Reservations are required for the 22 rooms. Telephone: (540) 869-1797 or (tollfree) (877) 869-1797. Nearby attractions include historic tours, golf, fishing, caverns, hiking, and a host of other outdoor attractions. Web site: www.alongthewayside.com.

Near the inn, at 7853 Main Street, is the **Wayside Theater,** the second-oldest professional theater in Virginia. The season runs year-round, offering 8 productions in various genres. Telephone: (540) 869-1776. Web site: www.waysidetheater.org.

Belle Grove, about a mile south of Middletown on U.S. Route 11, is a one-story structure of hewn limestone, built by Maj. Isaac Hite, Jr., in 1794. It served as headquarters for Gen. Philip Sheridan during the Civil War, and many interesting historical episodes occurred there. Belle Grove has been restored by the National Trust for Historic Preservation as a working farm and American folk-culture center. Several types of tours are offered, including one that is followed by "a stylish afternoon tea." Belle Grove is open Monday through Saturday, April through October, 10 A.M. to 4 P.M.; Sunday, 1 to 5 P.M. Admission charge. Telephone: (540) 869-2028. Web site: www.bellegrove.org.

Front Royal

Front Royal is 16 miles south of Winchester via Route 522. The vast Shenandoah National Park begins at the southern limits of town.

Front Royal was the home of Belle Boyd, the celebrated Confederate spy, and the **Warren Rifles Confederate Museum** is located here at 95 Chester Street. Open April 15 to October 31, Monday through Saturday, 9 A.M. to 4 P.M.; Sunday, 12:30 P.M. to 4 P.M. By appointment the rest of the year. Admission charge. Telephone: (540) 636-6982, 635-2219, or 635-3463. Web site: vaudc.org/museum.html.

Skyline Caverns features rainbow and brook trout in a cavern stream, a 37-foot waterfall, snow-white flowstone and unique "anthodites," flowerlike calcite formations, among other geological oddities. Picnic facilities are available, and there is a miniature railroad. Open daily, except Christmas; first daily tour at 9 A.M. Admission charge. Telephone: (800) 296-4545. Web site: www.skylinecaverns.com.

A few miles southeast of Front Royal off Route 522 is the **Smithsonian Institution's Conservation and Research Center.** A 3,200-acre annex to Washington's National Zoological Park is located in the Blue Ridge

Mountains about 75 miles west of Washington. Here scientists study the ecology of native wildlife and habitats within the Appalachian ecosystem. The center is not open to the public, but all kinds of animals can frequently be seen from the road. Don't be surprised when you look out your car window and see camels and zebras grazing in the Virginia countryside. To learn more, visit the center's Web site: nationalzoo.si.edu/SCBI/default.cfm.

Nestled in the mountains one-half mile north of Strasburg on Route 11 are the 250 wooded acres of **the Wayside Foundation of American History and Arts, Inc.,** a public nonprofit organization. The area includes three sites and links to other attractions in the area. First is **Crystal Caverns at Hupp's Hill,** discovered in 1755, the oldest-documented and northernmost show cave in Virginia. Located in Strasburg at 33231 Old Valley Pike. Admission charge. Telephone: (540) 465-5884.

The **Museum of American Presidents,** 130 North Massanutten Street in Strasburg, contains an impressive display of presidential portraits, signatures, artifacts, and memorabilia from a 60-year private collection. Admission charge. Telephone: (540) 465-5999. Web site: www.waysideofva.com.

The **Stonewall Jackson Museum at Hupp's Hill** serves as an interpretive center for the Civil War in the Shenandoah Valley. It exhibits Jackson's 1862 Valley campaign with a fine collection of Civil War artifacts and hands-on reproductions. Admission charge. Telephone: (540) 465-5884.

The Wayside Museums are open Monday through Saturday, 10 A.M. to 5 P.M.; Sunday, noon to 5 P.M. Closed New Year's Day, Easter Sunday, Thanksgiving, and Christmas. Admission charge. Web site: www.waysideofva.com.

Off Route 81 in Edinburg are the **Shenandoah Vineyards,** the oldest winery in Virginia. You can join a free wine tasting or stroll through the vineyards and winery. Open daily, 10 A.M. to 6 P.M.; January through February, 10 A.M. to 5 P.M. Need a minimum of 10 for tours. Closed New Year's Day, Easter, Thanksgiving, and Christmas. Free admission. Telephone: (540) 984-8699. Web site includes links to all other Virginia wineries: www.shentel.net/shenvine.

Basye is a small community perched on the edge of the George Washington National Forest and is the home of one of the larger Virginia ski operations. **Bryce Mountain** is on the western edge of the Shenandoah Valley, located near Orkney Springs, where the Annual Shenandoah Valley Music Festival is held in late July. The acreage includes a 45-acre lake with a beach and an 18-hole championship golf course. It is almost due west from Washington and is reached from Mt. Jackson (U.S. Route 11 or I-81) via Virginia Route 263. This mountainous area has an average of 90 inches of snowfall, which, coupled with Bryce's snow-making installation, makes it a popular winter as well as summer resort. Telephone: (540) 856-2121. Web site: www.bryceresort.com.

Shenandoah Caverns are just off I-81, exit 269, or U.S. 11, midway between Mt. Jackson and New Market. Shenandoah Caverns' distinction is its sparkling "diamond," glittering masses of flowstone shot with crystals, truly reflecting the name Shenandoah, "Daughter of the Stars." It also features a unique elevator service and animated window displays celebrating America. Admission charge. Open spring and fall, 9 A.M. to 6 P.M.; winter, 9 A.M. to 4 P.M.; summer 9 A.M. to 7 P.M. Telephone: (540) 477-3115. Web site: www.shenandoahcaverns.com.

At Exit 68 on Interstate 81, you will find **Tuttle & Spice General Store and Free Village Museum.** A vast and unique collection of early Americana items are on display in 10 separate turn-of-the-century shops: toy store, drug store and soda fountain, clothing store, clock, jewelry and lamp shop, tobacco shop, doctor's office and an educational exhibit of American Indian art and artifacts. There is a large gift shop and hundreds of general store items in the main building. Open daily, 9 A.M. Closing hours vary by season from 4:15 P.M. in winter to 6:15 P.M. in early summer. Admission charge. Telephone: (540) 477-3115 or (toll free) (888) 4-CAVERN. Web site offers discount on admission fee: www.shenandoahcaverns.com.

New Market to Luray

New Market is located at the junction of Routes 81, 11, and 211, in the heart of the Shenandoah Valley, 15 miles west of Luray. Here, where Indian trails crossed, the town was established in 1765 by Gen. John Sevier, who was Governor of Tennessee six times and also U.S. Senator from Tennessee.

The New Market area was the scene of Civil War battles that were featured in Gen. Stonewall Jackson's Valley campaign. Here the young Virginia Military Institute cadets made their famous charge on May 15, 1864. The **New Market Battlefield Park** is located one mile north of the town. The well-preserved, 260-acre battlefield park and its monuments are visited each year by thousands of students of the Civil War. Visitors can trace the path of the V.M.I. cadets and see the restored, historic Bushong House and its nine dependencies. From the battlefield there are scenic overlooks 200 feet above the Shenandoah River. Each year, on the weekend closest to the anniversary of the battle, which is May 15, the Battle of New Market is reenacted before crowds of observers.

The impressive **Hall of Valor,** a visitor center and museum, displays exhibits that depict the entire Civil War. In its two-story Virginia Room there are three-dimensional exhibits and a panoramic survey of all the major campaigns of the War. Two award-winning films are also shown. The park is open daily year-round, except New Year's Day, Thanksgiving, Christmas Eve, and Christmas, from 9 A.M. to 5 P.M. Admission charge. Telephone: (866) 515-1864. Web site: www2.vmi.edu/museum/nm/hov.html.

The **Shenandoah Valley Travel Association Information Center,** at 277 West Old Cross Road, New Market, is open daily, 9 A.M. to 5 P.M., for free information and literature about tours and points of interest in the Shenandoah Valley. Closed Thanksgiving, Christmas, and New Year's. It is just off I-81, exit 264. Telephone: (540) 847-4878. Web site: www.visitshenandoah.org.

Luray Caverns, at 970 U.S. Highway 211 West, is one of the largest and most popular caves in the eastern United States and is a major Virginia natural wonder. Special lighting has been installed to enable visitors to photograph the interior of this cavern with any type of camera. Guided tours allow time in the itinerary for those wishing to take pictures. The Great Stalacpipe Organ permits visitors to hear the only organ in the world playing musical selections of concert quality on stone formations.

Another interesting attraction on the grounds of Luray Caverns is the **Car and Carriage Caravan,** a museum featuring nearly 100 carts, carriages, and cars in the story of transportation. There is a general admission charge that includes both caverns and caravan. Open daily at 9 A.M., closing varies with the season. Admission charge. Telephone: (540) 743-6551. Web site: www.luraycaverns.com.

The **Luray Singing Tower** nearby has a 47-bell carillon. Carillon recitals are given on Tuesdays, Thursdays, Saturdays, and Sundays, from April 1 to mid-November. The tower is located at the intersection of Highway 211 and Route 340 bypass.

Shenandoah National Park

The 194,596-acre **Shenandoah National Park** stretches along the crest of the Blue Ridge Mountains from Front Royal south to

Waynesboro, VA. It features more than 500 miles of foot trails, 40 kinds of mammals, 200 species of birds, with elevations ranging from 600 to 4,000 feet. About 95 percent of the park area is forested. Set in the heart of the Blue Ridge Mountains of Virginia, its most celebrated features are the succession of panoramas from the crest of the ridge, enabling visitors to view the checkerboard beauty of the Shenandoah Valley.

The **Skyline Drive** ribbons its way through the park for 105 miles, providing 72 overlooks along the way for views of the Piedmont to the east and the Shenandoah River Valley to the west. From Hogback Overlook on a clear day, one may count 11 bends in the river and see panoramic views of the fertile valley areas where Indian villages once stood. Shenandoah National Park is open year-round. Occasionally Skyline Drive is closed for short periods during periods of ice and snow. Some visitor facilities such as camping, picnic areas, food, lodging, and service stations are open March through December. Big Meadows campground is open all year, and lodge and cottage accommodations are available from April through October.

Dickey Ridge Visitor Center (Mile 4.6) and **Harry F. Byrd, Sr. Visitor Center** (Mile 51) provide general park information, exhibits, orientation films, postcards, maps, back-country camping permits, and Eagle and Golden Access Passports. Dickey Ridge and Byrd are open daily during the season. Telephone: (540) 999-3500. Web site: www.nps.gov/shen.

Picnic facilities with tables, fireplaces, water, and toilets are found at Dickey Ridge (Mile 4.6), Pinnacles (Mile 36.7), Big Meadows (Mile 51), Lewis Mountain (Mile 57.5), South River (Mile 62.8), and Loft Mountain (Mile 79.5). Open fires are permitted in fireplaces, but wood is not always available. Visitors are advised to bring their own fuel.

All lodging, food facilities, gift shops, and service stations in the Shenandoah National Park are operated by ARAMARK, P.O. Box 727, Luray, VA 22835, with whom reservations should be made by visitors desiring overnight lodge, cabin, or hotel accommodations. Telephone: (888) 896-3833. Web site: www.visitshenandoah.com.

Shenandoah National Park has over 500 miles of trails, including 101 miles of the Appalachian Trail. Many trails are accessed from Skyline Drive. Some short trails lead to a waterfall or viewpoint; longer and more difficult trails penetrate deep into the forest and wilderness.

Many naturalist-led nature walks and programs are conducted on trails throughout the park. Check program schedules in the "Shenandoah Overlook," at visitor-information desks, or on bulletin boards. Camping in the back country is allowed by permit only. Permits are available at entrance stations, visitor centers, park headquarters, or trailhead self-registration stations. Campers must demonstrate knowledge of park camping regulations.

There is a series of 3-sided, trail-side camping shelters, each sleeping between 7 and 11 people, 12 to 20 miles apart along the Appalachian Trail. These huts are operated by the Potomac Appalachian Trail Club and are intended for use by long-distance Appalachian Trail hikers or campers with back-country permits for three or more days. Cabins are located in back-country areas of the park. These cabins will accommodate as many as 12 people and are fully equipped, except for food. Reservations may be made by contacting the Potomac Appalachian Trail Club. Telephone: (703) 242-0315. Web site: www.patc.net.

Entrance fees to Shenandoah National Park are per vehicle, per hiker, bicycle, or bus passenger over 12 and under 62 years of age. This fee is good for seven consecutive days. An annual Park Pass is available at entrance stations or at park headquarters.

George Washington National Forest

The largest national forest in the eastern United States, George Washington National Forest, a recreational area of more than one million acres, lies to either side of the well-known Shenandoah National Park and is within easy driving distance of the Baltimore-Washington-Richmond areas. The forest embraces three mountain ranges in western Virginia and part of West Virginia—the Blue Ridge, Massanutten, and Shenandoah Mountains. Visitors come here to enjoy picnicking, camping, fishing, hiking, backpacking, water sports, hunting, and nature study. Many come simply to enjoy the quiet scenic beauty away from the noise, bustle, and pollution of the cities.

For convenience of visitors, there are 13 developed campgrounds and numerous picnic areas. Many early historic sites are preserved. Of six iron furnaces, two, Elizabeth and Catherine Furnaces, are easily accessible and worthy of a visit. Many hikers visit the remnants of **Signal Knob,** an observation point used by both sides in the Civil War. There is good blueberry picking along the trail in midsummer.

Among spectacular natural phenomena are caves, rock slides, and "lost" rivers. There is **Ramsey's Draft Wilderness,** over 6,500 acres of old growth timber, including oak, hemlock, and other species spared from the woodman's ax. In the fall, thousands visit the forest to view the spectacular colorful foliage and to avoid the traffic jams in nearby Shenandoah National Park. Plan your forest trip carefully. Request copies of maps, historic and descriptive booklets, and a list of developed recreational sites, all obtainable from the National Forest Headquarters, 5162 Valleypointe Parkway, Roanoke, VA 24099. Telephone: (800) 832-1355 or (404) 347-4095. Web site: www.southernregion.fs.fed.us/gwj. You can also get more detailed information about fishing, hiking, food and supply sources, motels, historic sites, etc., by writing the District Ranger's Office in the area you plan to visit. Browse the Web site listed above or call the listed numbers.

Harrisonburg to Lexington

The Harrisonburg to Lexington route is a continuation of the tour of the Valley of Virginia, which began at Winchester. Routes 81 and 11 are the main arteries. Intersecting main east-west roads are Route 33 at Harrisonburg, Route 250 at Staunton, and Route 60 at Lexington.

Harrisonburg is the home of James Madison University and Eastern Mennonite College. A visitor center is located at the corner of North Main and East Gay Street in downtown Harrisonburg. Open daily, 9 A.M. to 5 P.M. Telephone: (540) 432-8935. Web site: www.harrisonburgtourism.com.

Just 10 miles east of Harrisonburg, on Route 33, is **Massanutten Resort,** a four-season resort that offers activities from golf to skiing, mountain biking to fishing, and antique shopping to arts and crafts. One of the more popular attractions is the snow-tubing facility. There are hotel accommodations and condominium rentals available. Telephone: (540) 289-9441. Web site: www.massresort.com.

Grand Caverns, at 5 Grand Caverns Drive, were the first discovered in Virginia and are situated near the town of Grottoes at the junction of routes 340 and 256. Open to the public since 1806, Grand Caverns is historic as well as scenic. Stonewall Jackson quartered his troops in the Grand Ballroom, so named because dances had been held there over the years. Its unique shield formations, projecting from the walls, are of special interest. Open daily, 9 A.M. to 5 P.M. Admission charge. Telephone: (540) 249-5705. Web site: www.grandcaverns.com.

Mount Solon is the locale of the **Natural Chimneys,** at 94 Natural Chimneys Lane. The park name comes from seven massive towers of colorful stone that rise majestically for more than 100 feet above their naturally tunneled bases. Formed under an inland sea in the Cambrian Period of the Paleozoic Era, at least 500 million years ago, one "chimney" stands 107 feet high and leans from the perpendicular 13-and-one-half feet, nearly the same as that of the Leaning Tower of Pisa. Admission charge. Telephone: (540) 350-2510.

The park offers camping facilities, including use of water and electricity (limited December through March). There is a camping charge. The park is the home of the oldest continuously held sporting event in the United States, the annual Jousting Tournament, first held in 1821. There are picnicking facilities, a pool, a camp store, a playground, a gift shop, and nature and bicycle trails.

Staunton, 24 miles south of Harrisonburg, on routes 11 and 81, is scenically situated in the heart of a prosperous agricultural, commercial, and educational area. Mary Baldwin College and Stuart Hall are located here. There are two visitor centers in the area. The Staunton Visitors Center at the New Street Parking Garage is open daily 9:30 A.M. to 5:30 P.M., November through March, and 9 A.M. to 6:30 P.M. April through October. Telephone: (540) 332-3971. The Staunton-Augusta Travel Information Center is located at the Frontier Culture Museum, exit 222 off of I-81. Open daily, 9 A.M. to 5 P.M. Closed Thanksgiving, Christmas, and New Year's. Telephone: (540) 332-3972 or (800) 332-5219. Web site: www.visitstaunton.com.

The goal of the **Frontier Culture Museum,** 1290 Richmond Avenue, on the outskirts of Staunton, is to "bring the past to life" by showing how people of various farming heritages lived and worked and raised their families. The museum currently includes 4 farms on its 80 acres, each built with original materials. The four farms are German, English, Irish, and early American.

Plans are currently underway to double the size of the state-owned museum, adding an eighteenth-century American-Indian hunting camp, a pioneer farm, and a West African model, as well as indoor exhibits. The projected date for completion of the $10.5 million expansion is 2007. The museum will continue to be open daily, 9 A.M. to 5 P.M.; winter hours (December 1 to mid-March) 10 A.M. to 4 P.M. Closed Thanksgiving, Christmas, and New Year's Day. Admission charge. Telephone: (540) 332-7850.
Web site: www.frontiermuseum.org.

Woodrow Wilson Birthplace is where the 28th president of the United States was born in what was then the Presbyterian Manse at 24 North Coalter Street. The dignity and simplicity of the furnishings and the appealing nursery never fail to charm the visitor to this national shrine. A documentary film on the life of President Wilson is shown. The garden at the rear of the house was restored by the Garden Club of Virginia. Open March through October, 10 A.M. to 5 P.M., Monday through Saturday; 12 P.M. to 5 P.M. Sundays; November through February, 10 A.M. to 4 P.M., Monday through Saturday; 12 P.M. to 4 P.M. Sundays. Closed Thanksgiving, Christmas, and New Year's Day. Admission charge. Telephone: (540) 885-0897. Web site: www.woodrowwilson.org.

Waynesboro, 11 miles east of Staunton, is an industrial city at the foot of the western slope of the Blue Ridge Mountains, the southern entrance to Shenandoah National Park, and the northern entrance to the Blue Ridge Parkway. It is beautifully located in the rolling plain of the Shenandoah Valley, with rich farmlands surrounding it. The Waynesboro Tourism Office is located at 301 West Main Street in downtown Waynesboro. Open daily 8 A.M. to 5 P.M. Telephone: (540) 942-6644. Web site: www.waynesboro.va.us/tourism.html.

Lexington is 34 miles south of Staunton, on Routes 11 and 81. This charming old town is the seat of two of Virginia's most distinguished colleges. **Washington and Lee University** was founded in 1749 and later took the name of Washington upon its endowment in 1782 by George Washington. Robert E. Lee served as its president, following the surrender at Appomattox, and at his death in 1870 his name was added. The **Lee Chapel,** in which Robert E. Lee is buried, contains many famous works of art associated with George Washington and Robert E. Lee. Open April 1 through October 31, Monday through Saturday, 9 A.M. to 5 P.M.; Sunday, 1 to 5 P.M.; and November 1 through March 31, Monday through Saturday, 9 A.M. to 4 P.M., Sunday, 1 to 4 P.M. Telephone: (540) 458-8768. Web site: leechapel.wlu.edu.

The **Virginia Military Institute** was founded in 1839 and is known today as the "West Point of the South." Among its distinguished faculty members was Thomas J. "Stonewall" Jackson, and it numbers among its alumni the late general George Marshall. A mural depicting the charge of the V.M.I. Cadets at the Battle of New Market and flags of all states are contained in the chapel. Retreat Parade is held each Friday at 4:15 P.M. on the V.M.I. Parade Ground during the school year. The **V.M.I. Museum,** in Jackson Memorial Hall, is open daily, 9 A.M. to 5 P.M.

Guides are available, but please call ahead. Free admission. Telephone: (540) 464-7334. Web site: www.vmi.edu/museum. The **George C. Marshall Research Museum** is a handsome structure located at the west end of the V.M.I. Parade Ground. The museum, a memorial to the General of the Armies and World War II's Chief of Staff, houses Marshall's personal papers as well as a collection of material relating to the United States military and diplomatic history. The museum is open to the public daily, from 9 A.M. to 5 P.M. Closed Thanksgiving, Christmas, and New Year's. Admission charge. Telephone: (540) 463-7103. Web site: www.marshallfoundation.org/museum/.

Stonewall Jackson House, at 8 East Washington Street in Lexington, is open Monday through Saturday, 9 A.M. to 5 P.M.; Sunday, 1 to 5 P.M.. Last tour begins at 4:30 P.M. Admission charge. Telephone: (540) 464-7704. Web site: www.stonewalljackson.org.

In and around Lexington are many other historic buildings and sites. Among them are the **"Castle"** and a number of historic churches and homes, most of which are on self-conducted tour routes. Also **Lawyers Row, Court Square,** and **Goshen Pass,** which leads, via the Virginia Byway (Route 39), to Warm Springs and Hot Springs. You can get more information on these and other sites at the Lexington and the Rockbridge Area Visitor Center, 106 East Washington Street, Lexington, VA 24450. Telephone: (540) 463-3777. Web site: www.lexingtonvirginia.com.

One of America's great natural wonders is 14 miles south of Lexington on Route 11, just off I-81, exits 49 or 50. An arch of stone, created by the action of water over millions of years, **Natural Bridge** stands 215 feet above Cedar Creek and is 90 feet long and from 50 to 150 feet wide. It was worshipped by the Indians as "the Bridge of God" long before the white man came.

About 1750, a youthful George Washington surveyed the towering stone archway, climbed up its side and cut his initials, which may be seen today. In 1774 Thomas Jefferson bought it and the surrounding 157 acres from King George III of England for 20 shillings. The grounds are open from 8 A.M. until dark. An outdoor pageant, "The Drama of Creation," a symphonic sound and light show is conducted under the bridge. Seasonal show times. Admission charge. Combination tickets that include some or all of the following attractions are available. Telephone: (800) 533-1410. Web site: www.naturalbridgeva.com.

Adjacent to the entrance to Natural Bridge is **Natural Bridge Wax Museum,** with a self-guided tour of more than 150 life replicas of folklore and personalities of early American history. Open year-round. Seasonal hours apply. Admission charge. **Natural Bridge Caverns** are open March through November. Admission charge.

Hot Springs and Warm Springs

The history of the "Springs of Virginia" is a rich and varied one—and one that reflects the development of social customs and fashions from the earliest days of the nation.

In the late 1700s, the aristocracy of Virginia discovered the pleasures of going up to the springs in the early summer and disporting in pleasant company for several months before retiring, as colder weather came on, to the Lowlands again. It was fashionable, in those days, to move from one spring to another: from the Warm to the Hot, from the Hot to the Sweet, etc., in a group composed of the highest society of the times. Originally valued for medicinal purposes, the springs became more and more sought after as centers of pleasure and activity, including gambling.

Hot Springs, where the **Homestead** has, for more than a century, catered to its discriminating clientele, was one of the most prominent of these springs in Virginia and has withstood the test of time. The Homestead is set within 16,000 Allegheny acres. It reflects a style and grandeur that may still be enjoyed in this day and time.

The Homestead provides a wealth of outlets for your energies: championship golf on three 18-hole courses, tennis on 8 courts, fishing in its own mountain streams, horseback riding, skeet and trap shooting, walks through the Virginia countryside, and an outdoor pool are among its numerous activities and attractions. During the winter season skiing and ice skating are offered.

There is a complete health spa at the Homestead, as well as an indoor pool and eight 10-pin bowling alleys. In the evening, dining, dancing, concerts, and movies are a tradition. There is a supervised playground and indoor playroom for children. Telephone: (540) 839-1766 or (800) 838-1766. Web site: www.thehomestead.com.

The **Warm Springs,** located five miles from the Homestead, were the gateway to the tour of the springs (which included White Sulphur Springs, now in nearby West Virginia). No properly mannered Virginian would have dreamed of beginning the round at any other point. The approach was from Lexington and the Goshen Pass, over what, in the present day, is Route 39, the Virginia Byway.

Life at Warm Springs centered around two covered pools and the sheltered "drinking spring." They have been preserved in their natural, if not their original, condition. The scene is not far from that which greeted the eyes of visitors even before the first Homestead was built at Hot Springs.

And perhaps most interesting of all, the same warm crystal waters fill the pools. Bathers still enjoy them in large numbers. Occasionally the pools are rented for private parties, where some of the old customs, such as floating mint juleps out to the bathers on cork trays, are still observed. There are large numbers who swear by the waters' curative properties, in addition to the many who find in them an opportunity for superlative physical luxury.

Roanoke Valley

Animals were attracted to salt deposits, giving the name "Big Lick" to the first settlement here. **Roanoke** began as a crossroads from the first movement of Indians, explorers, and settlers. Today Roanoke is the principal city in the Valley.

Scotch-Irish and Germans made their way here from Pennsylvania through the Shenandoah Valley in the 1700s, followed later by English settlers from Eastern Virginia. Salem, the first town in the Valley, was formed in 1802, and Roanoke County was formed from Boteourt County in 1838.

A new era began in 1882 when the Shenandoah Valley Railroad connected with the Norfolk and Western here and the town of Roanoke was formed from Big Lick. It became a boomtown, spurred by the coal-hauling railroad and the iron-ore industry. Because of the rapid progress it made after World War II, Roanoke is called "the Star City of the South," symbolized by a 100-foot-high neon star atop nearby Mill Mountain.

Roanoke's heritage as a crossroads for transportation and commerce is evident in the Farmers Market, where area farmers have sold their produce since the 1870s. At the corner of Campbell Avenue and First Street, SE, you will find local farmers selling produce throughout most of the year. The market is also the site of a wide variety of restaurants and boutiques.

For more information about regional attractions, you can visit the Roanoke Valley Convention & Visitors Bureau at 114 Market Street in downtown Roanoke. Telephone: (540) 342-6025 or (800) 635-5535. Web site: www.visitroanokeva.com.

Begin your tour of Roanoke with a stop at the **Center in the Square,** at One Market Square, a restored 1914 warehouse housing three museums, a planetarium, a theater, a tea room, and the Arts Council of the Roanoke Valley and is surrounded by Roanoke's historic farmers' market. Open Tuesday through Saturday, 10 A.M. to 5 P.M.; Sunday, 1 to 5 P.M. Telephone: (540) 342-5700 . Web site: www.centerinthesquare.org.

The **Science Museum of Western Virginia,** located in Center in the Square, features changing exhibits about the scientific wonders of the world. The museum offers many programs, activities, and services, including the Science Spectacular in February and the Wildflower Pilgrimage in April. The museum's centerpiece is the 120-seat **William B. Hopkins Planetarium.** Open daily Tuesday through Saturday, 10 A.M. to 5 P.M.; Sunday, 1 to 5 P.M. Admission charge. Telephone: (540) 342-5710. Web site: www.smwv.org.

Also located at Center in the Square is the **History Museum and Historical Society of Western Virginia.** The heritage of the Roanoke area unfolds before visitors in the galleries and library of the Roanoke Valley Historical Society. Exhibits document Indian life before colonial settlement, the Revolutionary and Civil wars, and Reconstruction. Of special note are the recreation of an 1890 country store and an exhibit of fashions from the 1700s to the 1940s. During the Christmas season, there is a Fantasyland Holiday display. Open year-round, Tuesday through Friday, 10 A.M. to 4 P.M.; Saturday, 10 A.M. to 5 P.M.; Sunday, 1 to 5 P.M. Admission charge. Telephone: (540) 342-8634 . Web site: www.history-museum.org.

The third museum at Center in the Square is the **Art Museum of Western Virginia,** where visitors will find a permanent collection of nineteenth- and twentieth-century American art, decorative arts, and works by Southern artists. Changing exhibitions of regional and national art are featured at the museum year-round. There is also an interactive center for both children and adults. Admission charge. Open Tuesday through Saturday, 10 A.M. to 5 P.M.; Sunday, 1 to 5 P.M. Closed major holidays. Telephone: (540) 342-5760. Web site: www.artmuseumroanoke.org.

Founded in 1963, **Mill Mountain Theater** enjoys a permanent home at Center in the Square. The theater provides year-round, live, professional entertainment in two separate theaters, a 400-seat proscenium theater and a 125-seat black-box theater. Telephone: (540) 342-5749. Web site: www.millmountain.org. After leaving Center in the Square, travel six blocks west to the **Virginia Museum of Transportation.** Located in a restored railway freight station, at 303 Norfolk Avenue, the museum actively honors Roanoke's great transportation heritage. There are displays of steam, electric, and diesel locomotives. A walk down the museum's Main Street allows visitors to discover early automotive history. Open year-round, Monday through Friday, 11 A.M. to 4 P.M.; Saturday, 10 A.M. to 5 P.M.; Sunday, 1 P.M. to 5 P.M. Closed on Mondays in January and February. Admission charge. Telephone: (540) 342-5670. Web site: www.vmt.org.

The **Harrison Museum of African Culture** is located at 523 Harrison Avenue, NW. The Harrison School building, home of the first high school for blacks in southwest Virginia, now houses the cultural center. The primary focus of the center is the documentation and preservation of black heritage in the Roanoke Valley. Art exhibits, manuscript collections, films, workshops, and dramatic presentations are open to the public. Hosts the Henry Street Festival in September and a Soulful Christmas in December. Open Tuesday through Friday, 10 A.M. to 5 P.M.; Saturday and Sunday, 1 to 5 P.M. Free admission. Telephone: (540) 345-4818. Web site: www.harrisonmuseum.org.

Visible from the market is Mill Mountain, home of **Mill Mountain Zoo,** which has been in existence since the 1950s. The park exhibits 50 species of exotic and native animals on a 3½-acre site. The zoo demonstrates the beauty of nature in many forms. It is open daily, 10 A.M. to 4:30 P.M. Admission charge. Telephone: (540) 343-3241. Web site: www.mmzoo.org.

In nearby Salem is **Dixie Caverns,** the only caverns in southwest Virginia. Admission charge. Year-round camping available. Open daily, 9:30 A.M. to 5 P.M. Telephone: (540) 380-2085. Web site: www.dixiecaverns.com.

Smith Mountain Lake State Park, southeast of Roanoke, via Route 122, is the second largest body of fresh water in the state of Virginia. It borders four counties, and is comprised of 20,000 acres of water and 500 miles of shoreline. The park encompasses 16 miles of shoreline and 1,200 acres of land. Fishing, boating, hiking, mountain biking, picnicking, and swimming available. There is a boat ramp and fishing pier. The beach has a concession stand in the summer. There are 20 cabins available for rent, and they sleep 4-6 and 6-8. Call for hours of operation of the visitor center. Telephone: (540) 297-6066. Web site: www.dcr.virginia.gov/state_parks/smi.shtml.

FREDERICKSBURG AND THE NORTHERN NECK

Fredericksburg Area

The Fredericksburg area is just off I-95 about halfway between Washington and Richmond. No community can claim a closer association with the Washington family than **Fredericksburg.** When George Washington was seven years old, his parents moved to **Ferry Farm,** directly across the Rappahannock River. This is where the story of Washington and the cherry tree took place. Also the site of where he threw (so legend says) the silver dollar across the river. During the Civil War, Union soldiers camped on the fields and crossed the river here on December 1, 1862, under heavy Confederate fire. The old ferry landing on the plantation was the site of a Union pontoon bridge that was used by the Army of the Potomac on its way to the First Battle of Fredericksburg. Open daily March through December, 10 A.M. to 5 P.M.; in January and February on Saturday and Sunday, 10 A.M. to 5 P.M. Closed New Year's Eve, New Year's Day, Thanksgiving Day, Christmas Eve, and Christmas Day. Free admission. Telephone: (540) 371-3363. Web site: www.kenmore.org/.

Besides Washington, many other illustrious names contributed to Fredericksburg's niche in the history of our nation, including Thomas Jefferson, James Madison, James Monroe, John Marshall, Patrick Henry, and Admiral John Paul Jones. Commodore Matthew Fontaine Maury, the great naval scientist who plotted the currents of the Atlantic Ocean, conducted much of his work while living in Fredericksburg. Fredericksburg sent six generals into the Continental Army. During the Civil War, it changed hands seven times and was the scene of several battles.

Start your tour at the **Fredericksburg Visitor Center** on 706 Caroline Street. You can watch a free 13-minute film on the history of the city, pick up maps for the walking tour, and get a pass good for free parking throughout Fredericksburg during your visit. Admission to most of the sites in town is free, except for eight historic homes. You can save on admission by purchasing a Hospitality Pass, good for seven homes. The visitor center is open daily, 9 A.M. to 5 P.M. Summer hours are extended. Free admission. Telephone: (540) 373-1776 or (800) 678-4748. Web site: www.visitfred.com.

A must-see on a walking tour of downtown Fredericksburg is **Hugh Mercer's Apothecary Shop,** at 1020 Caroline Street. Dr. Mercer operated this shop from 1771 to 1776. His drugstore includes a physician's office. You can see such oddities as an apothecary jar decorated from the inside, silver-plated pills, and an eighteenth-century operating room. Guides in period dress explain why you might wish to have some spider webs in your first-aid kit and why complaints might call for remedies such as a dose of ground oyster shells. Mercer served as a brigadier general in the Revolutionary War and was mortally wounded at the Battle of Princeton. Open Monday through Saturday, 9 A.M. to 5 P.M.; Sunday, 11 A.M. to 5 P.M. In December, January, and February, open 10 A.M. to 4 P.M., Monday through Saturday; noon to 4 P.M. on Sunday. Admission charge. Telephone: (540) 373-1776. Web site: preservationvirginia.org/visit/historic-properties/hugh-mercer-apothecary-shop.

At 1304 Caroline Street is the **Rising Sun Tavern,** which was built by Washington's brother Charles about 1760. About two years after the Washingtons moved out, it became a tavern. It was an early post office and stagecoach stop. Modern visitors can now sample interpretive, historical entertainment as might have been enjoyed by stagecoach travelers of days gone by. Open March 1 through November 30 on Monday through Saturday, 9 A.M. to 5 P.M.; Sunday, 11 A.M. to 5 P.M. In December, January, and February, the tavern is open on Monday through Saturday from 10 A.M. to 4 P.M.; Sunday, noon to 4 P.M. Telephone: (540) 373-1776. Web site: preservationvirginia.org/visit/historic-properties/rising-sun-tavern.

Take a left on Princess Anne Street, passing the **Baptist Church,** built in 1857. Continue to the intersection with William Street, to **City Hall.** Built in 1814, it was the site of a reception for Lafayette in 1824. It served as a market house and as the city's municipal headquarters until 1983. It is now open as the **Fredericksburg Area Museum,** featuring temporary exhibits, permanent exhibits about Fredericksburg's colorful past, and a museum shop. Open March 1 through November 30 on Monday through Saturday, 10 A.M. to 5 P.M.; Sunday, 1 to 5 P.M. In December, January, and February, the museum is open on Monday through Saturday from 10 A.M. to 4 P.M.; Sunday, 1 to 4 P.M. Admission charge. Telephone: (540) 371-3037. Web site: www.famcc.org.

A block further is **St. George's Episcopal Church and Graveyard,** at 905 Princess Anne Street. Buried in the graveyard are Fredericksburg notables, including John Dandridge, father of Martha Washington.

St. George's served as the Washington family's church. Open Monday through Saturday, 8 A.M. to 10 P.M.; Sunday, 8 A.M. to 8 P.M. Telephone: (540) 373-4133.

George Washington was initiated a Mason on November 4, 1752, at the **Masonic Lodge** No. 4, at 900 Princess Anne Street. Inside hangs an original Gilbert Stuart portrait of the country's founding father. Outside is the oldest Masonic cemetery in America. Admission charge to lodge. Open Monday through Saturday, 9 A.M. to 4 P.M.; Sunday, 1 to 4 P.M. Continue right on George Street, passing the **Presbyterian Church.** Built in 1833, in Greek revival style, it is the oldest church in Fredericksburg. Clara Barton served here during the Civil War when it was used as a hospital. Turn right on Charles Street, passing another **Masonic Cemetery,** this one dating from 1784. Continue to number 908C, the **James Monroe Museum and Memorial Library.** The building was used by Monroe as his law office from 1786 to 1789, and contains furniture he and his wife purchased in Paris, including the Louis XVI desk on which he signed the Monroe Doctrine. Reproductions of many of these pieces are now used in the White House. The library wing has over 10,000 volumes on Monroe's life. Open Monday through Saturday, March 1 through November 30, 10 A.M. to 5 P.M.; Sunday, 1 to 5 P.M. December 1 through February 28, open Monday through Saturday, 10 A.M. to 4 P.M.; Sunday, 1 to 4 P.M. Closed New Year's Eve, New Year's Day, Thanksgiving, Christmas Eve, and Christmas Day. Admission charge. Telephone: (540) 654-1043. Web site: http://jamesmonroemuseum.umw.edu/.

Continue down Charles Street, passing the old **Slave Auction Block,** to **Mary Washington's House.** "All that I am, I owe to my mother," said George Washington of his beloved mother, Mary. He bought this home and enlarged it for her. Mary happily spent the last seventeen years of her life here. In 1968, the Garden Club of Virginia restored the gardens, which remain beautifully maintained. Open Monday through Saturday, March through November, 9 A.M. to 5 P.M.; Sunday, 11 A.M. to 5 P.M. December through February open Monday through Saturday 10 A.M. to 4 P.M.; Sunday, noon to 4 P.M. Admission charge. Telephone: (540) 373-1569. Web site: http://preservationvirginia.org/visit.

The **St. James House,** at the corner of Charles and Fauquier streets, is only open to the public during Historic Garden Week and during the first week in October. The cottage was once owned James Mercer, who had partial ownership of a Revolutionary War gunnery. Telephone: (800) 678-4748.

You can continue your tour on foot or by car. The next stop is three blocks further down Fauquier at the intersection with Washington Avenue. **Kenmore** was the magnificent tobacco plantation of Colonel Fielding Lewis and his wife, Betty Washington Lewis, the only sister of George. In a listing of the 100 most beautiful rooms in America, one of Kenmore's rooms is included. The home, built in 1752, is famous for its intricate ornamental ceilings. Tea and fragrant gingerbread from a Mary Washington recipe are served to visitors in the colonial kitchen. Open daily March through December, 10 A.M. to 5 P.M. Open Saturday and Sunday in January and February, 10 A.M. to 5 P.M. Admission charge. Telephone: (540) 373-3381. Web site: www.kenmore.org.

Three monuments are along Washington Avenue. Near the river is the **Thomas Jefferson Religious Freedom Monument,** commemorating a meeting he attended in 1777 in Fredericksburg to review the laws of Virginia. The results served as the basis for the religious freedom clauses in the Bill of Rights. The **Mary Washington Monument and Grave** were built with donations given by women from all over the country. The **Hugh Mercer Monument** was given to the City of Fredericksburg by the United States in 1906 to honor this colonial doctor. Further down Washington Avenue is the **Confederate Cemetery,** where unknown Confederate soldiers from the battles around Fredericksburg are buried.

Elsewhere in the city are other important sites. Near Mary Washington College is the graceful **Brompton,** now the private home of the college's president. It served as Lee's headquarters during the Battle of Fredericksburg. A monument nearby commemorates Richard Kirkland, a man lovingly called by many the "angel of Marye's Heights." A Confederate sergeant from South Carolina, Kirkland asked, and was given permission, to give water to the thirsty and dying Union troops. The powerful monument was designed by the same sculptor, Felix de Weldon, who did the Iwo Jima Memorial in Washington.

South of Route 17, at 224 Washington Street in nearby Falmouth, is **Belmont,** the **Gari Melchers' Estate and Gardens,** an eighteenth-century 27-acre estate. The home is furnished with fine antiques. Open daily, 10 A.M. to 5 P.M. Admission charge. Telephone: (540) 654-1015. Web site: http://garimelchers.umw.edu/.

Fredericksburg and Spotsylvania National Military Park, near Fredericksburg, at 120 Chatham Lane, encompasses four Civil War battlefields: Fredericksburg, Chancellorsville, the Wilderness, and Spotsylvania Court House. On December 13, 1862, Union general A. E. Burnside's troops crossed the Rappahannock River on pontoon bridges. His attack on Lee's heavily fortified position was a disastrous and bloody failure. West of Fredericksburg were fought the Battles of Chancellorsville, April 27-May 6, 1863; the Wilderness, May 5-6, 1864; and Spotsylvania Court House, May 8-21, 1864. Throughout the park, you will see miles of trenches and gun pits, the Sunken Road, and Marye's Heights. At Chancellorsville, you may follow the route over which Jackson marched to attack the exposed right flank of Gen. J. Hooker's army. At Guinea Station is the Stonewall Jackson Shrine, the house in which he died. The **visitor center,** located at Fredericksburg, features a diorama, an electric map, and collections of arms and photographs and other relics. Maps to the various battlefields also are available. There is another visitor center at Chancellorsville. The park is open daily, 9 A.M. to 5 P.M., with expanded hours during the summer. Admission charge. Telephone: (540) 371-6122. Web site: www.nps.gov/frsp.

Also a part of the Fredericksburg Battlefield Tour is **Chatham,** a magnificent Georgian mansion built circa 1770 and once known for its luxurious gardens and extensive grounds. In 1862-64, when the Confederates utilized the Rappahannock River as their northern frontier, Union armies used this house as headquarters for federal commanders, a communications center, an artillery position, and a field hospital. It was here that Clara Barton and Walt Whitman nursed the wounded. Visitors can see five rooms of the mansion and museum exhibits as well as the grounds and garden. Open daily, 9 A.M. to 5 P.M. Closed Christmas and New Year's. Admission charge. Telephone: (540) 654-5121.

The Northern Neck

A popular Rappahannock River resort town and county seat of Essex County, **Tappahannock** was founded as a river port in 1680. Today it is an important crossroads of US 17 and US 360, gateway from Richmond to the historic Northern Neck. Among its famous old colonial dwellings is the **Ritchie House,** on Courthouse Square. Many colonial homes are nearby. An **old customhouse** (closed to the public) is still standing, as well as the first brick courthouse, the **clerk's office,** and the **debtor's prison,** all erected between 1728 and 1750.

Seven miles to the east, across the Rappahannock River, is Warsaw, seat of Richmond County. The **County Courthouse,** on the green off Wallace Street, was built in 1748, as was the nearby **Clerk's Office.** Many old colonial records and wills are stored here. Both buildings open Monday through Friday, 9 A.M. to 5 P.M. Free admission. Telephone: (804) 333-3415.

Historic Christ Church, in Irvington, was built in 1732 by Col. Robert ("King") Carter, proprietor of the Northern Neck. The church is in the form of a Latin cross, and the interior has the only original high-back pews in the state. Ornate Carter tombs may be seen outside the eastern end of the church. The Reception Center, offering a museum, guided tours, and a slide program, is open April 1 through November 30, Monday to Saturday, 10 A.M. to 4 P.M.; Sunday, 2 to 5 P.M. Closed Thanksgiving, Christmas, and New Year's. Free admission. Telephone: (804) 438-6855. Web site: www.christchurch1735.org.

Surrounded by broad meadows and commanding a superb view of the Potomac River, **Stratford Hall** remains today as it was when built by Thomas Lee around 1725-30. The Great Mansion sheltered four generations of Lees, including two signers of the Declaration of Independence, Richard Henry Lee and Francis Lightfoot Lee. One of Washington's favorite officers was the dashing "Light Horse Harry" Lee. His son, Robert E. Lee, lived here as a small boy and went on to command the Confederate Army during the Civil War.

In 1929 Stratford Hall was purchased by the Robert E. Lee Memorial Foundation, which carefully restored the Great Mansion and other buildings, while the East Garden with its eighteenth-century boxwoods was restored by the Garden Club of Virginia according to original plan. Today Stratford Hall is a completely restored, working plantation.

The four massive chimneys on the east and west wings of the Mansion are connected to form tower platforms, a rare architectural feature which makes this handsome structure unlike any other building of its period in Virginia. The mansion's attractive brick dependencies include the kitchen, wash house, and plantation office. The same type of brick, fired in an adjoining field, was used for the Ha-Ha Wall, which kept livestock off the mansion's lawns and gardens. Today, cattle are again raised on the plantation.

The Grist Mill, where cornmeal is still ground, has been rebuilt on its original foundations. Celebrated also for its ancient beech trees and great forests, the setting of Stratford affords splendid vistas of the Potomac River. Open daily, 9:30 A.M. to 4:00 P.M. Closed

Thanksgiving, Christmas Eve, Christmas Day, New Year's Eve, and New Year's Day. Admission charge. Telephone: (804) 493-8038. Web site: www.stratfordhall.org.

The 1,295-acre **Westmoreland State Park** has a water frontage of 13 miles on the Potomac River. It is seven miles north of Montross on Route 3. Visitors to the park can swim at the pool. Trees fringe the water's edge, merging with a background of picturesque sandstone cliffs. On the beach are a modern bathhouse, parking area, picnic shelters, modern sanitation, and excellent facilities for boating and fishing. A popular pastime is hunting for shark teeth on the beach. Benches located on strategic sites afford gorgeous views of the Potomac River. Located on the cliffs above the beach are 25 housekeeping cabins. The self-guiding nature trail shows how a forest restores itself on abandoned farmland. Evening programs are held two nights a week.

The park has 118 campsites and 24 cabins. Cabin reservations can be made 51 weeks ahead of time, while campsite reservations should be made 90 days in advance. Telephone: (800) 933-PARK; in Richmond, (804) 225-3867. Call the park or visit the Web site for information on hours of the park and the visitor center, which vary throughout the year. Nominal parking charge. Telephone: (804) 493-8821. Web site: www.dcr.virginia.gov/state_parks/wes.shtml.

George Washington Birthplace National Monument is on the Potomac River, 38 miles east of Fredericksburg, on Route 204 off Route 3. Here on his father's plantation, Pope's Creek, George Washington was born and spent the first three years of his life. The **Memorial Mansion** represents a Virginia plantation house of the eighteenth century. Tradition and surviving houses of the period were used as a basis for its design. It is a house of eight rooms, four downstairs and four in the half-story upstairs, with a central hallway on each floor. The bricks used in its construction were made by hand from clay obtained in a nearby field.

Situated about 50 feet from the Memorial Mansion is the **Kitchen-House,** a typical colonial-period frame kitchen built on the traditional site of the old kitchen. It has been furnished to represent a plantation cooking establishment of the period of Washington's youth. In the Colonial Herb and Flower Garden are found only those flowers, vines, herbs, and berries that were common to Virginia gardens during that period.

About one mile northwest of the Memorial Mansion, on the banks of Bridges Creek, is the site of the 1664 home of Col. John Washington and the burying ground where members of the Washington family are interred.

Across Dancing Marsh are a walking trail and a picnic area that overlooks Pope's Creek. Light refreshments and souvenirs are for sale in the gift shop at the main parking area. Monument open daily, 9 A.M. to 5 P.M. Closed Christmas and New Year's. Admission charge. Telephone: (804) 224-1732. Web site: www.nps.gov/gewa.

GREATER RICHMOND AREA AND TIDEWATER

Visitors have been coming to the Tidewater area of Virginia for nearly four centuries. Capt. John Smith started a trend when he arrived in 1607, and it's been a popular spot ever since. Richmond, the former capital of the Confederate States of America, is in the center of the Tidewater area. Flowing through the area is the historic James River which provides a stunning backdrop for the plantation country to the southwest.

Greater Richmond Area

In Hanover County, about 25 miles north of Richmond in Beaverdam, at 16120 Chiswell Lane, is **Scotchtown,** the home Patrick Henry bought at an auction in 1771. The patriot lived here for seven years while he was a delegate to the First Continental Congress and later as first governor of the independent Commonwealth of Virginia. Scotchtown was built in 1719 and was also the childhood home of Dolley Payne, who married James Madison. The home is now a registered National Historic Landmark. Open April through October, Tuesday through Saturday, 10 A.M. to 4:00 P.M.; Sunday, 1:30 to 4:30 P.M. Admission charge. Telephone: (804) 227-3500. Web site: preservation-virginia.org/visit/historic-properties/patrick-henrys-scotchtown.

Paramount's **Kings Dominion** is a 400-acre theme park located 20 miles north of Richmond and 75 miles south of Washington, DC, in Doswell, VA, exit 98, off I-95. The park features one of the largest roller coaster collections on the east coast, including the world's first air-launched coaster. The park hosts more than 2 million guests annually. In 2003 the park added the Drop Zone Stunt Tower, the tallest drop ride in North America, a 305-foot tower of thrills that promises daring riders a 272-foot descent at 72 miles per hour. For the kids, there's Nickelodeon Central, where they can get behind the wheel of their very own automobile on the Rugrats™ Toonpike, solve the day's puzzle and meet Blue™, or soar above the treetops on the Nickelodeon™ Space Surfer. King's Dominion also includes Water Works, a water park that includes a 650,000-gallon wave pool. Life-size walk-around characters include Chuckie, Tommy and Angelica from the Rugrats™, Eliza and Donnie from the Wild Thornberrys™, Dora the Explorer™, and Jimmy Neutron™ from Nickelodeon™, as well as Hanna-Barberä favorites, including Scooby-Doo™. In 2003, the park added SpongeBob SquarePants™. Summer, open daily end of May through beginning of September; fall, open Saturdays and Sundays in September and mid-October; spring, open Saturdays and Sundays, end of March through end of May. Telephone: (804) 876-5000. Web site: www.kingsdominion.com.

As the former capital of the confederacy, Richmond holds an understandable attraction for Civil War buffs. But many visitors are surprised to learn that Richmond also played a significant role in the American Revolution. In fact, a local advertising agency recently suggested that instead of "Easy to Love" (Richmond's current slogan), it might be more apt to say, "Where America began."

The basis for the claim? It was in Richmond that Patrick Henry delivered the speech that some historians say made all the difference. Up to that point, some might have viewed the conflict as a squabble between some rowdy Bostonians and their king. But once the Virginians threw in their lot, well, then you had a revolution.

Less that a hundred years later, Richmond was at the center of yet another rebellion—which locals supported by the same reasoning that led them to declare independence from King George. Between 1861 and 1865, Richmond was the capital of the Confederate States of America, making it a natural target for Union armies who hoped to capture it to end the Civil War. Three of those campaigns came within a few miles of the city. The Richmond National Battlefield Park encompasses 10 large battlefields (and several smaller ones) all around the Greater Richmond area. It includes some of the most hotly contested land in the Civil War. Here Gen. George B. McClellan's Peninsula Campaign culminated in the Battle of Seven Pines, and the famous Seven Days Battle, which embraced Mechanicsville, Gaines Mill, Savage Station, Frayser's Farm and Malvern Hill. In this area, the dashing Confederate cavalry leader Gen. J. E. B. Stuart made his famous ride around McClellan. Here, Robert E. Lee assumed command of the Army of Northern Virginia for the first time.

Tredegar Iron Works, the site of the **Richmond National Battlefield Civil War Visitor Center,** at 470 Tredegar Street in downtown Richmond along the Canal Walk, is a good starting point for tours of Richmond and the surrounding battlefields. Here you can obtain information on all the attractions in the Greater Richmond area, not just those related to battlefields. The 21 buildings that once comprised **Tredegar Iron Works,** named for an ironworks in Wales, operated day and night during the Civil War in the attempt to meet Confederate demands for artillery, ammunition, and war-related materials. In the one remaining building, three floors of exhibits and artifacts are on display, and an orientation film is shown throughout the day. Open daily, 9 A.M. to 5 P.M. Closed Thanksgiving, Christmas, and New Year's. Individual battlefields open daily, dawn to dusk. Free admission. Telephone: (804) 226-1981. Web site: www.nps.gov/rich.

Richmond's **Canal Walk** is a pedestrian path that meanders 1.25 miles through downtown Richmond from the Tredegar Iron Works along the banks of the restored and renovated Haxall Canal and the James River and Kanawha Canal. Originally envisioned by George Washington as a link to the West, the canals and the James River provide glimpses of Richmond's 400-year history. Open 24 hours a day, 365 days a year. Nearby Brown's Island, once known as the Confederate States Laboratory, is now a waterfront park used in summer as a gathering place for concerts and other special events.

Belle Isle, located in the James River west of the city, and accessible by footbridge near Oregon Hill Park, was a prison for captured Union soldiers during the Civil War. By 1863, some 10,000 men were held here. A hospital for prisoners and an iron factory also occupied the island. The men were allowed to swim in the river, and some attempted to escape in this manner. Treatment of the prisoners remains a controversial issue, as is the number of deaths on Belle Isle when it was used as a prison camp. Web site: www.censusdiggins.com/prison_bellisle.html.

Visits to the following battlefields will take you outside the city limits. If you wish to explore the downtown area in more detail before venturing outside it to explore battlefields, skip ahead to the entry identified as "Monument Avenue" and those immediately following. Otherwise, see below and proceed north of the city to Cold Harbor Battlefield.

Cold Harbor Battlefield and Cemetery, northeast of the city and five miles southeast of Mechanicsville on Route 156, is where Grant hurled his men against the Confederates in June 1864. He not only lost the battle, but nearly 6,000 of his men were killed or wounded, most of them in one violent hour. A 56-mile drive will take you on a tour of the fields of combat, the forts and intricate field fortifications, and the historic old houses on the battlefields. Begin at the visitor center, where you will see graphic exhibits.

At **Fort Harrison,** a museum and a small visitor center on Battlefield Park Road off Route 5 (open during the summer) provide background information on, and an explanation of what went on around, Richmond's defenses. Other battlefields belonging to the park include the spectacular **Fort Darling** on Drewry's Bluff, where Confederate gunners halted Union efforts to ascend the James River to Richmond; **Beaverdam Creek and Malvern Hill,** where the Confederates unsuccessfully attacked the Union forces on two separate occasions during the Seven Days Campaign; and **Gaines Mill.** A small visitor center (open only on weekends) at **Glendale National Cemetery** offers an electric map program and exhibits that interpret the final half of the Seven Days Campaign. Telephone for all of the battlefield visitor centers: (804) 226-1981. Web site: www.nps.gov/rich.

Monument Avenue in downtown Richmond has been praised as "one of America's most beautiful streets." Hurricane Isabel did considerable damage to some of the stately trees in September 2003, and the loss of any notable trees, especially those that were flourishing in a city setting, is keenly felt. But, thankfully, most residences were spared. Grand, turn-of-the-century homes, many of them lovingly restored with authentic period details, line the avenue for several miles. The "monument" in Monument Avenue refers to the statues of Richmond heroes, beginning with Confederate heroes, strategically located in the center of the avenue.

The procession begins with the dashing figure of flamboyant and much-beloved J. E. B. Stuart (complete with plumed hat) and continues with Robert E. Lee (known to some locals as "Saint Robert"), Jefferson Davis, "Stonewall" Jackson, and Matthew Fontaine Maury, the astronomer, hydrographer, and commander in the Confederate navy who was also known as the "Pathfinder of the Seas." The most recent addition to Monument Avenue's procession of worthies is tennis legend and Richmond native Arthur Ashe.

Maymont, located at 1700 Hampton Street, is a 100-acre, turn-of-the-century estate that is graced by a Victorian Romanesque mansion built in 1893. The estate also boasts a nature center and children's zoo, an extensive working carriage collection, and beautiful gardens and grounds. The river otters in the nature center are worth a trip themselves. Thanks to Plexiglass, you can watch the playful creatures swim, dive, and cavort underwater. Maymont grounds are open daily, 10 A.M. to 5 P.M. Sloping lawns and wonderful shade trees make wonderful picnic areas or places to kick back and meditate on passing clouds. Maymont House, nature center, and children's farm are open Tuesday through Sunday, noon to 5 P.M. Guided house tours every hour on the half hour; last tour leaves at 4:30 P.M. Admission charge. Call or check online for special, themed tours (such as "Below Stairs," which explains servants' roles in the house) or events (such as an annual herb festival). Telephone: (804) 358-7166. Web site: www.maymont.org.

Hollywood Cemetery, 412 South Cherry Street, is situated on hilly land bordering the James River. It is considered by some to be America's most beautiful "garden" cemetery. If visiting graves isn't usually on your list of tourist attractions, and the whole idea sounds a little stuffy, fear not. Guided tours are so animated they feel like living history. And anyone interested in landscape design or symbolic arts will find many delights. Hollywood Cemetery is the final resting place of two U.S. presidents, James Monroe and John Tyler; Confederate president Jefferson Davis; and more than 18,000 Confederate soldiers. Open daily. Telephone: (804) 648-8501. Web site: www.hollywoodcemetery.org (includes a virtual tour).

One of the best ways to experience Hollywood Cemetery is the Historic Walking Tour "Highlights of Hollywood Cemetery," offered Monday through Saturday at 10 A.M., April through October. Tour charge. Reservations for the walking tour can be made by calling the Valentine Richmond History Center at (804) 649-0711, ext. 334.

Lewis Ginter Botanical Garden, 1800 Lakeside Avenue, includes more than 30 acres of gardens designed to highlight the horticultural displays of each season and a new (2003), 16,617-square-foot glass conservatory that houses exotic and unusual plants from tropical and subtropical regions of the world. The structure is the only classical, domed conservatory open to the public in the mid-Atlantic region.

The grounds include a perennial garden, a Victorian-style garden, an exotic Asian garden, a wetland environment garden, a children's garden specifically designed to attract butterflies and birds, a study garden of daffodils and daylilies, and a conifer garden featuring dwarf conifers. Lunch and snacks may be purchased in the Garden Café, open 10 A.M. to 4 P.M.; lunch is also available in the Tea House by reservation. Other facilities and the gardens are open daily, 9 A.M. to 5 P.M. Garden Shop opens at 10 A.M., Monday through Saturday; 1 P.M. on Sunday. Closed Thanksgiving, Christmas Eve, Christmas Day, and New Year's. Admission charge. Telephone: (804) 262-9887. Web site: www.lewisginter.org.

Richmond's pivotal role as capital of the Confederate States of America during the Civil War is brought to life at the **Museum & White House of the Confederacy,** 12th & E. Clay streets. The museum houses the world's largest collection of Civil War memorabilia. The White House was home to Pres. Jefferson Davis and his family during the Civil War and has been restored to the period of their residency. The buildings are located next to each other. In the lobby of the museum, you may purchase tickets to visit the White House, the museum, or both. Open Monday through Saturday, 10 A.M. to 5 P.M.; Sunday, noon to 5 P.M. Closed Thanksgiving, Christmas, and New Year's. Admission charge. Telephone: (804) 649-1861. Web site: www.moc.org.

Just a short walk from the White House of the Confederacy, the **Valentine Richmond History Center,** 1015 East Clay Street, has collected, preserved, and interpreted the materials of the life and history of Richmond for more than 100 years. The Valentine Center offers tours of the Wickham House (1812), educational programs for the public as well as school groups, 14 different 2-hour walking tours (Hollywood Cemetery being only one), a dozen guided driving tours, and the opportunity to have a tour customized to your group's needs and interests. The Wickham House is a spectacular example of nineteenth-century Federal architecture. Tours are included with paid admission to the Valentine Richmond History Center's gallery and exhibits. Separate fees for guided walking/driving tours and courses. Open Tuesday through Saturday, 10 A.M. to 5 P.M.; Sunday, noon to 5 P.M. Telephone: (804) 649-0711. Web site: www.richmondhistorycenter.com.

The **Virginia Museum of Fine Arts,** Grove Avenue and the Boulevard, is the largest art museum in the southeastern United States. It is noted for its Fabergé holdings (including five Russian Imperial Easter eggs), its Renaissance paintings, and its art nouveau and art deco decorative arts collection. Open Wednesday through Sunday, 11 A.M. to 5 P.M. Closed New Year's, the Fourth of July,

Thanksgiving, and Christmas. Admission charge. Telephone: (804) 340-1400. Web site: www.vmfa.state.va.us.

No visit to downtown Richmond would be complete without a visit to the **Virginia State Capitol.** In 1785 Thomas Jefferson was asked to design a capitol building for the Commonwealth of Virginia, which had moved its center of government from Williamsburg to Richmond in 1780. At the time, Jefferson was serving as minister to France, and the legislators were meeting in a converted tobacco warehouse. Jefferson created a magnificent domed structure based on the design of a Roman temple. The first neoclassical public building in America, it is splendidly situated on a hill at Ninth and Grace streets.

The building is still in use, though the legislators outgrew their original chambers and now conduct their legislative business in wings that were added to Jefferson's original structure many years later. But visitors to Richmond will see the old chambers on the excellent guided tour offered several times daily at no charge. One of many notable art works on the tour—and worth a visit itself—is Jean-Antoine Houdon's exquisite life-size sculpture of George Washington, which has been in the capitol since 1796.

On April 17, 1861, the Virginia General Assembly met in the Thomas Jefferson-designed capitol and voted to secede from the Union that he had helped create. In that same capitol Robert E. Lee accepted command of the military forces in Virginia. As the war came to an end, much of Richmond was burned, but the capitol survived. Also in the Capitol Complex is the recently restored Executive Mansion, which dates from 1813 and was the residence of the governor and his family. Tours are offered Monday through Friday, 9 A.M. to 5 P.M.; Saturday, 10 A.M. to 5 P.M.; Sunday, 1 to 4 P.M. Final tour begins one hour prior to closing. Free admission; no charge for tours. Call for entrance information or visit Web site. Closed Thanksgiving, Christmas, and New Year's Day. Telephone: (804) 698-1788. For a more detailed history of the building, and an on-line virtual tour, visit the Virginia Assembly Web site: http://legis.virginia.gov/1_vis_guide/vis_welcome.html.

John Marshall built his home at 818 East Marshall Street in 1790, when he was a member of the Virginia Assembly, 11 years prior to becoming the third justice of the U.S. Supreme Court. The Federal-style brick house contains the largest collection of Marshall family furnishings and memorabilia in America. In the early 1900s the house was slated to be torn down and a high school honoring Marshall built in its place. When this plan was opposed, the house was entrusted to the Association for the Preservation of Virginia Antiquities (APVA), which restored the house and made it available for public education and viewing. To learn more about the nonprofit APVA, its mission (to preserve, interpret, and promote historic Virginia), and the properties under its protection, you can visit its Web site: preservationvirginia.org. The John Marshall House is open Tuesday through Saturday, 10 A.M. to 4:30 P.M. (last tour at 4); Sunday, noon to 5 P.M. Telephone: (804) 648-7998. Web site: preservationvirginia.org/visit/historic-properties/the-john-marshall-house On another hill, approximately one mile from the capitol, is **St. John's Church.** Built in 1742, St John's (2401 East Broad Street) is the only surviving Colonial-era building in the Church Hill District of Richmond and is home to an active, present-day Episcopalian parish. Even beyond its age, St. John's is historically significant because it was the site of the Second Virginia Convention in 1775, where, on March 23, Patrick Henry delivered his "Give me liberty or give me death" speech. In March of each year, on the Sunday closest to the anniversary of the speech, and on Sunday afternoons from Memorial Day through Labor Day, history comes to life with a reenactment of the convention and Henry's stirring speech. Call to confirm the starting time (usually 2 P.M.) and when the doors will open. Plan to arrive early; no seats are reserved. The reenactment is sometimes preceded by an organ recital that will give you a chance to soak in the ambiance of the place where some say "America really began." Richmond's oldest cemetery surrounds the church. Edgar Allan Poe's mother and other notables are buried there. If you cannot attend a reenactment, the church and cemetery are still well worth a visit. Tours are offered, Monday through Saturday, 10 A.M. to 3:30 P.M.; Sunday, 1 to 3:30 P.M. Admission charge. Telephone: (804) 648-5015, Web site: www.historicstjohnschurch.org.

Children and adults alike can explore the wonders of science at the **Science Museum of Virginia,** 2500 West Broad Street. In addition to its hands-on exhibits, the museum has an IMAX Dome theater and a planetarium. Open Monday through Saturday, 9:30 A.M. to 5 P.M.; Sunday; 11:30 A.M. to 5 P.M. Admission charge. Telephone: (804) 864-1400. Web site: www.smv.org.

The **Virginia Aviation Museum,** 5701 Huntsman Road, is a division of the Science Museum of Virginia. Located at Richmond

International Airport, this shrine to the "Golden Age of Aviation" includes an extensive collection of vintage flying machines. Call or check Web site for information about programs. Telephone: (804) 236-3622. Web site: vam.smv.org.

Another favorite spot for youngsters from ages 2 to 12 is the **Children's Museum of Richmond,** right next door to the Science Museum of Virginia, at 2626 West Broad. (They share parking lots.) The museum, recognized in 2002 by *Child Magazine* as the "11th best Children's Museum in America," features interactive learning environments, including an art studio, a climb-in model of the digestive system, a "How It Works" exhibit, a kid-sized cave, and lots of other see, do, experiment, and explore activities. Open Tuesday through Saturday, 9:30 A.M. to 5 P.M.; Sunday, noon to 5 P.M. Closed Thanksgiving, Christmas Eve, Christmas Day, and New Year's. Admission charge. Telephone: (804) 474-7000. Web site: www.c-mor.org.

The **Virginia Holocaust Museum,** 2000 East Cary Street, is dedicated to increasing "tolerance through education." Its mission includes remembering victims of the Holocaust, combating intolerance, providing educational materials on the Holocaust, and increasing public awareness and understanding of the Holocaust. The 120,000-square-foot facility, which opened at its Cary Street location in April 2003, occupies a renovated, turn-of the century tobacco factory. Many visitors have observed that from the outside the former factory looks like a concentration-camp building. Its proximity to train tracks adds to the atmosphere. Open Monday through Friday, 9 A.M. to 5 P.M.; Saturday, 2 P.M. to 5 P.M.; and Sunday, 11 A.M. to 5 P.M. Free admission. Telephone: (804) 257-5400. Web site: www.va-holocaust.com.

Richmond's **Main Street Station,** 1520 East Main Street, was built in 1901, when passenger trains were king, and has recently been restored to its rightful place: a handsome architectural landmark. A gem of the Shockoe Valley District of Richmond, the Beaux Arts masterpiece has the largest intact train trestle in the United States. Web site: www.richmondgov.com/MainStreetStation/index.aspx.

The renovation of Main Street Station is symbolic of the renaissance underway in the Shockoe District (sometimes referred to as "Shockoe Slip" and sometimes "Shockoe Bottom"), named after the creek that bordered Richmond to the west, where William Byrd, II established a warehouse in the mid-eighteenth century. Huge tobacco warehouses, factories, shop fronts, and the 17th Street Farmer's Market, which has been in continuous operation since the 1780s, made this a thriving area until tobacco companies left the city. The area has now been revitalized, and the formerly abandoned buildings given new life as restaurants, apartments, and modern businesses. For more about revitalization and preservation in the city (including Jackson Ward, mentioned in the next entry) and walking tours, contact the Historic Richmond Foundation, whose efforts have saved approximately 200 structures important to Richmond's history. Telephone: (804) 643-7407. Web site: www.historicrichmond.com.

African American presence in Richmond can be traced to 1671, when William Byrd brought black laborers with him to the frontier territory that encompassed what later became Richmond. In 1860, more than 2,500 free blacks lived in Richmond, making it one of the largest populations of free blacks in the antebellum South. Several black units fought as colored troops for the Union army. After the war, Jackson Ward emerged as a center of African American culture, business, politics, and entertainment. The area is now preserved as a historic district. The architecture features some of the finest wrought-ironwork in America.

The **Black History Museum and Cultural Center of Virginia** at 00 Clay Street is the primary source for information on Jackson Ward and other noteworthy Richmond sites with links to African American heritage. Telephone: (804) 780-9093. Web site: www.blackhistorymuseum.org.

Nearby, at 110 East Leigh Street, is the **Maggie L. Walker National Historic Site.** In spite of many adversities, Ms. Walker, an African American, founded the Saint Luke Penny Savings Bank in 1903 and was the first woman bank president in America. Her home has been restored to its 1930s appearance, with many of the furnishings from the Walker family. The site is now operated by the National Park Service. Open Monday through Sunday, 9 A.M. to 5 P.M. Telephone: (804) 771-2017. Web site: www.nps.gov/malw.

Virginia House, 4301 Sulgrave Road, off Cary Street, in the Windsor Farms section of the city, was constructed from the materials of a sixteenth-century manor house. Completed in 1929, just a few months before the historic stock-market crash that ushered in the Great Depression, the Virginia House was deeded to the Historical Society, which now maintains it and makes it available for public tours, by its owners. Grounds and gardens are open Monday through

Saturday, 10 A.M. to 4 P.M.; Sunday, 12:30 to 4 P.M. Walk-in house tours, Friday and Saturday, 10 A.M. to 4 P.M.; Sunday 12:30 P.M. to 4 P.M. Last tours one hour before closing. Other days by appointment. Admission charge. Telephone: (804) 353-4251. Web site: www.vahistorical.org/vh/virginia_house01.htm.

Agecroft Hall, a manor house built in Lancaster, England, in the late fifteenth century, was purchased by Richmonder Thomas C. Williams in 1925. He had it dismantled, shipped across the Atlantic, and painstakingly reassembled at its current location—4305 Sulgrave Road in the Windsor Farms section of Richmond. The museum and gardens are open Tuesday through Saturday, 10 A.M. to 4 P.M.; Sunday, 12:30 to 5 P.M. Admission charge. Telephone: (804) 353-4241. Web site: www.agecrofthall.com.

Southwest of Richmond, in the town of Chesterfield, at 10301 State Park Road, is **Pocahontas State Park,** one of the largest in Virginia. Within its 1,700 acres are two freshwater lakes and a variety of facilities: hiking trails, fishing and boat rentals, playgrounds, camping, cabins, lake swimming, bike paths, a self-guided nature trail, and evening programs. The **Civilian Conservation Corps Museum** has displays on the plant and animal life of the Piedmont region. Season: Memorial Day to Labor Day. Telephone: (804) 796-4255. Web site: www.dcr.virginia.gov/state_parks/poc.shtml.

Also south of the city, the 809-acre **Dutch Gap Conservation Area** features an active great blue heron rookery, tidal and nontidal marshes, freshwater ponds, open fields, a tidal lagoon, trails for hiking and biking, and scenic areas for fishing. It is known as one of the foremost birding areas in the mid-Atlantic, "an orthinologist's dream." Take exit 61B from I-95, travel east on Route 10 to the first stoplight, then north on Route 732 to Route 615, and right on Route 615 to Henricus Road. Open during daylight hours. Telephone: (804) 706-9690. Web site: www.chesterfield.gov/visitors.aspx?id=3009. Also see "Birding" in the "Special-Interest Sections" chapter of this book.

Also within the Dutch Gap Conservation area is the **Citie of Henricus,** from which Chesterfield evolved. Here, in 1611, according to the county's Henricus Park Web site, Sir Thomas Dale, following instructions from the London Company to find a more suitable location for a colony than the Jamestown site, led 350 settlers in the building of Virginia's second permanent English settlement in the New World. The location was described as "convenient, strong, healthie and a sweete seate to plant a new Towne in." It was here that Pocahontas resided at Rock Hall, the home of the Reverend Alexander Whitaker, converted to Christianity, and was courted by John Rolfe. The Citie's history also boasts the first private ownership of land and the development of the American system of free enterprise. It was at Henricus that tobacco crops were first grown and cultivated for sale in Europe and where the large self-sustaining plantations, for which Virginia is famous, found their beginnings. In addition, here the first university was chartered; the first hospital, Mt. Malady, was built and operated; and the industries of ironworks and brickmaking were first successfully practiced in the New World.

The Citie is being reconstructed. A partial reconstruction is open to the public. A visitor center with gift shop is also open. Visitors can watch living history unfold as interpreters wearing period clothing reenact life from four centuries ago, as they tend gardens, establish dwellings, and guard the Citie. The Citie of Henricus and Henricus Historical Park are operated by the Henricus Foundation. Follow above directions to Dutch Gap, then follow the signs to Henricus. Open Tuesday through Sunday, 10 A.M. to 4 P.M. Free admission. See Web site or call for information about special events. Telephone: (804) 748-1613. Web site: www.henricus.org.

Petersburg

One of Virginia's oldest and most historic cities, **Petersburg,** located 30 miles south of Richmond (exit 3 off I-95), received its name from Peter Jones, who opened a trading post with the Indians in 1645. It was here that Cornwallis organized his British troops to prepare for the Yorktown campaign. Petersburg is best known, however, as the site of the largest battleground of the Civil War. The siege of Petersburg, lasting 10 months, was the longest battle of the war. Throughout the city, you will see evidence of cotton and tobacco trade, foundries, grand old homes, and artistic heritage. Do not miss the restored areas, little shops and restaurants in Old Towne, around Sycamore and Old streets.

The city of Petersburg maintains an **Information Center** at 425 Cockade Alley in Old Town Petersburg and another at the Carson Rest area on I-95. Both centers are open 9 A.M. to 5 P.M. daily. Telephone: (804) 733-2400 or (800) 368-3595. Web site: www.petersburg-va.org/tourism/vcenter.asp.

You can pick up maps leading you to the start of the self-guided tour. Points of interest near the downtown information center are the **Court House** (1839), **Cockade Alley, Farmers Market** (1876), **Peter Jones Trading Station, Lace Iron Work, Trapezium House** (1817), and two old churches.

Old Blandford Church, at 111 Rochelle Lane, was built in 1735 and has 15 memorial windows, designed by Louis Tiffany. Soldiers of six wars rest in adjoining Blandford Cemetery, among them 30,000 Confederates. It was here in 1886 that Memorial Day began. Admission charge. Open daily, 10 A.M. to 5 P.M. Telephone: (804) 733-2396.

Centre Hill Mansion, at Centre Hill Court, completed in 1823, illustrates the elegant living of both the antebellum and postbellum eras. Later remodeling makes the house museum and its more than 25 rooms an evolution of the Federal, Greek Revival, Victorian, and Colonial revival styles. Period wallpaper, textiles, and furnishings re-create the elegance of the nineteenth century. Admission charge. Open daily, 10 A.M. to 5 P.M. Telephone: (804) 733-2401.

Farmers Bank Visitor Center, at 19 Bollingbrook Street, built in 1817, displays press and plates used to print the bank's paper currency, examples of currency, and an audiovisual account of nineteenth-century banking. Admission charge. Open daily, 10 A.M. to 5 P.M., April through October. Telephone: (804) 733-2400.

At Petersburg, the hard-pressed Confederates withstood a siege lasting from June 15, 1864, to April 2, 1865, with the two armies in almost constant contact. It was the longest siege in American history. **Siege Museum** is housed in the attractive Greek Revival Exchange Building at 15 W. Bank Street. Its exhibits explore everyday life in Petersburg before the Civil War and during the 10 long months of siege. Admission charge. Open daily, 10 A.M. to 5 P.M. Telephone: (804) 733-2404.

Just outside of town, at 1539 Hickory Hill Road, is **Petersburg National Battlefield,** which contains many well-preserved fortifications, trenches, and gun pits. Here occurred the famous Battle of the Crater, in which the Federal army exploded a huge mine beneath the Confederate fortifications but failed to penetrate the Confederate lines. A replica of the giant mortar, the **Dictator,** used to shell Petersburg is in the original location. You may visit Fort Stedman, Battery #5, and the Crater. Audio recordings at sites of interest help visualize the battles. At the **visitor center** an audiovisual presentation of the 10-month siege, as well as maps, dioramas, photographs, and displays, will give more meaning to your trip. Open daily, 9 A.M. to 5 P.M. Admission charge. Telephone: (804) 732-3531. Web site: www.nps.gov/pete.

Located at 7 Old Street, the **Petersburg Area Art League** displays works of its 750 members as well as visiting exhibitions. You can watch craftsmen at work and listen to lectures on photography, ceramics, watercolor, and oil painting. Open Tuesday through Saturday, 10:30 A.M. to 2:30 P.M.; Sundays, 1 to 4 P.M. Telephone: (804) 861-4611.

At **Fort Lee,** northwest of Petersburg off Route 36, at 1201 22nd Street, is the **Quartermaster Museum,** which houses a large collection of uniforms, insignia, rations, and flags used by soldiers from the Revolutionary War to the present. The most extensive displays relate to the Civil War. Visitors are subject to force protection procedures. When visiting the Quartermaster Museum, you must present photo identification to gate personnel at the entrance to Fort Lee and identify your destination. Open Tuesday through Friday, 10 A.M. to 5 P.M.; Saturday and Sunday, 11 A.M. to 5 P.M. Closed New Year's, Thanksgiving, and Christmas. Free admission. Telephone: (804) 734-4203. Web site: www.qmmuseum.lee.army.mil.

Historic James River Plantations

Virginia was the largest and wealthiest of the British colonies, and remained largely rural for over 300 years. Thanks to the efforts of state and local preservation groups, many of the great homes of Virginia's early years are still standing restored to their former splendor.

Along both sides of the James River you may visit plantation homes of early leaders, patriots, presidents, and others who set their mark in history. From their wharves, ships departed with tobacco and other farm products, and returned with goods needed by the colonists. The James River was a source of fish, oysters, and other seafood as well as a means of easy communication among the planters. Between Richmond and Williamsburg on Routes 5 and 10, on both sides of the James, markers guide the tourist onto roads leading directly to plantations, gardens, and old churches. Several distinctive homes are open year-round, though some are only open during Historic Garden Week (last week in April). To get from one side of the James to the other, take the Jamestown-Scotland Ferry, or the bridge at Hopewell from Route 5 to Route 10.

On the south bank of the James is the city of Hopewell. It is an outgrowth of the second English settlement in America. **Weston Manor,** off 21st Avenue along the Appomattox River, is an eighteenth-century Georgian manor with a mixture of antiques and fine reproductions. More than 85 percent of the wood flooring and molding is original. All three floors are open to the public. Open daily April through October, 10:00 A.M. to 4:30 P.M. Admission charged. Telephone: (804) 458-4682.

Web site: www.nps.gov/nr/travel/jamesriver/wsm.htm.

Also in Hopewell is **Appomattox Manor,** at the corner of Cedar Lane and Pecan Avenue. It is part of a grant patented in 1632 by Capt. Francis Eppes. The main section of the house dates from 1763; the dairy kitchen and smokehouse date from 1700. It was headquarters of General Grant from June 1864 to April 1865, when he directed his armies from the present dining room. The home was also used by President Lincoln to direct affairs of the Federal Union during his stay in City Point in 1865. A National Park Service site, visitors can view a 15-minute video as well as the parlor, library, Grant's cabi, and outbuildings. The site is open daily from 9 A.M. to 5 P.M. Admission charged. Telephone: (804) 458-9504.

Web site: www.nps.gov/nr/travel/jamesriver/app.htm.

Merchant's Hope Church, five miles east of Hopewell, at 11500 Merchant Hope Road, was completed in 1657 and is the oldest Protestant church in America still standing and used as a house of worship. It takes its name from Merchant's Hope Plantation (1635). Its interior was destroyed by Federal troops during the Civil War when it was used as a picket station. The exterior is practically the same as when built and has been declared the "most beautiful Colonial brickwork in America." A legacy left in 1657 includes a "great Bible," still in possession of the church. No set hours. Telephone: (804) 458-1356.

Brandon Church, 19 miles from Hopewell at Claremont, 18721 James River Drive, is part of the original Martin's-Brandon Parish founded in 1616. The present building was erected in 1865 to replace earlier churches. The communion silver, given to the parish by John Westrope in 1757, is displayed during Historic Garden Week. Telephone: (757) 866-8977.

Brandon Plantation, 23500 Brandon Road in Spring Grove, was designed by Thomas Jefferson, and its gardens extending to the riverfront are among the loveliest in Virginia. Cultivated since 1614, it may be the longest continuous farming enterprise in the United

States. This vast plantation was once owned by John Martin, friend of Capt. John Smith, and later by Benjamin Harrison. The estate comprises more than 5,000 acres, planted mostly in small grains and pasture. Admission charge. Gardens open daily, 9 A.M. to 5:30 P.M. House open during Historic Garden Week and otherwise by appointment only. Telephone: (757) 866-8486.

The town of Surry is the home of **Smith's Fort Plantation,** located just off Route 31. Here in 1609, Capt. John Smith built a "New Fort" to defend Jamestown directly across the river. Land was given in 1614 by Chief Powhatan to John Rolfe on the occasion of Rolfe's marriage to Pocahontas, daughter of Powhatan. Deep in what was then a hostile wilderness, in 1652, Thomas Warren "did begin to build a fifty-foot brick house." The house was restored in 1935 and furnished with authentic period furniture and furnishings. Open daily April through October, Tuesday through Saturday, 10 A.M. to 4 P.M.; Sundays, 12 to 4 P.M. Weekends only, March and November. Admission charge. Telephone: (757) 294-3872. Web site: preservationvirginia.org/visit/historic-properties/smiths-fort-plantation.

Also in Surry is **Chippokes Plantation State Park,** at 695 Chippokes Park Road. Across the river from Jamestown, Chippokes has been farmed continuously since 1616. The existing house was built about 1854, and has many original furnishings. Its gardens are resplendent with flowering crepe myrtle, azaleas, towering cedars, and gnarled paper mulberry trees. Sheep and cattle graze and soybeans, peanuts and corn are grown on the 1,683-acre plantation, which is operated by the Virginia Division of Parks. The visitors center is open year-round, Monday through Friday, 8 A.M. to 4:30 P.M. Plantation Mansion tours are offered Friday through Monday, 1 to 5 P.M. from Memorial Day to Labor Day, and on Saturday and Sundays only in April, May, September, and October, 1 to 5 P.M. Nominal parking charge. The park also offers a campground from March through November, with Olympic-sized pool from Memorial Day weekend to Labor Day weekend, and three cabins year-round. Park information telephone: (757) 294-3625. Camping reservations telephone: (800) 933-PARK. Web site: www.dcr.virginia.gov/state_parks/chi.shtml.

The north bank of the James River is dotted with equally lovely plantations, most of them along Route 5 in Charles City County. **Shirley Plantation,** 18 miles east of Richmond, at 501 Shirley Plantation Road, has been the home of the Carter family since 1723. Furnishings include the original family portraits, English silver, superb paneling, and carved walnut stairway. Shirley was the home so often visited by Robert E. Lee, whose mother was Anne Hill Carter. The present owners are the ninth generation to operate the plantation. A complete set of eighteenth-century buildings form a Queen Anne forecourt. Open daily, 9 A.M. to 5 P.M. The last tour begins at 4:30 P.M. Closed Thanksgiving and Christmas. Admission charge. Telephone: (804) 829-5121. Web site: www.shirleyplantation.com.

Berkeley, on Virginia Route 5 at 12602 Harrison Landing Road, is one of the most visited and historic of the great James River plantations. It was the site of the first official American Thanksgiving in 1619, the birthplace of Pres. William Henry Harrison, and the ancestral home of Pres. Benjamin Harrison. "Taps" was composed here in 1862. The plantation mansion was built in 1726, and its grounds include terraced boxwood gardens, a restaurant, and gift shop. Admission charge. Open daily, 8:00 A.M. to 5 P.M. Telephone: (804) 829-6018. Web site: www.berkeleyplantation.com.

Westover was built in 1730 by William Byrd II, a founder of Richmond and Petersburg, and is located at 7000 Westover Road in Charles City. It is one of the notable plantations between Richmond and Williamsburg and an outstanding example of Georgian architecture. It boasts one of the finest eighteenth-century gates made in England and the most copied doorway in America. The grounds and garden are open to the public daily, 9 A.M. to 6 P.M. House itself is open some days during Historic Garden Week and for groups of 12 or more by appointment. Admission charge. Telephone: (804) 829-2882.

Westover Church was erected in 1737. The families of William Byrd of Westover and two presidents of the United States, William Henry Harrison and John Tyler, have worshipped in this building. The earlier church of this name was on the Westover estate. In this ancient churchyard was located the oldest recorded tombstone in Virginia. Its inscription, now weathered away, bore the date 1637 in memory of Capt. William Perry. Open daily, 9 A.M. to 5 P.M. Telephone: (804) 829-2488. Web site: http://westoverepiscopalchurch.org.

Pres. John Tyler purchased **Sherwood Forest Plantation** in 1842. He doubled the size of the original house, which had been built in 1780 and today is believed to be the longest frame dwelling in the United States. The home is of the Greek Revival period and contains many effects and furnishings of the late president. Two important features are its unusual woodwork and a unique arched ceiling in the ballroom. Since 1845, Sherwood Forest has been the home of the Tyler family. The grounds are open daily, 9 A.M. to 5 P.M. Telephone: (804) 829-5377. Web site: www.sherwoodforest.org.

Belle Air plantation house, built around 1670, located at 11800 John Tyler Highway, is one of the oldest frame dwellings in America. As the only survivor of its kind in Virginia, it is an important architectural monument. Original heart pine timbers still serve ingeniously as both sturdy structure and interior decorative trim. Plainly visible are huge hand-carved summer beams, expressed sills, intermediate and corner posts, and the finest Jacobean staircase in America. Though elegant for its period, Belle Air reflects the simplicity in which even wealthy pioneer planters lived. It has been restored and beautifully decorated in fabrics and furnishings of the eighteenth century. First and second floors, smokehouse, laundry, kitchen, and herb garden are open to group tours of 20 or more by appointment. Admission charge. Telephone: (804) 829-2431. Web site: www.nps.gov/nr/travel/jamesriver/bel.htm.

Eastern Shore of Virginia

To reach the Eastern Shore of Virginia from the Capital Beltway, take exit 19 (Route 50) east across the Chesapeake Bay Bridge to Salisbury (almost 90 miles), then south on Route 13. From the Baltimore Beltway, take exit 4 (Route I-97 south) to Route 50 east, continuing as above. From Richmond, follow I-64 south to Norfolk, then take the Chesapeake Bay Bridge-Tunnel to Route 13. A Virginia welcome center is located in New Church, on Route 13, one mile south of the Virginia/Maryland state line. State Web site: www.esvatourism.org.

The original name of Virginia's Eastern Shore was "Accomack," an Indian name meaning "across the water place." It is a narrow peninsula between the bay and the ocean, with one through highway, Route 13, running down the middle from Maryland to the bridge-tunnel. The region is noted for its excellent fishing, swimming, boating, and seventeenth- and eighteenth-century historic buildings. Visitors can watch thousands of waterfowl feeding or resting in game preserves or see the wild ponies grazing on Chincoteague salt marshes.

The ancient fishing village of **Chincoteague** is reached from Route 13 via Route 175 and a causeway. Close to the Gulf Stream, it is a major fishing port with many sport-fishing boats available. A visitor center is located at 6733 Maddox Boulevard. Telephone: (757) 336-6161. Web site: chincoteaguechamber.com.

The **Oyster and Maritime Museum of Chincoteague,** at 7125 Maddox Boulevard, has live exhibits of all kinds of shellfish, including seahorses and clams, as well as maritime artifacts and implements of the seafood industry. Open daily May through September, 10 A.M. to 5 P.M.; open weekends, 10 A.M. to 5 P.M. in March, April, October, and November. Closed December through February. Admission charge. Telephone: (757) 336-6117. Web site: www.chincoteaguemuseum.com.

Refuge Waterfowl Museum is at Maddox Boulevard and Beach Road. There are exhibits of boats, weapons, traps, antique decoys, carvings, and art, all relating to the hunting of waterfowl. Open daily, except Wednesdays, Memorial Day through Labor Day. Closed January through March. Other times of the year call for information. Admission charge. Telephone: (757) 336-5800.

A free causeway takes the visitor to **Assateague Island National Seashore,** a narrow, 33-mile-long island, where you can see the wild ponies and three-foot high Sitka deer in their natural habitat. Camping and pavilions are available, and you need to make reservations for their use. Admission charge. Telephone: (410) 641-1441or (757) 336-6577. Web site: www.nps.gov/asis.

The **Chincoteague National Wildlife Refuge,** on Assateague, is an area set aside to protect wildlife and their habitat. Special emphasis is placed on protecting threatened and endangered species, such as the Delmarva Peninsula fox squirrel. Hiking, biking, fishing, and crabbing are permitted. The visitor center is open daily, 9 A.M. to 4 P.M. Closed Christmas and New Year's. Telephone: (757) 336-6122.

Six miles from Chincoteague off Route 13 is the **NASA Wallops Visitor Center Flight Facility.** Information on self-guided walking tours is available at the visitor center, where exhibits commemorate America's space program. Open Thursday through Monday, 10 A.M. to 4 P.M. Closed Thanksgiving, Christmas, and New Year's. Free admission. Telephone: (757) 824-2298. Web site: www.wff.nasa.gov.

Tangier, a get-away-from-it-all island in the middle of the Chesapeake Bay west of Chincoteague, was chartered by Capt. John Smith in 1607. Almost 80 years later, it was settled by John Crockett and his family—and little has changed since. In fact, some claim the townspeople still speak with an Elizabethan accent. You will enjoy strolling quaint, car-less streets; visiting the crab shanties at the harbor; and filling up on seafood. Web site: www.tangierisland-va.com.

The only way to get to Tangier is by boat. If you don't have your own, hop aboard one of the two regular cruise ships serving Tangier. Tangier Onancock Cruises leave from the Onancock, Virginia, at 10 A.M., returning at 3:30 P.M., daily, May 1 through October 15. Reservations required. Charge per passenger. Telephone: (757) 891-2505. Tangier Island Transportation leaves from Crisfield, Maryland, daily, departing 12:30 P.M. and returning at 8 A.M. the following morning. Additional late afternoon departures from May through October. No reservations needed. Charge per person. Children no charge when accompanied by parent. Telephone: (757) 891-2440.

Accomac, charming town and county seat, is noted for its many well-preserved federal buildings. The county was formed in 1634, one of the original "shires" of Virginia. Its most famous shrine is the **Debtor's Prison,** built in 1782. In nearby **Makemie Park** stands a monument to Francis Makemie, father of Presbyterianism in America. To him is attributed the Act of Toleration of 1699.

Onancock, founded in 1680, is the site of **Ker Place,** at 69 Market Street, built in the 1790s and now the local historical society's museum. Open Tuesday through Saturday, 10 A.M. to 4 P.M. Closed January and February, except for group tours. Telephone: (757) 787-8012.

Eight miles south, on Route 718, is **Pungoteague.** The first English-spoken play acted in America, "Ye Beare and Ye Cubb," was performed here in 1665. The third-oldest church in the country, established in 1662, stands here. The present structure was built in 1738, replacing an earlier wooden building.

Wachapreague fishing resort is on Route 180, five miles east of Route 13. The fishing season extends from April through October. Among game fish caught in the waters here are croakers, sea bass, white marlin, bluefish, and black drum. Wachapreague also claims the title "flounder fishing capital of the world."

The **Locustville Academy,** in the town of the same name, is the only survivor of the many schools built during the 1800s. This stately, white-framed building was used between 1859 and 1873. Arrangements for visits may be made by calling (757) 787-7480. Free admission.

Nassawadox was established by Quaker dissenters in the mid-1600s. Three miles to the south, just east of Birdsnest, is **Hungar's Church,** built in 1751. It is a rectangular structure of old rose brick in Flemish bond, covered with ivy. Its unique feature is a twin entrance with semicircular brick arches.

Eastville, town and county seat, dating from 1680, has several noteworthy buildings. The ivy-covered **Clerk's Office** was built in 1731. Nearby is the **Debtor's Prison** and the old whipping post. Christ Church was built in 1826, and Taylor Tavern dates back to pre-Revolutionary days.

Virginia Coast Reserve, near Nassawadox, contains about 35,000 acres of islands and salt marshes that extend to the mouth of Chesapeake Bay. The area is renowned for large concentrations of shore birds, sea birds, and migrating and wintering waterfowl. Visitors come here to see the cormorant, snow goose, egret, heron, ibis, sandpiper, and 10 species of hawk, including the rare falcon. There is a bird trail that is open to the public.

East of Oyster is **Wreck Island Natural Area,** an island some seven miles offshore that forms a link in the chain of barrier islands separating the Eastern Shore from the Atlantic. Only one-fifth of the island is high ground; the rest is salt marsh interlaced with a maze of pools and creeks. As with all the barrier islands, Wreck is a haven for flora and fauna. It is accessible only by boat from Oyster.

The **Eastern Shore of Virginia Tourism Commission** can provide additional information. Telephone: (757) 787-8268. Web site: www.esvatourism.org.

Tourists who wish to link a trip to the Eastern Shores of Maryland and Virginia with a visit to the Norfolk and Williamsburg areas should take the **Chesapeake Bay Bridge Tunnel.** Consisting of bridges, tunnels, and man-made islands, the 17.6-mile span crosses the lower Chesapeake Bay, connecting the tip of Cape Charles with the southern Virginia mainland. At the Sea Gull Fishing Pier and Snack Bar, located on the island of Thimble Shoal Tunnel (the first tunnel from the south), parking, meals and sandwiches, and bait and fishing tackle are available. Driving time from shore to shore is 20 to 25 minutes. There is a toll charge. Web site: www.cbbt.com.

JAMESTOWN-WILLIAMSBURG-YORKTOWN

This historic area can be reached by taking I-64 east from Richmond approximately 50 miles. More than 350 years of our nation's history are preserved within the span of the 23-mile-long Colonial Parkway linking three of America's greatest shrines—Jamestown, Williamsburg, and Yorktown. The river and woodland parkway moves, as did history itself, from Jamestown, the first permanent English settlement (1607), to Williamsburg, the colonial capital (1699), and from there to Yorktown, where American independence was won (1781). Crucial milestones in American history are crammed into the triangle formed by these three cities. The parkway begins at the Jamestown Visitor Center, passes near the door of the Williamsburg Information Center, and concludes at the Yorktown Visitor Center.

Jamestown

Statues of John Smith and Pocahontas welcome the visitor to the 1,500-acre **Jamestown Island,** operated by the National Park Service. This is the original site where the English landed, May 13, 1607. A tangible reminder of old Jamestown is the ancient tower with its reconstructed church, the location of the first representative legislative assembly in the New World, which met in 1619. For 92 years (1607-1699) Jamestown was the capital city of Virginia. For 13 of those years, it constituted the lone English toehold along the Atlantic seaboard. Now the National Park Service manages the Jamestown Settlement and nearby Yorktown. Web sites: www.historyisfun.org or www.nps.gov/jame/index.htm.

The first point to visit at Jamestown is the modern **visitor center** building just across the footbridge from the parking area. Interpretative theater programs and dioramas of Jamestown activities are constantly shown. In addition, many objects once used by the settlers have been unearthed from ruins and are on display. From the center a walking tour extends over the town site along the old streets and paths to the Church, the statehouse sites, and the ruins of old houses, taverns, and other buildings. The **Old Church Tower** is the only seventeenth-century ruin standing above ground at Jamestown. Paintings, markers, and recorded messages along the way describe life in the colony. The original landing site and the fort have long since been lost to the river's ebb and flow, but you can see pieces of original pottery and other seventeenth-century archaeological finds on display at Dale House. Lovely side excursions are the self-guided island loop drives through the wilderness section of the island.

Another road across a sandbar leads to **Glasshouse Point.** An isthmus, which later washed away, existed there in colonial times, when the glasshouse was built in 1608 "in the woods near a mile from

James Towne." The present house is a reconstruction, but some of the original ruins are still on the site. You can watch with fascination as craftsmen blow hot glass into bottles and pitchers with the same skill as their colleagues of 350 years ago. Examples of their work are available for purchase.

The visitor center and Glasshouse Point are open daily, 9 A.M. to 5 P.M. Closed Christmas and New Year's Day. Admission charge. Telephone: (757) 856-1200.

Nearby **Jamestown Settlement** commemorates the first permanent English settlement in the New World in 1607. The festival park was built in 1957 by the Commonwealth of Virginia as a reconstruction of that settlement. The **Old Pavilion** dramatizes the heritage transmitted from Great Britain to Jamestown, and the **New Pavilion** emphasizes the evolution of our democratic form of government from the first representative assembly held at Jamestown.

At reconstructed **James Fort,** the visitor may climb the ramparts of the palisade fort with its seventeenth-century costumed halberdier guides, pose for pictures in the stocks, and visit the thatch and clay houses similar to those in which the first settlers lived. One may watch the changing of the guard, see Chief Powhatan's Lodge, and complete the illusion by clambering aboard three little ships that are full-scale sailing replicas of the *Susan Constant, Godspeed,* and *Discovery.* Craftsmen demonstrate pottery, spinning, basketmaking, woodworking, and other colonial handiwork. Seventeenth-century farming methods are also displayed including plots of tobacco and corn.

Added attractions at Jamestown Settlement are **Mermaid Tavern,** a gift shop, and spacious picnic grounds with running water, soft drink machines, picnic tables, and benches. All exhibits are identified by labels and signs, and the Settlement provides hostesses and interpreters in the pavilions and reconstructed sites. Admission charge. Same hours as the visitor center.

Williamsburg

Many places around the country call themselves shrines of American democracy, but **Colonial Williamsburg** can accurately claim that title. It was here that such patriots as Thomas Jefferson and Patrick Henry forged ideas into ideals that became the American dream.

Today Williamsburg is restored to resemble its appearance from

1699 to 1780, when it served as capital of Great Britain's largest and most prosperous colony in the New World. During that time, it was the center of activity-political, social, economic, and cultural-in the Old Dominion. A succession of seven royal governors lived in the Palace, the symbol of the power and prestige of the Crown in Virginia. The General Assembly convened and held discussion in the Capitol. Twice a year during the "Publick Times," when the general court was in session and people were in town to conduct business, the town's population doubled and the taverns were crowded. A cross-section of Virginians went up and down Duke of Gloucester Street on foot, on horseback, and in carriages, where today's sightseers can observe various aspects of eighteenth-century life. Now they come to Williamsburg from all corners of the world not only to view the restored eighteenth-century city, but also to return home with a renewed appreciation of the precepts, ideals, and traditions upon which our democracy was founded.

Colonial Williamsburg's Historic Area portrays eighteenth-century Williamsburg as it appeared on the eve of the American Revolution. Historic trade demonstrations, dramatic vignettes, interactive programs and encounters with "People of the Past" take place at numerous exhibition sites and historic shops throughout the Historic Area. A large percentage of eighteenth-century Williamsburg was black, and there are some programs that will be of particular interest to African Americans. (Some are identified later in this section; more are discussed in the "Special-Interest Sections" chapter.) Telephone: (800) HISTORY. Web site: www.history.org.

Begin your visit at the **visitor center,** where a film will make what happened in Williamsburg come alive for you. *Williamsburg—The Story of a Patriot* is shown throughout the day. Those who visited Williamsburg a generation ago will note that the 40-minute film is the same. Few would dispute its claim as the longest-running movie in the U.S. Admission charge.

The Historic Area encompasses 90 acres of greens and gardens that range from the formal splendor of the Governor's Palace garden to the utilitarian kitchen garden of the James Geddy site. To protect the eighteenth-century ambiance, Duke of Gloucester and adjacent streets are closed to motor vehicles daily from 8 A.M. to 10 P.M.

The grounds and shops are open to the public, but to enter any of the historic buildings, you will need an admission ticket, which can be purchased at the visitor center. The ticket also entitles you to unlimited use of the shuttle buses that circle the entire Historic Area. Major exhibition buildings in Williamsburg include the **Raleigh Tavern,** a center of social and political life, where Virginia patriots met to discuss independence in open defiance of the Crown; the **Capitol,** the seat of colonial power and site of Virginia's vote for independence, May 15; **Governor's Palace,** the symbol of British authority in the colony; **Magazine and Guardhouse** (1715), from which Lord Dunmore's removal of the powder was a signal to revolution; and such unpretentious but inviting homes as **Brush-Everard House** (1717) and **George Wythe House** (c. 1760).

Throughout the Historic Area are 17 restored and reconstructed shops exhibiting more than 30 colonial crafts. They include **Anderson Forge, Boot Shop, Printing Office and Bookbindery, Millinery Shop, Silversmith Shop, Apothecary Shop, Wig Shop, Cabinet Shop, Windmill, Gunsmith, and Candle Maker.** Other important exhibition buildings are **Wetherburn's Tavern,** and the shops of the **blacksmith, cooper, pewter, music teacher, harnessmaker, and shinglemaker.**

At the **Peyton Randolph** site, historic trade carpenters have reconstructed Randolph's urban "plantation." The **James Geddy House and Foundry** is the site of an up-and-coming family business.

One of the most photographed spots in America is the **Public Gaol,** near the Capitol, with pillories and stocks for debtors and criminals. The **Sir Christopher Wren Building** (1695) is the oldest academic building in America and stands on the campus of the College of William and Mary, the second oldest college in the United States.

Also of interest is **Bruton Parish Church** (completed in 1715), the court church of the Virginia Colony. Regular services are held in this lovely church that contains the font and communion silver of the Jamestown church. The bell, installed in 1761, has rung for many historic events and may be heard each Sunday. Especially fascinating is the beautiful churchyard, which contains a number of early tombstones.

The **Public Hospital** on Francis Street was the first American institution devoted exclusively to the treatment of the mentally ill, when it was completed in 1773. Destroyed by fire in 1885, the hospital was meticulously rebuilt on original foundations after more than 12 years of research. Adjacent to the Public Hospital is the **DeWitt Wallace Decorative Arts Gallery,** a contemporary bi-level museum opened in 1985 and funded by the late DeWitt Wallace, founder of *The Reader's*

Digest. The Gallery displays a broad range of English and American decorative arts—furniture, metals, ceramics, glass, paintings, prints, maps, and textiles-dating from about 1600 through 1830. Weary visitors can find respite in the **Lila Acheson Wallace Memorial Garden,** part of the Gallery/Public Hospital complex. This contemporary formal garden, designed by British landscape architect Sir Peter Shepheard, combines permanent plantings with many seasonal ones and features native materials.

There are a number of interesting sites nearby operated by the Colonial Williamsburg Foundation. On Francis Street near the Capitol is **Bassett Hall,** the former eighteenth-century home of Mr. and Mrs. John D. Rockefeller, Jr. The family lovingly restored it during the 1930s, and it is handsomely furnished with many of their possessions and artwork. A more recent restoration was completed in 2002. Open daily, 10 A.M. to 5 P.M. Closed Wednesdays. Admission with Colonial Williamsburg ticket.

Housed in a nineteenth-century building next to the Williamsburg Inn is the largest collection of American primitive paintings and other objects of folk art in the country. The **Abby Aldrich Rockefeller Folk Art Center** is the gift of Mrs. John D. Rockefeller, Jr., who presented it to Colonial Williamsburg in 1939. Its nine galleries suggest the kind of domestic interiors in which folk art was originally displayed. Hours of operation change seasonally. Admission with Colonial Williamsburg ticket.

Carter's Grove, a James River plantation spanning nearly 400 years of Virginia history, is the site of two Colonial Williamsburg museum facilities—the **plantation mansion** and the **Winthrop Rockefeller Archaeology Museum,** a permanent exhibition of the early seventeenth-century and Native American artifacts excavated from the **Wolstenholme Town** site at Carter's Grove. Until 2005, these sites are closed to the public for a two-year assessment on the property, grounds, and programs. The popular interpretation of slave family life exhibit at Carter's Grove has been relocated to the Historic Area. For information on the reopening of these sites, call (800) HISTORY or visit the Web site at www.history.org.

During the eighteenth century, half of Williamsburg's population was black. The lives of the slaves and free blacks in this Virginia colonial capitol are presented in reenactments and programs throughout the Historic Area.

The **Other Half: A History Walk** is an hour-long walking tour that gives visitors an in-depth look at the African-Virginian experience in the eighteenth century and how the Revolution changed the face of slavery up to the Civil War. Daily tours begin at the Greenhow Lumber House ticket office, where reservations can be made.

Order in the Court allows visitors to observe or participate in reenactments of eighteenth-century court cases, some of which involved free and enslaved blacks at the Courthouse of 1770.

In the evening enjoy dramatic re-enactments, which include slave weddings, elderly enslaved Africans remembering their journey and "people of the past." For more information on program times, telephone (800) HISTORY. Web site: www.history.org.

Located three miles east of Williamsburg, on Route 60, is **Busch Gardens.** It is considered one of America's favorite theme parks, with more than 40 exciting rides and some of the world's top-rated roller coasters. Enjoy live entertainment, authentic European cuisine, and a children's adventure area, Land of the Dragons. Open weekends spring and fall; daily, from mid-May through Labor Day. Hours vary. Admission charge. Telephone: (800) 343-7946. Web site: www.buschgardens.com.

Yorktown

Leaving the Colonial Williamsburg Visitor Center, the parkway leads to Yorktown. There are scenic markers and stopping points at strategic spots along the parkway. The road hugs the riverbank for six miles and ends on the bluffs of **Yorktown Battlefield.**

All through the eighteenth century, Yorktown was a busy port. The town's "port facilities and good harbor" held a fatal attraction for the British General Cornwallis in the last major battle of the American Revolutionary War. Cornwallis and his British Army were bottled up by George Washington's allied American and French forces and were forced to surrender on October 19, 1781.

The **Yorktown Visitor Center and Battlefield** is operated by the National Park Service. Climb to the **Siege Line Overlook,** where the strategic area of the famous battle can be seen. The view affords a tremendous sweep of the harbor and toward the Chesapeake Bay where Comte de Grasse with his French fleet held the blockade of the British in Yorktown. Special exhibits at the Yorktown Visitor Center trace the story of the Town of York and events of the decisive three-week siege. On the wall is a mural that depicts the American and French Commanders as they plan the attack on the Redoubts 9 and 10. Among the displays are a partially reconstructed British frigate, bottles, and other artifacts recovered from the river bottom. A number of dioramas depict scenes of the battle, and a six-panel exhibit interprets the role of African Americans at Yorktown before, during and after the revolution. Visitor center open daily, 9 A.M. to 5 P.M. Closed Christmas Day. Admission charge. Telephone: (757) 898-2410. Web site: www.nps.gov/york/historyculture/historic-yorktown.htm. Two separate **Loop Drives** leave from the visitor center; one is seven miles long, the other is nine. Taped narration and recorders are available for rent from the bookstore. You will drive past redoubts, cannons, twisting fortifications, **Surrender Field** and by **Washington's Headquarters.** A visit to the **Moore House** will enlighten visitors about the process of surrender negotiations. Open seasonally; call for dates and hours. Admission included in battlefield fee.

Yorktown's famous citizen, Thomas Nelson, Jr., a signer of the Declaration of Independence and wartime governor of Virginia, lived in the early eighteenth-century Georgian home now called **Nelson House.** Some historians believe that the home served as Cornwallis's headquarters during the siege. The house is open daily mid-June to mid-August, from 10 A.M. to 5 P.M. During the spring and fall, the house is open 10 A.M. to 4:30 P.M. on weekends, and from 1 to 4:30 P.M. on weekdays, as staffing permits. Call for hours of operation during the winter months. Admission included in battlefield fee.

The nearby **Yorktown Victory Center** houses over 500 artifacts from the period, including maps, books, documents, currency, clothing, personal effects, and household objects. A **Children's Kaleidoscope** discovery room offers youngsters the opportunity to learn about the Revolutionary era through participatory activities. Open daily, 9 A.M. to 5 P.M. Closed New Year's and Christmas days. Admission charge. Telephone: (757) 253-4838 or (888) 593-4682. Web site: www.historyisfun.org.

North of Historical Area

North of the colonial historic area are a number of places that should interest visitors. **York River State Park,** about one and one-half miles off Route 607 at 5526 Riverview Road, has an excellent interpretive program, organized canoe trips on Taskinas Creek, and hikes through the rare and delicate ecological environment that constitutes coastal Virginia. The visitor information center has exhibits, an audiovisual presentation, playground and picnic facilities, and a boat ramp. Park and visitor center open daily, 8 A.M. to dusk. Free admission, small parking fee. Telephone: (757) 566-3036. Web site: www.dcr.virginia.gov/state_parks/yor.shtml.

Mattaponi Indian Reservation is located in King William County, 13 miles west of West Point. It consists of 125 acres. Visitors can use the wooded picnic grounds, spring, and a hard slope into the Mattaponi River that is suitable as a boat ramp. There is a museum, trading post, and craft shop, where pottery is sold. Open Saturday and Sunday, 2 to 5 P.M. Admission charge. Telephone: (804) 769-2194.

King William County Courthouse, about 18 miles from West Point, at 227 Courthouse Lane, was built in 1725 and has been in continuous use since its first occupancy. It is one of the few buildings in the nation of that date that still serves its original purpose today and is a fine example of colonial architecture. The brickwork is Flemish bond. Open Monday through Friday, 8:30 A.M. to 4:30 P.M. Closed national holidays. Free admission. Telephone: (804) 769-4947.

On Route 602 (just off Route 17), **Urbanna** is a mecca for fishing, boating, and crabbing enthusiasts who enjoy sailing and yachting on the Rappahannock and Piankatank rivers and on the Chesapeake Bay. Boat and yacht harbors abound on Urbanna Creek, Fishing Bay, at Deltaville in Middlesex County, and the area is headquarters for a large crab and oyster fleet. Throughout the season, Urbanna is a popular place for regattas, motorboat and sailing races. Each summer and early fall, local boat owners arrange fishing parties and cruises (especially to Tangier Island), and the town sponsors an Oyster Festival the first weekend in November. Sportsmen also come for the fine quail and duck hunting in the area.

Among historic buildings in Urbanna are the **Old Tobacco Warehouse,** built circa 1763, now serving as a public library, and the **Old Court House.** Other noted colonial landmarks are Rosegill, home of a colonial governor, the **Old Tavern** (1742), and **Hewick** (1675). The **Custom House** dates from about 1695.

NORFOLK-HAMPTON ROADS AREA

Reach this southeastern part of Virginia from Richmond via I-64 east about 90 miles. From Washington and Baltimore, take I-95 south and proceed as above. The seaports clustered around the mouth of the James River are only about a half hour's drive beyond

Williamsburg. The area has long been known as one of the world's finest natural harbors, and is justifiably an important entry in both history and guide books. Hampton Roads has been a major anchorage since colonial times and has extensive harbor facilities and shipyards. The term "Hampton Roads" actually refers to the roadstead or four-mile passageway through which the waters of the James, Nansemond, and Elizabeth rivers pass into Chesapeake Bay. It is often used to designate the harbors and cities that surround the area: Hampton and Newport News on the north shore, and Norfolk and Portsmouth on the south. Route I-64 and its arteries connect the various cities, and its Hampton Roads Bridge-Tunnel (toll charge) has one of the longest vehicular tunnels (nearly one-and-a-half miles) in the United States.

Hampton

First stop should be the **Hampton Visitors Center** in the Hampton History Museum at 120 Old Hampton Lane, where you can obtain information on the self-guided driving tour. Open daily, 9 A.M. to 5 P.M. Closed major holidays. Free admission. Telephone: (800) 800-2202. Web site: www.hamptoncvb.com.

The best way to get an idea of the size of the giant Hampton Roads harbor area is to take the harbor cruise, which will take you past Norfolk Naval Base and the water side of Newport News Shipbuilding and Dry Dock Company. The cruises are run by Venture Inn Charters, located at 4330-C Kecoughtan Road, Sunset Boating Center, Hampton. There is a full departure schedule that varies with the season. Telephone: (800) 853-5002 or (757) 850-8960. Web site: www.ventureinncharters.com.

Air Power Park, at 413 West Mercury Boulevard, displays vintage jet aircraft. Open daily, 9 A.M. to 4:30 P.M. Closed New Year's, Thanksgiving, and Christmas. Free admission. Telephone: (757) 726-0650 .

Old downtown Hampton, around King and Queen streets, will give you the flavor of this 350-year-old city. Stroll along the docks, visit the many fine shops, and (if you time it right) watch the fishing boats and crabbers unloading their catch.

At the corner of Queens Way and High Court Lane is **St. John's Church.** Established in 1610, it is the oldest English-speaking parish in the country. The present church was built in 1728, and the communion silver, prized possession of the parish, is from London (1618). Tours by appointment only. Free admission. Telephone: (757) 722-2567.

The **Virginia Air & Space Center** at 600 Settlers Landing Road displays the full range of America's space program. "Hands on" exhibits feature lots of buttons to press and levers to pull, a real treat for children. The center also is loaded with space vehicles, paraphernalia transported to the moon, and satellite equipment. Hours of operation: Memorial Day-Labor Day, Monday-Wednesday, 10 A.M. to 5 P.M.; Thursday-Sunday, 10 A.M. to 7 P.M.; Labor Day-Memorial Day, Monday-Sunday, 10 A.M. to 5 P.M. Closed Thanksgiving and Christmas Day. Admission charge. Telephone: (757) 727-0900.

A highlight of your visit to this area is a walking tour of **Fort Monroe,** which is located at CM 20 Bernard Road (obtain maps at the Hampton Visitor Center). Forts have occupied this land since 1609, and the present, moat-encircled facility remained a Union stronghold throughout the Civil War. It was here at Hampton Roads on March 9, 1862, that the ironclad warships, the Monitor and the Merrimack (more correctly known as the Virginia), engaged in a historic four-hour battle. Located within the old fort's walls is the **Casemate Museum,** displaying the cell that held Jefferson Davis prisoner. The ramparts provide panoramic views of the Chesapeake Bay. Open daily, 10:30 A.M. to 4:30 P.M. Closed Thanksgiving, Christmas, and New Year's. Free admission. Telephone: (757) 788-3391.

Other points of interest in the Hampton area include the 11,000-seat **Hampton Roads Coliseum; Buckroe Beach,** a family amusement and recreation area on Chesapeake Bay; **Bluebird Gap Farm,** a livestock zoo for children; **Big Bethel Battlefield,** where the first major land battle of the Civil War was fought on June 10, 1861; **Hampton University,** established 1868 and dedicated to the education of freed slaves; and **Hampton University Museum,** with an excellent collection of ethnic art.

Newport News

The main thoroughfare into **Newport News** is I-64. A good place to start your visit is the visitor center at 13560 Jefferson Avenue, Newport News, VA 23603. Telephone: (757) 886-7777 or (888) 493-7386. Web site: www.newport-news.org.

Right next door to the visitor center is the wooded **Newport News Park,** at 13564 Jefferson Avenue. The park's attractions include nature trails, picnic facilities, a playground, two golf courses, a fishing lake, archery, and 180 campsites. Newport News Park is one of the largest city/municipal parks east of the Mississippi. Open daily, dawn to dusk. Free admission, though there is a charge for campsites. Telephone: (757) 886-7912. Within the gates of Fort Eustis at 300 Washington Boulevard, Besson Hall, is the fascinating **U.S. Army Transportation Museum** depicting the extensive history of military transportation. "Nothing happens until something moves" is a military slogan that unfolds here. Exhibits feature overland vehicles, helicopters, fixed-wing aircraft, and rail systems which the Army operated in Europe, North Africa, and the Far East. One of the more unusual displays is the world's only captive "flying saucer." Fort Eustis is a limited access post. This means that you will need to stop at the Guard House near the gate and inform them of your desire to visit the museum. They will issue you a Visitor's Pass. Open Tuesday through Sunday, 9 A.M. to 4:30 P.M. Closed on all federal holidays and Easter. Free admission. Telephone: (757) 878-1115. Web site: www.transchool.lee.army.mil/Museum/Transportation%20Museum/museum.htm

The **Virginia Living Museum,** at 524 J. Clyde Morris Boulevard, interprets land, sea, and sky with native annual exhibits from bullfrog to bobcat. Daily planetarium programs and observatory viewings are available, as well as a native botanical garden. The natural history exhibits explore the area's unique habitat, while an aquarium has displays of local sea life. Open daily, 9 A.M. to 6 P.M., Memorial Day to Labor Day, and the rest of the year Monday through Saturday, 9 A.M. to 5 P.M.; Sunday, noon to 5 P.M. Admission charge. Telephone: (757) 595-1900. Web site: www.valivingmuseum.org.

Turn right on Clyde Morris Boulevard for the **Mariner's Museum,** a top area attraction located at 100 Museum Drive. Here the visitor can see the world's foremost collection of ships, ship models, naval weapons, figureheads, and maritime art, as well as the story of whaling and the history of the Chesapeake Bay. Open daily, 10 A.M. to 5 P.M. Closed Thanksgiving and Christmas. Admission charge. Telephone: (757) 596-2222. Web site: www.marinersmuseum.org.

The **Virginia War Museum,** at 9285 Warwick Boulevard, contains a vast collection of more than 60,000 artifacts tracing American combat from 1775 to the present: uniforms, weapons, posters, vehicles, and insignia. Open Monday through Saturday, 9 A.M. to 5 P.M.; Sunday, 1 to 5 P.M. Admission charge. Telephone: (757) 247-8523. Web site: www.warmuseum.org.

As you head downtown on Warwick Boulevard, you will pass the giant **Newport News Shipbuilding and Dry Dock Company,** the world's largest privately owned shipyard. Because of its many top-secret projects, it is closed to the public. You can, however, see some of the facility from the water by taking a harbor cruise. Continue south past **Christopher Newport Park**, located at 26th Street and West Avenue. This is a worthwhile stop if you are interested in a stroll through formal gardens or a sweeping view of the waterfront. **Victory Arch**, a short distance beyond, at the corner of West Avenue and 25th Street, honors Peninsula servicemen of all wars who marched through the arch on their way to and from warships.

Norfolk

Maps and other information for your tour of Norfolk are available at the **Norfolk Convention and Visitors Bureau**, 232 East Main Street. Open weekdays, 8:30 A.M. to 5 P.M. Telephone: (757) 664-6620 or (800) 368-3097. The Oceanview Information Center is at 9401 Fourth View Street, Exit 273 off I-64 West). Open 9 A.M. to 5 P.M. Closed Thanksgiving, Christmas, and New Year's. Telephone: (757) 480-9206. Web site: www.visitnorfolktoday.com.

There are five sites worthy of a visit in downtown Norfolk. The **Douglas MacArthur Memorial** on MacArthur Square serves as the final resting place of Gen. Douglas MacArthur. Located in the nineteenth-century city hall, it has several galleries of exhibits tracing the career of the illustrious military leader. Visitors are invited to see a film on the general's life and achievements. Open Monday through Saturday, 10 A.M. to 5 P.M.; Sunday, 11 A.M. to 5 P.M. Closed Thanksgiving, Christmas, and New Year's. Free admission. Telephone: (757) 441-2965. Web site: www.macarthurmemorial.org.

Nearby is **St. Paul's Church**, at St. Paul's Boulevard and City Hall Avenue, the only building left standing in Norfolk after the British bombardment of 1776. Today you can still see a cannonball from that battle lodged in the southeast wall. Guided tours available for large groups if scheduled in advance. Open Monday through Friday, 10 A.M. to 4 P.M. Sunday services, call for times. Free admission. Telephone: (757) 627-4353.

The **Chrysler Museum** is at the corner of Olney Road and Mowbray Arch. Founded in 1933 as the Norfolk Museum of Arts and Sciences, it was greatly expanded in 1971 when Walter P. Chrysler, Jr., donated his magnificent art collection. The galleries represent many works from 2500 B.C. Chinese bronzes, to major European paintings, to the latest in contemporary American art. Its Institute of Glass, acknowledged as one of the most comprehensive collections in the nation, displays thousands of pieces from Tiffany to Sandwich to rare Persian. Open Wednesday, 10 A.M. to 9 P.M.; Thursday through Saturday, 10 A.M. to 5 P.M.; Sunday, 1 to 5 P.M. Closed Thanksgiving, Christmas, and New Year's. Admission charge. Telephone: (757) 664-6200. Web site: www.chrysler.org.

The **Willoughby-Baylor House,** 601 E. Freemason Street, is a brick townhouse built in 1794. The authentic period furnishings were collected according to an inventory made after Captain Willoughby's death in 1800. Just down the street at Number 323 is the **Moses Myers House,** built shortly after the Revolution by Myers, one of America's "merchant princes." It is a classic example of an eighteenth-century townhouse, and is superbly preserved. About half the furnishings are original. Visitors are guided through the elegant home by costumed hostesses. An adjacent, colonial, rose garden reflects the tastes of the eighteenth century. Both homes are administered by the Chrysler Museum. Tours are offered when the museum is open.

An enjoyable diversion is a drive around Colley and Colonial avenues through **Ghent,** a turn-of-the-century residential area undergoing restoration. Afterwards, consider a stop at the **Hermitage Foundation Museum** at 7637 North Shore Road. Occupying a wooded estate overlooking Lafayette River, the Tudor mansion has a renowned collection of Oriental and medieval art, including wood paneling and bas-relief carvings. Open Monday through Saturday, 10 A.M. to 5 P.M.; Sunday, 1 to 5 P.M. Admission charge. Telephone: (757) 423-2052. Web site: www.hermitagefoundation.org.

Naval Station Norfolk, near the junction of routes 337 and 170, is the world's largest naval base and home port of more than 130 ships of the Atlantic and Mediterranean fleets. The tour office is located at 9079 Hampton Boulevard. Buses leave the tour office at frequent intervals daily. Admission charge. You can usually see submarines, aircraft carriers, and destroyers at anchor. Telephone: (757) 444-7955. Web site: www.cnic.navy.mil/norfolksta/.

At 6700 Azalea Gardens Road, the **Norfolk Botanical Gardens** embraces 175 acres of flowers blooming almost year-round: azaleas, camellias, dogwood, roses, rhododendron, and many other beauties. Trackless trains and canal boats offer visitors a memorable trip through miles of roadways and waterways. Open 9 A.M. to

7 P.M., April 15 to October 15; 9 A.M. to 5 P.M., October 16 to April 14. Admission charge. Telephone: (757) 441-5830. Web site: www.norfolkbotanicalgarden.org/home. Norfolk also boasts the largest zoo in Virginia. **Virginia Zoological Park,** 3500 Granby Street, has exhibits of more than 350 animals and a Public Plant Conservatory with tropical and desert displays. A new, 10-acre, African exhibit opened in 2002. Open daily, 10 A.M. to 5 P.M. Closed New Year's, Thanksgiving, and Christmas. Telephone: (757) 441-2374. Web site: www.virginiazoo.org.

As in Hampton, there are **harbor tours** offered in Norfolk. Departing from the Otter Berth next to the Waterside Mall, Spirit Cruises offers lunch, dinner, and moonlight cruises with entertainment and dancing. April through December. Call for schedules, rates, and reservations. Telephone: (866) 304-2469. Web site: www.spiritofnorfolk.com.

If you prefer sailing under wind rather than power, you can take a two- or three-hour sailing tour of Norfolk harbor aboard the 135-foot topsail schooner *American Rover.* Trips leave daily from the Waterside Festival Marketplace, April through October, call for schedule. Special charters are available at other times of the year. Admission charge. Telephone: (757) 627-7245. Web site: www.americanrover.com.

Portsmouth and Suffolk

This historic seaport was first explored in 1608 and has a wealth of modern and historic attractions and undiscovered treasures, making it an especially appealing getaway destination. As with the other cities in the area, its past revolves around the sea. Pick up maps and sightseeing information at the **Portsmouth Visitor Information Center,** 6 Crawford Parkway at the North Ferry Landing. Open daily, 9 A.M. to 5 P.M. Telephone: (757) 393-5111. Web site: www.visitportsva.com.

You can begin your tour of downtown Portsmouth at the Spanish-American War Monument on Crawford Parkway at North Street. The visitor center can give you a brochure for a self-guided walking tour of Olde Towne, which takes you to 45 sites in the historic district—about one mile total. Two of the many interesting historic homes on the Olde Towne walking tour are the **Watts House** at 516 North St. and the **Ball-Nivison House** at 417 Middle St. Both homes are privately owned, and therefore not open to the public, but are worth close observation from the street.

The **Watts House** is a fine example of the Federal style. Built in 1799 by Col. Dempsey Watts, this house was originally constructed on a hill one block east of its current site and was moved to its present location at North and Dinwiddie streets in 1808. Congressman Henry Clay, Chief Black Hawk, and Pres. Andrew Jackson have visited this house.

The **Ball-Nivison House** at 417 Middle Street was built around 1780 and is an ideal example of a "tax-dodger" house. Houses like these were built with a gambrel roof—a roof with two slopes on each side, the lower slope steeper than the upper slope—to avoid paying the heavy English taxes on a two-story house. The roof comes down to the first floor and, along with the dormer windows, gives the illusion of a one-story home. These houses are an example of Dutch Colonial architecture and became popular in Williamsburg and throughout the Virginia Colony in the eighteenth century because they allowed for more space upstairs while avoiding the higher taxes imposed on two-story homes.

While on the walking tour, be sure to visit the fine collection of museums in Olde Towne. The **Courthouse Galleries,** located in the city's historic 1846 Courthouse at High and Court streets, features the works of international as well as regional and local artists. Open Tuesday through Saturday, 10 A.M. to 5 P.M.; Sunday, 1 to 5 P.M. Closed Mondays. Admission charge. Telephone: (757) 393-8543. Web site: www.courthousegalleries.com.

Next door to the Courthouse Galleries, at 420 High Street, you'll find the **Virginia Sports Hall of Fame and Museum,** which contains mementos of more than 160 athletes who are natives of Virginia or who have made a significant contribution to sports in the state. This museum will be of particular interest to sports enthusiasts of all types. The Hall of Fame honors Virginia sports heroes ranging from golfer Sam Snead and baseball player Cy Young to tennis star Arthur Ashe. Open Tuesday through Saturday, 10 A.M. to 5 P.M. Free admission. Telephone: (757) 393-8031. Web site: http://vshfm.com/.

Continue down High Street to find the **Children's Museum of Virginia,** the largest museum of its kind in the state, with more than 80 hands-on exhibits for children and adults. The museum, which draws more than a quarter million visitors each year, also features a $1 million antique toy and model train collection, as well as a state-of-the-art planetarium. From Labor Day to Memorial Day, the museum is open Tuesday through Saturday, 9 A.M. to 5 P.M.; Sunday, 11

A.M. to 5 P.M. Closed Mondays, except during observed holidays such as Memorial Day and Presidents' Day. From Memorial Day to Labor Day, the museum is open Monday through Saturday, 9 A.M. to 5 P.M.; Sunday, 11 A.M. to 5 P.M. Closed Thanksgiving, Christmas, and New Year's. Admission charge. Telephone: (757) 393-5258. Web site: www.childrensmuseumva.com.

At the foot of High Street, you'll find artifacts depicting the city's rich history in the **Portsmouth Naval Shipyard Museum,** which has an outstanding collection of models of famous naval vessels, relics, trophies, old weapons, flags, and maps. Several exhibits are devoted to the Civil War battle between the Monitor and the Virginia, formally known as the Merrimac. Admission charge. Telephone: (757) 393-8591. Web site: www.portsnavalmuseums.com.

Where London Street meets the waterfront, get a glimpse of how turn-of-the-century mariners lived and worked by visiting the **Lightship Portsmouth Museum,** a lightship restored to its original condition. A National Historic Landmark, the Lightship *Portsmouth* was commissioned in 1915 to guide ships through treacherous waters. This 101-foot ship, the last of its class, contains all types of Coast Guard equipment and historical exhibits. The Portsmouth Naval Museum and the Lightship Museum have the same hours. From Labor Day to Memorial Day, the museums are open Tuesday through Saturday, 9 A.M. to 5 P.M.; Sunday, 11 A.M. to 5 P.M. Closed Mondays, except during observed holidays such as Memorial Day and Presidents' Day. From Memorial Day to Labor Day, the museums are open Monday through Saturday, 9 A.M. to 5 P.M.; Sunday, 11 A.M. to 5 P.M. Closed Thanksgiving, Christmas, and New Year's. Admission charge. Telephone: (757) 393-8591. Web site: www.portsnavalmuseums.com.

The **Hill House,** the only home of its kind open for guided tours in the Olde Towne Historic District, is a four-story English basement dwelling. Built in the early 1800s, it contains the original furnishings collected by generations of the same family. Located at 221 North Street, the house is open April through December, Wednesdays, 12:30 to 4:30 P.M.; Saturday and Sunday, 1 to 5 P.M. Admission charge. Telephone: (757) 393-0241.

Beginning in late May and continuing through September, Tidewater Regional Transit offers the **Olde Towne Portsmouth Discovery Tour** (conducted by a guide in period costume), which lasts about 45 minutes. The trolley tour follows a route similar to that found on the walking tour. The trolleys depart from the Portsmouth Visitor Information Center, 6 Crawford Parkway, on Wednesdays at 9:30 A.M. and Sundays at 10:45 A.M. Call (757) 393-5111 for more information.

To learn more about Portsmouth's rich ethnic heritage, the city's Convention & Visitors Bureau can arrange a special tour for groups of 25 or more interested in learning more about the contributions of African Americans to the early history of Portsmouth. Called the African American Heritage Trolley Tour, the tour is also offered during the Umoja Festival, an African American cultural celebration held annually in Portsmouth. Through narrated commentary, visitors learn about such notables as Sissieretta Matilda Jones, the Portsmouth-born African American soprano who was invited to sing at the White House in 1892 by Pres. Benjamin Harrison, and James Lafayette, a slave who became a Revolutionary War spy. Lafayette discovered when and where the Redcoats would strike at Yorktown. Along the tour route, the trolley makes two stops to allow passengers to venture inside **Emanuel AME Church,** which was built by slaves, and the **Art Atrium II Gallery,** which features exhibitions by regional black artists, as well as arts and crafts from Africa. Call (757) 393-5111 for information.

Increasing in popularity each year is the Olde Towne Lantern Tour, a twilight walking tour of the historic district led by escorts in period attire. On this one-hour tour, from 8:30 to 9:30 P.M. on Tuesdays, visitors get a taste of Olde Towne legends and folklore, but also get a quick lesson in the district's unique architectural styles, which include Colonial, Federal, Greek Revival, Georgian and Victorian. An interesting stop on the Olde Towne Lantern Tour is the house at 367 Middle St., built in 1859. This was the home of Pres. Grover Cleveland's parents before he was born. The Lantern Tours are available June through September and begin in the lobby of the Holiday Inn, 8 Crawford Parkway. For more information, call (757) 393-5111.

To enjoy the richness of the Portsmouth waterfront, a cruise by day or evening aboard the *Carrie B*, an exact replica of a nineteenth-century Mississippi riverboat, provides panoramic views of the nation's oldest shipyard, its first U.S. Naval hospital and the world's largest naval base. On the *Carrie B*, visitors can explore the world's largest natural harbor and cruise the site of the battle between the Monitor and the Merrimac. The *Carrie B* can be boarded in Portsmouth at the landing adjacent to the Portsmouth Visitor Information Center at 6

Crawford Parkway. Cruises are available April through mid-October only. Daytime tours depart at 12:10 P.M. (90-minute cruise) and at 2:10 P.M. (2½-hour cruise). Sunset cruises, available June 1 through Labor Day, leave Portsmouth at 6:10 P.M. and last 2½ hours. Telephone: (954) 609-4735. Web site: www.carrieb.com.

Another popular cruise, on board the *Capt. Rudy Thomas*, brings visitors to Portsmouth from the Eastern Shore for a delightful overnight stay at the Holiday Inn-Olde Towne. During their visit, guests discover the charm of Olde Towne on trolley tours or evening lantern tours. This scenic Chesapeake Bay cruise also departs from Olde Towne to take visitors to Tangier Island and Crisfield, Maryland, for an overnight excursion that includes a seafood feast before returning to Portsmouth the following day.

The package from Crisfield, Maryland, to Portsmouth is offered two days a week. One departs on a Saturday; the other departs on a Tuesday. Both trips return the following day and include round-trip cruise, lunch on vessel both days, overnight accommodations, and a breakfast buffet. The package from Portsmouth to Crisfield, Maryland, includes round-trip cruise, lunch on vessel both days, trip to Tangier Island, crab feast, overnight motel accommodations, and a breakfast buffet. Telephone: (410) 968-2338 or (800) 863-2338. Web site: www.tangiercruise.com.

Another way to enjoy the Portsmouth waterfront is to take a ride on the charming paddlewheel pedestrian ferry for a short (5-minute) trip across the Elizabeth River to Norfolk. The ferry operates seven days a week, takes bicycles, and departs from High Street Landing on the hour and the half-hour, and from the Portsmouth Visitor Information Center at North Landing at 5 minutes after the hour and half-hour. Admission charge. Telephone: (757) 222-6100. Web site: www.hrtransit.org.

The **Suffolk** area is southwest of Portsmouth via routes 58, 13, or 460. Suffolk dates from 1608, when Capt. John Smith sailed and mapped the Nansemond River. A year later a settlement was founded here. Today, Suffolk has a number of claims to fame: it is the world's leading peanut market (home of Planter's Peanuts), and thanks to its 1974 merger with Nansemond County, it is the largest city (430 square miles) in Virginia and the sixth largest in the nation.

The seven freshwater lakes situated to the west and north of the city offer fine fishing year-round including bass, pike, crappie, and bream. A city or state fishing license is obtainable from the clerk of the court, 150 N. Main Street. Open Monday through Friday, 9 A.M. to 5 P.M. Telephone: (804) 923-2251.

Riddick's Folly, an 1837 Greek Revival house, is one of the city's most interesting attractions. It was the home of merchant Mills Riddick and his descendants for 130 years and is now a museum and cultural center. Located at 510 N. Main Street. Open Tuesday through Friday, 10 A.M. to 5 P.M.; Sunday, 1 P.M. to 5 P.M. Telephone: (757) 934-0822.

The **Suffolk Museum,** at 118 Bosley Street, features changing art exhibits and an annual concert series. Open Tuesday to Saturday, 10 A.M. to 5 P.M.; Sunday, 1 to 5 P.M. Free admission. Telephone: (757) 514-7284. Web site: www.suffolk-fun.com/artsculture.html.

Great Dismal Swamp National Wildlife Refuge is an exciting and unusual area beginning about five miles east of Suffolk and extending south to the state line. The swamp covers about 200 square miles and includes many waterways, canals, and Lake Drummond. Cypress and pine forests, heavy moss, coffee-colored water, and a lush growth give this area a unique appearance. The abundant wildlife attracts naturalists: 207 species of birds, 40 species of trees, and numerous bears, wildcats, foxes, and raccoons. The self-guided Boardwalk Trail provides a close look at the ecology. There are 100 miles of hiking and biking trails. The Great Dismal Swamp was a haven for runaway slaves and has recently been recognized by the National Park Service as a link in the Underground Railroad Network to Freedom. Access into the refuge is by foot or bicycle only; automobiles must be parked at the main gate. The refuge itself is open daily, dawn to dusk. Free admission. Telephone: (757) 986-3705.

Virginia Beach Area

The Virginia Beach area is about fifteen miles east of Norfolk, accessible via routes 58, 60, or 44. The **Virginia Beach Visitor Information Center,** 2100 Parks Avenue, can provide more information on what to see in and around the resort. Open daily, 9 A.M. to 8 P.M., from June 15 through the day after Labor Day, and from 9 A.M. to 5 P.M. the rest of the year. Telephone: (800) VA-BEACH. Web site: www.visitvirginiabeach.com.

If you are traveling from Norfolk via Route 60, you can stop at **First Landing State Park** on Cape Henry. The 2,770-acre park offers a glimpse of almost semitropical lagoons with aged trees gracefully festooned with Spanish moss. The natural dunes area is preserved in its original state with a variety of unusual plant and animal life. Activities include biking, hiking, fishing, sailing, camping, water skiing, nature programs, and tours of the museum. The visitor center can provide more information, including an illustrated guide to Bald Cypress Nature Trail. Park open daily, 8 A.M. to sunset. Free admission. Telephone: (757) 412-2300.

Cape Henry Cross, to the east of the park in Fort Story Military Reservation, marks the landing site of the first English settlers in America in 1607. They went on to found Jamestown as the first settlement. Cape Henry Lighthouse, built in 1791 as an improvement over the inland fires colonists used to build, is the oldest structure of its kind in the United States. Open 10 A.M. to 5 P.M., March 16 to October 31; 10 A.M. to 4 P.M., November 1 to March 15. Closed Thanksgiving and December 5 through January 4. Admission charge. Telephone: (757) 422-9421. Web site: preservationvirginia.org/visit/historic-properties/cape-henry-lighthouse.

Virginia Beach itself is a popular seaside resort with modern motels, hotels, apartments, and cottages to accommodate the large numbers of summer visitors who come here to enjoy the beach, boating, fishing, and other sports. There is also a two-mile biking trail parallel to the Boardwalk, and colorful trolleys you can ride up and down Atlantic Avenue. The **Old Coast Guard Station,** at the corner of 24th and Atlantic, has displays of maritime history and a gift shop. Open Memorial Day through September, Monday through Saturday, 10 A.M. to 5 P.M.; Sunday, noon to 5 P.M. October to Memorial Day, Tuesday to Saturday; 10 A.M. to 5 P.M.; Sunday, noon to 5 P.M. Closed Thanksgiving, Christmas, New Year's Eve, and New Year's Day. Admission charge. Telephone: (757) 422-1587. Web site: www.oldcoastguardstation.com.

The **Virginia Marine Science Museum,** 717 General Booth Blvd., is the state's largest aquarium and home to sharks, sea turtles, stingrays, and fish. Virginia's marine environment is represented by 800,000 gallons of aquariums, live animal habitats, an outdoor aviary, ten acres of outdoor marsh habitat, a nature walk, and over 300 interactive exhibits. You can experience "larger-than-life" nature and marine movies on a screen six stories high in an IMAX 3-D theater. Seasonal boat trips are offered. Open 9 A.M. to 5 P.M. in the winter; 9 A.M. to 7 P.M. in the summer. Telephone: (757) 385-FISH. Web site: www.virginiaaquarium.com.

The **Adam Thoroughgood House,** 1636 Parrish Road, built around 1680, is an exceptionally well-preserved example of English colonial architecture. The interior has been restored, complete with period furnishings. Costumed guides conduct visits through the house.

Open Tuesday through Saturday, 10 A.M. to 5 P.M.; Sunday, 1 P.M. to 5 P.M. Last tour starts at 4:30 P.M. Closed Thanksgiving, Christmas, and New Year's. Admission charge. Telephone: (757) 460-7588.

An intact survivor of the eighteenth century, the **Lynnhaven House,** 4405 Wishart Road, is a brick plantation house dating from about 1725. Its Jacobean staircase is one of only two in the state. Open May and October, weekends only, noon to 4 P.M.; June through September, Tuesday through Saturday, noon to 4 P.M. Admission charge. Telephone: (757) 431-4000.

The **Francis Land House,** 3131 Virginia Beach Boulevard, is believed to have been built about 1732, and is a fine example of Dutch gambrel roof structure. The city of Virginia Beach saved the house from demolition in 1975 and has renovated the building. Open Tuesday through Saturday, 9 A.M. to 5 P.M.; Sunday, 1 P.M. to 5 P.M. Last tour starts at 4:30 P.M. Telephone: (757) 431-4000.

One of the more remarkable sights in Virginia Beach is **Mt. Trashmore,** a popular park and picnic area built on the site of a former solid-waste disposal facility at 310 Edwin Drive. The 162-acre park, complete with bike trails and soapbox derby ramp, has been lauded here and abroad as a creative solution to a ubiquitous problem. Telephone: (757) 473-5237.

South of Virginia Beach, along the coast, is an area so unique in its ecology that it is preserved by local, state, and federal governments: **Back Bay National Wildlife Refuge** is an 8,000-acre refuge made up of dunes, beaches, marshes, and woodlands. It provides habitats for loggerhead sea turtles, piping glovers, peregrine falcons, and bald eagles. Enjoy hiking, canoeing, kayaking, mountain biking, fresh- and saltwater fishing, and bird watching. The visitor center is open Monday through Friday, 8 A.M. to 4 P.M.; Saturday and Sunday, 9 A.M. to 4 P.M. Admission charge. Telephone: (757) 721-7329. Web site: www.fws.gov/backbay.

False Cape State Park is a mile-wide embankment between Back Bay and the Atlantic Ocean. It is made up of 4,321 acres, with almost 6 miles of beaches. Indulge in fishing, boating, swimming, hiking, biking, picnicking, and camping. Telephone: (757) 426-7128, camping reservations (800) 933-PARK. Web site: www.dcr.virginia.gov/state_parks/fal.shtml.

For more information, log onto Virginia's official Web site: www.virginia.org.

MARYLAND

In a tourism campaign some years ago, **Maryland** called itself "little America," suggesting that in a compact area it contained samples of all the most desirable geographies. And so it does. From above, the state's most prominent feature is the Chesapeake Bay. This great, protected body of water accounts in part for Maryland's early settlement. But so do the rich lands that line its shores and coves. These lands became tobacco plantations and farms. To the east is the Atlantic Ocean and its beaches; to the west, mountains that once marked the beginning of the American frontier. From colonial days to the present, history has left her footprints in many places throughout the state.

The following information highlights some of its many attractions. It is organized by region and then counties or categories within that region. Most counties have visitor centers where one can call or visit for additional information. The state of Maryland has an Internet site that includes links to nearly all counties and Maryland attractions of interest. Web site: www.mdisfun.org. The Maryland Department of Natural Resources has a site where you will find links to state parks. Web site: www.dnr.state.md.us. Camping reservations may be made online or by calling, toll free (888) 432-CAMP.

CENTRAL MARYLAND

Baltimore County

The county of Baltimore surrounds the city of Baltimore, but the two are separate political entities. The county extends north to the Pennsylvania state line and encompasses rolling farmlands dotted with scenic horse farms, the suburbs of Baltimore, and 173 miles of Chesapeake Bay shoreline.

Historic sites such as **Towson,** the county seat, and **Reisterstown** give the traveler a picturesque glimpse into the past. In Towson, one can see the **Sheppard-Pratt Hospital Buildings** (c. 1862) on North Charles Street. On the grounds on Osler Drive is a house in which F. Scott Fitzgerald stayed while visiting his wife, Zelda, when she was at Sheppard-Pratt Hospital. Reisterstown, which is northwest of Baltimore, was founded in 1758 and still has many well-maintained homes of the Revolutionary War era, and Main Street has a block of shops for antique shoppers.

The **Benjamin Banneker Historical Park & Museum,** at 300 Oella Avenue in Catonsville, honors the free black American who was commissioned by Thomas Jefferson to help survey and lay out the new capital city of Washington. Benjamin Banneker was born in 1731 near Ellicott City and was a self-educated scientist. Open Tuesday through Saturday, 10 A.M. to 4 P.M. The Mount Gilboa Church houses the Banneker Memorial Obelisk. The church is located in the picturesque Historic Register milltown of Oella, built on the banks of the Patapsco River, at 1221 Westchester Avenue in Catonsville. Open during services. Grounds may be visited at any time.

The **Maryland State Police Headquarters,** at 1201 Reisterstown Road in Pikesville, is housed in a historic structure. It was built as an arsenal after the War of 1812 to protect the route to Washington. After the Civil War, it served as a home for Confederate veterans, and in recent years has served as police headquarters. The building has a venerable exterior appearance. Low walls surround the quadrangle, and a fine wrought-iron fence gives the effect of great age. The museum on the site displays artifacts, photographs, equipment, memorabilia, and a history of the Maryland State Police. Open weekdays. Telephone: (410) 653-4200.

The **Cloisters,** at 10440 Falls Road South in Brooklandville, is housed in a large French Gothic Tudor Revival castle built in 1930. Many of the doorways and doors, however, are original. The castle is located on a 53-acre wooded park with nature trails and may be rented for special events. Call or visit the Web site for information about the open house schedule. Telephone: (410) 821-7448 or (888) 330-9571. Web site: www.cloisterscastle.com.

The **Fire Museum of Maryland,** at 1305 York Road in Lutherville, displays more than 42 antique fire-fighting vehicles dating from 1806 to 1960. In addition to the vehicles, there is other fire-fighting equipment on display, as well as a photographic exhibit. Open Tuesday through Saturday, 11 A.M. to 4 P.M., in June, July, and August; Saturdays only, May, September, October, November, and December. Admission charge. Telephone: (410) 321-7500. Web site: www.firemuseummd.org.

Hampton National Historic Site, just north of Towson at Exit 27B off I-695, includes one of the largest and most ornate Georgian mansions constructed in America during the 1780s and 90s. Built by Charles Ridgely, Hampton House was the home of the Ridgely family for 158 years. The family owned the Northampton Ironworks, which supplied cannon and shot to the Continental Army during the Revolutionary War. Almost all of the elegant furnishings are original. The 63-acre park contains 27 buildings, including an overseer's house, slave quarters, stables, and a reconstructed orangerie. Hampton is administered by the National Park Service. The farmhouse is the oldest building on the site and is among the oldest in Baltimore County (c. 1725). Hampton's stone slave quarters, unique in construction and decoration, date from the 1840s and illustrate living conditions for African American slaves and later, tenant farm workers. The mansion is open year round except Thanksgiving, Christmas, and New Year's. Tours hourly, 9 A.M. to 4 P.M. Admission charge. Telephone: (410) 823-1309. Web site: www.nps.gov/hamp.

Gunpowder Falls State Park has several tracts encompassing 16,000 acres in Baltimore and Harford Counties. As the Big and Little Gunpowder Rivers approach the Chesapeake Bay, they merge and become one body of water, the Gunpowder River, which flows for eight miles until it meets the waters of the Chesapeake Bay. Gunpowder State Park lies in this stream valley. The "Falls" appellation comes from the fact that the two Gunpowder Rivers cross the fall line between the piedmont and tidewater area. The tidewater extends north of I-95 above the point where the two rivers merge. Prosperous mills and factories sprang up along the river's banks during the eighteenth and nineteenth centuries, and the sites or remains of some of these institutions may still be seen, although the industry ceased many years ago. Along the Old Post Road, the river enters into Long Calm Ford, one of the famous fording places for colonial travelers en route from Philadelphia to Annapolis. The park is located at 2813

Jerusalem Road in Kingsville, Maryland. Telephone: (410) 592-2897. The main areas are the Hammerman Area, a developed area at the mouth of the Gunpowder River, undeveloped central areas along the Little Gunpowder and Big Gunpowder Rivers, and the undeveloped Hereford area astride Route 83 in the northern section of Baltimore County. About 100 miles of hiking trails are located throughout the park. Unsupervised swimming opportunities are available along sections of the river. Permits are required for freshwater fishing, tidewater fishing, and crabbing. Note that this is a day-use park, not a camping park. In addition to the natural beauty of the park, there are some manmade sites worth seeing. The **Jericho Covered Bridge** is east of Route 1, approximately two miles north of Kingsville. The bridge may be reached on Jericho Road off Jerusalem Road or from Joppa Road to West Franklinville Road. This 88-foot, Howe truss bridge was built around 1860. Nearby is the **Jerusalem Village** on the banks of the Little Gunpowder adjacent to Jerusalem Road. A mill was constructed in here 1772 by David Lee, a Quaker from Bucks County, Pennsylvania. The mill is a unique example of early American architecture and is believed to be the only double-dormed mill in the United States. Behind the mill is a two-story house where David Lee manufactured gun stocks during the Revolutionary War. The village also has a blacksmith shop, a small museum, and park offices. Telephone: (410) 592-2897.

Frederick County

Frederick, the largest Maryland county, is now an outlying suburb of Washington, D.C., although farming is still a part of its economy. The county ranges from the Piedmont Plateau region in the east and the beginning of the Appalachians in the west. Its many public parks make it a pleasant driving area throughout the year. The presidential retreat, Camp David, is located in Frederick County's Catoctin Mountains. During World War II and the Vietnam War, chemical and biological weapons research was conducted at Fort Detrick near the city of Frederick. Today, under the U.S. Army Health Services Command, studies on infectious diseases, toxins, and recombinant DNA are conducted there. The Frederick Cancer Research Center of the National Institutes of Health is also located at Fort Detrick. In recent years Frederick County achieved notoriety in some circles because the tiny town of Burkittsville (population 214) was the setting for the movie *The Blair Witch Project*.

Frederick County was settled in the early 1700s by German farmers from Pennsylvania, as well as by Scots and English settlers. Both town and county were named in honor of Frederick Calvert, the sixth and last Lord Baltimore. Frederick County was formed in 1748 and, because of its productive iron furnaces, played an important part in both the Revolutionary and Civil wars. From its earliest days, transportation was important, as the National Road route cut through the county, and today much of the busy interstate traffic from Baltimore and Washington passes through it to the west. The main artery to/from Washington is I-270; from Baltimore, I-70 west. Web sites: (Frederick County) www.fredericktourism.org; (city of Frederick) www.cityoffrederick.com.

Sugarloaf Mountain is surrounded by a privately owned 3,000-acre park in Dickerson, Maryland, near Comus. To visit Sugarloaf, take exit 22 (Route 109, south) off I-270, about midway between Rockville and Frederick, follow Route 109 for 5 miles to State Route 95, then take a right and follow Route 95 for 4.2 miles to the Stronghold entrance. **Sugarloaf Mountain,** a national landmark, rises to a height of 1,283 feet above sea level and stands out strikingly above the surrounding countryside. The solitary mountain was named by the early settlers because of its shape, which reminded them of sugar, then commonly stored in a loaf.

A winding paved road leads up the mountain for about a mile to a parking area near the top. Visitors may stop at several lookout points cut out of the natural stands of pine and oak. Over an acre of level ground at the summit supports a scattered growth of stunted, windblown oaks. On clear days the Bull Run Mountains can be seen far off to the south. The view is unobstructed, since the mountain breaks off into a sheer cliff on both the south and west sides. Sugarloaf Mountain Park is open daily, 8 A.M. to sunset. Admission charge. Motorcycles are prohibited; buses are barred on weekends and holidays. Telephone: (301) 869-7846 or (301) 874-2024. Web site: www.patc.us/hiking/destinations/sug_loaf.html.

Brunswick, about 20 miles southwest of Frederick off Route 340, was originally named Berlin in 1787. The area, bounded by the Potomac River; Central, Park, and Tenth avenues; and C Street, has been designated a National Historic District. The Chesapeake & Ohio Canal and the Baltimore & Ohio Railroad reached the town about the same time in 1834. However, the influence of the canal displaced that of the railroad for nearly 70 years by providing work for residents and business for warehouses and shopkeepers as barge and packet boat trade increased. It was during the Civil War that the railroad took on a new, more active role. Brunswick's proximity to Washington on a rail line made it an ideal supply depot and guard outpost for the Federal Army. Confederate troops repeatedly sabotaged the railroad and canal properties. The year 1890 brought the new name and the start of one of our nation's industrial "boomtowns." The B&O Railroad began developing a freight classification yard that by 1907 was one-half mile across, eight miles in length, and contained over 100 miles of track. The expansion eventually wiped out all of old Berlin along the canal, pushing the newly built "Victorian" style homes and businesses upward into the hills overlooking the river. Web site: www.brunswickmd.gov.

The **Brunswick Railroad Museum,** at 40 West Potomac Street, features a huge, visitor interactive, model railroad and emphasizes the area's role in transportation. It has collections of railroad and canal tools, uniforms, documents, and pictures. The third floor of the museum is devoted to a scale model of the railroad system from Brunswick to Washington, D.C.'s Union Station. There are also exhibits of Indian artifacts, Civil War relics, farmers' tools, home furnishings, and utensils. The visitor may also see train engines being changed in a 180-degree direction at the **Roundhouse and Turntable.** Steam engines were housed for repair in this 1907 brick roundhouse, but today diesels dominate the scene. The **B&O Railroad Station,** built in 1891, still serves passengers. An annual Railroad Days, featuring bus and walking tours, old trains, films, and food, is held the first weekend in October. The museum is open January to April on Fridays 10 A.M. to 2 P.M., Saturdays 10 A.M. to 4 P.M., and Sundays 1 to 4 P.M.; from April to January it is also open on Thursdays 10 A.M. to 2 P.M. Admission charge. Telephone: (301) 834-7100. Web site: http://brrm.net.

Point of Rocks is at the intersection of routes 28 and 15, which crosses the bridge over the Potomac River into Virginia. A court battle was waged between the C&O Canal Companies and the B&O Railroad over rights to a strip of land bordering the river. The historical highlight of the town is the **B&O Railroad Station,** located just east of town on Route 15 south then state Route 28. The Victorian railroad station is listed on the National Register of Historic Places and is now used as a MARC transit stop. Telephone: (301) 600-2888.

Frederick is noted for its architectural charms as well as its historical associations. The city was founded in 1745 by English and

German settlers. In 1765, the first organized community resistance to British rule in the colonies occurred in its Court House Square, when Frederick citizenry burned the Stamp Act in effigy.

Francis Scott Key lived here and the Stars and Stripes flies over his tomb. During the Civil War, the city figured prominently in the Antietam and Gettysburg campaigns. The restored home of Barbara Fritchie, legendary heroine of Whittier's patriotic poem, is here.

Three old covered bridges can be found on country roads in the area. While driving, look for characteristic brick-end barns, a type found along the northern border of Carroll and Frederick counties. Their end walls of brick have decorative designs in the openwork. They date from the late eighteenth century.

Monocacy National Battlefield is south of Frederick in the area near the Monocacy River Bridge on I-270. On July 9, 1864, a bloody battle took place here between Union forces under Gen. Lew Wallace and 18,000 Confederate troops under Gen. Jubal A. Early. Just prior to the battle of Monocacy on July 9, 1864, Confederate general Early demanded and received from the city of Frederick the sum of $200,000. The banks loyally supported the city authorities who feared the result of a refusal to meet the demand. Early proceeded to the Monocacy River, where his troops were engaged by Union soldiers commanded by General Wallace. The Union forces delayed Early's advance toward Washington for 24 hours, which gave General Grant enough time to reinforce the defenses around Washington. This battle probably prevented the Capital from falling into rebel hands. It was not until 1951 that final repayment was made to the Frederick banks.

Several monuments have been erected to commemorate the action that took place on the banks of the Monocacy, and a visitor center at 4801 Urbana Pike provides a good overview of the battle. Telephone: (301) 662-3515. Web site: www.nps.gov/mono.

Frederick Historic District, a 50-block area, contains many interesting and historic structures that are well preserved and restored. It is best to park your car and see historic Frederick on foot. The Tourism Council and Visitors Center office is at 19 East Church Street, where the visitor may pick up detailed information on walking tours, driving tours, and bicycling tours. One-and-a-half-hour guided tours of the city are available April through December on Saturdays and Sundays at 1:30 P.M., as well as some Monday holidays. The visitors center is open daily. Telephone: (301) 600-2888.

On East Church Street, across from the Tourism Council offices, the county administrative offices are housed in **Winchester Hall.** These stately Greek Revival buildings were built in 1843 to house the Frederick Female Seminary, which was later renamed **Hood College** (now located on Rosemont Avenue).

The **Evangelical Lutheran Church,** 31 East Church Street, is opposite Winchester Hall. A log church was first built on this site in 1738 and was replaced in 1752 by the stone rear section of the present church. The twin spires of this Norman Gothic church were added in 1854 and they have been described as the best-matched pair of spires in the United States. The five buildings and gardens are open to the public during the day. Telephone: (301) 663-6361. Web site: http://twinspires.org.

The **Historical Society of Frederick County Museum** is at 24 East Church Street. This house was built in 1820 by John Baltzell. Later the house was owned by John Loats, who bequeathed it to the Lutheran Church for use as an orphanage. The Loats Orphanage occupied the house from the late 1870s to 1958. It now contains an excellent collection of historical objects of early Frederick. The museum has large collections of lustreware. The Society library also is a good resource for local historical and genealogical materials. Open Monday through Saturday, 10:30 A.M. to 4 P.M.; Sunday, 1 to 4 P.M. Admission charge. Telephone: (301) 663-1188. Web site: www.hsfcinfo.org.

Court House Square, surrounded by late eighteenth- and early nineteenth-century dwellings and law offices, is located at the corner of Church and Court streets. In 1765 it was the scene of the first official repudiation of the hated British Stamp Act. The red brick Court House, erected in 1862, replaced the colonial building destroyed by fire. Busts of Maryland's first governor, Thomas Johnson, and chief justice of the United States Supreme Court, Roger Brooke Taney, both members of the Frederick Bar, stand before the courthouse.

The **Barbara Fritchie House,** 154 West Patrick Street, is a restoration of the home and glove shop of John Casper Fritchie and his wife, Barbara. Barbara Fritchie, a devoted Unionist of Civil War days, has been immortalized in the poem by John Greenleaf Whittier with the lines, "Shoot if you must, this old grey head, but spare your country's flag." The legendary confrontation between the fiery heroine in her nineties and Confederate Gen. Stonewall Jackson occurred here in 1862. The privately owned museum displays some of Barbara

Fritchie's furniture and clothes. Open April through September, Monday, Thursday through Saturday, 10 A.M. to 4 P.M.; Sunday, 1 to 4 P.M. Open October and November, Saturday, 10 A.M. to 4 P.M. and Sunday, 1 to 4 P.M. Closed December through March. Admission charge. Telephone: (301) 698-8992.

The **Roger Brooke Taney House and Francis Scott Key Museum,** at 123 South Bentz Street near Patrick Street, was built in 1799. This was Taney's farm and summer place during his residence in Frederick, 1801-1823. As Chief Justice of the United States Supreme Court, Taney is well known for the *Dred Scott* decision, which ruled that Congress had no power to prohibit slavery. He also administered the presidential oath to Abraham Lincoln, as well as to six previous presidents at their inaugurations.

The Taney House is furnished with period pieces and the museum contains Taney and Key memorabilia. The building is a fine example of late eighteenth-century architecture with its slave quarters behind the house. The Francis Scott Key Foundation maintains the buildings and the public is invited to visit by appointment. Telephone: (301) 663-7880.

Schifferstadt Architectural Museum, built in 1756, at 1110 Rosemont Avenue near Route 15, is an early German, three-story, sandstone farmhouse that is considered to be one of the finest examples of early German Colonial architecture. The old section of the house is unfurnished in order that visitors may see the construction methods. The farmhouse features two unusual old Colonial stoves— a five-plate, cast-iron "jamb" stove and a six-foot squirrel-tail oven. The eighteenth-century gardens feature plant and fruit trees from the period of the house. The newer section, built in the early 1800s, houses the sales shop, and there are outdoor special events throughout the summer and fall. Open April through mid-December, Monday through Friday, 10 A.M. to 4 P.M.; Saturday and Sunday, noon to 4 P.M. Admission charge. Telephone: (301) 663-3885. Web site: www.frederickcountylandmarksfoundation.org.

The **Children's Museum of Rose Hill Manor Park,** at 1611 North Market Street, is a "touch and see" museum for children and adults. The museum is a 1790s manor house built by John Graham, son-in-law of Thomas Johnson, Maryland governor and friend of George Washington. The museum features exhibits that children may touch and work with, such as adding stitches to a quilt. Costumed guides add a period flavor to the visit. On the grounds of the 43-acre park are an icehouse, carriage museums, a log cabin, and a blacksmith shop. Open April through mid-December, Monday through Saturday, 10 A.M. to 4 P.M. Admission charge. Telephone: (301) 600-1650. The **National Museum of Civil War Medicine** is dedicated to telling the medical story of the Civil War. The museum's exhibits feature scenes from a soldier's life in the armies of the North and South, recruitment, life in camps, the hospitals, and the home front. Open Monday through Saturday, 10 A.M. to 5 P.M.; Sunday, 11 A.M. to 5 P.M. Admission charge. Telephone: (301) 695-1864. Web site: www.CivilWarMed.org.

Mountaindale is an out-of-the-way village which lies in the deep, hemlock-clad valley of Fishing Creek, off Route 15 north of Frederick. Turn onto Mountaindale Road (which is well marked) then proceed past modern houses for about 3 miles. Cross a small creek into the historic village and turn left. The village has been described as an austere community of a bygone era. Almost all the homes are built of squared chestnut logs, chinked with white mortar. It was constructed in the early 1940s by Civilian Conservation Corps youth, who salvaged dead chestnut trees from the nearby mountainside and built this unique village. Houses are privately owned, often passed down generation to generation.

Maryland visitors often go to **New Market** seeking treasures. This antiquarian's mecca is located seven miles east of Frederick on Route 144, off Routes 40/70 at the intersection of Route 75. The town, dating back to 1793, has a population of fewer than 500, and thrives on one business—antique shops. Approximately 30 shops line its main street, and tourists make up almost all of its customers. New Market was one of the stops on the National Pike that ran from Baltimore to Cumberland. Until the end of the horse and buggy age, the town served travelers, providing hotel rooms and food for passengers and the services of wheelwrights and blacksmiths for stagecoaches and six-horse Conestoga wagons on their way to the Ohio Country and beyond. The hotels and taverns lining Main Street provided travelers with a night's lodging for 25 cents and a glass of whiskey for 5 cents. Off Main Street were resting pens for livestock being herded to market. In the 1930s, the first antique shop was opened as a part-time venture, and New Market grew to be the "antiques capital of the mid-Atlantic." Hours of shops vary, but the local custom is that a flag flying out front signals an open shop. Web site: www.townofnewmarket.org.

Catoctin Wildlife Preserve and Zoo, at 13019A Catoctin Furnace Road in Thurmont, provides ways to meet, feed, and touch exotic animals. There are over 300 animals of over 100 varieties to discover—bears, boas, big cats, small mammals, reptiles, and petting zoo. The grounds also include 26 beautiful acres of flowers, bamboo, and trees. Open daily, April 1 through October 31; open weekends in March and November. Hours and admission change seasonally. Telephone: (301) 271-3180. Web site: www.CWPZoo.com.

Gambrill State Park, six miles northwest of Frederick off Route 40 on Gambrill Park Road, attracts visitors interested in hiking, picnicking, camping, fishing, and nature study. Some simply enjoy the drive to the mountaintop, with three outlook points on High Knob at the top of Catoctin Mountain. Among attractions are dogwood and wildflowers in spring, and later, mountain laurel and azalea.

Take the self-guided Lost Chestnut Nature Trail to become acquainted with the plant and animal life of the area. During the summer, nature walks and campfire programs are scheduled. There are 35 family camping areas with showers, laundry tubs, and hot water. The park is open year round. Telephone: (301) 271-7574. Web site: www.dnr.state.md.us/publiclands/western/gambrill.asp.

Catoctin Furnace is located near Cunningham Falls State Park, on Catoctin Furnace Road south of Thurmont. Catoctin Furnace is a National Register historic landmark. Built in 1774 by Thomas Johnson, first governor of Maryland, it continued in operation until 1903. Iron ore was extracted from nearby iron ore banks, lime was brought in from the Frederick area, and charcoal, the other ingredient in iron production, was made in the nearby hollows from the plentiful supply of hardwoods. The furnace had been in operation only a few years when it was called upon to supply cannon ball, armor plate, and other materials to the Continental Army. During the Civil War the furnace produced plates for the ironclad ship *Monitor.* Over the years it produced stoves, kitchen ironware, and other iron products for which there was a demand.

Today, one can stroll around the partly restored furnace that dates from 1857, see the ruins of the once-elegant superintendent's residence, and the workers' stone cottages along the road. Admission charge. Telephone: (301) 271-7574. Web site: www.dnr.state.md.us/publiclands/western/catoctinfurnace.asp.

Cunningham Falls State Park, in the beautiful Catoctin Mountains, is named for a scenic 78-foot-drop cascade that extends over a 220-foot area of Big Hunting Creek. The 5,000-acre park has two developed areas—**Manor Area,** which may be reached from Route 15, 3 miles south of Thurmont, and the **Houck Area,** which is located off Route 77 approximately 4 miles west of Thurmont.

Park facilities include a 43-acre stocked lake, picnicking and camping areas, and hiking trails. Trails lead to scenic mountain overlooks such as Cat Rock and Bobs Hill. Visitors may swim, boat, and fish in Hunting Creek Lake, which has two sandy beaches and a bathhouse nearby. During the winter snowshoeing and cross-country skiing are permitted.

The park is open year round. Campgrounds open mid-April through October with hot water showers, toilets, tables, and fireplaces provided. Trout fishing is permitted year round, except for a one-month period that varies annually. Maryland State fishing license required. Admission charge. Telephone: (301) 271-7574. Web site: www.dnr.state.md.us/publiclands/western/catoctinfurnace.asp.

Catoctin Mountain Park, operated by the National Park Service, adjoins Cunningham Falls State Park and is 65 miles from Washington and 55 miles from Baltimore. It is west of Thurmont, bounded by Route 81 on the north and Route 77 on the south. The Visitor's Center is located on Route 77 at Park Central Road. **Camp David,** the mountain retreat of presidents, is located here, but is not open to the public. Most of the park (except for the Camp David area) is open to the public for recreational use year round. Interpretive programs offered during the summer months include guided walks, lectures, and campfire programs. Talks about the whiskey-making industry are held at the **Blue Blazes Whiskey Still,** a Prohibition-era still that was relocated to the park. Please check the calendar of events for specific dates and times. Family camping is available in the Owens Creek Campground from mid-April through the third Sunday in November. There are 51 sites with central comfort stations. Fee charged for sites. The park also offers bridle trails, a five-mile scenic drive on Park Central Road, self-guided nature trails, and picnicking areas. In the spring and fall there are orienteering lectures that focus on compass use. In the winter, ski-touring lectures are given. Telephone: (301) 663-9388. Web site: www.nps.gov/cato.

There is an old church in **Thurmont** that is of more than passing interest. **Apples United Church of Christ,** built in 1826, is one of the oldest in Frederick County. Located at 7908 Apples Church Road, this historic one room church with a high pulpit features a gun corner where worshippers stacked their guns in case of an unexpected Indian attack. An Indian graveyard is nearby. To reach the church, go one mile out Main Street, then left on Apples Church Road. Open to public during services. Telephone: (301) 271-2087.

Frederick County maintains three lovely covered bridges, which are still in use in the Frederick/Thurmont area. Although the original trusses are in place, they have been reinforced with concrete piers and steel beam supports. The **Utica Bridge** (c. 1850) is the largest of the three bridges. It spans Fishing Creek for 100 feet, with a 17.5-foot roadway, and its original Burr arch and trusses are still in place. The Utica Bridge was originally over the Monocacy River, but was moved to Fishing Creek when half of the bridge was destroyed in the 1889 Johnstown Flood. It was during this flood that most of the 52 covered bridges in Maryland were destroyed. The bridge can be found on Utica Road, about 1 1/2 miles from the point where Old Frederick Road forks to the right from Route 15, about four miles north of Frederick. **Loys Station Covered Bridge** has a 90-foot span and a 12.5-foot roadway. It is located 4 or 5 miles north of Utica Bridge on Old Frederick Road, near its junction with Route 77. This multiple Kingpost truss bridge was originally constructed in 1850. It was destroyed by fire in the 1990s. Local people raised funds to have it rebuilt using aged materials from a covered bridge in Pennsylvania. The county maintains a park and picnicking facilities near the bridge. The **Roddy Road Covered Bridge** is the smallest covered bridge in Maryland and is of the single Kingpost truss type. It is 40 feet long, spans Owen's Creek, and was built around 1856. Heading north out of Thurmont on Route 15, turn right at the large road sign indicating a single lane bridge. The bridge is surrounded by a 17-acre natural area.

Eight miles north of Thurmont on Route 15, at 16300 Old Emmitsburg Road, is the campus of **Mount St. Mary's College and Seminary** and the **Grotto of Lourdes Replica.** The Grotto is the first such replica of the famed Grotto of Lourdes in France and is located on the mountainside above the campus of Mount St. Mary's College. The statue of the Virgin Mary, containing a carillon, highlights the setting. Paths through the garden feature Stations of the Cross and Stations of the Rosary. Mount St. Mary's College, founded in 1808, is the second oldest Roman Catholic College in the United States. The Grotto is open daily, 7 A.M. to 7:30 P.M., April through September; 7

A.M. to 5:30 P.M., October through March. Telephone: (301) 447-5330. Web site: www.msmary.edu/grotto. The National Shrine of St. Elizabeth Ann Seton, located off Route 15 in Emmitsburg, at 333 South Seton Avenue, commemorates the life of St. Elizabeth Ann Seton (1774-1821), who, in 1975, became the first native-born American to be canonized by the Catholic Church. On the beautiful grounds are located the Stone House (c. 1750), the White House (c. 1810), and the Seton Shrine Chapel in St. Joseph's Provincial House. Mother Seton and her companions opened the first Catholic parochial school in the United States at the "White House" in Emmitsburg. A visitors center and gift shop are located on the grounds. Open Tuesday through Sunday, 10 A.M. to 4:30 P.M. Free admission. Telephone: (301) 447-6606. Web site: www.setonshrine.org.

Carroll County

This county, named for Charles Carroll of Carrollton, is located in north central Maryland and borders the Mason-Dixon line. It is rich in beautiful scenery and prosperous farms, and offers many historic attractions. Carroll County is part of the Piedmont Plateau and the county seat at Westminster is 56 miles northwest of Washington and 31 miles northwest of Baltimore. The county was first settled in 1723 by English and Scotch-Irish families from the Baltimore and Annapolis areas. In the mid-eighteenth-century German, Swiss, and Scotch-Irish settlers from Pennsylvania moved to the county.

Some prominent Carroll County natives have been Francis Scott Key and Revolutionary War hero Mordecai Gist. Another Carroll County native was Jacob R. Thomas of Union Bridge, who in 1809 invented a harvester and reaping machine. The invention was later perfected and marketed by Obed Hussey and his cousin, Cyrus McCormick.

Agriculture remains an important aspect of the economy of Carroll County. Brick-end barns are a local architectural feature that the visitor to Carroll and Frederick counties may observe. The side walls of the barns were made of brick with designs fashioned by leaving out some of the brick in order to provide ventilation.

Your first stop in Carroll County should be **Westminster.** Tourist information may be obtained from the Carroll County Visitor Center at 210 East Main Street. The office is open year round, Monday to Saturday, 9 A.M. to 5 P.M.; Sundays and most holidays, 10 A.M. to 2 P.M. Closed on

Easter, Thanksgiving, Christmas, and New Year's. Telephone: (410) 848-1388 or (800) 272-1933. Web site: www.carrollcountytourism.org.

The **Sherman-Fisher-Shellman House** and the **Kimmey House,** next door, 206-210 East Main Street, are the chief attractions of Westminster. The Kimmey House is headquarters of the county historical society. The society maintains a collection of about 150 examples of early nineteenth-century dolls; a unique collection of American flags, maps, and fans; and the hobnail glass collection of the late Mrs. H. L. Mencken. The basement rooms have an exceptional collection of tools and implements used before the machine age.

The **County Courthouse** (1838), still in use, is on Court Street, one block off Main Street. It is a Greek Revival building with a two-story portico. **Western Maryland College,** on West Main Street, was founded as a private academy in 1860 and reorganized in 1867 as a college. It was the first coeducational college south of the Mason-Dixon line.

The **Pennsylvania Dutch Farmers' Market of Westminster** is located just east of downtown on Route 140 and 97 South, in the Crossroads Square Shopping Center. It is well known for its fresh produce and baked goods. Open year round, Thursday, 10 A.M. to 6 P.M.; Friday, 10 A.M. to 8 P.M.; and Saturday, 10 A.M. to 4 P.M. Telephone: (410) 876-8100. Web site: www.carr.org/ccg/tourism/d-market.htm.

The **Union Mills Homestead,** built in 1797, is located at 3311 Littlestown Pike on Route 97, seven miles north of Westminster. The rambling clapboard farm home and gristmill overlook picturesque Big Pipe Creek. At various times it served as an inn, stagecoach office, post office, schoolhouse, and magistrate's office. The old mill alongside Big Pipe Creek has been restored to operating condition, and visitors may purchase grain produced by the mill. The homestead today is a museum of eighteenth- and early nineteenth-century Americana. Its 23 rooms are filled with the furnishings and household articles used by the six generations of the Shriver family, who lived here. The visitor will see the old postmaster's desk, a ballroom, kitchen, guest room, and dining room; it also has collections of toys, business documents, and family heirlooms.

The homestead, mill, and gift shop are open May and September, weekends only, noon to 4 P.M.; June through August, Tuesday through Friday, 10 A.M. to 4 P.M.; weekends, noon to 4 P.M. Admission charge.

For further information, contact the Union Mills Foundation, 3311 Littlestown Pike, Westminster, MD 21158. Telephone: (410) 848-2288. Website: www.unionmills.org. The **Carroll County Farm Museum** is located one mile south of Westminster at 500 South Center Street, off Route 140. This 140-acre facility features life on the farm in the late 1800s. Guides in period costumes give tours through the farmhouse. Antique farm machinery and early transportation exhibits are on display. Volunteer museum artisans present demonstrations of the various nineteenth-century skills. There is a Living History Center featuring a quilting room, a general store, a veterinary surgeon's office, and more. A walking tour can be taken of the other out buildings, such as the blacksmith's shop, "Horsing Around" exhibit, and one-room schoolhouse. Admission charge. Open May through October, Saturday and Sunday, noon to 4 P.M.; July and August, Tuesday through Friday, 10 A.M. to 4 P.M. Extended weekend hours in July and August, and a special holiday visit is offered in December. Telephone: (410) 848-7775 Web site: ccgovernment.carr.org/ccg/farmmus.

In Union Bridge on Route 75 at 410 N. Main Street is the **Western Maryland Railway Historical Society Museum.** It contains artifacts of the Western Maryland Railroad and numerous other railroad memorabilia, such as one of the first pay phones, an old telegraph set, and HO models. This red brick building with white marble keystones, built in 1902, was saved from demolition and has been completely restored. Open Sundays, noon to 4 P.M., and by appointment. Telephone: (410) 775-0150. Web site: moosevalley.org/wmrhs/wmrhshistory.htm.

Near the town of Keymar, on the Bruceville Road, is the sleepy village of **Bruceville,** which virtually died when the highway was rerouted. Most of its old stone houses were once occupied by workers in a nearby grist mill and fertilizer plant. The single street of Bruceville overlooks the Monocacy River. This "ghost town" should be a delight for antiquarians and photographers.

The village of **Uniontown** has been listed on the National Register of Historic Places and is a typical small Carroll County town of more than 100 years ago. It is six miles east of Middleburg on Route 77. The town of **New Windsor** is three miles from Uniontown, on Route 84. At New Windsor the **Strawbridge Shrine,** 2650 Strawbridge Lane, includes a log house like one built here in the 1760s by Robert Strawbridge, thought to be the first Methodist preacher in the

United States. Tours are available by appointment. Telephone: (410) 635-2600. Web site: www.strawbridgeshrine.org.

Montgomery County

Most of this county's attractions are within a 30- or 40-minute drive from Washington and an additional 40 minutes from the Baltimore area. Scattered through the county are a number of regional and state parks, each with a variety of recreational facilities and nature centers offering educational nature programs. For more information about attractions in the county, contact the **Montgomery County Conference and Visitors Bureau,** 11820 Parklawn Drive, Suite 380, Rockville, MD. Telephone: (240) 777-2060 or (877) 789-6904. Web site: www.visitmontgomery.com.

Glen Echo National Park, 7300 MacArthur Blvd (off I-495 north of Washington at Exit 40), was a Chautauqua meeting ground in the late nineteenth century. It was turned into a popular amusement park that continued until 1968. The present park is an active art and dance center. Local artists rent space in the center and surrounding yurts; the gallery exhibits and sells the creations of the resident and teaching artists. The art-deco Spanish ballroom was restored in 2003, thanks to a cooperative agreement between the National Park Service and a local nonprofit group, the Glen Echo Park Partnership for Arts and Culture, Inc. The Partnership will manage the park facilities and programs for at least the next decade. The gallery is open year round, Tuesday through Saturday, noon to 5 P.M.

A children's adventure theater offers theatrical and puppet performances on a year-round basis. In the summer, children can ride on the historic Dentzel carousel, and adults can attend free outdoor concerts. Small charge for carousel. Picnic areas are on a first-come, first-served basis. No camping facilities are available. Call or visit the Web site for a full list of programs and hours. The park is open daily, 6 A.M. to 1 A.M. Telephone: (301) 320-1400; events hot line: (301) 634-2222. Web site: www.nps.gov/glec.

Clara Barton National Historic Site is near Glen Echo at 5801 Oxford Road. This unique, 38-room Victorian house was the home of Clara Barton, founder of the American Red Cross, and headquarters of that organization from 1897 to 1904. Miss Barton was a humanitarian known for her relief work during and after the Civil War and for her support of African Americans and women's rights. She moved to Glen Echo in 1897 and lived there until her death in 1912.

The house was patterned after the Red Cross Relief Hotel erected in Johnstown, Pennsylvania, after the flood of 1889. The architectural style of the interior of the present building follows the style of that hotel. The house is not a typical home and, in fact, Clara Barton broke many Victorian decorating rules. The central hall rises up three stories with galleries from which one can peer over the balustrades. Although the Park Service refutes the allusion, many have noted the resemblance to a Mississippi River sternwheeler. Clara Barton built a utilitarian home and warehouse for her work. Her housekeeping was extremely casual for the times. The wooden paneling was selected because it was cheaper than the plaster used in upper-class homes and even cheaper than the wallpaper used in middle-class homes. She even had muslin wall coverings, normally used as a base for wallpaper.

The Park Service continues to restore the house, and the tour given by the service gives a fascinating insight into an unusual woman. Open daily, with tours on the hour from 10 A.M. to 4 P.M. Closed Thanksgiving, Christmas, and New Year's. Free admission. Telephone: (301) 320-1410. Web site: www.nps.gov/clba.

The **Cabin John Regional Park,** at 7400 Tuckerman Lane in Rockville, has two areas—the park and the nature center. The park offers a variety of attractions for all ages—picnic tables, camping sites, nature trails, and an ice-skating rink. A marked nature trail, maintained by the Potomac Appalachian Trail Club, starts north of the park and winds along Cabin John Creek to the Potomac River. Approximately four miles of the trail are in the park itself. A miniature railroad offers a one-mile ride through woods and fields. On the playground, children will delight in the slides and climbing areas. Open daily, dawn to dusk. Telephone: (301) 299-0024. The ice-skating rink is open all year. Rink telephone: (301) 765-8620. Web site: www.montgomeryparks.org/facilities/regional_parks/cabinjohn.

The **Meadowside Nature Center** is located at 5100 Meadowside Lane in Rockville. The center offers nature programs for families and groups and a small collection of live animals, such as snakes, turtles, and spiders, are on display. Open Tuesday through Saturday, 9 A.M. to 5 P.M. Telephone: (301) 258-4030. Web site: www.montgomeryparks.org/nature_centers/meadow.

The **National Institutes of Health** is the principal medical research arm of the federal government, whose mission is to improve the health of the nation by increasing our understanding of the processes underlying human health and by acquiring new knowledge to help prevent, detect, diagnose, and treat disease. NIH is located on a 300-acre campus in Bethesda. Most NIH divisions maintain their own laboratory and clinical research programs. Well over two thousand research projects are in progress at all times on the Bethesda site, making NIH one of the largest research centers in the world. The NIH Visitors' Center, in the Natcher Conference Center, Building 45, is open Monday through Friday, 8:30 A.M. to 4:30 P.M., with general overviews every Monday, Wednesday, and Friday at 11 A.M. Telephone: (301) 496-1776. Web site: www.NIH.gov. Because of increased security, please call the visitor center or check the Web site for identification requirements, restrictions, and specific directions before visiting NIH.

The NIH **National Library of Medicine** in the Lister Hill Center, Building 38A, is the world's largest reference center devoted to a single subject. Currently, the Library's collection includes 5,000,000 items. As one of its services, the Library produces and publishes the *Index Medicus,* an indispensable reference journal for investigators and practitioners throughout the world. The library tour includes a video overview of NLM programs and services, a computer search of MEDLINE © database, and a stop in the computer room, reading room, audiovisual learning center, online public catalog, and a history of the medical division. Tours of the library are given at 1:30 P.M. each weekday. Special tours arranged on request. Telephone: (301) 594-5983 or (888) 346-3656. Web site: www.nlm.nih.gov.

The **Beall-Dawson House and Doctors' Museum,** 111 West Montgomery Avenue, Rockville, is headquarters of the Montgomery County Historical Society. The house was built in 1815 by Upton Beall, the second clerk of the Montgomery County Court. Constructed of red brick with a main section and a wing, it is a fine example of the Federal style of architecture. There are extensive grounds with many box bushes.

The interior is beautifully designed in the neo-classic style of Robert Adam, with a wide entrance hall and staircase. It is furnished with pieces from the period 1815-60. The drawing room, with its lovely Adam mantel, is furnished with many pieces of pre-1890 furniture such as a Duncan Phyfe sofa, Sheraton Empire chairs, early Victorian chairs, lamps, and bric-a-brac. The dining room is furnished in the Empire style with a formal banquet table. A collection of china and glassware is on display. There are interesting portraits and pictures pertaining to Montgomery County and Maryland history. The Society has a collection of period clothes, which is on display from time to time. The house is open Tuesday through Saturday, noon to 4 P.M. Admission charge. Telephone: (301) 340-2825. Web site: www.montgomeryhistory.org/beall-dawson-historic-park.

Wheaton Regional Park, at 2000 Shorefield Road in Wheaton, offers a variety of recreational opportunities that appeal to young and old. The lake is well stocked with fish, and visitors are welcome to try their skill with rod and reel. The park offers bike and bridle trails, with bike rentals and a riding stable. Open daily, sunrise to sunset. Telephone: (301) 905-3045. Web site: www.montgomeryparks.org/facilities/regional_parks/wheaton/index. shtm.

The **Brookside Nature Center** is located at 1500 Glenallan Avenue, at the north end of the park. It can be reached by a foot trail from the park. One can also reach the small museum and nature trail by returning to Georgia Avenue, turning right, then right again on Randolph Road for less than a mile to Glenallen Avenue on the right. A naturalist is generally on duty during the week to conduct groups on nature walks or in special programs. Open Tuesday to Saturday, 9 A.M. to 5 P.M.; Sunday, 1 to 5 P.M. Web site: www.montgomeryparks.org/nature_centers/brookside.

Brookside Gardens, adjacent to the Nature Center at 1800 Glenallan, is a 50-acre public display garden featuring two indoor conservatories where lush green tropical plants accent colorful seasonal displays and special exhibits year round. Outside, 11 specialty gardens are dazzling in color and variety, including a rose garden, an azalea garden, a fragrance gardern, an herb garden, gude garden, and the trial garden. The visitors center houses a 3,000-volume horticulture reference library, which is aimed at the home gardener. Free admission. The gardens are open year round, 9 A.M. to sunset, except Christmas Day. The conservatories are open daily, 10 A.M. to 5 P.M. Call for information about special lectures and tours. Telephone: (301) 962-1400. Web site: www.montgomeryparks.org/brookside.

The **National Capital Trolley Museum,** located at 1313 Bonifant Road in Colesville, was founded in 1959 after the abandonment of streetcar service in the District of Columbia had become a certainty. The collection consists of 17 streetcars from DC and other cities. Many of these are operational on a one-mile demonstration railway. In addition, there is a zero-scale model layout representing a

Washington streetscape from the 1930's, a film program, and traditional exhibits of street railway artifacts and photographs. Open January through November, weekends, noon to 5 P.M.; additional Thursday and Friday operations, June 15 through August 15, from 11 A.M. to 3 P.M.; additional Thursday and Friday operations, October 1 through November 15, from 10 A.M. to 2 P.M.; Holly Trolley Festival in December, weekends, 5 to 9 P.M. Free admission. Nominal charge for trolley rides. Telephone: (301) 384-6088. Web site: www.dctrolley.org.

Rock Creek Regional Park in Rockville offers many recreational facilities, including a picnic area, playgrounds, an archery range, boat rental, hiking trails, and a horse trail. Open daily, sunrise to sunset. A boat ride on Needwood Lake aboard the *Needwood Queen*, replica of a nineteenth-century Mississippi sternwheeler. The 15-minute cruise is available on weekends and holidays from May through September. For reservations and fees call (301) 762-1888. Rowboats, canoes, and pedal boats may be rented from May through September. Fishing is good in the stocked lake, and visitors may buy supplies in the bait-and-tackle shop. Maryland fishing permits are required and may be purchased in the shop. Telephone: (301) 948-5053. Web site: www.montgomeryparks.org/facilities/regional_parks/rockcreek/ind ex.shtm.

Most of the Patuxent River Valley, from Rocky Gorge Dam above Laurel to Route 97 above Sunshine, is under the jurisdiction of the Washington Suburban Sanitary Commission and called **Patuxent River Recreational Areas.** The two large reservoirs along this river are a major source of water for the suburban Washington area. The Commission has set aside seven recreational areas for public use for fishing, boating, picnicking, hunting, and horseback riding. The recreation areas are open during daylight hours. Boating and fishing activities are allowed from March to December. Picnicking is permitted from April to October. The specific Patuxent River Recreation Areas include **Brighton Dam** (with its lovely Azalea Gardens), **Green's Bridge Fishing Area, Triadelphia Lake Picnic and Fishing Area, Pigtail Branch Fishing Area, Brown's Bridge Fishing Area, T. Howard Duckett Reservoir** (Rocky Gorge), and **Scott's Cove.** Reservoir-use permits are issued by the commission. The permits cover all activities—fishing, boating, boat mooring, hunting, and horseback riding. For hunting and fishing, state permits, in addition to the WSSC permits, are necessary. Hunting is limited to bow only and is permitted in designated areas along Triadelphia Lake. Check with the Brighton Dam Information Office (2 Brighton Dam Road in Brookville), which is open daily for permit purchases, 8 A.M. to 8 P.M. Telephone: (301) 774-9124.

Except for the 600-acre, developed Clopper area, **Seneca Creek State Park,** at 11950 Clopper Road in Gaithersburg, has a rustic, wild atmosphere in its 6,200 acres. One can follow streamside trails, which afford an opportunity to observe abundant and varied wildlife and to enjoy the scenic beauty of this primitive area close to the Washington suburbs. Wild ducks and muskrats in the creek, and deer, squirrel, wild turkey, quail, rabbit, and woodchuck may be seen in the forests and meadows. Wild flowers are abundant along the woodland trails, especially in spring and early summer. A visitor center is located at the entrance to the park, where summer programs are offered. Open daily, 8 A.M. to sunset. Admission charge on weekends and holidays. Telephone: (301) 924-2127.

Web site: www.dnr.state.md.us/publiclands/central/seneca.asp.

C&O Canal National Historical Park

One of the most popular weekend escapes for city folks is the 184.5 miles of the Chesapeake and Ohio Canal, paralleling the Potomac River from Washington to Cumberland, Maryland. The canal and its towpath make an enjoyable spot for a picnic, an afternoon bike or hiking trip, or even a more ambitious field trip exploring the ecology, geology, and culture of the towns along its banks. The canal was an engineering feat when it was first built, and today it is no less a marvel.

As early as 1753, George Washington envisioned a waterway connecting the Ohio Valley and the Chesapeake Bay. Three decades later, a start was made on his ambitious plan when he and other like-minded Virginia gentlemen chartered the Patowmack Company. Plans were made to cut "skirting" canals around five falls along the Virginia side of the river at what is now Great Falls National Park. Though Washington resigned from the company in 1789 when he became the first U.S. president, his interest in the project never lessened. The skirting canals were finally completed in 1802, three years after his death, although the rest of the plan was never carried out.

Merchants still dreamed of a completed canal across the Alleghenies providing a more economic means of transportation. Expanding the Patowmack Company's canal was the only answer. Construction of what was known as the Chesapeake and Ohio Canal began on July 4, 1828, when Pres. John Quincy Adams removed the first spade full of dirt of what was dubbed the "magnificent ditch." As if to predict the eventual fate of the canal, that same day construction was begun in Baltimore of the Baltimore & Ohio Railroad. The race for the west across the Alleghenies was on.

Problems plagued the C&O Canal Company from the beginning. Supplies were scarce, excavation much more difficult than originally imagined, and skilled labor virtually unavailable. To complicate matters, a feud to obtain land rights developed between the Canal Company and the B&O Railroad. Because the bluffs come so close to the river, there was often room for only one right of way. The canal company fought a bitter court battle, and finally reached Cumberland, Maryland, in 1850—eight years after the railroad had arrived. By then it was an accepted fact of life that trains were faster and less expensive than canal travel. Regrettably, plans to continue the canal to Pittsburgh were finally dropped.

Although the canal never achieved the economic success George Washington had dreamed of, for 75 years the completed portion of the canal saw active traffic along its waters. Mules walking along the towpath pulled barges at the rate of four miles per hour. The 184.5 miles of the canal consisted of 74 lift locks, which raised barges from sea level at Georgetown to 605 feet at Cumberland. Eleven stone aqueducts carried the canal over major Potomac tributaries, and seven dams supplied water for the canal. There were also a number of waste weirs to control the water level, hundreds of culverts to carry roads and streams under the canal, a 3,118-foot tunnel to take it under a mountain, and a variety of stop locks, river locks, bridges, section houses, and lock houses.

In 1889, an enormous flood swept the Potomac Valley, leaving the canal in ruin. It was rebuilt and used until 1924 when another flood seriously harmed the already financially troubled canal company. It was again damaged by Hurricane Agnes in 1972, and has undergone extensive repairs in recent years. Since 1971, the canal has been a national park.

Because of the amount of territory the C&O Canal traverses, there is a wide variety of recreational activities for visitors. Backpacking, biking, bird watching, boating, camping, climbing, cross-country skiing, fishing, hiking, horseback riding, kayaking, nature walks, and wildlife viewing are the most popular activities. Interpretive programs are offered at each of the visitors centers along the canal. The

Georgetown Visitor Center is a good starting point for your tour of the C&O Canal. It is located at 1057 Thomas Jefferson Street, near 30th and M streets in Washington, D.C. Telephone: (202) 653-5190. You can also check the C&O Canal Web site at www.nps.gov/choh.

In addition to the Georgetown Visitor Center, there are five other visitor centers that can provide detailed information on the particular canal activities that are nearby. The centers are as follows: Brunswick Visitor Center, 40 West Potomac Street, Brunswick, MD 21716, Telephone: (301) 834-7100; Cumberland Visitor Center/Western Maryland Station, Room 304, 13 Canal Street, Cumberland, MD 21502, Telephone: (301) 722-8226; Great Falls Tavern Visitor Center, 11710 MacArthur Boulevard, Potomac, MD 20854, Telephone: (301) 767-3714; Hancock Visitor Center, 326 East Main Street, Hancock, MD 21750, Telephone: (301) 745-5877; and Williamsport Visitor Center, 205 West Potomac Street, Williamsport, MD 21795, Telephone: (301) 582-0813.

Howard County

Howard County, in the western corridor between Baltimore and Washington, is still a somewhat rural area, although its eastern portion has become a suburb of both cities. There are several historic towns in Howard County—such as Ellicott City, Elkridge, and Savage—that provide a pleasant visit for the weekend traveler.

John Smith is said to have explored the Patapsco River near the location of **Elkridge,** which is the oldest settlement in the county. Elkridge, originally named Elk Ridge Landing in colonial times, was settled early in the eighteenth century by tobacco farmers who were attracted to the area's rich soil and the accessibility of the Patapsco River. By 1746 the settlement rivaled Annapolis as a port and commercial center. Ships sailed from Elk Ridge Landing for the markets in England loaded with hogsheads of tobacco, iron ore, lumber, and flour from the Ellicott mills.

Ellicott City, south of Baltimore near the intersection of Routes 29 and 144, is a truly unique town. It is nestled between two gorges, the narrow Tiber Creek and the rocky valley into which the Patapsco River flows. Many of the old houses, built of a dark local granite, seem to be wedged into the rocky hillside. A number of old buildings on Main Street actually straddle Tiber Creek.

The town was founded by three Quaker brothers from Bucks County, Pennsylvania—Joseph, John, and Andrew Ellicott. They helped revolutionize the economy of Maryland by persuading farmers to grow wheat instead of tobacco and by introducing fertilizer. Ellicott City developed around Ellicott's grist and flourmill, established in 1772 on the east bank of the river, and grew with the building of the Cumberland Road and the coming of the B&O Railroad in 1830.

For more information about county and Ellicott City attractions, you can visit the Howard County Tourism Council at 8267 Main Street, Ellicott City, MD 21041. Telephone: (410) 313-1900 or (800) 288-TRIP. Web sites: visitmaryland.org/Pages/MarylandHome.aspx. or www.visithowardcounty.com.

The **Ellicott City B&O Railroad Station Museum** is located at 2711 Maryland Avenue. The Ellicott City station was the first terminus to be built outside Baltimore. It was on the Ellicott City-Baltimore route that the famous race between the steam engine "Tom Thumb" and a horse-drawn carriage occurred in 1830. The horse won the race because of a mechanical failure on the "Tom Thumb." The museum offers a tour of the 1831 stone building, a multimedia presentation of the history of railroading as it began in America, and a 45-foot model of the railroad in the Patapsco Valley from Baltimore to Ellicott City as it was in the 1870s. Admission charge. Open Fridays, Saturdays, and Mondays, 11 A.M. to 4 P.M.; Sundays, noon to 5 P.M. Telephone: (410) 461-1945. Web site: www.borail.org/Ellicott-City-Station.aspx.

The little village of Savage is tucked away between two busy highways, I-95 and Route 1, and is equidistant from Baltimore and Washington, just east of the point where I-95 and I-97 cross. Savage was a hub of textile activity in the nineteenth century. The mill, developed by John Savage of Philadelphia in 1816, operated constantly from 1816 to 1945.

In its heyday, the mill manufactured cotton duck that was made into sails for the clipper ships that sailed from nearby Baltimore harbor. One of the first hydroelectric generating plants was constructed on this site in 1918. The mill provided electricity for the village, as well as providing other services such as a company store, for which the workers were paid in scrip currency printed by the company. In the village of Savage the visitor may still see the white cottages built for the mill workers, and at the corner of Baltimore and Foundry streets is a privately owned stone building that houses the county library. Called **Carroll Baldwin Hall,** the building and the small park behind it are early examples of community planning by the industrialists who ran the town.

Historic Savage Mill's buildings have been fully restored. Located at 800 Foundry Street, the almost-200-year-old mill has been renovated into a marketplace featuring specialty and antique shops, artists' studios, and galleries. Throughout the mill historical panels and museum displays describe mill life and the technology of the weaving industry. **Historic Savage Mill** has purchased the manor house, built in 1840 for the Cotton Mill's first manager. Open Monday through Wednesday, 10 A.M. to 6 P.M.; Thursday through Saturday, 10 A.M. to 9 P.M.; Sunday, 11 A.M. to 7 P.M. Telephone: (800) 788-6455. Web site: www.savagemill.com.

The last standing **Bollman Truss semisuspension bridge** in the world can be visited in Savage Mill and is recognized as a national treasure. The bridge spans the Little Patuxent River and was brought to Savage in 1860 when the B&O Railroad serviced the Mill. This style of bridge was used all over the United States and Europe, but was made of wrought and cast iron which rusted out in all locations but this one. You can cross the bridge on foot for scenic views of the mill complex.

Patapsco Valley State Park is located at 8020 Baltimore National Pike in Ellicott City. The park extends along 32 miles of the Patapsco River, encompassing 14,000 acres and five developed areas. Recreational opportunities include hiking, fishing, camping, canoeing, horseback and mountain bike trails, as well as picnicking for individuals or large groups in the park's many popular pavilions. The Avalon Visitor Center houses exhibits spanning over 300 years of history along the Patapsco River. Housed in a nineteenth-century stone dwelling in the Avalon Area, the center includes a re-creation of a 1930s forest warden's office. Telephone: (410) 461-5670. Web site: www.dnr.state.md.us/publiclands/central/patapsco.asp.

Columbia is a planned city embracing over 15,000 acres. About one-fifth of the area has been set aside for parks, lakes, woodlands, and other recreational purposes. It consists of planned villages grouped around a shopping mall, between Baltimore and Washington off Route 29. Or follow signs from I-95. Columbia offers many recreational facilities, most of which are open to visitors. Among these, in season, are boating on the downtown lake, outdoor skating on two lakes, indoor ice skating and swimming, horseback riding, golfing on two courses, and hiking. Cultural activities include music, theater, and art. The Merriweather Post Pavilion of Music, at 10475 Little Patuxent Parkway, in a beautiful woodland setting, draws topflight summertime entertainment. For more information, telephone (410) 715.5550 or visit the Merriweather Post Pavilion Web site: www.merriweathermusic.com/contact.

WESTERN MARYLAND

Garrett County

Garrett County, the westernmost area of Maryland, lies within the Allegheny plateau and contains the highest point in the state—Backbone Mountain, 3,360 feet. It is the only county in Maryland where the rivers do not flow entirely eastward into the Potomac. From the crest of Backbone Mountain, the waters flow northward toward the Ohio and Mississippi rivers. The Youghiogheny River, which has been designated a Wild and Scenic River, begins in Garrett. More than half the county is forest area. Garrett County was created in 1872 and was named for John W. Garrett, who was president of the Baltimore and Ohio Railroad and had done much to further the development of the area.

In the early 1880s, it was the western frontier of the United States. Today it is one of Maryland's most sparsely populated counties. For more information about the county and its many attractions, contact the Garrett County Chamber of Commerce. Telephone: (301) 387-4FUN. Web site: www.garrettchamber.com.

Begin your tour of Garrett County in Grantsville. The **Casselman Inn** (c. 1824) was built to serve the travelers on the National Road. Many of the early features of the building have been preserved. One of the three dining rooms was originally used during the stagecoach days and diners may see the original fireplace where food was prepared. The building has been in continuous use for more than 175 years and is still serving as a hotel. The hotel is listed on the National Register of Historic Places. The restaurant is open year round but is closed on Sundays. Located at 113 East Main Street (Alt. U.S. Route 40) in Grantsville. Telephone: (301) 895-5055 (lodging) or (301) 895-5266 (restaurant). Web Site: www.thecasselman.com.

Casselman Bridge State Park is probably the smallest state park in Maryland. When it was built in 1813, the stone bridge was the longest single-span bridge (80 feet) in the United States. It was built to link Cumberland, Maryland, to Wheeling, West Virginia, on the National Pike (Route 40). It was in use until 1953 and has been designated a National Historic Landmark. The bridge is located one mile east of

Grantsville on Route 40. Its five-acre park has picnicking facilities. Telephone: (301) 895-5453. Web site: www.dnr.state.md.us/publiclands/western/casselman.asp.

Nearby in the shadow of the stone bridge is **Penn Alps,** a remodeled log stagecoach stop that serves as a restaurant and crafts shop. The main building was constructed in 1818 and diners will see the stones of the huge fireplace that date back to the days when stagecoach travelers used the Cumberland Road to Wheeling. Another relocated log stagecoach stop (c. 1818) serves as a demonstration center for spinners, weavers, potters, a bird carver, a blacksmith, and a Tiffany stained-glass craftsman. The craft shop also sells the handiwork of local craftsmen. The adjacent Spruce Forest Artisan Village is open Monday through Saturday, 8 A.M. to 5 P.M.; year round. Telephone: (301) 895-5985. Web site: www.pennalps.com.

Braddock's Trail, built by British general Edward Braddock's army in 1755, was an improvement of the old Indian route, Nemacolin Trail. The trail was a major route west until it was abandoned in the nineteenth century with the construction of the National Road (Route 40). The trail can be seen at Little Meadows, one of Braddock's most important encampments and a site used by George Washington. It is four miles east of Grantsville on the north side of Route 40.

Nearby is **Savage River State Forest,** off I-68 via exit 22, route 219/Chestnut Ridge Road or exit 24 on Lower New Germany Road. Savage River State Forest is the largest Maryland state forest covering three mountain ridges. Many visitors come here to walk the 18-mile Savage Trail, which follows the ridge of Big Savage Mountain from near route 40 southward to the Savage River Dam. The two state parks, **New Germany State Park** and **Big Run State Park,** are located in the larger (eastern) portion of the forest. The forest contains a 360-acre reservoir with limited boating use; no motorized boats are allowed. The damming of the Savage River has enabled control of a 5.2-mile whitewater-canoeing course where competitions are periodically held. In other non-wilderness areas, the forest offers a 12-mile snowmobile trail, 50 miles of moderately difficult hiking, trails and 26 designated primitive camping sites. A daily service charge is required for the campsites, which are on a first-come, first-served basis. Telephone: (301) 895-5759. Web site: dnr.maryland.gov/publiclands/western/savageriverforest.asp.

New Germany State Park is located on the site of a once-prosperous milling center. The 13-acre lake was formed by damming the river in operation of the mills. New Germany is a large cross-country ski center. It has camping, hiking, picnicking, trailer camping, boating, fishing, and swimming facilities, as well as vending concession, toilets, and showers. Eleven cabins are completely furnished. The lake is stocked with game fish. Numerous hiking trails take one through the old hemlock grove and along Poplar Lick Run. All reservations for cabins, camping and pavilions are handled through a central reservation system. Camping facilities are available April through October. Camping charge; weekend day-use park charge. Telephone: (301) 895-5453 or, for reservations, (888) 432-CAMP. Web site: www.dnr.state.md.us/publiclands/western/newgermany.asp.

Big Run State Park is 300 acres which lie wholly within the Savage River State Forest, at the north end of the Savage River reservoir. Big Run attracts the backpacker and canoeist who seek the peace and quiet of the backwoods. There is excellent fishing, notably for bass and trout. Camping sites are available with nearby composting toilets and drinking water. The park is open year round. Day use admission charge. Campsite and pavilion service charge. Telephone: (301) 895-5453. Reservations: (888) 432-CAMP. Web site: www.dnr.state.md.us/publiclands/western/bigrun.asp.

Deep Creek Lake State Park and Deep Creek Lake are near McHenry, Maryland. Deep Creek Lake is the largest freshwater lake in Maryland. It is 12 miles in length, with a shoreline of 65 miles covering nearly 3,900 acres. A wide variety of activities abound, including boating, water skiing, fishing, swimming, hiking, picnicking, mountain biking, golf, sailing, downhill and cross country skiing and snowmobiling. There are a number of campgrounds in the area. Motels, rental homes, condos, and bed-and-breakfast accommodations also dot the shoreline. Some provide dock facilities, sandy beaches, and swimming areas.

Built in 1925 by the Youghiogheny Electric Company, the lake was purchased by the Pennsylvania Electric Company in 1942. The state park is located in the northeastern section of the lake and includes hiking and snowmobile trails, swimming, boat launching, biking and 112 campsites. A discovery center offers year-round programming. Service charge applies to day-use area. Reservations are required for sites and pavilions. Telephone: (301) 387-5563. For camping reservations: (888) 432-CAMP. Web site: www.dnr.state.md.us/publiclands/western/deepcreek.asp.

Garrett State Forest, near Oakland, Maryland, is suggestive of the Rocky Mountains, though it attains only a fraction of their altitude. Its many peaks and ridges are about 3,000 feet in elevation. The ridge called Backbone Mountain is located here, and an eastern "continental divide" occurs, causing waters from the western slopes to flow toward the Mississippi River. You can enjoy hiking, camping, fishing, and hunting in season, and snowmobiling in winter. There are 35 primitive campsites available without hookups or showers. Deer, small game, grouse, and turkey lure the hunter. Many abandoned coal mines may be seen in and near the forest. Free admission; small charge for camping sites. Telephone: (301) 334-2038 or (888) 432-CAMP, for reservations.
Web site: dnr.maryland.gov/publiclands/western/garrettforest.asp.

Oakland, the county seat, sits on a plateau of 2,650 feet above sea level. The coming of the railroad at the end of the nineteenth century encouraged development of the Deer Park/Oakland area. It was known for its clean air and beautiful scenery and had a Chautauqua meeting ground.

The **Garrett County Historical Society Museum,** located at 107 S. Second Street, is devoted to county-related historical and cultural events. The museum displays artifacts depicting lifestyles in Garrett County from 1872 to present day. The museum also has many items from the grand old hotels—Glades, Oakland, Deer Park, and Mountain Lake Park hotels—from the Victorian era. None of these frame structures have survived. The museum is open various hours; it is best to call before stopping by. Free admission. Telephone: (301) 334-3226. Web site: www.deepcreekhospitality.com/fr_gc_historical.asp.

One block away at the corner of Liberty and Second streets is the **B&O Railroad Station** (c. 1884). The station is a picturesque remainder of the nineteenth-century resort community. This Queen Anne-style building is composed of incised brick and has a round tower with a conical roof and arched windows. The station has been placed on the National Register of Historic Places. Across the street at Second and Liberty, one can visit **St. Matthew's Episcopal Church,** the church of the presidents. The church was attended during their summer vacations by presidents Grant, Harrison, and Cleveland. This handsome building was built in 1868 by John Garrett as a memorial to his brother, Henry, and has been restored by the St. Matthew's congregation. Telephone: (301) 334-2510.

Swallow Falls State Park and **Herrington Manor State Park** are both located at the southwestern end of the state, three miles east of West Virginia. Both parks offer picnicking areas and interpretive programs during the summer season. Telephone: (301) 387-6938 or (301) 334-9180. Web sites: dnr.maryland.gov/publiclands/western/swallowfalls.asp or dnr.maryland.gov/publiclands/western/herrington.asp.

One of the most beautiful sites in the county, the 55-foot **Muddy Creek Falls,** is the tallest in the state. **Swallow Falls State Park** is a scenic paradise of rushing water and towering trees, cliffs, narrow gorges, and misty glens. Maryland's last virgin forest is found in the park, with giant pines and hemlocks that rise more than 100 feet. Muddy Creek Falls is located near the confluence of Muddy Creek and the Youghiogheny River. Hiking trails along the Youghiogheny skirt the rapids, and one trail features a swinging bridge across Muddy Creek above the falls. The park was the site of summer vacation camps in 1918 and 1921 of Henry Ford, Thomas Edison, and Harvey Firestone. The park has 64 campsites near a washhouse with running water, laundry tubs, showers, and toilets. Campsites are closed from the last day of deer season to April 1.

Herrington Manor State Park surrounds a 53-acre lake with housekeeping cabins. Forest plantations around the lake, representing Maryland state reforestation practices, may be seen via easily accessible trails in the 365-acre park. Twenty cabins may be rented year round for a 2-night minimum in the winter and a 7-night minimum in the summer. Camping, swimming, boating, and fishing are allowed on the lake. Only electric motors of one horsepower or less are permitted. Canoes, rowboats and paddleboats are available for rent. Three of the tent sites have hookups and there are 3 large youth group sites. During the winter the park offers five miles of cross-country skiing trails and has skis for rent. Reservations for the cabins are accepted one year in advance. Telephone: (301) 334-9180. For camping reservations: (888) 432-2267. Web site: dnr.maryland.gov/publiclands/western/herrington.asp.

Cranesville Swamp, bridging the Maryland-West Virginia border, is a rare pocket of sub-Arctic swamp surviving from the Ice Age. The swamp has been designated a National Natural Landmark and is owned and administered by The Nature Conservancy, a nonprofit private organization. The boreal bog preserves a rare assemblage of plant life that is typical of colder Canadian climates. The preserve presently covers 560 acres of swampland and is the southernmost tamarack forest in the United States. There is no resident naturalist on the site, but the Herrington Manor State Park rangers will assist visitors in getting to the swamp. Free admission. The Nature Conservancy periodically conducts guided tours for its members. Telephone: (301) 897-8570. Web site: www.nature.org.

Allegany County

Allegany County was formed in 1789, and its first settlers in the mid-eighteenth century were English. Later immigrants came from Scotland, Wales, Ireland, and Germany. Unlike other sections of Maryland, Allegany is not an agricultural area. During the nineteenth century, bituminous coal and iron ore mining and the glass-making industry developed. Those industries declined in the twentieth century, and Allegany County has had difficulty replacing the jobs lost.

Allegany County is located in the heart of the Allegany plateau, with elevations ranging from 2,850 feet near Frostburg to Cumberland's 620 feet. For more about local attractions in "the mountain side of Maryland," stop by the visitors center in Cumberland at 13 Canal Street. Telephone: (800) 425-2067. Web site: www.mdmountainside.com.

Allegany County has a small African American population but a rich historical and cultural presence. The Potomac Cultural Group, 804 Buckingham Road in Cumberland, specializes in African American historical and cultural events. Telephone: (301) 759-6446.

The **Green Ridge State Forest** is 43,000 acres located about 22 miles east of Cumberland. Chief attractions are rugged scenery, 92 primitive campsites, 8 primitive group sites, picnicking, hiking, biking, riding trails, shooting range, hunting, fishing, and, in the winter, snowmobiling. Four streams in the forest are stocked with fish.

Other unique features include **Old Stone Furnace** at Chimney Hollow and the 3,080-mile-long **Paw Paw Tunnel,** part of the historic C&O Canal. The forest also features large plantations of red, white, and Scotch pine. Nearby are **Sideling Hill Wildlife Management Area,** and the **Billmeyer/Belle Wildlife Management.** Telephone: (301) 478-3124. Camping reservations: (888) 432-CAMP. Web site: http://www.dnr.state.md.us/publiclands/western/greenridgeforest.asp.

Rocky Gap State Park is near Flintstone, west of Green Ridge, about seven miles east of Cumberland. Rocky Gap lies in an area of impressive scenic beauty. Rugged mountains surround it, and a splendid mile-long gorge, descending to Rocky Gap Run, displays sheer cliffs, rock slides, and dense forests. The road which bisects the day-use area was once the first wagon road westward through this vicinity, in use long before the National Pike was developed. Known as the "Old Hancock Road," its construction was authorized by the Maryland Assembly in 1791. The 243-acre, man-made lake has three bathing beaches, modern bathhouses, drinking fountains, and boating and food concessions. Picnic areas have charcoal grills. Visitors may enjoy swimming, boating, nature study, fishing, or hiking on the park's winding trails. The campground consists of 278 wooded campsites with washhouses and hot showers. Interpretative programs such as films, nature-study hikes, and crafts exhibits are scheduled year round in the park. Telephone: (301) 722-1480. Web site: http://www.dnr.state.md.us/publiclands/western/rockygap.asp.

Cumberland, once known as Wills Creek, took its present name from Fort Cumberland, located here during the French and Indian Wars. It was the western terminus of the Chesapeake and Ohio Canal. Cumberland was also the starting point of the historic National Road, the first federally funded highway in the U.S.; it helped open to settlement the area west of the Alleghenies. Between Hancock and Cumberland, the motorist crosses five mountains. A stop can be made at each overlook for a scene of grandeur and beauty. The mountain views, from east to west, are: Sideling Hill (1,600 feet), Town Hill (1,600 feet), Green Ridge (1,575 feet), Polish Mountain (1,340 feet), and Martin's Mountain (1,695 feet).

Cumberland offers visitors a walking tour of its historic places. One can also take a motor tour of the area to visit points within several miles of the city. Maps and directions may be obtained free of charge from the Allegany County Visitors Center, 13 Canal Street in Cumberland. Telephone: (301) (800) 425-2067. Web site: www.mdmountinside.com.

Baltimore Street, the city's main street, is now a pedestrian mall. Walking west across the bridge over **Wills Creek** and up the hill you enter the beautiful and historic **Washington Street District.** Up to the 600 block it is listed on the National Register of Historic Places. At the beginning of the street you will see **Emmanuel Episcopal Church** (c. 1848), built on the site of **Fort Cumberland** (1753). The Fort Cumberland tunnels under the church are open for touring during Allegany County's official Heritage Days Festival the second weekend of June. They were used to obtain water from Wills Creek, as an escape route, and for storage of ammunition. Washington Street traverses the oldest and finest residential area in the city. As you climb the hill, the **First Presbyterian Church** is on the right. Beyond, where the street levels off, is the **Allegany County Library** (c. 1849), once an academy. Directly across the street is the impressive **Allegany County Court House** (c. 1893). This **Prospect Square** area was the parade ground for Fort Cumberland, during its occupancy by General Braddock and his aide, George Washington. The first fort was built on this site in 1750 and was the scene of Washington's first military command in 1754, during the French and Indian Wars. It was here also that Washington, in 1794, made his last military appearance in a review of troops called out to suppress the Whiskey Rebellion.

A block farther up the street is **St. Paul's Lutheran Church** (c. 1958). Its history goes back to 1795 when a log church was built on this site. On Fayette Street, behind St. Paul's, is **St. Peter and Paul Church and Monastery.** The monastery, built in 1849 by the Redemptorists, was taken over by the Carmelites in 1866. Cross the street and proceed to **History House** (c. 1867), at 218 Washington Street. This old home is headquarters of the Allegany County Historical Society. Many interesting exhibits of the early history of the area can be seen here. At 108 Washington Street is the old **Walsh Home** built in 1866, now occupied by the Board of Education, and the birthplace of Bishop James Walsh, a missionary in China imprisoned for many years by the Chinese Communists. This historic district maintains a uniformity of architectural quality that is tied together by the tree-shaded street where coal and rail barons in another era lived in ornate mansions, many of which are now restored.

One block to the left of Washington Street is Greene Street, where **Riverside Park** and **George Washington's Headquarters** (c. 1755) are located. This building was used by Washington during the French and Indian Wars and again during the Whiskey Rebellion. Also in the park is the **Thomas Cresap Monument,** erected to the memory of a noted pioneer and patriot. In the **Oldtown** area in 1740, Cresap built the first home and fort and laid out the first trail to lands west of the Alleghenies. Opposite Washington's Headquarters is the starting point of the **Old Cumberland Road** (also known as Braddock Road) to the west. A plaque marks the ground-zero mile marker. Below the Western Maryland Railway Station is the western terminus for the famous **Chesapeake and Ohio Canal,** opened in 1850.

A few miles farther down Route 220 south is **Cresaptown,** named for sons of the Cresap pioneer settler family. Turn right on Route 53, a picturesque road which leads to Route 40. Just west of the intersection of Routes 53 and 40 is the restored **Old Toll House,** erected in 1835, the first toll house on the Old Cumberland Road. A picnic spot invites you to read the rates collected.

On the western outskirts of the city following Alternate Route 40 you will pass through the famous **"Narrows."** The "Narrows" is a natural 1,000-foot breach between Haystack and Wills Mountain. Known as the "Gateway to the West," this transportation route played an important part in the development of the west. The picturesque gap in the Allegheny Mountains has been designated a Natural Landmark. The Narrows also boasts a "Lover's Leap" legend—an Indian princess and her lover, an English trapper, are said to have leaped to their deaths from here.

A detour off Interstate 68 on Route 220 north will bring you to Nave's Crossroads. Turn right for a short distance to Route 40 and head east. At this area sits the 1810 Brew House, a local microbrewery originally known as **Turkey Flight Manor.** It is the oldest brick house in the Cumberland area, built in 1758. Soldiers were hospitalized here during the Civil War.

Frostburg is about 15 miles west of Cumberland on Alternate Route 40. It began with the log home Meshach Frost built for his bride in 1812. When the National Road brought stagecoach service, their home became an inn, **Highland Hall.** During the 1840s Frostburg became a commercial mining, brick, and lumber center. These industries declined during the late nineteenth and early twentieth centuries. Today, Frostburg's biggest employer is Frostburg University. The town retains many of its old historic homes, which may be seen on a walking tour of Main Street. A map and description of the homes may be obtained from the Allegany County Visitors Center in Cumberland. Some of the homes date from the National Road days, as well as from the Civil War and Victorian eras.

Washington County

Washington County lies in the Hagerstown Valley, between two ridges. This valley is a continuation of the Shenandoah Valley of Virginia. The Appalachian Trail runs along the entire eastern boundary of the county. The early eighteenth-century settlements in Washington County began as frontier outposts. In 1756, the

Maryland General Assembly authorized the construction of Fort Frederick to provide a base for British military operations and protection for local homesteaders against the Indians, who were allied with the French. In 1776 the county was founded and named for Gen. George Washington. During the Civil War, Washington County was the scene of several significant and bloody battles—South Mountain, Harpers Ferry, and Antietam.

For more about regional attractions, you can visit the Washington County Convention and Visitors Bureau at Elizabeth Hager Center, 16 Public Square, Hagerstown, MD 21740. Telephone: (301) 791-3246. Web site: www.marylandmemories.org.

Antietam National Battlefield, near Sharpsburg, where Routes 34 and 65 meet, is the site of the bloodiest single-day battle in the Civil War. The battle, which took place on September 17, 1862, greatly altered the course of the Civil War, although neither side gained the upper hand at Antietam. Gen. George B. McClellan and the Federal forces prevented the Confederates under Gen. Robert E. Lee from carrying the war effectively into the North and caused Great Britain to postpone recognition of the Confederate government. Of almost equal importance was the long-awaited opportunity given President Lincoln to issue the Emancipation Proclamation. Five days after the Federal victory, Lincoln issued his preliminary proclamation, which warned the South that, on January 1, 1863, he would declare free all slaves in territory still in rebellion against the United States. Henceforth, the war would have a dual purpose: to preserve the Union and to end slavery.

At the visitor center, exhibits and an explanatory slide show tell the story of the campaign. Pick up a map and directions for a self-guided tour of the battlefield. The battlefield site contains a national cemetery of Federal soldiers from the Civil War and some from later wars. The remains of Confederate soldiers are scattered in private cemeteries in the area. The Antietam National Battlefield Site and Cemetery, administered by the National Park Service, is open daily, 8:30 A.M. to 6 P.M. from June through August; 8:30 A.M. to 5 P.M. from September through May. Closed Thanksgiving, Christmas, and New Year's. Admission charge. Telephone: (301) 432-5124. Web site: www.nps.gov/anti.

Burnside Bridge, over Antietam Creek, is probably the most famous of the Washington County bridges. It figured prominently in the Battle of Antietam for it was where a few hundred Georgia riflemen held off four Federal divisions for hours, changing the outcome of the battle. This beautiful three-arch, 12-foot-wide bridge was built in 1836.

The stone bridges in Washington County were built between 1819 and 1863, in part spurred by the National Road project. The 23 remaining bridges are a result of the pride that Marylanders, and particularly natives of Washington County, displayed in building bridges to endure. The Scotch, German, and Irish immigrants to the area were skilled stonemasons, and the native limestone was an ideal building material. When the secretary of war suggested building covered wooden bridges as a cost-cutting measure, Maryland refused to comply and continued to use stone in Washington County. The Washington County Convention and Visitors Bureau, 16 Public Square (Potomac & Washington Streets) in Hagerstown can provide directions to bridges and information about other attractions in the county. Telephone: (301) 791-3246. Web site: www.marylandmemories.org.

South Mountain State Park is comprised of over 10,000 acres, offering year-round hiking along the Appalachian Trail. South Mountain rises from about 200 feet above sea level in the south by the Potomac River to nearly 2,000 feet at High Rock, almost 40 miles north. There are a number of neighboring state parks on South Mountain: **Gathland, Greenbrier,** and **Washington Monument.** Information about each park is accessible through links on the Maryland State Department of Natural Resources Web site:
www.dnr.state.md.us.

Gathland State Park is the site of the **George Alfred Townsend Museum** located at Arnoldstown Road, Burkittsville. Gathland was the estate of George Alfred Townsend, war correspondent of the Civil War, who became an important journalist and novelist of the Reconstruction Era. His pen name, Gath, was formed by adding an "H" to his initials and was inspired by a biblical passage: "Tell it not in Gath, publish it not in the streets of Askalon." The museum is located at Crampton's Gap, one of three gaps comprising the Battle of South Mountain in September 1862. The museum chronicles Townsend's life and the past splendor of the estate. Civil War weaponry and uniform are on display. The **War Correspondents Memorial Arch,** a 50-foot stone arch, the only known memorial to correspondents of any war, is the centerpiece of the park.

Within the park you can enjoy a hike on the Appalachian Trail, picnic, or participate in periodic Civil War encampments and special events. The park is open daily, year round. The small museum, staffed by docents, is opened seasonally during the summer. Call for days and times. Telephone: (301) 791-4767. Web site: www.dnr.state.md.us/publiclands/western/gathland.asp.

Greenbrier State Park is just off I-70 on South Mountain, 10 miles southeast of Hagerstown on Route 40. The park is near the scene of several Civil War engagements. The area was first settled in 1754 and was the scene of Indian raids during the French and Indian War. Local furnaces furnished the iron for cannons during the Revolutionary War. The Appalachian Trail, an attraction for hikers and campers, passes through the park. A 42-acre lake, fed by forest springs, is used for swimming and fishing. The park offers hiking trails, picnicking, boating facilities, and 165 campsites with showers and flush toilets. The park is open during daylight hours. Admission charge. Telephone: (301) 791-4767. Web site: www.dnr.state.md.us/publiclands/western/greenbrier.asp.

Washington Monument State Park is off Alternate Route 40, two miles southeast of Boonsboro. Originally constructed in 1827, this rugged stone tower was the first memorial dedicated to George Washington. It was built on the summit of South Mountain by citizens of nearby Boonsboro from materials picked up at the site. Three states are visible from the top of the Monument—Maryland, Virginia, and West Virginia—as well as such historical sites as Antietam, Harpers Ferry, and Winchester.

The park museum highlights the historic interest of the region, with displays of firearms, Indian relics, and Civil War mementos. The famous Appalachian Trail winds through the park and past the base of the Monument. The Cumberland Valley is a flyway for migratory birds, and an annual count of migrating hawks and eagles is made at the Monument by ornithologists.

There is an accessible picnic area and four camping sites for youth groups. Free admission; charge for campsites. Telephone: (301) 791-4767. Web site: www.dnr.state.md.us/publiclands/western/washington.asp.

Crystal Grottoes Caverns are located near Boonsboro, west on Route 34. An underground limestone cavern of beauty and enchantment, Crystal Grottoes contains corridors of jeweled stalactites and stalagmites of unusual design and formation. The cavern was discovered in 1920 in the course of excavating a rock quarry. A sheltered pavilion is available for picnicking. Open April through October 31, daily, 10 A.M. to 5 P.M.; November through March, weekends, 11 A.M. to 4 P.M. Admission charge. Telephone: (301) 432-6336. Web site: www.crystalgrottoescaverns.com.

Also in Boonsboro is the privately owned **Boonsborough Museum of History,** which contains Civil War memorabilia and Indian artifacts. It is located at 113 North Main Street and can be identified by the five cannons sitting on the front yard. Open May to September, Sunday, 1 to 5 P.M. or by appointment. Admission charge. Telephone: (301) 432-6969.

Fort Frederick State Park is on Route 56, two miles east of I-70's Big Pool Exit between Hagerstown and Hancock. Fort Frederick is a beautifully preserved, historic fort erected in the 1750s during the French and Indian Wars. Fort Frederick and a chain of smaller forts protected the Maryland frontier. A classic fort of that period, it was designed by skilled military engineers. The massive stone walls provided protection for hundreds of settlers. It served as a barracks for captured British and Hessian troops during the American Revolution, and figured as an outpost in the Civil War.

The C&O Canal runs through the southern end of the park. A museum on the grounds displays relics found at Fort Frederick. The park has camping, fishing, picnicking, hiking, and boating facilities. There are 29 primitive campsites, and permits are issued on a first-come, first-served basis. Open daily Memorial Day through Labor Day; weekends only in April, May, September, and October. Admission charge to tour the fort and to enter the park on special-event weekends. Telephone: (301) 842-2155. Web site: www.dnr.state.md.us/publiclands/western/fortfrederick.asp.

Hagerstown, the seat of Washington County, is at the junction of Interstates 70 and 81. It was in 1739 that Jonathan Hager, a German immigrant, settled on his first tract of land, "Hager's Fancy." Hager's original homestead, built over natural springs to provide a water supply safe from Indian attack, survives.

Today, Hagerstown reflects the artistic skill of Hagerstown's eighteenth-century German, Scotch, and Irish stonemasons. The city offers many points of interest for visitors to see.

A few of the most prominent are: The **Zion Reformed Church,** at Potomac and Church streets, was originally built in 1774, but extensive renovations were made to the stone structure in the nineteenth century. It is the oldest building in the city. Jonathan Hager (1719-75), founder of Hagerstown, is buried in the graveyard behind the church.

The **Miller House,** a typical townhouse of the late Federal period (built early 1820s), is at 135 West Washington Street. The Miller House is headquarters of the Washington County Historical Society. The elegant interior is noteworthy for its original hanging stairway rising in a graceful curve to the third floor and for its spacious, high-ceilinged drawing rooms. On exhibit are period furniture pieces; a collection of early photographs, papers, and artifacts of the C&O Canal and of the Civil War; a doll and antique clock collection; and Hagerstown's first fire engine and first taxi. Open Thursday through Saturday, 1 to 4 P.M. Telephone: (301) 797-8782. Web site: www.washcomdhistoricalsociety.org/miller-house.php#.

Jonathan **Hager House Museum,** the home of Jonathan Hager, was built in 1739 and is located at 110 Key Street in Hagerstown City Park. The house was originally one-and-a-half stories high. Built as a fort home and a fur-trading post, the Germanic floor plan spans two springs of water. Hager wanted to assure fresh water within his stronghold, in case of Indian attacks. He used the basement as a blacksmith shop and the upper floors for living quarters. Restored in 1953, today it is owned by the City of Hagerstown and furnished by the Washington County Historical Society. Open to the public, April to December, Tuesday through Saturday, 10 A.M. to 4 P.M.; Sunday, 2 to 5 P.M. Admission charge. Telephone: (301) (301) 739-8577 ext. 169. Web site: www.hagerstownmd.org/index.aspx?NID=309.

Of special interest to visitors is the national award-winning City Park, noted for its beautiful design. The **Washington County Museum of Fine Arts,** located at the lakeside in City Park, contains a notable collection of sculpture, paintings, and graphic arts, including examples of works of foremost artists of America and Europe. Open Tuesday through Saturday, 10 A.M. to 5 P.M.; Sunday, 1 to 5 P.M. Donation. Telephone: (301) 739-5727. Web site: www.wcmfa.org.

The **Rose Hill Cemetery** is located on Memorial Boulevard and Potomac Street. Located within Rose Hill is a five-acre section called Washington Cemetery, dedicated to the Confederate soldiers who died in the battles of Antietam and South Mountain. The cemetery was the result of the work of Henry Kyd Douglas, a Hagerstown native and the youngest officer on Gen. Stonewall Jackson's staff. Feeling the injustice of the neglect of Southern Civil War dead, Douglas gathered the remains of many Confederate soldiers from the local countryside. Washington Cemetery is a flat, grassy area with a plaque listing the names of the known dead buried there. To the east is the **Thomas Kennedy Monument,** which marks the grave of the noted merchant-lawyer who spent almost two decades fighting for the passage of the "Jew Bill," which would grant Jews the same civil rights enjoyed by all other citizens. Kennedy won his fight in 1826. The monument was erected in 1919 by prominent Maryland Jews.

The **Maryland Theatre,** near the city's Public Square, was designed by a famous New York theater architect, Thomas W. Lamb. It was constructed in 1915 in neoclassical style and has flawless acoustic qualities. Slated for demolition after a 1974 fire destroyed the theater's lobby, the building was purchased by a concerned citizen who formed a committee to preserve and restore this architectural work of art. It now features a full calendar of events. Call or visit the Web site for directions and coming attractions. Telephone: (301) 790-3500. Web site: www.mdtheatre.org.

Williamsport, an old town on the historic Chesapeake and Ohio Canal, is southwest of Hagerstown on Route 11 at the intersection of Route 68. The town was laid out in 1786 by Gen. O. H. Williams, for whom it is named. West of town is the old Conococheague Creek Bridge. The Chesapeake and Ohio Canal crosses the creek by means of a long stone aqueduct.

UPPER CHESAPEAKE

Harford and Cecil Counties

Harford County, lying between Pennsylvania and the Chesapeake Bay, was established in 1773 and named for Henry Harford, the son of the last Lord Baltimore. The county boasts 38.9 miles of Chesapeake Bay shoreline and ranges from the coastal plain area at sea level to 750 feet in the Piedmont Plateau. For information on Harford County visit the Harford County Tourism Council at 3 West Bel Air Avenue, Aberdeen, MD 21001. Web site: www.harfordmd.com.

Ladew Topiary Gardens are famous for topiary sculptures. The garden is located at 3535 Jarrettsville Pike in Monkton. The 22 acres contain life-size figures of many types of birds and animals and sculptured hedges that reflect the versatile artistry of Harvey Ladew. Flowers bloom throughout the growing season, including roses, azaleas, dogwood, hydrangea, and irises. The manor house contains a museum displaying a collection of English antiques, fox hunting memorabilia, and a library. Also on the grounds is a Carriage museum, self-guided nature walk trail, café and gift shop. The garden is open mid-April through October, Monday through Friday, 10 A.M. to 4 P.M.; Saturday and Sunday, 10:30 A.M. to 5 P.M. Group tours available. There are workshops and lectures held throughout the year, as well as a summer concert series and Christmas Open House. Admission charge. Telephone: (410) 557-9570. Web site: www.ladewgardens.com.

Rocks State Park is in Jarrettsville, at 3318 Rocks Chrome Hill Road, off Route 24, eight miles northwest of Bel Air. This area is an imposing scenic site, with lofty and rugged rock formations separated by the deep valley of Deer Creek. Several trails lead from the park headquarters and from the picnic area to the famous King and Queen Seats, 94 feet high. The cliffs overlooking the valley below are 190 feet high. An old iron mill, established early in the nineteenth century, once stood in the area. The power for the water wheel came from Deer Creek. Pig iron from this mill was used in building the Civil War warship *Monitor*. The 2,200-acre park has facilities for picnicking, boating, hiking, fishing, horseback riding, and camping. A nature trail will interest students of natural history. The shad run in April, in addition to the pike, perch, and bass, makes this one of the best fishing grounds in the state. The park is open year round. The camping area is open May through October. Free admission; charge for campsites. Telephone: (410) 557-7994. Web site: www.dnr.state.md.us/publiclands/central/rocks.asp.

The nearby area encompassing **Susquehanna State Park** was settled more than 200 years ago, and many early structures built by the first settlers may be visited. The park publishes a self-guided-walking-tour brochure of a historic trail that includes restored canal and mill structures. The imposing four-story **Rock Run Grist Mill** was built in 1794 and has been restored to operating condition. Visitors receive a package of meal as a souvenir of their visit. The mill operates in summer and on weekends and holidays, 1 to 4 P.M. Other sights in the park include the Jersey Toll House, Rock Run House, Steppingstone Museum, and the community of Lapidum. Telephone: (410) 557-7994. Web site: www.dnr.state.md.us/publiclands/central/susquehanna.asp.

The **Jersey Toll House Visitors Center,** near the mill, was originally built as a residence for the tollkeeper of the Rock Run covered bridge, which was the first bridge built over the turbulent Susquehanna River. This bridge was destroyed in 1854. This structure is now a private residence for park personnel.

Steppingstone Museum, administered by a nonprofit organization, is located in Susquehanna State Park on the bluffs above the river at 461 Quaker Bottom Road. It is an outdoor agricultural museum devoted to preservation and demonstration of the rural arts and crafts of the 1880-1920 period. An eighteenth-century stone farmhouse is furnished with period furniture and outlying buildings contain a replica of a country store and a cooper shop, woodworking shop, and a working blacksmith shop. Open May through the first Sunday in October, Saturday and Sunday, 1 to 5 P.M. By appointment only during the week. Admission charge. Telephone: (410) 939-2299. Web site: www.steppingstonemuseum.org.

Students of military history will find the **U.S. Army Ordnance Museum** of interest. It is readily accessible from Routes 95 and 40, east of the town of Aberdeen, which is northeast about 30 miles from the center of Baltimore. Along Maryland Boulevard, leading to the museum, is a two-mile-long display of tanks and self-propelled artillery. Visitors can also see guns, tanks, and other weapons used in all wars to World War II and the Vietnam War, including captured German and Viet Cong weapons. The U.S. Army Ordnance Museum has the most complete collection of weapons in the world and is a resource for students at the Army Ordnance Center and school.

The museum, which covers 20 acres, originated around 1918 when the Army convened a commission to study the use of weapons in World War I. In order to make technical evaluations, the commission utilized the Aberdeen Proving Ground facilities. Because of heightened security at the Aberdeen Proving Ground, the base is no longer open to the public. Access to the museum may be limited, so call first to verify museum access. Telephone: (410) 278-3602.

The historic town of **Havre de Grace** calls itself the "water sports capital of the upper Chesapeake Bay." It derives its name from an incident in 1782 when a Frenchman in the entourage of the Marquis de Lafayette exclaimed upon seeing the Susquehanna shoreline, "Ah, c'est Le Havre—Le Havre de Grace!"

Havre de Grace, located off Route 40 and I-95 on the southern banks of the Susquehanna River, is a delightful old town that has been designated a National Historic District. It was settled in 1658 and has many historic ties as it lies on the Old Post Road between Philadelphia and Williamsburg. In addition to the many large, historic houses, there is Antique Row, a collection of antique and gift shops. Stop by the visitor center at 450 Pennington Avenue; call or visit the city Web site for more details about what to see and do in the area. Telephone: (410) 939-2100 or (800) 851-7756. Web site: www.hdgtourism.com.

The **Susquehanna Museum,** 817 Conesteo Street, is housed in the old lock house of the **Susquehanna and Tidewater Canal.** The canal began operations in 1840 and mule-driven barges transported boats of 150-ton capacity 45 miles through a system of 29 locks from Havre de Grace to Wrightsville, Pennsylvania. The lockhouse served as the home and office of the lockmaster and is decorated with 1840-75 period furniture. Open Friday through Sunday, May through October, 1 to 5 P.M. Telephone: (410) 939-5780. Web site: www.thelockhousemuseum.org.

The **Concord Point Lighthouse** is located at the Foot of Lafayette Street on the south end of town, where the Susquehanna River empties into the Chesapeake Bay. It was built in 1827 and is one of the oldest lighthouses on the East Coast. The light keeper's former home, an eighteenth-century structure, is across the road from the light. It was once a stagecoach station and an inn. The lighthouse is open April to October on Sundays, 1 to 5 P.M., and by appointment. Free admission. Telephone: (410) 939-3213 Web site: www.concordpointlighthouse.org.

Cecil County is in the upper northeast corner of the state. Capt. John Smith first visited the area in 1608. **Perryville,** one of the major towns in the county, was settled in 1622, when Edward Palmer was granted a patent for settlement in what is now Garrett Island. Before incorporation in 1882, Perryville was known as Lower Ferry and then Susquehana. Web site: www.seececil.org

The three-story **Rodgers Tavern** is located at 259 Broad Street, at the north side of the toll bridge over the Susquehanna River. It served as a stopping place for travelers on the Post Road who were waiting for the ferry. It was built in 1666. The tavern was operated by Col. John Rodgers, who fought under Gen. George Washington during the Revolutionary War. His son, also named John, was a naval hero of the War of 1812. It has been verified that the tavern was patronized by such illustrious persons as Martha and George Washington, Thomas Jefferson, James Madison, and the Marquis de Lafayette. Open May through October, Saturday and Sunday, 1 to 4 P.M. Telephone: (410) 642-6066. Web site: www.perryvillemd.org/about.html#Tavern.

Principio Iron Works is located two miles east of Perryville on Route 7. The original works were built before 1719, the first in the

British colonies. Later, they supplied cannon balls and cannons for the Revolution. During the War of 1812, the furnace was destroyed by the British. In 1836, a new furnace was in operation and continued in business until 1886. The scenery around the area is very beautiful. Principio Creek follows a winding course through the primeval, wooded valley. Tours by appointment only. Telephone: (410) 642-2358.

Elk Neck State Park is located at 4395 Turkey Point Road, in North East, Maryland, at the northern end of Chesapeake Bay, at the tip of the narrow peninsula between the Elk and Northeast rivers. Its varied topography—heavily wooded bluffs, marshes and beaches—offers unusual opportunities for nature walks and observation of wildlife. The park is a wildlife sanctuary and visitors may see white-tailed deer and other woodland animals. Bird watchers will also enjoy the spring and autumn migrations of waterfowl, as the park is located on the Atlantic flyway. The park offers swimming, camping, boating, fishing, crabbing, and picnicking opportunities. A concession supplies food and refreshments. Fully furnished housekeeping cabins are available from spring to fall. There is one boat launch ramp and a boat rental concession where boaters may also purchase gasoline. The park offers year-round camping, and there are areas set aside for youth groups and for pet owners. Telephone: (410) 287-5333. Web site: www.dnr.state.md.us/publiclands/central/elkneck.asp.

The historic tree **Richards Oak** is located on Route 1 at Richardsmere, one-and-a-half miles west of Rising Sun, close to the highway. A roadside marker tells the story. General Lafayette, en route with his army to Yorktown, camped under this tree on April 12, 1781. The venerable oak is estimated to be about 500 years old. It is 80 feet high, with a 115-foot branch spread, and its trunk is 24 feet around.

Gilpin Falls Covered Bridge is north of North East, near the town of Bay View. It is easily accessible from Routes 95 or 40, 1.5 miles north on Route 272. The bridge crosses North East Creek and is a 119-foot, Burr truss bridge built around 1860.

The **West Nottingham Academy** campus is in the town of Colora, at 1079 Firetower Road. The academy was founded in 1744 by the Reverend Samuel Finley, who later became president of the College of New Jersey (now Princeton University). Finley was an Irish-Presbyterian minister who preached at revivals known as "the Great Awakening." The school, the oldest continuously operating boarding school in the United States, is now a nonsectarian school. Its distinguished graduates include two signers of the Declaration of Independence—Richard Stockton of New Jersey and Benjamin Rush of Pennsylvania. The campus is extremely attractive, with its complex of old buildings and an unusual variety of different types of trees. Most of the buildings date from the nineteenth century, but portions of the headmaster's house are said to predate the school and may date from as early as 1688. Telephone: (410) 658-5556. Web site: www.wna.org.

St. Mary Anne's Episcopal Church, located at 315 S. Main Street in North East, was built in 1742. The churchyard contains the graves of a number of Indian converts. The church has a Dutch gambrel roof and an unusual bell tower. The original Bible and communion silver were gifts from Queen Anne, who had actively supported the original St. Mary's parish. The church was renamed in her honor. The church welcomes visitors; inquire at the rectory. Telephone: (410) 287-5522. Web site: www.stmaryanne.org.

The **Old Bohemia Mission,** or St. Francis Xavier Church, is off Route 282, two miles north of Warwick. Founded in 1704, it was one of the earliest Catholic churches in the colonies. The present church dates from 1792. During the eighteenth century, the Jesuits developed a mission, which included a self-supporting plantation. Graduates of the school operated by the Jesuits included John Carroll, the first U.S. Catholic bishop, and Charles Carroll, signer of the Declaration of Independence. Many early church relics and old farm equipment are exhibited in the rectory museum and a farm building nearby. The Old Bohemia Society maintains the church. Mass celebrated the third Sunday of April, May, September, and October at 4 P.M.

Elkton is on Route 40, 51 miles from Baltimore. The **Cecil County Library** and the **Historical Society of Cecil County** are housed in a beautiful nineteenth-century house located at 135 E. Main Street in Elkton. The society has restored the original basement kitchen, a country-store exhibit, an early firehouse, and a log-cabin schoolhouse. The museum includes a collection of Indian artifacts. Free admission. Open Monday, noon to 4 P.M.; Tuesday, 6 to 8 P.M.; Thursday, 10 A.M. to 4 P.M.; and the fourth Saturday of each month, 10 A.M. to 2 P.M. Web site: www.cecilhistory.org.

There are several other historic buildings in Elkton. Inquire at the library or the historical society.

An interesting short side trip is along a rural road from Elkton to the old port of entry, **Head of Elk,** just south of town. In colonial days ships from overseas put in at this port, and it was here that troops from the south came ashore during the Revolutionary War.

Chesapeake City, five miles south of Elkton on Route 213, is the western terminus of the Chesapeake and Delaware Canal. The 14-mile canal, which connects the Chesapeake Bay with the Delaware River, is administered by the U.S. Corps of Engineers. Picnicking areas are located along the canal, where visitors can observe a variety of ocean-going ships as well as smaller pleasure craft.

South Chesapeake City, one of the few remaining canal towns in the United States, has been listed as a National Historic District. The **C&D Canal Museum,** located in the **Old Lock Pump House** at Second Street and Bethel Road, highlights the history of one of the busiest canals ever built. The 38-foot **C&D Canal Waterwheel,** built in 1837, has been preserved in the museum. The wooden wheel, equipped with buckets, was used to raise the water level of the canal above the locks. The water was lifted from Back Creek and dumped into the canal at a rate of 1,200,000 gallons an hour. Two steam engines, which may still be seen in a stone house, provided the power. In 1910 the Corps enlarged the canal and removed the locks, making the canal a free-flowing waterway. The museum also includes exhibits on the development of the Chesapeake and Delaware Canal and there are two working models, one with the locks. Open Monday through Saturday, 10 A.M. to 4 P.M. Free admission. Telephone: (410) 885-5621.

Charlestown, located on the Northeast River on Route 267 off of Route 40, was created by an act of the Maryland General Assembly in 1742 to provide a shipping port at the head of the Chesapeake Bay. Its port activity and position along the Philadelphia-Baltimore Post Road contributed to a busy town during the mid-eighteenth century. However, with the predominance of Baltimore as the Chesapeake shipping port and the removal of the county seat in the 1780s to Elkton, Charlestown was bypassed. Many citizens moved away and some even dismantled their homes and rebuilt them in Baltimore.

During the Revolutionary War, Charlestown was an important supply area. Because it was on the post road, the town served as a stage-coach stop. At that time, Charlestown had 10 taverns located within a four-block area. Today, the historic district of Charlestown contains an assortment of eighteenth-century architecture, much of it in various stages of restoration. Most buildings are occupied, preserving the atmosphere and charm of a small eighteenth-century port town. A 150-acre portion of the town has been established as a historic district. The **107 House (Tory House)** on Market Street is one of the historic buildings that is open to the public. This olive-colored frame house was built in 1810 on the foundations of an earlier building, constructed in 1750. The house was believed to have been confiscated by the state from a loyalist after the Revolutionary War, but later research proved this to be incorrect. The basement of the former tavern contains a Colonial kitchen and had a separate entrance. Visitors may also tour the upper floors, where a small museum is located. The communal sleeping room may also be seen, although it is used today for community activities. Open May through September, third Sundays, 2 to 4 P.M. and by appointment. Free admission. Telephone: (410) 287-8262.

Less than a block away on Market Street are **Indian Queen Tavern, Red Lyon Tavern,** and the **Linton House,** all built around 1755. When what is now known as Linton House operated as a tavern, George Washington noted in his diary that he stopped there. The **Paca House,** also on Market Street, was the home of John Paca, father of William Paca, signer of the Declaration of Independence. The frame section of the house is partly of log construction and is the oldest section, while the newer stone section was added later in 1750.

The **Colonial Wharf,** authorized by the General Assembly in 1742, was built of heavy logs and stone ship ballast. It was wide enough for two wagons and extended 300 feet out into the river. During the Revolutionary War, Charlestown was a supply depot for the Continental Army and a massive stone warehouse stored grains near the wharf. The town commissioners have extended the original wharf to include a fishing pier at the end.

Mt. Harmon Plantation, on Grove Neck Road in Earleville, about 30 miles from Charlestown, is an eighteenth-century tobacco plantation located on the banks of the Sassafras River. The house is furnished with period American and English antiques and is complemented by a formal boxwood garden. There is a tobacco prize house on the grounds. Call for the varied hours of operation and appointments. Telephone: (410) 275-8819. Web site: www.mountharmon.org.

Kent County

Kent County was established in 1642 and at that time encompassed the whole of the Maryland section of the Eastern Shore. **Chestertown,** the county seat, rivals Annapolis for its preservation of eighteenth-century buildings and was known for its lavish and extravagant life-style, which reached its height in the decade before the Revolutionary War. However, the independent and egalitarian spirit of the Eastern Shore character was observed by an Englishman who remarked "that the inferior order of people pay but little external respect to those who occupy superior station."

Chestertown is the foremost historic attraction of the northern Eastern Shore. The spirit of the eighteenth century lives in this well-kept community, with its many buildings that date back to the 1700s. While many of these historic buildings are privately owned and not open to the public, the historic district lends itself to a walking tour.

Chestertown was founded in 1698 and has served as the Kent County seat since 1706. This aura of the past pervades **Town Square** with its cast-iron fountain, old lamps, and colonial-style storefronts. Chestertown is the home of **Washington College,** the only college having a direct association with George Washington. Chartered in 1782, it is the nation's tenth oldest institution of higher learning.

For more information about area sites and tours, visit the Kent County Office of Tourism Development, 400 High Street, Chestertown, MD 21620. Telephone: (410) 778-0416. There is also a new Kent County Visitor Center at the intersection of Maryland Route 213 and Cross Street in Chestertown.

Web sites: www.kentcounty.com. or www.chestertown.com.

The **Hynson-Ringgold House** is rich in historical and architectural interest. The rear section dates from 1735, while the front was designed by the noted English architect William Buckland and built in 1771. The mansion, surrounded by a walled garden, is now the home of the president of Washington College.

The **Customs House,** at Front and High streets, dates from the 1730s. It was the center of the rich trade with the sugar plantations of the British West Indies in colonial days. Near this site, on May 23, 1774, irate citizens boarded the brigantine *William Geddes* and threw the detested tea into the Chester River. In this way the citizenry expressed their anger over passage of the "Intolerable Acts" by the British Parliament.

Widehall, at 101 Water Street, is an elaborate merchant's house built about 1770. This beautiful Georgian home was built by Thomas Smythe, head of Maryland's government from 1774 until 1776. Most of the town's historic buildings are on or near Water Street. Six other Water Street structures, at numbers 103, 107, 109, 110, 115, and 201, were eighteenth-century merchants' homes. The **Nicholson House,** at 111 Queen Street, was built in 1788 by Capt. John Nicholson of the Continental navy. The houses at 102 and 105 Queen Street date back to the early 1700s. Across the street at 101 Church Alley is the only local example of a Philadelphia town house. It is the **Geddes-Piper House,** a three-and-one-half story home that was once owned by William Geddes, the port's customs collector, of Chestertown Tea Party fame. The house serves as the headquarters of the Kent County Historical Society. Admission charge. Open May through October, Wednesday through Friday, 10 A.M. to 4 P.M.; Saturday and Sunday, 1 to 4 P.M. and by appointment. Telephone: (410) 778-3499. Web site: www.kentcountyhistory.org.

A right on High Street will lead to the **White Swan Tavern** (c. 1733) at 231. The tavern has been restored to appear as it would have looked in 1795. It is now a bed and breakfast. Telephone: (410) 778-2300. At the corner of Cross Street is **Emmanuel P. E. Church,** erected in 1768. Its rector, Rev. Dr. William Smith, was the founder of Washington College. The nearby **Court House** dates from 1860.

Around the corner to the left, on Mill Street (numbers 101-103), is a three-sectioned "telescope" house, the last of its kind in the area. One section was once a tavern. The gardens in the rear are a notable feature of this landmark. At 107 Mill Street is a small dormered tradesman's house (c.1750s).

Continue west on High Street past 411 and 414, both mid-eighteenth-century homes. At 532 High Street is the **"Rock of Ages" House,** built entirely of stone. It is believed that the stone was brought over as ship's ballast by Captain Palmer, who erected the house.

The final stop is at **Washington College.** Go right on College Avenue to Campus Avenue, a short drive. Here the visitor can see Middle, East, and West halls, which date from 1845. They replace an earlier structure, built between 1783-88 and destroyed by fire in 1827. George Washington was one of the college's first governors and took part in a meeting at which the building's design was determined and a fund-raising lottery approved. Today the visitor, strolling about the campus of this small, historic, liberal arts college (enrollment is 1,300 men and women) will note buildings in many styles of architecture, including the very modern. Telephone: (410) 778-2800 or (800) 422-1782. Web site: www.washcoll.edu/.

A side trip to **Rock Hall** from Chestertown on Route 20 west will bring the traveler past **St. Paul's Church** at the intersection of Routes 20 and 21. St. Paul's was established in 1692, and the present edifice was built in 1711. It is one of the oldest Episcopal churches in Maryland. The church is surrounded by old oak trees, some about 400 years old. Tallulah Bankhead, the actress, is buried in St. Paul's graveyard. Rock Hall is a charming colonial town memorable for a historic trip by Col. Tench Tilghman, aide to General Washington. He stopped off at Rock Hall on his way from Yorktown to Philadelphia, carrying the news to the Continental Congress of Cornwallis's surrender. When Tilghman arrived at an inn to rest and change horses, he shouted, "A horse for the Congress! Cornwallis is taken!" More recently Rock Hall was best known as a fishing center serving areas as far away as New England with fresh Bay seafood. Be sure to take the waterfront walk at the deep sea port to view the fishing fleet and pleasure craft. And enjoy the seafood restaurants. Telephone: (401) 639-7611 Web site: www.rockhallmd.com.

The **Rock Hall Museum** moved to new quarters in 2003. It is now located in the Rock Hall Municipal Building on South Main Street. Hours vary. Web site: www.rockhallmd.com/museum/index.php. The **Waterman's Museum** at 20880 Rock Hall Avenue is a salute to those who have worked the Chesapeake Bay. It includes exhibits on the art and skills of oystering, crabbing, and fishing. Donations welcome.

Eastern Neck National Wildlife Refuge, located eight miles south of Rock Hall on Route 445, teems with wildlife, especially deer, waterfowl, and small game. Explore along automobile and walking trails, or take the Boardwalk Trail across a marsh to an observation platform. There are various game animals along the Wildlife Trail. This 2,285-acre island refuge has an undeveloped 400-acre section open to nature-lovers and photographers on foot. Open year round, dawn to dusk. Headquarters building open Monday through Friday, 7:30 A.M. to 4 P.M. Free admission. Telephone: (410) 639-7056. Web site: www.fws.gov/northeast/easternneck.

North, on Route 213, are the historic towns of **Galena** and **Georgetown.** The latter was once a busy port of entry and a popular stop on the post road between Annapolis and Philadelphia. During the War of 1812 the town was almost totally destroyed by a landing party from Admiral Cockburn's fleet. The **Kitty Knight House** was spared when Kitty prevailed on the admiral to save the house because a bedridden old lady lived there. This old home is now a country inn and bed and breakfast. Today Georgetown is a busy yachting center.

Upper Eastern Shore: A Small-Town Tour

Queen Anne's and Caroline County have a number of historic small towns, and the counties are small enough to lend themselves to a scenic driving tour. As always, a good starting point is the county tourism office. The Queen Anne's County Department of Tourism is located at 425 Piney Narrows Road in Chester. Telephone: (410) 604-2100. Web site: www.qac.org/default.aspx?pageid=76&template=3&toplevel=34.

Kent Island is the gateway to the Eastern Shore from the west. The island was settled by Virginians in 1631 and claims its antiquity in friendly rivalry disputes with St. Mary's, which was established in 1634 by Lord Baltimore's settlers. William Claiborne, Virginia secretary of state, established an Indian trading post on Kent Island and his claim led to armed encounters with Maryland officials who were determined to retain their legal hold on the Eastern Shore.

Kent Island today is the eastern terminus of the William Preston Lane Jr. Memorial Bridge, commonly known as the **Bay Bridge.** The twin spans of the bridge are each 4.3 miles long and 186.5 feet high above mean water. In May of each year, except when prohibited by security concerns, the Maryland Transportation Authority closes one span to vehicles for the annual Chesapeake Bay Bridge Walk. The walk is free. A small donation is requested for buses from central parking areas. Telephone: 866-713-1596. An excellent view of the bridge may be enjoyed from a small fishing pier and parking lot area in **Matapeake County Park.** It is on Route 8, just south of the bridge from Route 50.

Wye Mills, on the Queen Anne's and Talbot county line on Route 50, is a picturesque village. The visitor may see an authentic replica of a colonial school as well as a church and mill. Nearby **Wye Plantation** was the summer home of William Paca, a signer of the Declaration of Independence. The original plantation mansion was demolished, but William Paca's grave site is marked. The plantation site is now used as a conference center.

A 450-year-old white oak, known as the **Wye Oak,** was once in the 21-acre state park near the village. With a height of 95 feet and a crown spread of almost half an acre, until toppled by high winds on June 6, 2002, it was believed to be the largest of its species in the United States. Its circumference exceeded 37 feet, and it was Maryland's official state tree.

Horses were tied to the massive tree in Colonial times. The Wye Oak survived all manner of human and natural forces as it bore silent witness to the founding of a new nation. But in recent years, time began to take its toll. Its trunk was hollow, creating a space large enough for a family of four to set up a table and dine within its ancient bark. In April 2002, a cloned twig from the giant oak was planted at George Washington's home at Mt. Vernon. A more complete history of the great tree is included on the following Web site, which reads like a reverent obituary. Web site: www.dnr.state.md.us/forests/trees/giant.asp.

Wye Church, a small brick structure, was consecrated on October 18, 1721. It was built on the foundations of an earlier church. Among interesting features are the high box pews, the hanging pulpit, the west gallery bearing the Royal Arms of England, and the original 1737 communion service in silver. Nearby are Wye Vestry House and Parish House, which were built in 1948-58 to appear as they would have in the early eighteenth-century.

The **Wye Grist Mill** stands on land that was patented in 1664. The mill itself was built in 1660 and moved to its present location in 1682. Flour for Washington's troops at Valley Forge was produced here. The owner of the mill, Col. William Hemsley, received an open-ended contract from the Continental Congress to provision the army during the Revolutionary War. Admission charge. Open mid-April through mid-November, Monday through Thursday, 10 A.M. to 1 P.M.; Friday and Saturday, 10 A.M. to 4 P.M. Call to inquire about grindings and other seasonal festivities and events. Telephone: (410) 827-6909. Web site: www.oldwyemill.org.

Tuckahoe State Park, embracing the meandering Tuckahoe Creek stream valley, affords visitors a chance to fish, canoe, and hike. It is located seven miles west of Denton, off Maryland route 404. Campers will find Tuckahoe State Park a convenient base for short trips to Annapolis, Easton, St. Michaels, and Chestertown.

The park has 51 campsites with a central bathhouse and four youth group sites with a central bathhouse that has showers and toilets, as well as picnicking and hiking facilities. A 60-acre lake offers boating and fishing opportunities. **Adkins Arboretum** is a 500-acre natural wooded setting that has almost three miles of surfaced walkways leading through tagged native species of trees and shrubs. The highlight of a trip here is the opportunity to inspect the largest overcup oak in the nation, a 235-year-old tree with a height of 118 feet and a spread of 120 feet. Telephone: (410) 820-1668.

Web site: www.dnr.state.md.us/publiclands/eastern/tuckahoe.asp.

Centreville, the county seat of Queen Anne's County, is on Route 213 off of Route 301. The chief attraction here is the attractive eighteenth-century town green with the courthouse (1792), which was moved from Queenstown to its current location at 100 Courthouse Square and is the oldest county courthouse in continuous use in Maryland. A statue of Queen Anne, dedicated by Princess Anne in 1977, stands on the square. On the southern side of the square, a row of nineteenth- and early twentieth-century houses make up **Lawyer's Row.**

At 119 South Commerce Street the visitor will see **Wright's Chance** (c. 1744), the Queen Anne's County Historical Society headquarters, and **Tucker House** (c. 1792), the society's museum. Both houses are representative Eastern Shore plantation homes. Wright's Chance is furnished with Chippendale and Hepplewhite pieces. Tucker House is the repository for county and state historical information. Donations requested. Open by appointment and on Saturdays from May through October, 2 to 4 P.M. Telephone: (410) 758-3010. Web site: www.historicqac.org/Centreville.htm.

Nearby at 126 Dulin Clark Road is the **Queen Anne's Museum of Eastern Shore Life,** dedicated to preserving and displaying artifacts relating to the Eastern Shore. Telephone: (410) 758-8641. Web site: www.historicqac.org/sites/mesl.htm.

Church Hill is eight miles north of the county seat on Route 19. It is named for **St. Luke's Episcopal Church,** which dates from 1732. This is an impressive church, with gambrel roof, arched windows, and Flemish bond brick walls. Inside, on either side of the chancel, hang two tablets, one the Lord's Prayer, the other the Ten Commandments. Tradition says these were gifts from Queen Anne. The **Academy,** on the church grounds, served as an elementary school in the early nineteenth century before the days of public education. This small brick building dates from 1817, and is still used by St. Luke's. The original cost of the church building was 140,000 pounds of tobacco. The church is open by appointment only, Monday through Friday. Telephone: (410) 556-6644.

Caroline County is the only Eastern Shore county with no bay or ocean shoreline, although the Choptank River is navigable up to Denton. On the east it borders Delaware and on the west Talbot County. On the north and south are Queen Anne's and Dorchester counties, from which it was created in 1773. The county was named in honor of the sister of the sixth Lord Baltimore. She was also the wife of Governor Eden, the last colonial governor of Maryland. The county prides itself on its agricultural production, primarily grain and vegetables for marketing and processing. Web site: tourcaroline.com.

On the Delaware-Maryland state line at Marydel, near the convergence of Routes 454 and 311, the visitor will see a **Mason-Dixon Crownstone,** which was erected in 1765. Crownstones were placed every 100 miles on the line and few have survived. The Marydel crownstone is an elaborately carved English limestone post bearing Lord Baltimore's coat of arms on the Maryland side and William Penn's on the Delaware side.

Two miles south of Denton on Route 404 is the 107-acre **Martinak State Park.** This park has facilities for picnicking, camping, boating, fishing, playgrounds and walking paths. There are 63 improved camping sites, 30 of which have hookups. The wreck of a **pungy,** a type of Chesapeake Bay sailing vessel no longer used, is on display in the park. Telephone: (410) 802-1668. Web site: www.dnr.state.md.us/publiclands/eastern/martinak.asp.

On Route 16, the motorist traveling south reaches the town of **Choptank** on the Choptank River. The Choptank River is one of the longest rivers on the Eastern Shore and is navigable up to Denton.

East on Route 318 is **Federalsburg.** The town is located on the Marshyhope Creek, a tributary of the Nanticoke River. North of Federalsburg, off Route 306, the municipally owned, six-acre **Chambers Lake** offers bass, pickerel, and sunfish fishing.

Talbot County

Talbot County has 602 miles of waterfront. The extensive shoreline, believed to be the longest of any county in the country, is a result of the many tidal rivers and creeks that intersperse the landmass. The county has several historic towns—St. Michaels, Oxford, and Easton—which have old buildings and also many picturesque maritime locales where the visitor can observe and participate in fishing and oystering activities. Oxford is known as a yachting port and the area is one of the oldest settlements in the state. In addition to the English settlers, French Acadians from Canada settled in this area leaving a slight French influence. Web site: www.tourtalbot.org.

Easton is 12 miles south of Wye Mills on Route 50. It is the county seat of Talbot County, and dates its origin from a Quaker meetinghouse built in the 1680s. A dozen places of historic interest can be seen on a walking tour of about one mile. A walking tour and map brochure may be obtained from the Easton Business Management Association.

Telephone: (410) 770-8000. Web site: www.eastonmd.org. Or you can pick up a map at the Easton Welcome and Resource Center at 11 S. Harrison Street.

The **Talbot County Court House** stands on Washington Street between Dover and Federal streets. The original building (c. 1789) was replaced in 1794 and again enlarged and remodeled in 1958. It was on these grounds on May 24, 1774, that the "Talbot Resolves" were adopted. The sentiments of the resolves were later incorporated into the Declaration of Independence.

Guided walking tours are conducted by the Historical Society of Talbot County, 25 South Washington Street, which was built in the 1790s. Telephone: (410) 822-0773. Web site: www.hstc.org. Number 29 South Washington Street is a Federal-style townhouse, dating from 1804-10, with a garden in the rear. In addition, the society complex houses a three-room gallery that exhibits rotating collections, and there is a museum shop. Open year round, Monday through Saturday, 10 to 4 P.M. Free admission.

At 106 South Street is the **Academy Art Museum,** housed in a nineteenth-century primary school. The exhibits of the academy range from the visual arts to dance and music performances. Film and concert series are presented throughout the year. Visitors can see works of local artists as well as the permanent art collection. Open year round, Monday through Saturday, 10 to 4 P.M. On Wednesday the museum is open until 9 P.M. Admission charge. Telephone: (410) 822-2787. Web site: www.academyartmuseum.org.

Turn left on Talbot Lane to South Lane, then to **Talbot County Women's Club.** The frame portion of this house dates from the eighteenth century. The brick section dates from 1843 and is an example of the early Federal period. The Women's Club purchased the property in 1943 and has restored it. Continue on Talbot Lane to Dover Street, left to Harrison Street. The **Bullitt House,** one of Easton's oldest and most beautiful homes, was built in 1790. It is now occupied by a real estate company.

Turn left on Goldsborough to Washington Street. On the right, at the corner, is a 150-year-old building, formerly the **Frame Hotel,** now an office building. Across the street at 119 is the **Smith-Perrin House,** built in 1803. The building served as both the home of Thomas P. Smith and the office of the newspaper from which the Easton *Star-Democrat* grew. In 1912 the Chesapeake Bay Yacht Club acquired the property and still occupies the building.

The **Brick Hotel** at Washington and Federal streets was built in 1812 and was Easton's leading hotel, the scene of important civic events and balls. The facade has been altered from its original appearance and now the building houses offices.

Near the south edge of town, on Washington Street beyond Brookletts Avenue, is the **Third Haven Meeting House,** built in 1682. It is believed to be the oldest frame church building in Maryland still in use. Built at the headwaters of the Tred Avon River, worshippers came by boat to attend services. Visitors may inquire at the residence on the grounds regarding visiting the building. Usually open from 9 to 5 P.M. Telephone: (410) 822-0293. Web site: www.thirdhaven.org.

No Corner for the Devil (c. 1881), a hexagonal structure originally used as a Methodist church, is located three miles south of Easton on Route 50. The wide angles were devised, so a story goes, "to give the Devil no corner on which to sit to hatch evil." The ruins of **White Marsh Church** are about two miles beyond, to the left on Route 50. The churchyard contains the grave of Robert Morris, who died on July 22, 1750. He was the father of the Revolutionary War financier.

St. Michaels, a picturesque old seaport, is near Easton on Route 33. The town was settled in the 1670s and during the Colonial period was an important port and shipbuilding center. The Baltimore clipper ship is said to have been conceived here. St. Michael's is also known as the "Town that Fooled the British" with a strategy that caused British naval forces to overshoot the town on the morning of August 13, 1813, during the War of 1812. The residents of the town hoisted lanterns to the masts of ships and placed them in the tops of trees, causing the British cannons to overshoot the town. Telephone: (800) 808-7622. Web site: www.stmichaelsmd.org.

Situated on the harbor in historic St. Michaels, the **Chesapeake Bay Maritime Museum**'s nine exhibit buildings and floating fleet bring to life the story of the Bay and its inhabitants. Visitors can venture into the fully restored 1879 **Hooper Strait Lighthouse,** observe a working boat yard with the world's largest collection of Chesapeake Bay boats, pull up crab pots or nipper for oysters in a re-created waterman's wharf, and explore impressive exhibits depicting the golden age of steamboats and the sport and art of Chesapeake decoys. Open March through May, 9 A.M. to 5 P.M.; June through September, 9 A.M. to 6 P.M.; fall, 9 A.M. to 5 P.M.; winter, 9 A.M. to 4 P.M. Closed Thanksgiving, Christmas, and New Year's. Admission charge. Telephone: (410) 745-2916. Web site: www.cbmm.org.

There are a half-dozen other very old homes that one can see on a stroll down the six blocks of the village. Pleasure boaters and other watermen still use its harbor daily. Visitors to St. Michaels may cruise aboard the *Patriot* on the Miles River, St. Michaels harbor, and past many historic homes and plantations. Fare charge. Call for fees and schedule. Telephone: (410) 745-3100. Web site: www.patriotcruises.com.

The **Old Inn,** at Talbot and Mulberry streets, was built in 1817 and has an overhanging porch typical of the inns of the period. The **Cannonball House,** at the north end of the green, is so called because of its connection to the War of 1812. A cannonball from a British warship hit the chimney of this house and rolled down the attic stairway, endangering the lives of the occupants. This was the only building struck during the British bombardment of Easton. Both the Old Inn and the Cannonball House are private residences, not open to the public.

St. Mary's Square Museum is located in two old buildings on the Green. The main building is a log house built in the late 1600s or early 1700s, while the square frame building is at least 100 years younger. The frame house is called a "teetotum" building because it is an absolute square. The explanation and history of the term are not known. The museum exhibits include St. Michaels' memorabilia, such as old household items, furniture, and photographs. Open May through October, Saturday and Sunday, 10 to 4 P.M. Admission charge. Telephone: (410) 745-9561. Web site: www.stmichaelsmuseum.org.

Tilghman Island lies at the end of Route 33, 22 miles from Easton. The focal point of the island is the counter balance drawbridge at Knapps Narrows, built in 1932 and still in use today. Tilghman Island is home to the largest remaining fleet of skipjacks on the Chesapeake Bay. Visitors may charter fishing boats, tour the oyster processing plants, and accompany a working skipjack. There are many fishing charters to choose from, including those for novice fishermen, who will be given instruction and guidance by the crew. Web site: www.tilghmanisland.com.

Oxford existed as a port of entry as early as 1694. It has long been important in boat building and as the home of watermen whose livelihood was harvesting oysters, crabs, clams, and fish. It remains a charming residential town where locals mix with those from Washington, D.C., and other cities that use the area as a getaway. Web site: wwwoxfordmd.net.

In Oxford Cemetery, near the entrance to town on Route 333, stands the **Tench Tilghman Monument,** erected in honor of the Revolutionary War hero. On entering town, the first stop is the **Oxford Museum.** Open April 15 to October 15, Friday, Saturday, and Sunday, 2 to 5 P.M., and at other times by appointment. Telephone: (410) 226-0191. Web site: www.oxfordmuseum.org. In the next block are three notable private residences. On the left side is the **Academy House,** built in 1848, and once officers' quarters of the Maryland Military Academy. Across the street is the **Barnaby House,** built in the 1770s. The **Grapevine House,** not far from The Strand, is recognized by the grapevine in the front yard. The vine was brought here from the Isle of Jersey in 1810 by a sea captain. It still bears fruit.

Another private residence with deep historic roots is **Byeberry,** facing Town Creek. Records show Byeberry existed in 1695. It can be viewed from the end of Tilghman Street.

The **Robert Morris Inn,** on the corner of The Strand and Morris Street, was built about 1710. The house was the home of Robert Morris, Sr., the father of the man who became known as the Philadelphia financier of the Revolutionary War. The original house has been expanded, although the original ornate staircase can be seen in the inn and restaurant. The restaurant is open April through November, daily, 8 to 9 P.M. The inn is open April through November; weekends only in March. Telephone: (410) 226-5111. Web site: www.robertmorrisinn.com.

The **Oxford/Bellevue Ferry** connects Oxford with Bellevue by crossing the Tred Avon River and leaves from a pier near the Robert Morris Inn. It was started in 1683 and is believed to be the oldest private ferry crossing in the United States. Currently, the ferry is powered by diesel engines and can accommodate vehicles up to 12,000 pounds and foot passengers. The ferry operates year round. Schedules vary. Fare charged. Telephone: (410) 745-9023. Web site: www.oxfordbellevueferry.com.

SOUTHERN MARYLAND, EASTERN SHORE

Dorchester County

Dorchester County, established in 1669, is very much bound to the seafood industry, but also possesses some of Maryland's most productive agricultural lands. Crops such as soybeans, barley, corn, wheat, pickling cucumbers, and tomatoes are produced for packing plants and for fresh consumption. Detailed tourist information and self-directed walking tours of Cambridge, East New Market, and Vienna may be obtained from Dorchester County Tourism, 2 Rose Hill Place, Cambridge, Maryland. Telephone: (410) 228-1000 or (800) 522-TOUR. Web site: www.tourdorchester.org.

The **Cambridge** area of Dorchester County is bounded by the broad Choptank River and Chesapeake Bay, and is known as the "Sportmen's Paradise." The area beckons visitors interested in fishing, boating, swimming, water skiing, and crabbing. Hunting (deer and waterfowl) also is popular in this area. Visitors wishing to learn more of the past will find scores of homes and churches dating back 200 years or more. Cambridge was established in 1686; other nearby communities are even older. There are also a number of antique shops in the area.

The **Meredith House and Neild Museum,** at 902 LaGrange Avenue, is the home of the **Dorchester County Historical Society.** The Meredith House, built in 1760, contains exhibits related to Dorchester County and includes a Governor's Room honoring six Maryland governors who were born in Dorchester County. The **Neild Museum** houses social history exhibits such as the county's maritime and industrial development and Indian artifacts. Also on exhibit are an original 1834 McCormick reaper and an eighteenth-century smokehouse. On the grounds of the museum is a typical eighteenth-century formal garden. Open Tuesday through Friday, 10 A.M. to 1 P.M.; Saturday, 10 A.M. to 4 P.M. Telephone: (410) 228-7953. Web site: www.intercom.net/npo/dchs/neild.html.

On historic High Street you can begin a walking tour of Cambridge. This tour of historic Cambridge on foot is less than one mile. The walking tour extends from the **County Court House** at High Street and Court Lane to the **Long Wharf** on the Choptank River. The present Court House was completed in 1852 on the site of the original 1687 building.

Diagonally across the street is the **Christ P. E. Church,** a nineteenth-century edifice on the site of the first church, built in 1693. Notable Revolutionary War soldiers and other war heroes and statesmen are buried in the adjoining graveyard. Many old gravestones have dates in the 1600s. At the north end of the brick wall around the cemetery, on High Street, is the former office of **Josiah Bayly,** tenth attorney general of Maryland, and adjoining it is his old home, both dating from the 1790s. Most of the nearby houses on High Street, from the Court House to the River, were constructed in the 1700s. **Long Wharf,** at the foot of High Street, was the site of the old steamboat wharf. A city park with picnic tables and a public boat basin are now located here. One can see the **Roosevelt Memorial, war memorials, Cambridge Yacht Club and Basin.** Seafood processing plants were long the landmarks of this location.

Your tour of Cambridge should include a drive along Water Street and Hambrooks Avenue and Boulevard. Begin on Water Street where it joins High Street at the Yacht Club. **Glasgow,** a large brick house painted white, dates from 1760. The **Annie Oakley House,** near the end of Hambrooks Boulevard, and **Hambrooks,** built about 1803, are two other notable mansions in this area of palatial homes. Annie Oakley and her husband built their house at 28 Bellevue Avenue in 1913 after touring the world with the Wild West Show and deciding Cambridge was the most delightful place to live.

Located at 210 Talbot Avenue, the **Brannock Maritime Museum** houses collections of marine artifacts which illuminate the rich heritage of the Chesapeake Bay. The museum library features a growing collection of books, magazines, pamphlets, diaries, letters, and photographs documenting the history of the Cambridge area. Open Friday through Saturday, 10 A.M. to 4 P.M.; Sunday, 1 to 4 P.M. Telephone: (410) 228-6938.

The **Dorchester Heritage Museum** is located a few miles west of Cambridge on Horn Point Road, off Route 343. Four areas of county historical significance are highlighted in the Heritage Room, the Watermen Room, Aviation Hall, and Archaeology Room. Located on the Horn Point property of the University of Maryland, the museum is a working museum for local school children who are involved in construction of exhibits and in archaeological digs. Open Saturday and Sunday, 1 to 4 P.M., April 15 through October 30, and by appointment anytime. Free admission. Telephone: (410) 228-5530 or (410) 228-1899.

Also west of town is **Spocott Windmill,** six miles from Cambridge on Route 343. This is the only existing post windmill for grinding grain in Maryland. Open for tours year round, it is most exciting during the annual "Spocott Windmill Day," when grinding occurs. Also on the grounds are a tenant farmhouse and a one-room school. Telephone: (410) 228-7670. Web site: spocottwindmill.org.

The University of Maryland's **Horn Point Environmental Laboratories** are best known for their research on oysters and the blue crab, one of Maryland's major resources. The laboratories also conduct research to develop new seafood products and new processing methods. Tours of the laboratories are available. Open year round, Monday through Friday, 8:30 A.M. to 4:30 P.M. Call ahead for guided tours. Telephone: (410) 221-8483. Web site: www.umces.edu/hpl.

Take Route 16 southwest of Cambridge to visit the Church Creek area. **Old Trinity Church,** built about 1690, has been restored. Many notables, including members of the Carroll family, are buried in the churchyard. Anna Ella Carroll, who contributed to the Tennessee campaign strategy planning for Abraham Lincoln, is buried here. The miller's grave is marked with old millstones. There are many old houses in this area, and the **Old Baptist Meeting House,** at Woolford, two miles west of Church Creek, is a landmark. It is also known as the Old Woolford Mace Burying Ground, with gravestones dating back to the late 1600s.

Continue 10 miles west to **Taylor's Island.** Here, near Mulberry Grove, is the first schoolhouse built in Dorchester County. The **LeCompte House,** erected in 1710, was used as a Methodist meeting house until the chapel was built. The **Old Brick Church,** also Methodist, dates from 1787.

From Taylor's Island, you can return to Church Creek, then proceed south on Route 355, then left toward Seward and Bucktown. On Green Briar Road, east of Seward, one can see a marker identifying the site where Harriet Tubman lived and worked as a slave. **Harriet Tubman** is known for her work in freeing 300 slaves through the Underground Railroad. Continuing on Green Briar Road, turn right to Bestpitch Ferry Road, south one mile to **Bazel Church** where Harriet Tubman worshipped. For additional information and to arrange guided tours of sites that figured in Tubman's life, contact the Harriet Tubman Organization. Telephone: (410) 228-0401. Web site: www.intercom.net/npo/tubman.

Three miles farther, at Bucktown, you can see **Yarmouth,** or White House, built in 1735. Continue left to Airey and U.S. 50, where a one-mile jog to the right brings you to Route 16, and then to **East New Market,** settled in 1660. The East part of the name was added in 1827 to distinguish this town from the "New Markets" in Western Maryland and Virginia.

On Main Street are five old buildings noted for their architecture: **House of Hinges, Manning House, Edmondson House, Collins**

House, and Smith Cottage. Several are more than 200 years old. Traveling west toward the town of Secretary you will pass **Maurice Hall,** which is a fine two-and-a-half-story brick structure, circa 1740, with pilasters on the front and two oval windows in the pediment of the west gable end. **Friendship Hall,** now a private residence, is noted especially for the original raised paneling, cornices, mantels, and floors throughout the house, plus the lovely gardens and boxwood surrounding it. At Secretary is the Trippe House, also known as **My Lady Sewall's Manor,** erected in 1662 for Lord Sewall, secretary of the Province of Maryland. The house is in disrepair; the land is now owned by a hunting lodge.

The **Blackwater National Wildlife Refuge** is located at 2145 Key Wallace Road off of Route 335, south of Cambridge. The over-24,000-acre refuge is a wintering place for a great variety of waterfowl and other bird species. Tours can be planned and guides are available at the visitor center.

In the late fall many large flocks of Canada geese and ducks can be observed on the refuge. The official bird list shows that 240 different species of birds have been observed, and approximately 15,000 ducks winter in the area, and 35,000 to 50,000 geese migrate through the area. Dozens of species nest here in the spring and early summer. Two short hiking trails and a 3.5-mile wildlife drive are open from dawn to dusk throughout the year.

The visitor center offers interpretive films and exhibits. Open Monday to Friday, 8 A.M. to 4 P.M.; Saturday and Sunday, 9 A.M. to 5 P.M. Admission charge. Telephone: (410) 228-2677. Web site: www.fws.gov/blackwater.

Wicomico County

Wicomico County and its county seat, Salisbury, are nestled in the heart of the famous Eastern Shore, where opportunities for boating, fishing, and hunting abound. Many historic and scenic places beckon the visitor interested in reliving American history. Although the county was only created in 1867 from Somerset and Worcester counties, the city of Salisbury was chartered in 1732. All through the area the sightseer can visit picturesque waterfront towns and villages, where there are oystering, crabbing, and fishing boats alongside the piers. The Eastern Shore's large poultry industry is centered here.

A driving tour of approximately 40 miles around the Salisbury area takes about two hours. It covers historical points of interest and a cable ferry. Begin at the town of **Delmar,** seven miles north of Salisbury. It is situated on Routes 13 and 54, the dividing line between Maryland and Delaware. On the right, just before you cross the railroad tracks, is the original High Ball, one of the earliest of railroad signals which has been restored to its original condition, along with a restored caboose. Railroad enthusiasts will also enjoy the railroad museum at the Delmar Public Library.

Stop at the **Wicomico County Tourism Office** at Leonard Mill Pond, located on Route 13 just south of Delmar, for additional information about area sites, including a brochure on antique hunting in the area. Telephone: (800) 332-TOUR. Web site: www.wicomicotourism.org.

From the tourism office, continue west on Maryland 54 about seven miles, following the tour signs to the double crownstone marker of the Mason-Dixon line. This marker, dating from 1768, has the coat of arms of Lord Baltimore on the Maryland side and that of William Penn on the Delaware side. It is located on the north side of the road and is well marked.

Continue west on Route 54, crossing Route 50 to Mardela Springs. On the left is **"Spring House."** This is an old health spa of the early 1800s. When you leave here, backtrack to the junction of Route 50 and Route 54. Turn right onto 50 and continue approximately 4½ miles. On your left is the old **Spring Hill Church,** which was built in the 1700s and is one of the early Episcopal churches of the area.

Leaving Spring Hill Church, take Route 347 for 5½ miles, passing through Hebron to Quantico. After Quantico, about a mile-and-a-half farther, is the junction of 347 and 349. Cross the highway and turn south onto Route 352. After about 4½ miles turn left to old **Green Hill Church.** This church was built in 1782 from bricks and material shipped over from England. It has the original box pews, wine cup, pulpit, and brick floor.

Upon leaving Green Hill Church, continue south on Route 352. Bear left to the town of Whitehaven, an eighteenth-century ship-building and waterman's town. This village located on the Wicomico River is on the National Historic Register and was chartered in 1686. This quaint village is the home of the Whitehaven Bed and Breakfast, which occupies two historic properties—the Charles Leatherbury House and the Otis Lloyd House, both of which offer Victorian rooms with views of the river and marsh.

The Whitehaven Hotel (c. 1880), 2685 Whitehaven Road, was saved from the wrecking ball in 1999 through the cooperative efforts of local residents, the Maryland Historic trust, and friends of the village of Whitehaven. Restore and renovated, the hotel, which once provided lodging for those traveling by horse or steamship, reopened for those seeking a charming getaway in the spring of 2002. Telephone: (410) 873-3099 or (877) 233-8203. Web site: whitehaven.tripod.com/index.htm.

At Whitehaven you cross over the Wicomico River on the **Whitehaven Ferry,** which provides free, on-demand services for cars, passengers, and bikers between Wicomico and Somerset counties. (Also see entry in the section on Somerset County.) From the Whitehaven Ferry follow signs to Allen Road, then turn right to Route 13, then left (north) eight miles to Salisbury's city limits. In Salisbury you will find the Salisbury Zoological Park, the Ward Museum of Wildfowl Art, Salisbury's Historic Downtown Plaza, and a variety of antique shops, galleries, and eateries. Salisbury State University and the headquarters of Perdue Farms, Inc., are also located in Salisbury. Web site: www.salisburyarea.com.

The Ward Museum of Wildfowl Art, located at 909 S. Schumaker Drive in Salisbury, has the world's largest collection of bird carvings. The 2,300 pieces date back to 1870. The museum presents an 18-minute, audio-visual show with a setting of the Eastern Shore marshlands. Because bird carving is Maryland's official pastime, the museum sponsors an annual wildfowl art exhibit as well as a bird-carving competition in the spring. Open year round, Monday to Saturday, 10 to 5 P.M.; Sunday, noon to 5 P.M. Closed Thanksgiving, Easter, and Christmas. Admission charge. Telephone: (410) 742-4988. Web site: www.wardmuseum.org.

Poplar Hill Mansion, at 117 Elizabeth Street in Salisbury's Newtown Historic District, was built in 1805 and is the oldest house in Salisbury. It features pilasters in the main entrance, Palladian windows, outstanding cornice work, the original floors, and some of the original windows. The large mansion is furnished with eighteenth- and nineteenth-century furniture. Open year round, Sunday, 1 to 4 P.M., and by appointment. Telephone: (410) 749-1776. Web site: www.poplarhillmansion.org.

The **Salisbury Zoological Park,** on South Park Drive in the City Park, is one of the finest small zoos in the country. The park emphasizes a natural setting for the 350 animals. While the zoo concentrates on waterfowl species, it also has some rare animals. Open year round, Memorial Day to Labor Day, 8 A.M. to 7:30 P.M., September to May, 8 A.M. to 4:30 P.M. Free admission. Telephone: (410) 548-3188. Web site: www.salisburyzoo.org.

Worcester County

Worcester County is the easternmost county in Maryland and the only one facing the Atlantic Ocean. Although the county is known today for the beaches at Ocean City and on Assateague Island, the county seat, Snow Hill, was a thriving colonial commercial center. Snow Hill, on the Pocomoke River, was once a main port and a tobacco inspection station. Tobacco, grain, and livestock were shipped to English and West Indian ports until Baltimore overshadowed the Eastern Shore ports.

For additional information about county attractions, contact the Worcester County Tourism Office, 113 Franklin Street, Unit 1, Snow Hill, Maryland. The county has produced a number of guidance brochures on such subjects as African American heritage, birding, biking, golfing, attractions (especially for kids), bed-and-breakfast inns, museums, and nature trails. Telephone: (410) 632-3110 or (800) 852-0335. Web site: www.visitworcester.org.

Snow Hill, county seat of Worcester County, was founded in 1642. It is on Route 12, about 18 miles south of Salisbury, six miles from the Sinepuxent Bay, and on the Pocomoke River. Although the Pocomoke is too narrow for modern ships, its navigability from the Chesapeake Bay in earlier times made Snow Hill a natural early settlement. Snow Hill was made a royal port in 1694 and was a thriving shipping port until Baltimore eclipsed all the Maryland port towns. Snow Hill, which is relatively flat and generally snow-free, was named for a London suburb and retains a quiet, brick-sidewalked, tree-lined atmosphere with homes dating from the eighteenth century. The older houses are frame, with large outside chimneys, separate kitchens, and often with colonnades. Some have second-story galleries. A walking tour brochure may be obtained from the Julia A. Purnell Museum. Web site: www.snowhillmd.com.

The **Julia A. Purnell Museum,** at 208 W. Market Street, is housed in a small, white frame building that was built as a Catholic Church in 1891. The museum contains a unique collection of Americana—tools for tobacco processing, for crop farming, and for household chores. The exhibits range from Indian artifacts to Victorian era costumes and furnishings. Workshops, craft classes, and clinics are held by the museum. A shop offering the work of local craftsmen is also open during museum hours. Open April through October, Tuesday through Saturday, 10 A.M. to 4 P.M.; Sunday, 1 to 4 P.M. Admission charge. Telephone: (410) 632-0515. Web site: www.purnellmuseum.com. The **Mt. Zion One-Room Schoolhouse,** at the corner of Ironshire and Church streets, has been restored and is complete with tin lunch pails, recitation bench, double slates, a school bell, and a good collection of antique texts. Open mid-June through the first week in September, Tuesday through Saturday, 1 to 4 P.M. Admission charge. Telephone: (410) 632-0669. Web site: www.octhebeach.com/museum/Zion.html.

All Hallows Episcopal Church, at Market and Church streets, was constructed in 1748 at a cost of 120,000 pounds of tobacco. Gifts from Queen Anne to the church included a Bible dated "London, 1701," and a bell, hanging in the churchyard. An unusual feature of the church is the 15-foot-high windows. The stained glass of the windows dates from 1890 and replaced the original clear glass. The church may be viewed by appointment. Telephone: (410) 632-2327.

Four miles northwest of Snow Hill, off Route 12 on Old Furnace Road, the visitor may see **Furnace Town.** The grounds include the remains of the **Nassawango Furnace,** a significant iron ore smelting enterprise started in 1832. For 15 years iron ore was taken from the nearby swamp and smelted into iron bars. The operation was then recognized as an unprofitable one, and the works were abandoned. People moved away; the town fell into decay and disappeared through the years. The 30-foot furnace tower has been repaired, and excavation has disclosed the dam, spillway, and foundations of homes. The grounds include eleven nineteenth-century exhibit buildings, including a church, blacksmith shop, smokehouse, broom house, print shop, woodworking shop, weaving house, farm implement house, and museum. Demonstrations of blacksmithing, printing, broom making, weaving, and gardening are held daily in period dress.

The public is also invited to participate in archeological digs of nineteenth-century structures, held seasonally. Grounds include picnic areas, nature trails, and a nineteenth-century kitchen garden. Open April through October, daily, 10 A.M. to 5 P.M. Admission charge. Call or visit the Web site for a schedule of yearly festivals and events or for further information. Telephone: (410) 632-2032. Web site: www.furnacetown.com.

Furnace Town is the entrance to the Nature Conservancy's Paul

Leifer Trail featuring boardwalks over and through the Nassawango Cypress Swamp, which includes 3,000 acres of wilderness along Nassawango Creek. The primeval bald cypress-gum swamp, home to swamp species of deer, otter, nesting wood duck, and many reptiles, is located between Furnace Road and Red House Road.

Pocomoke River State Park is located within the Pocomoke State Forest and has two separate areas, the Shad Landing and Milburn Landing areas. The park, and the adjacent forest, are a paradise for nature enthusiasts. Roads and trails through the area provide access to a region typical of a Deep South swamp, as well as upland loblolly pine stands. The combination of swamp and upland makes for a great variety in plant and animal life. During the Civil War era, the swamps of this area provided hiding places for runaway slaves and for Southern sympathizers. During Prohibition, illegal whiskey stills flourished in the dense woods.

Bird watchers and hunters are attracted here because of the great variety and abundance of bird life. Pocomoke is said to support a greater number of bird species than any other Atlantic inland area. The fishing in Pocomoke River State Park requires no license because the Pocomoke River is considered tidal waters up to Snow Hill. Hunting is allowed in the State Forest area. Interpretive programs are offered during the summer at both Shad Landing and Milburn Landing. Activities include nature walks, evening campfire talks, canoe and fishing trips, and junior park ranger programs.

The **Shad Landing Area** is located 3.5 miles south of Snow Hill, on Route 113. It borders the Pocomoke River and Corkers Creek. The waterways, winding through a cypress swamp, remind one of the Florida Everglades. Facilities include picnicking, playground, shelter, restroom, boat launch, bathhouse, camping, hiking, marina, youth group camping, dumping station, ball field, and swimming. The river offers good bass fishing, and boating facilities are available. Bike, canoe, and rowboat rentals are available. A "fish for fun" pond is available for young people. The young anglers are encouraged to return the fish to the pond. No pets allowed in this area.

The **Milburn Landing Area** is 7 miles northeast of Pocomoke City via Route 364 or Route 12. It is also situated on the north bank of the Pocomoke River. This section has a picnic area, playground, shelter, restroom, boat launch, bathhouse, and facilities for camping and fishing. Telephone: (410) 632-2566. Web site: www.dnr.state.md.us/publiclands/eastern/pocomokeriver.asp.

In downtown Pocomoke, which is about 6 miles south of Milburn Landing on Route 113, the **Costen House Museum** on Market Street features a late Victorian house with period furniture and intimate memorial gardens. Admission charge. Open May through October, Wednesday through Saturday, 1 to 4 P.M. Telephone: (410) 957-3110. Web site: pocomokeriver.org/Costenhouse.html. Also in Pocomoke is the recently restored **Sturgis School House,** which was one room school for African American children in the early twentieth-century. Open May through October, Wednesdays and Saturdays, 1 to 4 P.M. or by appointment. Telephone: (410) 957-1913. Web site: www.octhebeach.com/museum/Sturgis.html.

The **Calvin B. Taylor House Museum** at N. Main and Baker streets is located in Berlin's National Register Historic District. It includes both a house museum and a display gallery of local memorabilia. Open Memorial Day through September, Monday, Wednesday, Friday, and Saturday, 1 to 4 P.M. Telephone: (410) 641-1019. Web site: www.octhebeach.com/museum/Taylor.html.

At 2 N. Main Street is the **Atlantic Hotel.** Included in the Great Inns of America, the meticulously refurbished Victorian hotel features a lounge, parlors, a fine dining room, and a long front porch. Telephone: (410) 641-3589. Web site: www.atlantichotel.com.

Assateague is a barrier island, a narrow strip of land extending 33 miles, from the Ocean City inlet to the Virginia end of the peninsula. At its southern tip, the Virginia Island of Chincoteague is located on the Chincoteague Bay side of Assateague. The island is divided into different areas administered by the Maryland and U.S. Park Services and the U.S. Fish and Wildlife Service. The Maryland section, reached via Route 611, which joins Route 50 about two miles east of Ocean City, contains Assateague State Park and the U.S. Assateague Island National Seashore.

The island once extended from Virginia to Delaware, but in a 1933 storm, an inlet was cut through at Ocean City. The island varies in width from one-third of a mile to about one mile. The low sand dunes are constantly changing because of storms and the normal action of tides, waves, and winds.

The island affords swimming and bird watching opportunities at an unspoiled, quiet beach. The park is very popular in the summer; its sand beach is considered one of the finest on the East Coast. Bird watchers come in fall to observe the flocks of waterfowl in Sinepuxent Bay and its shallow tributaries.

The **Assateague Island National Seashore,** administered by the U.S. National Park Service, is composed of two sections, the area north of Assateague State Park and the area south of the state park to the Virginia state line. Camping, swimming, bay canoeing, crabbing, fishing, and hiking opportunities are available in the National Seashore area. Over-sand vehicles are also allowed on a 14-mile stretch of beach. Permits are required for both over-sand vehicle use and for camping. The park is open year round. May 15 through October 15 camping reservations are required, the rest of the year is first come, first serve. Admission charge. The **Barrier Island Visitors Center** on Route 611, just before the bridge to Assateague, shows a nature film and can provide an auto cassette tape tour. Telephone: (410) 641-1441, for camping reservations: (800) 365-2267. Web site: www.nps.gov/asis.

Assateague State Park encompasses a two-mile strip at the northern tip of the island. The beach is divided into separate areas for swimming, surfing, and surf fishing. A one-mile Oceanic Trail is available for self-guided walks. During the summer the park offers body surfing demonstrations, salt marsh walks, nature discussions, and awards weekly surf fishing certificates for the largest fish caught in six categories. The campsites are open year round, although the washhouses are closed from November to Easter. Telephone: (410) 641-2918. Web site: www.dnr.state.md.us/publiclands/eastern/assateaguecamping.asp.

Ocean City is a popular seaside family resort which attracts thousands of visitors all year long, drawn to its 10 miles of white sand beaches, three-mile world-famous Boardwalk and numerous recreational opportunities. Ocean City offers seventeen 18-hole championship golf courses, boating, bay and deep sea fishing, nature tours, water sports, antique and outlet shopping.

Ocean City sponsors special events each season, including festivals and concerts, antique shows, and arts and crafts offerings. Popular annual events include Springfest in May, with four days of arts, crafts and music, Sunfest in September, and Winterfest of Lights in November and December. Visit the Ocean City Visitors Center, 4001 Coastal Hwy, Ocean City, Maryland. Telephone: (800) OC-OCEAN or (800) 626-2326. Web sites: www.ocean-city.com (or) www.ococean.com.

The **Ocean City Life-Saving Station Museum,** at South Boardwalk and the Inlet, was a life saving station built by the U.S. Treasury Department and used to house the U.S. Life Saving Service crew. It was used from 1878 to 1962. Today the museum houses Ocean City historical memorabilia. Exhibits include doll house models of the resort's old hotels, shipwreck artifacts, saltwater aquariums, and the history of the Life Saving Service. A museum shop sells souvenirs. Open June through September, daily, 11 A.M. to 10 P.M.; May and October, daily, 11 A.M. to 4 P.M.; November, December and April, 11 A.M. to 4 P.M. on weekends only; January through March, call for hours. Admission charge. Telephone: (410) 289-4991. Web site: www.ocmuseum.org.

Somerset County

Somerset County is the southernmost Maryland county on the Eastern Shore, and was established in 1666. The Somerset area was a religious haven for dissident Virginians and also was the area in great dispute between Lord Baltimore and the royal colony of Virginia. For an overview of county attractions or to request fishing, driving walking brochures, use Web site: www.visitsomerset.com.

Princess Anne, the county seat, is 12 miles south of Salisbury on Route 13. This town, laid out in 1733, was named in honor of Anne, daughter of King George II. For a walking tour brochure and other information, contact Somerset County Tourism, PO Box 243, Princess Anne, MD 21853. Telephones: (410) 651-2968 or (toll free) (800) 521-9189. The walking tour is also available on the town's Web site: www.townofprincessanne.com. For an overview of county attractions or to request fishing, driving walking brochures, use Web site: www.visitsomerset.com.

The Lower Shore Heritage Committee, 11696 Church Street, Princess Anne, MD 21853 is a grassroots, nonprofit organization dedicated to preserving and protecting the historical heritage of Somerset, Worcester, and Wicomico Counties. Telephone: (410) 651-4420. Web site: Link through Lower Shore at www.mdisfun.org.

The Princess Anne walking tour includes 40 notable structures dating from 1744. Four are described below. **Teackle Mansion,** 11736 Mansion Street, headquarters of Old Princess Anne Days, Inc., and the Somerset County Historical Society, is an elaborate example of Federal-style architecture. Built in 1802 the home is furnished with period furniture and contains historical exhibits. George A. Townsend, author of the famous nineteenth-century novel *The Entailed Hat,* used the mansion as the setting for the home of the novel's heroine. The house is at the end of Prince William Street.

Open April through mid-December, Wednesday, Saturday, and Sunday, 1 to 3 P.M.; January through March, Sunday 1 to 3 P.M. Other times by appointment. Admission charge. Telephone: (410) 651-2238. The **Washington Hotel,** 11784 Somerset Avenue in the center of town, dates from the 1740s and has operated as an inn since 1797. **St. Andrew's Episcopal Church,** 11700 Church Street, was built in the 1770s and reconstructed twice. One of its treasures is the communion silver dating from 1717. **Manokin Presbyterian Church** (1756) is located at 11890 Somerset Avenue, north of the bridge. The tower was added in 1888. Presbyterian meetings have been held on this site since 1672, and its congregation was organized in 1683.

Just north of Princess Anne turn off Route 13 onto Route 362 west to the village of Mt.Vernon. The local fire company, now housed in what was the elementary school in former days, holds an annual biking outing as a fundraiser each April. According to A. W. Carey, a former resident, "Years ago before cars were as omnipresent as today, what were known as 'down the road' people never met the 'up the road' people until we all converged at the elementary school which was roughly in the middle." The flat back roads offer a variety of interesting routes and scenery, including the work boats and pleasure craft moored at towns like Mt. Vernon. Nearby you can take the White Haven Ferry, which has been in operation for 300+ years, to Wicomico County and the picturesque village of Whitehaven.

The parish for **Old Rehoboth Presbyterian Church** was founded in 1672 and became official when Francis Mackemie arrived in 1683. Under his direction, the current building was erected in 1706, and the same sanctuary is used for worship today. Francis Mackemie is the founder of Presbyterianism in America. "Old Rehoboth" is the oldest continually active Presbyterian Church in America today. A lobby tape recording provides visitors with church history. It is south of Princess Anne on Route 13, then right on Route 667, five miles to Rehobeth (spelled different due to an error long ago) on Route 406. The ruins of **Coventry Episcopal Church,** built in 1740, are across the road in back of the parsonage. Check there about gaining admittance to Old Rehoboth Presbyterian. Telephone: (410) 957-4143.

The motorist who wishes to take side trips to get a glimpse of secluded villages and beautiful scenery can visit **Deal Island** at the west end of Route 363 from Princess Anne or four small villages on Route 361 further south. Deal Island is connected to the mainland by bridge and has two quaint fishing villages—Deal Island and Wenona. The island is an ideal place to observe the maritime activities on Tangier Sound. Wenona is the home port of a portion of the last remaining skipjack fleet. In Deal Island village is the grave of Joshua Thomas, the evangelical minister who converted many bay islanders to Methodism and who resisted the British invaders during the War of 1812.

Returning to Route 13, the motorist may take the second side trip to the small communities of **Manokin, Upper Fairmont, and Rumbley.** These villages are south from Princess Anne on Routes 13 and 413, west on Route 361. Upper Fairmont is located on a peninsula between the Manokin and Big Annemessex rivers. The community is a cluster of farmhouses, Victorian homes, cottages, and several churches, served by a single old-time country store. The Fairmont Academy, in Upper Fairmont, was founded in 1839 and was in continuous use as a school until 1968. Now a firehouse and community center, several rooms have been set up to reflect classrooms of bygone days, and it is also used for community activities. Open by appointment. Write: Fairmont Academy Historical Association, Upper Fairmont, MD 21867.

Crisfield, terminus of Route 413, derives its livelihood from oysters, crabs, and fish. It is the self-styled "Sea Food Capital." Scores of boats come and go, bringing tons of marine edibles from every direction. The lower waterfront part of town gives Crisfield its character. Many structures are built on oyster shells deposited over the decades on marshland. Here one finds seafood processing plants and piers. Crisfield also manufactures oyster tongs, knives, dredges, muskrat traps, and packing cases. It has skilled craftsmen who make sails and duck decoys. For further information contact the Crisfield Area Chamber of Commerce, 906 W. Main Street (PO Box 292), Crisfield, MD 21817. The offices are open Monday through Friday, 9 A.M. to 5 P.M. Telephones: (410) 968-2500 or (800) 782-3913. Web site: www.crisfield.org.

The **Crisfield Historical Museum** also known as the **J. Millard Tawes Museum,** one block from the city wharf, has exhibits of early Indian inhabitants, maritime history of Somerset County, and prominent county residents, such as former Governor J. Millard Tawes. Hours vary. Telephone: (410) 968-2501.

Crisfield is the mainland port from which visitors can take ferries and cruises to **Smith Island** and also to Tangier Island in Virginia. (Also see Virginia section and Web site: www.smithislandcruises.com/crisfield-maryland-cruises.).
Smith Island Web site: www.smithisland.org.

Smith Island in reality is a group of about four large islands, including the one designated as Martin National Wildlife Refuge. The islands straddle the Maryland-Virginia State Line, although the three villages of Smith Island are in the Maryland section. The Martin Wildlife refuge is, for the most part, closed to the public because of the fragile nature of the waterfowl population inhabiting the island. Even scientific studies have disturbed the heron rookeries there.

Smith Island is Maryland's only inhabited island accessible exclusively by boat. Comprised of three separate villages, Ewell, Tylerton, and Rhodes Point, Smith Island lies in the Chesapeake Bay 12 miles west of Crisfield. When Capt. John Smith explored the Chesapeake Bay in 1608, he gave this island his name. Captain Smith wrote in his log, "Heaven and earth seemed never to have agreed better for man's commodious and delightful habitation."

The direct descendants of the original settlers from England and Cornwall in 1657 inhabit Smith Island, a quiet, peaceful land. Most of its citizens derive their livelihood from the unpredictable waters of the Chesapeake. The **Smith Island Center** is a visitor center and cultural museum in Ewell, one of three villages on the Island. There is a twenty-minute film entitled, *Land, Water, People, and Time,* and exhibits depicting the history, economy, and social life of the area. Open daily, April through October, noon to 4 P.M. Other times by appointment. Telephone: (410) 425-3351.

Year-round ferries, *Captain Jason* and *Island Belle II,* leave daily from Crisfield carrying freight and mail, but passengers are welcome. The *Captain Tyler* cruise line operates Memorial Day to September. Overnight cruises are also available. Fare charge. Call for schedule. Telephone: (410) 425-2771. Passenger ferries to Tangier Island also leave from the City Dock. Telephone: (410) 968-2338 or (800) 863-2338.

Janes Island State Park is located at the mouth of Crisfield Harbor, two miles north of Crisfield on Route 358. The original inhabitants were Native Americans of the Annemessex Nation. The park is composed of two topographically separate areas: a small developed portion on the mainland, known as the **Hodson Area,** which may be reached by automobile, and an island area of several thousand acres, entirely separated from the mainland by the Annemessex Canal, and bordered by waters of the Big and Little Annemessex rivers and the Tangier Sound. The island portion of the park is accessible only by boat.

The mainland portion of the park has camping and picnic areas, cabins, boat rental, and a boat launching ramp. The island portion offers swimming, crabbing, fishing, canoeing, kayaking, camping, and picnicking. The miles of shoreline and marsh areas and the inland ponds abound in waterfowl and birds. For further information, contact: Janes Island State Park, 26280 Alfred Lawson Drive, Crisfield, MD 21817. Telephone: (410) 968-1565; camping reservations (888) 432-CAMP. Web site: www.dnr.state.md.us/publiclands.

SOUTHERN MARYLAND, WESTERN SHORE

Five counties comprise the peninsula known as the western shore of Southern Maryland: Anne Arundel, Calvert, Prince George's, Charles, and St. Mary's. The area is bounded on the east by the Chesapeake Bay and on the west by the Potomac River, which separates it from Virginia. The area is home to some of the earliest settlements in America as well as some of the oldest churches, some of which still have active parishes. Since water surrounds the area, and its irregular shore line makes for countless coves and hideaways, it is no surprise that boats, sailing, and related industries figure in its history. As does agriculture, since early settlers discovered some of the richest farmland on the East Coast within its borders.

"Since the early 1600s, tobacco has been the cultural mainstay and primary source of income for Southern Maryland. In 2001, the State of Maryland instituted a Tobacco Buyout to encourage farmers to transition away from tobacco production for human consumption," according to the Southern Maryland Agricultural Development Commission, which was created to promote "diverse, market-driven, agricultural enterprises." The group produces a guide book of such enterprises, ranging from bees to Christmas trees, hay, fishing, 4-H Clubs and Local Farmers' Markets. The Commission can be reached at the Tri-County Council for Southern Maryland. Telephone: (301) 274-1922 or (301) 301-870-2520. Web site: www.tccsmd.org.

Anne Arundel

The Anne Arundel County area, named after Lady Anne of Arundell, wife of Cecilius Calvert, second Lord Baltimore, was settled by Puritans from Virginia and the county was created in 1650. The provincial capital was moved from St. Mary's City because of its inaccessibility to Arundell Towne, which was renamed Annapolis in 1695. Annapolis was convenient both for English ships and as a meeting place for tobacco planters and politicians. In 1699, an observer noted that there were "fourty dwelling houses" in Annapolis. A French traveler described the elegant society of Annapolis in 1781, noting that "a French hair dresser is a man of importance among... the fine women" and it was said he commanded "a thousand crowns a year salary."

Anne Arundel County, bordering on the western shore of the Chesapeake Bay, has 437 miles of shoreline, which makes it perfect for "gunk holing," as the locals call exploring the small coves of the Bay in boats. The area is a mecca for sailing and boating enthusiasts who moor their craft at the many deepwater piers of the Severn, South, Rhode, and Magothy rivers. The northwestern portion of the county is situated in the Baltimore-Washington corridor and is largely suburban.

For more information about county attractions, as well as walking and driving tours, contact the Annapolis and Anne Arundel County Convention and Visitors Bureau, 26 West Street in Annapolis. Brochures are available, including one highlighting the region's African American heritage. Telephone: (410) 280-0445. Web site: www.visit-annapolis.org. Or visit the Chamber of Commerce Web site: www.ci.annapolis.md.us/visitors.

The city of **Annapolis** is a National Historic Landmark with more surviving Colonial (eighteenth-century) buildings than any other city in the county. Because there are so many noteworthy historical buildings, it would be impossible to list and describe them all. Consider this section a broad brush overview. Visit or contact a local information center to get a full sense of the many interesting sites and historical treasures that await your discovery.

Annapolis is the capital of the state, the home of the **U.S. Naval Academy,** and a base for many sailing and boating activities. It is also on the busy ocean shipping route from Hampton Roads in Virginia to Baltimore and is near the western approach to the **Chesapeake Bay Bridge,** which connects the Eastern and Western Shores of the state.

In planning a visit to Annapolis, it is well worthwhile for visitors to consider a guided walking tour. **Three Centuries Tours of Annapolis,** 48 Maryland Avenue, offer walking tours of the city and give informative lectures of 90 minutes to two hours. Prearranged tours, such as the two-hour "Early Bird" walking tour and a "Colonial Life" tour for young people, as well as group tours by arrangement. All Three

Centuries tour guides wear period costumes. Telephone: (410) 260-7601. Web site: http://annapolistours.com. Other companies offering guided tours are listed on the Chamber of Commerce Web site under Visitor Information: www.ci.annapolis.md.us/visitors. **Historic Annapolis Foundation** also offers walking tours and lectures. The administrative offices are located in the **Shiplap House** (c. 1715), originally a tavern. For walking tour information, stop first at 77 Main Street. Or, for more information contact: Historic Annapolis Foundation, 18 Pinkney Street, Annapolis, MD 21401. Telephone: (410) 267-7619. Web site: www.annapolis.org.

The Historic Annapolis Foundation owns and/or manages six historic properties in Annapolis. Start your tour at the **Victualling Warehouse,** at 77 Main Street. This is their museum store and welcome center. This well-restored structure stored provisions for local troops during the Revolutionary war. Burned in 1790, it was rebuilt about 1815. Here you can rent a Historic Annapolis cassette Walking Tour. Open daily, 10 A.M. to 5 P.M. Telephone: (410) 268-5576.

Entrance to the **William Paca House** (c. 1765) and **Garden** is located at 186 Prince George Street. This elegant Georgian mansion, home of Declaration of Independence signer and three-term Maryland governor, has been authentically restored. The reconstructed garden features a Chinese-trellis bridge, domed pavilion, and fish-shaped pond. House and garden open March 17 through December 30, Monday through Saturday, 10 A.M. to 5 P.M. (first tour starts at 10:30 A.M., then every half hour); Sunday, noon to 5 P.M. January and February, weekends only, Saturday,10 A.M. to 4 P.M.; Sunday, noon to 4 P.M. Admission charge, combined garden and house or separately. Telephone: (410) 990-4543.

The **Maynard-Burgess House,** across from City Hall at 163 Duke of Gloucester Street, was the home of two successive African American families from 1847 to 1900. It is a tribute to the aspirations of the free black population of Annapolis in the 1800s. The house is currently under restoration but may be viewed from without. Check with the Historic Annapolis Foundation for completion date.

Highlights of the walking tour include the **State House,** the oldest state capitol in continuous legislative use in the country. Construction began in 1772. No nails were used in building the large wooden dome. Here George Washington resigned his commission, and here the fledgling U.S. Congress ratified the Treaty of Paris ending the Revolutionary War. Inquire in the State House about guided tours. Nearby on School Street just off State Circle is the **Government House,** which was completed in 1870 but has since been remodeled to the Georgian style of the Colonial period. **St. John's College** campus, which is bordered by St. John's Street and College Avenue, is a four-year, liberal arts college, third oldest in the United States. It was chartered in 1784, but traces its beginnings to King William School that opened in 1696. The curriculum is organized around great books, tutorials, and seminars. On the campus grounds is a descendent of the famous 400-year-old tulip poplar known as the Liberty Tree. The original tree expired and was removed in 1999, but one of its offspring, planted in 1889 continues to thrive. Also on campus is **McDowell Hall** (1742) and the French Monument, erected in honor of the French soldiers and sailors who died en route to Yorktown during the American Revolution and are buried on campus. This was one of the first U.S. monuments to unknown and unnamed soldiers. Telephone: (410) 263-2371. The Web site includes a virtual tour: www.sjca.edu.

A walk down to 247 King George Street offers views of **Ogle Hall** (U.S. Naval Academy Alumni House, c. 1739), and the **Chase-Lloyd House** (c. 1769) at 22 Maryland Avenue where Francis Scott Key was married. The Chase-Lloyd House, begun by Samuel Chase, signer of the Declaration of Independence, was one of the first three-story townhouses built in Annapolis. It is now a home for the elderly, but the first floor is open to the public (except January and February), Monday through Saturday, 2 to 4 P.M. Admission charge. Telephone: (410) 263-2723. Web site: www.dnr.state.md.us/forests/programs/urban/toa/site5.html.

Across the street is the **Hammond-Harwood House** (1774), an outstanding example of Georgian colonial architecture located at 19 Maryland Avenue. It is a beautifully furnished museum of decorative arts. Open Wednesday through Sunday, noon to 5 P.M. Closed New Year's Day, Christmas, Thanksgiving and for occasional special events. Admission charge. Telephone: (410) 263-4683. Web site includes a virtual tour: www.hammondharwoodhouse.org.

At this point you may enter the **U.S. Naval Academy** through Gate #3 to visit the **museum,** and the beautiful **Chapel.** (Photo identification is required to enter the campus.) The Chapel contains the **crypt of John Paul Jones,** whose body was transferred in 1905 from an abandoned cemetery in Paris where he had died in 1792. Visitors may see the **Bancroft Hall Memorial Hall** collection of Naval memorabilia.

Naval Academy tours leave from the Visitors Center inside Gate #1. Times vary depending upon the season. Advance tour arrangements are advised. Telephone: (410) 293-2292. Web site: www.usna.edu. At 42 East Street stands **Brice House,** a magnificent eighteenth-century mansion. This National Historic Landmark is not open to the public but may be viewed from without. Left on Prince George Street to Randall Street will bring you to the Market Space and inner harbor area. Here in the picturesque **City Market House,** built in 1858 and restored in 1970, several landscaped areas are ideal for sitting, eating, and people watching.

At 84 Franklin Street, the **Banneker-Douglas Museum** is housed in the former **Mount Moriah African Methodist Episcopal Church.** It is an official repository of regional African American history and culture. Open Tuesday through Friday, 10 A.M. to 3 P.M.; Saturday, noon to 4 P.M. Free admission. Telephone: (410) 216-6180. Web site: www.bdmuseum.com.

One can stroll along the waterfront to see an occasional skipjack oyster boat or a clam boat, as well as the many yachts that tie up at **City Dock.** A further walk (or drive) is past the Annapolis Yacht Club across Spa Creek to **Eastport,** the sailing center of the Chesapeake Bay. This is a picturesque locale for photographers.

Visitors may also take cruises on several vessels. There is a 40-minute guided tour of the bay on the *Harbor Queen* and a 40-minute guided tour of the tidewater areas on the *Miss Anne,* as well as an all-day cruise to St. Michaels on the *Annapotitan II.* A 90-minute eco-cruise of the Severn River and Chesapeake Bay to Thomas Point Light House on the *Rebecca Forbush* takes visitors on a different route. The cruises are operated by Chesapeake Marine Tours on the City Dock, from mid-May to early October. For fare information and schedules, telephone: (410) 268-7601. Web site: www.annapoliscruises.com.

Another beautiful spot in Annapolis is the **Helen Avalynne Tawes Garden** at 580 Taylor Avenue. This award-winning botanical garden features representations of Maryland's natural resources. They include a Western Maryland forest, a streamside environment, and an Eastern Shore peninsula, in addition to pleasant ponds. Open daily, dawn to dusk. Gift shop, cafeteria, and guided tours by reservation, Monday through Friday until 3 P.M. Last tour at 2 P.M. Admission charge. Telephone: (410) 260-8189. Web site: www.dnr.state.md.us/publiclands/tawesgarden.asp.

Across the South River from Annapolis, by boat or by Route 252, is the **London Town Publik House** (c. 1760), 839 Londontown Road in Edgewater, which served as a stopping place for travelers who used the Annapolis-Londontown ferry on their way between Williamsburg and Philadelphia. The Publik House is the only remnant of the once-prosperous tobacco inspection town of the eighteenth century, which was eclipsed by Annapolis when it became the state capital. The Publik House is furnished with mid-eighteenth-century antiques and is surrounded by eight acres of gardens. A relocated log tobacco barn is open to the public and a portion of the garden is devoted to crops and plants grown in the nineteenth century. The grounds are the largest ongoing archeological excavations in the state of Maryland. During the summer, demonstration programs are offered. Open Monday through Saturday, 10 A.M. to 4 P.M.; Sunday, noon to 4 P.M. Last tours begin at 3 P.M. Admission charge. Telephone: (410) 222-1919. Web site: www.historiclondontown.com.

Sandy Point State Park is located, off US 50/301, about eight miles east of Annapolis, in view of the Chesapeake Bay Bridge. This 786-acre park is famous for its sandy bathing beaches, fishing, crabbing, boating wind surfing and bird watching. The park is located on the Atlantic Flyway, the migratory route of eastern birds, and autumn finds bird-lovers enjoying the splendid spectacle provided by the profusion of wild geese and ducks overhead. The **Sandy Point Farmhouse,** an early nineteenth-century building, is centrally located in the park. It has been placed on the National Register of Historic Places. The park offers picnicking facilities, toilets, showers, a playground, hiking trails, boat rentals, a boat launch; areas suitable for crabbing, birding, swimming, windsurfing, and kayaking, and a refreshment stand. From May 15 to October 31, the park is open 6 A.M. to sunset, although boat launching and fishing are available 24 hours a day, mid-May through mid-September. For further information and off season hours, contact Sandy Point State Park, 1100 East College Parkway, Annapolis, MD 21401. Telephone: (410) 974-2149. Web site: www.dnr.state.md.us/publiclands/southern/sandypoint.asp.

Calvert County

Calvert County is almost completely surrounded by water—on the east by the Chesapeake Bay and on the west by the Patuxent River. Calvert Cliffs, famous for its Miocene Age fossil deposits, form the bay coastline for 30 miles from Chesapeake Beach to Solomons Island. In 1608 when he first explored the bay, Capt. John Smith wrote in his diary: "The Western Shore, by which we sailed, we found well watered. But very mountainous and barren, the valleys were fertile, but extremely thick of small woods, as well as trees and much frequented with wolves, bears, deer, and other wild beasts. The streams were crystal clear and full of fish." From June to September Calvert County beaches are popular for their gradual sloping sandy bottoms, light wave action, and warm salt water. Calvert County has a wonderful Web site that will provide you with information on special events, beaches, museums, and other attractions. Or you may write or call Calvert County Department of Economic Development Visitor Information, Courthouse, 175 Main Street, Prince Frederick 20678. Telephone: (410) 535-1600 or (301) 855-1243. Web site: www.co.cal.md.us. Or, as an additional source for Calvert, Charles, and St. Mary's Counties: www.tccsmd.org.

Breezy Point may be reached from Chesapeake Beach on Route 261 south to Breezy Point Road. There is a half-mile sandy beach with netted swimming area for protection from sea nettles, a bathhouse, playground, picnic tables, marina, boat ramps, and fishing pier. Rental cottages, camp sites, and group picnic facilities are available. Open daily from May 1 through October 31. Admission charge. Telephone: (410) 535-0259. Web site: www.co.cal.md.us/visitors/beaches.

The **Chesapeake Beach Railway Museum** on Route 261 at 4155 Mears Avenue features exhibits on the resort town that was constructed in the 1890s. The Chesapeake Beach Railway Company ran between Washington, D.C. and Chesapeake Beach from 1900 to 1935. The museum is housed in a restored railway station. Open May through September, daily, 1 to 4 P.M.; April and October, weekends, 1 to 4 P.M. Closed November through March but prescheduled visits are encouraged. Free admission; donations welcome. Telephone: (410) 257-3892. Web site: www.cbrm.org.

Historic Lower Marlboro can be reached from Route 4 by turning right on Route 523 and going approximately four miles. It is one of the oldest towns in Maryland and was an important port until the Patuxent River silted over. One can browse through this settlement, once a British port, which saw the building of one of Maryland's oldest schools, the Marlboro Academy, the early establishment of a ferry service, and later, a steamboat wharf. Several eighteenth-century homes are still a part of the community. Web site: calvert-county.com/communities/lowermarlboro/lowermarlboro.html.

Return on Route 262 to where Routes 2 and 4 join, at Sunderland. At the junction is **All Saints Church,** founded in1692 and rebuilt in 1774 with Flemish bond brick walls. The baptismal font and paneling were brought from England in 1735. Telephone: (410) 257 6306. Web site: www.allsaints1692.org.

Prince Frederick has been the seat of Calvert County since 1723. From Prince Frederick continue south on Route 2/4 to the **Battle Creek Cypress Swamp Sanctuary,** on Gray's Road off Route 506. This 100-acre Nature Conservancy preserve contains one of the last remaining sites where bald cypress is to be found occurring naturally in the state of Maryland, and it is one of the northernmost significant stands of bald cypress in the United States. Although cypress were once widespread in the Chesapeake Bay region, they are now reduced to the Pocomoke River on the Eastern Shore of Maryland, Battle Creek, and a few scattered small occurrences. Just why the cypress stand at Battle Creek has survived is not fully understood. The cypress in the swamp are up to four feet in diameter and 100 feet high. The wet habitat formed by periodic flooding creates an important breeding area for several species of salamanders and tree frogs. A quarter-mile boardwalk trail provides easy access to the most interesting part of the swamp. The Nature Center features exhibits and natural history lectures. Open April through September, Tuesday through Saturday, 8:30 A.M. to 4:30 P.M. Call to confirm Sunday and seasonal hours. Free admission. Telephone: (410) 535-5327. Web site: calvert-county.com/cypress.htm.

On Route 264 it is ½ mile to **Old Christ Episcopal Church** (3100 Broomes Island Road in Port Republic). Although the present building dates from 1769, the original log structure was built in 1672. Telephone: (410) 586-0565. There is a **One-Room Schoolhouse** on the grounds and a unique blend of Biblical plants. Telephone: (410) 535-3334. Route 264 continues for four miles to Broomes Island, a small community of oystermen and fishermen.

On Route 4 South, 10 miles south of Prince Frederick, look for the sign and turn left to **Flag Ponds Nature Park.** Once a pound-net fishing station on the Chesapeake Bay, Flag Ponds Nature Park displays a remarkable variety of natural environments—from sandy beaches to freshwater ponds and the forested heights of Calvert Cliffs. There are hiking trails, observation platforms, a wetlands boardwalk, a fishing pier, the beach and a visitor center with wildlife exhibits. You can hunt for fossils, picnic on the beach or swim (no life guards) in the

Chesapeake Bay. The park is open Memorial Day through Labor Day, Monday through Friday, 9 A.M. to 6 P.M., Saturday and Sunday, 9 A.M. to 8 P.M.; Labor Day through Memorial Day, weekends only, 9 A.M. to 6 P.M. Admission charge. Telephone: (410) 586-1477 or (410) 535-5327. Web site: www.calvertparks.org/Parks/FlagPonds/FPhome.htm.

The Visitors Center, high on an observation platform, affords a view of the **Calvert Cliffs Nuclear Power Plant** and the majestic Chesapeake Bay. In March 2002, Calvert Cliffs became the first plant in the U.S. to earn 20-year extensions of its operating license from the U.S. Nuclear Regulatory Commission.

Jefferson Patterson Park & Museum is off Route 4 at 10515 Mackall Road in St. Leonard. Take Route 4 South approximately 3 south of Prince Frederick, turn right on Broomes Island Road and follow Mackall Road 6 miles to the park. This Maryland State museum of history and archeology is located on a 544-acre property on the scenic Patuxent River. The visitor center houses a permanent exhibit, "12,000 Years in the Chesapeake," a family Discovery Room and gift shop. The Farm Exhibit building displays historical farm equipment from the region. The Park also features a Woodland Nature Train and a Riverside Archeology Trail, picnic areas and a covered pavilion. The park is home to the Maryland Archeological Conservation Laboratory, which houses the state's extensive archeological collections. Free admission. Telephone: (410) 586-8501. Web site: www.jefpat.org.

Calvert Cliffs State Park in Lusby (approximately 14 miles south of Prince Frederick on Routes 2/4) offers extensive hiking and nature trails, many beautiful picnic areas, and a youth camping area. The unique feature of this park is its miles of cliffs, rising in places to 100 feet, containing visible beds of fossils, some estimated to be over 15 million years old. Fossils of more than 600 species of mollusks and fish can be found here. There is a 2-mile walk one-way to the beach. Picnic tables and grills are provided, there is a playground and fishing is allowed. Note that digging in the cliffs is dangerous and prohibited. Open daily, sunrise to sunset. Donation requested. Telephone: (310) 743-7613. Web site: www.dnr.state.md.us/publiclands/southern/calvertcliffs.asp.

Middleham Chapel, the oldest cruciform-designed church in Maryland, is on Route 2/4 at Lusby. Near the present building (1748) lie many gravestones from the early 1700s. A memorial plaque to the Parrans, an old Maryland family, is dated 1729. Telephone: (410) 326-4948. Web site: www.middlehamandstpeters.org/directions.html.

The **Cove Point Light Station** is located on a two-acre lot at the end of Route 497, which intersects with Route 2/4, two miles below Lusby. This 51-foot structure is the oldest brick tower lighthouse in the Chesapeake Bay area. The Coast Guard lighthouse has been in continuous use from 1828 to the present. Until 1877 the lights were fueled by whale, coal, and lard oils. There is an excellent view from the top of the lighthouse. Open weekends and holidays, May through September, and daily June, July, and August, 10 A.M. to 4:30 P.M. Access is via shuttle bus from the Calvert Marine Museum in Solomons. Admission charge. Telephone: (410) 326-2042. Website: www.calvertmarinemuseum.com/exhibits/cove-point-lighthouse.php.

Just north of **Solomons** on Dowell Road is Annmarie Garden on St. John. This outstanding outdoor sculpture garden is being developed along the St. Johns Creek to allow for the experience of museum quality outdoor artwork in combination with the unique, tranquil setting of a natural garden. Sculpture, flora, fauna, and cultural programs enhance one's background for reflection. From Route 4 South, turn left on Dowell Road at Solomons Firehouse. The Garden is located on the left less than one quarter mile. Admission charge. Open 10 A.M. to 4 P.M. daily. Telephone: (410) 326-4640. Web site: www.annmariegarden.org.

The tiny tidewater town of **Solomons** is almost completely surrounded by water. It lies between the Chesapeake Bay and the mouth of the Patuxent River, which is two miles wide at this point. Once a thriving center for oyster processing and the construction and repair of oystering vessels, Solomons is now a lovely resort community where restaurants and gift stores have replaced general stores and groceries of former years. Modern hotels and quaint Bed and Breakfast inns have replaced much of the old landscape. Solomons' focus still lies with the water as nearby marinas, marine suppliers, charter boat operators and other water-related businesses thrive in this sleepy waterside town. Web site: www.solomonsmaryland.com.

Located at the southern tip of Calvert County, at Solomons, the **Calvert Marine Museum** offers educational exhibits, programs, and publications relating to marine paleontology the Calvert Cliffs, estuarine biology of the Patuxent River, and local marine history. The museum may be reached on Route 2 or by boat.

The visitor can see artifacts, exhibits, and documents in the Maritime History, Aquatic, and Waterman's Rooms; stroll through the small craft shed; and visit the woodcarver's shop, marine art gallery, and exhibits on area marine life and fossil remains. You can also climb through the hatch of the **Drum Point Lighthouse,** now located at the museum. The lighthouse was moved six miles to its present location and restored and furnished in an early 1900s style. Built in 1883, it is a cottage lighthouse with screw-type piles. The museum and lighthouse are open daily, 10 A.M. to 5 P.M. Admission charge. The museum also offers cruises of the Patuxent River estuary on a chunk-built, log canoe, the *Wm. B. Tennison,* the oldest Coast Guard-licensed passenger-carrying vessel on the Chesapeake. Built in 1899, this boat, converted from a sailboat to a powerboat is described as an oyster buy-boat of the bugeye class. The *Wm. B. Tennison* operates one-hour cruises, May to October, Wednesday through Sunday, at 2 P.M. In July and August, an additional cruise is offered on Saturday and Sunday at 12:30 P.M. Fare charge. Telephone: (410) 326-2042. Web site: www.calvertmarinemuseum.com/exhibits/drum-point-lighthouse.php.

Here you can also visit the J.C. Lore & Sons Oyster House, only one-half mile south of the main museum. Learn about the boom and decline of the region's commercial seafood industries and see the tools and gear used by local watermen to harvest fish, soft-shelled clams, eels, crabs, and oysters. Open daily June through August, and weekends only in May and September, 10 A.M. to 4:30 P.M.

Prince George's County

The eastern Washington suburbs of Prince George's County offer tour opportunities ranging from the history of space travel at the National Aeronautics and Space Administration's Goddard Space Flight Center to the history of agriculture, an expansive equestrian center, and an important wildlife sanctuary. The county also has a long and varied history, which can still be seen in the rural tobacco-growing regions in the southern portion of the county and in its many historical mansions.

The county was created in 1696, and it was named in honor of Prince George of Denmark, husband of Princess Anne (Queen of England from 1702-14). At the time, Prince George's included all the western portion of the state and it was not until 1748 that the present boundaries were fixed. Much of Washington, D.C. was originally part of Prince George's. Another historical event was the invasion of Washington in 1814, when the British troops marched through Prince George's from the Chesapeake Bay to burn the capital city. The county government is very active in attempting to preserve historical sites and many new sites are being restored and made available for public use.

For additional information about local attractions, contact the Prince George's County Convention and Visitors Bureau, 9200 Basil Court, #101, Largo, MD 20774. Telephone: (301) 925-8300. The Maryland National Capital Park and Planning Commission, 6611 Kenilworth Avenue, Riverdale, MD 20737 is another good source. Telephone: (301) 454-1740. Web site: www.mncppc.org. Regional Web sites: www.co.pg.md.us or search for Prince George's County on the state Web site: www.mdisfun.org.

The **Montpelier Mansion,** 9401 Montpelier Drive in Laurel, owned by the Maryland National Capital Park and Planning Commission, was constructed circa 1783, and is an excellent example of eighteenth-century Georgian architecture. Officially designated as a Registered National Historic Landmark, the Mansion contains 22 rooms, 10 fireplaces, and seven baths. Many of the rooms have impressive decorative features: columns, plaster scrolls and entablature, ornamental fireplaces and mantels. The wings of the Mansion have an unusual semi-octagonal design. A permanent exhibit is on display on the history of Montpelier.

The visitor to Montpelier may inspect the Mansion as well as the magnificent boxwood gardens and a variety of stately trees, including an unusual triple flowering dogwood. Staff and volunteers offer tours, concerts, teas, re-enactments, festivals, lectures and seminars. The Little Teapot Gift Shop is open Tuesday through Saturday, 10 A.M. to 6 P.M.; Sunday, noon to 4 P.M. The Mansion is on Route 197, one mile west of the Baltimore-Washington Parkway, which separates it from the Patuxent Wildlife Research Center.

Tours are given on the hour, Sunday through Thursday, noon to 3 P.M., March through November. December through February, Sundays only, 1 and 2 P.M. Special tours of 10 or more may be arranged at other times. Admission charge. Telephone: (301) 377-7817. Web site: www.pgparks.com/places/eleganthistoric/montpelier_intro.html.

The **Montpelier Cultural Arts Center,** located on the grounds of the Mansion, houses three art galleries. and is Prince George's County's premier multifaceted arts facility. Work by artists of regional and national acclaim is featured. Various styles are represented among the resident artists who have studios at the Art Center, including prints, sculpture, and ceramics. The public is welcome daily except holidays, 10 to 5 P.M. Telephone: (301) 377-7800 or (410) 792-0664. Consult the

Web site for a list of classes and programs: arts.pgparks.com/Our_Facilities/Montpelier_Arts_Center.htm. **Beltsville Agricultural Research Center** of the U.S. Department of Agriculture covers 7,200 acres of land 15 miles north of Washington. The Agricultural Research Service is America's foremost single agency for food and farm sciences. The exhibits and comprehensive information at the National Visitor Center (housed in a large, attractive log structure built by the WPA) offers many opportunities to learn about research to protect the environment, provide wholesome and safe supplies of food, and to improve agricultural fibers—cotton, wool and leather. The Beltsville Center, a highly diversified research facility, includes laboratories, greenhouses, and hundreds of barns for animals and poultry. It is the largest of the ARS' 100+ sites. In the late 1930s, the Center developed the Beltsville small white turkey to provide the American people with a small turkey that would fit into a refrigerator and could be eaten at one sitting by a small family. The Visitors Center is open year round. Reservations must be made in advance for tours. Web site: www.ars.usda.gov/main/site_main.htm?modecode=12-00-00-00.

The **National Agricultural Library,** the world's largest life sciences library, is also open to the public. The library was founded in 1862 at the request of Abraham Lincoln and has a collection of 1.5 million volumes, including rare books dating back to the fifteenth-century. The library also subscribes to 23,000 serial publications. Telephone: (301) 504-5755. Web site: www.nalusda.gov.

The **Goddard Space Flight Center,** one of the largest research and development facilities of the National Aeronautics and Space Administration, is responsible for scientific and environmental satellites, tracking, and communications. The Center is named in honor of Robert H. Goddard, recognized as the "father of American rocketry." Visitors will see the collection of spacecraft and flight articles, as well as exhibits about America's Space Flight Program in the NASA/Goddard Visitor's Center and Museum. Open Monday Through Friday, 9 A.M. to 4 P.M., except Thanksgiving, Christmas, and New Year's. Model rocket launches on the first Sunday of each month. Free admission. Telephone: (301) 286-3978. Web site: www.gsfc.nasa.gov./vc/index.html.

College Park is the largest of the 11 **University of Maryland** campuses and is the main campus where its president resides. The University was chartered in 1856 and offers many activities that are open to the public. Only a few of them are mentioned below. The Conference and Visitor Center, located on U.S. Route 1 (Baltimore Avenue), 2.2 miles south of Exit 25 off Interstate 95, is open Monday through Friday, 8 to 5 P.M. when the University is open. Telephone: (301)314-7777. Web site: www.cvs.umd.edu.

The **University Dairy** located between Campus Drive and Knox Road on the west side of Route 1, in the historic Turner Hall, has been a tradition for more than 75 years. Renovated in 1998 it now offers a "witty mix of retro...and a touch of [cow] kitsch." In addition to the famous University of Maryland ice cream (alumni are promised it's "still as sinfully rich as you remember"), the Dairy also features lunch fare. Open summer, Monday through Friday 11 A.M. to 4 P.M.; other seasons, call for hours. Telephone: (301) 405-1415.

The **Astronomical Observatory** is open to the public on the 5th and 20th of each month. The program consists of short, non-specialist talks beginning at 8 P.M. in the winter, 9 P.M. in the summer. (Call to confirm hours.) Weather permitting, the audience may look through the telescopes. The largest is 20 inches in diameter. Advance reservations requested for large groups. Contact the visitors center for directions and more information. Telephone: (301) 405-6555.

The **Art Gallery** is located near the intersection of University Boulevard and Adelphi Road on the second floor of the Arts and Sociology Building. The Gallery has a permanent collection of twentieth-century American prints, paintings and photographs, African art, including traditional African sculpture, American Social Realist and Regionalist work, early Chinese Ceramic vessels, a government-sponsored 1930's Mural (on long-term loan from the General Services Administration, Smithsonian American Art Museum), and Mid-twentieth-century Japanese prints. Exhibitions of national and international artists. Open only during academic year, Monday through Saturday, 11 to 4 P.M. with later (7 P.M.) closing on Thursdays. Telephone: (301) 405-2763. Web site: www.artgallery.umd.edu.

The **Glenn L. Martin Wind Tunnel** is one of the largest in the eastern United States and performs aerodynamic testing of airplanes, trucks, automobiles, ships, garbage cans, and many other items. Tours are by advance appointment only. Web site: www.eng.umd.edu/facilities/windtunnel.

Belair Mansion, a beautiful five-part Georgian plantation house originally built for Governor Samuel Ogle, is an eighteenth-century mansion that belongs to the nearby town of Bowie. Visitors can stroll around the grounds and note the architectural features of this ornate structure, erected circa 1745, and the 20 varieties of trees on the grounds. The additional wings were added in 1914. Governor Ogle was interested in race horses and brought to this country the original thoroughbreds from which have descended much of the stock which has made Maryland famous in American horse-racing history. Open Thursday through Sunday, 1 to 4 P.M. Donation requested. Telephone: (301) 809-3088. Web site: www.cityofbowie.org/leisureactivities/museum/belair_mansion.asp. Belair can be reached from the Capital Beltway (I-95/495) via Exit 19 (Route 50) to Route 197, left to Route 450, and on to Tulip Grove Road.

The **Belair Stables Museum,** 2835 Belair Drive (at Tulip Grove Road), preserves the stables owned by William B. Woodward in its heyday. These stables produced two Triple Crown winners, Gallant Fox in 1930 and Omaha in 1935, as well as Nashua who won two of the Triple Crown races in 1954. The museum has a carriage room, a tack room, and collections of photographs, racing silks, and farm tools on exhibit. Open year round, Thursday through Sunday, 1 to 4 P.M. Free admission. Telephone: (301) 809-3088. Web site: www.cityofbowie.org/LeisureActivities/Museum/stable.asp.

Robert M. Watkins Regional Park is a 1,000-acre regional park centrally located in Prince George's County at 301 Watkins Park Drive in Upper Marlboro. It is owned and operated by the Maryland National Capital Park and Planning Commission. A variety of both active and passive recreational facilities are designed to keep every member of the family occupied. Telephone: (301) 218-6700. Web site: www.pgparks.com/Things_To_Do/Nature/Watkins_Regional_Park.htm.

The Chesapeake Beach carousel has been delighting children for almost 100 years. A miniature train chugs through the wooded countryside of the park Tuesday through Sunday during the summer months. A nominal fee is charged for both. An old farm with resident animals is situated behind the carousel.

In addition to these seasonal attractions, there are over more than 200 picnic tables located conveniently near an extensive children's playground area, plus miniature golf and group picnic areas. These tables are by reservation only on weekends. Senior citizen and handicapped picnic areas may be reserved. Telephone: (301) 918-8111.

Adjacent to the train ride and near the playground is a snack bar. Football, baseball, and softball fields are available, plus eight tennis courts. In the athletic field area is an Administration-Visitors Center

Building. During summer evenings free concerts are held in the park. The park also hosts the "Festival of Lights" each December. Thirty-four first-come, first-served campsites are available. Two group sites (10 persons or more) are available on a reserved basis. Campers may use tennis courts, showers, and toilets. Open all year. Reservations and information telephone: (301) 218-6700. Web site: www.pgparks.com/Things_To_Do/Nature/Watkins_Regional_Park.htm. The **Watkins Nature Center,** one mile west of Six Flags, is open daily 8:30 A.M. to 5 P.M.; Sunday 11 A.M. to 4 P.M. It features native wildlife, butterfly and herb gardens, indoor and outdoor ponds, and amphitheater for evening campers. Call for information on programs and nature trails. Telephone: (301) 218-6702.

The city of **Upper Marlboro** is accessible from Baltimore via Routes 3 and 301. From the Capital Beltway (I-95) take Exit 11 to Route 4 nine miles to Upper Marlboro. Founded in 1706, the town was named for the Duke of Marlborough. It is the seat of Prince George's County and has been an important tobacco center since its founding.

A walk or drive through Upper Marlboro affords the visitor the opportunity to see many early homes spanning the period from before the eighteenth century to the Victorian era. Three blocks off the main street, near the public school, is a small graveyard on what was once the Beane property. Located here is the tomb of Dr. William Beane and his wife, who were lifelong residents of the town. Dr. Beane's arrest by the British in 1814 caused Francis Scott Key to protest to the British admiral on his flagship in Baltimore harbor. During the subsequent bombardment of Fort McHenry, Key was inspired to compose our national anthem.

Among other historical attractions is **Trinity Church,** founded in 1810 by Thomas Claggett of Croome, who in 1802 became the first person to be consecrated an Episcopal bishop in America. The present brick edifice dates from 1846. Trinity is located at 14519 Church Street, just off Main Street near the courthouse. Nearby is a large marker commemorating the site of the birthplace of John Carroll, first bishop and archbishop of the Catholic Church in the United States. Telephone: (301) 627-2636.

The **Prince George's Equestrian Center,** at 14900 Pennsylvania Avenue in Upper Marlboro, is a training facility for licensed registered thoroughbred trainers. Many special events take place throughout the year, including horse shows, dog shows, and antique car shows. Telephone: (301) 952-7900. Web site: www.showplacearena.com.

One can combine a tour of Upper Marlboro with a visit to several unique Episcopalian churches, which date back 150 years or more. Most of them are located in western and southern Prince George's County.

St. Barnabas Episcopal Church of Leeland at 14111 Oak Grove Road in Upper Marlboro is a brick edifice, dating from 1773, that was a replacement for the church built in 1710. The parish itself was founded in 1704 or possibly earlier. A painting over the altar, *The Last Supper* (1722), is the work of Gustavus Hesselius, a noted Swedish artist who painted in America from 1711 to 1775. It was the first commissioned religious painting in the American colonies. The parish communion vessels are dated 1714. The building is open during services or by special arrangement. Telephone: (301) 249-5000.

St. Thomas Episcopal, 14300 St. Thomas Road in Croom, is accessible via Route 301, then east on Route 382 to Croom Road, then left to Croom. The church is on a hilltop at the edge of the village. The church was built in 1742-45, with a bell tower added in 1888 honoring Bishop Claggett. The parish itself was founded in 1674. Interior features include traditional box pews, a balcony, and stained-glass windows. The edifice is surrounded by venerable oaks and an old graveyard bearing some famous Maryland names: Calvert, Bowie, Oden, and Carr. Tours by appointment. Telephone: (301)627-8469. Web site: www.stthomascroom.org.

St. Paul's Parish at 13500 Baden-Westwood Road in Brandywine was founded in 1692 and was also served by Rev. Claggett from 1780 to 1786. The present building dates from 1735. A sundial was added on the front wall in 1753. The church is cruciform and constructed of very old brick. The interior has plain pews and a balcony; the one memorial window is in Bishop Claggett's honor. A very old model pipe organ is adjacent to the choir room. Telephone: (301) 579-2643. The parish Web site also contains information about St. Mary's Chapel in nearby Aquasco. Web site: www.stpaulsbaden.org

An air of antiquity surrounds **St. John's** at Broad Creek, 9801 Livingston Road in Ft. Washington near Silesia. The parish was established in 1695 and the current church erected in 1766. George Washington is said to have worshipped at Broad Creek Church because it was accessible by boat when his own church was snowed in. It has a number of lovely stained-glass windows. The church bell is hung from a heavy log frame in the churchyard. Telephone: (301) 248-4290. Web site: www.stjohnsbroadcreek.org.

Six Flags near Largo is a family recreation theme park with water attractions and amusement park rides. Six Flags is located on Route 214, the Central Avenue exit west of I-95/I-495. Open daily, 10:30 A.M. to 10 P.M., from Memorial Day until Labor Day; open weekends only in other months, weather permitting. Admission charge. Telephone: (301) 249-1500. Web site: www.sixflags.com.

Artifacts formerly stored in the **Paul E. Garber Preservation, Restoration and Storage Facility** were moved to the **Steven F. Udvar-Hazy Center,** which opened in December 2003. Located at Dulles International Airport in Virginia, the new museum houses the National Air and Space Museum's collection of historic aviation and space artifacts. See Web site for admission hours and special programs: airandspace.si.edu/udvarhazy.

The **Mary Surratt House** is located at 9118 Brandywine Road in Clinton. Built in 1852, this wood-frame house served as a tavern and meeting place for the community of Surrattsville (now called Clinton), as well as the home of the John Surratt family. It is recognized as being significant in U.S. history because of the controversy surrounding the assassination of President Lincoln in 1865.

The widow Mary Surratt was implicated in the assassination plot against Abraham Lincoln because the assassin John Wilkes Booth was known to have visited her boarding house in Washington, D.C. He also used Surratt House in southern Prince George's County as a resupply point in his escape after the assassination of Lincoln on the evening of April 14, 1865. Mary Surratt and three others were convicted for complicity in the assassination and were hanged on July 7, 1865. She was the first woman to be hanged by order of the U.S. government. Today the museum presents a variety of programs and events, recapturing the history of the mid-nineteenth-century life and focusing on the mysterious web of the Lincoln conspiracy

The house is open for public tours mid-January through mid-December, Thursday and Friday, 11 A.M. to 3 P.M., and Saturday and Sunday, from noon to 4 P.M. Closed Easter Sunday and Fourth of July. Admission charge. Telephone: (301) 868-1121. Web site: www.surratt.org.

Louise F. Cosca Regional Park and its **Clearwater Nature Center** are located on a 500-acre park in southern Prince George's County. The park is owned and maintained by the Maryland National Capital Park and Planning Commission. The Nature Center staff offers a varied natural history program. Highlights of the park include the 14-acre artificial Lake Clinton, where fishing and boating equipment can be rented; an extensive children's play area featuring a pioneer camp; nearly 200 picnic tables; nine picnic shelters; plus baseball and softball fields. An adjacent field house is located near the 10 public tennis courts and athletic area. Twenty-four campsites are available on a first-come, first-served basis with showers, water, and electricity hookups; and more than three miles of nature trails weave their way throughout the park. A tram train ride, in operation during the summer months, and weekends at other times (weather permitting), gives park visitors the opportunity to take a leisurely park tour, sit-down fashion.

The wooded park is bisected by Butler's Branch, a main waterway draining into Piscataway Creek. The nature trails, and the path along the electrical power line right-of-way, afford an opportunity for the study of the rich and diverse natural history of the area.

Admission is free for Prince George's and Montgomery county residents. There is a charge for out-of-county residents on weekends and holidays. A small fee is charged for all camping hookups. Telephones: For general information: (301) 868-1397; for Nature Center: (301) 297-4575; for picnic shelter/pavilion reservations: (301) 699-2400. Web site: www.pgparks.com/Things_To_Do/Nature/Cosca_Regional_Park.htm.

The **National Colonial Farm Museum** is a cooperative project of the Accokeek Foundation and the National Park Service. It is an operating example of a middle-class, eighteenth-century, Tidewater tobacco plantation. The farm is planted with various crops and orchards grown there in colonial times, and is stocked with Heritage breed sheep, hogs, cattle, horses, and poultry. The farmhouse and tobacco barn are authentic restorations. Other buildings are recreations of structures typical of a colonial plantation. From the Capital Beltway (I-95) take Exit 3A (Indian Head Highway) south about 10 miles to Bryan Point Road and follow signs.

The park is open daily, dawn to dusk. The Colonial site is open Tuesday through Sunday, 10 A.M. to 4:30 P.M., March 15 to December 15; mid-December to mid-March weekends only. Telephone: (301) 283-2113, ext. 28. Web site: accokeekfoundation.org.

Oxon Hill Farm, 6411 Oxon Hill Road in Oxon Hill, is a demonstration farm for children is like many farms found in the Maryland and Virginia countryside around Washington at the end of the nineteenth century. A former wheat plantation, much of the farm work here is done just as it was then—the family cow is milked by hand and the horse team earns its keep by plowing the fields and hauling wag-onloads of corn, wheat, oats, and other things. Special demonstra-tions are given throughout the year. Open daily, year round, 8 A.M. to 4 P.M. Free admission. Telephone: (301) 839-1176. Web site: www.nps.gov/oxhi/index.htm.

Fort Washington Military Historical Park, 13551 Fort Washington Road, is under jurisdiction of the National Park Service and is a notable example of an early nineteenth-century coastal defense. It is on the same site as the earliest fort erected for the defense of the nation's capital. It was begun late in 1814, as a replacement for the first fort, destroyed during the War of 1812. The new fort was built between 1814 and 1824.

Little altered since it was rebuilt, it is an enclosed masonry fortifi-cation, entered by a drawbridge across the dry moat at the main entrance. Two half-bastions overlook the river above and below the fort. At three levels—water battery, casemate positions, and ram-parts—guns could deliver heavy fire on an enemy fleet in the river.

On the parade ground visitors can see the officers' quarters and the soldiers' barracks. Near each is a magazine and guardroom. During the Civil War, Union troops manned the fort, but it was never attacked. One can spend a good part of a day, and walk about three miles, if interested, in touring the old fort and the eight batteries that surround it on the Potomac side and along Piscataway Creek. Admission charge. Explore on your own or call for a schedule of guided tours. Picnic areas are available in various parts of the park. Renovations on the visitor center began in summer 2003. Call to check on status. The fort and park are open year round, daily, 9 A.M. to 4:30 P.M. Telephone: (301) 763-4600. Web site: www.nps.gov/fowa/index.htm.

Another attraction in Prince George's County is the **Merkle Wildlife Sanctuary and Visitor Center,** 11704 Fenno Road in Croom (Upper Marlboro). Located on the Patuxent River in the southern part of the county, it was established in 1932 by Edgar Merkle as a breeding and nesting ground for Canada geese. The Merkles sold the land to the Maryland Department of Natural Resources in 1970, with the understanding that the 1,600-acre tract would be main-tained as a sanctuary for Canada geese.

The visitor center offers scheduled interpretive nature programs during the week, and special programs on weekends. Some of the pro-grams require payment of a nominal fee, and all require reservations.

The sanctuary is open daily, year round, 7 A.M. to sunset. The visitor center is open daily in summer, 10 A.M. until 5 P.M. Hours vary the rest of the year. Admission charge. Telephone: (301) 888-1410 or (301) 888-1377 Web site: www.dnr.state.md.us/publiclands/southern/merkle.asp.

Charles County

Charles County, with its southwestern shoreline facing Virginia across the Potomac River, was long considered a frontier area and has had ties with Virginia throughout its history. Roads were bad and river transport was more reliable in sailing craft. Several sailboats were developed on the river, such as the bugeye, a sophisticated version of the Indian log canoe, the "Black Nancy," and the Potomac River dory-boat (flat-bottom boats with sails that were used for oyster tonging, crab dredging, and fishing).

The post road between Philadelphia and Williamsburg ran through Charles County and the necessity for ferrying passengers across the Potomac River fostered close communication with Virginia. During the Civil War, there were many Southern sympathizers among the slave-owning tobacco planters in Charles County. Tobacco growing was the most important livelihood for county residents and continues to be a significant part of the economy. Much of the county remains rural with many small towns.

Charles County's slogan is "the wild side of the Potomac . . . where eagles soar." A tour of Charles County may be made in one day, covering a few of the historic sites with a stop to eat at one of the "crab houses" at Popes Creek on the Potomac River. Or there's plenty to keep you busy for a week. The following entries are just a small sample of the range of things to see and do. For more information Contact the Charles County Office of Tourism in La Plata. Telephone: (301) 645-0558 or 301-645-0550. Brochures about local sights of interest may be requested by phone or online. The county Web site is also rich in local lore and ghost stories as well as historical and recreational information. Web site: www.charlescountymd.gov/for-visitors. There's also a "Religious Freedom" Driving tour of Southern Maryland. Web site: byways.org/explore/byways/40532.

Smallwood State Park, 2750 Sweden Point Road in Marbury, is located four miles west of Mason Springs on the Mattawoman Creek, which empties into the Potomac River. Route 224, which leads to the park, may be reached via Route 225 from either Routes 210 or 301. This 628-acre area is centered around the manor house of

Revolutionary War hero Gen. William Smallwood, who also served as governor of Maryland from 1785 to 1788. The general is buried on the slope below his house, which has been restored and furnished with eighteenth-century period furniture. During the summer, demonstrations are given of candle dipping, cooking, and other eighteenth-century domestic activities. The manor house is open May through September, Sunday, 1 to 5 P.M. and by appointment during the rest of the year.

Picnicking facilities are available for visitors to the park, and there is a two-and-a-half mile hiking trail. There are 16 camping sites, four with hookups and 4 mini cabins. The park also has six boat launching ramps at Sweden Point Marina. The marina wet-slip area has been renovated and is schedules to re-open in summer 2004. All other marina facilities are open. There is also a boat concession for boaters and fishermen and a snack bar. The park is open all year, daily, April through October, 6 A.M. to sunset, rest of the year, 8 A.M. to sunset. Telephone: (301) 743-7613; or (888) 432-CAMP for camping reservations, which may also be made online. Web site: www.dnr.state.md.us/publiclands/southern/smallwood.asp.

Old Durham Episcopal Church (Christ Church, Durham Parish), 8685 Ironsides Road, is located one mile south of Ironsides in Nanjemoy. The original log church was built in 1692 and was one of the original Anglican parishes created in southern Maryland. (Although the Maryland proprietorship was the personal domain of Catholic Lord Baltimore, the Anglicans were able to persuade the government to establish official Church of England parishes with government perquisites.) The present brick building was begun in 1732 and subsequently has been enlarged many times. An ancient sundial near the front gate and graves dating from 1695 make this old church an interesting stop for the tourist. It is open to the public by request. Telephone: (301) 743-7099. Web site: www.christchurcholddurhamparish.com/About_Us.html.

Nanjemoy Baptist Church, 3030 Baptist Church Road, is one of the oldest continuously active Baptist churches in Maryland. In 1790 four Baptist men fled from religious persecution in Virginia to Charles County and established the Nanjemoy church in 1791. Telephone: (301)246-4926. Web site: www.nanjemoybaptist.com.

One of the oldest cities on the East Coast, **Port Tobacco,** was originally a Potopaco Indian village where Capt. John Smith stopped and

Jesuit Father White taught Indian children. Port Tobacco became a major seaport during the late 1600s, and in colonial days it bustled the varied activities of wharves, warehouses, a customhouse, hotels, churches, and inns. During the Civil War it was known as a hot spot for Confederate conspiracy and it noted as being a part of John Wilkes Booth's escape route. It was the county seat until replaced by La Plata. A springhouse containing the original town well occupies the middle of the square. The nearby part of the river on which the town depended for its commerce has been long since silted up. The old **Court House** on Chapel Point Road (off Route 6, West) and a number of eighteenth-century houses were restored around Court House Square. The original courthouse was built in 1719, destroyed in 1808, and rebuilt in 1819. The second courthouse was destroyed in 1892 and in 1973 there was a reconstruction of the 1819 building. The first floor is a display of the 1819 courthouse. In the second floor museum colonial artifacts unearthed during excavation of the site and exhibits on the role of tobacco in the region are on display. Costumed docents are sometimes on hand to help bring the history of Port Tobacco to life. The courthouse and museum are open, Saturday through Monday, 11 A.M. to 4 P.M. Admission charge. Telephone: (301) 934-4313.

Web site: www.somd.com/Detailed/2118.php.

Charles County is home to some of the oldest churches in the nation, a few of which are described below. For a complete listing, call the tourism office or visit the Web site: maryland.hometownlocator.com/md/charles.

At **Chapel Point** two historic religious sites, **St. Ignatius Church** and **St. Thomas Manor,** stand on a hilltop overlooking the Potomac and Port Tobacco rivers. Located at 8855 Chapel Point Road, the Catholic parish dates from 1641, though the present building was erected in 1798. St. Ignatius is the oldest continuously active Roman Catholic church in the United States. The beautiful interior of the church is dominated by eighteenth-century architecture. The manor, built in 1741, is occupied by the Jesuits and is not open to visitors. From Chapel Point, the idyllic view of the two rivers is one never to be forgotten. Telephone: (301) 934-8245. Click on "history" on the following Web site for more detailed information on the two buildings.

Web site: www.chapelpoint.org.

The tiny community of **Popes Creek** off Route 301 is known for its homey atmosphere and good crab houses, and is a favorite stop for lovers of Southern Maryland seafood. The crab houses are built on piles over the Potomac River, with plenty of windows to provide a good view of the broad river. Pope's Creek is also the point where John Wilkes Booth crossed the Potomac after the assassination of President Lincoln.

Further south on Route 301 at Newburg, turn east on Route 257 to **Christ Church, William and Mary Parish, Wayside,** an original parish of Maryland, dating from 1692. The present brick church dates from the early eighteenth century and there are tall cedars and ancient gravestones in the adjacent burial ground. Valued possessions of the church include a silver Queen Anne chalice and paten dated 1700. Telephone: (301) 259-4327.
Web site: christchurchwayside.edow.org.

La Plata, whose existence is due to the railroad, is now the county seat. West of La Plata off Route 225, on Mitchell Road one mile from the Port Tobacco Court House, is **Mt. Carmel Convent,** 5678 Mount Carmel Road, the first Carmelite convent in America. Two original structures of the convent have been restored. The chapel, open to the public, and the new convent buildings are located beyond the original buildings. There is a small gift shop of handcrafted items, which may also be viewed and ordered online. The historic buildings are open to the public daily, May to October. The gift store is open 7 A.M. to to 5 P.M. For further information and a schedule of Masses, visit the Web site. Telephone: (301) 934-1654.
Web site: www.carmelofporttobacco.com.

The **Dr. Samuel A. Mudd Home Museum,** is located near Waldorf at 14940 Hoffman Road. Call or visit Web site for specific directions. After shooting President Lincoln on April 14, 1865, actor John Wilkes Booth escaped from Washington to the home of Dr. Mudd who treated him. Dr. Mudd was charged with conspiracy in the assassination and was convicted and imprisoned but was pardoned in 1869. The house has been restored by the Mudd Society. Open April through November, weekends, 11 A.M. to 4 P.M., Wednesday, 11 A.M. to 3:30 P.M. Admission charge. Telephone: (301) 274-9358.
Web site: drmudd.org.

North of Waldorf is **Cedarville State Forest** at 10201 Bee Oak Road in Brandywine, which can be reached from Route 301 via the Cedarville Road. This park has facilities for picnicking, fishing, hiking, and camping including 130 campsites with toilets, showers, laundry tubs, and fireplaces. There are also 14 miles of marked foot trails for hiking, off-road biking, and equestrians. There are many springs in the park and trails are sometimes wet. Some areas are designated for hunting during appropriate seasons. There is also a Visitors Center at the state's only warm water fish hatchery. Telephone: (301) 888-1410; or (888) 432-CAMP for camping reservations, which may also be made online. Web site: www.dnr.state.md.us/publiclands/southern/cedarville.asp.

The headwaters of the **Zekiah Swamp** are located in the Brandywine area and rare plants such as the sundew and carnivorous pitcher plant may be observed. A wide variety of wildlife may also be seen, including the bald eagle. The swamp, a natural greenway running the length of Charles County before it empties into the Wicomico River to the south, has been recognized by numerous authorities as one of the most significant ecological features in the Chesapeake Bay watershed. The swamp also played an important part in the Civil War when the swamp was used by Southern sympathizers for clandestine activities. For more information, check at the visitors center for Cedarville State Forest.

St. Mary's County

The first English-speaking Catholic settlers, under Governor Leonard Calvert, landed at St. Clement's Island in the Potomac River to found the colony of Maryland. The first colonists who arrived on the *Ark* and *Dove* numbered two Jesuit priests, a lay brother, and 140 men. After celebrating Mass at St. Clement's on March 25, 1634, and re-supplying, the settlers moved to their permanent settlement on the banks of St. Mary's River and established the capital of the Maryland colony there. St. Mary's is thus the oldest official county in the state.

St. Mary's County is located at the southern tip on the western shore and may be reached from Charles County on Route 5, from Calvert County on Route 2/4 crossing at Solomons over the Governor Johnson Bridge to Route 235, and from Virginia over the Governor Nice Bridge (toll) on Route 301 to Route 234.

The St. Mary's County Chamber of Commerce Information Center is located in the center of Mechanicsville on Route 5, south of Charlotte Hall. Visitors may get information on St. Mary's as well as on the neighboring counties of Calvert and Charles. Open March through October, Monday through Friday, 9 A.M. to 5 P.M.; Saturday and Sunday, 10 A.M. to 3 P.M. Contact the Chamber of Commerce, 28290 Three Notch Road, Mechanicsville, MD 20659. Telephone: (301) 737-3001. Web site: www.smcchamber.com.

A popular **Farmers' Market** is located on Route 5 at Charlotte Hall. It is open Wednesdays and Saturdays throughout the year. Here tourists will find real bargains in the flea market, produce stalls, the Amish food and produce stands, and in the antique and used household goods shops. The office opens at 8 A.M.; vendors are in place by 9 A.M. Telephone: (301) 475-4200.

Many Amish farmers have settled in the area south of Charlotte Hall. A trip through countryside includes many picturesque small farms. A suggested trip is along Route 236 from New Market to Budd's Creek.

Sotterley, built in 1717, is an outstanding Georgian-style mansion in Hollywood, Maryland. It exemplifies the colonial plantation way of life. In one of the most beautiful settings in the state, it commands a sweeping view of the Patuxent River. The estate is an on-going example of America from the eighteenth-century to the twentieth-century. Open May through October, Tuesday through Saturday, 10 A.M. to 4 P.M.; Sunday, noon to 4 P.M. Admission charge. Telephone: (301) 373-2280. Web site: www.sotterley.com.

In Leonardtown, one can view **Tudor Hall,** which is now owned by the St. Mary's Historical Society, is near the Court House. This 1756 Georgian mansion overlooks Breton Bay. The mansion features a hanging staircase and a widow's walk. It also features the research center for the historical society. Telephone: (301) 475-2467 or (301) 475-9455.

St. Mary's County "Old" Jail Museum is now the headquarters for the St. Mary's Historical Society. The museum exhibits artifacts relating to the county. One of the rooms is furnished as a woman's jail cell as it would have appeared in 1857, when the jail was built, and another is furnished as a physician's office as it appeared in the early twentieth century. Open Wednesday through Friday, 12 to 2 P.M. Telephone: (301) 475-2467. Web site: home.md.metrocast.net/~smchs/index.htm.

Piney Point is four miles south of Valley Lee on Route 5. The first summer White House—during Monroe's term—was in this locality. The primary attraction here is the **Paul Hall Center for Marine Training and Education.** The training school was formerly called the Leadership School of Seamanship. It is the nation's largest facility for preparing men and women to sail aboard U.S. flag, commercial, deep sea, inland and Great Lakes vessels as well as upgrading and teaching veterans new skills. The Paul Hall library and museum contains more than 8,000 volumes on maritime history, including some eighteenth-century manuscripts. Telephone: (301) 994-0010. Web site: www.seafarers.org.

The **Patuxent River Naval Air Museum** is being moved to a new location at the intersection of Route 235 and Pegg Road in Lexington Park, Maryland. The museum is the only museum in the U.S. dedicated to telling the extraordinary story of the U.S. Navy's aviation research, development, testing and evaluation. . Aircraft, such as the F-18 Hornet, the F-14 Tomcat, and the S-2 Tracker, plus many more, are on display outside the museum. Inside exhibits include a photographic survey of naval air history, the technological development of computers, wind tunnel models, and aircraft carrier testing equipment. Call or visit the Web site for new hours and special programs. Telephone: (301) 863-7418. Web site: paxmuseum.com.

Maryland was established in 1634 when the first European settlers started a permanent settlement on the banks of St. Mary's River and called it **St. Mary's City.** Here, in 1649, the Assembly decreed religious toleration for the first time in America. At the entrance to the town is a monument commemorating the Act. Today St. Mary's City is a small, unincorporated rural town with St. Mary's College located there.

The state has developed an 800-acre park, an outdoor museum called **Historic St. Mary's City,** which is a partial reconstruction of the seventeenth-century town. Archaeological excavations of the colonial site are in progress during the summer and may be observed by the public. A replica of Maryland's **State House of 1676,** which served as the Capitol until 1694, has been reconstructed on the site. This two-story Jacobean structure contains historic exhibits. The visitor center is open Wednesday through Sunday, in summer 10 to 5 P.M. Check Web site or call for hours/details in other seasons. Closed Thanksgiving, Christmas, and New Year's. Telephone: (800) 762-1634 or (240) 895-4990 or (240) 895-4960. Web site: www.stmaryscity.org.

"The Maryland Dove," a representation of one of the ships that transported Maryland's first settlers, is moored near the State House. The *Dove* was the smaller of the two ships that brought the settlers from England in 1634. Although there is no exact description of the *Dove,* the replica is the same type and approximate size as the original. The present *Dove* was designed by William A. Baker and was built by James Richardson, who employed methods and tools used in the seventeenth century.

The **Godiah Spray Plantation,** a working seventeenth-century tobacco plantation, has been reconstructed as part of the **St. Mary's Museum.** Farthing's Ordinary, an inn of the period, is nearby in the same living history museum setting, which includes the Woodland Indian Hamlet. Farthing's Kitchen provides food service for visitors and other amenities are provided by the Brome-Howard County Inn & Restaurant, located in a building dating from about 1841. Exhibits under construction include various structures in the Town Center of Maryland's first capital, and the museum plans to reconstruct the Brick Chapel, located on the site of the first English Catholic Chapel in the New World. A five mile trail links the sites at the museum, taking visitors and recreational walkers along the shoreline of the St. Mary's River and into the woods and fields around the National Historic Landmark site. Further plans call for an inn and maritime exhibit complex to be built. St. Mary's Museum Complex is located on Route 5, just past the College. Admission Charge. Call the Visitors Center for hours. Telephone: (800) 762-1634 or (240) 895-4990. Web site: http://www.stmaryscity.org/Virtual%20Tour/Virtual%20tour.html.

Nearby is **Trinity Church,** erected in 1829 with bricks taken from ruins of the original State House. The **Leonard Calvert Monument,** in the churchyard, marks the site where the colonists first assembled in 1634 to establish a government for the colony.

St. Ignatius Church, at St. Inigoes on Villa Road, off Route 5, dates from 1785 and is on the site of the original church, built in 1641. Its boxwood hedges, more than 300 years old, are a notable feature of the setting.

Point Lookout State Park on Route 5 is at the tip of St. Mary's County, where the Potomac River empties into the Chesapeake Bay. During the Civil War, more than 52,000 Confederate prisoners were held under appalling conditions at Camp Hoffman, which stood on this site. Today, at Scotland, Maryland, one mile north of the park, one can visit the monument commemorating the Confederate soldiers. It is the only federal memorial to Confederate soldiers. The Visitor's Center offers interpretive lectures on the Civil War historical background of Point Lookout as well as natural history lectures.

The state park offers facilities for swimming, picnicking, oystering, fishing, crabbing, boating, and camping, and there are three miles of shoreline. There are 147 campsites, including 27 that have full hookup facilities. Rental boats are available for those wishing to take advantage of one of the best fishing and crabbing spots in Maryland.

Hiking and biking trails are located in the park. Open year round, daily, 8 to sunset. Campsites are also open year round. Further information on facilities and fees is available on the Web site. Telephone: (301) 872-5688; (888) 432-CAMP for camping reservations, which may also be made online. Web site: www.dnr.state.md.us/publiclands/southern/pointlookout.asp.

To reach **St. Clement's Island** the visitor must go to Colton's Point and take a boat to the island where Lord Baltimore's first settlers landed in Maryland. To reach Colton's Point, go south on Route 5, west and south on Route 242 to end of road. From Virginia, take the Governor Nice Bridge (toll) on Route 301 to Route 234, right at Route 242 to the end of the road. Call Point Lookout State Park (301) 872-5688 or visit the St. Clements Web site for the water taxi schedule. Web site: www.dnr.state.md.us/publiclands/southern/stclements.asp.

The **St. Clement's Island-Potomac River Museum** at Colton's Point overlooks St. Clement's Island. The museum exhibits depict the history of man in this area from the days of the original Indians. Included are exhibits of Indian and colonial artifacts unearthed nearby. Other exhibits concern the activities and lives of the farmers and watermen of the region. Open March 25 (Maryland Day) through September, Monday through Friday, 9 A.M. to 5 P.M.; Saturday and Sunday, noon to 5 P.M.; October 1 through March 24, Wednesday through Sunday, noon to 4 P.M. Admission charge.

On the island of St. Clement's a 40-foot cross marks the first landing and celebration of the mass in Maryland. Although inhabited at one time, today the 40-acre island is uninhabited. Boat trips to the island may be arranged by appointment. The state-owned island has picnicking facilities with drinking water. Boat captains conduct guided tours or visitors may take their own self-guided tour. Telephone: (301) 769-2222. Web site: www.co.saint-marys.md.us/recreate/stclementsisland.asp.

DELAWARE

This second smallest state in the Union is called the "Diamond State" because of its value as a state and its position in history compared with its size. Delaware is also called the "First State" because it was the first to ratify the Constitution. It was claimed by Henry Hudson for the Dutch in 1609, but in 1638 the Dutch formed a joint venture with the Swedes. Fort Christina is a monument to the first major Swedish settlement. In 1664 the area was seized by the British and incorporated in the lands held by the Duke of York, and then, in 1682, it was given to William Penn. In 1704 the three counties of Delaware established a separate legislature, but remained technically under the control of the Governor of Pennsylvania until the colony became a state in 1776.

The state travel and tourism office and information centers in each of Delaware's three counties—New Castle, Kent, and Sussex—provide travel guides on request. All the information is also available online. Delaware Tourism Office, 99 Kings Highway, Dover, DE 19901. Telephone: (866) 2-VisitD. Web site: www.visitdelaware.com. Web site for information on Delaware's state parks: www.destateparks.com. (This web site has a feature that allows you to translate the information into any of eight languages.) Web site for information on museums: www.destatemuseums.org.

The state has an excellent system of natural waterways, which has helped the development of its economy. The 14-mile **Chesapeake and Delaware Canal** connects the upper Chesapeake Bay with the Delaware River. The actual excavation and construction, begun in 1804, were delayed and not completed until 1829. Originally the canal had four locks. It has been both deepened and widened several times in its history, and is now an open waterway. Although the canal faced competition from the railroads as early as 1832, almost as soon as it opened, it was a major economic and social phenomenon in the life of the state. Showboats brought entertainment; floating stores sold goods and carried the informal news of the day. During World War II the canal was used as an alternate route for vessels in order to avoid German submarines that patrolled the Atlantic from Virginia to the Delaware capes.

Delaware City now contains the only lock left from the old canal. There and in other towns you can walk along the edge of the canal as it exists today. The only other landmark of the original canal is the old stone pump house in Chesapeake City, Maryland. From Delaware City it is possible to visit **Fort Delaware State Park**, a granite and brick fortress located on Pea Patch Island in the Delaware River. The fort, built in 1859, served as a prison for Confederate soldiers in the Civil War. Visitors can inspect the old fort and experience a living history program with guides in period costume. Delaware City is on Route 79, two miles east of Route 13, and 10 miles south of New Castle. The marshes surrounding Pea Patch Island are an excellent bird habitat. A hiking training and observation platform provide numerous vantages for photography and nature study. The park is open weekends from the end of April through September, 10 A.M. to 6 P.M.; mid-June through Labor Day weekend, Wednesday through Sunday, 10 A.M. to 6 P.M. Catch the *Three Fort Ferry* from Delaware City or New Jersey. Fare charge, which also includes a stop at Fort Mott State Park on the New Jersey side of the river. Telephone: (302) 834-7941. Web site: www.destateparks.com.

SOUTHERN DELAWARE: SUSSEX COUNTY AND ITS BEACHES

There are numerous, well-maintained historic and cultural sites in southern Delaware. Of particular note is the first stone positioned by the surveyors of the Mason-Dixon line at the extreme southwest corner of the state off Route 54. (It is literally a corner.) For additional information on state attractions, contact the state tourism office listed above, or for Sussex County, contact Southern Delaware Tourism, PO Box 240, 103 W. Pine Street, Georgetown, DE 19947. Telephone: (800) 357-1818 or (302) 357-1818. Web sites: www.visitdelaware.net (specify southern region in search) or www.visitsoutherndelaware.com.

Old Christ Church at Broad Creek, three miles east of Laurel on Route 24 near the southwest corner of the state, was erected in 1771. It is a fine example of early church architecture with an unpainted heart-of-pine interior. It is open Sunday afternoons in summer. Telephone: (302) 875-3644.

Continue east on Route 24, then east on Route 26 to the intersection with Route 382 in Dagsboro. Here a stop can be made at Prince George's Chapel, an Anglican church built in 1757, restored in the 1920s, and now maintained as a museum. Part of the original pine interior can still be seen. Open July 1 through October, weekends only, 1 to 4:30 P.M. Free admission. Telephone: (302) 732-3551. Web Site: www.sussexcountyonline.com/towns/dagsboro/princegeorges.html.

Continuing east on Route 26 the traveler passes the **Blackwater Presbyterian Church**, one mile west of Clarksville on Route 54. Organized in 1667, the present edifice was built 1767.

Continuing east on Route 26, will take you into **Bethany Beach**, one of Delaware's many excellent summer resorts. Bethany and Fenwick take special pride in being able to offer visitors peaceful, quiet getaways as well as surf, sun, and sand, and advertise themselves with pride as "The Quiet Resorts" (without disparaging the louder entertainments of Ocean City, Maryland, to the south). A drive-up/walk-in Chamber of Commerce center with additional information about the Bethany-Fenwick area is located on Route 1 between Bethany and Fenwick. Telephone: (302) 539-2100 or (800) 962-7873 (SURF). Web sites: www.visitdelaware.com (search Southern Section under "Things to Do") or www.bethany-fenwick.org.

Six miles south of Bethany on Route 54 at 146th Street, just north Ocean City, Maryland, is the **Fenwick Island Lighthouse**, built in 1859. At the base of the 87-foot tower is a marker for the Trans-Peninsula Line, the south boundary between Maryland and Delaware established by surveyors in 1751. The lighthouse was recently renovated and is open on select days throughout the summer. Call for hours. Telephone: (302) 436-8100 . For photos, visit: www.octhebeach.com/lighthouse.

Traveling north on Route 1, the tourist has an additional choice of **Delaware Seashore State Park**, which offers ocean swimming, surf fishing, camping with hookups, and a marina with two boat ramps. Telephone: (302) 227-2800. Web site: www.destateparks.com.

Between Bethany and Dewey Beach on Route 1, in the Delaware Seashore State Park, one mile north of the Indian River Inlet bridge, is the recently restored **Indian River Life Saving Station**. Originally built in 1876, the site is one of the few remaining "life rescue" stations still at its original location on the East Coast. It now includes a maritime museum and educational facility restored and preserved by The Delaware Seashore Preservation Foundation. Open daily, Memorial Day through Labor Day, 10 A.M. to 5 P.M.; in May, 10 A.M. to 3 P.M., weekdays; 10 A.M. to 4 P.M. weekends. Call for off-season hours. Admission charge. Telephone: (302) 227-6991. Web site: www.destateparks.com/attractions/life-saving-station.

North on Route 1, **Rehoboth Beach, Dewey Beach**, and **Cape Henlopen State Park** all offer ocean bathing, surf fishing, and picnicking. A walk-in center providing visitor information is operated by the **Rehobeth-Bethany Chamber of Commerce** and located at 501 Rehobeth Ave. (PO Box 216) in Rehobeth Beach, DE 19971. Telephone: (800) 441-1329 or (302) 227-2233. Web site: www.beach-fun.com.

Five miles north of Rehoboth, turn right from Route 1 to Route 9 to reach Lewes and Cape Henlopen State Park. **Cape Henlopen State Park** occupies a sandy hook with ocean and bay views on three sides. Excellent recreation facilities are available, including basketball courts, a parade field, and an 18-hole Frisbee golf course. A picnic area as well as a camping area for tents and self-contained units (no hookups) are available. There is a pier for crabbing and fishing. Special areas have been designated for ocean swimming and surf fishing. A paved trail loop leads to a World War II Observation Tower with spectacular views. The state park is also of interest because of its rare plants and waterfowl. Canadian and snow geese pass through on migration routes, and there are numerous terns. Porpoises are often viewed offshore. Lilies, beach plums, and cranberry bogs, as well as the natural habitats of small animals, can be seen from two carefully marked nature trails. Admission charge. For further information contact the park at 42 Cape Henlopen Drive, Lewes, DE 19958. Telephone: (302) 645-8983; camping information: (877) 987-2757. Web site: www.destateparks.com.

The Dutch were the first to establish a settlement in 1631 near present-day Lewes. They were followed by the English in the 1660s. Throughout the area, visitors can see monuments, museums, and buildings devoted to these pioneer settlers.

Exhibits at the **Zwaanendael Museum**, 102 Kings Highway in Lewes, include a model of the Swaanendael settlement, Delaware's first

European settlement, a 1631 whaling colony. Artifacts recovered from the *H.M. Brig DeBraak*, a British warship that sank off Cape Henlopen in 1798 are on display. This exhibit also includes information regarding ship life during the period and an archival of Naval dress. Open Tuesday through Saturday, 10 A.M. to 4:30 P.M.; Sunday, 1:30 to 4:30 P.M. Closed Monday and state holidays. Admission charge. Telephone: (302) 645-1148. Web site: http://history.delaware.gov/museums/zm/zm_main.shtml.
1812 Memorial Park, on Front Street, is the site of a defense battery during the War of 1812. Lewes was heavily bombarded by the British during the spring of 1813. The site is marked by a granite monument placed by the National Society, U.S. Daughters of 1812. Several naval guns are also on display, including a three-inch gun used during World War I. **The deVries Monument and Fort Site** marks the site of a Dutch whaling colony established in 1631 and the fort they erected. Many old homes and churches are preserved in Lewes. Among them are the Episcopal, Presbyterian, and Methodist churches.

The **Lewes Historical Complex**, a collection of restored and reconstructed buildings that have been brought together to give visitors a feel for the past, is located at Third and Shipcarpenter streets. The Lewes Historical Society is located at 110 Shipcarpenter Street. The complex includes the **Thompson Country Store**, which dates from 1800 and still has the original lights, shelves, and cabinets, as well as the old Post Office counter. Other museums in the complex include the **Ellegood House and Blacksmith Shop, the Old Doctor's Office, Midway School**,the **Plank House** (c. 1700), **The Cannonball House** (c. 1760, so named by locals in honor of its scars from being struck by British Cannon fire during the War of 1812), the **Rabbit's Ferry House** (an 18th-century farmhouse), the inviting shingled **The Burton-Ingram House**, and the splendid **Hiram Rodney Burton House** (c. 1780). The Lewes Historical Society also owns the **Lewes Life-Saving Station**(1884). The museums are open from mid June through Labor Day, Tuesday to Friday, 11 A.M. to 4 P.M.; Saturday, 10 A.M. to 12:30 P.M. The museum gift shops are open all day on Saturday. Self-guided tours are offered during the season. Admission charge. Telephone: (302) 645-7670. Web site: www.historiclewes.org.

In 1999 the Lewes Historical Society sold the **"Overfalls" Lightship** (a ship that functions like a lighthouse—one of only 15 remaining in the U.S.) to a group of local citizens who then formed the Overfalls

Maritime Museum Foundation. The organization welcomes supporters and volunteers to assist in the restoration of the Lightship. Currently located at the foot of Shipcarpenter Street while in search of a permanent home (brown signs in Lewes point the way). The Lightship is open Friday and Saturday 11 A.M. to 4 P.M.; Sunday, 1-4 P.M., June through October 5. Thursdays are added during July and August. Best to communicate by e-mail via the web site, but you may call and leave a message. Telephone: (302) 644-8050. Web site: www.overfalls.org.

Among the interesting annual events in Lewes are: A Christmas Fair and House Tour held on the first Saturday in December; craft fairs held the second Saturday in July and the first Saturday in October, and summer Antique and Marts, usually held in late June and early August. For details, contact the **Lewes Historical Society**, Third and Shipcarpenter Streets, Lewes, DE 19958. Telephone: (302) 645-7670. Web site: www.historiclewes.org/events.

Lewes area lighthouses have been a long-standing testament to its origins as a nautical center. The oldest, **Breakwater Light**, which can be viewed off the coast, was commissioned by John Quincy Adams in 1828 and remained in service until 1994. The **Harbor of Refuge Lighthouse** was built off the coast of Lewes in 1901 and is the only lighthouse still in operation on the Delaware coast. Web Site: www.delawarebaylights.org.

The privately owned **Mispillion Lighthouse** was commissioned in 1831. It was located where the Mispillion River meets the Delaware Bay. There it was struck by lightning on May 2, 2002, and the resulting fire destroyed most of the tower portion of the lighthouse. The remains have been removed. A campaign is underway to urge construction of a replica. See web site for details. Web site: www.lighthousefriends.com.

The **Cape May-Lewes Ferry**, one mile east of Lewes, 43 Henlopen Drive, offers year-round transportation between Lewes, Delaware and Cape May, New Jersey for cars, bikers, and foot passengers. The scenic crossing takes about 90 minutes. Fare charge. Call for more information, directions, fares, and a schedule of departures. Telephone: (800) 643-3779 (Lewes Terminal) or (800) 643-3779 (Cape May Terminal). Web site: www.capemaylewesferry.com.

The 8,839-acre **Prime Hook National Wildlife Refuge** is five miles northwest of Lewes. Its marshes, freshwater ponds, brush, and upland attract over more than 260 species of birds and about 25 kinds of mammals and reptiles. Migratory waterfowl populations reach their peak from October to December. In summer the visitor can enjoy hiking, fishing, canoeing, and nature study. Two wildlife trails traverse several habitats, and 15 miles of waterways are open to canoeists. The hunting of deer, waterfowl, and upland game is permitted in season by special regulations. For further information, contact the Refuge Manager, RD 3, Box 195, Milton, DE 19968. Telephone: (302) 684-8419. Web site: www.fws.gov/northeast/primehook/.

CENTRAL DELAWARE: KENT COUNTY

Kent County marks the central portion of the state. Dover, the state capital, is located in Kent County some miles north of Milford, which is at the southern border. The Kent County Tourism Convention and Visitors Bureau is located at 435 North DuPont Highway Dover. Telephone: (800) 233 KENT or (302) 734-1736. Web sites: www.visitdover.com or www.co.kent.de.us.

To explore Kent County, take Route 113 to Frederica. Once known as Johnny Cake Landing, Frederica dates back to 1770. One mile north of town at 6362 Bay Road is **Barratt's Chapel**, built in 1780, and called the "Cradle of Methodism in America." Here the first sacrament of communion was administered by a Methodist clergyman. It is the oldest standing Methodist church in America built by Methodists. Visitors are welcome to the chapel and adjoining museum. Open Saturday and Sunday, 2 to 4 P.M. Other times by appointment. Free admission; donations appreciated. Telephone: (302) 335-5544. Web site: www.barrattschapel.org.

John Dickinson Plantation, 340 Kitts Hummock Road, a National Historic Landmark, is five miles north of Frederica then east on Kitts-Hummock Road, on the fringes of Dover Airforce Base via US 113 or Route 9. It is the boyhood home of the "Penman of the Revolution." Dickinson, a framer and signer of the U.S. Constitution, was called upon to write many political documents as a member of the Continental Congress. The 18-acre Plantation along the St. Jones River includes the brick mansion, reconstructed farm outbuildings, a log dwelling, and a slave/tenant house. Exhibits, a 20-minute historical video, and costumed guides are on site. Open Tuesday through Saturday, 10 A.M. to 3:30 P.M.; Sunday, 1:30 to 4:30 P.M. Closed Mondays, state holidays, and Sundays in January and February. Free admission; donations appreciated. Telephone: (302) 739-3277. Web site: www.history.delaware.gov/museums/jdp/jdp_main.shtml.

The **Camden Friends Meeting House** (1805), west of Route 13 at 122 E. Wyoming Avenue in nearby Camden, is open to the public and still in use. Telephone: (302) 698-3324.

Continue into Dover, the state capital, via Route 113A, stopping at **The Green**, a public area designated by William Penn in 1683 and laid out in the center of the city in 1717. Be sure to visit the **State House** at 406 Federal Street. Constructed in 1791, and now used only for ceremonial occasions, it is a splendid Georgian building. Open Tuesday through Saturday, 10 A.M. to 4:30 P.M.; Sunday, 1:30 to 4:30 P.M. Closed Mondays and state holidays. Telephone: (302) 744-5055. Web site: www.history.delaware.gov/museums/sh/sh_main.shtml.

The **Delaware State Visitors Center**, 406 Federal Street (at the end of the Duke of York Street and, behind the State House) has extensive visitor information and changing exhibits on Delaware history and a visual exhibition on the Delaware State Museum System. The Biggs Museum of American Art is located on the second and third floors above the Visitor Center. Open Monday to Saturday, 8:30 A.M. to 4:30 P.M.; Sunday, 1:30 to 4:30 P.M. Free admission; donations appreciated. Telephone: (302) 674-2111. Web Site: www.biggsmuseum.org.

On Legislative Avenue is **Legislative Hall**, which houses the General Assembly, the Governor's offices, and, at 121 Duke of York Street, a new building housing the **Delaware Public Archives**. Preserved here is the original royal grant from Charles II to the Duke of York (1682) as well as extensive genealogical records, from both private and public sources. Open Monday through Saturday, 8 A.M. to 4:30 P.M., with evening hours on Wednesday until 8 P.M. Telephone: (302) 739-9194. Web site: legis.delaware.gov/legislature.nsf/Lookup/Leghall_Tours?open.

Woodburn, Governor's House, at 151 Kings Highway, built in 1790, is still used as the Governor's Mansion. It is said to be a stopping point of the "Underground Railroad" in pre-Civil War days and legend says it is also inhabited by several ghosts. Open weekdays by appointment only. Free admission. Telephone: (302) 739-5656. Web site: woodburn.delaware.gov.

Delaware Archaeology Museum, Museum of Small Town Life, and the **Johnson Victrola Museum** at 316 S. Governor's Avenue (corner of Bank Street) contain exhibits dealing with the history of the state. This complex occupies a Presbyterian Church built in 1790 and its adjacent Sunday school building in Meeting House Square. The Square was part of the original plan of Dover developed by William Penn in 1683. Models of Victor Talking Machines are exhibited in the Johnson Victrola Museum. E. R. Johnson, founder of the company, was a Delaware native. The Museum of Small Town Life is a museum of early Delaware business. Vignettes of a post office, general store, pharmacy and print shop show how life was in small town Delaware around the turn of the century (1900). The Delaware Archaeology Museum houses an exhibit on Delaware archaeology and shows how we discover information on Delaware's Native American population. Open Tuesday through Saturday, 10 A.M. to 3:30 P.M. Closed Sunday, Monday, and state holidays. Free admission; donations appreciated. Telephone: (302) 734-1736. Web site: www.visitdover.com/museums.htm.

Christ Episcopal Church, built in 1734, is at Water and South State streets. There is a monument to Caesar Rodney, signer of the Declaration of Independence, in the churchyard. Open Monday through Friday, 9 A.M. to 3 P.M. Telephone: (302) 734-5731.

The Delaware Agricultural Museum and Village at 866 N. Dupont Highway (just south of Delaware State University on Route 13 in Dover) is dedicated to the preservation of the agricultural heritage of Delaware and the Delmarva Peninsula. A complete calendar of events, exhibits, and workshops is available on-line. Admission charge. Open January through March, Monday through Friday, 10 A.M. to 4 P.M.; April through December, Tuesday through Saturday 10 A.M. to 4 P.M., Sunday 1 to 4 P.M. Telephone: (302) 734-1618. Web site: www.agriculturalmuseum.org.

Smyrna began in 1700 as an English Settlement called Duck Creek Village. Several historic sites and parks in the **Smyrna Area** are worthy of visitation. The Allee House and Bombay Hook are described below. For information about others, contact the Kent County Convention and Visitor's Bureau. Telephone: (800) 233-KENT or (203) 734-1736. Web site: www.visitdover.com.

The **Allee House**, built by a Huguenot family in 1753, is part of Bombay Hook National Wildlife Refuge. It is a fine example of the Queen Anne style, with interesting architectural details including an original kitchen fireplace with lugpole and trammel. Free admission. Open Saturdays and Sundays, spring and fall, from 1 to 4 P.M. This home is located on Dutch Neck Road, 2½ miles north of Leipsic off Route 9. Telephone: (302) 653-6872. Web site: www.friendsofbombayhook.org/alleehouse.html.

Bombay Hook National Wildlife Refuge (off Route 9, east of Smyrna) is a very popular location for studying waterfowl and animal life. It includes over 13,000 acres of tidal marsh and 1,100 acres of freshwater ponds. The combination of swamp, upland, tidal marsh, and thicket provides diversity of habitat, accounting for 260 bird species observed here, as well as 35 species of mammals and 31 kinds of reptiles and amphibians. You can take the tour route, walk the nature trails, or climb up the observation towers in order to see waterfowl and wildlife. Tours, trail walks, outdoor classroom studies, movies, and slide shows are offered with advance reservations. For more information, visit the web site or contact the Refuge Manager, 2591 Whitehill Road, Smyrna, DE 19977. Telephone: (302) 653-9345. Web Site: bombayhook.fws.gov.

NORTHERN DELAWARE: NEW CASTLE COUNTY

The historic district of **Odessa**, in New Castle County about 15 miles north of Smyrna on Route 13 and 25 miles south of Wilmington, is on the National Register. Originally known as Appoquinimink because it is located near a creek of that name, Odessa was settled by the Dutch in the 17th century.

Old Union Methodist Church, four miles south of Odessa on Route 13, was built in 1847. Four historic houses in town that are owned and operated by the Winterthur Museum and Gardens merit special attention. Once available for tours, they closed to the public in May 2003. You can read about the sites below and on the related web site. Call Winterthur for more information. Telephone: (800) 448-3883.

Corbit-Sharp House (1774) is a beautiful example of Georgian colonial architecture. It now contains numerous fine antiques from the state of Delaware, as well as original furnishings belonging to the Corbit family. A formal garden and an herb garden adjoin the mansion. Another Georgian home is the **Wilson-Warner House** (1769), also a museum, furnished with period furniture and antiquities. The third museum is **Brick Hotel Gallery** (1822). This early 19th century hotel opened as a modern exhibition gallery in 1980. Victorian furniture by John Henry Belter, a gift of the Manney Foundation, is on permanent display. The fourth museum is the gable-roofed **Collins-Sharp House**, (1700) one of the earliest structures still standing in Delaware. Its frame construction and relatively large size (five rooms) made it quite fashionable for its time. It most recently served as the museum's center for educational programming, including open hearth cooking demonstrations and other hands-on programs.

Outbuildings include stables and a muskrat skinning station.
Web site: www.winterthur.org.

The **Appoquinimink Friends Meeting House** in Odessa is only 20 feet square, probably the smallest brick house of worship in the country. Located on route 299, west of U.S. 13, the church, built in 1783, is open by appointment only. Telephone: (302) 652-4491. Web site: www.cr.nps.gov/nr/travel/underground/de1.htm

St. Anne's Episcopal Church at 15 East Green Street in Middletown is dated 1768. It has original box pews and a Palladian window, as well as a classic example of a wineglass pulpit with clerk's desk, lectern, and pulpit in three tiers. The church grounds contain lovely boxwood and numerous colonial graves near a 300-year-old William Penn Oak, one of the few in the country. Call for Sunday and special services. Telephone: (302) 378-2401.

Old Drawyers Presbyterian Church, north of Odessa, is a brick structure erected in 1773 on the site of an earlier church. The interior was completed sixty years later. This historic shrine has an adjoining graveyard and beautiful grounds.

To the west, **Lums Pond State Park**, 1068 Howell School Road in Bear, contains the largest inland lake in the state (200 acres), built many decades ago to supply water for the locks of the Chesapeake and Delaware Canal. The park is accessible from the Washington area and Baltimore via I-95 exit 1A. You may want to spend some time here enjoying the many outdoor activities, while planning short excursions to any of the historic-cultural sites within an hour's drive.

Among summer activities, which extend from Memorial Day to Labor Day, are: hiking, fishing, camping, canoeing, sailing, power boating, swimming, and rowing. There are 72 camping sites, (no hookups) with a central bathhouse that is open April 1 through November 1. Athletic facilities include those for baseball, basketball, volleyball, tennis, lacrosse, and soccer. Nature study and evening programs are offered during summer months. Admission charge. For further information, visit the web site or contact the Park Manager, 1068 Howell School Road, Bear, DE 19701. Telephone: (302) 368-6989. Web site: www.destateparks.com.

Nearby on Route 72 at Cooch's Bridge, a few miles south of Newark, is **Welsh Tract Baptist Church,** which was founded in the early 1700s by Welsh settlers. The brick church, the oldest Old School Baptist church in America, was built in 1746 and bears marks of cannonballs used in a skirmish between Washington's and Cornwallis's troops in 1777.

Web site: www.newrivernotes.com/de/wt.htm.

To the east, **New Castle** on the Delaware Bay dates back to 1651 when Fort Casimir was built here under order of Governor Stuyvesant of New Amsterdam. The English gained control from the Dutch in 1664, which was when the town received its present name. New Castle is located at the convergence of Routes 9 and 73. Web site: http://newcastlecity.delaware.gov/.

Many historic points surround **the Green**, formerly the Public Square, between Delaware and Market streets at Third Street. The **New Castle Courthouse Museum** (1732), 211 Delaware Street, was Delaware's colonial capitol, and the first state capitol and county seat until 1881. Now a museum, it features several portraits of signers of the Declaration of Independence, restored courtrooms and assembly rooms, as well as changing exhibits. Open Tuesday through Saturday, 10 A.M. to 3:30 P.M.; Sunday, 1:30 to 4:30 P.M. Free admission; donations appreciated. Telephone: (302) 323-4453. Web site: www.history.delaware.gov/museums/ncch/ncch_main.shtml.

Town Hall (1832) and **Market Place** (1682) are at Second and Delaware streets. The **New Castle and Frenchtown Railroad Ticket Office** (1832) is at Battery Park. It was one of America's oldest railroads. A section of track is nearby. The exteriors of these sites and of the **New Castle Academy** (opened in 1798, on the Green, as a public school) can be viewed on a walking tour.

Amstel House (1738), at 2 E. Fourth Street (corner of Delaware Street), now a museum, provides a glimpse of New Castle life in the eighteenth and nineteenth centuries. Displayed are colonial arts, handicrafts, and furnishings. Open daily except Monday, March through December, 11 A.M. to 4 P.M; Sunday 1 A.M. to 4 P.M. Admission charge. Telephone: (302) 322-2794.

New Castle Presbyterian Church (1707), at 25 E. Third Street, was originally a Dutch church, built in 1657, rebuilt in 1707. This is believed to be the oldest Presbyterian church in the United States. Free admission. Telephone: (302) 328-3279. Web site: www.newcastlepreschurch.org.

Dutch House, 32 East Third Street, is one of the oldest houses in the state, and reflects the 1651 founding of New Castle by the Dutch. Open March 1 through December 31, Tuesday through Sunday, 11 A.M. to 4 P.M. Closed November to April. Nominal admission charge. Telephone: (302) 322-2794. Web site: www.newcastlehistory.org/houses/dutch.html.

The **George Read II House and Gardens** at 42 the Strand is a fine example of late Georgian/early Federal architecture. It was built between 1797 and 1804 by George Read I, a signer of the Declaration of Independence and the U.S. Constitution. It has been restored under the auspices of the Historical Society of Delaware. Thirteen rooms are open to the public, including a tap room, servants' quarters, a parlor, kitchen, and dining room, Tuesday through Thursday, and Sunday, 11 A.M. to 4 P.M.; Friday and Saturday, 10 A.M. to 4 P.M. Admission charge. Telephone: (302) 322-8411. Web site: www.hsd.org/read.htm. Check with the the Delaware Historical Society or Read House guides about walking tours through the New Castle Historic District and other notable sites and events.

The town of New Castle, which dates from 1651, occasionally hosts special events. Chief among them is an annual "Day in Old New Castle" on the third Saturday of May. Twenty private houses and some lovely old gardens are opened to the public at this time. Residents wear colonial costume. There is a single admission charge to all the events. For information, contact: "A Day in Old New Castle," Box 166, New Castle, DE 19720. New Castle also hosts special Christmas events. Check with the New Castle Historical Society. Telephone: (877) 496-9498 .

Wilmington is seven miles north of New Castle, via Route 9. Several historic landmarks in the city are worthy of visits. A suggested tour route in Wilmington begins at the **Friends Meetinghouse** (1816) at Fourth and West streets. Go east to Market Street, and north to Sixth, to **Old Town Hall**. Proceed east to **Old Swede's Church** at Seventh and Church, and then east into **Fort Christina State Park**. Nearby is Delaware's Tall Ship, *Kalmar Nyckel*. You may the go north on Locust to 11th Street, left to Market Street to **Free Library** at corner of Tenth Street. Continue on 11th Street and on Pennsylvania Avenue to Union Street, turning right to Lovering Avenue, site of the **Delaware Academy of Medicine**.

Holy Trinity Old Swede's Church (1698) and Hendrickson House Museum (1690) at 606 Church Street commemorate where the early Swedes landed and the hardships of colonial life. Open Wednesday through Saturday, 10 A.M. to 4 P.M. Small admission charge. Telephone: (302) 652-5629. Web site (with virtual tour): www.oldswedes.org.

Fort Christina Monument is located in a small park at the foot of Seventh Street close to Old Swede's Church. It commemorates the landing of Swedish colonists at the Rocks in 1638.

The **Delaware History Center** dominates the 500 block of Market Street Mall in downtown Wilmington and is composed of the Delaware History Museum, Old Town Hall (1798), Wilmington Square, and the Historical Society of Delaware's Research Library. The Complex was built on land given by John Dickinson, signer of the Declaration of Independence. Inside there are exhibits of 18th- and 19th-century decorative arts, antique toys, restored jail cells, and changing exhibits on the history of Delaware. Open Monday through Friday, noon to 4 P.M.; Saturday, 10 A.M. to 4 P.M. Admission charge. Telephone: (302) 656-0637. Web site: www.hsd.org/dhm.htm.

Across the Mall is **Willingtown Square**, a group of six restored 18th-century homes that can be viewed from the outside. The Historical Society of Delaware has its offices here in the library at 505 Market Street. **The library** contains excellent material on the history of Delaware and the mid-Atlantic area from colonial times to the present day, as well as unique material on genealogy and local history. There is an emphasis on political, legal, economic, and social history, including books, manuscripts, pamphlets (including some from the famous "pamphleteers" of the American Revolution), ledgers, maps, charts, sketches, deeds, wills, reports, "broadsides" (early printed political posters), photographs, and newspaper collections, including the printed and private papers of Delaware families. Open Monday, 1 to 9 P.M.; Tuesday through Friday, 9 A.M. to 5 P.M. Closed major holidays. Telephone: (302) 655-7161. Web site: www.hsd.org.

Nearby is at 818 Market Street is the **Grand Opera House** (1871). Now known as the Delaware Center for Performing Arts, it is a National Historic Landmark. It was restored as closely as possible to its original elegance. The brick building displays an ornate facade of white-painted, finely-finished cast iron that imitates chiseled marble. Call for information regarding performances. Telephone: (800) 37-GRAND or (302) 652-5577. Web site: www.thegrandwilmington.org.

Delaware Academy of Medicine, 1925 Lovering Avenue (at Union Street), has the largest medical library in the state as well as an interesting collection of early medical and dental instruments. The building (1816) originally housed the bank of Delaware. It was disassembled brick by brick and rebuilt in its present location in 1930. Open Monday through Friday, 8:30 A.M. to 4:30 P.M. Telephone: (302) 733-3900. Check web site for on-line services. Reference Desk for medical information: (302) 733-3952. Web site: www.delamed.org.

Tourists interested in art may wish to see the permanent collection at the recently expanded **Delaware Art Museum**, 2301 Kentmere Parkway. The museum, scheduled to re-open in fall 2004, possesses several major collections, including the largest collection of English Pre-Raphaelite paintings and decorative arts in the United States, 19th-and 20th-century American painting collections, and important works by Howard Pyle and other well-known illustrators. Changing exhibits are also featured, receiving triple the space (12,000 square feet) in the expanded museum than in the previous structure. The museum contains a library, a sales and rental gallery, and a museum store. While renovations continue, the museum is exhibiting at the Bank One Center on Riverfront, Tuesday through Saturday, 10 A.M. to 4 P.M.; Wednesday 10 A.M. to 5 P.M.; Saturday and Sunday, 1 to 5 P.M. Admission charge. Telephone: (302) 571-9590. Web site: www.delart.org.

Rockwood Mansion Park, a country estate built in the 1850s three miles north of Wilmington at 610 Shipley Road, is a fine example of rural Gothic architecture. Furnishings range from the 18th century to the Victorian period, reflecting ways of life of five generations of one family. Open daily 7 A.M. to 7 P.M. Closed major holidays. There is a gift shop and garden tours are also available. Telephone: (302) 761-4340. Web site: www.nccde.org/rockwood/.

The **Henry Francis Dupont Winterthur Museum, Gardens, and Library** are major attractions in the Wilmington area. They are located on Route 52, five miles west of the city, and contain more than 100 period rooms reflecting the American domestic scene between 1640 and 1840. The *New York Times* described the collection as being so fine that "no other collection comes even close in matching its range, its richness, and its quality." Open Tuesday through Sunday, 10 A.M. to 5 p.m. Admission charge. Special events and tours, such as the Labor Day Craft Festival, the Delaware Antiques Show in November, Yuletide Tours, November through mid-January, and the Point-to-Point Races in May, are scheduled throughout the year. Reservations needed for some tours and events. Detailed information and discount coupons available on web site. Telephone: (302) 888-4600 or (800) 448-3883. Web site: www.winterthur.org.

The impressive **Winterthur Gardens**, a major accomplishment in themselves, boast unusual flowers from all over the world interspersed with stands of trees, winding brooks, and broad vistas. Garden tours are self-guided unless the visitor chooses a tram tour, available mid-April through mid-November, for an extra charge. Open year round, except Mondays and major holidays. Same schedule as museum.

Admission charge. Lunch, Sunday brunch, and snacks are served in the Garden Cafeteria and the Cappuccino Café. Contact information in previous entry.

The **Delaware Museum of Natural History**, 4840 Kennett Pike, is five miles north of Wilmington and three miles south of the Pennsylvania border. It is the first institution in Delaware dedicated to the study and interpretation of natural history. Experience nature from the wilds of Africa to the quiet restfulness of the local area in dioramas, exhibits, and special programs. Permanent exhibits include Delaware's only dinosaurs, a walk across the Great Barrier Reef, and a 500-lb clam. The interactive Discovery Room offers families new worlds to explore. Open Monday through Saturday, 9:30 A.M. to 4:30 P.M.; Sunday, noon to 4:30 P.M. Admission charge. Telephone: (302) 658-9111. Web site: www.delmnh.org.

The **Hagley Museum**, the original du Pont mills, estate, and gardens, is located on a 235-acre site on Brandywine River at 298 Buck Road East. The museum grounds are three miles north of Wilmington via Routes 52 and 141. This is a National Historic Landmark. Daily demonstrations and exhibits depict American home and work life in the 19th century. You may visit the museum buildings, tour Eleutherian Mills (see below), and take a bus ride along the Brandywine. Open daily, March 15 through December, 9:30 A.M. to 4:30 P.M. January through March hours vary. Admission charge. Telephone: (302) 658-2400. Web site: www.hagley.lib.de.us.

Eleutherian Mills, the Georgian residence built by E. I. du Pont in 1803 overlooking his powder yards, and the First Office of the Du Pont Company, are open the same hours as The Hagley Museum (1837). There is Lammot du Pont's Workshop, and a Barn containing displays of 19th-century vehicles, a 20th-century du Pont motor car and weathervanes. There is also an excellent library of business and economic history. Visitors must board a bus at The Hagley Museum for the trip to this area. No extra admission charge. Telephone: (302) 658-2400.

Nemours Mansion, named for the original duPont residence in north central France, was built by Alfred I. DuPont in 1910 at 1600 Rockland Road. A fine example of a modified Louis XVI French chateau, the mansion contains 102 rooms. The public can view many of them and their fine rugs, tapestries, art, and furniture. One-third of a mile of French-style gardens extends along the main vista from the house. Visitors must be over 12 years of age. Reservations are recommended for individuals and required for groups. Tours are offered May through October, Tuesdays through Saturdays, 9 A.M., 11 A.M., 1 P.M., 3 P.M.; Sundays, 11 A.M., 1 P.M., 3 P.M. Admission charge. For reservations or additional information, contact: Nemours Mansion, PO Box 109, Wilmington, DE 19899. Telephone: (302) 651-6912. Web site (with virtual photo tour): www.nemoursmansion.org.

Note that Nemours' mission is children's health, and in that connection, the organization owns and operates the Alfred I. duPont Hospital for Children, as well as four other pediatric specialty centers in the U.S.

For a change in scenery, enjoy a ride on the **Wilmington and Western Railroad**, an old steam rail line that chugs through scenic Red Clay Valley. The depot is on Route 41, four miles west of Wilmington, at 2201 Newport Gap Pike. A lay-over is permitted at the Mt. Cuba picnic grounds. Open May through December. Schedule varies. Admission charge. Telephone: (302) 998-1930. Web site: www.wwrr.com.

Only two covered bridges remain in Delaware. **Wooddale Bridge** is located off Rolling Mill Road, which can be approached from Route 48 and then turning north. Wooddale links a few houses from the west side of Red Clay Creek with east side. **Ashland Covered Bridge** is on Route 82 in the village of Ashland (in the northwestern part of the state near the Pennsylvania border). The bridge is a 52-foot Town lattice bridge, built around 1870. It is about a half-hour drive from Wilmington. Web site: www.bridges-covered.com/delaware.htm.

PENNSYLVANIA

The Keystone State was settled first by the Swedes and Dutch, and then by the British. William Penn landed at Chester, Delaware, at the head of a band of Quakers and Friends more than 300 years ago, in 1682. He had accepted, in the New World, the largest grant of land ever given to a British subject (in payment of a debt owed by the Crown to his family). By 1700 the areas presently known as Philadelphia and Bucks, Chester, Delaware, and Montgomery counties had been settled.

The city of Philadelphia, which served as the state capital until the end of the 1700s, has played an illustrious role in the history of the nation. In addition to hosting the First Continental Congress at which the Declaration of Independence was written and adopted, and providing the lion's share of financial backing for the Revolution, the city served as the new nation's first capital from 1775 to 1789, and (after surrendering its position to New York for one year) again from 1790 to 1800. During the Civil War it threw in its lot with the North. Early in its history it became a vital shipping center. During and after World War I it became a major industrial city. We know it today as a city important in manufacturing and commerce, as well as one of the richest historical sites in the country.

In the southeastern Pennsylvania counties near Philadelphia there is much to see that is unique to each of the many national, cultural, and religious groups that settled here. William Penn considered religious freedom the pivotal one, and Pennsylvania boasts a particularly large and varied trove of very lovely churches. Almost everything one might wish to see, from world-famous Longwood Gardens to a number of the oldest houses, stores, inns, museums, and places of work in the country, can be visited. Here, too, are some of the nation's loveliest residential areas, most fashionable shopping streets, most creative artists' colonies, best nightclubs, and the single largest civic park (Philadelphia's Fairmount Park) in the world.

As we travel westward into the state, one of the major sites is Valley Forge. Here Washington's army encamped from December 13, 1777, to June 19, 1778, having crossed from New Jersey to avoid the British and regroup during a hard winter. Approximately 11,000 strong, the Continental Army spent a bitter, under-clothed and under-fed winter. Many soldiers did not even have boots. The suffering was overwhelming, so terrible, in fact, that Washington almost decided to abandon the cause. It is impossible to visit here and not be moved by the sacrifices that helped to purchase our freedom.

Even farther west we come to the famous Pennsylvania Dutch country, famous for delicious food, beautiful farms, magnificent examples of trades and handicrafts, and distinctive, immaculate houses. The word *Dutch* actually was a mispronunciation of the word *Deutsch*, meaning "German," but the usage has survived.

The unique architecture of each barn in Montgomery County, the art shows of Bucks County, the marvelous antique shops, and hostelries which have catered to travelers for two centuries are only a few of the discoveries to be made in Pennsylvania.

The Pennsylvania state tourism web site is very comprehensive, and includes sections on nature, arts and entertainment, historic sites, accommodations and dining, and children.
Web site: www.visitpa.com.

Though each Pennsylvania state park has its own phone number for information, one central line is used to make camping reservations. Telephone for camping reservations: (888) PA-PARKS. Online, you can find additional information about all the state parks at a central site. Web site: www.dcnr.state.pa.us. The central source for an overview of historic sites within the state is www.phmc.state.pa.us.

PHILADELPHIA

Philadelphia, the "Cradle of Liberty" and birthplace of our nation, deserves a place on every weekender's itinerary. This city and surrounding counties north, south, and west of the city offer a panorama of historic landmarks, picturesque countryside, and beautiful homes, gardens, and parks. In planning a trip to the area, you may wish to contact the Philadelphia Convention and Visitors Bureau, 1515 Market Street, Suite 2020, Philadelphia, PA 19102. Telephone: (800) 225-5745 ext. 1 to request a destination planning guide which would reach you in about a week or (215) 636-3300. Web site: www.pcvb.org.

Begin your tour of the city with a visit to **Independence National Historical Park**, under the jurisdiction of the National Park Service. This park area includes some forty historical sites located between Front and Seventh Streets, and Pine and Market from Second to Sixth Streets. A walk of about two miles, which begins and ends at or near Independence Hall, passes most of the Independence Park sites in the heart of Philadelphia. Many are open to the public. Information on all sites (and a walking tour map) can be obtained at the new Visitors Center, One North Independence Mall West (Sixth and Market Streets). Hours are 8:30 A.M. to 5:00 P.M. (6:00 P.M. July 1- September 1). Verify hours and security procedures by calling the Independence Park Visitors Center or visiting its web site. A few of the more important landmarks are mentioned immediately below. Admission to the park is free; charge for some sites, as noted. Telephone: (800) 537-7676 or (215) 965-2305. Web sites: www.nps.gov/inde/index.htm or www.independencevisitorcenter.com.

Independence Hall enjoys a gracious setting on a broad green mall. As you step inside the front door, you imagine the Revolutionary War patriots in the Assembly Room signing the Declaration of Independence, or debating the provisions of the Constitution. Special tours, just for this building, depart every 15 minutes from the east wing. In front of Independence Hall, across Chestnut Street, is **Liberty Bell Pavilion**, home of the famed Liberty Bell. Read the words cast deep into the metal around the top: "Proclaim Liberty Throughout All the Land Unto All the Inhabitants Thereof." It was this bell's deep voice that summoned the people of Philadelphia to the first public reading of the Declaration of Independence on that hot eighth of July 1776. A recorded voice tells the history of the bell.

Adjoining Independence Hall is **Congress Hall**, a bustling place from 1790 to 1800, when Philadelphia was the national capital and both houses of Congress met in this building. Here Washington was inaugurated for his second term. Behind the Hall to the south is **Independence Mall.** Around the corner at 420 Chestnut Street (between South 4th and South 5th) is the **Second Bank of the United States/Portrait Gallery**, built in 1824. This building, a fine example of Greek revival architecture, houses an exhibit of portraits, many by Charles Wilson Pearle, featuring important early Americans. Open Tuesday through Sunday, 10 A.M. to 3 P.M. Admission charge. Web site: www.ushistory.org/tour/second-bank.htm.

The **Fireman's Hall Museum** is located at 147 North Second Street. The museum depicts over 300 years of fire-fighting history with authentic examples of equipment, tools, and fire fighters' regalia, including a hand engine used by Benjamin Franklin in 1731. Open Tuesday through Sunday, 9 A.M. to 5 P.M. Free admission. Telephone: (215) 923-1438. Web site: www.ushistory.org/tour/firemans-hall.htm.

At 239 Arch Street is the **Betsy Ross House.** This tiny brick residence with the Stars and Stripes flying in front is where (according to tradition) Ross lived and made the first American flag with its circle of 13 stars. The house has been restored and furnished with authentic pieces from the Revolutionary period. In addition to the Flag Room there is a room where the Ross family is supposed to have had its upholstery shop. Open Memorial Day through Labor Day, daily 10 A.M. to 5 P.M.; rest of the year, Tuesday through Saturday, 10 A.M. to 5 P.M. Tours are self-guided. Free admission; donations requested. Telephone: (215) 629-4026. Web site: historicphiladelphia.org/betsy-ross-house/what-to-see/.

The **Arch Street Friends Meeting House** at 320 Arch Street between Third and Fourth Streets is the oldest Friends meeting house still in use in Philadelphia and the largest in the world. It was built in 1804 and enlarged in 1811. Monthly meetings are still conducted here, as they have been since the 19th century. The ground around the meeting house was used for burial purposes under a patent issued to William Penn in 1701. Burials continued until 1803 and included many victims of the yellow fever epidemic of 1793. Open Monday through Saturday, 10 A.M. to 4 P.M. Free admission; donation requested. Telephone: (215) 627-2667.

At the corner of Fifth and Arch Streets is the **Christ Church Burial Ground**, which was re-opened to the public in spring 2003 after being closed for twenty-five years. Five signers of the Declaration of Independence are buried here, including Benjamin Franklin and Benjamin Rush. The grounds are also the final resting places for more Revolutionary war heroes than any other nonmilitary cemetery. Open Monday through Saturday, 10 A.M. to 4 P.M.; Sunday noon to 4 P.M., weather permitting. Donation requested. Voice telephone: (215) 922-1695. Web site: www.oldchristchurch.org/burial/.

On Independence Mall, at 55 North Fifth Street, across from the new Constitution Center, is the **National Museum of American Jewish History**. Its permanent exhibition, *Creating American Jews,* explores the evolution of Jewish identity in America. It shares its location with historic **Congregation Mikveh Israel**, the synagogue of the American Revolution. The historic synagogue will remain, but much of the existing structure will be replaced by a new, five-story glass and stone building at the same location which is schedule for completion in 2006. The museum is open Monday through Thursday, 10 A.M. to 5 P.M., Friday, 10 A.M. to 3 P.M., Sunday, noon to 5 P.M. Free admission. Telephone: (215) 923-3811. Web site: www.nmajh.org.

On Second Street between Market and Arch streets stands one of America's most beautiful religious buildings, **Christ Church**, built between 1727 and 1754. (The congregation was founded in 1695.) There, row upon row, are the straight-backed pews where George Washington, John Adams, Benjamin Franklin, and many other patriots worshipped. It has one of North America's oldest Palladian windows and a notable wine glass pulpit, as well as the font where William Penn was baptized. Telephone: 215- 922-1695.

Between Third and Fourth streets at 314 Market is **Franklin Court**, site of Benjamin Franklin's home. There is an underground museum, an 18th-century printing exhibit, a U.S. Post Office and an architectural-cultural exhibit. Open daily. Call Visitors Center or check online for hours. Telephone: (215) 965-2305. Web site: www.nps.gov/inde/franklin-court.htm.

Across the street at 320 Chestnut is the **New Hall Military Museum**, which is housed in a replica of the building constructed on the site in 1791. The museum features a large collection of memorabilia for the military buff. Exhibits feature weapons, uniforms, battle flags, and as well as depictions of a soldier's life. Open Saturday and Sunday, 9 A.M. to 5 P.M. Telephone: (215) 965-2305. Web site: www.nps.gov/inde/new-hall.htm. Next door is **Carpenter's Hall,** site of the meeting of the First Continental Congress, held September 1774, where Washington, Patrick Henry, and others denounced British colonial policies. Although located physically in the park, the building is privately owned by the Carpenters Association. The museum is devoted to 18th-century building procedures and the early decades of the Carpenter Company, the oldest trade guild in America, which was formed by a group of master builder-designers who banded together to protect their trade and assist each other in times of need. Open Tuesday through Sunday, 10 A.M. to 4 P.M. Closed Mondays. Free admission. Telephone: (215) 925-0167. Web site: www.ushistory.org/tour/carpenters-hall.htm.

The Physick House, at 321 South Fourth Street, was the home of Philip Syng Physick, who is considered the "Father of American Surgery." The Physick House, constructed in 1786, is the only free-standing federal-style house in Society Hill. Open September through May, Thursday, Friday, and Saturday, 11 A.M. to 3 P.M.; June through August, Thursday, Friday and Saturday, noon to 4 P.M. Closed holidays and for special functions. Admission charge. Telephone: (215) 925-7866. Web site: www.philalandmarks.org/.

At the corner of Walnut and Fourth Streets is the **Todd House** (1776) where Dolley Todd, who was to become Dolley Madison, one of the most famous first ladies, once lived. Today the house is a museum depicting a middle-class Quaker home of the late 1700s. Free tickets to the Todd House and the neighboring **Bishop William White House,** the restored home of the "Father of the American Protestant Episcopal Church" are available through the Independence Visitor Center. Telephone: (215) 597-8974. Web Site: www.ushistory.org/tour/todd-house.htm.

Across Walnut Street at 321 Willings Alley is Old **St. Joseph's Church,** first built in 1733, and the oldest Catholic church in Philadelphia. Call for a schedule of Masses or stop by the rector's office to request entrance. Free admission. Telephone: (215) 923-1733. Web site: www.oldstjoseph.org.

At the corner of Third and Walnut Streets is the old Philadelphia Stock Exchange, built in 1832. In the middle of the next block at 244 South Third is **Powel House,** built in 1765 by Samuel Powel, the first mayor of Philadelphia. The house was a social center during the Revolutionary period. Many of our nation's founding fathers and other notables were entertained here, including George and Martha Washington, John Adams, and Benjamin Franklin. In fact, the Washingtons celebrated their 20th wedding anniversary at the Powel House. The Powel House Museum is furnished in 18th and 19th-century furniture, including some pieces owned by the Powels. Attractive gardens. Open Thursday through Saturday, noon to 5 P.M.; Sunday, 1 to 5 P.M. Admission charge. Telephone: (215) 627-0364. Web site: www.philalandmarks.org.

Thaddeus Kosciusko National Memorial (1775), at 301 Pine Street (corner of Third), is the 1797-98 residence of the Polish military engineer who fought for the American cause during the Revolution. Open daily, 9 A.M. to 5 P.M. Telephone : (215) 597-9618. Web site: www.ushistory.org/tour/kosciuszko.htm.

Other notable historic attractions in the city beyond Independence Park include **Penn's Landing®** at Columbus Boulevard and Spring Garden Street. Here on Philadelphia's urban waterfront is where Philadelphia founder William Penn landed his ship in 1682. Majestic sailing vessels, unique floating restaurants, museums, and landscaped gardens offer visitors a recreational paradise. Telephone: (215) 928-8801 or (215) 922 2FUN. Web site: www.pennslandingcorp.com.

Located in the heart of the Penn's Landing Waterfront at 211 Columbus Boulevard at Walnut Street is the Independence Seaport Museum. It captures the Philadelphia region's maritime heritage with family oriented interactive exhibits, ship models, artifacts and art. Open daily, 10 A.M. to 5 P.M. Closed Thanksgiving, Christmas and New Year's Day. Admission charge. Telephone: (215) 413-8655. Web site: http://phillyseaport.org.

The *USS Olympia,* the flagship of Admiral Dewey at the Battle of Manila Bay in the Spanish-American War, and *USS Becuna,* a Guppy Class World War II submarine, which are owned by the Seaport Museum are also docked at Penn's Landing and may be visited. Aboard you can see the big guns, the torpedo tubes, and the Admiral's quarters. Open daily, 10 A.M. to 5 P.M. Closed Thanksgiving, Christmas and New Year's. Admission charge (one fee for both ships). Telephone: (215) 413-8655. Web site: http://phillyseaport.org.

The center city area of Philadelphia, which begins at City Hall includes **Penn Center, Centre Square,** and **Dilworth Plaza,** an ultra-modern city-within-a-city. Here, Swedish artist Claes Oldenburg's forty-five-foot-high "Clothespin" sculpture stands at South 15th and Market Streets before forty-story buildings gleaming in aluminum, enamel, and stainless steel. Also nearby at John F. Kennedy Plaza, John F Kennedy Boulevard and North 15th Street, is the LOVE sculpture that has been featured on popular U.S. postage stamps. Telephone: (215) 636-1666.

City Hall, the world's largest municipal building, towers 510 feet above the intersection of Broad and Market streets, the exact geographical center of William Penn's original plan for Philadelphia, and is topped by a 37-foot statue of William Penn. A circular observation platform at the base of the statue gives visitors a full circle of spectacular views. Open Monday through Friday, 9:30 A.M. to 4:15 P.M.

Admission free, donations requested. Telephone: (215) 686-2840. Web site with virtual tour: www.phila.gov/virtualch/body_pages/visitorinfo.html. For shopping, there's Philadelphia's **Gallery Malls I and II** more than 250 indoor stores in the heart of downtown. In the city's renovated Society Hill area is **Head House Square** and **Newmarket,** an architectural wonderland of unique glass boutiques. The area has become a prototype for urban restoration projects across the United States.

You can spend days visiting museums and galleries in the Philadelphia area. Some of the major ones are described below.

Visitors can delight in the **Philadelphia Museum of Art,** at 26th Street and Benjamin Franklin Parkway, with its priceless collections of paintings by American and European masters. Lovers of antiques will enjoy visiting the period rooms and exhibits of oriental rugs and objets d'art. Open Tuesday through Sunday, 10 A.M. to 5 P.M. Wednesday and Friday evenings until 8:45 P.M. Admission charge. Telephone: Main number (215) 763-8100. Web site: www.philamuseum.org.

Also administered by the Philadelphia Museum of Art is **The Rodin Museum,** located on the North side of the Benjamin Franklin Parkway at 22nd Street. The museum houses the largest public collection of sculptures by Auguste Rodin, the celebrated late 19th-century French sculptor, outside of Paris. The collection was given to the city by Jules E. Mastbaum, a Philadelphia motion picture magnate and philanthropist. The collection includes casts of many of Rodin's best known work as well as drawings, letters, books and a variety of documentary material. Open Tuesday through Sunday, 10 A.M. to 5 P.M. Donations suggested. Telephone: (215) 568-6026. Web site: www.rodinmuseum.org.

The University of Pennsylvania Museum of Archaeology and Anthropology located at 33rd and Spruce Streets, houses an internationally renowned collection of materials from ancient and traditional cultures around the world. Major Ancient Egyptian, Mesopotamian, Mayan and Meso-American, North American, Greco-Roman, Polynesian, Chinese, and African exhibits are displayed here. In addition special exhibits, cultural events, workshops films, talks and tours are scheduled for adults and children. Open Tuesday through Saturday, 10 A.M. to 4:15 P.M.; Sunday, 1 to 4:45 P.M. Closed on summer Sundays. Telephone: (215) 746-4174. Web site: www.penn.museum.

The **Please Touch Museum,** The **Children's Museum of Philadelphia** at 210 North 21st Street, is dedicated to enriching the lives of children, ages one to seven. Highlights include "Alice's Adventure in Wonderland." Open Tuesday to Saturday, 10 A.M. to 4:30 P.M.; Sunday, 12:30 to 4:30 P.M. Admission charge. Telephone: (215) 581-3181. Web site: www.pleasetouchmuseum.org.

The **United States Mint,** located at 151 North Independence Mall East, may be toured by students, youth groups, and organized military and veterans groups if appointments are scheduled at least two weeks in advance through the Office of Exhibits and Public Services. Groups of four to six citizens may also arrange tours by contacting their Senators or Congressional Representatives. The visitor entrance is located on Fifth Street, in front of the building. Telephone: (215) 408-0112. Web site: www.usmint.gov.

At 15 South Seventh Street, just around the corner from Independence Hall, is the **Atwater Kent Museum.** The museum, the first home of the Franklin Institute, displays artifacts and memorabilia reflecting the social and cultural history of Philadelphia. It is one of only two places in the country that has among its collections, all of the *Saturday Evening Post* covers. Its extensive holdings also include more than 3,000 textiles and costumes (half reflecting Quaker dress from 1740-1920), political memorabilia, an extensive toy collection, artifacts from The First African Baptist Church in Philadelphia, and from Philadelphia industries such as the Stetson Hat Company and Baldwin Locomotive. Open daily, though exhibitions are closed on Tuesday, 10 A.M. to 5 P.M. Admission charge. Telephone: (215) 685-4830. Web site: www.philadelphiahistory.org.

The **African American Historical Cultural Museum** at Seventh and Arch streets opened in 1976. Exhibits in its 400,000 piece permanent collection trace black history from its African heritage, through the Revolutionary and Civil wars, and up to the present day. Another gallery is devoted to art and photographs by black artists. Open Tuesday through Saturday, 10 A.M. to 5 P.M.; Sunday, noon to 5 P.M. Admission charge. Telephone: (215) 574-0380. Web site: www.aampmuseum.org/.

For both adults and children the oldest natural history museum in the United States is a must. Here at the **Academy of Natural Sciences Museum** located at 1900 Benjamin Franklin Parkway, is an international museum of natural history in operation since 1812. Permanent exhibits include "Discovering Dinosaurs," which allows visitor to explore the ancient world through video, interactive displays and fossils, some of which you may handle. The North American Hall shows the great variety of environments throughout the United States, and Live Butterflies features butterflies raised on farms in Costa Rica, Malaysia and Africa. It is the only indoor butterfly house in the region. Open Monday through Friday, 10 A.M. to 4:30 P.M.; Saturday, Sunday and holidays, 10 A.M. to 5 P.M. Admission charge. Telephone: (215) 299-1000. Web site: www.acnatsci.org.

The **Franklin Institute Science Museum** interprets scientific facts in simple and dramatic form. The museum has four floors of interactive exhibits about science and technology, such as astronomy, chemistry, aviation, transportation, computers, meteorology, math, electricity, and communications, that inspire visitors to "learn by doing." It is located at 222 North 20th Street (where 20th joins Benjamin Franklin Parkway). Home of the **Benjamin Franklin National Memorial,** the Franklin Institute also features the **Fels Planetarium,** where the universe unfolds before your eyes and the four-story, wrap-around **Tuttle Omniverse Theater.** Open daily, except major holidays, 9:30 A.M. to 5 P.M. Admission charge. Call to reserve tickets and confirm show times for the planetarium and theater. Telephone: (215) 448-1200. Web site: www.fi.edu.

Declaration (Graff) House, on the southwest corner of Seventh and Market, is a reconstruction of the house where Jefferson wrote the Declaration of Independence. Open daily, 10 A.M. to 3 P.M. Telephone: (215) 965-2305. Web site: www.visitphilly.com/history.

The **Mummers Museum,** located at 1100 South 2nd Street, gives visitors a chance to see flamboyant exhibits highlighting the historical tradition of the Philadelphia Mummers Parade. The costume displays are accompanied by videotapes of the parades. Open Tuesday to Saturday, 9:30 A.M. to 4:30 P.M.; Sunday, noon to 4:30 P.M. Admission charge. Telephone: (215) 336-3050. Web site: www.mummersmuseum.com/home.html.

For the gourmet or gourmand there is a delightful open-air Italian market which extends from Ninth and Christian to Ninth and Wharton streets. Philadelphia's Italian Market is the oldest and largest working outdoor market in the U.S. The booths are set up beginning at dawn, and are laden with fruit and vegetables, meat and fish, homemade pastries, and imported cheeses and oils. Some handicrafts are displayed in the section near Federal Street. Open Tuesday through Friday, 8 A.M. to 5 P.M.; Saturday, 7 A.M. to 5 P.M.. Web site: www.phillyitalianmarket.com.

On the Delaware River just beside the airport is **Old Fort Mifflin,** the only fort in Philadelphia. This fort figured in the Revolutionary War and was again manned in the War of 1812. During the Civil War it was used as a prison camp. Although de-armed in 1904, it has been restored as it would have appeared in 1834. Visitors may participate in tours, weapons demonstrations and special events with costumed guides. Open April through November, Wednesday through Sunday, 9 A.M. to 5 P.M. Admission charge. Telephone: (215) 685-4167. Web site: www.fortmifflin.com.

Fairmount Park System comprises more than 8,000 acres of rolling countryside, flower gardens, woods, sparkling streams, a bicycle path, and a hundred miles of bridle paths. This is the largest civic park in the world. Winding through the park is the Schuylkill River, edged with hundred-year-old boat clubs and dotted with sailboats and the fragile rowing shells of college and club crews. The park contains 23 historical houses, once the country homes of early Philadelphians. Eight of the most interesting houses have been restored and are open to the public. They are: Cedar Grove, Laurel Hill, Lemon Hill, Mount Pleasant, Solitude, Strawberry Mansion, Sweetbriar, and Woodford. Hours vary. It is best to telephone in advance for times as well as information on available bus tours. Admission charge. Combination house tour tickets available. Telephone: (215) 683-0200. W eb site: www.fairmountpark.org.

The park offers "Under the Stars" free summer concerts at **Fredric R. Mann Music Center** and **Robin Hood Dell East.**

The **Zoological Garden of Philadelphia,** also in the park, is the oldest zoo in the United States, housing more than 2,000 birds, animals, primates, and reptiles. Open daily, 9:30 A.M. to 5 P.M. except December and January, when it closes at 4 P.M.. Closed June 12, Thanksgiving, Christmas Eve, Christmas Day, and New Year's Eve and New Year's Day. Admission charge. Telephone: (215) 243-1100. Web site: www.philadelphiazoo.org.

On the far side of the Schuylkill River in Germantown there are two places of interest not very far from each other. **Deshler-Morris House** (1772), 5442 Germantown Avenue, was used by George Washington from 1793 to 1794. It is where the President held cabinet meetings and where his family escaped the devastating yellow fever epidemic in Philadelphia in 1794. Open April through mid-December, Friday through Sunday 1 to 4 P.M. Closed legal holidays. Free admission. Telephone: (215) 965-2305. Web site: www.nps.gov/demo/.

At 6401 Germantown Avenue is **Cliveden** (1763-67), which was built as the country residence of Chief Justice Benjamin Chew, a lawyer, jurist, and political figure from Philadelphia. Shortly after it was completed, it was the scene of a battle between the Continental Army under Washington, and British troops who had taken the house. The grounds still show the marks of fighting. The Chew family lived here for another 200 years before the house was turned into a museum. Throughout the house there are examples of some of the finest 18th- and 19th-century furniture built in Philadelphia, as well as family portraits, and Chinese porcelain made specifically for the Chews. Cliveden is the only Pennsylvania property of the National Trust for Historic Preservation. Open April through December, Thursday to Saturday, noon to 4 P.M. Admission charge. Telephone: (215) 848-1777. Web site: www.cliveden.org.

CHESTER AND DELAWARE COUNTIES

The following web sites and phone numbers may be useful in planning a trip to Chester and Delaware Counties which are part of Pennsylvania's Brandywine Valley. The Delaware County Tourist Information office in Chadds Ford will mail free visitors' guides on request, or you can view highlights online. Telephone: (800)-343-3983.Web site: www.brandywinecvb.org. The Chester County Tourist Bureau in Exton also provides information by phone and on line. Telephone: (610) 719-1730 or (800)-228-9933. Web site: www.brandywinevalley.com.

If you enter the Brandywine Valley via Route 1 into West Grove, the initial point of interest on Route 1 is the **Red Rose Inn,** 804 West Baltimore Pike near West Grove in Jennersville. This inn, founded in 1740, has served travelers for more than 250 years. It was established at the crossroads of the only colonial road connecting Baltimore and Philadelphia (now Route 1/Baltimore Pike) and a former Indian Trail (now Route 796). The Inn is one of several "red rose rent" buildings in the area. Tradition says that for many years on the first Saturday after Labor Day, a rent of one red rose was duly paid by the inn owners to a descendant of William Penn in accordance with the original deed. Call or visit web site for hours and menu offerings. Telephone: (610)) 869-3003. Web site: www.1740redroseinn.com.

Continue north for three miles on Route 796 and then right on Route 926 to Route 841 and left half a mile to **Primitive Hall and Library,** a lesser known but outstanding example of early 18th century architecture. For more about the history of the house, which was begun in 1738, its preservation, restoration, and completion, visit the Primitive Hall Foundation web site. Telephone: (610) 909.3324. Web site: www.primitivehall.org.

Kennett Square is said to be the "Mushroom capitol of the world." Here you can visit the **Phillips Mushroom Place and Museum** at 909 East Baltimore Pike. Learn about the history and love of mushrooms. There are also scale model mushroom houses that depict each phase of growing. Open year-round, hours vary.

Longwood Gardens, two miles east of Kennett Square, is considered one of the world's premier horticultural display gardens on 1,050 acres. Four acres are under glass in greenhouses, and more than 350 acres comprise waterfalls, display gardens, and fountains. Visitors may stroll through the flower, hillside and vegetable gardens. One of the notable areas is the Italian Water Garden. Colored fountain displays in the evenings Memorial Day through Labor Day, Tuesday, Thursday and Saturday. Open daily, 9 A.M. to 5 P.M. with later hours on fountain nights and for special events. Admission charge. Telephone: (610) 388-1000. Web site: www.longwoodgardens.org.

Brandywine River Museum, which features regional and American art, is housed in a Civil War-period grist mill. The museum is a study and display center for the tradition of Brandywine art, especially the work of Howard Pyle, his students, and the members of the Wyeth family. The museum is located on Route 1, just east of Chadds Ford, at intersection of Route 100. Open daily, 9:30 A.M. to 4:30 P.M. Admission charge. Telephone: (610) 388-2700. Web site: www.brandywinemuseum.org.

Nearby, also on Route 1, is **Barnes Brinton House** (1714), restored and furnished as an early 18th-century tavern. Open May through September, weekends only, noon to 5 P.M.; the rest of year by appointment. Colonial cooking demonstrations during open hours on weekends. Admission charge. Telephone: (610) 388-7376. Web site: www.chaddsfordhistory.org/historically-speaking/our-houses.

John Chads House (c.1725), home of the farmer, Brandywine River ferryman, and tavern keeper for whom Chadds Ford was named, is located on Route 100, one-quarter mile north of Route 1. It has been furnished in early 18th-century style. Beehive-oven bread-baking exhibitions are held some weekends. Open May through September, weekends only, noon to 5 P.M.; the rest of the year by appointment. Admission charge. Telephone: (610) 388-7376. Web site: www.chaddsfordhistory.org/historically-speaking/our-houses.

The **Christian C. Sanderson Museum** is located near the Brandywine River Museum, on Route 100 north near Route 1 in Chadds Ford. It includes a collection of old time toys, telegrams, and Valentines, early Wyeth family art, many mementos from the Battle of Brandywine and both World Wars, a collection of presidential autographs, exhibits of Indian artifacts, and all sorts of Americana that belonged to the Sanderson family. The Barn Shops and Chadds Ford Inn are adjacent. Open weekends, 1 to 4:30 P.M. Telephone: (610) 388-6545. Web site: www.sandersonmuseum.org.

Brandywine Battlefield is located one mile west of Chadds Ford. The battle, fought on September 11, 1777, was the largest engagement of the Revolutionary War and resulted in the British capture of Philadelphia, at that time the U.S. capital. The headquarters of Gen. George Washington and Marquis de Lafayette's quarters were located here. The museum and visitor center will help you get a feel for the human aspects of the engagement and its historical importance with many artifacts from the battle, rotating exhibits, and an audio-visual program. Tickets needed to visit the historic houses where interpretive guides provide background. Maps available on the web site and in the visitor center for self-guided driving tours. Open Tuesday through Saturday, 9 A.M. to 5 P.M.; Sunday, noon to 5 P.M. Telephone: (610) 459-3342.
Web site: www.ushistory.org/BRANDYWINE.

At Painter's Crossroads, take Route 202 North to the second light, then left onto Oakland Road for a stop at the **Brinton 1704 House and Historic Site,** 1435 Oakland Road. This Quaker home has been restored to its original simple elegance by descendants of the builders. Open May 1 through October 31, Monday through Friday 10 a.m. to 2 P.M. Saturday and Sunday, 11 A.M. to 6 P.M.; other seasons, tours by appointment. Admission charge. Telephone: (610) 399-0913. Web site: www.brintonfamily.org.

Continue north on Route 202 to **West Chester** and **The History Center,** home of the Chester County Historical Society (CCHS), located at 225 North High Street. Six of its galleries offer exhibits that highlight Chester County's fascinating past. They draw on collections that span more than three centuries in southeastern Pennsylvania, interpreting daily life and work from 1680 to the present. There are furnished period rooms, and collections of silver, glass, china, pewter, and needlework. The CCHS also features exhibits on special topics, some of which may be previewed on line with text, photos, and interactive games. A recent example was "Just Over the Line," which explored Chester County's role as a junction on the Underground Railroad. Open Monday through Saturday, 9:30 A.M. to 4:30 P.M. Admission charge. Telephone: (610) 692-4800. Web site: www.chestercohistorical.org. Obtain information on location and hours of additional historic sites from the Chester County Tourist Bureau on line or by phone. Telephone: (610) 719-1730 or (800) 228-9933. Web site: www.brandywinevalley.com. West Chester State University of Pennsylvania is also located here, and one may wish to drive through the grounds en route to other points of interest. West Chester State University evolved from an academy founded on the same grounds in 1817. The West Chester State College Quadrangle Historical District is listed on the National Register of Historic Places.

Tyler Arboretum, 515 Painter Road in Media, has 650 acres with hundreds of species of trees and shrubs, all labeled, from many parts of the world. There is about twenty miles of trails for hikers, naturalist and bird watchers. Labels are duplicated in Braille. The grounds are open daily, dawn to dusk, the office, 10 A.M. to 4 P.M., in winter, midweek, later on weekends and other seasons. Admission charge. Telephone: (610) 566-9134. Web site: www.tylerarboretum.org.

The **Franklin Mint Museum** is located on Route 1 south of Media, five miles north of Chester. The museum contains collections of porcelain dolls, precision die-cast model vehicles of all types, collector plates and much more. Special events and exhibits are held throughout the year. Open Monday through Saturday, 9:30 A.M. to 4:30 P.M.; Sunday, 1 to 4:30 P.M. Closed Christmas, New Year's, Easter, and Thanksgiving. Groups of 15 or more require reservations Admission free. Web site: www.franklinmint.com.

The Delaware County Convention and Visitors Bureau is located at One Beaver Valley Road in Chadds Ford. Open Monday through Friday, 8:30 A.M. to 4:30 P.M. Telephone: (610) 565-3679 or (800) 343 3983. Web site: www.brandywinecvb.org.

In Chester, you may wish to inspect the **Caleb Pusey House** (c. 1683) at 15 Race Street. It is the oldest English-built house in Pennsylvania. Turn right on Upland Avenue soon after entering city limits of Chester. Caleb Pusey was a friend and business associate of William Penn and operated the first gristmill in the colony. The Pusey House is part of the Landingford Plantation, which includes the Log House, the Mill, the Barn, and mill houses. A nearby schoolhouse built about 1849 has been acquired and is being developed as a museum in which hundreds of artifacts, unearthed in the area, will be displayed. The house is open on weekends, May to September, 1 to 4 P.M. Admission charge. Telephone: (610) 874-5665. Web site: www.delcohistory.org/fcph.

Old **St. Paul's Churchyard,** on Third Street between Market and Welsh streets in Chester, is one of the oldest Swedish burial place in the United States. A marble shaft marks the grave of John Morton, signer of the Declaration of Independence. The **Penn Memorial Landing Stone** marks the spot where William Penn first set foot on his colony, October 28, 1682. It is located at Front and Penn streets.

The **Delaware County Historical Society** was founded in 1895. Its historical library, containing local records, documents, newspapers, and genealogical material, is located at Wolfgram Memorial Library at Widener University in Chester, but is now in temporary quarters at the Malin Road Center of Delaware County Community College in Broomall. A new Museum of the History of Delaware County is being constructed in a wonderful old bank building at the corner of the Avenue of the State and Fourth Street. Call library for status of museum renovations, hours, and exhibits. Telephone: (610) 872-0502. Web site: www.dchs-pa.org.

The **Old Court House,** built for Governor William Penn in 1724, is the oldest building in the U.S. in continuous use. It is located at Fifth and Market streets and can be viewed from the outside only.

The permanent art collections at the **Widener University Art Gallery,** located on the main campus between Walnut and Melrose, include the Alfred O. Deshong Collection of 19th and 20th century American and European paintings and 18th and 19th-century Asian art objects. Open during the academic year, Tuesday, 10 A.M. to 7 P.M., Wednesday through Saturday, 10 A.M. to 4:30 P.M. Call or check web site for summer hours. Free admission. Telephone: (610) 499-1189. Web site: www.widener.edu/about/artgallery.

Taylor Memorial Arboretum, 10 Ridley Drive, Wallingford, offers guided tours through its grounds. Noted for its collection of heather, camellias, and ornamentals. Open Monday through Saturday, 9 A.M. to 4 P.M. Free admission. Telephone: (610) 876-2649.

Governor Printz Park and **Morton Homestead** in Essington are both historic shrines of New Sweden. These historic places, built by Swedish settlers before Pennsylvania's founding as an English colony, are administered by the state Historical and Museum Commission. Turn right on Wanamaker Avenue to enter **Governor Printz Park** at Second and Taylor Avenue in Essington. In 1643, Johan Printz, Royal Governor of New Sweden, built his capital on Tinicum Island in the Delaware River. This structure and others were destroyed by fire. Today visitors can see the remains of the capital, the first permanent European settlement in Pennsylvania established by Swedish and Finnish colonists, and Indian relics. The park is open weekdays, 8 A.M. to 5 P.M. and Sunday afternoons. Call to verify hours. Telephone: (610) 583 7221.

Web site: http://explorepahistory.com/attraction.php?id=1-B-AF2.

About a mile north of the park, on the banks of Darby Creek, at 100 Lincoln Avenue, which can be reached via Route 420, stands the **Morton Homestead.** It is among the earliest documented log cabins in the U.S. This Swedish log house, built circa 1650, was the home of John Morton, a signer of the Declaration of Independence. Tradition has it that Morton was born here in 1725, the great-grandson of Morton Mortenson, one of the colonists of the New Sweden Colony. The log house is typical of those built by early Swedish settlers whose primary purpose in establishing the New Sweden Colony was to trade with Native Americans. Open Wednesday, Thursday and Saturday, 9:30 A.M. to 3 P.M.; Friday 9:30 A.M. to 5 P.M.; June to August open only on Sundays, by appointment. Free admission. Telephone: (610) 583-7221. Web site: http://explorepahistory.com/attraction.php?id=1-B-AF2.

The original structure for the **Darby Friends' Meeting House** on Main Street was built in 1684. This one, the third on the site, was erected in 1805.

At 9 Creek Road in nearby Upper Darby, which is located north-west of Darby on Route 3 (ask locally for directions), is another log structure of Scandinavian construction. Open weekend afternoons. Call for hours. Telephone: (610) 623-1650.

BUCKS COUNTY

Bucks County, adjoining Philadelphia on the north, is steeped in early American history. The area is noted for its scenery, artists, and lovely old inns. For additional information about the area in advance of a visit, call ahead or look on line. Telephone: (215) 348-6000. Web site: www.buckscounty.org.

For a tour of Lower Bucks County of approximately 65 miles, leave

Philadelphia on Bristol Pike (1675). Two miles east of the Cornwell Heights city line at Cornwells Avenue is Vandegrift Burying Ground (1776).

Bristol, founded in 1681, has several historic buildings. **King George II Inn,** dating from 1765, is the nation's oldest inn in continuous operation. In the course of its history the inn, located at 102 Radcliffe Street, has had four presidents of the United States as guests. Telephone: (215) 788-5536. Web site: www.kginn.com. **Bristol Friends Meeting House Cemetery,** Walnut and Wood Streets, has many soldiers from the Revolutionary War. (The meetinghouse is no longer there.) Nearby at 225 Walnut Street in Bristol is the old **St. James Episcopal Church** and cemetery, whose parish was established around 1712. The cemetery is always open to the public; inquire at the parish house to view the inside of the church, which was built in 1857. For information regarding Sunday services and special events, telephone: (215) 788-2228. Web site: www.stjamesbristol.org.

Go north on Radcliffe Street to 610, the Victorian home of the late Joseph R. Grundy, manufacturer and U.S. senator. Now called the **Margaret R. Grundy Museum,** the house is a fine example of Victorian architecture. It has been furnished with antiques which belonged to the Grundy family. Open Monday through Friday, 1 to 4 P.M.; Saturday, 1 to 3 P.M. Closed Saturdays in July and August. Group tours by appointment. Free admission. Telephone: (215) 788-7891 .

Attached to the museum by underground passage is a library. An interesting building in itself, the contemporary library was constructed with one wall of windows offering a splendid view of the Delaware River. Web site: www.grundymuseum.org.

Every year on the third Saturday of October, a Historic Bristol Day is held featuring tours of all these historic buildings as well as a number of privately owned old houses opened especially for the occasion. For more information about the area and walking tours, contact Bristol Historic Preservation Inc. at 100 Prospect Street in Bristol. Telephone: (215) 826-8159.

Pennsbury Manor is the 17th-century reconstructed country home built by **William Penn** in 1681, 26 miles from Philadelphia. The manor, located at 400 Pennsbury Memorial Road, is just off Bordentown Road, about one mile outside Tullytown on the outskirts of Morrisville. Pennsbury Manor, deserted and neglected by 1800, was completely restored in the 1930s on the basis of historical and archaeological research. Tourists may visit the manor house, bake house, brew house, stables, worker's cottage and gardens. Guided tours are available. Special events and activities are scheduled from time to time. Open Tuesday through Saturday, 9 A.M. to 5 P.M.; Sunday, noon to 5 P.M. The last tour begins at 3:30 P.M. Closed Mondays and most state holidays. Open Memorial Day, Fourth of July, and Labor Day. Admission charge. Telephone: (215) 946-0400. Web site: www.pennsburymanor.org.

Fallsington is a colonial village built around the **Friends Meeting House** in which William Penn worshipped. Although the original meetinghouse is no longer standing, three meeting houses built in 1728, 1789, and 1841 still are and can be viewed from the exterior. The last is still in use by the Friends. The original meeting house was built in 1690. It is located three miles southwest of Trenton, only a few miles from the intersection of Route 1 and Tyburn Road.

Homes have been restored to original condition by a nonprofit organization. The **Burges-Lippincott House** is a fine example of 18th-century colonial architecture, and the **Stagecoach Tavern** has been restored as an 18th-century stage stop. Altogether, more than 25 pre-Revolutionary War buildings are clustered around Meetinghouse Square. The **Schoolmaster's House** (1757) provides a gateway to the square. The **Moon-Williamson House,** one section of which shows evidence of Swedish occupancy, is believed to be the oldest structure in the village. Guided walking tours cover Meetinghouse Square and the interiors of the Moon-Williamson Log House, the Burges-Lippincott House, and the Stagecoach Tavern. The one-hour tour focuses on historic architecture, material culture, and local history. Open mid-May through October, Monday through Saturday, 10:30 A.M. to 3:30 P.M. Groups of nine or more must make reservations. Admission charge. A self-guided walking tour map is also available from Historic Fallsington, 4 Yardley Avenue, Fallsington, PA 19054. Telephone: (215) 295-6567. Web site: www.historicfallsington.org.

West of Yardley on Route 332 is **Newtown,** one of Bucks County's most beautiful and picturesque colonial towns. More than three dozen colonial buildings have been preserved. The **Brick Hotel** has been serving three meals a day continuously since 1740 and is noted as a restaurant that usually requires reservations on the weekend. In the lobby is a mural depicting a colonial scene, painted by well-known artist Edward Hicks. Telephone: (215) 860-8313. The **Old Newtown Presbyterian Church** was erected in 1769, replacing an earlier structure. **Court Inn,** on Court Street at Centre Avenue, headquarters of the Newtown Historic Association, was a noted tavern built in 1733. Telephone: (215) 968-4004. Web site: www.newtownhistoric.org. A free brochure, *Walking Tour of Newtown,* is available. The **Hicks House,** 122 Penn Street, was the home of the noted colonial painter. This is a private residence. **Temperance House** (1722), 5 South State Street, was named for a sign painted by Edward Hicks. It is now a small hotel and four-star restaurant. Telephone: (215) 860-9975. **Bird-in-Hand House,** built in 1690, is the oldest frame building in the state. It served as an Army clothing depot during the Revolution. This house, now a private home, derives its name from a Hicks sign of Franklin's famous adage: "A bird in the hand is worth two in the bush."

The village of **Langhorne,** which is south on Route 413, also has some pre-Revolutionary War homes. Another **Hicks House,** Bellevue and Maple avenues, was built by Edward Hicks' grandfather. The **Richardson House** (1737), across the street, was once a general store. It is now a community center. The **Friends Meeting,** on Maple Avenue, was built in 1731.

Playwicki County Park, which is west on Route 213, is a mecca for bird watchers, botanists, and fishermen. It also offers picnicking, hiking, biking, playgrounds and ball fields. Two old stone-arched railroad bridges are favorite subjects of artists and camera fans. Telephone: (215) 757-0571 or (215) 348-6114. Web site: www.buckscounty.org/government/departments/parksandrec/Parks/Playwicki.aspx.

The **Buck Hotel,** at 1200 Buck Road in Feasterville (junction of Routes 213 and 532), was opened in 1735. It achieved fame as a meeting place of politicans. It is now known for its bands. Telephone: (215) 396-2002. Web site: www.thebuckhotel.com/ordereze/default.aspx.

For another tour take Route 532 from Philadelphia about 15 miles to **Washington Crossing.** This national shrine, now a state park, is located at 1112 River Road, three miles north of I-95 exit 31. The historic park is noted for the 22-foot, famed painting of Leutze's *Washington Crossing the Delaware,* which is housed in a memorial building. This is an exact copy by Robert B. Williams, a noted artist of Washington, D.C. Narration and music accompany the exhibit. Visitors can stand at the point of embarkation from which General Washington and his 2,400 men boarded boats on Christmas night, 1776. Their dramatic crossing marked the turning point of the American Revolution.

Among other places of interest in the park are the **Thompson-Neely**

House, furnished with pre-Revolutionary pieces; the **Johnson Ferry House,** which was occupied by Washington and his staff while the American Army regrouped after successfully crossing the Delaware. It is interpreted as an 18th century ferry keeper's family farm residence. The **Taylor House** and the **gristmill,** built about 1740, provided meal and flour for Continental troops. A nearby cemetery has unmarked headstones for the graves of some of America's first unknown soldiers. Admission charge. Groups may rent picnic pavilions. The Visitor Center/Museum is open Tuesday to Saturday, 9 A.M. to 5 P.M.; Sunday, noon to 5 P.M. Telephone: (215) 493-4076. Web site: www.cr.nps.gov/NR/travel/delaware/was.htm or www.phmc.state.pa.us.

Bowman's Hill Wildflower Preserve is located 2½ miles south of New Hope on River Road This preserve is best visited during the spring and summer months. Nearly 1000 species of Pennsylvania native wildflowers, trees, shrubs, and ferns be seen in naturalistic settings along 15 nature trails, excellent for birding, photography, exercise, and contemplation. Open daily, 8:30 A.M. to sundown. The visitor center and Twinleaf Shop are open daily, 9 A.M. to 5 P.M. Free admission. Virtual tour on web site. Mailing address: Bowman's Hill Wildflower Preserve, PO Box 685, New Hope, PA 18977. Telephone: (215) 862-2924. Web site: www.bhwp.org.

A detour to the **Van Sant Covered Bridge** built in 1875 may be of interest. Take Aquetong Road past Thompson Memorial Church, then left on Covered Bridge Road.

The main route is north to the **New Hope** area. This town is an internationally-known artists' center, with many galleries and frequent art shows. It is also replete with points of historic interest, and has many antique and gift shops, fine restaurants, and unusual specialty shops. A new Visitor Center is located at 1 West Mechanic, corner of Main and Mechanic Streets. Open Monday through Thursday 10 A.M. to 5 P.M., Friday and Sunday, 10 A.M. to 6 P.M., and Saturday, 10 A.M. to 7 P.M. Telephone: (215) 862-5030. Web site: www.newhopevisitorcenter.org.

New Hope is nestled along the banks of the Delaware River (northwest of Washington Crossing on Route 32) and dates from the 19th century. The **New Hope Town Hall** (1839) is open to visitors during regular business hours. The New Hope Library (c. 1750) on Ferry Street, which was in a converted church, is now a restaurant. Many old homes have been converted into shops, such as **Vansant House** on Mechanic Street (probably the oldest house in New Hope) and **Flood House** on South Main Street.

Leisurely sightseeing trips on mule-drawn barges are offered on the historic **Delaware Canal,** by the New Hope Canal Boat Company, 149 South Main Street. Canal boats are located at Lock #11 along the canal. Trips are offered weekends in April; several times daily May 1 through October 31. Fare charge. Telephone: (215) 862-0758.

For an interesting 10-mile side trip, go north on Route 32 along the old canal to **Center Bridge,** a town popularized by artist E. W. Redfield, whose stone home is at the left of the bridge. At Lumberville is the noted **Hard Times Tavern,** now a private home. From Cuttalossa Road, turn left past Solebury School, built in 1755. In Lahaska, off Route 263, there are many fine antique shops. A charming shopping area, **Peddler's Village** is made up of about 46 boutiques scattered about a village green. They specialize in arts and crafts and imported wares. Continuing west on Route 202, pass the **Buckingham Friends Meeting,** built in 1768 and used as a hospital during the Revolution.

The Bucks County Playhouse, located at 70 South Main Street, is a professional theatre with a season that runs from April through December. It was originally the Parry Mills, destroyed by fire in 1790 and rebuilt. Admission charge. For information regarding performances, call or visit their web site. Telephone: (215) 315-7788. Web site: www.bcptheater.org.

The nearby **Parry Mansion** (c. 1784) at 45 South Main, houses a small museum with five different rooms, each set in a different period from 1775-1900. It is maintained by New Hope Historical Society. Open for tours, Saturday and Sunday from late April through early December. Admission charge. Call for hours. Telephone: (215) 862-5652. Web site: newhopehs.org/guidedtours.html.

Doylestown is farther west on Route 202. **The Mercer Museum,** 84 South Pine Street, was built by Dr. Henry Mercer in 1916. The museum houses a vast collection of more than 50,000 objects depicting everyday life and work in pre-industrial America. Housed in a towering castle that is worth a trip in itself, the museum displays such treasures as a Conestoga wagon, a whaling boat, and antique fire engines. The Spruance Library, with its enormous number of books and manuscripts, is a gold mine for historical researchers and genealogists.

Original paintings by Edward Hicks, Jonathan and William Trego, and other famous artists are on display; also folk art, crafts, and ceramics. Open year round, Monday through Saturday, 10 A.M. to 5 P.M.; Tuesday 10 A.M. to 9 p.m, and Sunday, noon to 5 P.M. Admission charge. Telephone: (215) 345-0210. Web site: www.mercermuseum.org.

Fonthill, East Court Street and Route 313, houses a collection of paintings, antiques, and Mercer tiles that were made on the premises. Tour reservations are suggested. Open Monday through Saturday, 10 a.m. to 5 P.M. Sunday, noon to 5 P.M. Last tour starts at 4 P.M. Admission charge. Telephone: (215) 345-0210. Web site: www.mercermuseum.org.

The **Moravian Pottery and Tileworks,** 130 Swamp Road, is a working pottery, where tiles for the State Capitol buildings were made. It is a National Historic Landmark and handmade tiles are still produced in a manner similar to that developed by the founder and builder, Dr. Henry Mercer. Tours available. Open daily, 10 A.M. to 4:45 P.M. Admission charge. Telephone: (215) 348.6098. Web site: www.buckscounty.org/government/departments/Tileworks/index.aspx.

From Doylestown the direct route to Philadelphia is south on Route 611. One may also visit other historic sites in **Wrightstown,** which would add a few miles to the tour. The township was first settled in 1684, and its boundaries date from 1692. Go east on Route 202 to Buckingham and right on Route 413 to Wrightstown. Telephone: (215) 598-3313. Web site: www.wrightstownpa.org.

Wrightstown is the site of **The Octagonal Schoolhouse** (1802) on Swamp Road, off Route 232, and the **Walking Purchase Monument,** on the Friends Meeting House grounds. It recalls the "walk" planned by Thomas Penn, whereby the land over which a man could walk in a day and a half could be purchased from the Indians. Three men started at sunrise, September 1737, and practically ran 100 miles, thus gaining 500,000 acres of the Indians' best land for a trifle.

South of Wrightstown, is **Tyler State Park.** The park encompasses 1,711 acres that offer picnicking, hiking, biking, horseback riding, disc golf, playgrounds, sports fields, fishing, and boating. Winter fun includes ice skating and fishing, sledding, tobogganing, and cross-country skiing. The nearby **Schofield Ford Covered Bridge,** was built over the Neshaminy Creek in 1874. At 181 feet, the hemlock construction was the longest covered bridge in the country until it burned in 1991. It was rebuilt through volunteer efforts and rededicated in September 1997. The dimensions of the new version are some 15 feet shorter than the original, but the restoration of this treasured landmark is was a community service that surpasses all measure. For an on-line map of other covered bridges in Bucks County, visit www.livingplaces.net/pa/bucks/coveredbridges/coveredbridgemap.htm. Or contact Tyler State Park, 101 Swamp Road, Newtown, PA 18940. Telephone: (215) 968-2021. Web site: www.dcnr.state.pa.us. You can also link to additional information about covered bridges in Bucks County through www.bctc.org. For more on covered bridges, also see the "Special Interest Section." To conclude your tour at this point, return to Route 232 and head south into Philadelphia.

For an 80-mile extension to Upper Bucks County continue on Route 611 and turn right on Pt. Pleasant Road, to River Road along the Delaware River. The **Delaware Canal,** opened in 1830 and operated for a century, lies between the highway and river.

A splendid panoramic view of **Tohickon Creek Valley** is your reward for ascending **Boileau Rock,** a 200-foot cliff at Horseshoe Bend. Nearby, off Dark Hollow Road, are **Loux Covered Bridge,** built in 1874 and **Cabin Run Covered Bridge,** built in 1871. Proceed north on Route 32 to Tinicum Creek. The **Erwinna Covered Bridge** is a short distance to the left.

Tinicum County Park, up Route 32 a half mile, offers 126 acres for picnicking, hiking, biking, playgrounds, ball fields, boating, fishing, ice skating, eight sites for group and individual camping, and includes the old John Stover residence. Telephone: (215) 757-0571 or (215) 348-6114. Web site: www.buckscounty.org/government/departments/parksandrec/Parks/Tinicum.aspx.

Ralph Stover State Park, which marks the site of a former grist mill, is located in central Bucks County, two miles off Route 32. It provides tourist cabins and facilities for hiking, fishing, swimming, whitewater canoeing and kayaking, nature study, and athletics. There is a mile-long trail to High Rocks, a scenic outlook point. Call or visit web site for further information. Telephone: (610) 982-5560. Web site: www.dcnr.state.pa.us/stateparks/findapark/ralphstover/index.htm.

The **Uhlerstown Covered Bridge,** built in 1832 over the Delaware Canal, is unique with its windows in midspan. Proceed to Upper Black Eddy, and turn left into **Ringing Rocks Park.** Rocks in this 3½-acre field of boulders, fragments of Triassic diabase, produce bell-like sounds when hit with a hammer. The park also offers picnicking and biking. Nearby is an attractive waterfall. Telephone (215) 757-0571.

Web site: www.buckscounty.org/government/departments/parksandrec/parks/ringingrocks.aspx.

A short distance west on Route 212 leads to **Durham,** which was organized in 1775. Here are ruins of **Durham Furnace** built in 1727. It produced chains, cannonballs, and small shot for the Continental Army. Web site: explorepahistory.com/hmarker.php?markerId=1-A-162. Just west of the furnace at 35 South Front Street in Catasauqua is the house of **George Taylor,** a signer of the Declaration of Independence and officer of the furnace company. The George Taylor Mansion is owned and operated by the Lehigh County Historical Society. Open June through October, Saturdays and Sundays, 1 to 4 P.M. Admission charge. Telephone: (610) 435-4664. Web site: www.nps.gov/nr/travel/delaware/tay.htm

About 1½ miles from Durham, on Route 212, is **Haupt's Mill Covered Bridge,** over Durham Creek. Ruins of an old mill are nearby. On Route 412, four-tenths of a mile west of Springtown, is the **Indian Walk Monument,** the midday stop of the group of men who made the "Walking Purchase" of 1737. **Pleasant Valley,** on Route 212, is a very old settlement with many old homes.

Continue to **Quakertown** seven miles south. This town's claim to fame rests on the legend that the Liberty Bell was hidden here in September 1777 after the British occupied Philadelphia. The bell was then kept in Allentown while the British occupied the capital of the young nation. The original **Friends Meeting House** in Quakertown was founded in 1730; the current one dates from 1862. **The Red Lion** (1748) is across the street from a former stagecoach stop on the route between Philadelphia and Bethlehem. The Red Lion provided lodging for travel-weary passengers and was one of the largest hotels in upper Bucks County. An event known as John Frye's Rebellion is said to have occurred in front of the Red Lion. The house was expanded in 1810 and the kitchen connected to the main building with further expansion in 1865. Now called Donzes Red Lion Inn, the two-hundred-year-old establishment continues to serve wayfarers and tourists with fine food and lodging. Telephone: 538.1776. Web site: www.mccoolesredlioninn.com.

The **Burgess-Foulke House Museum,** administered by the Quakertown Historical Society, 26 N. Main Street, is open summer weekends and by appointment. Call the Historical Society for further information about walking tours, either self-guided or by appointment, and other noteworthy attractions in the area. Telephone: (215) 536-3298.

Turn south on Route 313, to Route 563. To the left are two parks, **Nockamixon,** and **Lake Towhee. Nockamixon State Park** is a 5,283 acre day-use park. During the summer you can enjoy the swimming pool, boating picnicking, fishing, biking and horseback riding trails. In the winter the park offers ice skiing and fishing, cross-country skiing and sledding. There are ten cabins available for rent that sleep six to eight. Open April 1 through October 31, daily 8 A.M. to sunset. For more information contact: Nockamixon State Park, 1542 Mountain View Drive, Quakertown, PA 18951. Telephone: (215) 529-7300, reservations: (888) PA-PARKS. Web site: www.dcnr.state.pa.us.

The entrance to **Lake Towhee Park** is from Old Bethlehem Road. This 552 acre park with its 50 acre lake offers playgrounds, picnicking, ballfields, horseback, riding, biking, boating, fishing, camping, ice skating, nature study trails, and bird watching. There are also 17 campsites for groups and individuals. Visitors may have the experience of wild mallards, black ducks, and Canadian geese approaching them as they picnic. Posted nature trails have been developed in this park, with "walk books" available to interested visitors. Telephone: (215) 757-0571. Web site: www.buckscounty.org/government/ departments/parksandrec/Parks/Towhee.aspx.

Return to Route 313, turning south (left) to Route 113. To the left is **Irish Meeting House Cemetery** (1725). **Deep Run Mennonite Church,** on Deep Run Road, was established in the early 18th century. Return to Dublin, and Route 313. Of special interest to those of the Roman Catholic faith is the Shrine of the American **Czestochowa** in Doylestown. To reach the shrine, turn right on Ferry Road. The shrine houses a reproduction of the famous Black Madonna icon in the Shrine of Jasna Gora, Poland, which is believed to be more than 1,600 years old. The Shrine is open daily, 7:15 A.M. to 4:30 P.M., business office and monastery, Monday through Friday, 9 A.M. to 4:30 P.M. Free admission. Telephone: (215) 345-0600 or (215) 345-0601. Web site: www.czestochowa.us.

NORTHWEST OF PHILADELPHIA

The area northwest of Philadelphia is rich in historic sites connected with colonial America and the Revolutionary War period. Outstanding is **Valley Forge National Military Park,** one of the shrines of our war for independence. It is located on the Schuylkill River, between King of Prussia and Phoenixville on Route 23, near

Exit 24 of the Pennsylvania Turnpike and accessible from Philadelphia via the Schuylkill Expressway, Route 76. Washington's army was encamped here from December 19, 1777 until June 19, 1778. The 3,000-acre park comprises the major portion of the area occupied by the Continental Army. Begin your tour at the park's new Welcome Center (completed in 2002) located at the junction of Route 23 and North Gulf Road. Telephone: (610) 783-1099. Web site: www.nps.gov/vafo/index.htm.

Visitors can walk through **Washington's Headquarters,** the building in which he lived and conferred with such notables as Lafayette, Knox, Wayne, Greene, Hamilton, and von Steuben. Varnum's Quarters are sometimes open to the public, but check first at the Visitor's Center. Throughout the park are log huts, replicas of the quarters which housed Washington's soldiers during the bitter winter of 1777-78. Visitors may also see restored fortifications, redoubts, and numerous monuments. Special activities are planned throughout the year. Four special dates are celebrated annually: December 19, the day the Revolutionary army encamped here; the weekend nearest to the official observation of George Washington's birthday in February; the date of the American Alliance with France, May 6; and the day the army marched out, June 19. Troop musters are held periodically. Bus tours featuring a taped narration are available during the summer months, and on a limited basis in the fall. Bikes can be rented during the summer months and on fall weekends. New activities and programs are planned frequently. It is best to check with the park for specific, timely information. The hours specified below apply to the Visitor's Center and Washington's Headquarters. Open daily, 9 A.M. to 5 P.M. Closed Christmas Day. Free admission. Telephone: (610) 783-1099. Web site: www.nps.gov/vafo/index.htm.

The Valley Forge Historical Society is joining forces with the National Park Service to create the National Center for the American Revolution, said to be the nation's "premier educational, historical, and cultural institution concerning the American Revolution." The center is slated for completion in 2005 and will house the Historical Society's extensive collection of memorabilia as well as significant artifacts under the protection of the National Park Service, some of which have never been displayed. Telephone: (610) 975-4939. Web site: explorepahistory.com/attraction.php?id=1-B-273C.

The Washington Memorial Chapel, built in memory of George Washington, is nearby on Route 23, adjacent to Valley Forge Park.

Sunday services honor a different state of the Union each week. The Washington Memorial National Carillon, which has 58 bells, is used for recitals by guest carilloneurs from the United States and Europe. Souvenirs and homemade edibles are available at the Cabin Shop behind the chapel. Open Monday through Friday, 8 A.M. to 5 P.M.; Saturday, 8 A.M. to 5:30 P.M.; Sunday, 8 A.M. to 6 P.M. Free admission. Telephone: (610) 783-0120. Web site: 209.200.101.38/frontpage.cfm.

Mill Grove/Audubon Wildlife Sanctuary at Audobon and Pawlings Roads in Audubon was the first home in America of John James Audubon, the noted artist and naturalist. Audubon lived here from 1803 to 1806 and gained his first impressions of American birds and animals from trips into the nearby woods and fields. His art studio and taxidermy room have been restored in the mansion's attic. The interior decorations, collections of Audubon lithographs, and exhibits are notable memorials of his achievements. To reach Mill Grove from Valley Forge, go north on Route 363, across the Schuylkill River, and left on Audubon Road. From the Pennsylvania Turnpike, take Exit 24.

The 175-acre sanctuary at Mill Grove includes six miles of trails where visitors may observe wildlife, particularly the many species of birds attracted to the area. About 51 species nest in the sanctuary. Approximately 174 species pass through on migration Routes. The mansion is open Tuesday through Saturday, 10 A.M. to 4 P.M.; Sunday, 1 to 4 P.M. The sanctuary is open 7 A.M. to dusk, Tuesday through Sunday. The Mill Grove/Audubon Wildlife Sanctuary is closed on Monday. Free admission. Telephone: (610) 666-5593. Web site: pa.audubon.org/john-james-audubon-center-mill-grove.

Morgan Log House (c. 1700) at 850 Weikel Road, Kulpsville, west of Route 363 between Snyder and Allentown Roads, was built by Daniel Boone's grandparents. This two-story house set on two acres of land is listed on the National Register of Historic Places. It is a splendid example of early domestic log architecture and ninety percent of the structure is original. Decorated in the style of Welsh pioneer families in early Pennsylvania, the house contains fine antique furniture, metals and household implements, and 18th-century Pennsylvania decorative arts are exhibited. Gardens feature period herbs, flowers, native plants and a picnic grove. Guided tours, special programs and workshops are offered throughout the year. Open April 1 through December 30, Saturday and Sunday, noon to 5 P.M. Other tours

Monday through Friday by appointment only. Admission charge. Telephone: (215) 368-2480. Web site: www.morganloghouse.org.

Perkiomen Bridge, on Route 422 at Collegeville, is one of the oldest bridges still in use in the United States. It was built in 1799 at a cost of $20,000 with funds raised through a lottery. The **Perkiomen Bridge Hotel** was built in 1721 and still functions as a restaurant. The public rooms are decorated in part according to the period. Telephone: (610) 489-4546.

Augustus Lutheran Church at 717 West Main in Trappe is the oldest unaltered Lutheran church in America. Construction was begun in 1743 and the church was dedicated in 1745. The pastor was the Reverend Dr. Henry Melchoir Muhlenberg, noted theologian, who is recognized as the patriarch of American Lutheranism. He is buried in the churchyard. Tours are conducted by appointment. Telephone: (610) 489-9625. Web site: www.oldaugustus.org.

Muhlenberg House, home of Pastor Muhlenberg during his later years (1776-1787), 201 West Main Street, has been professionally restored by the Historical Society of Trappe. Open June through August on Sundays, 1:30 to 4 P.M. Other hours by appointment. Telephone: (610) 489-2624 or (610) 489-7622.   The **Peter Wentz Farmstead,** at Center Point (Worcester Township), is located on Route 73 east of the 363 intersection. Here General Washington established headquarters before and after the historic battle of Germantown. The house, which dates from 1758, has been restored and furnished according to the year 1777. The working farm includes crops representative of the colonial period such as flax, tobacco, oats, pumpkins, rye and brown corn. The barn, which is also open to the public, houses Durham cattle, horned Dorset sheep, a family of Morgan horses, and gray geese. Open Tuesday through Saturday, 10 A.M. to 4 P.M.; Sunday, 1 to 4 P.M. Closed Mondays and major holidays. Free Admission. Telephone: (610) 584-5104. Web site: www.peterwentzfarmsteadsociety.org.

Hope Lodge, at the intersection of Bethlehem Pike (old Route 309) and 73 in Whitemarsh, was built between 1743-1748 by Samuel Morris. During the Revolutionary War it was the headquarters for Surgeon General John Cochran and his officers. It is an architectural masterpiece in the finest Georgian tradition. The interior is very impressive with large fireplaces, classical pilasters and pediments, arched doorways, and exquisite 18th- and 19th-century furnishings. There is a notable collection of Chinese export porcelain, and the paintings in the house include portraits by Thomas Sully and Jacob Zicholtz. Open

Wednesday through Saturday, 9 A.M. to 5 P.M.; Sunday, noon to 5 P.M. Also open Memorial Day, Fourth of July, and Labor Day. Admission charge. Telephone: (215) 646-1595. Web site: www.ushistory.org/hope. The **Abington Art Center** is located at 515 Meetinghouse Road in Jenkintown. The art center is housed in the Lessing J. Rosenwald estate, and its art-deco style art gallery (one room of which has been recreated at the Library of Congress) dates from 1939. Now one of the largest fine arts centers in Pennsylvania, Abington Center features changing fine arts exhibits from the United States and abroad. In addition to its regular fine arts, dance, and crafts curricula, the center periodically holds, lectures, and workshops. Open Monday through Friday, 10 A.M. to 5 P.M.; Thursdays, 10 A.M. to 7 P.M. For special events, contact the center. Free admission. Charges for some tours and events, as well as for classes. Telephone: (215) 887-4882. Web site: www.abingtonartcenter.org.

Abington Friends Meeting, at 520 Meetinghouse Road in Jenkintown, has existed as a Quaker meetinghouse since 1697. Here, Benjamin Lay, in 1737, published his book against slavery.

Bryn Athyn Cathedral, on Route 232 at Bryn Athyn, is a Swedenborgian Center noted for its distinctive 14th-century Gothic and 12th-century Romanesque architecture. Tours are available by appointment for groups of five or more. Telephone: (267) 502-4600. Web site: www.brynathyncathedral.org.

Beth Sholom Synagogue, in Elkins Park, is the only synagogue ever designed by Frank Lloyd Wright, the distinguished architect. Call for information about hours of operation. Telephone: (215) 887-1342. Web site: bethsholomcongregation.org.

The Barnes Foundation, 300 North Latchs Lane, in Merion, contains a notable collection of Impressionist art. More than 1,000 paintings hang in this appropriately French mansion. Among the artists represented are: Cezanne, Picasso, Matisse, and Renoir; as well as Titian, El Greco, and Tintoretto. Advanced reservations are required for all visits. Open Friday through Sunday, 9:30 A.M. to 5 P.M. In July and August, open Wednesday through Friday, 9:30 A.M. to 5 P.M. Admission charge. Telephone: (610) 667-0290. Web site: www.barnesfoundation.org.

Old Gulph Schoolhouse, Matsonford Road, Upper Merion, was built circa 1696. It served as a rural schoolhouse but is now used for religious education. **Hanging Rock,** at Montgomery Avenue at Gulph Mills, has an unusual rock formation protruding over the highway. It is said that Washington's engineers shaped it.

Merion Meeting House, on Montgomery Avenue in Merion, was originally a log structure, replaced by a stone building in 1695. William Penn, founder of the Commonwealth, preached here. It is still used as a place of worship by the Quakers.

Old Roberts School in Upper Merion, built in 1848, is fully restored as a period schoolhouse. It has a small basement museum, and stands in front of the modern Roberts School.

Pottsgrove Manor, a state-administered historic site, is located on Route 422 at the west edge of Pottstown. Built in the 1750s by John Potts, the noted ironmaster, it is distinguished for its fine architectural features and elegant furnishings, especially its Philadelphia Chippendale furniture. The mansion is surrounded by beautifully landscaped grounds, and an 18th-century flower and herb garden. Open Tuesday through Saturday, 10 a. m. to 4 P.M.; Sunday, 1 to 4 P.M. Last tour begins at 3:30 P.M. Admission charge. Telephone: (610) 326-4014. Web site: www.montcopa.org/historicsites.

Northwest of Schwenksville, off Route 29, is **Green Lane Park.** This park features an 814-acre reservoir that is well stocked with game fish. Telephone: (215) 234-4528.

Web site: www2.montcopa.org/parks/cwp/view.asp?A=1516&Q=26377.

Nature study enthusiasts may be interested in visiting some of the areas described below. There is **Morris Arboretum,** at Chestnut Hill in West Philadelphia off Route 422, a 175-acre collection of over 12,000 native and exotic trees and shrubs. Special gardens include an English park, an oak alley, an azalea meadow, a swan pond, a Japanese garden, and a rose garden. Open April through October, Monday through Friday, 10 A.M. to 4 P.M., Saturday and Sunday, 10 A.M. to 5 P.M.; June through August, open Thursday open until 8:30 P.M.; November through March daily, 10 A.M. to 4 P.M. Admission charge. Telephone: (215) 247-5777. Web site: www.upenn.edu/arboretum.

Swiss Pines Japanese Garden, at Malvern, west of the Pennsylvania Turnpike and Route 29, offers picturesque outdoor Japanese and Polynesian gardens, a large rhododendron display, and several ponds with wildfowl. Open from the second Wednesday in May through the end of November, Wednesday through Friday, 10 A.M. to 3 P.M., Saturday, 9 A.M. to 1 P.M. Closed during inclement weather or if wet from heavy rain. Admission charge. Children under 12 not admitted. Telephone: (610) 935-3571.

The **Elmwood Park Zoo,** Norristown, displays more than 150 wild animals of North America including jaguars, cougars, elk otters, bobcats, alligators and many more. There is a barn exhibit of domesticated farm animals including gentle cow, goat and sheep. A "wild west" pony ride for kids, large shaded picnic grove and food concession. Open daily, 10 A.M. to 5 P.M.; extended hours July 4th through Labor Day to 8 P.M. Closed on major holidays and severe winter weather days. Admission charge. Telephone : (610) 277-3825. Web site: www.elmwoodparkzoo.org.

Reading-Berks Area

The Reading-Berks area offers visitors a wide array of activities and historical sites such as the Daniel Boone Homestead, Hopewell Village, the Crystal Cave, and the Conrad Weiser Homestead. Reading also established a reputation as the first "factory outlet capital of the U.S.A." Visitors to the area may also enjoy Pennsylvania Dutch meals and roam through any of its six picturesque farmers' markets. For additional information stop by the Reading & Berks County Visitors Center at 352 Penn Street in Reading. Telephone: (800) 443-6610 or (610) 375-4085. Web site: www.readingberkspa.com.

Reading and Vicinity

Hopewell Furnance National Historic Site, 2 Mark Bird Lane in Elverson, is administered by the National Park Service and is one of the oldest ironworks in the country. Life in Hopewell Village, from its origin during the Revolutionary decade to the last iron production over a century later, was dominated by the constant operation of its massive furnace. The furnace was established in 1770 to supply cast iron for Mark Bird's three forges in Birdsboro. A village grew up around the furnace, consisting of the families of more than 65 workmen. The furnace prospered, supplying pig iron for forges and red-hot iron for stoves, pots, and kettles. Hopewell's prosperity peaked in the mid-1830s, except for a brief boom during the Civil War. In 1883, the furnace "blew out" for the last time. On a fascinating walking tour, visitors can see a coaling shed, anthracite furnace, charcoal hearth, water wheel, and blacksmith machinery. Open daily, 9 A.M. to 5 P.M. Admission charge. Telephone: (610) 582-8773. Web site: www.nps.gov/hofu.

French Creek State Park adjoins Hopewell Village. The park has two lakes, Hopewell and Scotts Run, which are available for boating and fishing, a swimming pool, frisbee golf and orienteering/map classes. For the hiker and mountain biker, there are almost forty miles of marked trails accessible from the camping area. The park has 201 modern campsites with access to showers and flush toilets, and 10 furnished cabins that sleep six that are available for use year round. There are also primitive group tenting sites for thirty or more people. Telephone: (610) 582-9680, camping reservations: (888) PA-PARKS. Web site: www.dcnr.state.pa.us/stateparks/findapark/frenchcreek.

The **Daniel Boone Homestead** is where Daniel Boone was born in 1734. The homestead is located in Birdsboro, 400 Daniel Boone Road, and is now a museum depicting country life of 18th-century Pennsylvania. Near the restored house are a blacksmith shop, smokehouse, and barn. The homestead area is a state sanctuary for deer, raccoon, pheasants, quail, and other wildlife. A nearby lake offers public fishing. Open Tuesday to Saturday, 9 A.M. to 5 P.M.; Sunday, noon to 5 P.M. Closed Monday. Admission charge. Telephone: (610) 582-4900. Web site: www.danielboonehomestead.org.

The **Mary Merritt Doll Museum,** 843 Ben Franklin Highway West in Douglassville, has a display of more than 1,500 dolls—toys, miniatures, and antiques—some dating from the early 1700s. There are also miniature period rooms, furnished dollhouses, and a full-size replica of a mid-l9th-century Philadelphia toy shop. Open Monday through Saturday, 10 A.M. to 4:30 P.M.; Sunday, 1 to 5 P.M. Closed Tuesdays. Admission charge. Telephone: (610) 385-3809. Web site: www.merritts.com.

Adjacent is **Merritt's Museum of Childhood.** Here one can see rooms furnished with early Pennsylvania furniture, Stiegel glass, and cigar store Indians. There is a very large collection of iron and metal ware of all periods. The thousands of articles are well arranged to give the visitor a bird's-eye view of the whole panorama of 18th- and 19th- century life in America. Hours same as for doll museum.

The **Boyertown Museum of Historic Vehicles** is located at 85 South Walnut Street in Boyertown. The museum features a collection of about 80 vehicles, all of which were built in Southeastern Pennsylvania, dating from 1763 to 1982. Open Tuesday to Sunday, 9:30 a.m. to 4 P.M. Admission charge. Telephone: (610) 367-2090. Web site: www.boyertownmuseum.org.

Reading is the major city in the Berks County area. One of Reading's main tourist attractions is the **Pagoda,** located atop Mt. Penn (1,200 ft.). The pagoda is listed in the National Register of Historic Places. Visitors are afforded a wide view of the surrounding countryside from the Observation Tower. The Pagoda is open daily,

12 noon to 5 P.M. Free admission. Telephone: (610) 375-6399. Web site: www.berksweb.com/pagoda-skyline-inc/pagoda.

The **Reading Public Museum,** 500 Museum Road, has an unusual collection of art from the Early American and Hudson River schools, and Pennsylvania German folk art. Open Monday, 9 A.M. to 4 P.M. (group tours only), Tuesday, Thursday, Friday, and Saturday, 11 A.M. to 5 P.M., Wednesday, 11 A.M. to 8 P.M., Sunday, noon to 5 P.M. Holidays, noon to 4 P.M. Admission charge. Adjacent to the museum is the **Planetarium.** There are star shows and laser shows at different times. Call for a schedule. Admission charge. Telephone: (610) 371-5850. Web site: www.readingpublicmuseum.org.

The **Historical Society of Berks County** is located at 940 Centre Avenue in Reading. The museum contains artifacts of the 18th and 19th-centuries. Open Tuesday to Saturday, 9 A.M. to 4 P.M. Admission charge. Telephone: (610) 375-4375. Web site: www.berkshistory.org.

Other places of interest in and about the City of Reading include: **Angelica Park,** a 45-acre regional park south of Reading offering boating, fishing, picnicking, and sports facilities; **Antietam Lake,** part of the City of Reading water supply, offering fishing and picnicking; **Callowhill Historical District,** where many fine residences, churches, and commercial buildings are now preserved around Penn Square and along North and South Fifth Street as examples of Federal and Victorian period architecture; **City Park and Firemen's Bandshell,** a 33-acre park, also known as Penn's Commons, where music and cultural events are regularly scheduled throughout the summer; **Lake Ontelaunee** bird sanctuary, located east of Route 61 and north of Reading, near Leesport; and **Penn Square,** located at the center of downtown Reading. This historic square once contained public market houses. The square now hosts many cultural, social, and commercial festivities throughout the year.

Reading is famous as the original outlet shopping mecca of the eastern United States. In town, there are several outlets where shoppers can buy an assortment of merchandise, especially clothing, shoes, linen, leather goods, power tools, and outdoor furniture at bargain prices. For information about the outlets, contact the Reading Outlet Center. Telephone: (800) 5-OUTLET. Web site: www.outletsonline.com/roc.

St. Peter's Village, Route 23 and St. Peters Road in St. Peters, south of Reading, was owned by the Knauer family in 1731. The center of a former quarrying operation, the historic buildings now house shops of modern goods. The Inn at St. Peter's is open for meals

Wednesday through Sunday. The village is open year round; some shops closed Mondays. Telephone: (610) 469-2600.

Northern Berks County

You will find a substantial farmer's market and flea market on Fridays and Saturdays one mile south of Kutztown at **Renninger's Antique & Farmers Market,** 740 Noble Street. The Farmers Market is open 10 A.M. to 7 P.M. on Friday and 8 A.M. to 4 P.M. on Saturday. The Antique Market is open 8 A.M. to 4 P.M. on Saturday and the Flea Market is open 6 A.M. to 2 P.M. on Saturday. Telephone: (610) 683-6848. Web site: www.renningers.com.

As you head into downtown Kutztown, Route 222 becomes Main Street. You may wish take a ride back in time aboard the Kutztown Scenic Train. Originally a key transportation link to the area, the train has been in operation almost 150 years. Station located on Main Street. Fare charge. Call for departure times and rates. Telephone: (610) 756-6469. Web site: www.kemptontrain.com.

A worthwhile detour is the **Crystal Cave,** on Crystal Cave Road (Route 3), two miles west of Kutztown. Crystal Cave has been a tourist attraction ever since it was discovered in 1871. The cave has exquisite stalactite and stalagmite formations, enhanced by artificial lighting. Guides present an informative video explaining the history of cave formation. The cave is situated in a 125-acre park that includes a museum, picnic areas, hiking trails, miniature golf, panning for gold, and facilities for other family activities. Open March, October, and November daily, 9 A.M. to 5 P.M., May and September, extended weekend hours to 6 P.M., Memorial Day through Labor Day weekend hours extended to 7 P.M. and weekday hours extended to 6 P.M. Telephone: (610) 683-6765. Web site: www.crystalcavepa.com.

Blue Rocks, 341 Sousley Road in Lenhartsville, is a family campground that has an ice age fossil stretching a mile long and covering 15 acres. Blue Rocks offers camping, hiking, playground, gameroom and picnicking facilities as well as refreshments and supplies. There is also a swimming pool and catch and release fishing. Reservations required for more than 2 days of camping. Open daily, 9 A.M. to 5 P.M. Admission charge. Telephone: (610) 756-6366. Web site: www.bluerockscampground.com.

The little town of Kempton is also the headquarters for the **Wanamaker, Kempton and Southern Railroad,** 42 Community Center Drive. The trains take the Hawk Mountain Line, a scenic meandering route through woods and along the banks of Maiden Creek to the small town of Wanamaker and back to Kempton. At the Wanamaker end of the tour there is a shop that sells antiques and a trackside picnic grove with lovely nature trails. The W.K.&S. operates weekends, May through October, 1 to 4 P.M. Fare charge. Telephone: (610) 756-6469. Web site: www.kemptontrain.com.

Just outside Shartlesville is **Roadside America,** billed as "the World's Greatest Indoor Miniature Village." A total of 67 scenes make up this miniature panorama. Open July through Labor Day, weekdays, 9 A.M. to 6:30 P.M.; weekends, to 7 P.M.; September through June, weekdays, 10 A.M. to 5 P.M., weekends, to 6 P.M. Admission charge. Telephone: (610) 488-6241. Web site: www.roadsideamericainc.com.

Koziar's Christmas Village features a seasonal spectacle of more than a half million lights. It's located at 782 Christmas Village Road in Bernville. This enterprise also offers an unusual collection of Christmas gifts, decorations and ceramics. The special Christmas display is open November 1 to Thanksgiving, Friday, 6 to 9 P.M., Saturday and Sunday, 5:30 to 9:30 P.M. From Thanksgiving to January 1 the hours are extended, Monday to Friday, 6 to 9 P.M.; Saturday and Sundays, 5 to 9:30 P.M. Admission charge. Telephone: (610) 488-1110. Web site: www.koziarschristmasvillage.com.

From Bernville, travel to Womelsdorf to visit the **Conrad Weiser Homestead** at 28 Weiser Road. The simple stone house built by Weiser in 1729 (enlarged in 1751) is set in a beautiful wooded area. Conrad Weiser, a German immigrant, served as ambassador and interpreter to the Iroquois Nation. Weiser's knowledge of the Indians made him an adept negotiator and in part his efforts made Pennsylvania the last of the original colonies to experience warfare between Native Americans and European inhabitants.

The stone home, spring house, and gravesite are set in a beautiful 26-acre park with a museum and memorial to one of Pennsylvania's earliest peacekeepers. Open year round, Wednesday through Saturday, 9 A.M. to 5 P.M.; Sunday, noon to 5 P.M. Admission charge. Telephone: (610) 589-2934. Web site: conradweiserhomestead.org.

LANCASTER AREA

Lancaster and the surrounding **Pennsylvania Dutch country** comprise one of the nation's major tourist attractions. The city of Lancaster is located approximately 100 miles northeast of

Washington, D.C. One of America's oldest inland cities, Lancaster has many historic buildings in its downtown area, as well as the oldest continuously operating farmers' market in the United States. This city was the nation's capital for one day, September 27, 1777; it was the state capital from 1799 to 1812.

Visitors come to **Lancaster County** to visit the farms, homes, and workshops of the "plain people," members of the Amish, Mennonite, and Brethren religious sects. The Amish are of special interest because their dress and rejection of "worldly" devices has remained unchanged for more than 300 years. They cling to the horse and buggy and reject the use of all electric-powered devices and modern plumbing. However, it is now permissible for the Amish to use devices such as battery-operated saws, or electric saws with temporary hookups, for special circumstances as barn raising. Propane gas tanks are used to operate adapted modern appliances such as refrigerators and a few lamps. Water gravity systems have been developed to create bathrooms (with gas-heated hot water) that are in accordance with Amish beliefs and prohibitions.

Tourists come here to sample local delicacies, such as shoofly pie, and partake of meals served in the Pennsylvania Dutch style. It is advisable to make advance reservations for motel rooms, especially during the summer season. Visitors also will find it advantageous to stop first at the **Pennsylvania Dutch Convention and Visitors Bureau,** 501 Greenfield Road. This is the main visitor information center for all of Lancaster County. Telephone: (800) PADUTCH. Web site: www.padutchcountry.com.

It will take three days or longer to see all of the major attractions of the area. There are five suggested tours in this edition, each approximately one half-day's duration. The first covers historic Lancaster. It is followed by four motor tours, north, east, south, and west of the city. Other intriguing ways to see the countryside include tours in Amish buggies offered by various vendors in the area, and using an audio-tape guide. Audio-tape tours can be purchased or rented (the price is about the same) at Dutch Wonderland, described below. (You may enter the gift shop and find out about tapes without paying admission to the recreation area.)

For information on guided walking tours of historic sites, contact the Lancaster County Historical Society, which also offers a 12-minute slide show of local highlights. The Historical Society is located at the intersection of Marietta and North President Avenue. Open Tuesday and Thursday, 9:30 A.M. to 9:30 P.M.; Wednesday, Friday and Saturday, 9:30 A.M. to 4:30 P.M. Closed Sunday and Monday and all major holidays. Telephone: (717) 392-4633. Web site: www.lancasterhistory.org.

Our historical walking tour begins on Penn Square. Facing King Street is **Old City Hall,** built in 1795. Nearby is the **Lancaster Central Market,** 23 North Market Street, where many types of farm delicacies are sold by Amish and Mennonite farmers. Open Tuesday and Friday, 6 A.M. to 4 P.M.; Saturday, 6 A.M. to 2 P.M. Telephone: (717) 735-6890.

From the Central Market proceed across Penn Square, go south on Queen Street to the **Montgomery House** (1804), and then go to Vine Street. To the left is the **Lancaster County Art Center,** built about 1825. Follow Vine Street to Duke Street, and turn left. On your right is **Trinity Lutheran Church,** built in the 1760s. Diagonally across to the left, at the corner of King Street, is the **Court House,** erected in 1852. **The DeMuth House Museum** includes all of the properties from 114 to 120 East King Street. The house, studio and gardens have all been restored. The museum includes 25 pieces of original artwork by Charles DeMuth and a gallery with rotating exhibits. Open Tuesday through Saturday, 10 A.M. to 4 P.M.; Sunday, 1 P.M. to 4 P.M. Closed Monday and all of January. Telephone: (717) 299-9940. Web site: www.demuth.org.

Also on East King Street is the **Bowsman House** (1762), with a carved angel's head under the eaves; and the **Sign of Ship House** (1761).

Return to Duke Street, then north to the **Muhlenberg House,** the former Trinity Lutheran parsonage. Beyond the intersection, on the right, is the **schoolhouse of the First Reformed Church** (1760). At Orange Street is **St. James Episcopal Church,** founded in 1744. This present building was erected in 1820.

Proceed east on Orange Street to the middle of the block beyond Lime Street. On the left is the home of **Christopher Marshall,** noted diarist of the Revolutionary War era. Near the corner is the fine Georgian home of Lancaster's first mayor, John Passmore. Turn back on Orange Street; on the left, past Duke Street, is the **First Reformed Church.** The present building was erected in 1852 on the site of an 18th-century edifice. Turn right on reaching Prince Street, to the home of **Andrew Ellicott,** built in 1780. Ellicott was America's first native-born city planner. South on Prince Street, at the corner of King, is the **Fulton Opera House,** America's oldest living theater (1852), named in honor of inventor Robert Fulton. Turn left to return to the start of the walking tour.

There are many other points of interest in and around Lancaster. Here are a few of the notable attractions, all conveniently reached by automobile. At 400 College Avenue is the **North Museum of Natural History and Science.** The museum features exhibits on science and natural history. Open Tuesday through Saturday, 9 A.M. to 5 P.M.; Sunday, noon to 5 P.M. Admission charge. Telephone: (717) 291-3941. For information regarding the planetarium hours and shows telephone: (717) 291-4315. Web site: www.northmuseum.org.

Wheatland, a Greek revival mansion built in 1828, was owned by **James Buchanan** (15th president of the United States) from 1848 until his death in 1868. It is located at 1120 Marietta Avenue, next door to the Lancaster County Historical Society. The mansion, used by Buchanan in 1856 as his presidential campaign headquarters, has been restored to its mid-19th-century appearance. Period rooms contain outstanding collections of American Empire and Victorian decorative arts, many of which belonged to Buchanan. Tours of the 17-room house and grounds are conducted by guides wearing period costumes. Open daily April 1 through October 31, and Friday through Monday in November, 10 A.M. to 4 P.M. Open in December for candlelight tours; call or check the web site for specific dates. Admission charge. Telephone: (717) 392-4633. Web site: www.wheatland.org.

Hammond Pretzel Bakery, 716 South West End Avenue, is open 7 A.M. to 5 P.M., weekdays; 8 A.M. to noon on Saturdays. If you want to see pretzels being made, plan to arrive before 3:30 P.M. on weekdays. Telephone: (717) 392-7532. Web site: www.hammondspretzels.com.

Historic Rock Ford Plantation is located in Lancaster County Park, 881 Rockford Road. This is the restored 1794 estate of Edward Hand, Adjutant General during the Revolution and a member of the Continental Congress. It is an authentic example of refined country living in the late 18th century. Open April through October, Tuesday through Friday, 10 A.M. to 4 P.M.; Sunday, noon to 4 P.M. Admission charge. Telephone: (717) 392-7223. Web site www.rockfordplantation.org.

North of Lancaster

This circuit tour encompasses Route 272 (Oregon Pike) to Ephrata, Route 322 to Brickerville, Route 501 to Lititz, Route 772 to Manheim, and return via Route 72. The distance is approximately 38 miles.

First stop is the **Landis Valley Museum,** 2451 Kissel Hill Road. This museum complex includes a farm home, barns, a one-room school-house, and many outbuildings. On display are thousands of items reflecting rural life, culture, and the economy in the 18th and 19th centuries including a large collection of farm implements and vehicles, and tools of various rural crafts. Open daily, 9 A.M. to 5 P.M.; Sundays, noon to 5 P.M. Admission charge. Children under 6, free. Telephone: (717) 569-0401. Web site: www.landisvalleymuseum.org. Continue north on Kissel Hill Road approximately two miles to the second intersection. Turn right, then go less than a mile to a picturesque covered bridge across Conestoga Creek. Return to Route 222, and continue north to intersection of Route 322 at Ephrata.

The **Ephrata Cloister,** 632 West Main Street, was one of America's earliest communal societies, founded in 1732 by Conrad Beissel, a German Pietist. The society, which once numbered more than 300 members, dwindled and was finally disbanded in 1929. A visit to the Cloister reveals a unique and amazing expression of the religious fervor which was an outstanding characteristic of early Pennsylvania.

Charity, always a part of the Cloister way of life, was nobly demonstrated during the Revolution when approximately 250 wounded soldiers from the Battle of Brandywine were brought here in December 1777 to be nursed by the members. The buildings on Mt. Zion (the hill to the west), which served as a hospital, had to be burned following their occupation in order to arrest the spread of camp fever. A monument in the Mt. Zion Cemetery marks the graves of many soldiers who died here.

The surviving buildings, extensively restored, include the Meetinghouse (Saal), Saron (sisters' house), Almonry (alms and bake house), Beissel's log house, a householders' cabin, three cottages, and the 1837 Academy. Bethania (brothers' house), which stood nearby, was razed around 1910. In addition to self-disciplines, the celibate orders engaged in printing, illuminated calligraphy, composing music and singing, spinning, weaving, and papermaking.

The Visitor Center introduces the Ephrata Cloister with a slide show and exhibits. Open Monday through Saturday, 9 A.M. to 5 P.M.; Sundays, noon to 5 P.M. Admission charge. Telephone: (717) 733-6600. Web site: www.ephratacloister.org.

Another attraction in Ephrata is the **Green Dragon Farmer's Market,** 955 North State Street. Open Fridays, 9 A.M. to 9 P.M. Telephone: (717) 738-1117. Web site: www.greendragonmarket.com.

The tour route is west from Ephrata on Route 322 to Brickerville, then south on Route 501, past the **Speedwell Forge Fishing Lake.** Stop off in

Brickerville to stroll over the grounds of Elizabeth Furnace (1763), where Baron Stiegel operated the finest glassworks in the colonies. Continue on Route 501 to Lititz. The **Lititz Museum** is located in the **Johannes Mueller House,** (c. 1792) 137 East Main Street, where guides depict the way of life of a tradesman living during the late 18th and early 19th centuries. Johannes Mueller was a local tanner and dyer. Open Memorial Day through October, Monday through Saturday, 10 A.M. to 4 P.M. Telephone: (717) 627-4636. Web site: http://www.lititzmutual.com/public/lhf.nsf/Home.

The **Sturgis Pretzel House,** 219 East Main Street in Lititz, is believed to be America's earliest such firm. Here the visitor will see how pretzels are made today and how they were made in 1861. Open Monday through Saturday, 9 A.M. to 5 P.M. Admission charge. Telephone: (717) 626-4354. Web site: www.juliussturgis.com.

Continue west for five miles on Route 772 to Manheim. The town was founded by Baron Stiegel, who was noted for his famous glass products. The remains of his home are on Main Street. The **Manheim Historical Society Heritage Center,** 88 South Grant Street, is a museum of early American antiques and Stiegel glass. The nearby **Manheim Railway Station** has an original 19th-century Lancaster County trolley car and railroad memorabilia. Open Monday and Friday, 1 to 4 P.M.; Wednesday, 6 to 9 P.M., and Saturday, 9 A.M. to noon. Telephone: (717) 665-7989. At the **Red Rose Church** (c. 1772), at 2 South Hazel Street, a rent of "one red rose" is paid to Stiegel's heirs annually on the second Sunday in June.

Three **covered bridges** were built south of Manheim, each crossing Chickies Creek. Ask for directions locally. The tour continues south on Route 128 toward Lancaster. Two miles south of East Petersburg, at the village of McGovernville, is another covered bridge.

East of Lancaster

This circuit tour is east out of Lancaster returning via Route 772 and Hempstead Road, a distance of about 33 miles. Take Route 340 and then Route 30, east out of Lancaster. Look for pottery and craft outlets in Bridgeport. The **Amish Country Homestead,** on Route 340, is an authentic, 71-acre Amish farm, actually occupied and farmed by an Amish family. Guides help to interpret how the Amish live today. Open daily, but weekends only January through March. Hours vary seasonally. Admission charge. Telephone: (717) 768-8400. Web site: www.amishexperience.com.

The **Discover Lancaster County History Museum** is located nearby at 2249 Route 30 East. This wax museum presents life-size figures that recreate momentous events in Lancaster's history. Open daily, year-round; hours vary seasonally. Admission charge. Telephone (717) 393-3679. Web site: www.discoverlancaster.com.

Also nearby is the **Mennonite Information Center,** 2209 Millstream Road, a tourist information center for people visiting the Amish and Mennonite areas of Lancaster County. A walk through exhibit shows the suffering, change, faith and work in an Anabaptist community. The center also features the **Hebrew Tabernacle Reproduction,** a full scale model of Moses' Tabernacle in the Wilderness. Telephone: (717) 299-0954. Web site: www.mennoniteinfoctr.com.

Dutch Wonderland at 2249 Route 30 East, is a 48 acre amusement park designed for families with children 12 and under. Excellent audio tapes for driving tours are sold or rented in the gift shop, which may be accessed without entering the park itself. Open weekends spring and fall; daily, Memorial Day through Labor Day. Hours vary. Admission charge. Telephone: (866) 386-2839. Web site: www.dutchwonderland.com.

The **Amish Farm and House,** 2395 Route 30 East, is a working Amish farm that makes you think you have stepped back in time 200 years. Guided tours are available. Hearty food is sold at the Dutch Food Pavillion. Open daily year-round, hours vary seasonally. Admission charge. Telephone: (717) 394-6185. Web site: www.amishfarmandhouse.com.

The **Mill Bridge Village** at South Ronks Road in Paradise is the oldest continuously operated historic village in the Pennsylvania Dutch country. Three National Historic Landmarks are located here. The first is Herr's Mill double span covered bridge, built in 1844. Next is the Amish style 1812 historical home and last is the 1738 Grist Mill. There is also a typical Amish schoolhouse. In the 18th century, the mill was an important social center for the area. Here you could have your corn ground, purchase supplies, and exchange news. You can take a self-tour of the historic sites. Admission charge. Open daily 9 A.M. to 6 P.M. There are also campsites available in the village. Telephone: (800) 645-2744. Web site: www.millbridge.com.

At 3056 Route 30 East in Paradise is Will-Char, "The Hex Place," which was started by Jacob Zook, a 12th generation Dutchman and an authority on Pennsylvania Dutch folk art, especially Hex signs. In addition to Hex signs, the shop features Amish dolls, weather vanes, lawn ornaments, and Pennsylvania Dutch decorated ware. Telephone: (717) 687-8329. Web site: www.padutch.com/hexsigns.shtml.

After the Hex Shop, make a left turn onto the paved road leading to Intercourse at the junction of Routes 772 and 340. Pass a covered bridge en route. Less than a mile east on Route 340 is the **Plain and Fancy Farm.** The farm is mostly noted for **Miller's Smorgasbord,** a restaurant that serves Pennsylvania Dutch food in the family style. Visitors can take an Amish buggy ride on the farm. Open year round; hours vary. Admission charge. Telephone: (717) 687-6621. Web site: www.millerssmorgasbord.com.

In Bird-In-Hand, the **Old Village Store** is an authentic 19th-century store with a pot belly stove. Open daily, 10 A.M. to 5 P.M., mid-March through December. Closed Sundays. Telephone: (717) 397-1291. Visitors will also find other shops in the village featuring antiques, collectibles, furniture, candles, and metal items for home and garden.

At Monterey make a sharp left turn to **Heller's Church,** an old country church. Bear left to Route 340 towards Lancaster.

Mid-18th-century pioneers of the Jewish faith are buried in **Shaarai Shomayim Cemetery,** established in 1747, on the outskirts of Lancaster. Joseph Simon, trader, landholder, and businessman, who came to Lancaster in 1740, is buried here. He was a founder of the Union Fire Co. and the Lancaster Library Co., as well as a Conawago Canal Commissioner, and supplier to the Continental Army.

The **Bird-In-Hand Farmers Market** is located at Route 340 and Maple Avenue. Open year round, winter and early spring, Friday and Saturday, 8:30 A.M. to 5:30 P.M.; April through November, Wednesday, 8:30 A.M. to 5:30 P.M., July through October, Thursday, 8:30 A.M. to 5:30 P.M. Telephone: (717) 393-9674. Web site: www.800padutch.com/z/bihmarket.htm.

South of Lancaster

This circuit tour begins on Route 222, south to Penn Hill; then backtrack to Route 372, go east to Route 896, then north by various roads to Lancaster. The distance is 58 miles.

Follow Route 222 to the junction with Route 741, follow 741 for about a mile to Hans Herr Drive, then less than a mile down to the entrance of the **Hans Herr House,** the oldest area landmark, which was built in 1719 by the first Swiss German Mennonites. Guided tours. Open April 1 through November, Monday through Saturday, 9 A.M. to 4 P.M.; closed Sunday. Admission charge; children under 7 free. Telephone: (717) 464-4438. Web site: www.hansherr.org. Continue to Lime Valley. Two covered bridges to the east cross Pequa Creek. New Providence is the home of the Lime Valley Roller Mill, as well as a lime kiln and the Old Conowingo Ore Mill. Continue on Route 222 through Quarryville to the **Robert Fulton Birthplace,** near Bethel. This is a National Historic Landmark of the renowned inventor, engineer and artist born in 1765. The original structure was built in 1734 and was reconstructed in 1965. Exhibits interpret the history of river navigation in relationship to Fulton's invention of the steamship. Open Memorial Day through Labor Day, Saturday, 11 A.M. to 4 P.M. and Sunday 1 P.M. to 5 P.M. Telephone: (717) 548-2679. Web site: www.padutchcountry.com/member_pages/Robert_Fulton_Birthplace.asp. Two miles beyond is the **Penn Hill Meeting House,** a Quaker landmark.

Retrace your steps to Quarryville, turning right on Route 372. Four miles to the east is **Middle Octorara Presbyterian Church,** erected in 1754. Continue to **Green Tree Inn** (1763), where Route 896 intersects. This was the home of Robert Fulton's parents. Then follow 896 north into Strasburg.

Park your car and enjoy a ride on the **Strasburg Rail Road,** America's oldest operating short-line railroad, chartered in 1832, incorporated in 1851. The hour-long round trip to Paradise and back traverses picturesque Amish countryside. The line was chartered in 1832 and the equipment in use dates from the late 19th century. At the depot one can board an assortment of old railroad cars. Hours of operation and tours vary seasonally. Fare charge. Telephone: (717) 687-7522. Web site: www.strasburgrailroad.com.

East of Strasburg on Route 741 is the **Choo Choo Barn**. Here one sees, in miniature, scenes from daily life in the Pennsylvania Dutch country. Open April through December, daily 10 A.M. to 5 P.M., extended hours on Fridays in December. Last admission 30 minutes prior to closing. Admission charge. Telephone (717) 687-7911 or (800) 450-2920. Web site: www.choochoobarn.com.

The **National Toy Train Museum**, at 300 Paradise Lane in Strasburg, is the national headquarters for the Train Collectors Association. Here the visitor can enjoy toy trains in a turn of the century setting and a collection of trains and train-related accessories from the mid-1800's to the present. Open April, November, and

December, Saturday and Sunday, 10 A.M. to 5 P.M.; May through October, daily, 10 A.M. to 5 P.M. Admission charge. Telephone: (717) 687-8976. Web site: www.traincollectors.org.

West of Lancaster

This circuit tour goes west on Route 230 to Elizabethtown, south on Routes 743 and 441, and east on Route 30. Distance is 45 miles.

Begin on Route 222 north, turn left on Route 230 for six miles to an optional detour to the right to a covered bridge on the Mechanicsville Road. Continue on Route 230 to Mt. Joy. Here one can tour the **Bubes Brewery** located in the Central Hotel at 102 North Market Street, a 19th-century brewery complex with a museum, an art gallery, an outdoor biergarten and brewery store. Built by Alois Bube, it is the only brewery surviving intact from the 1800's in the United States. Telephone: (717) 653-2056. Web site: www.bubesbrewery.com.

The **Masonic Home**, with its noted formal gardens, is also located in Mt. Joy. Turn south on Route 743, one mile east on Route 230. Travel four miles on Route 743, turning left to **Donegal Presbyterian Church.** In 1777, the entire congregation gathered under a large oak tree and "bore witness" to their support of General Washington.

Proceed right on the road to Chickies, located on the Susquehanna River. The **Chickies Rock Observation Site** is a promontory that affords a sweeping view of the great river valley. Continue on Route 441 into Columbia at the Route 30 intersection. The **First National Bank Museum** is located 170 Locust Street. The 1814 bank is one of the country's only restored banks in its original setting. The colonial architecture, especially the original unsupported staircase, is very interesting. The museum features exhibits depicting the history of banks in the area. Telephone: (717) 684-8864. Web site: www.bankmuseum.org.

LEBANON AREA

This part of the Pennsylvania Dutch country was settled largely by German immigrants, beginning in the early 1700s. The city of Lebanon was founded in 1750.

First stop is the **Stoy Museum,** 924 Cumberland Street. Here the visitor can see exhibits that reflect more than 200 years of history of the area. The house itself belonged to a well-known Revolutionary War doctor, the Reverend Doctor William Henry Stoy. The building later served as Lebanon's first county courthouse. The museum includes recreated rooms with original equipment for a railroad watch box, drug store, physician's office, Victorian parlor, children's toy room, colonial kitchen, schoolhouse, clothing store, barbershop, and a weaver's establishment. There is an excellent museum shop open the same hours as the museum. Open Monday, 12:30 to 8 P.M., Tuesday through Friday, 12:30 to 4:30 P.M., Sunday 1 P.M. to 4:30 P.M. Closed Saturdays and holidays. Groups are asked to make appointments. Admission charge. Telephone: (717) 272-1473. Web site: lebanoncountyhistoricalsociety.org/stoy-museum.

Two blocks from the market is Willow Street, noted for two old churches. **Salem Lutheran Church**, at the corner of 8th Street, was built circa 1735. Telephone: (717) 272-6151. **Tabor United Church of Christ**, at the corner of 10th Street, dates from 1762, is one of the oldest churches in the Lebanon area. Telephone: (717) 273-4222.

Proceed north to Maple Street and turn left; proceed three miles on Route 72 to Tunnel Hill Road. The oldest transportation tunnel in the United States, the **Union Canal Tunnel**, was cut through a mountain in 1827 and used from 1832 to 1885.

Middle Creek Wildlife Area, 10 miles southeast of Lebanon near Newmanstown, is a 6,254-acre wildlife management area. Picnicking, fishing, boating, and in-season hunting are the featured activities. A visitors center and a museum containing mounted exhibits of all wildlife native to Pennsylvania are located here. Open March through November, Tuesday through Saturday, 8 A.M. to 4 P.M.; Sunday, noon to 5 P.M. Closed Mondays. The area itself is open all year. Telephone: (717) 733-1512. Web site: www.visitpa.com/middle-creek-wildlife-management-area.

Fort Zeller Museum is an 18th-century Indian fort off Route 419 near Newmanstown. It is the oldest existing fort in the state of Pennslyvania. Open all year for tours by appointment. Donations requested. Telephone: (717) 272-0662. Web site: fortzeller.com.

Several plants where Lebanon bologna is made are located nearby. Visitors are shown how the sausage is prepared, and are taken through the smokehouses where the meat is aged and seasoned. The area's most notable historical monument is **Cornwall Iron Furnace**, five miles south of Lebanon on Route 72, then left on Route 419 for a mile. In Cornwall follow signs to this unique, well-preserved iron furnace depicting the beginnings of Pennsylvania's iron and steel industry. It is administered by the state as an important historical site. Peter Grubb began mining the rich iron ore banks along Furnace

Creek in the 1730s. In 1742 he established a furnace at the present site, which continued in operation until 1883. The ore mines remained in operation until 1973. The sturdy stone miners' houses built over a century ago are still standing.

Cornwall Furnace played an important role in the production of cannons and other military equipment during the Revolution. Washington and Lafayette are said to have visited here during their encampment at Valley Forge to observe the casting of cannons. Hessian prisoners were used as laborers at the furnace. The visitor today can see all the equipment and buildings used in the production of iron and the casting of iron products—the charging platform, furnace and casting room, as well as the interesting blowing equipment and a steam engine dating from 1856 are on display. Open June through August, Tuesday through Saturday, 9 A.M. to 5 P.M.; Sunday, noon to 5 P.M. From September to May the museum closes one hour earlier. Admission charge. Telephone: (717) 272-9711. Web site: www.cornwallironfurnace.org.

From Cornwall, one can go west on Route 117 two miles to Mt. Gretna, or east on Route 419 through Pennsylvania Dutch farmlands to Schaefferstown. **Mt. Gretna** is a 100-year-old resort community with 6,000 acres of wooded parklands, lovely Victorian cottages, boating and swimming on Lake Conewago, golf, miniature golf and an excellent summer theater, which is one of the oldest in the country. There are also summer concerts in the park.

Historic **Schaefferstown** lies east of Lebanon on Route 501. The area has many lovely old stone houses, farmhouses, and churches with unique architectural details. Among them is the **Alexander Schaeffer Farm** with its 1736 Swiss-type bank house and bank barn. Artists, craftsmen, folklorists, and farmers gather on special festival weekends in June and September to share knowledge about local folklore, arts, and crafts. In the village center, two blocks east of the homestead, is a small museum that contains exhibits on spinning wheels, quilts, 18th- and 19th-century cookware, and the culture of tobacco. It is also the site of the first municipal waterworks in America, built in 1750. Open Memorial Day to Labor Day by appointment. Free admission for homestead and village museum. Admission charge for festivals. Telephone: (717) 949-2244.

York County

York, first capital of the United States, is located within two hours' drive of Gettysburg, Lancaster, Harrisburg, and Hershey. **York**

County offers a host of outdoor activities year round; the county is fortunate to have within its boundaries three state parks. Other York County attractions include farmers' markets, brick-end barns, outlet stores, and several Revolutionary sites.

There are four visitors centers in York County. The downtown visitors center is at 149 West Market Street in York. Open daily, 9:30 A.M. to 4 P.M. Call for information or check online for details about the other centers. Telephone: 717-852-9675. Web site: www.yorkpa.org.

We suggest three different motor tours, each covering 60 miles. Before getting in your car, a walking tour of historical downtown York is suggested. You can obtain a detailed walking tour map and guide from the downtown visitors center. Some of the sites visited on the tour are described below.

The **Museum and Library of the Historical Society of York County**, 250 East Market Street, features a comprehensive picture of daily life in 18th-century York County. The contents of the museum include a life-size village square display. The Society's library contains nearly 15,000 volumes and extensive genealogical holdings (including the histories of more than 1,200 regional families). Museum open, Monday through Saturday, 9 A.M. to 5 P.M.; Sunday, 1 to 4 P.M. Admission charge. Telephone: (717) 848-1587. Web site: www.yorkheritage.org.

The **Bonham House**, 152 East Market Street, reflects the life and times of the Bonham family during the late 19th century. The rooms are arranged to display different styles and fashions from the red Victorian parlor to the Federal dining room. Also exhibited are the genre paintings of Horace Bonham which have been cited as excellent examples of 19th-century American art. Tours by appointment only. Admission charge. Telephone: (717) 848-1587.

Next visit the **York County Colonial Court House**, a full-size reconstruction of the courthouse where the Articles of Confederation were adopted in 1776. The courthouse is located at the intersection of West Market Street and Pershing Avenue.

Nearby, at 34 West Philadelphia Street, is the **Central Market House**. Here county farmers sell their produce Tuesday, Thursday, and Saturday, 6 A.M. to 3 P.M. Telephone: (717) 848-2243. Web site: www.centralmarket-house.com. Should you wish to visit other markets in the area, there is the **Market and Penn Farmer's Market** at 380 West Market Street. Call for days and hours of operation. Telephone: (717) 848-1402. **New Eastern Market**, at 201 Memory Lane, is York's only air-conditioned farm market. Call for days and hours of operation. Telephone: (717) 755-5811.

The **Quaker Meeting House** at 135 West Philadelphia Street, built in 1766, is used for regular services. To the right, on Beaver Street, is **St. John's Episcopal Church**. The present structure includes part of the original brick church built in 1765. The bell, presented to the congregation by Queen Caroline of Denmark, can be seen in the vestibule.

To the south of the church at 157 West Market Street are three historical buildings currently maintained by the York County Historical Society: the **Golden Plough Tavern**, the **Gates House,** and **the Barnett Bobb Log House.** The Golden Plough Tavern, distinguished by its half-timber construction, is believed to have been built in 1741. Architectural historians note that the construction of the Plough reflects the medieval character of the Black Forest in the 18th century, making the structure an anachronism then and now. The tavern also is home to a fine collection of studied furnishings reflecting the William and Mary period. The Gates House (c. 1751) was rented by General Gates while he was in York. The house was the site of the famous, but unsuccessful, campaign to replace General Washington with Gates as the head of the Continental Army. It is authentically furnished with fine pieces spanning the country styles of Chippendale and Queen Anne. The Barnett Bobb Log House, which is more than 150 years old, is typical of houses built by early German settlers in the York area. The Golden Plough Tavern, General Gates' House, and Barnett Bobb Log House are open Tuesday through Saturday, 10 A.M. to 4 P.M. Admission charge. Telephone: (717) 845-2951. Web site: www.yorkheritage.org.

Close by, at 757 West Market Street, is the **Fire Museum.** Here you will see a restored turn-of-the-century firehouse and a collection of old equipment from all 72 fire companies in York County (some dating back to pre-Revolutionary days). Open Saturdays, 10 A.M. to 4 P.M. Admission charge. Telephone: (717) 848-1587. Web site: www.yorkheritage.org.

While in York, visitors may be interested in visiting some unique sites outside of the historical section of town. Physical culture fans may wish to visit the **York Barbell Company** located at 3300 Board Road. This is the location of the Weight Lifting Hall of Fame, and visitors can see exhibits on special events and people in the sport. Tours are available. Hours vary. Free admission. Telephone: (800) 358-YORK.

The **Harley-Davidson Motor Company** is a favorite of motorcycle enthusiasts. Motorcycles from 1903 to the present are on display in the museum. Tours of the assembly plant are also included. Open Monday through Friday, 9 A.M. to 2 P.M. Free admission. Telephone: (877) 883-1450. Web site: www.harley-davidson.com.

The following three motor tours cover major points of interest in York County.

York—Hanover Area

To begin, take Route 30 west out of York for approximately 15 miles to Route 194 south. The **Hanover Shoe Farms** are located on Route 194, approximately three miles south of Hanover. The farm is the largest in the world devoted to the breeding of harness race horses. There are no guided tours, but visitors are welcome to walk through the barns and visit with the horses in the paddocks. Telephone: (717) 637-8931. Web site: www.hanoverpa.com.

Retrace your Route to Hanover and turn left on High Street (Route 116) to McSherrytown. Drive through town, take the second road to the right, and turn left at the dead end to view **Conewago Chapel,** at 30 Basilica Drive. The chapel, high on the hillside, is significant for many reasons. It was the first Catholic Mission in Pennsylvania, established in 1730. The present structure, built in 1787, replaced the original log chapel constructed in 1741. The chapel is also the first parish church in America dedicated to the Sacred Heart of Jesus. The church was elevated to the eminence of a Minor Basilica by Pope John XXIII. Only a half dozen churches in the United States have been bestowed such an honor. Along with the church's exquisite Georgian architecture, visitors can see beautiful 19th-century murals by Austrian painters. Call for information regarding hours and services. Telephone: (717) 637-2721.

After leaving the chapel, you may want to visit the delightful town of New Oxford, on Route 30 west. The town is full of antique stores.

You will find the 3,320-acre **Codorus State Park** two miles off Route 216, three miles east of Hanover, and only three miles north of the Maryland line. Its address is 1066 Blooming Grove Road, Hanover. It boasts one of the largest outdoor swimming pools in the nation, plus a five-mile-long lake for swimming, boating, and fishing. In summer, visitors can enjoy hiking, nature study, camping, horseback riding, fishing, canoeing, sailing, and evening programs. In winter, there is ice skating and tobogganing. Telephone: (717) 637-2816.

Web site: www.dcnr.state.pa.us/stateparks/findapark/codorus.

York—Wellsville—Lewisberry

Leave York via Route 921, and follow the signs toward Rossville. On the way, you might be able to see an old **brick-end barn.** This type of barn was commonly built in the 1700s in Pennsylvania. The brick ends have openings, necessary for ventilation, in various patterns such as trees and birds.

Gifford Pinchot State Park is conveniently located between York and Harrisburg, off I-83, at 2200 Rosstown Road in Lewisberry. This 2,338-acre park offers year-round recreation. There is hiking, camping, cabins, nature study, fishing, canoeing, sailing, boating, and lake swimming. Winter activities include cross-country skiing and ice-skating. Telephone: (717) 432-5011. Web site: www.dcnr.state.pa.us/stateparks/findapark/index.htm.

Round Top, a noted ski resort, is located about four miles west of Wellsville on Route 74. Take Route 177 from Wellsville toward Lewisberry, then turn right on Route 382 before town. By taking this detour you will be able to view the **Redland Quaker Meeting House,** built in 1811. This road east of Lewisberry is paved with brick, one of the few remaining roads of this type. Continue on Route 382 and turn left on Route 111, then go north to Route 262 and follows the signs to **River View.** From this high vantage point, you will have a spectacular view of the Susquehanna River. Continue on Route 382 until you reach York Haven; then take Routes 181 and 92 to Mt. Wolf. Turn left toward Starview and follow the signs to **Codorus Furnace,** a Revolutionary-era smelting furnace which was originally owned by Pennsylvania's signer of the Declaration of Independence, Col. James Smith. The furnace is situated along a creek surrounded by rolling hills and is an ideal picnic spot.

Follow the signs to Highmount and to Route 30; then turn right for the return trip to York.

York to Indian Steps Museum

From York, go east on Prospect Street (Route 124) approximately eight miles, turn left, and then go three miles to **Samuel S. Lewis State Park.** The 71-acre park is open for day use only. The park offers picnicking, hiking and has pavilions for rent. For information telephone: (717) 252-1134. From the top of Mt. Pisgah (more than 1,000 feet above sea level), the visitor can see the broad expanse of York County, the multiple-arch concrete bridge over the Susquehanna River, and parts of Lancaster County across the river.

After leaving the park, follow the signs to Long Level, along Route 624, which is exceptionally scenic. At **Long Level** the traveler can inspect the ruins of the old Susquehanna Canal. At Craley, follow

Route 124 to York Furnace, and signs to **Indian Steps Museum,** located at 4923 Pleasant Valley Road in York. Dedicated to the American Indian, this museum displays great quantities of relics of the Susquehannock and other Indians who lived along the "long winding river." The exhibits are arranged in seven rooms in the old mansion which houses the collection. The museum is open mid-April through mid-October, Thursday and Friday, 10 A.M. to 4 P.M.; Saturday and Sunday, 10 A.M. to 5 P.M. Admission charge. Telephone: (717) 862-3948 or (717) 757-7858.

HARRISBURG AND HERSHEY

The major attractions in the Harrisburg-Hershey area are the public buildings and museums in the Capitol Hill area of **Harrisburg** and the many attractions that comprise "Chocolate Town, U.S.A.," as Hershey is called. Harrisburg is approximately 115 miles northeast of Washington, D.C., and 75 miles north of Baltimore. Hershey is 12 miles east of Harrisburg on Route 322. For more information stop by the Harrisburg/Hershey/Carlisle Tourism and Convention Bureau, 25 Front Street, in Harrisburg. Telephone: (717) 231-7788. Web site: www.visithhc.com. For touring of a more historic nature, visit the Historic Harrisburg Resource Center at 1230 Third Street in Harrisburg. Telephone: (717) 233-4646. Web site: www.visithhc.com/resource.html.

Harrisburg

Harrisburg, capital city of the Keystone State since 1812, is famed for its picturesque "front steps" leading down to the broad Susquehanna River. The city has many beautiful parkways and gardens and numerous old homes.

In the middle of the city, between North and Walnut streets, towers the 272-foot **State Capitol** building, of Italian Renaissance style, with a dome patterned after that of St. Peter's in Rome. At the entrance to the Capitol are 27 dynamic granite figures, sculptured by a Pennsylvanian, George Grey Barnard. The Rotunda, the Legislative Chambers, and the Governor's Suite are lavish with mahogany, marble, statuary, and paintings. The corridor floors contain more than 400 mosaics, which were designed and executed by Henry Mercer of Doylestown. Free conducted tours of the Capitol are offered every half hour Monday through Friday, 8:30 A.M. to 4 P.M.; on weekends and most holidays, tours are offered at 9 A.M., 11 A.M., 1 P.M., and 3

P.M. Telephone: (800) 868-7672.

Web site: www.pacapitol.com/tours.html. Please note to allow additional time because of enhanced security procedures at the Capitol.

The **Governor's Mansion,** located on North Second Street, is open to visitors April through June, as well as September and October, Tuesdays and Thursdays, 9:30 A.M. to 1:30 P.M. Free admission. Reservations required. Telephone: (717) 772-9130.

Directly north of the Capitol, on Third Street between North and Forster streets, is the **State Museum of Pennsylvania.** The main portion of the museum is the William Penn Memorial Hall. This impressive three-storied hall is dominated by an 18-foot stylized bronze statue of Penn created by the Pennsylvania sculptress, Janet de Coux. Exhibitions of works from the permanent Pennsylvania Collection of Fine Arts, along with changing art shows, are on display in the Fine Arts Galleries on the ground floor of the Museum. As many as 10 or 12 major exhibitions of historic and contemporary arts and crafts are presented annually, along with several small or special showings. In addition, the museum has exhibits on the decorative arts and history of the state; displays of fine furniture, glassware, pottery, pewter and other materials, a transportation exhibit in the Hall of Industry and Technology, a Hall of Anthropology, a Gallery of Military History, and a Planetarium. The museum is open Tuesday through Saturday, 9 A.M. to 5 P.M.; Sunday, noon to 5 P.M. Free admission. There is a nominal charge for the Planetarium and The Curiosity Corner. Telephone: (717) 787-4980. Web site: www.statemuseumpa.org.

To the north of the museum stands the tower of the **Pennsylvania State Archives.** Its 21 levels contain extensive collections of official public records, historical manuscripts, and microfilms for research and writing on the history of Pennsylvania from William Penn's time down to the present. The public entrance to the Search Room of the Archives Building is off Third Street through the ornamental gates and the west garden court. Visiting researchers may ask at the Search Room for the documentary materials they need, and may use the desks and other facilities of the room for their work. Open Tuesday through Friday, 9 A.M. to 4 P.M. Saturday (microfilm only) 9 A.M. to noon and 1 to 4 P.M. Telephone: (717) 783-3281.

West of Capitol Hill on Front Street, the gaily colored mansions of the Commonwealth's statesmen, reposing in the shadow of giant oaks and elms, look out on the glittering river beyond. In the middle of the river is lovely **City Island Park,** with a bathing beach, baseball

stadium, recreated 19th-century village, and facilities for motorboat-
ing, canoeing, sailing, and fishing. Telephone: (717) 255-6534. Web
site: www.visitpa.com/city-island-harrisburg-pa.

John Harris/Simon Cameron Mansion, 219 South Front Street, is
the home of the **Historical Society of Dauphin County.** The mansion
was built in 1766 by Harrisburg's founder and has since been
"Victorianized." The museum specializes in 19th-century Victorian
decorative arts. Researchers may be interested in the society's
archives, which date from 1750 to the present. Open Monday
through Thursday, 10 A.M. to 4 P.M. Tours by reservation only.
Admission charge. Telephone: (717) 233-3462.
Web site: www.dauphincountyhistoricalsociety.org.

Fort Hunter Mansion Museum (1814) is a 19th-century Federal-
style mansion located on the site of what once was an old French and
Indian War fort. From Harrisburg it is approximately six miles north
via Front Street. On the mansion tour, which lasts one hour, visitors
can see exhibits of antique furniture, costumes, pewter, glass, and
toys. Open May 1 through December, Tuesday through Saturday,
10:30 A.M. to 4:30 P.M.; Sunday, noon to 4:30 P.M. Admission charge.
Telephone: (717) 599-5751. Web site: www.forthunter.org.

There are several other interesting sites in the Harrisburg vicinity.
At the northern end of the city, the **Pennsylvania Farm Show
Complex,** 2301 North Cameron Street, with 13 acres under one continuous roof, is the site of the annual Pennsylvania Farm Show, held
annually in mid-January. The show is the largest of its kind in the
world, and the complex is one of the largest exhibit facilities in the
East. Telephone: (717) 787-5373.

The **Three Mile Island Visitors Center,** is located off Route 441
south, 10 miles outside of Harrisburg in Middletown. The center
offers exhibits as well as an informative film on nuclear power production. Call for days and hours of operation. Reservations required.
Free admission. Telephone: (717) 948-8829.

About 30 miles north of Harrisburg, at Front and North Streets in
Millersburg, travelers can take a 20-minute ride across the
Susquehanna River on the old **Millersburg Ferry.** Open seasonally,
May through October, as water conditions allow. Nominal fare.
Telephone (717) 692-2442. The **Millersburg Ferryboat Campsites** are
open in the summer for camping. They have tent sites, RV hookups
and cabins. There is volleyball, basketball, mini-golf and shuffleboard.
Telephone: (717) 444-3200. Web site: www.ferryboatcampsites.com.

Hershey

Hershey, with its wide variety of tourist attractions, is built around the world's largest chocolate factory. This community and showplace was created by Milton S. Hershey, more than 60 years ago. He founded the **Hershey Chocolate Company** on a site near his birthplace, and proceeded to build a world-famous chocolate business. By the early 1920s "Chocolate Town, U.S.A." had established itself as one of the most unique places to visit. The streetlights are shaped like candy kisses (some chocolate and others foil wrapped). Street names, such as Cocoa Street and Chocolate Avenue, won't let you forget where you are. The ambiance of the town is sweetened by the scent of chocolate. "Chocolate Town, U.S.A." is just two hours from the Washington Beltway. For information regarding Hershey telephone: (800) HERSHEY. Web site: www.hersheypa.com or www.thehersheycompany.com.

Chocolate World is the official visitors center for the Hershey Food Corporation. Here you will take a simulated tour of a tropical jungle where cocoa beans are harvested to an old seaport where they are shipped. You can also take a tour ride through a simulated Hershey's factory to learn the secrets of chocolate making. At Chocolate World, "chocoholics" will enjoy the wide variety of bizarre chocolate items for sale. Open daily. Hours vary. Free admission. Telephone: (800) HERSHEY. Web site: www.thehersheycompany.com.

The **Hershey Museum** tells the story of Milton Hershey. The exhibit includes original machinery, early Hershey products, antiques owned by Mr. Hershey, a Pennsylvania German collection, and a wonderful Native American collection. Open Memorial Day through Labor Day, daily, 10 A.M. to 6 P.M.; Labor Day through Memorial Day, daily, 10 A.M. to 5 P.M. Admission charge. Telephone: (717) 520-5596. Web site: www.hersheymuseum.org.

The **Hershey Gardens** cover 23 acres. The gardens originated in 1936, when Milton Hershey was asked to contribute one million dollars to a National Rosarium in Washington, but instead decided to beautify his own community. The recently restored gardens contain award-winning roses and an outdoor butterfly house with 400-500 species. Open daily, April through September, 9 A.M. to 6 P.M.; October, 9 A.M. to 5 P.M. Extended evening hours on Fridays, Saturdays, and Sundays in the summer. Admission charge. Telephone: (717) 534-3492. Web site: www.hersheygardens.org.

Hotel Hershey, where you may wish to stay or to dine, is a noteworthy example of the Spanish style of the 1930s. Telphone: (800)

HERSHEY. Web site: www.hersheypa.com/accommodations/ the_hotel_hershey. **Hersheypark** was founded in 1906. The theme park includes more than sixty amusement rides and attractions (some with water features), nine roller coasters, and twenty rides just for children. Open mid-May through mid-September, daily, hours vary. Admission charge. Telephone: (800) HERSHEY. Web site: www.hersheypa.com/attractions/hersheypark. **Zoo America** is an 11-acre complex featuring plants and over 200 animals representing five natural regions throughout North America. Open year round, hours vary. Admission to Zoo America is included in the Hersheypark admission fee.

Three miles outside of Hershey to the west off Route 322 are the **Indian Echo Caverns,** located at 369 Middletown Road in Hummelstown. The caverns were opened in 1783, and they contain beautiful displays of stalactite and stalagmite formations. The caverns are always 52 degrees, so carry a sweater! Open Memorial Day through Labor Day, daily, 9 A.M. to 6 P.M.; 10 A.M. to 4 P.M. the rest of the year. Admission charge. Telephone: (717) 566-8131. Web site: www.indianechocaverns.com.

SOUTH CENTRAL PENNSYLVANIA

Chambersburg Area

The **Chambersburg** area, 24 miles west of Gettysburg on Route 30, has a number of historic points of interest including memorials to the abolitionist John Brown, the birthplace of President James Buchanan, and Thaddeus Stevens' blacksmith shop and iron furnace. In addition, one can visit churches, covered bridges, and state parks in the area. For more information stop by the Chambersburg, Pennsylvania Visitors Council at 1235 Lincoln Way E., Chambersburg, PA 17201. Telephone: (717) 261-1200.

If you plan to visit the birthplace of our 15th president, James Buchanan, you need to go to Mercersburg, which is 11 miles west of Greencastle. At Greencastle, see **Martin's Mill Covered Bridge,** built in 1839 and the **Enoch Brown Park,** a memorial to a schoolmaster and his pupils, massacred in 1764. The **Brown's Mill School,** state-maintained, is an old one-room school in which early residents were educated.

Greencastle is noted for its many large colonies of purple martins which make their homes in boxes provided by the municipality. The birds are "at home" from March until early August. At **Mercersburg,** the restored log cabin in which President Buchanan was born can be seen at the Mercersburg Academy amidst the Gothic-style buildings. **Chambersburg** was laid out in 1763 on the site of Chambers Fort, one of 13 such forts in the area. The town grew, especially after the railroad arrived in 1837. A serious setback, however, occurred in 1864, when raiding Confederates burned the town, destroying 537 buildings. A monument in **Memorial Square** recalls this episode. The unusual fountain seen in Memorial Square was made in France for the Philadelphia Exposition of 1876. It was purchased and moved to its present site in 1877, serving as a memorial to local men who fought in the Union Army.

North of Memorial Square at 221 North Main Street is **Falling Spring Presbyterian Church,** established in 1739. Here a rose-rent ceremony takes place each year, in which a church elder pays the rent, one red rose, to a descendent of Benjamin Chambers. Behind the church lie buried many early pioneers, as well as Indians, who once lived in the area. Two other churches make annual rose payments to descendents of Benjamin Chambers. They are the First Evangelical Lutheran and Zion United Church of Christ. Also, in Chambersburg, a few blocks out Philadelphia Avenue, is **Wilson College,** a private women's college founded in 1869. Telephone: (717) 262-2003. Web site: www.wilson.edu.

Rocky Spring Presbyterian Church, founded in 1738, is a picturesque structure located a few miles northwest of the city. The church was constructed without a chimney so that smoke from the stoves would not attract the attention of Indians. Instead, the smoke was directed to the attic where it filtered through the cracks inconspicuously. Ask locally for directions.

Caledonia State Park is located 11 miles east of Chambersburg, on Route 30. The park includes the **Thaddeus Stevens Blacksmith Shop Museum.** Here one can inspect the iron furnace developed by Stevens, who was a noted abolitionist and advocate of free schooling of children by the state. The park has facilities for swimming, picnicking, camping, hiking, fishing, and golfing. The blacksmith museum is open only during summer months. The **Totem Pole Playhouse** is a summer stock theater within the park. Telephone: park: (717) 352-2161, playhouse: (888) 805-7056.

Web sites: www.dcnr.state.pa.us/stateparks/findapark/caledonia.

Cowans Gap State Park is located off Route 75, 18 miles from Chambersburg. It is nestled high in the Tuscarora Mountains. The lake in the park is a very popular fishing spot; there are also boating, swimming, and picnicking facilities. Winter sports include cross-country skiing and ice skating. Rental cabins and tent-camping sites are available. Telephone: (717) 485-3948. Web site: www.dcnr.state.pa.us/stateparks/findapark/cowansgap/index.htm.

Gettysburg

Gettysburg National Military Park is the site of what many historians consider the decisive battle of the Civil War, which took place on July 1-3, 1863. The National Park Service administers the nearly 35 miles of park roads that lead to various monuments, memorials, and landmarks such as Little Round Top and Cemetery Ridge.

The Battle of Gettysburg, one of the most important and hotly contested battles of the Civil War, resulted in 51,000 casualties, making it one of the war's bloodiest battles. At Gettysburg the Federal Army of the Potomac, under General Meade, met the invading Confederate Army.

On the third day, after a heavy two-hour artillery barrage, Confederate forces advanced in the face of deadly fire that shattered their ranks and spelled disaster for the Confederate Army. They retreated on the evening of July 4, ending the last major offensive of Lee's army and presaging the war's outcome.

On November 19, 1863, President Lincoln dedicated Soldier's National Cemetery on the battlefield, as he delivered his most famous speech, the Gettysburg Address.

The park is open year round. The **Visitor Center** is located at 97 Taneytown Road, just south of the city at the intersection of Routes 15 and 134. Here tourists can see an accurate and instructional orientation program as well as many exhibits created by the National Park Service. Open daily, 8 A.M. to 5 P.M., summer, daily, 8 A.M. to 6 P.M. Closed Thanksgiving, Christmas, and New Year's. Telephone: (717) 334-1124. Web site: www.nps.gov/gett.

Licensed guides conduct visitors on a complete two-hour tour of the park. A fee is charged per car or per chartered bus. If you wish to tour the battlefield at your own pace, however, you can do so easily with the help of the map and text of the park brochure available at the Visitor Center. A one-hour walking tour leading to **Meade's Headquarters** and the **High Water Mark** is also delineated in the brochure.

The **Gettysburg National Military Park Cyclorama Center** features a panoramic painting of the climax of Pickett's charge, by the French artist Paul Philippoteaux. It measures 356 feet by 26 feet. There is a sound and light program which helps recreate the battle and highlights points of interest on the canvas. Open daily, 9:00 A.M. to 5:00 P.M. Closed Thanksgiving, Christmas, and New Year's.

The **Gettysburg Battle Theatre,** opposite the Visitor Center, offers a film and diorama, "America at Gettysburg." Admission charge. Call for program hours. Telephone: (717) 334-6100.

There are also about 15 commercially operated tourist attractions in the surrounding area. They include wax museums, dioramas, collections of Civil War relics, and a fantasyland for youngsters.

Soldier's National Museum was General Howard's headquarters during the battle. It has 60 displays featuring 5000 military miniatures, actual headgear and weapons, and is located near the intersection of Routes 140 and 15. Admission charge. Call for hours of operation. Telephone: (717) 334-4890.

Lincoln Room Museum, in a building on Lincoln Square, exhibits the room where Lincoln spent the night before delivering the Gettysburg Address. A recording recreates the delivery of the famous speech. Admission charge. Call for hours. Telephone: (717) 334-8188.

Hall of Presidents and First Ladies is next to the National Cemetery on Baltimore Street. It is a display of life-size wax figures of the Presidents telling the story of America in their own voices and authentic reproductions of First Ladies' inaugural gowns. Admission charge. Call for hours. Telephone: (717) 334-5717.

Jenny Wade House and Olde Town, also on Baltimore Street, tells the story of Gettysburg's heroine, the only civilian killed during the battle, in an authentic setting. Admission charge. Call for hours. Telephone: (717) 334-4100.

The **National Civil War Wax Museum,** 297 Steinwehr Avenue, is an audio-visual presentation of the Civil War with 200 life-size figures in 30 scenes. There is also a battle-room auditorium and a re-enactment of the Battle of Gettysburg. Admission charge. Call for hours of operation. Telephone: (717) 334-6245.

The **Lincoln Train Museum,** also on Steinwehr Avenue, offers seven dioramas on the role of trains in the Civil War and exhibits a collection of more than 1,000 model trains. Admission charge. Call for hours of operation. Telephone: (717) 334-5678.

At the **Conflict Theater** on Steinwehr, visitors can view a multimedia image production and live shows. Through music and slides the history of the Civil War is retold. Call for additional information regarding hours, show times and admission. Telephone: (717) 334-8003 .

On the **Gettysburg Scenic Rail Tours,** you can take 90-minute and

4-hour trips on old coaches pulled by steam locomotive. Call for schedules and fares. Telephone: (717) 334-6932.

Two nearby attractions are especially geared toward children. The first is **East Coast Exotic Animal Rescue,** formerly the Gettysburg Game Park, located in Fairfield, nine miles southwest of Gettysburg on Route 116. Many of the animals are domesticated and can be fed and petted. The park is open Monday through Friday, 10 A.M. to 5:00 P.M., Saturday and Sunday, 10:00 A.M. to 6:00 P.M. Admission charge. Telephone: (717) 642-5229. Web site: www.eastcoastrescue.org.

The **Land of Little Horses** is a miniature horse farm at 125 Glenwood Drive in Gettysburg. At the farm you can see miniature thoroughbreds, Appaloosas, and draft horses. Many of these full-grown miniature horses weigh only 250 to 400 pounds. Hours vary seasonally. Telephone: (717) 334-7259. Web site: www.landoflittlehorses.com.

Also near Gettysburg is **Mister Ed's Elephant Museum,** on Route 30, 12 miles out of town, at 6019 Chambersburg Road. One man's personal collection of more than 5,000 elephant figures forms a unique attraction. Open daily, year-round, 10 A.M. to 5 P.M. Telephone: (717) 352-3792. Web site: www.mistereds-elephantmuseum.com.

For the visitor to Gettysburg, **The Eisenhower National Historic Site** is within easy reach by bus from the Visitor Center. Fare charge. Please note that you must purchase your ticket and take the bus in order to visit the site, it is not open to the public otherwise. This was the home and farm of President and Mrs. Dwight David Eisenhower. The 230 acre country estate was deeded to the United States in 1967. Open daily, 9 A.M. to 4 P.M. Telephone: (717) 338-9114. Web site: www.nps.gov/eise.

A motor tour covering some of Adams County's historic and scenic sites is outlined below. The tour, which starts and ends in Gettysburg, covers some 36 miles around the city. It includes many of the county's famous orchards.

The tour begins at the **Gettysburg Convention and Visitors Bureau,** at 35 Carlisle Street. The tourist office is housed in the old **Western Maryland Railroad Station** (1858), one of many historic buildings in Gettysburg. Drive south along Carlisle Street to what is now known as **Lincoln Square.** From the square, turn right onto Route 30 West (Chambersburg Street). As you continue along Chambersburg Street, **Christ Lutheran Church** (1863) will be on the left about one-half block beyond the square.

Continue west on Chambersburg Street for three blocks to the second traffic light. Keep in the left lane and continue straight ahead on Springs Avenue, where there are the first of a series of signs designating the "Scenic Valley Tour." At the intersection of Springs Avenue and Route 30 West is a monument commemorating the young men of Gettysburg who joined together in defense of Pennsylvania when the Confederate invasion began in June 1863. On Springs Avenue you will climb **Seminary Ridge,** at the top of which is the **Gettysburg Lutheran Theological Seminary** (1826). As you follow the Scenic Valley Tour signs you will take a right onto Waterworks Road and pass the entrance road to the Eisenhower National Historic Site. As you continue straight ahead you will then cross Marsh Creek via **Sauk's Covered Bridge.** This 150-year-old bridge has "lattice-work" siding, a unique form of bridge construction.

The Township after crossing Marsh Creek is called "Freedom." The whole area was once part of the **Manor of Maske,** a 43,500-acre plantation of the Proprietors of Pennsylvania (the William Penn family). In this area the Mason-Dixon Survey was undertaken between 1763 and 1767 in order to settle the boundary dispute between Maryland and Pennsylvania. There still remain in place a very few of the famous stone markers which traced the final **Mason-Dixon Line.** The tour Route intersects Route 116, which was the old "Hagerstown Road" out of Gettysburg. The road was used by Lee's troops as they retreated south in 1863.

When the route you are following ends at a stop sign, turn left toward **Orrtanna.** The orchards through which you are traveling once extended for miles and miles. You may see remnants of roadside camps set up to house migrant laborers. At the Peach Glen intersection you will see the **Knouse Food Cooperative,** which handles millions of apples, cherries, and other fruit produced in the area. Turn right at the intersection, cross the railroad tracks, and continue straight ahead up to the summit of **Mt. Newman.** You will arrive at the **Church of St. Ignatius Loyola,** built in 1816 by the Jesuits from Conewago Chapel. Both the church and its graveyard are worth a visit. From St. Ignatius Church, continue down the hill to the intersection with Route 234. This stretch of road provides a panoramic view of the Buchanan Valley. At the intersection, turn right onto Route 234 to Biglerville. Beyond **Camp Nawaka,** along Route 234, the road runs through what is known as **The Narrows** with **Conewago Creek** on your right. The Conewago is noted for its scenic beauty and its excellent trout. Hence, the Narrows is a favorite picnic spot.

As you approach Arendtsville, the **South Mountain Fairgrounds** are on your left. In addition to the annual fair in August, the grounds are headquarters for the Apple Blossom and Apple Harvest celebrations held each year. Call for information on the dates and times of these events. Telephone: 717-677-9663. In Arendtsville, you will pass two churches, **Trinity Lutheran** and **Zion United Church of Christ,** both of which have congregations dating back to about 1804.

Biglerville, once known as Middletown, was plotted in 1817 and now calls itself the "Apple Capital of the U.S.A." At the traffic light in Biglerville, turn onto Route 34 toward Gettysburg. One-fourth of a mile along the road to Mummasburg (the turnoff is approximately three miles south of Biglerville) look for a building once known as **Russell's Tavern.** This was Washington's stopping place one night in 1794, as he returned from quelling the so-called "Whiskey Rebellion." Washington actually did sleep in the tavern. Continue south on Route 34 seven miles to Gettysburg. As you come over Keckler's Hill into Gettysburg, you might imagine how Confederate General Jubal Early felt as he traveled over this hill with his troops in 1863. Route 34 becomes Carlisle Street as it enters the Borough of Gettysburg.

Carlisle Area

The year 1720 marked the coming of the white man to the Cumberland Valley, where Carlisle is located. The town, nestled in the Cumberland Mountains 29 miles north of Gettysburg, is off the main tourist track yet worth a visit.

The earliest settler in the valley was an Indian trader, James Le Tort, who arrived at Great Beaver Pond, two miles south of Carlisle. In the decade following 1720, Scotch-Irish settlers began arriving in considerable numbers.

Carlisle, named for Carlisle, England, was laid out in 1751. Like its namesake, the town is bound by streets North, South, East, and West. The intervening streets, Louther, High, and Pomfret, running east and west, and Bedford, Hanover, and Pitt, running north and south, were all named for streets in Carlisle, England.

The **First Presbyterian Church** (c.1757), and **Dickinson College,** chartered in 1783, are among Carlisle's interesting institutions. The courtroom on the second floor of the **Old Court House** is a classic example of early courtrooms. Carlisle was the home of Molly Pitcher, famed heroine of the Battle of Monmouth, and several monuments have been erected to her memory in the "Old Graveyard."

Other historical buildings include the **County Jail** (1854), noted for its Roman architecture, the **Duncan-Stiles House** (1815), and the **Ephraim Blame House** (1749). For more information and details on an interesting walking tour, stop at the Greater Carlisle Area Chamber of Commerce, 212 North Hanover Street, Carlisle, PA 17013. Telephone: (717) 243-4515. Web site: www.carlislechamber.org.

The **Cumberland County Historical Society** was founded in 1874 to gather and publish facts of regional history. The society maintains a library and museum which are open to the public, Monday, 7 to 9 P.M.; Tuesday through Friday, 10:00 A.M. to 4 P.M.; Saturday, 10;00 A.M. to 1 P.M. The library has newspapers dating back to 1785. Among attractions in the museum are the oldest American-made printing press in existence, the finest collection of Schimmel and Mountz woodcarvings in Pennsylvania, a notable collection of early mechanical banks, iron products of 18th-century forges, photos of Jim Thorpe and other great Carlisle Indian School athletes, and products of Cumberland County artisans and manufacturers. Telephone: (717) 249-7610. Web site: www.historicalsociety.com.

The Society also manages the **Two Mile House** at 1189 Walnut Bottom. The Two Mile House is open to the public from May thru September on Wednesday afternoon from 1:00 to 4:00 P.M., or by appointment. It is also the site of the annual Highland Festival, a celebration of Scottish heritage. For more information telephone: (717) 243-3437.

The **Village of Colonial Peddlers,** located in a picturesque setting along Letort Creek in Carlisle, has 18 specialty gift and collectibles shops all in the "Spirit of 1776." Shops open Monday through Saturday, 10 A.M. to 5 P.M.; Sundays, noon to 5 P.M. Closed major holidays. Telephone: (717) 243-9970.

The **Carlisle Barracks,** the second oldest military post in the United States, currently houses the **Army War College.** There are several interesting sites worth visiting on the base. **The Hessian Powder Magazine** (1777) was used in Revolutionary days, 1777-89, as a munitions post. Hessian prisoners were brought here from Trenton. Carlisle Barracks is also home to the U.S. Army Military History Institute, the Battle of the Bulge Grove and Monument, and the Carlisle Indian Industrial School. Telephone: (717) 245-4101. Allow extra time for security checks.

The Military History Institute houses the largest collection of materials related to U.S. army history dating from the French and Indian

War to the present. The **Omar N. Bradley Museum** houses General Bradley's collection of more than 200,000 books, 30,000 volumes of periodicals, a huge collection of personal papers, and military memorabilia. Both are open Monday through Friday, 10:15 A.M. to 4:15 P.M. Free admission. Telephone: (717) 245-3972. Web site: www.carlisle.army.mil/AHEC/AHM/BradleyExhibit/ bradleyhome.cfm.

Eight miles west of Carlisle, in Newville on Route 641, is **Laughlin Mill** (1763), a classic example of a mill village of the 18th century. Just west of Newville, near State Game Land, a sign directs the visitor to the **Thompson Covered Bridge,** built in 1853. Five miles south of Carlisle on Route 174 at Boiling Springs is a Broadway theater in a rural setting. **Allenberry Playhouse** is open April to November. Call for program information and reservations. Telephone: (800) 430-5468. Web site: www.allenberry.com.

An interesting scenic return Route is via Route 81, west to Centerville, then south on Route 233, which passes through Pine Grove Furnace State Park and Mont Alto State Park, then through Waynesboro and into Hagerstown. **Mont Alto State Park** is a lovely, out-of-the-way place for picnicking. The 24-acre park with a creek running through it is located approximately 20 miles north of Hagerstown. The park offers fishing, hiking, picnicking and in the winter, snowmobiling. For more information contact Mont Alto State Park, c/o Caledonia State Park, 40 Rocky Mountain Road, Fayetteville, PA 17222-9610. Telephone: (717) 352-2161. Web site: www.dcnr.state.pa.us/stateparks/findapark/montalto/index.htm.

NEW JERSEY

Parts of southern New Jersey fall within the scope of this book, which identifies some of the many attractions within a 200 mile radius of Washington, D.C. South Jersey offers a wide range of attractions, from historic sites and unspoiled **Pine Barrens** to the dazzling nightlife of Atlantic City. In addition to the Pine Barrens, the area divides readily into three tourist regions: the southern half of the **Delaware River Region,** which stretches up along the river from Salem in the south to Camden; **Atlantic City** and the **Shore,** which includes **Cape May** and other beaches; and the **Delaware Bay Area.** For information on travel to New Jersey contact the New Jersey Commerce & Economic Growth Commission, PO Box 820, 20 West State Street, Trenton, NJ 08625-0820. Telephone: literature request: (800) VISITNJ; general information: (609) 599-6540. Web site: www.visitnj.org.

South Jersey has a number of fine state forests and parks. Visitors are reminded that New Jersey State law prohibits pets and alcoholic beverages inside these areas. Fishing licenses are required for all freshwater fishing. (This includes fishing above the freshwater point on the Delaware River and other rivers that empty into the ocean.) Regulations vary for saltwater fishing. Additional information on licenses and fishing areas can be obtained from the New Jersey Division of Fish and Wildlife, PO BOX 400, Trenton, NJ 08625-0400. Telephone: general information: (609) 292-2965, southern region information: (856) 629-0090. Web site: www.state.nj.us/dep/fgw.

New Jersey is notable for historic sites relating to the colonial period, the Revolution, and even the Civil War. General Washington based his operations here because the dense forests hid more than

80 illegal iron foundries, which could produce essential guns and cannons. One of the major causes of the Revolution was the desire of the colonists to be allowed to manufacture their own goods. According to British law, all raw materials had to be exported to Britain and the finished products then imported at high prices. General Washington had to judge carefully which of the local residents were sympathetic to his cause and could be trusted to lead his men safely through the wooded countryside. At that time, only about one-third of the colonists supported the Revolution; another third, Tories, supported the British Crown, although many did not fight and after the war emigrated to Canada and the West Indies; the final third were indifferent. New Jersey has a large number of excellent historical societies and other groups. Today the societies are responsible for preserving many sites, and they often publish or distribute information on them.

PINE BARRENS

The New Jersey **Pine Barrens** extend through more than one million acres in the southern part of the state. Scientists say that this land was at the bottom of the sea many thousands of years ago. Today most of it is a densely wooded wilderness area often resembling a jungle. Marshy grassland, cedar groves, and lakes abound. Water is plentiful here, but the dry, sandy soil left during the glacial meltings of the last ice age makes the pine forests highly flammable and only fitfully hospitable to many delicate forms of plant life.

This part of New Jersey, largely because of the Pine Barrens, is sparsely inhabited. The absence of good dark earth, and the capricious appearance of rivulets, ponds, and bogs with water always near the surface but rarely reliable in one place, led the colonists who first settled South Jersey to avoid the Pine Barrens. The word "Barrens" reflects their assessment of its potential for farming.

The Barrens, however, teem with more tolerant species of plants and wildlife. Sand dunes, which would do credit to a beach or a desert alternate with pine, oak, and cedar, as well as with cranberry bogs. An enormous variety of flowers and about 20 species of orchids grow wild. Several hundred different kinds of birds either nest here or pass through on migration routes. There are deer and foxes as well as smaller animals like raccoons. In short, there is a great deal to interest both the tourist and the professional naturalist.

This sprawling, almost primeval forest enfolds numerous historic sites and extends through many of the southern New Jersey state parks mentioned in this section, among them Wharton, Green Bank, Bass River, and Lebanon. A large part of the over 100,000 acres of **Wharton State Forest** belongs to the Pine Barrens and is of interest primarily to campers who like wilderness areas. There are picnic areas, cabins, and campgrounds. Four rivers of varying sizes flow through the park: the Mullica River, the Batsto River, the Branch Wading River, and the East Oswego Branch. Swimming, boating, and fishing are permitted at Atsion Lake. Fishing is also allowed in the river and tidewater areas. The Batona Trail is open to hikers for forty-seven miles. (Visitors are reminded that licenses are required for all freshwater fishing.) The irregularly shaped park is so large—it extends from five miles west of the Garden State Parkway halfway across the state, and is about fifteen miles deep from Batsto in the south to one of its northernmost points—that it can be reached by numerous routes. Inside the forest there are shore resorts for your enjoyment or you can indulge in saltwater boating, fishing, supervised swimming, hiking, biking, horseback riding, picnicking and playground facilities. There are also facilities for tent and trailer camping, and cabins are available for rent. The Carranza Memorial Batonia Trail, which starts in Lebonon State Forest, continues through Wharton and Bass River State Forest for 49.5 miles. A trail map is available at the park office. For information write to the Wharton Superintendent, 4110 Nesco Road, Hammonton, NJ 08037. Telephone: (609) 561-0024. Web site: www.state.nj.us/dep/parksandforests/parks/wharton.html.

From the town of Greenbank, on Route 542, it is approximately four miles to the 200-acre **Batsto Historic Area,** located in Wharton State Park. This ironworks produced military equipment of great value to the cause of the American Revolution. It was considered the iron and glassmaking industrial center from 1766 to 1867. The 39 buildings include a 36-room mansion. Visitors may stroll freely about the village, but only guided tours are available for the mansion. Craft demonstrations are given on varying days of the week and weekends. Hours vary. Admission charge for mansion tour. Telephone: (609) 561-0024 or (609) 503-9377.

Continue east on Route 542 to Route 9, and turn south eight miles to **The Towne of Historic Smithville** and The Village Green at Smithville. This is a restoration of an 18th-and 19th-century New

Jersey village. Stroll along the main street and peer in the windows of these charming old buildings. Among the many buildings are a grist mill, furnished homes, craft shops, and a chapel. Over sixty old-fashioned shops offer visitors all types of arts, crafts, and souvenirs. There are several excellent restaurants, a carousel, paddleboats, steam train and miniature golf for your enjoyment. Admission free. Open daily except Christmas Day. Telephone: (609) 748-6160 or (609) 652-7777. Web site: www.smithvillenj.com.

CAMDEN AND HADDONFIELD

Upon entering New Jersey via the Delaware Memorial Bridge, go north on Route 551 to **Swedesboro**. The **Moravian Church** at Oldman's Creek, three miles south of town, was built between 1786 and 1789. It is the oldest Moravian church in South Jersey. **Trinity Episcopal (Old Swede's) Church** is on King's Highway and Church Street. Built in 1784, it is a fine example of Georgian architecture. It is open for worship and also by appointment. In 1989 the **Schorn Log Cabin** was moved to the grounds of the church. This 18th-century cabin was built by Swedish settlers and was probably used as a granary by the early settlers.

The **Hunter-Lawrence House,** at 58 North Broad Street in Woodbury, is headquarters of the Gloucester County Historical Society. It was the home of the Reverend Andrew Hunter, chaplain with Washington at Valley Forge, and of Captain James Lawrence of "Don't give up the ship" fame. Its museum displays 18th-century weapons, costumes, furniture, coins and manuscripts, and a collection of Indian relics. Open Monday, Wednesday and Friday, 1 to 4 P.M. Closed in August. Telephone: museum (856) 848-8531; historical society: (856) 845-7881. For more information on these sites visit the Gloucester County Historical Society web site at www.rootsweb.ancestry.com/~njgchs/.

The **Woodbury Friends' Meeting House,** on North Broad Street, was built in 1715, and was used as a hospital by Hessians during the Battle of Red Bank in 1777. Open by appointment. Telephone: (856) 845-5080.

Red Bank Battlefield Park is at 100 Hessian Avenue, the nearby town of National Park, along the Delaware River. It was here, in October 1777, that 400 colonial troops defeated 1,200 Hessian soldiers who were British mercenaries. This victory, and that at Saratoga, caused the French to enter the Revolutionary War, and thus helped turn the tide for a patriot victory. The fortifications were built to protect Philadelphia from British forces. The Battle of Fort Mercer is staged every October. Open daily, 9 A.M. to dusk. Admissions free. Telephone: (856) 853-5120. Web site: www.co.gloucester.nj.us/depts/p/parks/parkgolf/redbank/.

The **James and Ann Whitall Mansion** is located at 100 Hessian Avenue within the **Red Bank Battle Field Park.** Built in 1748, this home was in the midst of the engagement at Red Bank. Many cannonballs are still embedded in its walls. The home, which contains original furnishings, served as a temporary hospital after the battle. Web site: http://whitall.org/.

Camden, eight miles to the north via Route 30, was the home of poet **Walt Whitman.** His home at 328 Mickle Street contains original furnishings and Whitman memorabilia. Open Wednesday through Saturday, 10 A.M. to noon and 1 to 4 P.M., Sunday, 1 to 4 P.M. Free admission. Telephone: (856) 964-5383. Web site: www.ci.camden.nj.us/attractions/waltwhitman.html.

Whitman Cultural Arts Center, at Second and Cooper Streets in Camden, is a center for the fine and performing arts. It houses a poetry library and a gallery, which hosts paintings, sculpture, and photography exhibits. On weekends, and sometimes during the week, there are concerts and plays. No admission charge for library and exhibits. Admission charge for performances. Library and gallery open Monday through Friday, 9 A.M. to 4 P.M. Open evenings and weekends for performances. (Gallery shows may be viewed at intermission.) Telephone: (856) 964-1534. Web site: www.waltwhitmancenter.org.

The **New Jersey State Aquarium**, is located on the Delaware River at 1 Riverside Drive. The aquarium houses a 760,000 gallon open ocean tank with two dozen sharks and over 1400 species of fish. Get up close and personal with over 4,000 aquatic animals in 80 exhibits, which include interactive exhibits, a penguin area, a children's garden and horticultural playground. Open September 16 through April 15, Monday through Friday, 9:30 A.M. to 4:30 P.M., Saturday and Sunday, 10 A.M. to 5 P.M.; April 16 through September 15, daily, 9:30 A.M. to 5:30 P.M. Admission charge. Telephone: (609) 365-3300. Web site: www.adventureaquarium.com.

Haddonfield, six miles east on Route 561, is the locale of many historic houses. For information regarding walking tours and events contact the Haddonfield Visitor Information Center, 114 King Hwy

East, Haddonfield, NJ 08033. Telephone: (856) 216-7253. Web site: www.haddonfieldnj.org/borough_Dept_infocenter.php. **The noted** Indian King Tavern, which was prominent in New Jersey history, has been a central landmark for over 200 years. Located at 233 East King's Highway, this 18th-century colonial tavern was the meeting place of the legislature which in 1777 proclaimed New Jersey's independence from Britain. In 1903 it became New Jersey's first state historical site. Open Wednesday through Saturday, 10 A.M. to noon and 1 to 4 P.M., Sunday, 1 to 4 P.M. Call for appointment if possible as the site is closed occasionally for private events. Admission free. Telephone: (856) 429-6792. Web site: www.levins.com/tavern.html.

Most of the historic houses and buildings are within an area of a few blocks and are easily visited on a walking tour. Unless otherwise indicated, they are privately owned and can be viewed only from the outside. Begin at **Borough Hall** on King's Highway. (There is an all-day parking lot located in the rear.) To the left of Borough Hall is **Glover House,** built in 1816. Across the street to the right are several brick houses dating from the 1830s. Indian King Tavern (described above) is next, at 233 King's Highway. In the next block, at 255 are the **Hedry-Pennypacker Home,** and the **Alexander House** at the corner of Grove Street. There are four historical buildings to the right on Potter Street. The **Old Pottery,** at No. 50, dates from 1805. Return to the highway and cross over. The **Haddon Fortnightly Club House** (1857) has a balcony and stage. It is still used as a private clubhouse.

Greenfield Hall, at 343 Kings Highway, was built in 1841 and is the home of the Historical Society of Haddonfield. This Georgian-style building is home to an excellent collection of early American furniture, china, tools and other artifacts. Hessian soldiers camped here before the Battle of Fort Mercer in 1777. A boxwood garden started circa 1796 is still growing today. Hours vary. It is safest to telephone first. Telephone: (856) 429-7375. Next door is the **Samuel Mickle House (Hip Roof House),** which was built in the 1730's as a saddlery. It is now used as a research library and houses photos, maps, old books, wills and genealogical records. Open Tuesday and Thursday 9:30 A.M. to 11:30 am, and the first Sunday of each month, 10 A.M. to 3 P.M. At the corner of Hopkins Lane to the right is a **double house** (Nos. 438 and 444), erected in 1790. Return via Hopkins Lane past **Pope John Library** (just beyond Grove Street) on right and **Friends Meeting House** at Lake and Wood streets. A number of Hessian soldiers are buried in this Quaker cemetery. **Friends School,** built in 1789, is at the corner of Haddon Avenue. It still serves as a school. Several old houses can be seen on Haddon Avenue. **Haddonfield Public Library** is also here. The current building dates from 1917, but the library itself dates from 1803 and is one of the oldest in the state. It began as a private library, which was open to the public. Telephone: (856) 429-1304. Web site: www.haddonfieldlibrary.org.

Turn right on Clement Street, to the **Tanyard House** at 38 Tanner Street, built in 1739.

Return to King's Highway, turn right, and cross the railroad tracks. The **Willis-Stretch Home,** at No. 8, is famous for its boxwood garden. Return to the starting point and go left a half block on Haddon Avenue to **Haddon Fire Company No. 1,** which is the second oldest volunteer fire department in continuous service in the United States. It has a small museum housing antique fire-fighting vehicles and equipment. The original Fire Company was organized in 1764, and there have been three successive buildings on this site. Open daily, 8 A.M. to 8 P.M. Free admission. Telephone: (856) 429-4308. Web site: www.haddonfirecompany.org.

DELAWARE RIVER REGION

This region can be reached by taking I-95 north to the Delaware Memorial Bridge.

Salem is four miles to the southeast of the Delaware Memorial Bridge on Routes 45 and 49. This town was settled by Quakers in 1675. The **Friends Meetinghouse,** built in 1772, has excellent examples of old Wistarburg glass. It is on East Broadway Street and is still used for services. The **Friends Burial Ground,** a couple of blocks away on West Broadway, is the site of the famous 500-year-old **Old Salem Oak,** under which Salem's founder, John Fenwick, made his peaceful treaty with the Leni-Lenape Indians in 1681, according to local legend.

Fort Mott State Park, located in Pennsville at 454 Fort Mott Road, was built during the Civil War. Now a state park, its fortifications and tunnels are of interest to the tourist. Nearby more than 2,400 Confederate prisoners of war, and 300 Union soldiers, are buried at Finn's Point National Cemetery on the banks of the Delaware River. The Confederates had been interned at Fort Delaware on Pea Patch Island, called by many "The Andersonville of the North." Fort Mott has fishing, boating, and picnicking facilities. The **Delaware River**

Bridge is six miles north of the park. Telephone: (856) 935-3218. Web site: www.state.nj.us/dep/parksandforests/parks/fortmott.html.

The Alexander Grant House, at 79-83 Market Street, built in 1721, is now a museum and home of the Salem County Historical Society and Research Library. The Grant House contains period furnishings, including fine collections of china, Wistarburg glass, and old dolls. The octagon-shaped John Jones Law Office, built about 1735 and reported to be the oldest brick law office in the 13 colonies, was recently moved to its present site behind Alexander Grant House. A barn at the same site contains carriages, a large collection of 18th- and 19th-century farm implements, and Indian artifacts. All three buildings can be viewed at the same time. Open Tuesday through Saturday, noon to 4 P.M. Admission charge. Telephone: (856) 935-5004. Web site: www.salem-countyhistoricalsociety.com.

Dotting the countryside surrounding Salem City are more than sixty 18th-century homes, churches, and meeting-houses. Many of them have on their walls the most outstanding glazed brick designs found in America. Additional information can be obtained from the Salem County Historical Society, which also hosts two open houses each year. The Annual House and Garden Show on the 1st weekend in May and the Yuletide Tour of Historic Homes and Businesses the 1st Saturday in December. Telephone (856) 935-5004.

ATLANTIC CITY AND THE SHORE AREA

To reach this popular area, follow I-95 north to the Delaware Memorial Bridge, then take Route 40 east to the shore. Many New Jersey beaches charge admission fees and require display of "day use" or "resident" tags. The sands are beautiful, fees are modest, and tags may be purchased at many locations.

Atlantic City, the major New Jersey seaside resort, is noted for its popular Convention Hall, for its annual Miss America pageant in September, its six-mile Boardwalk, its casino gambling and Las Vegas-style entertainment, and its many recreational facilities and amusements, including the major resort hotels. Among the available activities are sailing, deep-sea fishing, boat and bus sightseeing, horseback riding, tennis, racquetball, squash, biking on the Boardwalk, surfing, swimming, and several amusement piers. Garden Pier has an art center; Central Pier has a sky tower as well as helicopter charter flights and sightseeing. Several other major piers have undergone or are slated for extensive remodeling.

Atlantic City is a year-round resort with 450 motels, hotels, and guesthouses, as well as a great many restaurants. Advance reservations are suggested for accommodations during the summer months. There are numerous casino resort hotels that offer visitors the opportunity to play baccarat, slot machines, craps, roulette, blackjack, and big six. Video blackjack and poker are also available. There is a great variety of entertainment including cabaret, nightclub, and dinner shows featuring major show-business personalities. These resorts offer health clubs as well as restaurants, bars, and boutiques. For more information on Atlantic City contact the Atlantic City Convention and Visitors Authority, 2314 Pacific Avenue, Atlantic City, NJ 08401. The Authority also maintains two visitor centers, one on the Atlantic City Expressway just before you enter town, and the other at the Boardwalk and Mississippi. Telephone: (609) 348-7100. Web site: www.atlanticcitynj.com. There are several other points of interest in the Atlantic City area. The Renault Winery, 72 North Bremen Avenue, Egg Harbor City, has 1,400 acres including vineyards, wine cellars, a glass museum, and a hospitality center where one can enjoy wine tasting. Open Monday through Friday, 10 A.M. to 4 P.M.; Saturday, 11 A.M. to 8 P.M.; Sunday, noon to 4 P.M. Guided tours. Admission charge. Telephone: (609) 965-2111. Web site: www.renaultwinery.com.

The **Atlantic City Race Course,** located at 4501 Blackhorse Pike in Mays Landing, holds live races about 10 days per year, and simulcasts from other tracks year round. Telephone: (609) 641-2190.

Historic Gardner's Basin, at the north end of North New Hampshire Avenue and the bay in Atlantic City, features the **Ocean Life Center Aquarium.** This eight-tank aquarium features fish of the New Jersey Coast and Gulf Stream. Enjoy touch tanks and view artifacts from the *Andria Doria.* There is an observation deck and guided tours of the beach and salt marshes. Open daily, 10 A.M. to 5 P.M. Admission charge. Telephone: (609) 348-2880. Web site: www.oceanlifecenter.com.

Atlantic City Cruises leaving from Historic Gardener's Basin offers narrated sightseeing cruises along the Atlantic City ocean front, along with dolphin and whale watching tours. Open daily, May through October. Departure and cruise times vary. Fare charge. Telephone: (609) 347-7600. Web site: www.atlanticcitycruises.com.

The **Somers Mansion** is in Somers Point, about 10 miles south of Atlantic City on Route 9. Built circa 1725, it is now administered by the state, and has been restored as closely as possible to the way it looked when the Somers family lived in it more than 250 years ago. Of particular interest is the 18th-century furniture. Open Wednesday through Saturday, 10 A.M. to noon and 1 to 4 P.M.; Sunday, 1 P.M. 4 P.M. Closed winter holidays. Admission charge. Telephone: (609) 927-2212.

Across the street from the mansion is the **Atlantic County Historical Society Library and Museum,** which contains exhibits on the history of the area. Open Wednesday through Saturday, 10 A.M. to 3:30 P.M. Free admission. Telephone: (609) 927-5218.

Bass River State Forest, 762 Stage Road in New Gretna, is about 25 miles north of Atlantic City and bisected by the Garden State Parkway. It can be reached by driving north on I-95, east on Route 40, or north on Routes 575 and 9 to New Gretna. It also is convenient to several other popular seashore resorts.

During summer months you can enjoy hiking, horseback-riding trails, fishing, canoeing, sailing, boating, swimming, and camping. The Absegami Natural Area is known for interesting nature walks through pine and oak woods and a white cedar bog. Telephone: (609) 296-1114. Web site: www.state.nj.us/dep/parksandforests/parks/bass.html.

Bass River also administers **Penn State Forest,** a few miles away on Lake Oswego Road in Jenkin's Neck. You can obtain more detailed driving directions from the staff at Bass River. Penn State Forest is a real wilderness area. Fishing and canoeing are allowed on the lake. There are a few picnic tables. Swimming is not allowed because there is no lifeguard. Cross-country skiing is allowed in the winter. For more information contact: Penn State Park, c/o Bass River State Forest, PO Box 118, New Grenta, NJ 08224. Telephone: (609) 296-1114. Web site: www.state.nj.us/dep/parksandforests/parks/penn.html.

Located about 10 miles northwest of Atlantic City, the **Edwin B. Forsythe National Wildlife Refuge's** Brigantine Division has approximately 24,000 acres of saltmarsh, open waterways, and woodlands. The refuge itself is by Oceanville (not in the city of Brigantine), approximately two miles south of Smithville on Route 9. As many as 100,000 migratory waterfowl stop off here in the early spring and late fall to feed and rest. More than 275 bird species have been observed.

Take the Wildlife Drive around the West Pool and East Pool, where you can observe the wildlife. You can walk the half-mile Leeds Eco-Trail or the shorter Akers Woodland Trail. Have an insect repellent handy if you plan a summer visit. Telephone: (609) 652-1665. Web site: www.fws.gov/northeast/forsythe/.

Brendan T. Byrne State Forest is located in New Lisbon, off Exit 7 of the New Jersey Turnpike. Within this recreational area of the famous pine barrens in Central New Jersey there are large Atlantic white cedar swamps and open bogs. In summer you can enjoy hiking, biking, horseback riding fishing, and swimming, as well as cross-country skiing in the winter. There are family campsites and cabins available, as well as riding trails if you bring your own horse. Telephone: (609) 726-1191.
Web site: www.state.nj.us/dep/parksandforests/parks/byrne.html.

Plan to visit other nearby points of interest, such as **Whitesbog Village,** 120-13 Whitesbog Road in Browns Mills. This was a cranberry and blueberry producing community in the 19th and 20th centuries and was once one of the largest cranberry producing area in the state. For information regarding the village and events telephone: (609) 893-4646. Web site: www.whitesbog.org.

OCEAN CITY—WILDWOOD—CAPE MAY

The ocean resorts are accessible via I-95 north to the Delaware Memorial Bridge and east on Route 40 to Routes 55 and 47. They can also be reached by ferry from Lewes, Delaware, to Cape May.

The Cape May County Department of Tourism is located at # 4 More Road, Crest Haven Complex in the Cape May Courthouse. For information regarding hours of operation telephone: (800) 227-2297 or (609) 463-6415.
Web site: www.thejerseycape.net.

Ocean City lies on an eight-mile-long island between the ocean and the Intercoastal Waterway. Visitors can choose among 100 hotels and motels, and from about 250 guesthouses, furnished apartments, and condominiums. Among its attractions are its 2½-mile Boardwalk, saltwater fishing, crabbing, boating, sailing, bicycling, and water skiing. Other outdoor activities include tennis, golf, softball, shuffleboard, and surfing. Telephone: (800) BEACH-NJ.
Web site: http://www.ocnj.us/.

The **Ocean City Historical Museum** is located at 1735 Simpson Avenue. Displays deal with the social history of the area between 1890 and 1910, and with the Indian life before the coming of the white man. There are ship models and other nautical memorabilia salvaged from the *Sindia,* a four-masted ship that went aground between 16th and 17th Streets in 1901. Open summers, Monday through

Friday, 10 A.M. to 4 P.M.; Saturday, 1 P.M. to 4 P.M.; winters, Tuesday through Saturday, 1 to 4 P.M. Free admission. Guided tours are available. Telephone: (609) 399-1801. Web site: www.ocnjmuseum.org.

Many fine resorts dot the coastline from Ocean City to Cape May along Ocean Drive. Among these are **Strathmere, Sea Isle City, Avalon, Stone Harbor,** and the **Wildwoods.** There are many motels and guesthouses to accommodate visitors. The fisherman has a choice of deep-sea fishing on daily charter boats, surf casting, and pier fishing. No licenses are required. Fishing is not permitted on bathing beaches while lifeguards are on duty, which is usually from 9 A.M. to 6 P.M. during June, July, and August.

The **Stone Harbor Bird Sanctuary** is a nesting ground for thousands of waterfowl, chiefly egrets and herons. The sanctuary is located on Third Avenue in the southern part of the town of Stone Harbor. Open dawn to dusk. Telephone: (609) 368-7447.

Wildwood is a popular summer resort with a fine beach and two mile long boardwalk. Ocean fishing from party boats is very popular here. There are shops and restaurants galore, as well as five amusement piers and water parks. Early morning bike rides are a favorite along the boardwalk. Enjoy beach concerts, kite festivals and many other events through out the summer season. For more information on Wildwood, telephone: (888) 729-4000. Web site: www.gwcoc.com.

A few miles to the south are the Cape May City and Cape May Point resorts, known for their beach promenade and many stately 19th- century homes. **Cape May** has long been called the "summer home of the Presidents." Brochures listing addresses of the numerous historic houses and inns, as well as special events like antique shows, band concerts, and dances, are readily available at hotels, motels, and shops. Web site: www.capemay.com.

There are a number of interesting shopping areas, including the **Washington Street Mall** on Washington Street with its old time Victorians and a variety of beachfront shops. A small tour trolley travels along streets, which are tree-shaded by day and illuminated by gaslights in the evening. A number of excellent marinas are at hand for those who want to sail, fish, or take a ride on a motorboat or cabin cruiser. The beaches are well supplied with lifeguards.

One of the major attractions, of which there are many at Cape May, is the **Emlen Physick Estate,** home of the **Mid-Atlantic Center for the Arts** (MAC), 1048 Washington Street. This 16-room mansion (1881), designed by the famous 19th-century architect Frank

Furness, is used today as a museum of Victorian toys, costumes, artifacts, and the **Balsberg** book collection. MAC is responsible for operating the estate as a community and cultural center. The museum is open daily, 10 A.M. to 4 P.M. Last tour leaves at 3 P.M. MAC also sponsors numerous tours of the area. Two major events are a Christmas tour of decorated private houses (held on the Saturday between Christmas and New Year's), and a Columbus Day Victorian Week (in October), which includes a house tour as well as many other tours and events. Admission charge. Telephone: (609) 884-5404. Web site: www.capemaymac.org.

The **Coast Guard Training Center Cape May,** located at 1 Munroe Avenue, may be of interest to visitors. This area has served as a naval base since the American Revolution when the Continental Navy used it. During the War of 1812, the British captured it briefly. Through the beginning of the 19th-century, pirates took refuge in the many sheltered coastal inlets. Since the middle of World War I, the Cape May area has been used either by the U.S. Navy or by the Coast Guard as a base and training facility, for both sea and air operations. The Training Center is only open for group tours, which must be pre-arranged through the Public Affairs Officer at telephone: (609) 898-6969. Web site: www.uscg.mil/hq/capemay.

Fisherman's Wharf, at Schellenger's Landing, is a local landmark. Dozens of commercial fishing boats come and go from 12 large docks.

Cape May Bird Observatory is on the shore of Lily Lake, at 701 East Lake Drive, Cape May Point. Its sand dunes, marshes, and holly woods attract over 400 species of birds which frequent Cape May County (the largest number of species reported in any county outside Florida and southern California). The Observatory holds an annual hawk watch from mid-August to mid-November. Eighty-nine thousand hawks, a national record for this kind of watch, were recorded in 1981. The observatory has a gift shop. Open daily, 9 A.M. to 4:30 P.M. Telephone: (609) 884-2736. Web site: www.birdcapemay.org.

Many old homes and churches can be seen along Route 9, on a drive north toward the town of Cape May Courthouse. The **Cold Spring Presbyterian Church** was established in 1714. The **Friends Meeting House,** built in 1716, is still in use. It is located in Seaville on Route 9. The **Capt. George Hildreth House,** at Cold Spring, was built in the mid-1800s. Behind this house is a restored group of houses and other buildings named **Historic Cold Spring Village.** Located on

Route 9, three miles north of Cape May City, this 22-acre site is a 19th-century living museum. Over twenty antique homes from the Cape May area have been moved to and restored on this site. There are craft shops such as a working blacksmith shop and old fashioned potter. Open Memorial Day Weekend through mid-June, Saturday and Sunday, 10 A.M. to 4:30 P.M.; mid-June through Labor Day, Tuesday through Sunday, 10 A.M. to 4:30 P.M.; Labor Day to mid-September, Saturday and Sunday, 10 A.M. to 4:30 P.M. Telephone: (609) 898-2300. Web site: www.hcsv.org.

The museum of the local historical society is located at the John Holmes House, in **Cape May Courthouse.** It contains displays of Indian relics, antique furniture and utensils, whaling equipment, ship models, old china, and glassware. Open 10 A.M. to 4 P.M., April through mid-June and mid-September through November, Tuesday through Saturday; mid-June through mid-September, Monday through Friday; December through March, Saturdays only. Last tour starts at 3 P.M. Admission charge. Telephone: (609) 465-3535.

The *Atlantus,* a sunken concrete ship, may be seen at Cape May Point at the foot of Sunset Boulevard. It was one of three experimental concrete ships built during World War I in an attempt to overcome the wartime steel shortage. It was blown aground in a storm in 1926. **Cape May Lighthouse** is also located at Cape May Point. The current lighthouse was built in 1859, but there has been a light here since 1744. It is operated by the Mid-Atlantic Center for the Arts. Open daily, April through November, and on weekends the rest of the year. Hours of operation vary. Admission charge. Telephone: (609) 884-5404. Web site: www.capemaymac.org/attractions/lighthouse.

Belleplain State Forest, County Route 550 in Woodbine, can be reached by way of Routes 9 and 550 and by the Garden State Parkway. This forest beckons the visitor looking for a change from ocean beach vacations. You will find a quiet rural atmosphere with lots of room to roam and two lakes that offer all kinds of diversions. In summer you can find hiking, fishing, camping, swimming, boating, sailing, and playground and athletic activities. Winter sports include ice fishing, snowmobiling and cross-country skiing. Telephone: (609) 861-2404. Web site: www.state.nj.us/dep/parksandforests/parks/belle.html.

DELAWARE BAY AREA

This area can be reached by taking I-95 north to the Delaware

Memorial Bridge, then going southeast on Route 49. **Wheaton Village,** 1501 Glasstown Road in Millville, is a restored 19th-century glass and crafts town. It is approximately one hour's drive from Cape May as well as from Philadelphia and from the Delaware Memorial Bridge. The village contains a replica of an 1888 glass factory, a museum of American glass, a craft demonstration building, a general store and an 1876 one-room schoolhouse. In the Down Jersey Life Center there are artifacts from eight south Jersey counties depicting life in the 19th- and early 20th-century. The village contains several gift shops and boasts its own small train. Open April through December, Tuesday through Sunday, 10 A.M. to 5 P.M., January through March, Friday through Sunday, 10 A.M. to 5 P.M.; Closed Thanksgiving, Christmas, New Year's, and Easter Sunday. Admission charge. Telephone: (800) 998-4552 or (856) 825-6800. Web site: www.wheatonvillage.org.

Cumberland County's Liberty Bell, which tolled freedom's cry on July 7, 1776, is one of only three Liberty Bells in America and the only one in New Jersey. It can be seen in the lobby of the courthouse in Bridgeton. For more information regarding the Liberty Bell, log on to web site www.discovercumberlandcounty.com/history/.

Greenwich is a very old village on the Cohansey River, six miles west of Bridgeton. A monument in the square commemorates the burning of a cargo of taxed tea in its harbor in 1774 by men disguised as Indians.

Gibbon House (1730), on Ye Greate Street, is the headquarters of the Cumberland County Historical Society and Genealogical Library. The house is furnished in the style of the period and is notable, among other things, for a fine old kitchen with a nine-foot fireplace. It also contains a museum with collections of 19th-century children's toys, samplers, Ware chairs, antique lighting devices, and glass. A major item here is the figurehead of the *Ship John,* which sank in Delaware Bay in 1797. It was carved by William Rush, one of the foremost figurehead artists of his day. Open April through mid-Decmeber, Tuesday through Saturday, noon to 4 P.M.; Sunday, 2 to 5 P.M. Admission charge and guided tours during the week. Telephone: (856) 455-4055. Web site: www.cchistsoc.org.

The town also hosts an annual Christmas in Greenwich, in mid-December. There are caroling and other festivities at the beautifully decorated Market Square, a Swedish ceremony at the Presbyterian Church, a harpist and freshly baked gingerbread men at Gibbon House, and special exhibits and entertainment through the town.

Further information can be obtained from the Historical Society. Telephone: (856) 455-4055.

The **Hancock House** at Hancock's Bridge was built in 1734 by Judge William Hancock and his wife Sarah. It features blue-glazed header bricks. During the American Revolution this house, closest to the bridge, was used as a barracks. It is the only house in the state of New Jersey in which a wholesale massacre occurred. On March 21, 1778, a party of patriots was killed here by the British under Major Simcoe. In 1932, in memory of these men, the house was turned into a shrine. The house contains a large collection of antiques which, while not original to the house, are of significance to Salem County. Adjacent to the Hancock House is a replica of a cedar plank house built by the Swedish settlers more than 200 years ago. Open Wednesday through Saturday, 10 A.M. to noon and 1 to 4 P.M.; Sunday, 1 to 4 P.M. Telephone: (856) 935-4373.

Parvin State Park, which centers around a lake on a branch of the Maurice River, is at 701 Almond Road in Pittsgrove, about halfway between the Delaware Memorial Bridge and Atlantic City, off Route 40. A special feature is a nature trail through a unique botanical area where swamp flowers not often seen elsewhere may be observed. The park offers fishing, hiking, camping, swimming, boating, playground activities, and evening hikes, lectures, and slide shows. The park often serves as a convenient base for short trips to nearby attractions, such as Ft. Mott Park, Wheaton Village, and the Cape May resort area. Telephone: (856) 358-8616.
Web site: www.state.nj.us/dep/parksandforests/parks/parvin.html.

WEST VIRGINIA

Parts of West Virginia fall within the scope of this book, which highlights attractions within a 200-mile radius of Washington, D.C. For a comprehensive overview of the cities and towns, attractions, and historical sites in West Virginia, with links to almost all that have their own Web sites, the following Web site is a good first stop: www.wvtourism.com. The Web site for West Virginia state parks is www.wvstateparks.com.

HARPERS FERRY AND EASTERN GATEWAY

In 1733 Peter Stephens set up a ferry service at the confluence of the Shenandoah and Potomac rivers. In 1747 Robert Harper took over the ferry service and later built a mill. After President George Washington recommended to Congress that a national armory be built at **Harpers Ferry,** construction of the arms factory began in 1796. By the 1830s, both the C&O Canal and B&O Railroad reached Harpers Ferry, making it an important transportation center. Thus began the river town of Harpers Ferry.

Harpers Ferry is particularly notable in American history for John Brown's Raid, a prelude to the Civil War. On October 16, 1859, Brown and 21 followers seized the U.S. Armory in an attempt to liberate slaves throughout the south. It was also the scene of several Civil War engagements and was occupied by both Union and Confederate forces. In 1862 General "Stonewall" Jackson captured the federal garrison of 12,000 men at Harpers Ferry, just prior to the Battle of Antietam. This is an area of unusual scenic beauty, where the Potomac and Shenandoah rivers have carved a passage through the Appalachian Mountains. Today one can visit mid-19th century buildings, as well as an old cemetery, museums, and the noted Jefferson Rock. The historic district of the town, **Harpers Ferry National Historical Park,** is administered by the U.S. Park Service. For more about the area and the Eastern Panhandle region, contact the Martinsburg-Berkley County Convention and Visitors Bureau, 208 Queen Street, Martinsburg, WV, 25401. Telephone: (304) 264-8801. Web site: www.travelwv.com.

The **Harpers Ferry National Historical Park** Visitor Center is located just off Route 340. Visitors may pick up self-guiding tour brochures and information on conducted tours. Park historical buildings are open year round, and in the summer costumed rangers are available for lectures and explanations. Hours are 8 A.M. to 5 P.M. Admission charge. Telephone: (304) 535-6029. Web site: www.nps.gov/hafe.

A variety of museums and exhibits explain various aspects of Harpers Ferry's rich history. **Stone Steps,** carved in the natural rock, lead uphill from High Street to the **Harper House** (1775-82), built by Robert Harper. It is the oldest surviving structure in Harpers Ferry and is furnished in mid-l9th-century style. Further up a steep trail to the left is **Jefferson Rock,** a huge balanced boulder from which Thomas Jefferson, in 1783, viewed the confluence of the Shenandoah and Potomac rivers. He described the view as "one of the most stupendous scenes in nature," and said the view was "worth a voyage across the Atlantic." A path continues from the rock to **Morrell House** (c. 1858), on Filmore Street. This was the paymaster's house and later was one of the buildings of Storer College.

Another park trail leads from Jefferson Rock across the bridge over the Shenandoah River and ascends **Loudoun Heights,** where it joins the **Appalachian Trail.** A three-mile circuit hike follows Loudoun Heights eastward to the point where it descends to Route 340 and back to the starting point.

Another three-mile hike leads to the stone fort ruins on **Maryland Heights.** To reach this trail, cross the Potomac River footbridge and walk up the C&O Canal towpath for approximately a half-mile. The 3½-hour hike begins ascends steeply to the overlook cliff. From the almost bare ridge one can get a spectacular view up the Shenandoah and the Potomac valleys.

In the private area of Harpers Ferry the visitor will find many restaurants and shops in which to browse. On High Street the visitor can visit the **John Brown Wax Museum,** which recreates the John Brown story. Admission charge. Open daily March 15 to December, 15, 9 A.M. to 5 P.M. Telephone: (304) 535-6342.

The **Appalachian Trail Conference,** founded in 1925, is located at 799 Washington Street. This is the headquarters for the volunteer groups who help maintain the 2,160 mile-long trail. A 10-foot-long contour map of the trail route along the eastern seaboard is on permanent display, along with photographs, citations and other memorabilia. Open Monday through Friday, 9 A.M. to 5 P.M. Telephone: (304) 535-6331 Web site: www.appalachiantrail.org.

A few miles west of Harpers Ferry on Route 340 is **Charles Town,** where in the evenings horse racing fans can watch thoroughbreds race at the Charles Town Races or enjoy the thrill of fast cars at Summit Point Raceway. Telephones: Charles Town Races (800) 795-7001; Summit Point Raceway (304) 725-8444. Web sites: Charles Town Races - www.hollywoodcasinocharlestown.com/Racing; Summit Point Raceway - www.summitpoint-raceway.com.

The Jefferson County Courthouse (1836), in the center of Charles Town at the corner of Washington and George streets, was the scene of John Brown's trial in 1859 before the outbreak of the Civil War. The courtroom in which John Brown was tried has been preserved and may be viewed. Call for hours of operation. Telephone: (304) 728-3215.

Also at the corner of George and Washington streets is the **Charles Town Post Office.** It was Charles Town Postmaster William Wilson who started the first Rural Free Delivery in the country, in 1896. It still operates as the main post office for Charles Town. The **Jefferson County Museum,** one block east of the courthouse, at 200 East Washington Street, contains John Brown memorabilia, including the wagon which carried John Brown to the place of his execution. There is also a collection of old guns and rifles and other Jefferson County-related items. Open April through November, Monday through Saturday, 10 A.M. to 4 P.M. Free admission. Telephone: (304) 725-8628. Web site: www.jeffctywvmuseum.org.

North on Routes 9 and 48 takes the visitor to **Shepherdstown** (1762), one of the oldest towns in West Virginia. Here were established West Virginia's first newspaper, first post office, and the first church west of the Blue Ridge. The area bounded by Mill, Rocky, Duke, and Washington streets has been designated a National Historic District.

At the north end of Mill Street stands the **James Rumsey Historical Monument,** overlooking the Potomac River. The monument commemorates James Rumsey's first public demonstration of a steam-powered boat in 1787. Alongside is the **James Rumsey Steamboat Museum** which houses a half-size working replica of the first steamboat invented by Rumsey. Call for hours of operation. Telephone: (304) 876-0910.

Eight miles west of Shepherdstown on Route 45 is **Martinsburg.** This city was founded by General Adam Stephen, who served in both the French and Indian and Revolutionary wars. He was also a member of the Virginia Legislature. The **General Adam Stephen House,** at 309 East John Street, is a limestone building situated on a hill overlooking Tuscarora Creek at the edge of the city. It has been restored with furnishings of the 1750-1820 era. A log cabin, smokehouse, and other outbuildings have also been restored on the three-acre estate. Open Saturday and Sunday, 2 to 5 P.M., May through October. Telephone: (304) 267-4434.

Within a two-block area are several other interesting buildings. A showplace of Martinsburg is **Boydville,** built in 1812 and home to some of the city's most distinguished citizens. The house at 601 South Queen Street is shaded by venerable trees and bordered by high boxwood hedges. The grave and monument to General Adam Stephen is in one corner of this property. Martinsburg was the birthplace of Belle Boyd, noted Confederate spy, and the scene of one of her most notable exploits. The **Old Stone Jail,** built in 1795, is a stone building that has served as a jail, hospital, and nurses' residence.

The **Boarman House** on Public Square is one of the oldest buildings in the city. It was built as a residence between 1778 and 1792 and later operated as a tavern. It now houses an art gallery that features exhibits and a wide range of art workshops and the Martinsburg-Berkeley County Convention and Visitors Bureau. The **Market House,** at Queen and Burke streets, well over a century old, was used as a market and housed municipal offices for many decades. On King Street is the **Tuscarora Presbyterian Church,** which was built in 1802. The church was established by Scotch-Irish settlers in 1740. Wooden pegs on which pioneers hung their guns during services can be seen in the vestibule.

Berkeley Springs State Park, 121 South Washington Street, is on Route 9 about 25 miles west of Martinsburg or may be reached from I-70 on Route 522 south from Hancock, Maryland. The four-acre state park is located in the center of the town and offers Roman baths, mineral water baths, massages, dry heat cabinets, steam cabinets, and a swimming pool. The mineral water of the springs has no sulphur content and is quite clear. These springs, famous for reputed curative properties, were given to the colony by Lord Fairfax and were used regularly by George Washington. The town was established as a health spa in 1776. Open year round; reservations necessary. Telephone: (304) 258-2711. Web site: www.berkeleyspringssp.com.

The 6,115-acre **Cacapon Resort State Park** is south of Berkeley Springs on Route 522. It offers a variety of facilities, a 47 room lodge, the Cacapon Inn, and 30 cabins. Swimming, fishing, row and paddle boat rentals, hiking, golfing, tennis, and horseback riding are available. In the winter there is cross-country skiing. Open year round. Telephone: (304) 258-1022. Web site: www.cacaponresort.com.

POTOMAC HIGHLANDS

Northeastern West Virginia is one of the few places east of the Mississippi that is still a primeval wilderness area. Good roads provide easy access to stately forests, scenic overlooks, streams, and lakes in the highlands. National and state forests provide campsites, roadside parks, scenic overlooks, and hundreds of miles of hiking trails. This part of West Virginia also provides rock climbing, hunting and fishing opportunities, ski slopes, and has much to offer the bird lover, botanist, and the history-minded visitor. The adventuresome will be attracted to the 262 known caves and the 24 whitewater streams located in the highlands area. For further information contact: West Virginia Mountain Highlands, P.O. Box 1456, Elkins, WV 26241. Telephone: (304) 636-8400. Web site: mountainhighlands.com.

There are many old houses in and near Romney, whose town charter dates from 1762. The **Woodrow-Mytinger House,** on Gravel Lane, is the oldest building in town—more than 200 years old. It consists of a log kitchen, dwelling, and an office building. It is now listed on the National Register of Historic Places. Other houses are of considerable architectural interest and date back to the mid-1700s.

Washington had surveyed the Potomac Highlands area as a young man for Lord Fairfax, whose six-million-acre grant extended to what is now the Maryland-West Virginia Line. The **Fairfax Stone** marking the state line as a result of a U.S. Supreme Court decision is located north of Thomas off Route 219. The present stone is one mile north of the original 1746 stone.

In this area is **Ice Mountain,** on the North River, three miles east of Slanesville on Route 29. Cold blasts of air come out of rock crevices even on the hottest summer days and ice is found 18 inches below the surface on the southern end of the mountain. The area is now owned by the Nature Conservancy. Call (304) 496-7359 to make an appointment for a tour, or call (304) 637-0160 for general information. The old **Iron Furnace,** east of Romney on Route 45, three miles west of the Bloomery post office, is built of cut stone blocks. It produced military items for the Confederate army during the Civil War. There is a picnic site on the grounds.

The central feature of the 132-acre **Cathedral State Park** is the majestic stand of ancient hardwoods and hemlocks, the only remaining virgin hardwood forests in West Virginia. This forest has been designated a Natural Landmark by the U.S. Department of Interior. It mirrors the American wilderness before the white settlement of the continent. Here you can see the state's largest hemlock, 21 feet in circumference and 90 feet high. The park is located in Preston County on Route 50, approximately three miles east of Aurora. In summer you can enjoy hiking and picnicking and in the winter cross-country skiing in this day-use park. Free admission. Telephone: (304) 735-3771. Web site: www.cathedralstatepark.com.

Petersburg, on Route 220, is accessible from Front Royal (75 miles), and is known as the "Trout Capital" of the state. Here the fisherman finds in abundance the rainbow, brown, brook, and golden trout, the latter unique to West Virginia. Bass fishing is tops in the South Branch of the Potomac. Hunting also is popular in the area, and portions of two national forests are open to hunting in season.

One fourth mile north of Petersburg on Route 42, look for remains of an old country store built with 100-year-old logs. The **Edray Trout Hatchery** is located 3 miles from Marliton on Route 219. The hatchery raises rainbow, brook, brown and golden trout for stocking state streams. Observe the trout in their natural habitat in various stages of growth and development. Open daily 7:30 A.M. to 3:30 P.M. Telephone: (304) 799-6461.

The **Smoke Hole Caverns** are located on Route 28, eight miles south of Petersburg. They contain the largest "ribbon" stalactite in the world. The name derives from the fact that the Seneca Indians used the cavern to smoke their meat. Open year round. Admission charge. Telephone: (304) 257-4442. Web site: www.smokehole.com.

Seneca Caverns were discovered in 1760 and claim to be West

Virginia's largest and most beautiful caverns. Located six miles east of Seneca Rocks on Route 33, they have been nicknamed "West Virginia's Underground Wonderland." Seneca Caverns, HC 78, Box 85, Riverton, WV 26814. Telephone: (800) 239-7647. Web site: www.senecacaverns.com.

The eastern slope of **Saddle Mountain,** a geologic feature in the shape of a saddle, was the birthplace of Nancy Hanks, mother of Abraham Lincoln. It is accessible from Route 50 near Antioch, west of Romney. The visitor can see a stone marker showing the location of her cabin.

Lost River State Park is 3,712 acres large and located about 23 miles south of Wardensville, off Route 259, four miles west of Mathias. Among the recreational facilities available are hiking/cross-country skiing trails, bridle paths, outdoor games, playground equipment, a swimming pool, and picnic tables. There is also a recreational building and museum. The park has 24 cabins and a restaurant. The park derives its name from the Lost River, which vanishes beneath mountains several times. About four miles south of Wardensville the river flows under Sandy Ridge and emerges on the north side of the mountain, where it is called Cacapon River. Telephone: (304) 897-5372. Web site: www.lostriversp.com.

Blackwater Falls State Park, a 1,688-acre park located within the northern boundaries of the Monongahela National Forest, is on Route 32, four miles southwest of Davis. It is accessible from Romney via Routes 50 and 93. The scenic falls are 65 feet high, and the gorge is about 500 feet deep. The Blackwater River winds down the canyon in a series of rapids and cascades with drops of 1,850 feet in 10 miles. A 200-step stairway leads from the parking area to the foot of the falls. There are 65 tent/trailer campsites, 25 cabins, and a 55-room lodge. Visitors can enjoy swimming, boating, horseback riding, fishing, hiking/cross-country skiing trails, a sled run, picnicking, and use of playground facilities. There is a restaurant and refreshment service. Open year round. Free admission. Telephone: (304) 259-5216. Web site: www.blackwaterfalls.com.

Canaan Valley Resort is a four-season resort south of Blackwater Falls State Park on Route 32. It is situated in a mountain valley, 3,000 feet above sea level. Surrounding peaks rise to 4,200 feet or more, providing spectacular rugged scenery. The resort offers 23 fully equipped cabins and a 250-room lodge, as well as 34 deluxe tent/trailer campsites year round. There is an 18-hole golf course and a nature center, as well as hiking and nature trails, indoor and outdoor swimming pools, fishing, tennis, and evening programs. In winter there is downhill/cross-country skiing with year-round lifts and ice skating. Telephone: (304) 866-4121 or (800) 622-4121. Web site: www.canaanresort.com.

Monongahela National Forest, an 851,000-acre recreation area located in the Allegheny Mountains near the eastern border of West Virginia, is accessible via Route 50, west to Route 220, then south past Petersburg to the forest boundary. The state's highest peak, **Spruce Knob** (4,862 feet), ascends from this mountainous forest, and nearby are **Seneca Rocks,** whose towering walls rise dramatically almost 1,000 feet above the forest below. Within the forest are many unique areas of special interest.

There are excellent opportunities for picnicking, fishing, hiking, boating, and whitewater canoeing. Since wild game finds the forest a sanctuary, you may get a glimpse of bear, deer, beaver, turkey, or grouse. There are 21 campgrounds, 850 miles of hiking trails, and 40 recreation sites in the forest.

Within this national forest are also state parks such as the Blackwater Falls State Park, Calvin Price State Forest, skiing resorts such as Snowshoe and Canaan Valley and the Cass Scenic Railroad. Telephone: (304) 636-1800. Web site: www.fs.usda.gov/mnf.

The **Dolly Sods Wilderness Area** is located in the Monongahela National Forest, about 15 miles west of Petersburg. This is an area of high elevation wind-swept plains on the Allegheny plateau. Elevations range from 2,000 to over 4,000 feet, which consist of extensive flat rocky plains, upland bogs, beaver ponds and sweeping vistas which puts one in mind of Northern Canada.

The **Gaudineer** scenic area within the Monongahela National Forest, located north of Route Huttonsville and Bartow, has a stand of uncut virgin red spruce, some over 300 years old. There are scenic trails and a picnic area for day use.

The **National Radio Astronomy Observatory,** at Green Bank on Route 92/28, is a national research center for a consortium of nine universities. The scientists at the observatory study the universe through radio waves. The observatory presents a one-hour tour that includes a movie and a bus trip of the complex, which has six telescopes ranging from 40 feet to 300 feet. Open Memorial Day through October, daily, 9 A.M. to 6 P.M. Free admission, although there is a charge for special group tours. Telephone: (304) 456-2011. Web site: www.nrao.edu.

The **Cass Scenic Railroad State Park** is a 1,089-acre complex that includes trips on the mountain railroad, wildlife and historical museums, a country store, and a restaurant. Picnicking and hiking facilities are available. Thirteen former company houses have been restored and are available for rent year-round. Cass is located off Route 28/92 between Dunmore and Green Back in Pocahontas County. Open May through October. Schedule varies. Fare charge. Telephone: (304) 456-4300. Web site: www.cassrailroad.com.

The **Cranberry Mountain Nature Center** is located in a scenic mountain spot of the Monongahela National Forest at the junction of Route 150 and Route 39/55. The Center offers interpretive programs on the **Cranberry Glades,** the **Falls of Hills Creek,** the **Cranberry Backcountry,** and the **Highland Scenic Highway.** The visitor center has an exhibit hall, auditorium, restroom facilities, nature trails, and limited picnicking outside the center. Open daily, April through November, 9 A.M. to 5 P.M. Telephone: (304) 653-4826.

The 750-acre **Cranberry Glades Botanical Area** is two miles from the Cranberry Mountain Nature Center. One can take a self-guided tour on a half-mile boardwalk to see the plants that are unusual so far south and are more native to the northern areas of Wisconsin and Canada.

Bordering on the glades, the **Cranberry Backcountry** is a northern hardwood area. This large area encompasses 26,000 acres of the forest and has 75 miles of hiking trails within it.

The 23-mile **Highland Scenic Highway** proceeds north from the Cranberry Mountain Nature Center through the Cranberry Back Country with many overlooks over 400 feet and picnicking areas along the way. The highway ends at Route 219 near Marlinton.

The three **Falls of the Hills Creek,** further west on Route 39 from the Cranberry Mountain Nature Center, is a beautiful scenic area with a very fragile ecosystem. A very steep three-quarter-mile trail takes the hiker 250 feet down a narrow ravine. The falls increase in length from 20 feet to 45 feet, to 65 feet at the lowest level. The trail has stops along the way and the hiker will see the unusual layering consisting of three layers of sandstone and three of shale. This geologic formation, unique to this spot, caused the erosion creating the falls. There is now a paved walkway to the first (smallest) of the falls, which improves access for those who may otherwise find the footing too challenging.

Beyond the Monongahela National Forest, the **Pearl S. Buck**

Birthplace museum is located in Hillsboro on Route 219. Pearl Buck was born in her grandparents' home in 1892. Mrs. Buck won both the Pulitzer and Nobel prizes for literature. Open May to November, Monday to Saturday, 9 A.M. to 4:30 P.M. Admission charge. Telephone: (304) 653-4430. Web site: www.pearlsbuckbirthplace.com.

Droop Mountain Battlefield is a 287-acre park on Route 219, five miles south of Hillsboro. The battle took place on November 6, 1863, and was the largest Civil War engagement in West Virginia. The park offers hiking trails, a playground, picnic tables, and a museum of Civil War artifacts. Telephone: (304) 653-4254. Web site: www.droopmountainbattlefield.com.

Approximately 25 miles farther north off Route 219, near Slatyfork, is **Snowshoe Mountain Resort**. It is an all-season resort at the top of Cheat Mountain, known as a mecca for skiers and snowboarders. For the price of one lift ticket you can experience 53 different slopes and trails at the Snowshow and Silver Creek ski areas. In summer, tennis, hiking, horseback riding, mountain biking, swimming, and a signature golf course. There is also a spa, as well as conference facilities, restaurants, and a variety of accommodations. Telephone: (877) 441-4386. Web site: www.snowshoemtn.com.

Beyond Elkins, where Routes 219 and 250 divide as they continue northward, is the longest two-lane covered bridge still in use on a federal highway. The original bridge was built in 1852. **Philippi Covered Bridge** spans the Tygart Valley River and was used by the armies of both the North and South. The original bridge burned in 1989 but has been completely restored. Philippi, 25 miles west of Elkins on Route 250, was the site of the first land battle of the Civil War.

NEW RIVER/GREENBRIER VALLEY AREA

The southeastern section of West Virginia offers visitors a diverse choice of activities ranging from a stay at a historically renowned mineral springs spa, the Greenbrier, to roughing it on a whitewater raft trip down the New or Gauley rivers. The visitor to this region may wish to see a coal mine or visit one of the many glass factories. Telephone: (304) 252-2244 or (800) 636-1460. Web site: www.visitwv.com.

The **Greenbrier** is a five star luxury hotel with a complex of shops situated within a 6,500-acre tract on Route 60, just off of I-64 at White Sulphur Springs. The resort was established in 1778, when Virginians escaped the hot, sultry summers of the Tidewater to take advantage of the mountain air and curative powers of the mineral waters. Other families from Southern plantations soon followed, and The Greenbrier became an important summer social center. The Greenbrier is one of only three remaining mineral spring resorts that were popular in the 18th and 19th centuries. (The others are Berkeley Springs, West Virginia, and The Homestead at Hot Springs, Virginia.)

The hotel has a complete year-round sports program including three 18-hole championship golf courses, riding stables, skeet and trap shooting, swimming, biking, ice skating and skiing, and hiking and jogging trails. Indoor facilities include shopping, theaters, and heated pools, as well as sulphur baths, saunas, whirlpools, and massage. The resort has a dining room, two restaurants, and a nightclub. Telephone: (800) 453-4858. Web site: www.greenbrier.com.

Lewisburg is a tranquil agricultural community that is the third oldest town in the state. The town was founded in 1782 and was named in honor of General Andrew Lewis. The **Fort Savannah Inn** on North Jefferson Street is part of an original fort from which General Lewis in 1774 mustered troops to Point Pleasant, near the confluence of the Kanawha and Ohio rivers. Lewis and his troops defeated the Shawnee Indians under Chief Cornstalk in what some historians consider the first battle of the Revolutionary War. The Inn now operates as a 67-unit motel. Telephone: (304) 645-3055.

Across the street is **Lewis Springs,** a part of **Andrew Lewis Park.** The springs were discovered in the 1750s by Andrew Lewis. The spring supplied the earliest settlers of Lewisburg and Fort Savannah. It is enclosed in a 200- year-old stone spring house.

At 200 Church Street, the **Old Stone Church,** built in 1796, is the oldest church in continuous use west of the Alleghenies. This restored Presbyterian church has a slave gallery and an adjoining cemetery where Civil War soldiers are buried.

The **Lost World Caverns** are located 1½ miles north of Lewisburg on Fairview Road. This private cavern features a cave 1,000 feet long and 75 feet wide with several waterfalls and many terraced stalagmites. Open year round; hours vary seasonally. Admission charge. Telephone: (304) 645-6677. Web site: www.lostworldcaverns.com.

At **Beckley** you can visit a vintage coal mine, the **Beckley Exhibition Coal Mine.** Visitors can ride through the mine in authentic "man cars" that carried the miners to work each day. The tours of the mine are guided by veteran miners. For the same admission charge, you can visit buildings from the mine village, including the superintendent's house, a coal miner's house, the Coal Camp Church, and the Coal Camp School. Open April through October, with tours from 10 A.M. to 5:30 P.M. Telephone: (304) 256-1747. Web site: www.beckley.org/exhibition_coal_mine/.

The 4,127-acre **Babcock State Park** features waterfalls, rugged scenery, and an operating grist mill. It is located at Clifftop on Route 41, off Route 60. Facilities include rental cabins, campsites, playgrounds, a swimming pool, boating, horseback riding, hiking/cross country ski trails, and fishing. There are more than 20 miles of trails, including the "Island in the Sky" trail where hikers must squeeze through a crevice and a cave. The **Glade Creek Grist Mill** is one of the most photographed buildings in the area. Telephone: (304) 438-3004. Web site: www.babcocksp.com.

Bluestone Lake is a 2,000-acre lake created by the damming of the New River near Hinton on Routes 20 and 3. The lake is the center of a recreation area that includes Bluestone and Pipestem state parks and five camping and fishing areas. Geologists consider the New River to be among the oldest rivers in the world, originating millions of years ago, and perhaps second only to the Nile in age. The **Bluestone Dam** is a concrete gravity dam that closes a 2,048-foot gap between mountains and rises 165 feet above the streambed. Tail waters below the dam challenge fishing and canoe buffs. The U.S. Corps of Engineers offers tours of the dam, Memorial Day through Labor Day, Wednesday and Thursday, 1:30 P.M.; Saturday and Sunday, 2 P.M. Telephone: (304) 466-1234.

Bluestone State Park offers rental cabins, campsites, swimming pool, boat launching facilities, boat rentals, fishing, playground, hiking and picnicking in a 2,155-acre setting. Telephone: (304) 466-2805. Web site: www.bluestonesp.com.

The 4,023 acres of **Pipestem Resort State Park** include two lodges, 25 cottages and 82 campsites. Picnicking, hiking, boating, fishing, swimming, horseback riding, playgrounds, miniature golf, and two golf courses offer summer recreation possibilities. In the winter, cross-country skiing trails and sled runs are open. Telephone: (304) 466-1800. Web site: www.pipestemresort.com.

The **North Bend Rail Trail,** (formally Big Bend Tunnels) a former main line of the B&O Railroad, covers 72 miles from Parkersburg to near Clarksburg. The trail, used by hikers, bikers, and horseback riders, travels through several towns and ten tunnels. The trail is part of the 5,500-mile American Discovery Trail. From Route 3 near Talcott, visitors can get a glimpse of twin tunnels, 6,500-feet long, in the distance. Telephone: (304) 628-3777. Web site: www.northbendrailtrail.net.

Also located on Route 3 near Talcott is the **John Henry Monument.** A statue of the "steel-driving" man stands in a small overlook. According to the legend, Henry worked on the Chesapeake and Ohio Railroad tunnels in 1873 and he died after competing with a steam-powered drill in an attempt to prove he could work faster than a machine.

On Route 19 between Hico and Fayetteville, the **New River Gorge Bridge** rises 876 feet above the river. This bridge is the highest span east of the Mississippi River and is one of the longest four-lane, steel arch bridges in the world. It is 3,030 feet long.

The New River and the nearby Gauley are also famous for whitewater rafting. Rafting companies and guides may be found in the following Web site: www.whitewater.com.

Hawks Nest State Park is a 276-acre park off Route 60 near Ansted which features a lodge built on the rim of the canyon near the New River Gorge Bridge. The park offers boating, fishing, picnicking, and hiking opportunities. An aerial tram carries visitors from the lodge to a marina in the gorge below, providing a wide view of the New River and surrounding mountains. Fare charge for the tram. **Hawks Nest State Park Museum** is perched on the mountain above the park and contains early pioneer, Civil War and Native American artifacts. Free admission. Telephone: (304) 658-5212. Web site: www.hawksnestsp.com.

NORTH CAROLINA

Kitty Hawk . . . Cape Hatteras . . . Albemarle Sound. The northeastern corner of North Carolina (which falls within the scope of this book) evokes images of a diverse vacation land that offers something for everyone: sun-lovers, history buffs, gourmets, and sailors, even hang gliders.

The history of the "Tar Heel State" dates back to the very beginnings of the country. Colonists settled in this area as early as the 16th century, and you can visit the towns and cities where they left their mark. The area is also famous for its water sports. No matter where you are in northeastern North Carolina, you are never far from a cove, swamp, bay, or the ocean itself. And where there is water, there is seafood. You will enjoy stopping at the many little restaurants and diners by the side of the road—all one-of-a-kind establishments serving seafood just barely out of the water.

The state of North Carolina has a wonderful Web site that is a good starting point for your visit: www.visitnc.com. The North Carolina State Park Web site is www.ncparks.gov.

ALBEMARLE SOUND

Often called the "Cradle of American History," **Albemarle** dates back to the 16th century. King Charles II deeded the land to eight Lord Proprietors, one of whom was George Monck, Duke of Albemarle. In 1665, the colony's first representative assembly met in this region. Two years later, the colony's first organized resistance to British authority, Culpeper's Rebellion, took place here.

This area also boasts the state's first school (in Pasquotank County, 1705), first church building (near Edenton, about 1705), and the oldest still-standing church (St. Thomas, in Bath, 1734). Throughout the region, you will see brown and yellow signs directing you along the Historic Albemarle self-guided driving tour. It will take you to towns in the area, and from there you can take the individual tours offered by the sites themselves. A map of the route is available from Historic Albemarle Tour, Inc., PO Box 1604, Washington, NC 27889. Telephone: (800) 734-1117. Web site: www.albemarle-nc.com/hat.

The **Great Dismal Swamp National Wildlife Refuge** preserves the historic natural area surrounding the Dismal Swamp, which was first surveyed by Colonial William Byrd II in 1728. The Refuge consists of 107,000+ acres, which include Lake Drummond, a natural lake of 3,100 acres in the middle of the swamp. George Washington was engaged to survey a portion of the swamp and supervised the digging of an extensive passageway ("Washington's Ditch") to facilitate barge travel through the area. He also invested (badly, as it turned out) in a company that proposed to harvest lumber from the Swamp. The Swamp offers hiking, biking, photography opportunities, wildlife observation, fishing, canoeing, kayaking, boating and a mile-long boardwalk. Telephone: (757) 986-3705. Web site: www.fws.gov/northeast/greatdismalswamp. At the **Dismal Swamp Canal Welcome Center,** located at 2356 Route 17 N, you can pick up brochures to learn more about the history, mystery, and lore of the swamp, as well as other attractions in the Albemarle region. There are also restrooms, picnic tables, and grills. Open Memorial Day through October 31, daily, 9 A.M. to 5 P.M.; November 1 to Memorial Day, Tuesday through Saturday, 9 A.M. to 5 P.M. Telephone: (252) 771-8333. Web site: www.dismalswamp.com.

Cypress swamps and massive gum trees dominate **Merchants Millpond State Park** (off Route 158 in Gates County). A unique mingling of coastal ponds and southern swamp forest help make up this 3,246 acre park. There are facilities for picnicking, camping, hiking, birding, and canoeing. Excellent fishing is available in Millpond for largemouth bass, crappie, catfish, chain pickerel, and shad. Telephone: (919) 357-1191. Web site: www.ncparks.gov/Visit/parks/memi/main.php.

On Route 17 is the Pasquotank County seat of **Elizabeth City.** A 33-block area in the heart of the city is included in the National Register of Historic Places. The district is architecturally distinguished by Greek revival, Queen Anne, and colonial revival houses, a charming Victorian courthouse, and many antebellum commercial buildings. **Christ Episcopal Church and Parish House** (c. 1856), 200 S. McMorrine Street, boasts a three-story corner stair tower in the church and stained glass windows that portray the life of Christ. The Parish House, built in 1925, is a two-story brick Tudor Revival style.

The **Elizabeth City Chamber of Commerce,** located at 502 East Ehringhaus, has brochures and maps of the Historic District. Open Monday through Friday, 9 A.M. to 5 P.M. Closed holidays. Free admission. Telephone: (252) 335-4365. Web site: www.elizabethcitychamber.org.

The area's history is well explained at Elizabeth City's **Museum of the Albemarle,** located at 1116 Route 17 South. There are exhibits of regional history, geography, religion, and economy. In addition to exhibits, the museum offers lectures, "touch talks," and audiovisual programs. Open Tuesday through Saturday, 9 A.M. to 5 P.M.; Sunday, 2 to 5 P.M. Closed Mondays and state holidays. Free admission. Telephone: (252) 335-1453. Web site: www.museumofthealbemarle.com.

The **Watermark Association of Artisans** is located on Route 158 East in Camden County. This is a member-owned, craft-producing cooperative which creates over 700 traditional and indigenous crafts to the area. Open daily, 10 A.M. to 6 P.M. Telephone: (800) 982-8337 or (252) 338-0853. Web site: www.elizcity.com/G-O-E/chamber/artcult.htm.

Visitors entering **Hertford** will cross a unique, S-shaped bridge. The town celebrated its Bicentennial in 1958, and is now approaching its 250th birthday. Many of the homes date to the 18th and 19th centuries, especially those along Front, Church, Grubb, Market, and Dobb streets. The **Newbold-White House,** on Harvey Point Road, was built in 1730 by Abraham Sander, replacing the one built by Joseph Scot almost a hundred years earlier. The oldest brick house in the state, it was restored to its original condition by the townspeople. Open March through the day before Thanksgiving, Tuesday through Saturday, 10 A.M. to 4:30 P.M.; Sunday, 2 to 5 P.M. Admission charge. Telephone: (252) 426-7567. Web site: www.albemarle-nc.com/newbold-white.

Hertford is the seat of Perquimans County, and the **County Courthouse,** on Church Street, is worth a visit. Built between 1823 and 1825 in a simplified Federal style, it has been enlarged over the years to double its original size. The oldest part is the two-story front section.

The **Perquimans Chamber of Commerce,** located at 118 West

Market Street in Hertford, can answer visitors' questions and provide flyers on the town. The Chamber of Commerce also has a walking tour featuring historic homes and buildings. Open Monday through Friday, 10 A.M. to 4 P.M.; Saturday, 10 A.M. to 1 P.M. Telephone: (252) 426-5657. Web site: visitperquimans.com.

Continuing southwest on Route 17, the road leads to Chowan County. The fertile lands of the Chowan River brought settlers to this area as early as 1658. They planned the town of **Edenton** in 1712, and 10 years later it was incorporated as the first capital of the province of North Carolina. The town served as a prosperous port in the 18th and early 19th centuries. This commercial activity rapidly turned Edenton into a center of learning, taste, and political activity within the colony. Many noted American patriots lived here including Joseph Hewes, a Revolutionary War leader and signer of the Declaration of Independence; Samuel Johnston, a governor of North Carolina; and James Iredell, Supreme Court justice and speaker of the General Assembly. Even the infamous pirate Blackbeard sailed from Edenton's port. Throughout the Revolutionary War, Edenton exporters defied British blockades by sending supplies to Washington's army and the besieged northern colonies. The ladies of Edenton also did their part to aid the war effort. On October 25, 1774, 51 local women decided to join their Boston peers in protest of the British tax on tea. They signed a resolution supporting the acts of the rebellious provincial Congress. Led by Penelope Barker, the women poured their tea for the last time, and agreed not to buy more until the tea tax was abolished by Parliament.

Today, three centuries of homes, a waterfront setting on Albemarle Sound, and resplendent gardens make any route through town a delight. The **Edenton Visitor Center,** located at 108 North Broad Street, has many resources and exhibits to help you explore historic Edenton. Tours are offered, fee charged. Hours vary seasonally. Telephone: (252) 482-2637. Web site: www.edenton.com.

On your own, you may wish to start your tour at the **Barker House** at 505 South Broad Street. Built in 1782, it was once home of Thomas Barker, colonial agent in England, and his wife Penelope of Edenton Tea Party fame. It is now administered by the Edenton Historical Commission, whose members conduct tours of the interior. Open Monday, through Saturday, 10 A.M. to 4 P.M., Sunday, 1 to 4 P.M. Telephone: (252) 482-7800.
Web site: www.edenton.com/history/barker.htm.

Besides the Barker house, other buildings on the Visitor Center guided tour are the Iredell House, St. Paul's Episcopal Church, the Cupola House, and the Chowan County Courthouse. Built around 1773, the **Iredell House** was the home of James Iredell, a British subject who came to America in 1768 as deputy collector for the Port of Roanoke. He was later named attorney general of North Carolina and then appointed to the first U.S. Supreme Court. The house is listed on the National Register of Historic Places, and now has a museum of late 18th- and early 19th-century furnishings as well as a charming one-room schoolhouse and other dependencies on the grounds.

St. Paul's Episcopal Church is just what you think of when you imagine a colonial brick church. In fact, it has been called an "ideal in village church architecture." Begun in 1736 and completed some 30 years later, it still has an active congregation and is listed on the National Register of Historic Places. Buried in the churchyard are colonial governors Charles Eden, Thomas Pollock, and Henderson Walker.

The **Cupola House,** a National Historic Landmark, is named for the small cupola rising above the roof which enabled sea captains to observe ships entering the bay. Built about 1725, it has rare Jacobean features such as large chimneys, decorative finials, and a second-story overhang. Part of the downstairs woodwork was sold to the Brooklyn Museum of Fine Arts, but has been carefully reproduced. You can even trace your finger over 150-year-old signatures scratched in the wavy glass window panes. The herb garden in back and the formal garden in front have been restored according to a 1769 map.

In the heart of the Historic District, the village green is framed by the **Chowan County Courthouse,** a fine example of Georgian architecture and a National Historic Landmark. Built in 1767, it has been in continuous use for more than 200 years. A beautifully paneled room above the courtroom served as a ballroom for dancing, classes, and public festivities, and as a banquet room during the visit of President James Monroe in 1819.

Also around the village green are the **Bond House,** built around 1805 for Joseph Blount Skinner; the **East Custom House**; a monument to Joseph Hewes, signer of the Declaration of Independence; three Revolutionary War cannons; and a bronze teapot commemorating the Edenton Tea Party. These properties are privately owned and not open to the public, but may be viewed from the outside. A map provided by the Visitor Center can also guide you to a dozen additional properties of note, historically and architecturally.

The Visitor Center can also provide more information about African American heritage and culture in the area. Among them are a black builder and his sons who were responsible for constructing many historic houses in Edenton, each with a characteristic circular "cuppola" porch. Harriet A. Jacobs, author of "Life of a Slave Girl" was also a resident of Edenton. Jacobs is said to have escaped from her master by hiding in the loft of a barn in the very town in which she was in bondage. From that vantage, she kept track of the local comings and goings and the growth of her children for more than two years.

On the third Friday and Saturday in April of odd-numbered years, the Edenton Woman's Club Pilgrimage allows visitors to tour many town and countryside homes and buildings not normally open to the public. Contact the Edenton Visitor Center for specific dates and times. Telephone: (252) 482-2637. Web site: www.edenton.com.

Cross Albemarle Sound, the largest freshwater sound in the world, on Route 37, then turn left on Route 64 into Creswell. Just south of town is the splendid 19th-century coastal plantation estate, **Somerset Place.** The Greek revival mansion was built about 1830 by Josiah Collins, who had come to America from Somerset, England. This merchant and prominent citizen of nearby Edenton worked long and hard to open up the swampy lands around Lake Scuppernong (now called Lake Phelps). His son, Josiah, Jr., also a successful merchant, manufacturer, and planter, joined him in business. The plantation grew, and about 1830 the mansion was built. The farm continued prospering until the time of the Civil War, which drove Josiah III from his home, ruined the magnificent estate, scattered the servants, and sent his sons into battle. His widow and sons attempted to revive the enterprise to no avail, and were finally forced to sell the plantation. Restoration work began in 1951 and still continues on the beautifully preserved mansion and outbuildings. The authentic restoration was accomplished through extensive documentary and archaeological research, which has exposed the remains of slave buildings, a hospital and chapel, an overseer's house, original brick walks, and the completely detailed formal garden layout. Hands on programs demonstrate the plantation system and daily life during the antebellum period, and helps visitors to feel the impact of African culture and traditions of the enslaved community on the

Collins family. Open November 1 through March 31, Tuesday to Saturday, 10 A.M. to 4 P.M.; Sunday, 1 to 4 P.M.; April 1 through October 31, Monday to Saturday, 9 A.M. to 5 P.M.; Sunday, 1 to 5 P.M. Free admission. Telephone: (252) 797-4560. Web site: www.albemarle-nc.com/somerset.

Somerset Place is within the boundaries of **Pettigrew State Park,** named for Confederate General James F. Pettigrew. The park also includes parts of the old Pettigrew and Bonarva plantations and the 16,000 acres of Lake Phelps. Lined with magnificent cypress trees, the spring-fed lake is an angler's paradise with largemouth bass, yellow perch, and various types of panfish. Wind conditions make it an ideal spot for sailing, and facilities include a boat ramp. Birders enjoy Pettigrew's reputation as a wintering area for Canada geese and several species of duck. It is also the site of the annual Indian Heritage Week held each September. There are also 13 tent and trailer campsites and picnic grounds. Free admission. Open daily at 8 A.M., closing hours vary seasonally. Telephone: (252) 797-4475. Web site: www.ncparks.gov/Visit/parks/pett/main.php.

About 18 miles south of Plymouth off Highway 45 is **Pungo National Wildlife Refuge.** The 12,000 acres are similar in terrain to Great Dismal Swamp, and in fact it is sometimes considered the southern end of the swamp. Pungo Lake makes up almost one-fourth of the refuge, and is a good spot to watch wintering birds such as swans, geese, and shallow-water ducks. There are no organized activities for visitors. Open daily, dawn to dusk. Free admission.

Off Route 94 about 1½ miles north of Route 264, between Swan Quarter and Engelhard, you will come to **Mattamuskeet National Wildlife Refuge,** also popular among bird watchers. This is in the middle of the Atlantic flyway, and Canada geese, snow geese, tundra swans and 22 species of ducks winter here annually. You can also spot southern bald and golden eagles, and during other times of the year, osprey, herons, and egrets. There is a walking trail, dikes along the marsh area (for foot traffic only), and a causeway over Lake Mattamuskeet, the largest natural lake in the state. Fishing is permitted from March through September, and a managed duck hunt is held annually, usually in early December. Telephone: (252) 926-4021. Web site: www.fws.gov/mattamuskeet.

Still another refuge administered by the Mattamusket National Wildlife refuge is south of Route 264 on Pamlico Sound. **Swanquarter Wildlife Refuge** has limited access via a marked gravel road. The bird watching is minor compared to Mattamuskeet because the marsh areas are inaccessible, but there is a fishing pier available on the sound. Swanquarter Refuge is open daily, dawn to dusk. Free admission.

You can continue north on Route 264 through the farms and swamplands of Hyde and Dare counties, crossing the Intracoastal Waterway to Nags Head, or take the ferryboat leaving Swanquarter for Ocracoke Island. The toll ferries take 2½ hours to cross Pamlico Sound, and leave Swanquarter daily at 7 A.M., 9:30 A.M. and 4 A.M. If you are coming from the opposite direction, ferries leave Ocracoke at 6:30 A.M., 12:30 P.M. and 4 P.M. Reservations are advisable. If departing from Swanquarter telephone: (800) 293-3779 or (252) 926-6401; if departing from Ocracoke telephone: (800) 293-3779 or (252) 928-1665. Web site: www.ncdot.gov/travel/ferryroutes.

OUTER BANKS

The famous **Outer Banks** of North Carolina are favorite spots for those who abhor crowded beaches with wall-to-wall condominiums. About the nearest the Outer Banks comes to this type of resort is Nags Head, which can still be relatively uncrowded. The further south you go along this 120-mile stretch of sand dune islands, the less crowded they become. It is entirely possible to be the only one on a beautiful beach in Hatteras—even on a holiday weekend. If you want nightlife, you can find it; if your tastes run more to quaint fishing villages, you will also be kept happily occupied.

The geography of the Outer Banks is rather unique, owing its landscape to storms, winds, and waves. Many geologists believe the ever-changing sand dunes are slowly moving towards the mainland. The inlets and sound have always had a strong maritime activity, and many of the residents have kept the "high tide" accent and customs of their 17th-century forefathers. The area is also noted for its superlative fishing. The Outer Banks Visitors Bureau is a good place to start planning your trip. Telephone: (877) 629-4386 or (252) 473-2138. Web site: www.outer-banks.com/visitor-info.

To reach the Outer Banks from Richmond, take I-64 southeast to the 168-South Exit, and continue to the junction with Route 158, proceeding east. From Baltimore and Washington, take I-95 south to Richmond, then proceed as above.

Driving south on Route 158, you will cross a bridge over Currituck

Sound onto Bodie (pronounced "body") Island, giving you your first glimpse of the Outer Banks sand dunes. The **Outer Banks Chamber of Commerce Welcome Center,** located on 101 Town Hall Drive in Kill Devil Hills, can provide you with a host of sightseeing information including maps, lodging and restaurant listings, and brochures. Open Monday through Friday, 8:30 A.M. to 5 A.M. Closed Thanksgiving, and from Christmas through New Year's. Telephone: (252) 441-8144. Web site: www.outerbankschamber.com.

Continuing south on Route 158, you will see looming in the distance the **Wright Brothers National Memorial** commemorating Orville and Wilbur's historic powered-aircraft flight on December 17, 1903. The actual location of the flight is about 300 yards from the monument, marked by a large pylon. Nearby are reconstructions of their launching apparatus, the hangar, and their living quarters. At the Visitor Center, the Wright brothers' story is told through exhibits and full-scale reproductions of their 1902 glider and 1903 flying machine. Open daily, 9 A.M. to 6 A.M. summer, closes at 5 A.M. the rest of the year. Closed Christmas. Free admission. Telephone: (252) 473-2111. Web site: www.nps.gov/wrbr.

If the Wright brothers inspire you to take flight yourself, you can try hang gliding in **Jockey's Ridge State Park.** Its sand dune is the highest on the east coast, currently at 85 feet (beginners start on the lower slopes). Even if you don't hang glide, the exhilarating view from atop the dune is well worth the climb. Open daily, 8 A.M. to dusk; June through August, 8 A.M. to 9 A.M. Free admission. Telephone: (252) 441-7132. Web site: www.jockeysridgestatepark.com.

Nags Head is a popular resort with excellent beaches and facilities for fishing. Local legend says the town's name stems from an old practice of tying lanterns to ponies' necks at night and walking them along the beach. Ship captains would spot the swinging lights, and thinking they were boats at anchor, would run their own ships aground where waiting pirates would seize the cargo.

Today's natives treat visitors with more respect, and in fact welcome them with open arms. Along the beach are hundreds of hotels, motels, and cottages. There is a local height restriction of three stories, so you will not find glaring concrete high-rises to spoil the atmosphere. Besides swimming, there are outfitters who can assist you with sailing, windsurfing, jet skiing, and even diving to local shipwrecks. Up and down Route 158 you will find the usual assortment of miniature golf courses, amusement parks, surf slides, and roller rinks.

South of Nags Head at Whalebone Junction, take a right on Route 64/264 to Manteo on **Roanoke Island.** Four miles west of town is **Fort Raleigh National Historic Site,** the scene of the first English colonizing attempt (1585-86) within the limits of the present-day United States. Originally built in 1585, the now-restored fort lends an understanding to Sir Walter Raleigh's attempt to start an English colony in America. The small earthworks structure was built by the colonists as a defense against possible attack. Signs along the historic area trail explain more about the colony, and a granite stone memorializes Virginia Dare, the first English child born in the New World. The colony was not to last, however, and the complete disappearance of the settlers remains a mystery to this day. At the Visitor Center, a 17-minute film speculates on the cause of the disappearance, and artifacts and a diorama of the town add to the intrigue. You can also see a model of the type of ship in which the settlers sailed. The story of the settlement is portrayed throughout the summer in the 2,000-seat Waterside Theater. A mixture of song, dance, sudden Indian attacks, and a tender love story, "The Lost Colony" will fuel your imagination as you try to answer the questions that have puzzled historians for centuries. Performances early June through late August, Monday through Saturday. Admission charge. Ticket information: (800) 488-5012 or (252) 473-3414. The park itself is open 24 hours a day; Visitor Center open daily, 9 A.M. to 6 A.M. in summer; 9 A.M. to 5 A.M. the rest of the year. Free admission. Telephone: Visitor Center: (252) 473-5772. Web site: www.nps.gov/fora.

Another memorial to the Elizabethan men and women sent by Sir Walter Raleigh, the **Elizabethan Gardens** are an imaginative concept of 16th-century style gardens. The formal and informal plantings include an herb garden, the Queen's Rose Garden, the Mount, and antique garden ornaments. Herbs and wildflowers are at their peak in May and June, and the gardens are even popular in the winter months. Open daily June through Labor Day, 9 A.M. to 8 A.M. The Gardens open at 9 A.M. the rest of the year, but close from 4 A.M. to 6 A.M., depending on the season. Admission charge. Telephone: (252) 473-3234. Web site: www.elizabethangardens.org.

The **North Carolina Aquarium on Roanoke Island** sits on 14 acres, which overlook the Croatan Sound. Visitors get a first-hand look at underwater archaeology. There are exhibits depicting trawling marine ecosystems, and shark exhibits, along with "Touch Tanks" and interactive exhibits. Enjoy nature trails and a shoreline boardwalk with observation decks. Open daily, 9 A.M. to 5 A.M. Admission charge. Telephone: (252) 473-3494. Web site: www.ncaquariums.com/roanoke-island.

Retrace your steps across Route 64/264 to Bodie Island, and turn right onto Route 12 at Whalebone, the northern end of **Cape Hatteras National Seashore,** which consist of over 70 miles of barrier islands that include Bodie, Hatteras and Ocracoke Islands. You can drive the length of the park on Highway 12, a relatively narrow paved road with soft shoulders. The various islands are connected by bridges and ferryboats, and the road passes through a number of quaint villages (not part of the park), reflecting the unique culture of the region. A stop at **Hatteras Island Visitor Center** can provide you with a map of the entire park and information on campsites and park programs. Open daily, 9 A.M. to 6 P.M. Telephone: (252) 473-2111. Web site: www.nps.gov/caha.

At nearby **Coquina Beach,** visitors will get a good idea of why this coast is often called the "Graveyard of the Atlantic." A combination of strong ocean currents, a narrow channel, treacherous shoals, and frequent storms have been responsible for more than 1,500 shipwrecks in the past 400 years. The remains of one such tragedy is accessible to visitors at Coquina Beach: the four-masted *Laura Barnes,* stranded on a sandbar of Bodie Island in 1921, is now displayed on the beach itself. There are other shipwrecks as well, but they are not always visible due to shifting sands.

Three lighthouses within the National Seashore have guided seafarers through the treacherous waters for centuries. The **Bodie Island Lighthouse,** built in 1872, is 4 miles north of the Oregon Inlet. The lighthouse is not open to the public, but a visitor center in an old keeper's quarters features exhibits. Open daily, 9 A.M. to 5 P.M.; closes at 6 P.M. in the summer. Telephone: (252) 473-2111. Web site: www.nps.gov/caha.

At the tip of the island is the **Oregon Inlet Fishing Center,** home of the largest and most modern fishing fleets on the eastern seaboard. You can arrange charters for inshore and offshore fishing trips to these justly famous, bountiful waters. In abundance are flounder, bluefish, marlin, dolphin fish, striped bass, tuna, and wahoo. Park facilities at the inlet include a public boat launching ramp, a restaurant, and a camp store. Telephone: (800) 272-5199 or (252) 441-6301. Web site: www.oregon-inlet.com.

Cross Oregon Inlet by bridge onto Hatteras Island, where you'll enter **Pea Island National Wildlife Refuge,** the winter home of the Greater Snow Goose and over 256 other species of birds. About five miles south of the Oregon Inlet Bridge are refuge observation platforms offering excellent views of wildlife, the ocean, and even shipwrecks along the shore. Beaches are open to the public. Beware of strong rip tides and littoral currents; walk, do not drive, across the barrier dunes to sand beaches. The Visitor Center has information on the refuge and wildlife, with exhibits on wildlife. Open daily, 9 A.M. to 4 P.M. Free admission. Telephone: (252) 473-1131. Web site: www.fws.gov/peaisland.

Continuing south, you will find untouched beaches, dunes, and occasional villages such as Rodanthe (with the Chicamacomico Lifesaving Station, which presents reenactments of lifesaving operations), Waves, Salvo (which has the country's second smallest post office), and Avon. Another Visitor Center is located at the often photographed, black-and-white striped **Cape Hatteras Lighthouse.** The 208-foot structure, tallest lighthouse in the United States, was built in 1870, and still warns ships off treacherous Diamond Shoals. When the lighthouse was built, the shoreline was more than 1,500 feet away, but constant erosion has brought the Atlantic to within 70 feet of its base. The "Save Cape Hatteras Lighthouse Campaign" is working to preserve the structure, and were significant forces in having it moved inland in 1999. Guides in the Visitor Center will tell you how you can become a "Keeper of the Light." Cape Hatteras Visitor Center is open daily, 9 A.M. to 6 P.M. in summer, 9 A.M. to 5 P.M. September through May. Telephone: (252) 473-2111. Web site: www.nps.gov/caha.

You can continue south on Highway 12 past more beaches and fishing areas, past the towns of Frisco and Hatteras, to the tip of the island. A free ferry takes cars across the Hatteras inlet to **Ocracoke Island.** Service is daily, 5 A.M. to midnight. The crossing takes about 40 minutes. Web site: www.ncdot.gov/travel/ferryroutes.

About 10 miles beyond the ferry docks is a platform over the marshland which enables you to see the small Ocracoke ponies, the remnants of a once larger herd. At the far end of the island, the tiny village of Ocracoke, in its isolation, has retained much of its early charm. The houses in this fishing village have pleasant yards with giant, moss-covered oaks and yaupon trees. In the early 1700s, the pirate Blackbeard sold his booty here. He and his crew were killed at Teach's Hole in 1718. As with the other villages along the Outer Banks, Ocracoke is a fishing haven.

The **Ocracoke Visitor Center** near the harbor has nature displays and seasonal organized activities such as walks through the small woods, and trips wading through the saltmarshes on the bay side of the island. Open daily, 9 A.M. to 6 P.M. in summer, 9 A.M. to 5 P.M. the rest of the year. Free admission. Telephone: (252) 473-2111. Web site: www.nps.gov/caha.

Four British soldiers, from the *HMC Bedfordshire,* which was torpedoed on May 14, 1942 with all hands perishing at sea, are buried in the **British Cemetery** in Ocracoke. The land in this tiny graveyard was officially declared British soil and today stands as a memorial to the Royal Navy.

The **Ocracoke Island Lighthouse,** built in 1823, is the oldest lighthouse still in use and the shortest of the lighthouses mentioned. It is a pleasant walk from the Visitor Center to tour the grounds, though the tower is closed to the public.

Throughout Cape Hatteras National Seashore, camping is permitted only in designated areas; campsites are at Oregon Inlet, Salvo, Cape Hatteras, Frisco, and Ocracoke. There are also a number of commercial campgrounds in the area. Telephone: (252) 473-2111. Web site: www.nps.gov/caha.

SPECIAL INTEREST SECTIONS

AFRICAN-AMERICAN HERITAGE ⸻

In the 30+ years since the TV miniseries based on Alex Haley's *Roots* captivated households of all races nationwide, interest in discovering and preserving African-American heritage has been steadily increasing. Here are just a few of the attractions within the mid-Atlantic region that reflect—and invite reflection upon—African-Americans' experiences in America. By dates alone, many of the historical sites seem recent, even in towns established in the Colonial era. Yet each holds symbolic significance as a testament to the hundreds of thousands of African-Americans who lived and died in anonymity in the years between the earliest settlements and the American Civil War. Most are buried in unmarked graves. Their presence was noted only in bills of sale and estate inventories where they were reduced to genders and numbers.

But thanks to preservation initiatives by historical foundations, and the revival interest in family reunions, many families have developed greater awareness of and appreciation for their personal and cultural roots. The following Web site, initially created to provide information about black history on the New Hampshire seacoast, also includes links to resources throughout the U.S., including the National Park Service site on the Underground Railroad: www.seacoastnh.com/blackhistory/hotlinks.html and www.cr.nps.gov/nr/travel/underground/.

The sites and attractions identified on the following pages are only a tiny sampling of what is now available. Many state and regional Web sites now list sites of special interest to African-Americans, and more are being added all the time. See the "Hotlines" section for phone numbers and Web sites of Visitor Centers in the states and regions you wish to visit. Pepper Bird Publications, a division of Pepper Bird Foundation, PO Box 1071 in Williamsburg, VA 23187-1071 produces annual listings of sites and events of special interest to African-Americans in Virginia and Georgia. These are usually organized by state and presented in a colorful, oversized, newspaper-format that is distributed free through schools and tourist information centers. Also check the Web site for heritage treasures in the area you'll be visiting. The Foundation also produces publications identifying sites of special interest to American Indians, Hispanic-Americans, and Asian-Americans, and has developed continuing education programs for teachers. Web site: www.coax.net/people/lwf/pepbird.htm.

Another useful publication is *Making Impressions,* a monthly journal and bulletin produced by TYPECAST editorial and design services. The journal is devoted to highlighting cultural events appealing to the African-American community. *Making Impressions* is available at no cost (while supplies last) in all District of Columbia and Prince George's County libraries, and in selected merchants and waiting rooms. To inquire about individual subscriptions, contact Rosenbloom, 3303 18th Street, NW, Washington, DC 20010. Telephone: (202) 265-3443, Fax: (202) 328-6836.

DELAWARE

Fort Delaware, Pea Patch Island

Dozens of African-Americans helped build and operate Fort Delaware during the Civil War. Skilled blacksmiths, carpenters, stone masons, and laborers worked throughout the war to complete the granite-walled Union fortress. Originally built as one of three forts to protect Wilmington and Philadelphia from invasion, Fort Delaware housed more than 3,000 Confederate prisoners. Though the walls stand 32 feet high and are up to 30 feet thick, some daring prisoners attempted escape. Summer activities include re-enactments and living history tours, some of which feature African-Americans. Call for additional information and news of special events. Telephone: (302) 834-7941. Web site: www.destateparks.com/park/fort-delaware. Other useful Web sites: "A History of African-Americans of Delaware and Maryland's Eastern Shore," edited by Carole Marks: www.udel.edu/BlackHistory/, which includes a chapter on "Black Women in Delaware's History."

The New Castle County Court House also figures in African-American history because it was here that Thomas Garrett, a prominent station master on the Underground Railroad, and a fellow abolitionist, John Hunn, stood trial for violating the Fugitive Slave Act of 1793. Web site: history.delaware.gov/museums/ncch/ncch_main.shtml. Another Web site that may be of interest was created by a private individual, who invites sharing of additional findings: www.russpickett.com/history/sites.htm.

MARYLAND

For anyone interested in African-American history in Maryland, the following Web site, an Archives of Maryland Electronic Publication, is an excellent first stop. It explains how the Underground Railroad worked in Maryland, provides maps, stories of flight, and resources for additional research and links to related projects. New information and case studies are added regularly. Web site: www.mdslavery.net/index.html.

Annapolis

The Banneker Douglass Museum is located at 84 Franklin Street in Annapolis, a former slave port. The museum is housed in the Old Mount Moriah AME Church just a five minute walk from the Maryland State Capitol and Governor's Mansion. Mt. Moriah is one of the oldest extant black churches in Annapolis, built in 1874-75 by a free black congregation begun in 1799. The building is listed on the National Register of Historic Places.

The purpose of the museum is to foster the preservation of and education about African-American history and art in Maryland. The museum houses collections of rare books, documents, artifacts, and photographs relevant to black life in Maryland as well as a library of books, manuscripts, oral histories, and video tapes for research (by appointment). The museum also sponsors exhibitions, programs, and workshops, and space is sometimes available for meetings or small special events. Open Tuesday through Friday, 10 A.M. to 3 P.M.; Saturday, noon to 4 P.M. Free admission. Telephone: (410) 216-6180. Web site: www.bdmuseum.com.

The following Web site includes interesting information about African-American life in 19th and 20th century Annapolis: http://visitmaryland.org/Pages/Attractions2.aspx.

Towson

Hampton in Towson, Maryland, is a national historic site that preserves a vast estate from the late 1700s. The centerpiece Georgian mansion, which was at one time the largest house in the United States, and the lifestyle attending it were made possible by the work of enslaved African-Americans, indentured servants, and hired craftsmen. Interpretive mansion tours are offered daily. Extensive research has been done on the slaves of Hampton and special tours that include the farm, garden, and slave quarters are available by appointment. Information about slavery at Hampton and ongoing research is also available on the Hampton Web site: www.nps.gov/hamp. Also see the entry titled the "Ridgely Compound of Hampton": www.mdslavery.net/html/casestudies/fifrh.html.

Cumberland

Allegany County has a small African-American presence but a rich historical and cultural presence. The Potomac Cultural Group, headed by Leontyne Peck, is the only firm in Western Maryland specializing in African-American history, culture, tourism, and education. The Group conducts tours and designs special events celebrating African-American Heritage. Telephone (301) 759-6446.

Dorchester and Talbot Counties

Two notable African-Americans were born into slavery between 1818 and 1820 within 40 miles of each other on Maryland's Eastern Shore. **Harriet Tubman,** who was named Araminta but called herself Harriet in honor of her mother, was born on a plantation in Bucktown, near Cambridge. In 1849 she escaped to the free state of Pennsylvania and went on to Canada, returning many times to lead others to freedom along the Underground Railroad. During the Civil War, she served the Union Army as a spy, scout, guide, nurse, and cook. Historical roadside markers on Route 50 in Cambridge will direct you to her birthplace. The farmhouse is now overgrown, abandoned, and in disrepair, but many pilgrims report that the drive from Route 50 and visits to the land she once tilled continue to inspire as if her spirit remained in the area. The Harriet Tubman Museum and Educational Center, Inc., 424 Race Street in Cambridge, strives to keep Harriet Tubman's legacy alive as an inspiration to people of all races. The staff can provide additional information about the life of this remarkable woman and arrange guided tours. The museum and gift shop are open Monday through Friday, 10 A.M. to 2 P.M., alternate Saturdays 10 A.M. to 2 P.M. and other times by special arrangement. The museum also leads a celebration of Harriet Tubman annually on March 10. Telephone: (410) 228-0401. For more about Harriet Tubman and her house in New York, consult these Web sites: www.nyhistory.com/harriettubman (and) www.nps.gov.

Frederick Douglass' birthplace is recorded in many guide books as Talbot County, Maryland, on "Matthewstown Road, on the banks of the Tuckahoe River." But as the Barkers explain in "The Search for Frederick Douglass' Birthplace," posted at www.easternshore.com, you won't find it there, even if you know that Matthewstown Road is the local name for Maryland Route 328. Maps and detailed directions to the cabin site can be found at: www.easternshore.com/esguide/douglass_birthplace.html.

Somerset and Worcester Counties

The Eastern Shore Heritage Committee, Inc. reports that African-Americans are an integral part of the culture and heritage of the Eastern Shore. Slave trade began in 1640, and the area also may have served as a "slave market" for buyers from other areas of the state.

Later, African-Americans were essential forces in the emergence of the seafood industry, both in the processing plants and as independent watermen. African-Americans have also contributed to the development of agricultural and educational resources in the region. Princess Anne houses the University of Maryland Eastern Shore, a historic land grant university established in 1886 to educate young black men and women.

Prominent blacks from the past include folk hero Sampson Harmon (who is immortalized as the character Sampson Hat in *The Entailed Hat*, a novel by George A. Townsend). Harmon lived to be 106 and is buried in Furnace Town with his cat Tom. Some claim their ghosts continue to visit the area. Baseball Hall of Famer William Julius ("Judy") Johnson of Snow Hill played more than 3,000 games for the Negro League between 1918 and 1939, earning recognition from his peers as the all-time best third baseman. The **Julia A. Purnell Museum** in Snow Hill displays memorabilia from his long career.

Worcester County Tourism Office at 104 West Market Street in Snow Hill has produced a richly documented color brochure of the African-American experience in Worcester County. The brochure includes a collage of photographs and artwork as well as a list of resources for additional reading or research. It is also available on the county tourism Web site with wonderful links to related sites. Telephone: (410) 632-3110 or (800) 852-0335. Web site: www.visit-worcester.org/index.php/site/pages_visitorguides/.

NEW JERSEY

The state of New Jersey's travel Web site acknowledges that "New Jersey's African-American experience is a proud legacy that spans from the Revolutionary War era to present day." Also posted on the Web site is a suggested tour of notable sites of special interest to African-Americans, including restaurants and jazz clubs. Web site: www.visitnj.org/african-american-visitor-guide. Also consult the following Web site for links to historical sites (and preservation/historical societies throughout the state): www.state.nj.us/nj/things/historical.

Among them are the **Lawnside Historic District,** including the **Peter Mott House,** which was officially dedicated as an Underground Railroad historic site and museum in 2001. Peter Mott was a freed slave and farmer from Delaware who later served as pastor of Lawnside's Mount Pisgah AME Church. His house is one of the few remaining Underground Railroad "stations." Telephone: 856-546-8850.

Lawnside, initially known as "Snow Hill" and later as "Free Haven," was New Jersey's first all-African-American community to be incorporated as a municipality. To inquire about guided tours, geneology sessions, and special events, contact the Lawnside Historical Society, Inc. Telephone: (856) 546-8850. Web sites: www.petermotthouse.org (about the Peter Mott House) or www.cchsnj.com or historiccamden-county.com (Camden county historical sites).

A map of African American Historic sites in Burlington County is available at the library Web site: http://explore.bcls.lib.nj.us/black-history. Other suggested stops on the New Jersey tour include the **New Jersey State Museum in Trenton,** which features permanent exhibits from well-known African-American artists. Telephone: (609) 292-6300 .

The **Historical Society of Princeton** offers self-guided and guided tours of Princeton's African-American District. Telephone: (609) 921-6748. Web site: www.princetonhistory.org.

NORTH CAROLINA

Edenton

Historic Edenton incorporates news of its notable African-American citizens in walking and trolley tours that originate from the Visitor Center at 108 N. Broad Street. Among them was **Harriet A. Jacobs,** a slave who escaped from her master and hid for seven years in the attic of her grandmother's house. She eventually managed to find her way to freedom with help from a maritime version of the Underground Railroad, through which African-American watermen assisted runaway slaves along the coastal areas.

Hannibal Badham and his son were much in demand as builders and craftsmen in the late 1800s and at the turn of the century when Victorian styles were especially popular. One can still observe a distinctive cupola feature incorporated into the porches of some of the houses they built throughout historic Edenton. In approximately the same period, Josephine Napoleon Leary distinguished herself as a successful businesswoman. Her name can be observed to this day atop the building that houses the local newspaper offices.

For more information about scheduled tours or to arrange group tours featuring a specific aspect of Edenten's history, contact the **Edenton Visitor Center,** PO Box 474, Edenton, NC 27932. Telephone: (252) 482-3400 or the Tourism Development Authority (800) 775-0111. Web sites: www.visitedenton.com or www.edenton.com.

Creswell

Somerset Place, at 2572 Lake Shore Road nine miles south of Creswell, NC, is an antebellum plantation built in 1830. It once encompassed as many as 100,000 acres and was one of North Carolina's most prosperous plantations. The plantation was home to more than 300 enslaved men, women, and children of African descent, 80 of whom were brought directly from their West African homeland in 1785. Slaves established thousands of acres of rice fields, built the "big house," their own quarters, and a hospital. Admission charge. Open April 1 through October 31, Monday through Saturday, 9 A.M. to 5 P.M.; Sunday 1 to 5 P.M.; November 1 through March 31, Tuesday through Saturday, 10 a.m to 4 P.M.; Sunday 1 to 4 P.M. Call about guided tours. Telephone: (252) 797-4560.

Web site: www.albemarle-nc.com/somerset/. The following Web site provides an account of archeological research into African-American life on the plantation: Web site: www.archaeology.ncdcr.gov.

PENNSYLVANIA

Pennsylvania has a long history of opposition to slavery, perhaps because of its Quaker roots. Pennsylvania was one of the early destinations and through routes of the **Underground Railroad.** Among the influential conductors in the secret network of cooperation that helped slaves escape to freedom, was former slave Richards Allen, who founded the influential **Mother Bethel A.M.E. Church** in Philadelphia. William Still, Lucretia Mott, and Frederick Douglass were among those who spoke out against slavery from the lectern at Mother Bethel. Web sites related to the Underground Railroad include: www.visitpa.com/history-heritage (click on "Historic Places," then "African-American Heritage") and http://undergroundrailroadconductor.com/UGRR_Links.htm and midatlantic.rootsweb.com/padutch/urailroad.html.

African-Americans founded a number of **all-black communities** in Pennsylvania after an 1842 Supreme Court ruling determined that states were not obligated to help slave catchers. Among them were "Africa" in Franklin County, "Hayti" in Chester County, and "Guinea Run" in Bucks County.

More than 10,000 African-Americans volunteered to serve in the Union forces during the Civil War. Many were recruited and trained at **Camp William Penn,** north of Philadelphia, established in the summer of 1863 as the first U.S. Government center for recruiting and training black soldiers. Many of its recruits distinguished themselves in battle and were decorated for their bravery and valor.
Web sites: www.historic-lamott-pa.com (and) americancivilwar.com/colored/colored_troops.html (and) afroamhistory.about.com/library/prm/blsoldiersinblue6.htm?terms =Donald+Scott.

VIRGINIA

The following site provides links related to information about African American history and culture in Virginia:

http://www.aaheritageva.org/ (and)
www.lva.lib.va.us/whatwedo/k12/vhr/afam.htm.

Alexandria and Mt. Vernon

The **Alexandria Black History Resource Center** is located at 638 North Alfred Street, Alexandria, VA 22314, but the entrance is around the corner on Wythe. The building is of historical significance because it was the "colored branch" of the local public library. Seed funds for this branch were allocated by the City Council in 1940 in response to a sit-in staged on August 21, 1939, at the Alexandria Free Library on Queen Street. More than two decades before the Freedom Rides, Samuel Wilbert Tucker, then age 26, organized the nonviolent protest. Participants included his brother Otto, 22, Edward Gaddis, 21, Morris Murray, 22, William Evans, 19, and Buck Strange, 20. The five men, dressed in suits and straw hats, entered the building and asked for library cards. When they were refused, each man sat reading quietly at a separate table until they were charged with trespassing and arrested. Alexandria libraries were not fully integrated until the 1960s, but thanks to the funding prompted by the protest, the black community had some access to books.

The Black History Resource Center houses the **Moss Kendrix Collection,** documents from an African-American public relations pioneer, as well as other exhibits. Center staff can also alert you to historical sites in the area, such as the building that housed the Franklin and Armfield Slave Market and neighborhoods established by free blacks. Telephone: (703) 838-4356.

Next door at 906 Wythe is the **Watson Reading Room,** a non-circulating research library of books and documents related to African-American history and culture. Telephone: (703) 746-4356 .

The **Alexandria African-American Heritage Park** on Holland Lane off Duke Street, is an eight-acre memorial park established on the site of a 19th century African-American Baptist Cemetery. On the grounds are four tree-like memorial sculptures. Research has established that there were at least 26 burials at the site, though only 6 headstones remain. The unmarked graves are particularly poignant in contrast to the many headstones in the adjoining (white) cemetery. For more information, call the Black History Resource Center. Web sites: alexandriava.gov/BlackHistory (and) www.prmuseum.com/kendrix/resouctr.html.

Archeological Exhibit at the Torpedo Factory Art Center, 105 N. Union St., Room #327. Alexandria had one of the largest populations

of free blacks in the antebellum South, and archeological excavations have unearthed artifacts that reveal much about daily life for African-Americans in early Alexandria. Exhibit and an informative brochure. Telephone: (703) 746-4399.
Web site: www.torpedofactory.org/archaeology.htm (click on "Research," then "Themes from the Past," then "Black History." Web site: www.mountvernon.org.

Gum Springs was the site of a community of free blacks established by West Ford, a former slave and plantation manager on George Washington's estate at Mt. Vernon. According to *Pepper Bird Pathways,* the property, acquired in 1833, "became a place for runaway and freed slaves to live. Helped by Quakers, freed slaves worked in the trades they had learned as estate slaves." Gum Springs now has more than 2,500 residents, 500 of whom are descendants of the original families. Look for historical markers on Route 1 South, near the intersection with Sherwood Hall Lane, and on the right side of Sherwood Hall Lane as you drive west (toward Route 1). Call for hours of the **Gum Springs Historical Society and Museum,** operated by the Gum Springs Historical Society, 8100 Fordson Road, in Fairfax County south of Alexandria. Telephone: (703) 799-1198.

George Washington's Estate at one time occupied the great majority of the land between Old Town Alexandria and **Mount Vernon** some seven miles south. A special, guided "Slave Life" tour that includes the slave quarters, the overseer's lodgings, the storehouse, and the slave burial ground as well as information about daily life and practices on the estate is held periodically. Additional information is also woven into the narrations of costumed characters in the kitchen, gardens, and barn. Call to see when the "Slave Life" tour is offered. Telephone: (703) 780-2000.

Arlington

Arlington House, also known as the Custis-Lee Mansion and the Robert E. Lee Memorial, which is now surrounded by Arlington National Cemetery, was a originally a plantation owned by the Custis family. It is also where Robert E. Lee lived after marriage and where his children were born. Although he became commander of the Confederate forces, Robert E. Lee did not believe in slavery and did not own any slaves himself. After the war, part of the plantation served as a Freedman's Village. The mansion is now operated by the National Park Service and can be viewed on visits to Arlington

Cemetery. Visitors Center telephone: (703) 235-1530 or 692-0931. Web site: www.nps.gov (or) www.arlingtoncemetery.net.

Charlottesville

Results of recent DNA tests have given more credence to both oral history and scholarship indicating that Thomas Jefferson fathered at least one child and possibly as many as four children with his much beloved slave companion Sally Hemings. Family reunions now include Jefferson's black as well as white descendents, though the issue of whom has rights to be buried in the **Monticello** family plot is still unresolved. Special tours of the **slave quarters (Mulberry Row)** are offered in addition to tours of the mansion. Artifacts from the slave quarters are included in exhibits at the Thomas Jefferson Visitor's Center and Museum. Telephone: (434) 984-9800 for recorded information. Web site: www.loc.gov/exhibits/jefferson/jefflife.html. Also click on the article "To Labour for Another" on the following Web site: www.monticello.org/site/jefferson/to-labour-another.

Tours of nearby **Ash Lawn-Highland,** 1000 James Monroe Parkway, the home of James Monroe, fifth president of the U.S., also include slave quarters. Monroe helped establish the African Republic of Liberia in 1817. Telephone: (434) 293-8000. Web site: www.ashlawnhighland.org.

Falls Church

A memorial archway made from stone mined from the quarry where **Joseph Tinner** once worked was dedicated in 1999 to honor his achievements as a civil right pioneer and those of **Dr. Edwin Bancroft Henderson.** The stone arch occupies a corner of what was once known as **Tinner Hill,** where Tinner and Dr. Henderson lived in January 1915 when the town council passed an ordinance requiring blacks to live in a restricted neighborhood. In spite of threats from the Ku Klux Klan and others, Henderson organized a branch of the NAACP and filed a lawsuit challenging the segregation ordinance. The law was nullified by court order in 1917. Tinner, who had headed the Falls Church Chapter, and Henderson went on to help form NAACP chapters in neighboring regions. A memorial arch at S. Washington Street was dedicated in his honor in 1999. In early 2003, city and county officials agreed to lease property to the Tinner Hill Heritage Foundation to build a replica of Tinner's home and establish a cultural center. Work is to be completed by 2008.

Fredericksburg

Brochures at the Visitor's Center, 706 Caroline Street, Fredericksburg, offer a self-guided walking tour of this former slave port. Vignettes of notable African-Americans are included in the historical perspectives. Also ask about the contributions of African-American troops to the Civil War battles at nearby **Fredericksburg, Spotsylvania, and Wilderness National Military Parks.** For the City of Fredericksburg Department of Tourism, Telephone: (540) 373-1776 or (800) 678-4748. A brochure that includes a street-by-street account of local black history can be found on this Web site: http://history.library-point.org/african_american_history_of_fredericksburg_virginia.

Hampton

The Hampton University was founded in 1868 to educate former slaves. **The Hampton University Museum** in the Huntington Building on the campus is the oldest African-American museum in the country. Its collections include almost 10,000 artifacts. To reach the campus, follow signs from exit 267 off I-64. Telephone: (757) 727-5000 . Web site: www.hamptonu.edu (click on "Hampton's Heritage").

The **Virginia Air and Space Center,** 600 Settlers Landing Road, includes periodic exhibits honoring the **Tuskegee Airmen of WWII.** Telephone: (800) 800-2202 or (757) 727-0900. Web site: www.vasc.org.

Petersburg

African-American heritage in Petersburg is rich and well documented. The most comprehensive source of information is the **Historic Old Towne Visitors Center,** 425 Cockade Alley. Some sites in the area are a house believed to be a stop on the Underground Railroad, Old Blandford Church (where a headstone indicates that slave Lucy Lockett was buried with her owner's family), the community of free blacks that was established on Pocahontas Island as early as 1800, a monument to **Joseph Jenkins** (a native of Petersburg who was the first president of Liberia), **Petersburg National Battlefield,** historic black churches, the Trapezium House, and Virginia State University. Visitors Center telephone: (804) 733-2400. Web site: www.petersburg-va.org.

Richmond

African-American presence in Richmond can be traced to 1671 when William Byrd brought black laborers with him to the frontier territory that encompassed what later became Richmond. In 1860, more than 2,500 free blacks lived in Richmond, making it one of the largest populations of free blacks in the antebellum South. Several black units fought as Colored Troops for the Union Army. After the war, **Jackson Ward** emerged as a center of African-American culture, business, politics, and entertainment. The area is now preserved as a historic district. The architecture features some of the finest wrought iron work in America.

The **Black History Museum and Cultural Center of Virginia** at 00 Clay Street is the primary source for information on Jackson Ward and other noteworthy Richmond sites with links to African-American heritage. Telephone: (804) 780-9093.

Web site: www.blackhistorymuseum.org.

Nearby at 110 East Leigh Street is the **Maggie L. Walker National Historic Site.** In spite of many adversities, Ms. Walker founded the Saint Luke Penny Savings Bank in 1903 and was the first woman bank president in America. Her home has been restored to its 1930's appearance with many of the furnishings from the Walker family. The site is now operated by the National Park Service. Open Monday through Sunday, 9 A.M. to 5 P.M. Telephone: (804) 771-2017.

Web site: www.nps.gov/mawa

Williamsburg

The **"Other Half" tour of Colonial Williamsburg** acknowledges and honors the African-American presence in the Colonial Capital. Skilled costumed re-enactors discuss dimensions of everyday life, work, love, and marriage among the "other half."

Nearby **Carter's Grove Plantation** includes reconstructed slave quarters. In the past, interpreters explained the arrival of slaves and how their daily lives on the plantation contrasted with that of their counterparts in town. As of January 2, 2003, the facility was closed for a "comprehensive facility, site, and program assessment." Programs aimed at preserving African-American heritage have been moved to the better known Central Historic Area of Williamsburg. For more information call (800) HISTORY.

Web site: www.nps.gov/nr/travel/jamesriver/car.htm.

WEST VIRGINIA

On October 16, 1859 abolitionist **John Brown** seized the armory and arsenal at Harpers Ferry in hopes of equipping an army that would then liberate slaves in the Deep South. Although the raid itself was a failure, some historians now conclude that it set in motion a chain of events that led to civil war. Among those who died in the raid was **Dangerfield Newby,** a former slave who was freed by his white father but had not been able to earn enough to liberate his wife and six children, still in bondage. A touching letter from his wife was found in his pocket and has been preserved. The text can be viewed on the National Park Service Web site for Harpers Ferry. Click on "Virtual Visitors Center," then scroll down to find Newby. Web site: www.nps.gov/hafe.

Harpers Ferry is nestled between the Potomac and Shenandoah Rivers near West Virginia's borders with Maryland and Virginia. During the war, Harpers Ferry was much battered by both armies, though federal troops occupied it most of the time. It was also a refugee camp for thousands of runaway slaves trying to make their way north. When Stonewall Jackson captured the federal garrison on September 15, 1862, hundreds of refugees were marched back into slavery. After the war a small church-owned school gave rise to **Storer College,** one of the first African-American coeducational colleges in the country. It was the site of a meeting of the Niagra Movement led by W.E.B. Du Bois, and on the 14th anniversary of its founding, May 30, 1881, Frederick Douglass gave his notable "John Brown" oration. Artifacts from the college have been preserved and are on display. The town is located 20 miles southwest of Frederick, Maryland and 6 miles northeast of Charles Town, West Virginia. Telephone: (304) 535-6029. Web site: www.nps.gov/hafe.

ANTIQUES AND AUCTIONS ─────────

Antique collecting in the mid-Atlantic states is an exciting and varied experience because the range of quality collectibles is broad, and because so much is available. Excellent examples of furnishings, art, utensils, maritime objects, glass, fittings, farm implements, toys, handcrafts, quilts, and fixtures are bought and sold in heavy trading throughout the region. Objects vary from English and Early American 16th and 17th century to Colonial, Appalachian, early 20th century, and the Depression. Fine examples and good buys of many periods can still be found at flea markets, garage sales and auctions by astute and lucky collectors. For the shopper who would like information or guidance, there is an abundance of stores. In fact there are so many stores that a listing of their names and addresses would comprise a book in itself.

The Antique Dealers in the USA Web site provides listings for every state. You can click on a state to view the number of antique shops in particular cities and towns. You can also click for further information on particular shops. Web site: http://www.antiquetheusa.com/.

If the thrill of bidding is more of what you had in mind, local auctions and estate sales can also be sources of antique treasures. Such sales are usually held on weekends and advertised in local newspapers on Thursday and Friday. Local people can tell you which publications are best. Or check the **National Auctioneers Association** Web site where auction sales are posted, and you can search by location, date, and type of merchandise. Also check Web sites of the auctioneers who work in a particular area. Web site: www.auctioneers.org.

No one knows exactly when auctions were invented, but scholars generally agree that the method of selling items to the highest bidder was an established business practice in Babylonian times. Early auctioneers sold slaves, agricultural products, and maidens as potential wives. In an article for Agorics, Inc. (www.cap-lore.com/Agorics/Library/auctions.html), Kate Reynolds reports that Roman soldiers sometimes offered their spoils of war at auctions.

As early as the seventh century, auctions were used by Buddhist temples and monasteries to dispose of the possessions of monks who had died. In the late seventeenth century, auctions were held in taverns and coffeehouses to sell art. Early English and French auction houses sold antiques for consignors who wished to remain anonymous.

In America, the auctions were used initially to liquidate goods at the end of a season. But they are no longer mere "fire sales." Holding an auction is widely viewed as a marketing method that will obtain the highest amount possible for an item or product in the shortest possible time while offering advantages to both buyers and sellers.

The mid-Atlantic region is highly auction-oriented. Check local papers in areas you are visiting for ads announcing auctions. Estate sales may include antiques, collectibles, household goods, jewelry, furniture, art work, and other treasures, as well as what some will regard as mere junk. There are always bargains to be found, and there's no extra charge for the entertainment of watching a skilled auctioneer in action.

A number of auctioneers offer guidance on how auctions work and how to bid at auctions. Check the Internet for an online orientation. If possible, arrive in advance of the sale to preview the items (or property) to be auctioned. Clarify bidding procedures, terms of payment, and by when the items you have purchased must be removed. At most sales you will have to sign in (and sometimes offer a method of payment) to receive a number that allows you to bid.

All of the towns in the following list have at least three antique shops or auctioneers and are worthy of an outing. Some of the antique shops at a single address are actually "mini-malls" of several antique dealers under one roof. Towns listed in bold face have at least eight stores, which may warrant a day of treasure hunting.

DELAWARE

The Delaware Tourism Office produces a comprehensive printed listing of antique shops in the state. Telephone: (866) 2-VISIT-D. State Web site: www.visitdelaware.com. The Kent County Convention and Visitors Bureau is also helpful. Telephone: (800)-233-KENT. Web site: www.visitdover.com.

Good towns for antique hunting include: Bridgeville, **Dover, Georgetown,** Greenville, Gumboro, **Laurel, Lewes,** Middletown, Millsboro, Millville, Milton, Newark, New Castle, Ocean View, **Rehoboth,** Seaford, Selbyville, **Smyrna,** and **Wilmington.**

MARYLAND

Several Web sites are useful sources of antiquing information within the state:

Antique Dealers Association of Maryland, Inc., Web site: www.antiquesinmd.com

Chesapeake Antique Center, Web site: www.visitchesapeake.com

Historic New Market, Web site: www.townofnewmarket.org

Historic Savage Mill, Web site: www.antique-cntr-savage.com

Good towns for antique hunting include: **Annapolis,** Bel Air, **Berlin,** Bethesda, Boonsboro, **Bowie,** Brunswick, Cambridge, **Chestertown,** Chevy Chase, Churchville, **Cockeysville, Cumberland,** Damascus, Denton, **Easton,** Edgewater, Eldersburg, Elkton, **Ellicott City,** Essex, **Frederick,** Funkstown, **Gaithersburg,** Glen Burnie, Grasonville, **Hagerstown, Havre de Grace,** Hughesville, Hyattsville,

Kensington, Knoxville, La Plata, **Laurel,** Laytonsville, Monktown, Mt. Airy,New Market,**Northeast, Ocean City,** Onley, Oxford, Parkville, Queenstown, **Reisterstown,** Rockville, Royal Oak, **Salisbury, Severna Park,** Silver Spring, Snow Hill, Solomons, **St. Michaels,** Stevensville, Sykesville, Takoma Park, Thurmont, Timonium, Trappe, Waldorf, **Westminster,** White Plains.

NEW JERSEY

Good towns for antique hunting in the southern part of the state include: Atlantic City, **Cape May, Cape May Court House,** Long Branch, Ocean View, Point Pleasant, Trenton.

NORTH CAROLINA

Good towns for antique hunting with 200 miles of Washington, D.C. include: Albemarle, Elizabeth City, Kill Devil Hills, Nag's Head.

PENNSYLVANIA

Good towns for antique hunting in the eastern part of the state include: Ardmore, Bala Cynwyd, Berwyn, Bird-in-Hand, Bryn Mawr, **Chadds Ford,** Chambersburg, **Doylestown, Downingtown,** Drexel Hill, East Stroudsburg, Emmaus, Ephrata, **Gettysburg,** Hanover, **Harrisburg,** Haverford, Hershey, Kennett Square, **Lancaster, Lebanon,** Manheim, **New Hope, New Oxford, Newtown,** Paradise, **Philadelphia,** Plymouth, Plymouth Meeting, Pottstown, **Reading,** Strasburg, **Stroudsburg,** Swarthmore, Unionville, Upper Darby, **Wayne, West Chester,** Yardley, and **York.**

VIRGINIA

Good towns for antique hunting include: **Abingdon, Alexandria,** Altavista, Amelia Courthouse, **Annandale,** Appomattox, **Arlington,** Ashland, Bedford, Blacksburg, Bland, **Bristol,** Buchanan, Burgess, **Charlottesville, Chesapeake,** Christiansburg, Clifton, Colonial Heights, **Culpeper,** Danville, Disputanta, Edinburg, Emporia, Fairfax, Fairfield, Falls Church, Farmville, **Fredericksburg, Front Royal,** Gate City, Glen Allen, Gloucester, Gordonsville, Great Falls, **Hampton,** Harrisonburg, Herndon, Highland Springs, **Hopewell,**

King George, **Leesburg,** Lexington, Lorton, Luray, **Lynchburg, Madison, Manassas,** McLean, **Mechanicsville, Middleburg,** Midlothian, Millwood, Mt. Sidney, New Church, New Market, **Newport, Newport News, Norfolk, Occoquan, Petersburg,** Poquoson, **Portsmouth,** Powhatan, **Purcellville, Richmond, Roanoke,** Rocky Mount, **Ruckersville, Salem,** Smithfield, **South Boston,** Sperryville, **Staunton, Strasburg,** Stuart, **Suffolk, Tappahannock,** Toano, Troutville, Verona, **Vienna,** Vinton, **Virginia Beach, Warrenton, Waynesboro,** Weyers Cave, Whitestone, **Williamsburg, Winchester,** Wytheville, and Yorktown.

WEST VIRGINIA

Good towns for antique hunting include: Buckhannon, Charles Town, Clarksburg, Elkins, Fairmont, Harpers Ferry, **Martinsburg,** Morgantown, White Sulphur Springs.

ARCHAEOLOGY ─────────────────

If you are an amateur archaeologist, or if you have always wanted to get down on all fours at a "dig," you'll find plenty of opportunities to get the dirt of eons past under your fingernails. The mid-Atlantic area abounds with archaeological treasures, but as elsewhere, many sites are being threatened by parking lots, convention centers, and condominium developments.

To keep pace with urban sprawl and to rescue archaeological artifacts before they are forever bulldozed from view, each state has an archaeologist on staff who, in addition to other tasks, is responsible for organizing digs. Often archaeologists race against time, bulldozers, and limited resources to rescue priceless treasures, so volunteers are usually welcomed with open arms. Some projects are done in conjunction with government programs such as the National Historic Preservation Act and the National Register Program, which require states to "accommodate" the public—a bureaucratic word that means "use volunteers."

Volunteers have helped at a prehistoric Indian site in Parkersburg, West Virginia, where a Japanese steel plant was about to be built. Amateur archaeologists in Wilmington, Delaware, surveyed along South Wilmington Boulevard and found artifacts dating to the early 18th century. In Alexandria, Virginia, volunteers at the Archaeology

Research Center dig on land once occupied by 18th- and 19th-century families. And an ongoing project along Maryland's Calvert Cliffs has unearthed a number of prehistoric fossils. Recent archaeological finds in Jamestown, Virginia, suggest that the settlement was even more significant than previously imagined. Most **state archaeology offices** maintain lists of willing volunteers. When a project surfaces, they call those on the list to give them opportunities to help. You can contact these offices in your state to sign up:

STATE ARCHEOLOGY OFFICES

Delaware:　Delaware State Historic Preservation Office
15 The Green
Dover, DE 19901
(302) 736-7400
history.delaware.gov/preservation/default.shtml

Maryland:　Richard Hughes
Office of Archaeology, Division of
Historical/Cultural Programs
100 Community Place
Crownsville, MD 21032
(410) 514-7600
http://mht.maryland.gov/

Emery T. Cleaves
Maryland Geological Survey
2300 North St. Paul Street
Baltimore, MD 21218
(410) 554-5500
www.mgs.md.gov

New Jersey:　New Jersey State Museum
205 West State Street, P.O. Box 530
Trenton, NJ 08625
(609) 292-6464
www.state.nj.us/state/museum/index.html

North Carolina: Stephen R. Claggett
Office of State Archaeology
421 North Blount Street

Raleigh, NC
Mailing Address:
4619 Mail Service Center
Raleigh, NC 27699-4619
(919) 807-6552
www.archaeology.ncdcr.gov

Archaelogical Research Center
4612 Mail Service Center
Raleigh, NC 27699
(919) 807-7280
www.history.ncdcr.gov

Pennsylvania: Stephen G. Warfel
Senior Curator and Supervisor, Archaelogy
State Museum of Pennsylvania
300 North Street
Harrisburg, PA 17120
(717) 705-0869
www.statemuseumpa.org/archc.html

Virginia: Department of Historic Resources
2801 Kennsington Avenue
Richmond, VA 23221
(804) 367-2323
www.dhr.virginia.gov

Office of Historic Alexandria
405 Cameron Street
Alexandria, VA 22314
(703) 746-4554
alexandriava.gov/historic/

West Virginia: West Virginia Division of Culture and History
The Cultural Center
Capitol Complex
1900 Kanawha Blvd. East
Charleston, WV 25305-0300
(304) 558-0220
www.wvculture.org

ARCHEOLOGICAL SOCIETIES

Many regions also have archaeology societies of amateurs and professionals. Chapters sponsor local digs—good opportunities to learn more about archaeology. Contact your state society for the chapter nearest you:

Maryland: Archaeological Society of Maryland, Inc.
Carol Ebnight, President
305 Wembley Road
Reisterstown, MD 21136
(301) 953-1947
www.marylandarcheology.org.

North Carolina: North Carolina Archaeological Society
4619 Mail Service Center
Raleigh, NC 27699-4619
(919) 807-6552
www.archaeology.ncdcr.gov

Pennsylvania: Society for Pennsylvania Archaeology
PO Box 10287
Pittsburgh, PA 15232-0287
www.pennsylvaniaarchaeology.com

Virginia: Archaeological Society of Virginia
PO Box 70395
Richmond, VA 23255
(804) 273-9291

Local universities sometimes need volunteers to help with their work. Contact area colleges to see if they have any digs planned or in process. Veteran volunteers advise wearing old clothes and shoes, a hat, and work gloves. At the end of your day of fieldwork you can expect to be hot, tired, and no doubt caked with dirt. But you'll have the satisfaction of having made a vital contribution to man's knowledge of his past.

If you do not fancy getting down on all fours in dirt, many museums need volunteers to help sort and identify artifacts. These can include museums specializing not only in prehistoric memorabilia, but "newer" artifacts as well. The Office of Historic Alexandria, for example, frequently needs volunteers to sort through papers pertaining to Virginia's colonial history, mark maps, and give talks to visitors and school groups.

BATTLEFIELDS ──────────────────────

Weekend Getaways around Washington, D.C. includes additional information on Valley Forge, Yorktown, and other areas associated with many of the scenes of important battles of the Revolutionary War in the text portion. It also covers much of the territory that was at the heart of the Civil War from the site of its first major land battle, Manassas, to the quiet village, Appomattox, where the war came to a close four years later.

Many locales in the mid-Atlantic states were involved in both wars. Battlefield locations listed here are, for the most part, those set aside by federal and state governments. A few private homes or sites of particular interest to the visitor are also included. You can find several organizations that work for the preservation of battlefields listed at one of the National Park Service Web sites: www.cr.nps.gov/hps/abpp.

Antietam National Battlefield, Maryland. Telephone: (301) 432-5124. Web site: www.nps.gov/ancm/.

Appomattox Court House National Historical Park, Virginia. Telephone: (434) 352-8987 ext. 226. Web site: www.nps.gov/apco.

Ball's Bluff Cemetery, Virginia. Telephone (703) 737-7800. Web site: www.nvrpa.org/park/ball_s_bluff.

Battle of Brandy Station, Virginia. Telephone: (540) 829-1749. Web site: www.culpepermuseum.com.

Brandywine Battlefield State Historical Park, Pennsylvania. Telephone: (610) 459-3342. Web site: www.ushistory.org/brandywine.

Chancellorsville Battlefield, Virginia. Telephone: (540) 786-2880. Web site: www.nps.gov/frsp/chanville.htm.

Cold Harbor Battlefield and Cemetery, Virginia. Telephone: (757) 723-7104. Web site: www.nps.gov/history/nr/travel/national_cemeteries/Virginia/Cold_Harbor_National_Cemetery.html.

Droop Mountain Battlefield, West Virginia. Telephone: (304) 653-4254. Web site: www.droopmountainbattlefield.com/.

Fort Washington Military Historical Park, Maryland.
Telephone: (301) 763-4600. Web site: www.nps.gov/fowa.
Fredericksburg and Spotsylvania Battlefield, Virginia.
Telephone: (540) 373-6122. Web site: www.nps.gov/frsp.
Gettysburg National Military Park, Pennsylvania.
Telephone: (717) 334-1124. Web site: www.nps.gov/gett.
Harpers Ferry Battles, West Virginia. Telephone: (304) 535-6029.
Web site: www.nps.gov/hafe.
Manassas National Battlefield Park, Virginia.
Telephone: (703) 361-1339. Web site: www.nps.gov/mana.
Monocacy Civil War Battlefield, Maryland
Telephone: (301) 662-3515. Web site: www.nps.gov/mono.
New Market Battlefield Park, Virginia. Telephone: (540)
740-3101. Web site: www2.vmi.edu/museum/nm/.
Petersburg National Battlefield, Virginia.
Telephone: (804) 732-3531. Web site: www.nps.gov/pete.
Red Bank Battlefield Park, New Jersey.
Telephone: (856) 853-5120.
Richmond National Battlefield Park, Virginia.
Telephone: (804) 226-1981. Web site: www.nps.gov/rich.
Sailor's Creek Battlefield Historic State Park, Virginia. Telephone:
(804) 561-7510. Web site: www.dcr.state.va.us/parks/sailorcr.htm.
Valley Forge National Military Park, Pennsylvania.
Telephone: (610) 783-1053. Web site: www.nps.gov/vafo.
Yorktown Battlefield, Virginia. Telephone: (757) 898-2410.
Web site: www.nps.gov/colo.

BIKING

The bicycle is rightly considered one of the higher forms of elementary technology. Easy to store, transport, and maneuver, as well as inexpensive to operate, the bicycle is an attractive means of getting or keeping fit as well as a way to help conserve fuel resources. The bicycle was developed in Europe and introduced into this country in approximately 1875. The essential construction has remained unchanged, yet a study by researchers at Johns Hopkins University found that a bicycle chain drive is so efficient it wastes almost no energy. Often less than 2 percent.

According to the *Encyclopedia Britannica,* the idea that such a machine could be built occurred to people long ago. Representations of a two-wheeled version (with no pedals) occur in the art left behind by the Babylonians, the Egyptians, and the residents of Pompeii. This kind of bicycle was built every so often in the centuries that followed, but major progress was made in 1839 when the Scotsman Kirkpatrick Macmillan built one with pedals. Soon there were other developments. Tandem bicycles that would seat two were built, and are still used today. Efforts to build tricycles resulted in inventions that made the automobile possible. This was particularly true of the hub brake and the differential (which, by allowing the two back wheels to rotate at different speeds, made it possible to go around a curve). The modern, lightweight, multi-speed, touring bicycles are a distinct improvement, making touring vastly easier and racing much more fun. Heavier "mountain bikes" which have wider tires and a more stable ride have also become popular in recent years, on paved trails as well as rough terrain. There are even groups for those who enjoy recumbent biking.

This section contains information on some national organizations, touring and racing clubs, as well as names of sources where route maps and tour information can be obtained.

MAJOR BICYCLE ORGANIZATIONS AND CLUBS

There are several national and regional **biking organizations,** which deserve special mention because of the wide range of services they provide.

The League of American Bicyclists (LAB), founded in 1880, is a national organization of bicyclists and bicycle clubs. Based in Washington, D.C. at 1612 K Street, NW, the **LAB** promotes bicycling for fun, fitness, and transportation and works through advocacy and education for a bicycle-friendly America. In addition, the League publishes information on more than 500 biking events, nationwide, every year. Members receive a directory services, an annual almanac, discounts on cycling products, and have access to extensive information on routes, accommodations, and points of interest and safety. The 40,000-member League provides biking courses and course materials through its 600 affiliates, and will provide assistance in starting a bicycle club. To contact the league, telephone 202-822-1333. Web site: www.bikeleague.org.

USA Cycling (formerly **the United States Cycling Federation**), is a family of organizations "that promote and govern different disciplines of the sport, and that work as one to build the sport of bicycle racing, assist with athlete development and sustain international competitive excellence." USA Cycling provides information on racing procedures, routes, and events, nationwide. Information of interest to mountain, road, track, cyclo-cross and BMX bikers is arranged by category on the Web site. Address: One Olympic Plaza, Colorado Springs, CO 80909-5775. Telephone: (719) 434-4200. Web site: www.usacycling.org.

Adventure Cycling Association understands that cyclists need quiet, scenic roads and trails to enjoy. The Association researches and develops intra- and interstate bicycle trail systems, sponsors extended trips along these trails, publishes *Adventure Cyclist Magazine,* and provides what many regard as "the finest maps for cycling in North America." The group also sponsors tours for all levels of cyclists. Address: PO Box 8308-W, Missoula, MT 59807. Telephone: (800) 755-2453. Web site: www.adventurecycling.org.

American Youth Hostels (AYH), Potomac Area Council, sponsors weekend trips year round, extended summer-trips program through the United States and Canada, and promotes the establishment of hosteling clubs which receive organizational support from the Council. AYH also provides extensive reference and resource material for trip planning and research, including bike routes and maps and backpacking and canoeing information. The Potomac Council, based in Silver Spring, Maryland, will provide information and addresses on all member hostels and area councils. Telephone: (301) 495-1240. Web site: hiusa.org.

STATE AND LOCAL BICYCLE ORGANIZATIONS AND CLUBS

Most local clubs do not need office space and may not have a fixed mailing address. Members take turns volunteering to serve as the information contact. So fax or e-mail may be provided but no address or phone. If a phone number is given, it could well be a member's home or business. Check Web sites for updated lists of contacts. Potomac Pedalers Touring Club Web site provides links to several dozen bicycle clubs within the scope of this book, including those listed below: www.potomacpedalers.org.   Also   try   www.geocities.com/colosseum/6213/ for a nationwide list of local clubs.

Delaware

White Clay Bicycle Club invites road/hybrid/mountain/tandem and recumbent bikers to join them on rides in the Delaware, Maryland, Pennsylvania and New Jersey area. Web site: www.whiteclaybicycleclub.org. Tandem enthusiasts are encouraged to check out the Toucans, a White Clay affiliate: toucans_de.tripod.com.

District of Columbia

Potomac Pedalers Touring Club (PPTC) is one of the largest bicycle clubs in the U.S, and the largest in the D.C. metro area. Its energies are directed primarily toward providing a weekly schedule to accommodate all levels of skills and experience, novice to veteran. The club also has a tandem group, called the Wabits. Web site includes information about biking events and overnight trips as well as links to other biking organizations, some of which are listed below: www.potomacpedalers.org.

Washington (D.C.) Area Bicyclist Association (WABA) is a nonprofit citizen's association devoted to getting a better deal for the bicyclist. WABA promotes safer cycling throughout the area, publishes a bi-monthly newsletter, coordinates a legal service to protect cyclists' rights; provides a pedal pool of biking routes, tips, maps, general biking information, lobbying efforts, testifying, and surveys; and serves as a clearinghouse for bicycle commuting information. Voice phone: (202) 518.0524. Web site (with links to maps and related organizations): www.waba.org.

Bike and Brunch (B&B). Telephone: (301)-881-BIKE. This organization has a Bethesda, Maryland, address and phone, but almost always appears under the District of Columbia on resource lists. B&B is a group of Jewish, mostly single, bicycle riders who enjoy fun Sunday rides in the greater D.C. metro area, April through late November. Web site: www.bikeandbrunch.com.

Bike Washington, the creation/hobby of James Menzies, includes lots of routes and tips for recreational and commuter biking in the D.C. area. Web site: bikewashington.org.

MORE, Mid-Atlantic Off Road Enthusiasts, is a Mountain Bike Advocacy group and clearinghouse for routes and activities in the Eastern U.S., primarily D.C, Maryland and Virginia. Web site: www.more-mtb.org.

WHIRL (Washington's Happily Independent Recumbent Lovers) keeps fans of the unconventional recumbent bikes apprised of rides, routes, and events for like-minded cyclists. Web site: www.recumbents.com/whirl.

Maryland

Annapolis Bicycle Club. Web site: www.annapolisbicycleclub.org.

Baltimore Bicycling Club. Telephone: (410) 857-3262. Web site: www.baltobikeclub.org

Chesapeake Wheelmen. Web site: www.chesapeakewheelmen.org.

College Park Area Bicycle Coalition. Web site: www.cpabc.org.

Cumberland Valley Cycling Club (CVCC). Web site: www.bikecvcc.com.

Frederick Pedalers. Web site: www.frederickpedalers.org.

Harford Velo Cycling Club (HVCC). Web site: www.harfordvelo.org.

Oxon Hill Bicycle and Trail Club. Web site: ohbike.org.

Patuxent Area Cycling Enthusiasts (PACE). Web site: somd.com/Detailed/2476.php.

New Jersey

Shore Cycle Club. Web site: www.shorecycleclub.org.

South Jersey Cyclists. Telephone: (856) 489-1341. Web site: www.sjworks.org/view/group/646.

South Jersey Wheelmen. Telephone: (856) 691-3936. Web site: www. sjwheelmen.org.

North Carolina

River City Cycling Club. Web site: www.rivercitycyclingclub.com.

Pennsylvania

Bicycle Club of Philadelphia. Telephone: (215) 913-3246. Web site: www.phillybikeclub.org.

Central Bucks Bicycle Club. Web site: www.cbbikeclub.org.

Harrisburg Bicycle Club. Web site: www.harrisburgbicycleclub.org.

Lancaster Bicycle Club. Web site: www.lancasterbikeclub.org.

Quaker City Wheelmen. Web site: qcwcycling.org.

Red Rose Rockets Cycling Club. Telephone (717) 468-8080.

Tandems of York Society, (TOYS). Web site: http://suburbancyclists.org/tops/TandemLinks.htm.

Virginia

Blue Ridge Bicycle Club. Web site: www.blueridgebicycleclub.org.

Milepost Zero Bicycle Club. Web site: milepostzero.homestead.com.
New River Valley Bicycle Association. Web site: www.nrvbike.com.
Richmond Area Bicycling Association. Web site: www.raba.org.
Tidewater Bicycle Association.
    Web site: www.tbarides.org.
Whole Wheel Velo Club. Web site: www.wwvc.org.

Route Information Contacts
    The League of American Bicyclists has a very good Web page that lists bicycling events, whom they are hosted by, and whom to contact. Web page: www.bikeleague.org. Also check state park Web sites, Departments of Natural Resources, and the National Park Service for biking opportunities. Maryland, for example lists parks where biking is offered and some routes. Web site: dnr.maryland.gov/land/md_trails/trails_in_md.asp. The following groups are also good sources for maps and routes:

* Chesapeake & Ohio Canal National Historic Park, Telephone: (202) 653-5190.
* Maryland State Highway Administration, Web site: www.roads.maryland.gov/Index.aspx?PageId=677&d=108.
* North Carolina Department of Transportation, Telephone: (877) 368-4968.
* Northern Virginia Regional Park Authority, Telephone: (703) 352-5900.
* Tourism Council of Frederick County, Telephone: (800) 999-3613.
* Virginia Department of Transportation, Telephone: (800) 367-7623.
* Virginia Tourism Corporation, Telephone: (804) 545-5500.
* Visitors Center, Colonial Williamsburg, Telephone: (757) 220-7645.
* Washington Area Bicyclist Association, Telephone: (202) 518.0524.
* WILMAPCO (Wilmington Area Planning Council). Telephone: (302) 737-6205.

BIRDING

Birding has enjoyed a surge in popularity in recent years. The birding associations included in this section are only a partial listing of the many groups and activities available from Cape May to Cape Hatteras. Birding, like many other pastimes, is primarily volunteer-oriented, and most local organizations do not have offices or staffs.

But many regional parks and nature centers as well as the associations listed below will give you a good start on learning about birding if you are new to the subject or new to the area. The weekend sections of your local newspapers should also be helpful in identifying other associations, classes, and outings. Local birdwalks are usually free of charge and open to everyone. Some longer trips may be on a membership-only basis, but inquire first. The trips listed below are open to everyone, although costs vary.

PARKS

Many parks and refuges in the Mid-Atlantic region offer exceptional opportunities to observe and enjoy birds. The Audubon Society of the Central Atlantic States, Inc., maintains an active "Voice of the Naturalist" line that reports on bird sightings in the region and upcoming birding trips. Telephone: (301) 652-1088. Locations of special note in the region include Bombay Hook and Prime Hook National Wildlife Refuges in Delaware; the Pine Barrens, Cape May, and Stone Harbor in New Jersey; Pettigrew State Park, Pugo, Nettmuskeet, and Pea Island in North Carolina; and three areas described below—Dyke Marsh and Huntley Meadows in Alexandria, Virginia, and Hawk Mountain in Pennsylvania. Check the index under "Birding" and "Wildlife Refuges and Sanctuaries" for more information about the prime birding spots mentioned above, and others.

Dyke Marsh, Alexandria, VA. Web site: www.nps.gov/gwmp/dyke-marsh.htm.

Located between the Potomac River and the George Washington Memorial Parkway just south of Old Town Alexandria, Dyke Marsh is the largest piece of freshwater tidal wetlands in the Washington metro area. It is administered by the National Park Service as one of a dozen intriguing sites along the Parkway. More than 300 species of birds have been sighted in Dyke Marsh. A paved path and varied terrain make for a variety of interesting viewpoints.

Huntley Meadows, Alexandria, VA. Telephone: (703) 768-2525. Web site: www.fairfaxcounty.gov/parks/huntley-meadows-park.

Follow Route 1 south of Alexandria to Lockheed Blvd. Turn right onto Lockheed, and turn left into Huntley Meadows at the juncture with Harrison Lane. Look carefully. The entrance and sign can be easily overlooked. Free admission. The Information Center is nestled in trees as you enter the main trail, which includes an extensive boardwalk, observation tower, and 1400 acres of forest and wetlands. More than 200 species of birds have been reported.

Dutch Gap Conservation Area, Chesterfield, VA. Telephone: (804) 748-1624. Web site: www.chesterfield.gov/Parks.aspx?id=6442454866.

From I-95 in either direction, take Exit 61B. Proceed East on Route 10 to first stoplight, North on Route 732 to Route 615, Right on Route 615 to Henricus Road, look for park signs. Dutch Gap is an ornithologist's dream, and is ranked as one of the top 10 birding areas in the mid-Atlantic states. A blue heron rookery looms high in the marsh along the entrance. Eagles and other rare birds can be viewed.

Hawk Mountain Sanctuary, 1700 Hawk Mountain Road, Kempton, PA 19529-9449. Telephone: (610) 756-6961. Web site: www.hawkmountain.org.

Hawk Mountain is 25 miles north of Reading, PA. Take Route 61 north to 895 east for two miles to the Hawk Mountain sign. Turn right onto Hawk Mountain Road and follow it for another two miles to the top of the mountain.

BIRDING ASSOCIATIONS

Delaware

- Delaware Audubon Society, PO Box 1713, Wilmington, DE 19899. Telephone: (302) 292-3970. Web site: www.delawareaudubon.org.
- Delmarva Ornithological Society, PO Box 4247, Greenville, DE 19807. No telephone listing. Web site: www.dosbirds.org.

Maryland

- Audubon Naturalist Society of the Central Atlantic States, Inc., 8940 Jones Mill Road, Chevy Chase, MARYLAND 20815. Telephone: (301) 652-9188. Web site: www.audubonnaturalist.org.
- Audubon Society of Central Maryland, PO Box 660, Mount Airy, MARYLAND 21771. No telephone listing.
  Web site: www.centralmdaudubon.org.
- Chesapeake Audubon Society, PO Box 3173, Baltimore, MD 21228. Telephone: (410) 203-1819. Web site: www.chesapeakeaudubon.org.

- Maryland Ornithological Society, 4915 Greenspring Avenue, Baltimore, MD 21209. Telephone: (800) 823-0050. Web site: www.mdbirds.org.
- Prince George's Audubon Society, P.O. Box 693, Bowie, MD 20718. No telephone listing. Web site: www.pgaudubon.org.
- Southern Maryland Audubon Society, PO Box 181, Bryans Road, MD 20616. Telephone: (240) 765-5192. Web site: somdaudubon.org.

New Jersey
- Cape May Bird Observatory, PO Box 3, Cape May Point, NJ 08212. Telephone: (609) 884-2736. Web site: www.cmbo.org.
- New Jersey Audubon Society. 11 Hardscrabble Road, PO Box 693, Bernardsville, NJ 07924. Telephone: (908) 766-5787. Web site: www.njaudubon.org.
- The Wetlands Institute, 1075 Stone Harbor Blvd., Stone Harbor, NJ 08247. Telephone: (609) 368-1211. Web site: www.wetlandsinstitute.org.

North Carolina
- Carolina Bird Club. No telephone listing. Web site: www.carolinabirdclub.org.

Pennsylvania
- Bucks County Audubon Society, 6324 Upper York Road, New Hope, PA 18938. Telephone: (215) 297-5880. Web site: www.bcas.org.
- Hawk Mountain Sanctuary, 1700 Hawk Mountain Road, Kempton, PA 19529-9449. Telephone: (610) 756-6961. Web site: www.hawkmountain.org.
- Lehigh Valley Audubon Society, PO Box 290, Emmaus, PA 18049. No telephone listing. Web site: www.lehigh.edu/~bcm0/lvas.html.
- South Mountain Audubon Society, PO Box 3671, Gettysburg, PA 17325. No telephone listing. No Web site.
- Valley Forge Audubon Society, PO Box 866, Paoli, PA 19301. Telephone: (610) 666-5593. Web site: www.valleyforgeaudubon.org.

- Wyncote Audubon Society. No telephone listing.
  Web site: www.wyncoteaudubon.org.

Virginia

- Cape Henry Audubon Society, PO Box 1533, Norfolk, VA 23501.
  No telephone listing. Web site: chasnorfolk.org.
- Fairfax Audubon Society, 4022 Hummer Road, Annandale, VA
  22003. Telephone: (703) 438-6008. Web site: www.audubonva.org.
- Northern Neck Audubon Society. No telephone listing.
  Web site: www.northernneckaudubon.org.
- Richmond Audubon Society, P.O. Box 804, Richmond, VA 23207.
  No telephone listing. Web site: www.richmondaudubon.org.
- Roanoke Valley Bird Club. No telephone listing.
  Web site: roanokevalleybirdclub.com.
- Virginia Beach Audubon Society, PO Box 1066, Virginia Beach, VA
  23451. No telephone listing. Web site: www.audubon.org/chapters/virginia-beach-audubon-society.
- Virginia Society of Ornithology, 1230 Viewmont Drive, Evington,
  VA 24550. No telephone listing. Web site: virginiabirds.net.

Virginia is the first state in the nation to map birding and wildlife trails throughout its borders. The coastal area guide was published in 2002, and the mountain guide was published in 2003. The final guide covering a small section of Piedmont is slated for publication in 2004. The spiral-bound books are free from the Virginia Department of Game and Inland Fisheries. Telephone: (804) 367-1000. Web site: www.dgif.virginia.gov.

West Virginia

- Potomac Valley Audubon Society, PO Box 578, Shepherdstown,
  WV 25443. No telephone listing. Web site:
  www.potomacaudubon.org.
- West Virginia Raptor Rehabilitation Center, PO Box 333,
  Morgantown, WV 26507. Telephone: (304) 366-2867.
  Web site: www.wvrrc.org.

BIRDING TRIPS

- Brian Patteson, Inc. Pelagics, PO Box 772, Hatteras, NC 27943.
  Telephone: (252) 986-1363. Web site: www.patteson.com. Birding
  trips to North Carolina Outer Banks and Virginia Beach, VA.

- Skimmer, Captain Bob and Linda Carlough, Wildlife Unlimited, Inc., 10 Wahl Avenue, Cape May Court House, NJ 08210. Telephone: (609) 884-3100. Web site: www.skimmer.com. Trips to explore the Cape May Coastal Wetlands Wildlife Management Area.

CAMPING

Within the states covered by *Weekend Getaways Around Washington, D.C.,* hundreds of thousands of acres of mountain, woodland, and shore are open to public use. Shenandoah National Park in Virginia draws large crowds, but Jefferson, Monongahela, and George Washington National Forests comprise even larger portions of these lands. Found throughout this book, however, are many smaller parks and forests that are open to the public for camping. Their varying facilities range from primitive campsites reached only on foot to areas approachable from main automobile routes that offer full trailer hookups and such amenities as laundry tubs, showers, and flush toilets. Overnight camping is permitted at the parks listed below. The Index at the back of the book will refer you to pages within the Geographical section that include a description of the camping facilities and nearby attractions.

A good place to start your trip is by checking the following main Web sites or reservations numbers:

- **National Park Service.** Web site: www.nps.gov. Reservations: (800) 365-CAMP.
- **USDA Forest Service.** Web site: www.fs.fed.us. Reservations: (877) 444-6777.
- **Virginia State Parks.** Web site: www.dcr.virginia.gov. Reservations: (800) 933-PARK.
- **Maryland State Parks.** Web site: www.dnr.state.md.us/publiclands. Reservations: (888) 432-CAMP.
- **Delaware State Parks.** Web site: www.destateparks.com. Reservations: (877) 98-PARKS.
- **Pennsylvania State Parks.** Web site: www.dcnr.state.pa.us. Reservations: (888) PA-PARKS.
- **New Jersey State Parks.** Web site: www.state.nj.us/dep/parksandforests/parks. Reservations: Contact the individual park.
- **North Carolina State Parks.** Web site: www.ncparks.gov. Reservations: Contact the individual park.

Telephone numbers and Web sites are provided for the following sampling of individual parks to help you get additional information or make reservations. They are listed alphabetically by park name, regardless of state:

- **Assateague Island National Seashore,** VA. Information: (410) 641-1441 or (757) 336-6577. Reservations: (410) 641-3030. Web site: www.nps.gov/asis.
- **Babcock State Park,** WV. Information: (304) 438-3004. Reservations (800) CALL-WVA. Web site: www.babcocksp.com.
- **Bass River State Forest,** NJ. Information: (609) 296-1114. Web site: www.state.nj.us/dep/parksandforests/parks/bass.
- **Bear Creek Lake State Park,** VA. Information: (804) 492-4410. Reservations: (800) 933-PARK (7275).
- **Belleplain State Forest,** NJ. Telephone: (609) 861-2404. Web site: www.state.nj.us/dep/parksandforests/parks/belle.html.
- **Big Run State Park,** MD. Information: (301) 895-5453. Reservations: (888) 432-CAMP (2267). Web site: www.dnr.state.md.us/publiclands/western/bigrun.asp.
- **Blackwater Falls State Park,** WV. Information: (304) 259-5216. Reservations: (800) CALL-WVA. Web site: www.blackwaterfalls.com.
- **Bluestone State Park,** WV. Telephone: (304) 466-2805. Web site: www.bluestonesp.com.
- **Brendan T. Byrne State Forest,** NJ. Telephone: (609) 726-1191. Web site: www.state.nj.us/dep/parksandforests/parks/byrne.html.
- **Bull Run Regional Park,** VA. Telephone: (703) 631-0550. Web site: www.nvrpa.org/park/bull_run.
- **Burke Lake Park,** VA. Telephone: (703) 323-6601. Web site: www.fairfaxcounty.gov/parks/wp-lakefront.htm.
- **Cabin John Regional Park,** MD. Telephone (301) 299-0024. Rink telephone: (301) 765-8626. Web site: www.montgomeryparks.org/facilities/regional_parks/cabinjohn/.
- **Caledonia State Park,** PA. Telephone—park: (717) 352-2161. Telephone—playhouse: (717) 352-2164. Reservations: (888) PA-PARKS. Web site: www.dcnr.state.pa.us/stateparks/findapark/caledonia.
- **Canaan Valley State Park,** WV. Telephone: (304) 866-4121 or (800) 622-4121. Web site: www.canaanresort.com.
- **C&O Canal National Historical Park,** MD. Telephone: (202) 653-5190. Web site: www.nps.gov/choh.
- **Cape Hatteras National Seashore,** NC. Information: (252) 473-2111. Reservations: (800) 365-CAMP. Web site: www.nps.gov/caha.

- **Cape Henlopen State Park,** DE. Information: (302) 645-8983. Reservations: (877) 98-PARKS. Web site: www.destateparks.com/park/cape-henlopen.
- **Catoctin Mountain Park,** MD. Telephone: (301) 663-9388. Web site: www.nps.gov/cato
- **Codorus State Park,** PA. Telephone: (717) 637-2816. Reservations: 888-PA-PARKS. Web site: www.dcnr.state.pa.us/stateparks/findapark/codorus.
- **Cowans Gap State Park,** PA. Telephone: (717) 485-3948. Reservations: (888) PA-PARKS. Web site: www.dcnr.state.pa.us/stateparks/findapark/cowansgap.
- **Cunningham Falls State Park,** MD. Telephone: (301) 271-7574. Web site: www.dnr.state.md.us/publiclands/western/cunningham.asp.
- **Deep Creek Lake,** MD. Information: (301) 387-5563. Reservations: (888) 432-CAMP. Web site: www.dnr.state.md.us/publiclands/western/deepcreek.asp.
- **Dixie Caverns,** VA. Telephone: (540) 380-2085. Web site: www.dixiecaverns.com.
- **Elk Neck State Park,** MD. Information: (410) 287-5333. Reservations: (888) 432-2267. Web site: www.dnr.state.md.us/publiclands/central/elkneck.asp.
- **False Cape State Park,** VA. Information (757) 426-7128. Reservations (800) 933-PARK. Web site: www.dcr.virginia.gov/state_parks/fal.shtml.
- **Fort Frederick State Park,** MD. Telephone: (301) 842-2155. Web site: www.dnr.state.md.us/publiclands/western/fortfrederick.asp.
- **Fountainhead Regional Park,** VA. Telephone: (703) 250-9124. Web site: www.nvrpa.org/park/fountainhead/.
- **French Creek State Park,** PA. Information: (610) 582-9680. Reservations: (888) PA-PARKS. Web site: www.dcnr.state.pa.us/stateparks/findapark/frenchcreek.
- **Gambrill State Park,** MD. Telephone: (301) 271-7574. Web site: www.dnr.state.md.us/publiclands/western/gambrill.asp.
- **Garrett State Forest,** MD. Telephone: (301) 334-2038. Reservations: (888) 432-CAMP. Web site: www.dnr.state.md.us/publiclands/western/garrettforest.asp.
- **Gifford Pinchot State Park,** PA. Information: (717) 432-5011. Reservations: 888-PA-PARKS. Web site: www.dcnr.state.pa.us/stateparks/findapark/giffordpinchot.
- **Greenbrier State Park,** MD. Telephone: (301) 791-4767. Reservations: (888) 432-CAMP. Web site: www.dnr.state.md.us/publiclands/western/greenbrier.asp.

- **Green Ridge State Forest,** MD. Information: (301) 478-3124. Reservations: (888) 432-CAMP. Web site: www.dnr.state.md.us/publiclands/western/greenridgeforest.asp.
- **Herrington Manor State Park,** MD. Telephone: (301) 334-9180. Reservations: (888) 432-2267. Web site: www.dnr.state.md.us/publiclands/western/herrington.asp.
- **Holliday Lake State Park,** VA. Information: (434) 248-6308. Reservations: (800) 933-7275. Web site: www.dcr.virginia.gov/state_parks/hol.shtml.
- **Janes Island State Park,** MD. Information: (410) 968-1565. Reservations (888) 432-CAMP. Web site: www.dnr.state.md.us/publiclands/eastern/janesisland.asp.
- **Lake Fairfax,** VA. Telephone: (703) 471-5415. Web site: www.fairfaxcounty.gov/parks/wp-lakefront.htm.
- **Louise F. Cosca Regional Park,** MD. Information: (301) 868-1397. Reservations: (301) 203-6030. Web site: www.pgparks.com/Things_To_Do/Nature/Cosca_Regional_Park.htm.
- **Lums Pond State Park,** DE. Telephone: (302) 368-6989. Web site: www.destateparks.com/park/lums-pond/.
- **Martinak State Park,** MD. Information: (410) 820-1668. Reservations (410) 432-CAMP. Web site: www.dnr.state.md.us/publiclands/eastern/martinak.asp.
- **Millersburg Ferryboat Campsites,** PA. Telephone: (717) 444-3200. Web site: www.ferryboatcampsites.com.
- **Monongahela National Forest,** WV. Information: (304) 636-1800. Web site: www.forestcamping.com/dow/eastern/moncmp.htm.
- **New Germany State Park,** MD. Telephone: (301) 895-5453. Reservations: (888) 432-CAMP. Web site: www.dnr.state.md.us/publiclands/western/newgermany.asp.
- **Parvin State Park,** NJ. Telephone: (856) 358-8616. Web site: www.state.nj.us/dep/parksandforests/parks/parvin.html.
- **Patapsco Valley State Park**, MD. Telephone: (410) 461-5005. Web site: www.dnr.state.md.us/publiclands/central/patapsco.asp.
- **Pettigrew Resort State Park,** NC. Telephone: (252) 797-4475. Web site: visitncne.com/Campground/pettigrew-state-park.html.
- **Pipestem State Park,** WV. Telephone: (304) 466-1800. Web site: www.pipestemresort.com.
- **Pocomoke River State Park,** MD. Telephone: (410) 632-2566. Web site: www.dnr.state.md.us/publiclands/eastern/pocomokeriver.asp.

- **Pohick Bay Regional Park, VA.** Information: (703) 339-6104. Web site: www.nvrpa.org/park/pohick_bay.
- **Point Lookout State Park, MD.** Telephone: (301) 872-5688. Reservations: (888) 432-CAMP. Web site: www.dnr.state.md.us/publiclands/southern/pointlookout.asp.
- **Prince William Forest Park, VA.** Information: (703) 221-7181. Reservations: (703) 221-5843. Web site: www.nps.gov/prwi.
- **Savage River State Forest, MD.** Telephone: (301) 895-5759. Web site: www.dnr.state.md.us/publiclands/western/savageriverforest.asp.
- **Shenandoah National Park, VA.** Telephone: (540) 999-3500. Reservations: (877) 444-6777. Web site: www.nps.gov/shen.
- **Susquehanna State Park, MD.** Information: (410) 557-7994. Reservations: (888) 432-CAMP. Web site: www.dnr.state.md.us/publiclands/central/susquehanna.asp.
- **Swallow Falls State Park, MD.** Telephone: (301) 387-6938. Web site: www.dnr.state.md.us/publiclands/western/swallowfalls.asp.
- **Tuckahoe State Park, MD.** Information: (410) 820-1668. Reservations: (410) 432-CAMP. Web site: www.dnr.state.md.us/publiclands/eastern/tuckahoe.asp.
- **Washington Monument State Park, MD.** Telephone: (301) 791-4767. Web site: www.dnr.state.md.us/publiclands/western/washington.asp.
- **Westmoreland State Park, VA.** Telephone: (804) 493-8821. Web site: www.dcr.virginia.gov/state_parks/wes.shtml.
- **Wharton State Forest, NJ.** Telephone: (609) 561-0024. Web site: www.state.nj.us/dep/parksandforests/parks/wharton.html.

CANOEING AND KAYAKING

Both canoeing and kayaking involve using various paddle strokes and the current to navigate around obstructions like rocks and overhanging limbs. Both sports have aspects that appeal to reflective nature lovers who prefer the glide of flat water and adventure lovers who prefer the thrills and churns of white water. The kinships among canoeists and kayakers have led many of them to join forces with whitewater rafters in associations and clubs that promote the health and benefits of "paddle" water sports and work together on safety and preservation issues. The oldest of these groups is the **American Canoe Association,** Inc., which was founded in 1880, and now provides a range of services to those interested in canoeing, kayaking, and rafting. The ACA sanctions more than 700 paddlesport events each year. The "Paddler's Resources" Section of its Web site lists local clubs, contacts in each state, weather and water updates, and tips for beginners. A quarterly publication *Paddler Magazine* is included in membership fees, and the ACA also maintains a good booklist of relevant titles. Contact: American Canoe Association, 7432 Alban Station Blvd, Suite B-232, Springfield, VA 22150. Telephone: (540) 907-4460. Web site: www.americancanoe.org.

Information on fluctuations in water currents and levels can be obtained by calling the **National Weather Service** at (757) 899-4200 for a tape recording of river stages in most of Maryland, Virginia, and West Virginia. The National Weather Service Web site (www.weather.gov) also provides this information online through its "rivers" link, which prepares summaries of hydrologic activity with emphasis on extreme conditions.

For information on river and streamflow conditions, water supply and hydrometeorological outlooks, contact the Office of Hydrologic Development, 1325 East-West Highway, SSMC2, Silver Spring, MD 20910. Telephone: (301) 713-1658. Or visit the OHD Web site. The infomation online compares existing water levels to established norms for each body of water and includes helpful maps: www.nws.noaa.gov/oh.

The main canoeing and kayacking season is from March to mid-November. Winter outings (because of the dangers of hypothermia in case of upset) are for experienced paddlers only—or those on guided trips with appropriate precautions. Many people learn the basics of flat water canoeing through informal instruction from friends. Kayaking and whitewater canoeing are more challenging and require specific skills that can have a real bearing on safety. For information on courses and other aspects of canoeing contact: Canoe Cruisers Association of Greater Washington, D.C., Inc., PO Box 3236, Merrifield, VA 22116. The main purpose of this 1000-member organization is to unite people interested in paddling the Potomac River Basin and adjacent watersheds. The group sponsors both events and trips, many of which are also open to nonmembers. Web site: ccadc.org.

Tidewater administrations, as well as State Forest and Park Services, and Departments of Natural Resources for the area you intend to visit are also good sources of information. For example, if you go to the Maryland Department of Natural Resources site (www.dnr.state.md.us), then click on "outdoors" or "nature tourism," you'll find canoeing and kayaking information including lists of all parks that offer these sports as well as where you can rent equipment and find guides or outfitters.

Additional Clubs and Organizations

Appalachian Mountain Club (AMC), founded in 1876, is America's oldest conservation and recreation organization. Its 90,000 members enjoy and help preserve and maintain the rivers, mountains, and trails of the Northeastern U.S. Membership includes a subscription to *AMC Outdoors.* Web site: www.outdoors.org. At this Web site you can obtain information on the regional chapters for the areas within the scope of this book, such as the Delaware Valley Chapter and the D.C. Chapter.

The Potomac Appalachian Trail Club (PATC) has more than 7,000 members in the region. Its main purpose is the upkeep and improvement of 970 miles of hiking trails, 30 shelters, and 28 cabins in Virginia, Maryland, West Virginia, Pennsylvania and the District of Columbia. Outings and activities include hiking, camping, climbing, canoeing, and kayaking. Events and outing are also open to non-members. PATC Offices in Vienna are open to the public Monday through Thursday evenings, 7 P.M. to 9 P.M., and on Thursdays and Friday, noon to 2 P.M. Telephone: (703) 242-0315. Web site: www.patc.net.

Outfitters

Look under "Canoe Rental" in your regional Yellow Pages (on paper or online) to see who rents canoes and kayaks in your area. Many are located near parks and popular push-off points. The same heading is also likely to include regional outfitters. Many of the outfitters listed in the "Special Interest Section" on Whitewater Rafting also handle canoe and kayaking equipment and lead outings or know of guides.

For information about canoeing in national parks, go to the main Web site: www.nps.gov. Using "canoe" to search will bring up relevant links such as a list of canoe rental liveries in and around the Delaware Gap National Recreation Area, or near the Assateague Island National Seashore.

The Web sites for the **Trade Association of Paddlesports** (www.gopaddle.org) can also be of value in planning your trip. Tips, lists of outfitters for various interests, rental information, and guidance are offered, as well as useful links to other Web sites. Trips are posted as well as offers to buy and sell various kinds of paddlesports equipment.

You can request an information packet on paddle sports in Virginia by calling (888) 42-FLOAT. The Web site for the Virginia Professional Paddlesports Association lists outfitters in good standing and the waters they work as well as phone numbers, emails, and web links. Web site: www.vappa.com.

CAT SHOWS

Cats have become as popular as dogs as household pets in recent years, and the interest in cat shows has increased accordingly. The **Cat Fanciers' Association** (CFA) is the world's largest registry of pedigreed cats. At present, 37 breeds of cats are recognized for championship competition. The CFA has 655 member clubs that sanction more than 380 shows worldwide, and it is the best source of information on cat shows. The Cat Fanciers' Association, Inc., P.O. Box 1005, Manasquan, NJ 08736-0805. Telephone: (732) 528-9797. Web site: www.cfainc.org.

Community groups also sponsor informal shows that are open to cats of all types, whether recognized breeds or mixed blessings. Such shows may have no official standing in the breeding world but give families a chance to show off their pets while serving as fund raisers for an organization or worthy cause—often the local humane society or animal shelter. The events are usually announced in local papers, and via fliers in pet stores and veterinarians' offices.

CAVERNS

Caverns hold a subtle fascination for many people. They provide an opportunity to see a part of our earth that sunlight does not touch, a netherworld where water flows and life has a toehold in total darkness. Throughout the area covered by *Weekend Getaways* are underground caverns or caves, major attractions that charge admission fees and that are usually open year round. The greatest number of them are concentrated in the Shenandoah Valley of Virginia. Most of these caverns maintain year-round temperatures in the low 50s, so bring a sweater. Almost all are well-lit artificially and offer guided tours through the subterranean wonderlands of stalactites, stalagmites, and shimmering rock formations. Nearly all also have gift shops, restaurants, and picnic grounds nearby. See the "Caverns" heading in this Index for page references in the Geographic Section, which provides more detailed information about and contact information for the following caverns.

MARYLAND

Crystal Grottoes Caverns.   Near Boonsboro, west on Route 34.

PENNSYLVANIA

Crystal Cave.   Near the Reading-Berks area.
Indian Echo Caverns.   Off Route 322, three miles outside of Hershey.

VIRGINIA

Crystal Caverns, Hupp's Hill.   Near Strasburg.
Dixie Caverns, Salem.
Grand Caverns.   Located near Grottoes, junction of Routes 340 and 256.
Luray Caverns,   near the town of Luray.
Natural Bridge Caverns,   near the town of Natural Bridge.
Shenandoah Caverns.   Off I-81, exit 269, or Route 11, midway between Mt. Jackson and New Market.
Skyline Caverns,   near the town of Skyline.

WEST VIRGINIA

Lost World Caverns,   about 1.5 miles north of Lewisburg on Fairview Road.
Seneca Caverns,   three miles southeast of Riverton, off Routes 33 and 28.
Smoke Hole Caverns,   on Route 28, eight miles south of Petersburg.

COVERED BRIDGES ————————————————

Covered bridges are curious yet picturesque reminders of a previous age. One often speculates fleetingly about the endurance of the structures when seeing them from a nearby highway. These bridges are fast disappearing, but some are being carefully preserved by devoted individuals who cherish these relics of the past. Some 19th-century covered bridges survive and some new covered bridges are still being constructed. The tourist may see covered bridges throughout the mid-Atlantic states. The Philippi Covered Bridge, for example, the longest two-lane covered bridge still in use on a federal highway, is located at Philippi on Route 250 in West Virginia, 27 miles east of Clarksburg.

The Society for the Preservation of Covered Bridges keeps track of the bridges and catalogues them in a "World Guide to Covered Bridges." A good Web site listing covered bridges by county and state in Delaware, Pennsylvania and Maryland is: faculty.lebow.drexel.edu/McCainR//top/bridge/CB1.html.

The following Web site lists the covered bridges in Virginia: www.virginiadot.org/info/resources/covered_bridges.pdf

North Carolina covered bridges are listed at: www.dalejtravis.com/bridge/bridgenc.htm. West Virginia covered bridges are described at: users.hrea.coop/post/.

The wooden covered bridge of the 19th century is an American phenomenon, although similar bridges are found throughout the world. However, Europeans generally built their bridges of stone because of the scarcity of wood. In the United States, with its abundant forests, the wooden bridge was the cheapest type to build. Once the principle of the truss was utilized for bridge building, bridges spanning the many rivers from Maine to Georgia were built.

In the United States the bridge-building boom was a result of ingenious carpenters and craftsmen who capitalized on their knowledge of building barn support systems. In 1792, Timothy Palmer built a two-arch truss bridge over the Merrimac River. Subsequently, bridges were covered to protect the trusses from the extremes of weather. Wood can survive being submerged in water, but it is the alternate wetting and drying that will quickly destroy the wooden trusses. In 1806, Palmer built his patented arch-truss bridge 550 feet over the Schuylkill River and then covered it. It was a two-lane bridge and lasted for 70 years until it was destroyed by fire. Bridges soon not only had roofs, but also side walls. The enclosure of the bridges protected the trusses, provided a reassuring covering for horses and cows, and served as signboards advertising messages such as "Dr. Parker's Indian Oil for Ills of Man and Beast" and religious messages such as "The wages of sin is death [*sic*]."

Bridges are formally described by the truss system used. A truss is a triangular support; a triangle can not be distorted, only broken. Various improvements were added to the basic truss to strengthen the supports. The following is a list of diagrams and descriptions of the main types of trusses one will find in the Middle Atlantic areas covered in *Weekend Getaways around Washington, D.C.*

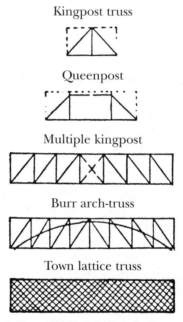

Kingpost truss

Queenpost

Multiple kingpost

Burr arch-truss

Town lattice truss

Long and Howe trusses (Howe truss substituted wrought-iron verticals)

With the coming of the railroad, wooden bridges proved inadequate because, under too much tension, the joints were pulled apart. Some of the covered bridges mentioned below are described in more detail in the geographic sections of this book.

DELAWARE

New Castle County
Ashland Bridge, 1870, Town lattice, Red Clay Creek.
Two miles southeast of the Pennsylvania state line on DE Rt. 82, then right to bridge.
Wooddale Bridge (private), 1870, Town lattice, Red Clay Creek.
Northwest of suburban Wilmington off DE Rt. 48.

MARYLAND

Baltimore County
Jericho Bridge, 1858, Burr arch, Gunpowder Creek.
East-northeast of Kingsville on Jericho Road.

Cecil County
Gilpin's Falls Bridge, (closed to motor traffic), 1860, Burr arch, Northeast Creek.
Northeast of Bayview off MD Rt. 272.
Foxcatcher Farms Bridge, 1860, Burr arch, Big Elk Creek.
Northeast off Fair Hill on the road to the Dupont Estate.

Frederick County
Utica Mills Bridge, 1850, restored 1997, Burr arch, Fishing Creek.
Southeast of Lewiston on Utica Road off MD Rt. 806.
Roddy Creek Bridge, 1850, Kingpost truss, Owens Creek.
Northern edge of Thurmont on Roddy Road.
Loy's Station Bridge, 1880, Kingspost truss, Owens Creek.
Northeast of Creagerstown on MD Rt. 550, then right on Old Frederick Road to bridge.

NEW JERSEY

Camden County
Scarborough Bridge, 1959, restored 1993, Town lattice with sidewalk, North Fork of Cooper River.
Located at Barclay Farm south of NJ Rt. 70, about one-half mile east of the junction with NJ Rt. 41 in the town of Cherry Hill.

Hunterton County
Green Sergeant's Bridge, 1866 Queen truss, Wickecheoke Creek.
West of Sergeantsville on CR 604.

PENNSYLVANIA

Adams County
Sach's Bridge, 1883, Town lattice, Marsh Creek.
Southwest of Gettysburg on Waterworks Road.

Bucks County
Van Sant Bridge, 1875, Town lattice, Pidcock Creek.
South of New Hope on TR 392, Soleburg Road.
Erwinna Bridge, 1871, Town lattice, Lodi Creek.
Two miles south of Ulherstown and bridge to New Jersey on PA Rt.
32, right on SR 1012 and right again on SR 1014 to bridge.
Ulherstown Bridge, 1832, Town lattice, Tinicum Creek (Delaware Canal).
South of bridge to New Jersey on PA Rt. 32 then right to bridge.
Cabin Run Bridge, 1871, Town lattice, Cabin Run.
East of Pipersville on SR 1011, Plumstead Turnpike.
Loux Bridge, 1874, Town lattice, Cabin Run.
East of Pipersville on SR 1003, Carversville Road.

Lancaster County
The Lancaster County area is a particularly rich one for covered bridges, with 28 still standing. The best way to find the bridges is to purchase a tourist information map that shows the location of the bridges. Or visit the Pennsylvania Dutch Country Welcome Center online: www.800padutch.com/covbrdg.shtml.

VIRGINIA

Alleghany County
Humpback Bridge, (closed to motor traffic), 1857, restored 1954, Multiple King truss, Dunlap Creek.
West of Covington off US Rt. 60 at roadside park.

Giles County
Sinking Creek Bridge, 1916, Modified Howe truss, Sinking Creek.
North edge of Newport off SR 601.
Link Farms Bridge, (private), 1912, Queen truss variant, Sinking Creek.
Northwestern edge of Newport off SR 700, Mountain Lake Road.
C. K. Reynolds Covered Bridge, (private, permission required), 1919, Queen truss variant, Sinking Creek.
Northeast of Newport off VA Rt. 42.

Patrick County
Bob White Bridge, (closed to motor traffic), 1921 Queen truss, Smith River.
Southeast of Woolwine off SR 618.
Jack's Creek Bridge, (closed to motor traffic), 1914, Queen truss, Smith River.
South of Woolwine off SR 615.

Rockingham County
Biedler Farm Bridge, (private), circa 1800, Burr variant, Smith Creek.
South of New Market off US 11.

Shenandoah County
Meem's Bottom Bridge, 1894, restored 1979, Burr arch, North Fork of the Shenandoah River.
South of Mount Jackson on SR 720.

WEST VIRGINIA

Barbour County
Philippi Bridge, 1852, Burr arch with cement deck, Tygart River.
Western edge of Philippi on US Rt. 250.
Carrollton Bridge, 1855, Burr arch with cement deck, Buckhannon River.
East of the village of Volga off US Rt. 119.

Greenbrier County
Herns Mill Bridge, 1884, Queen truss, Mulligans Creek.
Northwest of Lewisburg on CR 40.
Hokes Mill Bridge, 1884, Long truss variant, Second Creek.
Southwest of Ronceverte on CR 62, just north of Monroe County line.

Monroe County
Laurel Creek Bridge, 1911, Queen truss, Laurel Creek.
Southwest of Union on Rts. 219/11.
Indian Creek Bridge, 1903, Long truss, Indian Creek.
South-southwest of Union on old section of US Rt. 219.

CROSS-COUNTRY SKIING ━━━━━━━━━━━━━━━

Cross-country skiing is enjoying a great increase in popularity in the mid-Atlantic region. The flat and rolling contours of Virginia, Washington D.C., West Virginia, New Jersey, Maryland, and Pennsylvania offer an appealing variety of terrain for the novice to expert skier. This is a sport that is easy for most people to learn. All you need are skis, boots, poles, and a snow-covered area.

The following list includes the places within 200 miles of Washington and Baltimore where good skiing can be found. Rental equipment, food, and lodging are usually also available nearby, but it is wise to check on equipment rentals before venturing out. Recreational and day skiers should also check with local golf courses and regional parks for ski possibilities close to home. Areas which are not specifically designated for skiing, such as biking and bridle trails, logging and fire roads, and the rare but exquisite snow-covered beach, can also make fine ski areas.

Many of the locations listed, with the exception of private resort trails, are often left unplowed. Many trails in parks and forests are not marked. Skiers are well advised to obtain maps, including topographical maps, before leaving home for large park and wilderness areas. Park offices keep irregular hours during winter months and may be closed when you arrive. If you plan to ski in a wilderness area, it is a good idea to inform local authorities or friends of your plans and destination. Weather and snow conditions can make or break a holiday. Be sure to check the reports before taking off. The following numbers may be useful:

• Washington metropolitan area weather, hourly reports: (202) 936-1212.

• Maryland Department of Natural Resources recording (includes ski conditions for New Germany and Herrington Manor): (877) 620-8367 (Maryland only) or (410) 260-8100.

• West Virginia ski reports and transfers to major ski resorts: (800) 225-5982.

• The Internet provides immediate access to up-to-the-minute weather listings. You can see the desired region's forecast for the day or even for the whole week. The following are two very good sources:

• The Weather Channel: www.weather.com.

• The National Weather Service: www.weather.gov.

Several clubs and organizations sponsor cross country/Nordic style ski trips and races. Check the weekend section of your local newspaper, or call state and county parks or local ski equipment outfitters.

SKI OUTINGS

These organizations and outfitters provide planned ski tour packages that include instruction and rentals. Day and weekend tours are available.

Fairfax County Park Authority, VA: (703) 324-8702. Web site: www.fairfaxcounty.gov/parks/.

Montgomery County Recreation Department, MD: Web site: www6.montgomerycountymd.gov/rectmpl.asp?url=/content/rec/index.asp. Organized day trips offered January-March in MD, VA or WV. Telephone: (240) 777-6840.

Potomac Appalachian Trail Club has a Ski Touring Section which invites non-members to join them every ski season weekend to carpool to a ski area. Participants at all levels must get their own equipment. PATC Ski Touring Section, 118 Park Street, S.E., Vienna, Virginia 22180-4609. Telephone: (703) 242-0315. Web site: www.patc.net.

River and Trail Outfitters: 604 Valley Road, Knoxville, MD 21758. Telephone: (301) 695-5177. Web site: www.rivertrail.com. Tours to New Germany State Park in MD.

CROSS COUNTRY SKI AREAS

Maryland

C&O Canal National Historic Park. The park extends for 165 miles from Washington, DC, to Cumberland, MD. Camping allowed. For general information, telephone: (301) 739-4200. Web site: www.nps.gov/choh.

Catoctin Mountain Park (National Park), Thurmont, MD. Take Route 15 north out of Frederick to Route 77. Follow Route 77 to the park entrance. (Within 1½ hours of Washington, DC.) Catoctin Mountain Park and adjacent CUNNINGHAM FALLS STATE PARK have about 25 miles of marked trails. Terrain is hilly and rocky. Food and lodging nearby. Telephone: (301) 663-9388. Web site: www.nps.gov/cato.

Gambrill State Park and Frederick City Land, Frederick, MD. Take

270 to Frederick to Route 40. Follow signs off Route 40. (Close to Washington, D.C.) Gambrill is a park adjacent to Frederick and I-70 west. Park has no real ski trails but skiers follow the plowed road through the park to the ridgetop until Frederick City Watershed property. This area is full of short trails and skiable roads. Telephone: (301) 271-7574. Web site: www.dnr.state.md.us/publiclands/western/gambrill.asp.

Green Ridge State Forest, Flintstone, MD. Take Route 70 to Hancock, MD. Approximately three miles after Hancock exit take Route 40 exit towards Cumberland. Twenty miles after passing Cumberland exit take left on Fifteen Mile Creek Road. Difficult terrain. (The C&O towpath crosses through the southern end of the forest.) Telephone: (301) 478-3124. Web site: dnr.maryland.gov/publiclands/western/greenridgeforest.asp.

New Germany State Park, Grantsville, MD. In the Savage River State Forest, five miles south of Grantsville, MD. Take Route 48 west out of Cumberland to Lower New Germany Road. Exit and follow signs to the park. Easy to difficult, 15 miles of trails. Map, shelter, and wax available at the park headquarters. Lodging and food nearby. Telephone: (301) 895-5453. Web site: dnr.maryland.gov/publiclands/western/newgermany.asp.

Savage River State Forest, Grantsville, MD. Take Route 48 west out of Cumberland to Lower New Germany Road. Follow Lower New Germany Road to Big Run State Park. Information and maps available at park. To get to the **Savage Mountain hiking trail,** which is 16 miles of skiable trail along Big Savage mountain, take Exit 29 of Route 48 (Finzel Exit). Follow Old Frostburg Road south to the first stop. Turn left and go one more mile to the sign for the trail. Several other skiable trails and logging roads in the State Forest. Savage Run State Forest telephone: (301) 895-5759; Big Run State Park telephone: (301) 895-5453. Web site: dnr.maryland.gov/publiclands/western/savageriverforest.asp (or) dnr.maryland.gov/publiclands/western/bigrun.asp.

Seneca Creek State Park, 11950 Clopper Road, Gaithersburg, MD 20878. In Montgomery County, 20 miles northwest of Washington, DC. Drive south from I-270 near Gaithersburg on route 124 for one mile to Route 117 (Clopper Road); turn right (west) on Route 117 for two miles to park. Six miles of easy to difficult trails. Telephone: (301) 924-2127. Web site: dnr.maryland.gov/publiclands/central/seneca.asp.

Swallow Falls and Herrington Manor State Parks, Oakland, MD. These parks are side by side in western Maryland. Take I-270 north to Route 70 west to Route 40 west to 48 west to 219 south to Oakland, MD. At the far end of Oakland turn right on Route 20. Follow signs to parks. Swallow Falls offers a variety of long and short trails. Snowmobile trails in Potomac State Forest connect Swallow Falls with Herrington Manor. Herrington Manor has approximately five miles of trails. Telephone: (301) 387-6938. Web sites: dnr.maryland.gov/publiclands/western/swallowfalls.asp (or) dnr.maryland.gov/publiclands/western/herrington.asp.

New Jersey

Pine Barrens, Wharton State Forest, Hammonton, NJ. In Burlington County, south central New Jersey, 25 miles west of Camden. Drive east from Camden on Route 30 for 26 miles to Hammonton, turn left (east) on Route 542 for eight miles to Wharton State Forest, turn east from Camden on Route 70 for 27 miles to Route 72, turn right (east) on Route 72 for three miles to Lebanon State Forest office on left. Nine and a half miles of easy trails and 91 miles adjacent. Primitive camping available. Telephone: (609) 561-0024. Web site: www.state.nj.us/dep/parksandforests/parks/wharton.html.

Pennsylvania

Black Moshannon, Philipsburg, PA. In Centre County in central Pennsylvania. Drive south from I-80 on Route 220 for seven miles to Unionville and turn right on Route 504 for five miles. Ten miles of easy trails. Rentals, downhill skiing. Telephone: (814) 342-5960. Web site: www.dcnr.state.pa.us/stateparks/findapark/blackmoshannon/index.htm.

Caledonia State Park, Fayetteville, PA. In Franklin and Adams counties, south central Pennsylvania. From I-81 drive 10 miles east on Route 30 to park on left. From Gettysburg drive 15 miles west on Route 30 to park on right. Ten miles of trails, moderate to difficult. Lodging and camping nearby. Telephone: (717) 352-2161. Web site: www.dcnr.state.pa.us/stateparks/findapark/caledonia/index.htm.

Codorus State Park, Hanover, PA. In York County, south central Pennsylvania, 20 miles southwest of York. Drive west on Route 30 from York for six miles; turn left on Route 116 for 15 miles to Hanover; turn left on Route 216 at Hanover and go two miles south. Fifteen miles of trails and 300 acres of open fields and woodlands.

Telephone: (717) 637-2816. Web site:
www.dcnr.state.pa.us/stateparks/findapark/codorus/index.htm.
Cowans Gap State Park, Fort Loudon, PA. Near Chambersburg, PA,
off Route 75 in the Tuscarora Mountains. Easy to difficult, 7½ miles of
trails. Lodging nearby. Telephone: (717) 485-3948. Web site:
www.dcnr.state.pa.us/stateparks/findapark/cowansgap/index.htm.
Delaware Water Gap National Recreation Area, Shawnee, PA. In
Monroe and Northampton counties in northeastern Pennsylvania,
six miles south of Stroudsburg. Drive east from Stroudsburg on I-80
toward Water Gap and south at Exit 53 to Route 611. South on 611
for three miles to park on right at Slateford Farm. Five and a half
miles of easy to difficult trails. Telephone: (570) 828-2253 or (570)
426-2451. Web site: www.nps.gov/dewa.
Gettysburg National Military Park, Gettysburg, PA. Take I-270
north to Frederick; follow Route 15 north to the Battlefield. Food
and lodging available nearby. Maps available at the visitors center.
Telephone: (717) 334-1124. Web site: www.nps.gov/gett.
Gifford Pinchot State Park, Lewisberry, PA. In York County, 15 miles
northwest of York. Drive north on I-83 from York to Route 382 (west)
(Exit 13) for three miles to Route 177. Turn left into the park. Eight
miles of trails, easy to moderate. Rentals and instruction available.
Telephone: (717) 432-5011. Web site:
www.dcnr.state.pa.us/stateparks/findapark/giffordpinchot/index.htm.
Hickory Run State Park, Carbon County, 40 miles north of
Allentown. Drive west from Stroudsburg on I-80 for 38 miles to
Hickory Run Exit, then east on Route 534 for four miles. Thirteen
miles of easy to difficult trails. Rentals, instruction, food, and camp-
ing available. Some snowmobile trails. Telephone: (570) 443-0400.
Web site:
www.dcnr.state.pa.us/stateparks/findapark/hickoryrun/index.htm.
Ridley Creek State Park, East Sycamore Mills Road, Media, PA. In
Delaware County in southeast Pennsylvania. Drive west from
Philadelphia on Route 3 for 16 miles, through Newtown Square, to
park. Ten miles of multi-use trails. Telephone: (610) 892-3900. Web site:
www.dcnr.state.pa.us/stateparks/findapark/ridleycreek/index.htm.
Tyler State Park, Newtown, PA. In Bucks County in southeastern
Pennsylvania. Drive north from Philadelphia on I-95 to Newtown
exit. Go east on Route 322 for 4½ miles to park. Forty miles of multi-
use trails. Telephone: (215) 968-2021. Web site:
www.dcnr.state.pa.us/stateparks/findapark/tyler/index.htm.

Virginia

Blue Ridge Parkway. Take Route I-66 to 29 south to Charlottesville. Take 250 west to Waynesboro to the Blue Ridge Parkway. Parkway extends 469 miles from Waynesboro, VA, to Cherokee, NC. The parkway (except for the short section between Bedford, VA, and Apple Orchard Radar Station) and surrounding areas are excellent for ski touring. Telephone: (828) 298-0398. Web site: www.nps.gov/blri.

Fairfax County Parks. Fairfax County parks feature a variety of cross-country skiing trails near Washington, DC. For information on regional parks, telephone: (703) 352-5900. Web site: www.nvrpa.org.

Manassas National Battlefield Park. From Washington, DC, go west on I-66 to Route 234. Take Route 234 for two miles to the park office. (Thirty-eight miles west of Washington, DC.) Thirty miles of trails. Lodging and food nearby. Telephone: (703) 361-1339. Web site: www.nps.gov/mana.

Mount Rogers National Recreation Area/Jefferson National Forest, Marion, VA. Parking at Elk Garden Gap. Mount Rogers has several miles of designated trails, good elevation. Several skiable logging roads in the forest. Telephone: (276) 783-5196. Web site: www.fs.usda.gov/gwj.

Shenandoah National Park, Luray, VA. Park entrances: Front Royal (northern entrance); Thornton Gap off Route 211 (central entrance); or Route 29 south to Charlottesville to Route 250 west to Rockfish Gap (southern entrance). Ski touring unlimited in the 195,000 acre park. Parts of Skyline Drive are skiable; excellent touring on park roads. Intermediate to difficult. Camping allowed. Food and lodging nearby. Telephone: (540) 999-3500. Web site: www.nps.gov/shen/index.htm.

District of Columbia

Rock Creek Park, Washington, DC. In northwest Washington, DC, between Connecticut and Georgia avenues. Eleven miles of trails and golf course. Additional two miles of park roads closed for cross-country skiing when snow-covered. Telephone: (202) 895-6070. Web site: www.nps.gov/rocr.

West Virginia

Alpine Lake Resort and Conference Center, Terra Alta, WV. Northern West Virginia. Approximately nine miles of groomed and foot-packed trails, lodging, restaurants, heated swimming pools. Rentals and instruction. Telephone: (800) 752-7179 or (304) 789-2481. Web site: www.alpinelake.com.

Blackwater Nordic Center, Blackwater Falls State Park, Davis, WV. Fifteen and a half miles of maintained trails, six miles of machine-set track, ice-skating rink, lighted sled run, telemark slope with tow. Instruction, rentals, backcountry guides, food, and lodging. Telephone: (304) 259-5216. Web site: www.blackwaterfalls.com.

Canaan Valley Resort, Tucker County, 11 miles south of Thomas, WV. Proceed west from Cumberland, MD, on Route 48 for 31 miles, south on Route 219 through Oakland for 55 miles to Thomas, south on Route 32 from Thomas for 11 miles to park on right six miles. Rentals and instruction, lodging, camping, food, and downhill skiing available. Telephone: (304) 866-4121 or (800) 622-4121. Web site: www.canaanresort.com.

Cranberry Backcountry, near Richwood, WV. In Pocahontas and Webster counties, central West Virginia in the Monongahela National Forest, 26 miles east of Summersville. Drive west on I-64 and Route 60 from Lewisburg for 30 miles to Charmco, right (north) on Route 20 for 17 miles to Route 39, and right (east) for eight miles. Two trails of seven and 11 miles each, 70 miles of unplowed roads. Nine Adirondack shelters. Telephone: (304) 799-4334. Web site: www.fs.fed.us/r9/mnf/rec/xcountryski.html.

Elk River Touring Center, Slatyfork, WV. Twenty-five miles of trails, four miles of machine-groomed trails, and a mile of beginner loops which are lighted for night skiing. Food and lodging, instruction, telemark lessons and rentals, backcountry guided tours. Telephone: (304) 572-3771 or (866) 572-3771. Web site: www.ertc.com.

Pipestem Resort State Park, Pipestem, WV. Eastern West Virginia, 16 miles north of Princeton on Route 20 from Pipestem Exit off I-77. Twenty-five deluxe cabins, two lodges. Telephone: (304) 466-1800. Web site: www.pipestemresort.com.

Spruce Knob/Seneca Rocks, Seneca Rocks, WV. Randolph and Pendleton counties in the Monongahela National Forest. Drive west from Petersburg on Route 28 for 22 miles to Seneca Rocks; turn right (north) on Route 33 for six miles to road for Seneca Creek. Sixty miles of trails. Telephone: (304) 567-2827. Web sites: www.fs.usda.gov/recarea/mnf/recarea/?recid=9915 (or) www.fs.usda.gov/recarea/mnf/recarea/?recid=7050.

White Grass Ski Touring Center, Davis, WV. Adjacent to Canaan

Valley State Park. Three hundred forty miles of maintained trails, 12½ miles of machine-groomed trails, backcountry skiing in the Dolly Sods Wilderness area and in Monongahela National Forest. Instruction, rentals, sales, and guided tours available. Telephone: (304) 866-4114. Web site: www.whitegrass.com.

CRUISES AND FERRIES

Cruises around the Chesapeake Bay and the Inland Waterway are available by commercial boats. Some cruises are all-day outings, others an hour or less. Depending on the company, the boats may operate all year long or only from May through September. Ferry rides offer an alternative way to get from one point to another on the opposite side of a body of water. Sometimes ferries are of interest because they save time that would otherwise be spent driving a less direct route, or offer access to an area that can only be reached by boat. At other times their charm is as scenic reminder of a simpler time. Here is a sampling of what is available in the mid-Atlantic region:

DELAWARE

Cape May-Lewes Ferry, Lewes, DE and Cape May, NJ, a 70-minute ride between Cape May, NJ and Lewes, DE.
Telephone: (800) 64-FERRY (643-3779). Web site: www.capemaylewesferry.com

Three Forts Ferry, Fort Delaware State Park, DE, a ferry from the dock in Delaware City to Pea Patch Island in the Delaware River, where Fort Delaware State Park is located.
Telephone: (302) 834-7941. Web site: www.threeforts.com/fdel.html.

Dolphin/Whale Watching Cruises, Fisherman's Wharf by the Drawbridge-Anglers Road, Lewes, DE. Telephone: (302) 645-8862. Web site: fishlewes.com.

MARYLAND

Bay Queen, Ocean City Fishing Center, Ocean City, MD. Telephone: (410) 632-1415. Web site: www.thebayqueen.com.

Ocean City Rocket/Assateague Adventure Cruises, Talbot Street on the Bay, Downtown Ocean City, MD. Telephone: (410) 289-3500. Web site: www.ocean-city.com/listing-detail/Assateague-Adventure-Cruises.

Oxford/Bellevue Ferry, Royal Oak, MD, believed to be the nation's oldest privately operated ferry service, crosses the Tred Avon River between Oxford, Maryland and Bellevue, Maryland, a three-fourths of a mile trip that takes seven minutes, leaves each side every 25 minutes, and can accommodate nine vehicles. Telephone: (410) 745-9023. Web site: www.oxfordbellevueferry.com.

Patriot Cruises, St. Michaels, MD. Telephone: (410) 745-3100. Web site: www.patriotcruises.com.

Tangier Island Cruises, Crisfield, MD. Telephone: (410) 968-2338. Web site: www.tangierislandcruises.com.

White's Ferry is the only cable-guided (captive) fresh water ferry still operating on the East Coast. A ferry crossing has existed at this location in Dickerson, MD (4 miles from Leesburg, VA, 36 miles from Washington, D.C) since 1833. The ferry, which connects scenic areas of Poolesville, MD, and Leesburg, VA, also figured in the Civil War. The current ferry boat is named *General Jubal A. Early* in honor of this heritage. The ride across the Potomac takes 12 to 14 minutes. White's Ferry is located in a privately owned recreational area at Milepost 35.5 on the C&O Canal. Bikes, canoes, and Jon boats are available for rental. The ferry runs daily from 5 A.M. to 11 P.M. Fare charged. Located at 24801 White's Ferry Road, Dickerson, MD 20842. Telephone: (301) 349-5200.

NEW JERSEY

Atlantic City Cruises, Historic Gardener's Basin. Telephone: (609) 347-7600. Web site: www.atlanticcitycruises.com.

Starlight Fleet Whale and Dolphin Whale Tours, Wildwood Crest, NJ. Telephone: (609) 729-7776. Web site: www.jjcboats.com.

NORTH CAROLINA

A&A Atlantic Outer Banks Cruises, Manteo, NC. Telephone: (252) 480-9151. Web site: www.outerbankscruises.com.

North Carolina Department of Transportation, Ferry Information and Schedules, check Web site: www.ncferry.org.

VIRGINIA

Venture Inn Charters, Hampton, VA. Telephone: (757) 850-8960. Web site: www.ventureinncharters.com.

Reedville, VA. This small historic town includes an historic district of Victorian mansions and the Reedville Fishermen's Museum. It is a significant charter fishing center, especially for those seeking blue-fish and rockfish. More than 50 boats are available. Nearby back roads lead to the **Sunnybank Ferry,** established in 1906 and one of two remaining free ferries in Virginia. Blow your horn for ferry service, available from 7 A.M. to 7 P.M., Monday through Saturday.

CUT-YOUR-OWN CHRISTMAS TREES ———

Nothing says "Merry Christmas" better than the fragrance of a fresh Christmas tree, sparkling with lights and glittering with shiny tinsel. It is possible to relive the "good old days" when Grandpa used to lead the children through the woods to pick the biggest, greenest pine tree in the forest. Many farms allow customers to choose their own trees by tagging them, or by actually cutting or digging them. Be sure to know what size tree you want. The height of an in-the-ground tree can be deceptive.

The mid-Atlantic area has an abundance of Scotch pines. Other trees include white and Austrian pines, Douglas and Concolor firs, and Norway, blue, and white spruce. Be sure to ask if you must bring your own saw or shovel, if the farmer cuts or digs the tree, or if the task is up to you, and what facilities there are for preparing your tree for the trip home.

As soon as you arrive at the farm, check in and ask directions to the cutting, digging, or tagging area. Trees are usually less expensive than in a city-bound lot. And of course you have the pleasure of the outing at no extra charge!

Once you get your special tree home, follow a few rules to keep it fresh. Keep it in a cool spot as long as possible before bringing it in the house. If it is a cut tree, cut another inch off the main stem and place the tree in a clean pail of warm water in a shaded spot. Cut another inch off before you bring it into the house. Place it in a stand that can hold water or in a pail of clean sand to which water can be added. If it is a balled tree, be sure to keep the roots moist by placing it in a large tub of water. Add water daily. Some horticulturists also suggest adding a clear soft drink, such as 7-Up or Sprite, and a little bleach to the water to keep needles from drying out. Do not use diet brands of the soft drink. For each five gallons of water, use about one quart of soft drink, plus one tablespoon of bleach. Then trim your tree with your ornaments, sit back, and enjoy the best of nature in your home.

The following organizations can be helpful sources of information about **Christmas tree farms** in the region. They are followed by a list of farms, organized by state, where you can choose your own tree.

Growers' Associations

The Maryland Christmas Tree Association, 3501 Hanover Pike, Manchester, MD 21102. Web site: www.marylandchristmastrees.org.

The New Jersey Christmas Tree Growers Association, 805 Brookside Drive, Toms River, NJ 08753. Telephone: (609) 291-7855. Web site: www.njchristmastrees.org.

The Pennsylvania Christmas Tree Growers Association, 1924 North Second Street, Harrisburg, PA 17104. Telephone: (800) 547-2842. Web site: www.christmastrees.org.

The Virginia Christmas Tree Growers Association, PO Box 558, Rixeyville, VA 22737. Telephone: (540) 382-7310. Web site: www.virginiachristmastrees.org.

TREE FARMS IN THE REGION

Delaware

Coleman's Christmas Tree Farm, Middletown, DE. Telephone: (302) 378-8949 or (302) 378-1900.

Maryland

Baltimore County

All Timber Hill Farm, Parkton/White Hall, MD. Telephone: (410) 343-1940.

Elliott's Ventura Farm, Butler, MD. Telephone: (410) 771-4510.

Frostee Tree Farm, Perry Hall, MD. Telephone: (410) 391-5113 or (410) 256-5560. Web site: frosteetreefarm.com.

Green Hill Farm, Baldwin, MD. Telephone: (410) 592-7813.

Jones' Christmas Tree Plantation. Monkton, MD. Telephone: (410) 771-4346.

Martin's Tree Farm, Hampstead, MD. Telephone: (410) 374-2226. Web site: martintreefarm.com.

Mt. Carmel Tree Farm, Parkton, MD. Telephone: (443) 491-3323.
Ruhl's Tree Farm, Phoenix, MD. Telephone: (410) 666-2924.
Stansbury Christmas Tree Farm, Jacksonville, MD. Telephone:
(410) 666-2531.

Carroll County
Davidson Christmas Tree Farm, Upperco, MD. Telephone: (410)
239-6556.
Feldhof Farm, Westminster, MD. Telephone: (410) 876-7680.
Fra-mar Tree Farm, Hampstead, MD. Telephone: (410) 374-2868.
Hirt Tree Farm, Westminster, MD. Telephone: (410) 876-8839.
JCK Christmas Tree Farm, Taneytown, MD. Telephone: (410)
876-TREE or (410) 346-7597.
Judy's Nursery, Westminster, MD. Telephone: (410) 876-7647.
Otterdale View Christmas Tree Farm, Union Bridge, MD.
Telephone: (410) 775-0176.
Pine Valley Farms, Sykesville, MD. Telephone: (410) 795-8314.
Sewell's Farm, Taneytown, MD. Telephone: (410) 756-4397.
Silver Meadow Farm, Woodbine, MD. Telephone: (301) 829-9198.
Thomas Tree Farm, Manchester, MD. Telephone: (410) 374-9538.

Cecil County
Pusey Tree Plantation, Colora, MD. Telephone: (410) 658-6277.

Frederick County
Beaver Dam Tree Farm, Union Bridge, MD. Telephone: (410)
775-2661.
Clemsonville Christmas Tree Farm, Union Bridge, MD.
Telephone: (410) 848-6083.
Franz Tree Farm, Monrovia, MD. Telephone: (301) 865-1798.
Gaver Tree Farm, New Market, MD. Telephone: (301) 865-3515
or (301) 865-0747.
Hardee Farms, New Midway, MD. Telephone: (301) 384-6576 or
(301) 384-9455 or (301) 593-3990.
Mayne's Tree Farm, Buckeystown, MD. Telephone: (301) 662-
4320 or (301) 874-2665.
Unionville Tree Farm, Unionville, MD. Telephone: (301) 829-0604.

Garrett County
Mountain Top Tree Farm, Oakland, MD. Telephone: (301)
334-8342 or (301) 616-0488.

Harford County

Applewood Farm, Whiteford, MD. Telephone: (410) 836-1140.
Deer Creek Valley Tree Farm, Street, MD. Telephone: (410) 452-9793
Enviromental Evergreens Tree Farm, Darlington, MD. Telephone: (410) 457-4766 or (410) 457-4842.
Evergreen Farm, Harve De Grace, MD. Telephone: (410) 939-0659.
Jarrettsville Nurseries, Jarrettsville, MD. Telephone: (410) 557-9677 or (410) 838-3966.
Maranatha Tree Farm, White Hall, MD. Telephone: (410) 692-2517

Howard County

Greenway Farms, Woodbine, MD. Telephone: (410) 442-2388.
TLV Farm, Glenelg, MD. Telephone: (410) 489-4460 or (410) 489-0139.

Kent County

Simmons' Christmas Trees, Stillpond, MD. Telephone: (410) 778-0451 or (410) 348-5407.

Montgomery County

Buck Lodge Christmas Tree Farm, Boyds, MD. Telephone: (301) 349-5226.
Butler's Orchard, Germantown, MD. Telephone: (301) 972-3299.
King Farm, Clarksburg, MD. Telephone: (301) 253-4521.
R and K Trees, Boyds, MD 20841. Telephone: (301) 972-9355.

Prince George's County

Tanner's Enchanted Forest, Brandywine, MD. Telephone: (301) 579-2238.

Queen Anne's County

Blue Heron Tree Farm, Centerville, MD. Telephone: (410) 758-0405.

St. Mary's County

Evergreen Acres, Oakville, MD. Telephone: (301) 862-1597.

Talbot County

Hutchison's Christmas Forest, near Cordova, MD (between Easton and Denton). Telephone: (410) 820-2062.

Washington County
Mount Hope Farms, Hagerstown, MD. Telephone: (301) 790-2372.

New Jersey
Atlantic County
  Bill's Christmas Trees, Egg Harbor, NJ. Telephone: (609) 641-5459.
  Lanza's Tree Farm, Elwood, NJ. Telephone: (609) 567-3028.
  Petrongolo Evergreen Plantation, Hammonton, NJ. Telephone:
    (609) 567-0336.
  Winchelsea Farm, Port Republic, NJ. Telephone: (609) 652-6855

Burlington County
  Croshaw's Christmas Tree Farm, Columbus, NJ. Telephone: (609)
    298-0477.
  DeCou's Christmas Trees, Moorestown, NJ. Telephone: (856)
    234-0085.
  Haines Tree Farm, Burlington, NJ. Telephone: (609) 871-8755.
  Haines Farm, Tabernacle, NJ. Telephone: (609) 268-0484.
  Indian Acres Tree Farm, Medford, NJ. Telephone: (609) 953-0087.
  Kenlin Farm, Edgewater Park, NJ. Telephone: (609) 923-5254.
  Sandy Creek Christmas Tree Farm, Columbus, NJ. Telephone:
    (609) 261-8888.
  Spruce Goose Christmas Tree Farm, Chesterfield, NJ. Telephone:
    (609) 298-2498.
  Wading River Christmas Tree Farm, Wading River, NJ. Telephone:
    (609) 965-1601 or (609) 965-0565.

Camden County
  Culbertson's Nursery, Atco, NJ. Telephone: (856) 767-4839 or
    (856) 767-3221.
  Lucca's Christmas Tree Farm, Berlin, NJ. Telephone: (609)
    767-0189.

Cape May
  Eisele's Tree Farm, Petersburg, NJ. Telephone: (609) 628-2758.
  Fir-ee Holly Tree Farm, Burleigh, NJ. Telephone: (908) 835-7840.
  Krogman's Christmas Tree Farm, Dennisville, NJ. Telephone:
    (609) 861-5537.

Cumberland County
  Fisher's Tree Farm, Bridgeton, NJ. Telephone: (856) 451-2626.

Greenleaves Christmas Tree Farm, Newport, NJ. Telephone: (856) 447-3814.

Gloucester County
Belly Acres Christmas Tree Farm, Franklinville, NJ. Telephone: (856) 694-0350.
Exley's Country Lane Nursery, Sewell, NJ. Telephone: (856) 468-5949.

Ocean County
Christmas Time Tree Farm, Jackson, NJ. Telephone: (732) 929-0837.
Yuletide Christmas Tree Farm, New Egypt, NJ. Telephone: (732) 349-2705.

Pennsylvania
Berks County
Sheerlund Forests, Inc., Reading, PA. Telephone: (610) 777-9351.

Bucks County
Tuckamony Farm, Solebury, PA. Telephone: (215) 862-9510 .

Chester County
Schmidts' Tree Farm, Landenburg, PA. Telephone: (610) 274-8560.
Westlake Tree Farms, Pottstown, PA. Telephone: (800) 564 TREE.

Montgomery County
Hague's Christmas Trees, Hatfield, PA. Telephone: (215) 368-4542.
Varner's Farm, Collegeville, PA. Telephone: (610) 489-8878.

York County
Good's Christmas Tree Farm, Etters, PA. Telephone: (717) 938-1570.
Strathmeyer Forest, Inc., Dover, PA. Telephone: (800) 345-3406.

Virginia
Albemarle County
Indian Springs Farm, Earlysville, VA. Telephone: (804) 973-3459.
   The Annual "Cut Your Own Christmas Tree Festival" takes place at Ash Lawn, James Monroe's plantation near Charlottesville, every December. For more information, telephone: (434) 293-8000 or log on to the Ash Lawn Web site. Web site: www.ashlawnhighland.org/aboutus.htm.

Augusta County
Francisco Farms, Staunton, VA. Telephone: (540) 805-3008.

Hickory Hill Nursery Farm, West Augusta, VA. Telephone: (540) 943-6587.

Caroline County
Shephard Hill Christmas Tree Farm, Bowling Green, VA. Telephone: (804) 633-5133.

Chesterfield County
Ash Grove, Richmond, VA. Telephone: (804) 275-2204.

Clarke County
Ashcroft Farm, White Post, VA. Telephone: (540) 837-1240.
Oakland Tree Plantation, Berryville, VA. Telephone: (800) 727-XMAS or (540) 955-4495.

Craig County
Joe's Trees, Newport, VA. Telephone: (540) 544-7303.

Culpeper County
Glengary Christmas Tree Farm, Viewtown, VA. Telephone: (540) 937-4751.
Hinter Benedicten Conifers, Viewtown, VA. Telephone: (540) 937-6168.
Peper'mint Christmas Tree Farm, Culpeper, VA. Telephone: (540) 825-4693.

Fairfax and Fauquier Counties
Colline Farm, Warrenton, VA. Telephone: (540) 341-7342.
JB's Christmas Tree Farm, Midland, VA. Telephone: (540) 788-4035.
Stribling's Christmas Trees at Oldacre's Farm, Markham, VA. Telephone: (540) 364-1206.

Greene and Hanover Counties
Greene Meadows Tree Farm, Standardsville, VA 22973. Telephone: (434) 990-1999.
Gooseberry Tree Farm, Mechanicsville, VA. Telephone: (804) 781-0381.
Hanover Pine Christmas Tree Farm, Beaverdam, VA. Telephone: (804) 475-4094.

Windy Knoll Farm, Mechanicsville, VA. Telephone: (804) 730-8733.

Henrico, James City and Loudoun Counties
Rolling Oaks Farm, Mechanicsville, VA..
Jacobson's Tree Farm, Leesburg, VA. Telephone: (703) 777-9534.
Melody Farm, Chantilly, VA. Telephone: (703) 754-7905.
Middleburg Christmas Tree Farm, Middleburg, VA. Telephone: (540) 554-8625.
Snickers Gap Tree Farm, Bluemont, VA. Telephone: (540) 554-8323.
White Oak Farm, Middleburg, VA. Telephone: (540) 687-3260.

Louisa and Madison Counties
Claybrooke Christmas Tree Farm, Mineral, VA. Telephone: (540) 872-3817.
Windrush Farm, Mineral, VA. Telephone: (540) 872-5356.
Stonehearth Christmas Tree Farm, Leon, VA. Telephone: (301) 384-6215 or (540) 547-2576.

Middlesex, Montgomery, and Nelson Counties
Macey's Christmas Tree Farm, Hartfield, VA. Telephone: (804) 776-6043.

Orange, Powhatan, and Prince William Counties
Laron Christmas Tree Farm, Powhatan, VA. Telephone: (804) 598-7701.

Rappahannock, Roanoke, and Rockingham Counties
Conrad Jones Christmas Tree Farm, Bent Mountain, VA. Telephone: (540) 929-4770.
Evergreen Christmas Tree Farm, Keezletown, VA. Telephone: (540) 269-2691.

Shenandoah and Spotsylvania Counties
Blair Farms, Woodstock, VA. Telephone: (540) 459-2090.
Ralph's Christmas Trees, Spotsylvania, VA. Telephone: (540) 377-9490.

Warren County
   Quail Hollow Tree Farm, Bentonville, VA. Telephone: (540)
      635-9155.

West Virginia
   Bluestone Nursery, Camp Creek, WV. Telephone: (304) 425-5928.
   French Creek Farms, French Creek, WV. Telephone: (304)
      965-3108.
   May Christmas Tree Farm, Petersburg, WV. Telephone: (304)
      749-7294.
   Mount Teman Nursery, Camp Creek, WV. Telephone: (304)
      920-6308 or (304) 425-5182.
   Rolling Acres Tree Farm, Franklin, WV. Telephone: (304)
      358-2805.
   Shriver's Christmas Trees, Berkeley Springs, WV. Telephone:
      (304) 258-1159.

DOWNHILL SKIING AND
SNOWBOARDING

The terrain of the mid-Atlantic region is ideally suited to the beginning, novice, or intermediate skier or snowboarder. The abundance
of good areas only hours from the Baltimore-Washington-Richmond
area provides plentiful and varied terrain for learning how to ski or
snowboard, or for improving your skills. Advanced skiers and board-
ers accustomed to demanding slopes will find several ski centers with
sufficiently challenging runs for weekend trips. Large-scale snowmaking and the recent development of well-crafted trails in nearby
mountain areas are making downhill snow sports more attractive and
accessible.

Night skiing and the availability of equipment stores and ski clubs
in Washington, Baltimore, and Richmond are evidence of downhill's
popularity. Night skiing is particularly good on the gentler mid-
Atlantic slopes and far more popular than in New England or the
Western Rockies where temperatures drop drastically after the sun
goes down.

While most ski areas listed below are small, nearly all provide
instruction, rentals, repairs, and eating facilities. Many locations have
other outdoor sporting activities available, and some sort of après ski

life on site or nearby. Larger areas offer weekend and longer ski-and-stay packages that rival the better-known ski centers in New England and the West.

CLUBS

Ski clubs offer weekend and longer excursions during the season to local ski areas, to New England, and to the West. Throughout the year they sponsor weekly social gatherings with canoeing, hiking, and other sports outings as well as group ski and snowboarding trips. The major ski clubs are:

Baltimore Ski Club. Telephone: (410) 825-SNOW. (This is an answering service. Leave a message and they will send you literature.) Web site: www.baltimoreskiclub.com.

Black Ski of Washington, D.C. P.O. Box 90762, Washington, D.C. 20090-0762.

Columbia Ski Club. Web site: www.columbiaskiclub.org.

Crabtowne Skiers. Web site: www.clubcrabtowne.org. (Annapolis, MD)

Frederick Ski Club. Web site: www.frederickskiclub.com.

Fredericksburg Ski Club. Web site: www.fredericksburgskiclub.org.

NASA/Goddard Ski Club. Web site: gewa.gsfc.nasa.gov/clubs/ski.

Pentagon Ski Club. Web site: www.pentagonskiclub.org.

Richmond Ski Club. Web site: www.richmondskiclub.org.

Ski Club of Washington, D.C. Telephone: (703) 536-7776. (This is a recording of current events; you can also leave a message for more information.) Web site: www.scwdc.org.

DOWNHILL SKI RESORTS

Maryland
Wisp
Oakland, MD. Telephone: (301) 387-4000; Web site: www.wispresort.com. Season: Mid-December to early March.
Twelve miles of slopes and trails. Vertical rise 610 feet. Slopes are beginner, intermediate, advanced. Lift capacity 4,000 per hour. Snowmaking. Open all week, night skiing. Rentals, instruction, lodging, and food available. Cross-country skiing available. Three and a half to four hours from Washington and Baltimore, five hours from Richmond.

Pennsylvania

Big Boulder
Lake Harmony, PA. Telephone: (570) 443-8425. Web site: jfbb.com. Ski report: jfbb.com/explore/snow-reports.

Blue Knob
Claysburg, PA. Telephone: (814) 239-5111. Web site: www.blueknob.com. Season: December to mid-March. Seven miles of trails, 14 slopes. Vertical rise 1,052 feet. Slopes are beginner, intermediate, advanced. Lift capacity 3,000. Snowmaking. Open all week, night skiing. Rentals, repairs, instruction, lodging, and food available. Three and a half hours from Washington.

Blue Mountain
Palmerton, PA. Telephone: (610) 826-7700. Telephone for Ski Report: (877) SKI-BLUE. Web site: www.skibluemt.com.

Camelback
Tannersville, PA. Telephone: (570) 629-1661. Web site: www.skicamelback.com. Ski Report: (800) 233-8100.

Elk Mountain
Uniondale, PA. Telephone: (570) 679-4400. Web site: www.elkskier.com.

Jack Frost Mountain
White Haven, PA. Telephone: (570) 443-8425. Web site: jfbb.com.

Liberty Mountain Resort
Fairfield, PA. Telephone: (717) 642-8282. Web site: www.libertymountainresort.com. Season: Thanksgiving to March 15. Open daily. Night skiing. Vertical rise 600 feet. Fourteen trails. Beginner to advanced (mostly intermediate). Ski rentals and repair, instruction, lodging, and food. Seventy miles from Washington.

Montage
Scranton, PA. Telephone: (800) GOT-SNOW. Web site: www.snomtn.com.

Shawnee Mountain
Shawnee-on-Delaware, PA. Telephone: (570) 421-7231. Telephone for Ski Report: (800) 233-4218.

Web site: www.shawneemt.com. Season: Thanksgiving to March 30. Open daily. Vertical rise 700 feet. Eight miles of trails (11 trails and slopes). Instruction, rentals, ski shop, lodging, and food. Snowmaking covers 100 percent of area. Four miles outside of Stroudsburg, Pennsylvania.

Ski Roundtop
Lewisberry, PA. Telephone: (717) 432-9631. Web site: www.skiroundtop.com. Season: November 15 to March 15.
Open daily. Night skiing. Vertical rise 550 feet. Six trails, four slopes. Beginner to advanced (mostly beginner). Rentals, instruction, food, and lodging. Two and a half hours from Washington. One and a half hours from Baltimore.

Tamiment Resort and Country Club
Tamiment, PA. Telephone: (570) 588-6652. Web site: www.tamiment.com. Season: Late December to mid-March.
Open daily. Vertical rise 125 feet. Two slopes. Instruction, ski shop, lodging, and food. Snowmaking. Located near Bushkill and Route 209.

Virginia

Bryce Mountain Resort
Basye, VA. Telephone: (540) 856-2121.
Web site: www.bryceresort.com.
Season: Mid-December through mid-March.
Four slopes. Vertical rise 500 feet. Slopes are beginner, intermediate, advanced. Lift capacity 2,500 per hour. Snowmaking. Open all week, night skiing. Rentals, repairs, instruction, lodging, and food available. Two and a half to three hours from Baltimore/Richmond via 1-66.

The Homestead Ski Area
Hot Springs, VA. Telephone: (800) 838-1766.
Web site: www.thehomestead.com. Season: Mid-December through mid-March.
Six slopes and three trails. Vertical rise is 695 feet. Slopes are beginner, intermediate, advanced. Open all week. Rentals, repairs, instructions, lodging, and food available. Four hours from Baltimore/ Richmond.

Massanutten
Harrisonburg, VA. Telephone: (540) 289-9441. Web site: www.massresort.com. Season: Mid-December through mid-March.
Nine slopes. Vertical rise is 795 feet. Trails are beginner, intermediate,

advanced. Lift capacity 5,200 per hour. Open all week, night skiing. Rentals, repairs, instruction, lodging, and food available. Two hours from Baltimore/Richmond via I-66.

Wintergreen
Wintergreen, VA. Telephone: (800) 325-2200. Telephone for Ski Report: (800) 325-2100. Web site: www.wintergreenresort.com. Season: December 1 through late March. Ten slopes and 82 acres of skiing terrain. Vertical rise is 1,003 feet. Snowmaking. Beginner, intermediate, advanced slopes. Lift capacity 6,400 per hour. Open all week, night skiing. Rentals, repairs, instruction, lodging, and food available.

West Virginia
Canaan Valley Resort
Davis, WV. Telephone: (800) 622-4121. Web site: www.canaanresort.com. Season: Mid-December through mid-March. Six slopes, 14 trails. Slopes are beginner, intermediate, advanced. Lift capacity is 1,200 per hour. Snowmaking. Open all week, night skiing. Rentals, repairs, instruction, lodging, and food available. Four hours from Baltimore/Richmond.

Snowshoe Mountain
Snowshoe, WV. Telephone: (877) 441-4FUN. Web site: www.snowshoemtn.com. Season: Thanksgiving to Easter. One hundred fifty acres of slopes and trails; 11 major trails. Vertical rise 1,598 feet. Lift capacity 5,000 per hour. Snowmaking. Open all week. Rentals, repairs, instruction, lodging, and food available.

Timberline Four Seasons Resort
Canaan Valley, WV. Telephone: (800) SNOWING. Web site: www.timberlineresort.com. Season: December through March. Fourteen slopes and trails from beginner to expert. Vertical rise is 1,084. Longest run 10,640 feet. Lift capacity 3,000 per hour. Snowmaking. Lodging, food, instruction, and rentals.

Winterplace
Flat Top, WV. Telephone: (800) 607-SNOW. Web site: www.winterplace.com. Ski Report: (800) 258-3127.

FARMERS MARKETS

Farmers Markets allow consumers to purchase fresh fruit and vegetables from a variety of vendors at one location. Prices are often lower than at supermarkets. Some Farmers Markets are seasonal or operate only on certain days. Call for more information.

The following list of fruits and vegetables with harvest dates should provide an indication as to when these items might be available at Farmer's Markets throughout the mid-Atlantic region.

Fruits
Apples: August 15 to November 5
Blackberries: July 5 to August 1
Blackberries (Thornless): August 1 to September 10
Black Raspberries: June 15 to July 10
Red Raspberries: June 15 to July 10
Blueberries: June 20 to August 1
Cantaloupes: July 15 to September 15
Cider: July 21 to September 20
Grapes: August 15 to September 20
Nectarines: July 25 to August 25
Peaches: July 5 to September 20
Pears: August 15 to October 15
Plums: July 15 to September 15
Strawberries: May 15 to June 20
Sour Cherries: June 15 to July 15
Sweet Cherries: June 10 to July 10
Watermelon: August 1 to October 1
Watermelon (Sugar Babies): July 21 to October 1

Vegetables
Asparagus: April 25 to June 15
Beans (Green): June 10 to September 15
Beans (Lima): July 20 to September 1
Beans (Pole): June 24 to August 30
Beets: July 4 to September 1
Broccoli: July 10 to September 1
Cabbage: June 1 to September 15
Carrots: July 10 to September 15
Cauliflower: August 15   to November 1
Corn: July 4 to September 15
Cucumbers: July 1 to September 1
Cucumbers (Pickles): July 1 to August 1
Eggplant: July 25 to September 10
Gourds: August 15 to October 30
Okra: July 15 to August 30

Onion: June 25 to July 31
Peas (Green): June 10 to July 1
Peas (Blackeye): July 20 to August 30
Peppers: July 25 to September 15
Potatoes: July 1 to September 30
Potatoes (Sweet): September 5 to December 15
Pumpkins: September 10 to November 30
Spinach (Spring-Fall): May 1-30 to October 1-30
Squash (Summer): June 25 to September 1
Squash (Winter): August 1 to September 30
Tomatoes: July 4 to September 15
Turnips: August 15 to November 1

Delaware

- Lewes Terminal Green Market, Ferry Terminal Area, Lewes, DE. Telephone: (302) 739-4811.
- Wilmington Farmers Market, 8th and Orange Streets, Wilmington, DE. Telephone: (302) 571-9088.

Maryland

- Anne Arundel County Farmers Market, Riva Road and Harry S. Truman Pkwy, Annapolis, MD. Telephone: (410) 349-0317.
- Bowie Main Street Farmers Market, Bowie High School, 15200 Annapolis Road, Bowie, MD. Telephone: (301) 262-6200, ext.3076.
- Calvert County Farmers Market, Prince Frederick Shopping Center, Old Super Fresh Store, Prince Frederick, MD. Telephone: (443) 532-7479.
- Chestertown Farmers Market, Park Row on the Fountain Park, Chestertown, MD. Telephone:(410) 639-7217.
- Dorchester County Farmers Market, Sailwinds Park, Cambridge, MD. Telephone: (410) 228-8800.
- Easton Farmers Market, Harrison Street, Easton, MD. Telephone: (410) 822-0065.
- Frederick County Fairgrounds Market, East Patrick Street, Frederick, MD. Telephone: (301) 663-5895.
- Gaithersburg Farmers Market, East Cedar and South Frederick Avenues, Gaithersburg, MD. Telephone: (301) 590-2823.
- Hagerstown City Farmers Market, 25 West Church Street, Hagerstown, MD. Telephone: (301) 739-8577, ext. 190.
- Havre de Grace Farmers Market, Pennington Ave. at North Washington Street, Havre de Grace, MD. Telephone: (410) 939-2100.

- Ocean City Farmers Market, 42nd Street and Coastal Hwy., Phillips Restaurant parking lot, Ocean City, MD. Telephone: (410) 524-4647.
- Rockville Farmers Market, Rockville Town Center, Rockville, MD. Telephone: (240) 314-8605.
- Towson Farmers Market, Allegheny Avenue, Towson, MD. Telephone: (410) 825-1144.

New Jersey
- Atlantic City Farmers Market, Gordon's Alley parking lot, Atlantic City, NJ. Telephone: (609) 344-8338.
- Berlin Farmers Market, 41 Clemonton Road, Berlin, NJ. Telephone: (856) 767-1284.

North Carolina
- Chowan Farmers Market, North Granville Street and Virginia Road, Edenton, NC. Telephone: (252) 482-8431.
- Pasquotank County Farmers Market, Pritchard Street, Elizabeth City, NC. Telephone: (252) 338-3954.

Pennsylvania
- Allentown Fairgrounds Market, 17th and Chew Streets, Allentown, PA. Telephone: (610) 432-8425.
- Allentown Turnpike Service Plaza Farmers Market, Route 9—Northeast Extension, Allentown, PA. Telephone: (800) 331-3414.
- Bird-in-Hand Farmers Market, Maple Avenue, Bird-in-Hand, PA. Telephone: (717) 393-9674.
- Broad Street Farmers Market, 1233 North 3rd Street, Harrisburg, PA. Telephone: (717) 236-7923.
- Carlisle Farmers Market, 260 York Road, Carlisle, PA. Telephone: (717) 254-6457.
- Central Farmers Market, West King and Market Streets, Lancaster, PA. Telephone: (717) 735-6890.
- Central Market House, 34 West Philadelphia and Beaver Streets, York, PA. Telephone: (717) 848-2243.
- Clark Park Farmers Market, 43rd and Baltimore Avenue, Philadelphia, PA. Telephone: (215) 575-0444.
- Doylestown Farmers Market, State and Hamilton Streets, Doylestown, PA. Telephone: (215) 345-5355.
- Dutch Country Farmers Market, 2031 Cottman Avenue, Philadelphia, PA. Telephone: (215) 745-6008.

- Easton Farmers Market, Centre Square, Easton, PA. Telephone: (610) 330-9942
- Gettysburg Farmers Market, Lincoln Square, Gettysburg, PA. Telephone: (717) 334-8151.
- Green Dragon Farmers Market, Rural Delivery 4, Ephrata, PA. Telephone: (717) 738-1117.
- Hanover Farmers Market, 210 East Chestnut Street, Hanover, PA. Telephone: (717) 632-1353.
- Kline Village Farmers Market, 101 South 25th and Market Streets, Harrisburg, PA. Telephone: (717) 238-7788.
- Lancaster County Farmers Market II, 5942 Germantown Avenue, Philadelphia, PA. Telephone: (215) 843-9564.
- Market and Penn Street Farmers Market, 380 Market Street, York, PA. Telephone: (717) 848-1402.
- New Eastern Market, 201 Memory Lane, York, PA. Telephone: (717) 755-5811.
- Pennsylvania Open-Air Farmers Market, Farm Show parking lot, Harrisburg, PA. Telephone: (717) 697-9617.
- Reading Fairgrounds Farmers Market, 5th Street, Hwy. 222N, Reading, PA. Telephone: (610) 929-3429.
- Reading Farmers Market, 8th and Penn Street, Reading, PA. Telephone: (610) 898-5482.
- South Street West Farmers Market, 17th and South Streets, Philadelphia, PA. Telephone: (215) 568-0830.
- The Farm Market at Delaware Valley College, Route 202 and New Britain Road, Doylestown, PA. Telephone: (215) 230-7170.
- West Chester Growers' Market, Chestnut and Church Streets,West Chester, PA. Telephone: (610) 869-2791.

Virginia
- Annandale Farmers Market, Mason District Park, 6621 Columbia Pike, Annandale, VA. Telephone: (703) 642-0128.
- Arlington County Farmers Market, North 14th Street and North Courthouse Road, Arlington, VA. Telephone: (703) 228-6426.
- Cascades Farmers Market, Cascades Park and Ride, Leesburg, VA. Telephone: (540) 777-0426.
- Fredericksburg City Farmers Market, 900 Block, Prince Edward Street, Fredericksburg, VA. Telephone: (540) 847-2287.
- Harrisonburg Farmers Market, Water Street, Harrisonburg, VA. Telephone: (540) 476-3377.

- Lee District Farmers Market, Lee District Park, 6601 Telegraph Road, Alexandria, VA. Telephone: (703) 642-5173.
- Mount Vernon Farmers Market, 2501 Sherwood Hall Lane, Mount Vernon, VA. Telephone: (703) 642-0128.
- People's Market of Lebanon, Lebanon Elementary and Middle Schools, Lebanon, VA. Telephone: (540) 889-8056.
- 17th Street Farmers Market, 17th and Main Streets, Richmond, VA. Telephone: (804) 646-0477.
- Roanoke Historic City Farmers Market, Campbell Street Market Square, Roanoke, VA. Telephone: (540) 342-2028.
- Staunton-Augusta Farmers Market, Wharf parking lot, Johnston Street, Staunton, VA. Telephone: (540) 448-1937.
- Surry Farmers Market, Courthouse Square, Surry, VA. Telephone: (804) 294-5215.
- Virginia Beach Farmers Market, 1989 Landstown Road, Virginia Beach, VA. Telephone: (757) 385-4395.
- Warrenton Farmers Market, 5th and Lee Streets, Warrenton, VA. Telephone: (540) 347-6267.

West Virginia
- Elkins Farmers Market, Elkins City Park, Elkins, WV. Telephone: (304) 823-2960.
- Pendleton County Farmers Market, Fox's Pizza parking lot, Franklin, WV. Telephone: (304) 249-5817.

RESOURCES

For more information on farmers markets contact the following:

- Delaware Department of Agriculture, 2320 South Dupont Hwy., Dover, DE 19901. Telephone: (302) 698-4500. Web site: dda.delaware.gov.
- Maryland Department of Agriculture, 50 Harry S. Truman Parkway, Annapolis, MD 21401. Telephone: (410) 841-5700. Web site: www.mda.state.md.us.
- New Jersey Department of Agriculture. Web site: www.state.nj.us/agriculture.
- North Carolina Department of Agriculture, 2 West Edenton Street, Raleigh, NC 27601. Telephone: (919) 707-3000. Web site: www.ncagr.gov.

- Pennsylvania Department of Agriculture, 2301 North Cameron Street, Harrisburg, PA 17110. Telephone: (717) 787-4737. Web site: www.agriculture.state.pa.us.
- Virginia Department of Agriculture, 1100 Bank Street, Richmond, VA 23219. Telephone: (804) 786-3531. Web site: www.vdacs.virginia.gov.
- West Virginia Department of Agriculture, 1900 Kanawha Blvd., East, Charleston, WV 25305. Telephone: (304) 558-3550. Web site: www.wvagriculture.org.

FLOWER AND GARDEN SHOWS

The mid-Atlantic states host numerous diverse flower and garden shows, many of which are imaginatively planned. Most towns and cities have garden clubs which have at least one annual show, usually announced in the community Bulletin Board sections of local papers. The national association for virtually all these clubs is National Garden Clubs, Inc. Its Web site also includes links to all of the state and regional garden clubs that have Web sites. 4401 Magnolia Avenue, St. Louis, MO 63110. Telephone: (314) 776-7574. Web site: www.gardenclub.org.

Another helpful source of information is the Garden Club of America (Web site: www.gcamerica.org), which provides links to scores of related organizations such as the American Daffodil Society, the American Rose Society, and the American Horticultural Society. The American Horticultural Society (AHS), 7931 East Boulevard Dr., Alexandria, VA 22308, is a national, nonprofit, membership organization for gardeners founded in 1922. It can assist you in finding private and public organizations in your area, including garden clubs and centers, flower and garden shows, and other events. Telephone: (703) 768-5700. Web site: www.ahs.org.

Many of the historical sites and tourist attractions in the geographic sections of this book have excellent gardens. These sites frequently sponsor their own garden shows, and often employ horticultural or landscaping staff persons who can help you find regional or state-wide garden shows and clubs.

The following list features some of the organizations that sponsor or know about annual gardening events.

Delaware

Delaware Federation of Garden Clubs, P.O. Box 4643, Wilmington, DE 19807. Telephone: (302) 235-2226 or (302) 478-4719 .

Maryland
The Federated Garden Clubs of Maryland, Inc., 1105A Providence Road, Baltimore, MD 21286, Telephone: (410) 396-4842. Web site: http://fgcofmd.org.

New Jersey
Garden Club of New Jersey, 126 Ryders Lane, East Brunswick, NJ 08816. Telephone: (732) 249-0947. Web site: njclubs.esiteasp.com/gcnj/home.nxg.

Pennsylvania
Garden Club Federation of PA. 1525 Cedar Cliff Drive, Camp Hill, PA 17011. Telephone: (717) 737-8219. Web site: www.pagardenclubs.org.

Virginia
Virginia Federation of Garden Clubs, c/o Lewis Ginter Botanical Garden, 1800 Lakeside Avenue, Richmond, VA 23228. Telephone: (804) 262-9887. Web site: www.virginiagardenclubs.org.

Washington, D.C.
National Capitol Area Federation of Garden Clubs, Arbor House, U.S. National Arboretum, 3501 New York Avenue, N.E., Washington, DC 20002. Telephone: (202) 399-5958. Web site: http://ncagardenclubs.org.

West Virginia
West Virginia Garden Club, Web site: http://wvgardenclub.com/.

FLYING

When you have seen the sites from the ground level and want to get a different perspective on things, why not view them from the air? Hundreds of flying enthusiasts spend every weekend diving out of airplanes or hanging from kites. The sections here list chapters of national clubs and associations that can help you take flight.

HANG GLIDING
If you have ever dreamed of flying like a bird, **hang gliding** is the

nearest you'll come to fulfilling your fantasy. The U.S. Hang Gliding Association, P.O. Box 1330, Colorado Springs, CO 80901. Web site: www.ushpa.aero. Has affiliated clubs in the mid-Atlantic area, and members will be glad to show you the ropes.

Maryland

Maryland Hang Gliding Association, 703 Brickston Road, Reisterstown, MD 21136. Telephone: (410) 526-3987.

Capital Hang Gliding and Paragliding Association, 15914B Shady Grove Road # L-197, Gaithersburg, MD. Web site: www.chgpa.org.

Mountaineer Soaring Society, 13818 Florida Avenue, Cresaptown, MD 21502. Telephone: (301) 729-0773.

North Carolina

The Buzzard Club, 2546 Cedar Rock Circle, Lenoir, NC 28645. Web site: www.buzzardclub.com.

Central Carolina Tow to Soar Club, 5808 Tahoe Drive, Durham, NC 27713. Web site: www.ccttsc.org.

An inspiring place to learn hang gliding is on the site of the Wright Brothers' first flight at Kitty Hawk, NC. Kitty Hawk Kites runs the oldest hang gliding school on the East Coast of the U.S. and the largest school of its kind in the world. Kitty Hawk Kites, Inc., PO Box 1839, Nags Head, North Carolina 27959. Telephone: (252) 441-4127 or (877) 359-8447. Web site: www.kittyhawk.com.

Pennsylvania

Daedalus Hang Gliding Club, 145 Griffith Drive, Home, PA 15747. Telephone: (412) 661-3474.

Wind Riders Hang Gliding Club, 204 Hillock Drive, West Chester, PA 19380. Telephone: (610) 527-1687. Web site: www.wrhgc.org.

Hyner Hang Gliding Club, Inc., 1507 E. Newport Road, Lititz, PA. Telephone: (610) 488-9478. Web site: www.hynerclub.com.

Blue Ridge Hang Gliding Club, 349 Ontelaunee Drive, Shoemakerville, PA 19555. Telephone: (610) 916-1233.

Virginia

Capital Hang Gliding and Paragliding Association, 4403 Roundhill Road, Alexandria, VA 22310. Web site: www.chgpa.org.

Central Virginia Hang Gliding Association, P.O. Box 1268, Standardsville, VA 22937. Telephone: (434) 401-3434.

Mid Atlantic Paragliding Association, 3325 S. Stafford Street, Arlington, VA 22206. Telephone: (703) 824-3519. Southwest Virginia HG and PG, 306 Eakin Street, SE, Blacksburg, VA 24060. Telephone: (540) 961-6834.

PARACHUTING

Sport **parachuting** is a favorite pastime throughout the world. If you would like to see what you are getting into before you leap, attend one of the many shows and promotional events held throughout the year. Centers, also known as "drop zones," are affiliated with the U.S. Parachute Association, 1440 Duke Street, Alexandria, VA 22314. Telephone: (540) 604-9740. Web site: www.uspa.org. The centers or drop zones sponsor events and teach classes. Area drop zones are:

Delaware

Skydive Delmarva, Inc., Laurel Airport, Route 24W, Laurel, DE 19956. 15 miles north of Salisbury, MD. Telephone: (888) 875-3540.

Maryland

The Freefall Academy, Laurel Airport, Route 24W, Laurel, DE 19956. 15 miles north of Salisbury, MD. Telephone: (301) 261-6136. Web site: www.skydriven.com.

Ocean City Skydiving Center, Ocean City Municipal Airport, 12724 Airport Drive, Berlin, MD 21811. Telephone: (410) 213-1319 or (800) SKYDIVE. Web site: www.skydiveoc.com.

New Jersey

Freefall Adventures, Inc./Skydive Cross Keys, 300 Dahlia Ave., Williamstown, NJ 08094. Telephone: (856) 629-7553 or (888) 855 JUMP. Web site: www.freefalladventures.com.

Skydive Jersey Shore, Monmouth Executive Airport, Hwy. #34, Building #81-11, Farmingdale, NJ. Telephone: (732) 938-9002. Web site: www.skydivejerseyshore.com.

Pennsylvania

The Skydivin' Place, Kingsdale Airfield, LLC, 167 Ulricktown Road, Littlestown, PA 17340. 40 miles north of Baltimore.Telephone: (717) 359-8166. Web site: www.skydive-pa-md.com.

Chambersburg Skydiving Center, Chambersburg Municipal

Airport, 3506 Airport Road, Chambersburg, PA 17201. Telephone: (800) 526-3497. Web site: www.skydivingcenter.net.

Kutztown Skydiving Center, 113 Sharadin Road, Kutztown, PA 19530. Telephone: (610) 442-7500.

Web site: www.skydivekutztown.com.

Maytown Sport Parachute Club, Donegal Springs Airport, Marietta, PA. Telephone: (717) 653-0422.

Web site: www.maytownparachute.bizland.com.

Virginia

Hartwood Paracenter, Inc., Hartwood Airport, 194 Cropp Road, Hartwood, VA 22406. Telephone: (540) 752-4784.

Adrenaline Air Sports/Skydive Blue Ridge, Inc., Smith Mountain Lake Airport, 1092 Cutlass Road, Moneta, VA 24121. Telephone: (540) 296-1100. Web site: www.dcpages.com/Recreation/Skydiving/.

Skydive Orange, Inc., Orange County Airport, 11339 Bloomburg Road, Orange,VA 22960. Telephone: (540) 943-6587.

Web site: www.skydiveorange.com.

Skydive Suffolk, Inc., Suffolk Airport, 200 Airport Road, Suffolk, VA 23434. Telephone: (757) 539-3531.

Web site: www.skydivesuffolk.com.

Skydive The Point, Middle Peninsula Regional Airport, Airport Road, West Point, VA 23181. Telephone: (804) 785-4007.

Web site: www.skydivethepoint.com.

Skydive Virginia!, Louisa County Airport, Route 208, Louisa, VA. Telephone: (540) 967-3997.

Web site: www.skydivevirginia.com.

Westpoint SkydivingAdventures, Middle Regional Peninsula Airport, Airport Road, West Point, VA 23181. Telephone: (804) 785-9707.

Web site: www.skydivewestpoint.com.

SOARING

Soaring, or **gliding** as it is sometimes called, provides the thrill and freedom of silent flight. Sailplanes are towed by a powered airplane to a certain altitude; when they have caught a "thermal" or a "wave," the rope tow is released and the sailplane is on its own. The Soaring Society of America, Jack Gomez Blvd & Ave. A, P.O. Box 2100, Hobbs, NM 88241 (Telephone: (505) 392-1177. Web site: www.ssa.org) is the central information source for those interested in the sport. Its chapters can arrange lessons or just take you up for an afternoon of flying.

Delaware

Brandywine Soaring Association, P.O. Box 454, Wilmington, DE 19899. Located at New Garden Airport. Toughkenamon, PA. Web site: www.brandywinesoaring.org.

Maryland

Atlantic Soaring Club, 3536 Aldino Rd. Churchville, MD 21028, Harford County Airport—From I-95 Havre De Grace exit, north on MD Rt. 155, past blinking light, next left on MD Rt. 156, airport on right. Telephone: (410) 734-9170. Web site: atlanticsoaring.org.

Mid-Atlantic Soaring Association, C/O Hope Howard, 4823 Teen Barnes Rd., Frederick, MD 21703-6932. Web site: www.midatlanticsoaring.org/.

Delmarva Soaring Association, Ridgely Airpark, Rt. 1, Box 17, Ridgely, MD 21660. Telephone: (410) 228-0769. Web site: www.friend.ly.net/~soaring.

New Jersey

South Jersey Soaring Society, Landmark Inn, Rts. 73 and 38, Maple Shade, NJ 08052. Located at Hammonton Airport, Hammonton, NJ— ½ mile east of Rt. 206 and 2 miles north of Hammonton. Web site: sjsoaring.home.comcast.net/~sjsoaring/wsb/html/view.cgi-home. html-.html.

Pennsylvania

The Philadelphia Glider Council, 934 Route 152, Hilltown, PA 18927. Located 3 miles south of Route 113, 5 miles north of Route 202. Telephone: (215) 326 - 9263. Web site: pgcsoaring.org.

Kutztown Aviation, 15130 Kutztown Road, Kutztown, PA 19530. Telephone: (610) 683-5666. Web site: www.flyingclubs.us/ club_information.php?id=173.

Virginia

Blue Ridge Soaring Society, Inc., P.O. Box 369, New Castle, VA 24127. Located 25 miles north of Roanoke on Rt. 311, just outside of New Castle. Telephone: (540) 864-5800. Web site: www.brss.net.

Skyline Soaring Club, Front Royal, VA. Located at Front Royal-Warren County Airport, located 2 miles west of US 340, south of Front Royal. Web site: www.skylinesoaring.org.

Springwood Soaring Association, c/o Stover Accounting, 2518 Livingston Road SW, Roanoke, VA 24015. Telephone: (540) 463.3721.

Tidewater Soaring Society, 1412 Iron Mine Spring Road, Windsor, VA 23497. Telephone: (757) 357-3948. Web site: www.tidewatersoaring.org.

HORSE EVENTS

There are many opportunities for the weekend pleasure-seeker to attend horse shows and races throughout the mid-Atlantic area. In contrast to thoroughbred flat and standardbred harness races at commercial tracks, hunt club, steeplechase, and polo events also provide a chance for tailgating (picnicking from a car's trunk or the back of a station wagon, van, or sport utility vehicle) along the sidelines.

Steeplechase racing, sometimes called point-to-point racing, is a race over hurdles made of brush, timber, stone walls, or water obstacles. Generally the course covers two to four miles over open country. Records of the sport date back to Xenophon (431-355 B.C.). The name is derived from the use of church steeples as landmarks on a course.

Horse shows are held throughout the mid-Atlantic area and range from the prestigious Washington (D.C.) International to local 4-H pony shows. The shows have organized programs of exhibitions, demonstrations, and competitions of various types and breeds of horses and riding skills. The show divisions include hunter, jumper, saddle horses, pony (Shetland, Welsh, etc.), Appaloosa, cutting horses, quarter horses, and many others. The equitation events are a test of the rider's skill in controlling the horse. Dressage is a ring event where the horses are trained to execute intricate movements, such as changing gaits, pivoting, and moving laterally. Dressage is one of the three combined events that make up the Olympic equestrian competition. The other two events are cross-country and jumping. Hunters and jumpers are required to jump obstacles either in the ring or the open, and the test of the horse is to complete the course in the fastest time without knocking down obstacles, disobeying the rider, or falling. The jumper course and requirements are similar to the hunter's, except that the jumper has higher and wider obstacles to clear. The American Horse Shows Association sets standards for competition, licenses, judges, and stewards, and presents annual awards.

A representative sampling of the many equestrian events that the public can enjoy is listed below. Also check the weekend section of your local newspaper, especially in spring and fall. "Special Interest Sections" on jousting and polo follow.

Throughout the Year

Show Place Arena and the Prince George's Equestrian Center, 14900 Pennsylvania Avenue, Upper Marlboro, MD. Call for upcoming events; many are free. Telephone: (301) 952-7999. Web site: www.showplacearena.com.

Wicomico Equestian Center, Winter Place Farm, Route 50 East, Salisbury, MD. Call for upcoming events. Telephone: (410) 548-4900. Web site: www.horsenaround.org/wicomico.html.

Seasonal

Maryland Hunt Cup Race, Glyndon, MD, Worthington Valley. World's most difficult timber steeplechase race. (Winner eligible for English Grand National competition.) Last Saturday in April.

Fairfax Races, Leesburg, VA, Belmont Plantation. Timber and brush races. Third Saturday after Labor Day. Telephone: (703) 787-6673.

Frederick Horse Show, Ijamsville, MD, Moxley Field. Junior, hunter, and English equitation classes. Late August. Web site: frederick.ponyclub.org/.

Virginia Gold Cup, Warrenton, VA. Point-to-point steeplechase race. First Saturday in May. Telephone: (540) 347-2612. Web site: www.vagoldcup.com.

Winterthur Point-to-Point Steeplechase, Winterthur, DE, Winterthur Museum Grounds. Five steeplechase races and horse-drawn carriage parade. First Sunday in May. Telephone: (800) 448-3883. Web site: www.winterthur.org

Preakness Stakes, Baltimore, MD, Pimlico Race Course. Second race in Triple Crown of thoroughbred racing. Mid-May.

Fair Hill Races, Fair Hill, MD, Fair Hill Fairgrounds. Steeplechase races, pari-mutuel wagering, picnicking. Late May. Telephone: (410) 398-6565. Web site: www.fairhillraces.org.

Yearling Show, Maryland Horse Breeders Association, Timonium, MD, Timonium Fairgrounds. Yearling show of Maryland-bred thoroughbreds. Last Sunday in June. Telephone: (410) 252-2100.

Upperville Colt and Horse Show, Upperville, VA, Upperville Horse Show Grounds. Oldest horse show in U.S. Hunters, jumpers, juniors. First week in June. Web site: www.upperville.com.

Delaware State Fair, Harrington, DE, Harrington Fairgrounds. Four-day event, competition and show. Last week in July. Telephone: (302) 398-3269. Web site: www.delawarestatefair.com.

Howard County Fair, West Friendship, MD, Howard County Fairgrounds. Arabians, ponies, Appaloosas, hunters, quarter horses. August. Fairgrounds telephone: (410) 442-1022. Web site: www.howardcountyfair.com.

West Virginia State Fair, Lewisburg, WV, State Fairgrounds. Six-day event with 71 classes, including western, plantation, three-and five-gaited, harness, and walking horses. Third week of August. Web site: www.wvstatefair.com.

Maryland State Fair, Timonium, MD, Timonium Fairgrounds. Hunters, quarter horses, ponies. Late August. Fairgrounds telephone: (410) 252-0200. State Fair Web site: www.marylandstatefair.com.

Ludwig's Corner Horse Show, Chestertown, PA, Ludwig's Corner Horse Show Grounds. Two-day fair, includes hunter, jumper, and carriage competition. Labor Day weekend. Telephone: (610) 458-3344. Web site: www.ludwigshorseshow.org.

Great Frederick Fair, Frederick, MD, includes horse and pony shows, mule competitions, and pony and harness racing. Mid-to-late September. Telephone: (301) 663-5895. Web site: www.thegreatfrederickfair.com.

Morven Park Race Meet, Leesburg, VA, Morven Park. Steeplechase races: five brush and one flat race. Second Saturday in October. Telephone: (703) 777-2890. Web site: www.morvenpark.org.

Virginia Fall Race Meet, Middleburg, VA, Glenwood Park. Steeplechase races over brush and timber fences and a flat course. Early October. Telephone: (540) 687-5662. Web site: www.vafallraces.com.

Washington International Horse Show, Washington, D.C., MCI Center. More than 800 horses from all 50 states and foreign nations compete. Concession booths sell everything from horse-related gift items to antiques. Last week in October. Telephone: (202) 525-3679. Web site: www.wihs.org.

Carriage Parade, Frederick, MD, Rose Hill Manor. A parade of antique carriages. Late October. Telephone: (301) 600-1650.

Additional Resources

For further information on local clubs and associations, contact:

National Steeplechase Association, 400 Fair Hill Drive, Elkton, MD 21921. Telephone:(410) 392-0700. Web site: www.nationalsteeplechase.com.

United States Eventing Association, 525 Old Waterford Road, NW, Leesburg, VA 20176. Telephone: (703) 779-0440. Web site: www.useventing.com.
    U.S. Dressage Federation, Lexington, KY 40503. Telephone: (859) 971-2277. Web site: www.usdf.org.

HUNTING AND FISHING ─────────

Despite the traffic jams, high-rise apartment buildings, and crowds that seem to fill the lives of people living in the mid-Atlantic region, there is a great bounty of open lands, forests, rushing rivers, and clear lakes with fish and game to delight any sportsman or woman. In this region anglers can pit their skills against saltwater or freshwater fish. The small game populations provide the hunter with rabbit, raccoon, opossum, and many other small mammals. Bear and white-tailed deer will challenge even the experienced hunter's ability. Quail populations have declined in recent years because of changes in farming practices, especially the elimination of hedgerows between fields. Although their removal is agriculturally efficient, hedgerows were a favorite habitat for quail. But grouse, dove, and waterfowl continue to thrive in the region and can be hunted in almost all the areas open to the sport.

The Game and Fish Departments of each state have pamphlets and information that can be obtained free of charge. Useful local information can usually be obtained at any local sporting goods store, and online, often through state Web sites for departments of natural resources. (See Hotlines Section.)

Delaware

The state of Delaware hosts large concentrations of wintering waterfowl. Shifts in migration patterns have reduced the number of Canada geese traveling through the Maryland-Delaware area, but snow geese are abundant. The white-tailed deer herd is healthy and provides hours of pleasure for the big-game hunter. For the small-game enthusiast, squirrel, cottontail, woodcock, and raccoon provide excellent hunting throughout the state.

Delaware Bay is alive with sea trout and bluefish, while the lower bays provide small blues, flounder, tang, and rockfish. For the freshwater angler, the state offers over 30 state-owned millponds stocked with panfish, pickerel, and bass.

For further information concerning facilities, state regulations, seasons, limits, and directions to designated areas, contact: Division of Fish and Wildlife, 89 Kings Highway, Dover, DE 19901. Telephone: (302) 739-9910. Web site: www.dnrec.delaware.gov/fw/Pages/FWPortal.aspx

Maryland

Hunting in Maryland ranges from the delta regions of the Eastern Shore through the panhandle of central Maryland to the mountains of western Maryland. The list begins with white-tailed and sika deer. The white-tails are distributed abundantly throughout the state. Few areas of the Atlantic Flyway can match Maryland's nearly 4,000 miles of tidal marshlands, most of which are considered prime duck and goose hunting territory. As noted in Delaware, a change in migration patterns have reduced the numbers of Canada geese, but snow geese arrive in profusion. In the last 15 years, turkeys have been re-introduced in Maryland and Delaware, and there is now a population for spring hunting. In addition to turkeys, bird hunters will find ruffed grouse in western areas of the state. Central and southern Maryland host cottontail rabbits and squirrels as well as turkeys, and there are occasional sightings of ring-necked pheasant.

Maryland's Public Hunting Lands program, involving thousands of acres, encompasses the full spectrum of hunting opportunities. The list is swelled by annual migrations of mourning dove, king rail, clapper, sora and Virginia rail, woodcock, and snipe.

Mountain lake...reservoir...the Chesapeake Bay...wide rivers...tidal and marshy creeks...the Atlantic Ocean. That's Maryland fishing. Rockfish (striped bass), the state's official fish, are found in the tidal areas of the Chesapeake Bay. In fact, more than 200 species of fish frequent the Bay during a year. Flounder can be caught in Tangier Sound. Among the big battlers in the Bay are channel bass (red drum) and black drum.

For the saltwater angler, white marlin, blue marlin, dolphin, wahoo, and big bluefish are caught by cruisers running off Ocean City. Ocean fishing doesn't end on boats. Surf fishermen land bluefish, weakfish, channel bass, and kingfish at Assateague Island.

Freshwater anglers like Garrett County's huge Deep Creek Lake for exciting smallmouth bass fishing. The smallmouth join a good resident population of largemouth bass and walleye.

For additional information on hunting and fishing in the region, contact: Maryland Department of Natural Resources, 580 Taylor Avenue, Annapolis, MD 21401. Telephone: (877) 620-8367. Web site: www.dnr.state.md.us.

New Jersey

The southern counties of New Jersey offer a wide variety of hunting opportunities. This state's wildlife resources include deer and bear and small game such as turkey, rabbit, and squirrel, and waterfowl such as Canada and snow geese.

The New Jersey coast has provided big game fish for anglers since 1920, while sport-fishing trips to submarine canyons 70 to 90 miles offshore began in the mid-1950s. Yellowfin, bigeye, albacore tuna, and white and blue marlin inhabit these waters in abundance. Inland, there are more than 2,000 acres of warm water lakes and ponds and more than 100 miles of rivers and streams where trout and other warm water species are available.

For further information concerning facilities, state regulations, seasons, limits, and directions to designated areas, contact: Division of Fish and Wildlife, P.O. Box 402, Trenton, NJ 08625-0400. Walk-in at 501 E. State St., 3rd Floor. Telephone: (609) 292-2965.

Hunting in New Jersey can also be done on private property, state and national forests, and other public properties under certain circumstances. Inquire from the state office or county or local authorities.

North Carolina

The variety and excellence of North Carolina's sport fishing, both salt- and freshwater, is unmatched in the eastern United States. The Outer Banks region contains five sounds (Currituck, Albemarle, Pamlico, Core, and Bogue) and four inlets (Oregon, Hatteras, Ocracoke, and Beaufort) that provide excellent inland and offshore fishing. Due to this region's close proximity to the Gulf Stream (12 miles), there is year-round fishing. Offshore fishing is usually done from specialized sport-fishing cruisers equipped with twin engines, ship to shore radios, and other nautical accoutrements. These cruisers are manned by a captain and mate(s), many of whom developed big game fishing off the North Carolina coast. On an offshore fishing expedition, you can catch reef fish, sailfish, dolphin, blue marlin, and white marlin. The inlets provide another source of saltwater fishing. From trolling charters you can catch channel bass, bluefish, tarpon, trout, cobia, and several other species.

For further information on offshore and inland fishing, contact: North Carolina Wildlife Resources Commission, 1701 Mail Service Center, Raleigh, NC 27699-1701. Telephone: (919) 707-0010. Web site: www.ncwildlife.org.

Though eastern North Carolina is known primarily for its fishing,

there are some hunting opportunities available. Hunting in North Carolina is highly regulated; thus anyone interested in exploring hunting grounds should seek information from the County Attorney's Office, the Licenses Division, or the Law Enforcement Division (for seasons and locations) at: North Carolina Wildlife Resources Commission: 1701 Mail Service Center, Raleigh, NC 27699-1701. Telephone: (919) 707-0010. Web site: www.ncwildlife.org. State regulations and license requirements also apply to hunting on federal lands. For specific information related to the following coastal federal areas, contact:
Bodie Island (waterfowl): Superintendent, Cape Hatteras National Seashore, 1401 National Park Road, Manteo, NC 27954. Telephone: (252) 473-2111. Web site: www.nps.gov/caha/index.htm.

Pennsylvania

South central and southeastern Pennsylvania offer a wide variety of hunting for both big and small game.

The 11-county south central region, known for its rugged game-filled ridges, is abundant with deer, squirrel, grouse, dove, quail, woodchuck, and pheasant. Waterfowl can also be found throughout much of the area.

The 12-county area of southeastern Pennsylvania has excellent farm game hunting. This part of the state supports nearly one-third of the state hunting licenses with its abundant population of deer, ducks, geese, doves, squirrels, and rabbits. The Middle Creek Wildlife Management Area, located in this region, is one of Pennsylvania's finest facilities for waterfowl hunting and fishing. The lakes, rivers, and streams of this region provide anglers with plenty of varied fishing excitement.

Some waters of Pennsylvania are designated fly fishing only open to youth and handicapped, or catch and release only. Always check the rules governing the area where you intend to fish or hunt. For further information and specific details concerning licensing, facilities, state regulations, seasons, limits, and directions to designated areas, contact: Pennsylvania Game Commission License Division, 2001 Elmerton Avenue, Harrisburg, PA 17110. Telephone: (717) 787-2084. Web site: www.pgc.state.pa.us.

Virginia

Sometimes running furiously, other times meandering quietly

through the silent Civil War battlefields are some of Virginia's best known and most loved fishing waters. From the Back Bay of Virginia Beach to Lee County Lake, the angler can pit his ability against the small mouth bass, blue marlin, channel cat, or any one of 35 species of freshwater fish or 32 species of saltwater fish.

This state is also blessed with a variety of terrain which offers an excellent selection of mammals. National forests and state parks allow hunting at designated times in specific regions. The Virginia Department of Game and Inland Fisheries is your best guide to times and places as well as current information concerning licensing, facilities, hunting seasons, and regulations. Virginia Department of Game and Inland Fisheries, 4010 West Broad Street, Richmond, VA 23230. Telephone: (804) 367-1000. Web site: www.dgif.virginia.gov/.

West Virginia

West Virginia's streams and lakes host all of the best freshwater fish including bass, trout, pike, walleye, bluegill, and catfish. The eastern region of the state is a fisherman's delight. The once nearly extinct trout population now thrives. Today six hatcheries stock the ponds and streams throughout the state with beautiful specimens of rainbow, golden, and brown trout. Some waters are designated "Flyfishing Only" or "Catch and Release Only." Please be sure to check all regulations governing the area where you intend to fish.

Large populations of rabbits, woodchucks, migratory and nonmigratory birds, and deer inhabit the eastern portion of West Virginia. Only the eastern region permits hunting of black bear and turkey. For further information, contact: West Virginia Division of Natural Resources, State Capitol, Building 3, Room 812, Charleston, WV 25305. Telephone: (304) 588-2771. Web site: www.wvdnr.gov.

JOUSTING

Jousting, was a favorite pastime of Eastern Shore settlers in the 17th century and is still practiced at tournaments held in Maryland, Virginia and West Virginia. In fact, it is the official sport of the state of Maryland. In modern competitions, jousters wear jeans and boots rather than armor, but even in modern dress, competitors ride under Medieval-sounding titles as a nod to the long history of the sport.

The goal these days is not to topple another rider but to spear rings—ranging from 1.75" down to a scant quarter of an inch in diameter—with a six or seven foot steel-tipped lance while riding on horseback. This requires excellent hand-eye coordination, the ability to keep the upper body on course, and a compatible horse. Competitors are both male and female and range in age from teens to septuagenarians.

The jousting tournament at Natural Chimneys, VA has been held annually since 1821 and is the oldest continuously held sporting event in the United States.

A list of annual area jousting tournaments follows. Several are associated with county fairs. Others are organized by club members and volunteers. Some act as fundraisers or benefits. Contact people vary. Watch local papers for more details, or check club sites online for times, exact locations and directions.

Maryland
Maryland's state tourism site includes links to each county site. Web site: visitmaryland.org.
Caroline Country Fair—August
Queen Anne's County Fair Joust—August
St. Margaret's Church Joust, Annapolis—August
St. Mary's Church Joust, Pylesville—August
Fairplay Day's Tournament, Fairplay—August
Western Maryland Jousting Club Picnic Tournament—August
Calvert County Jousting Tournament—August
Tuckahoe Night Joust, Tuckahoe State Park Equestrian Center, Queen Anne—September
Saddle Friends Joust, Easton—September
Western Maryland Jousting Club Championship Joust—September
Ridgely Joust, Martin Sutton Memorial Park, Ridgely—September
Frederick Fair Exposition—September
St. Mary's Country Fair Tournament—September
Eastern Shore Jousting Association, Championship Joust, Tuckahoe State Park, Queen Anne—September
Amateur Jousting Club Championship Joust, Glenarm Field, Glenarm—September
Maryland State Jousting Championship, Darlington, MD —October

Virginia
Hall of Fame Tournament, Mt. Solon—June
Natural Chimneys Regional Park—August

Triple Crown Tournament, Tappanannock—October
National Jousting Tournament Morvan Park, Leesburg—October

Clubs

Central Maryland Jousting Club. Web site: www.nationaljousting.com.
Amateur Jousting Association of Maryland, Inc.
Web site: ajc.psyberia.com.

POLO ─────────────────────────

Polo is becoming an increasingly popular sport throughout the
country and Virginia, Maryland, and eastern Pennsylvania provide
excellent opportunities to sample the game at high quality levels.
Polo is an exciting sport, and fast, competitive, colorful, and dangerous. You need only to see one game to appreciate the thrill of eight
horses thundering across three football fields in pursuit of a baseball-
sized object that can soar at 70 m.p.h.

Polo is also an excellent family outing event. Most games allow tailgating (picnicking from the back of a pickup truck, car, or sport utility vehicle) along the sidelines, and there is usually plenty to watch
even when the game is not going on: the bustle of grooms, riders,
ponies and spectators, private parties, dogs, and a menagerie of
tents, pick-up trucks, and horse trailers vying for space and adding
flavor to the setting.

Polo matches in your area are often listed in the *Weekend* section of
your local newspaper under *Sports*. Bring your binoculars to better
follow the game and your own refreshments for warm summer days.
It is a good idea to call ahead for exact time and directions if you
have never been to a particular site before.

The speed and rapid changes of position of the players appear to
make the game more complex than it actually is to the observer. The
rules are easy to master, and knowing them will of course enhance
the pleasure of watching. Playing polo is a challenge since you need
to learn to ride first, and is extremely expensive. Still, you need not
own your own horse or have a polo-playing buddy to learn the basics.
The Potomac Polo Club in Poolesville, MD, offers a full curriculum
of lessons for every level of rider and player. Potomac Polo Club, P.O.
Box 35, Poolesville, MD. Telephone: (301) 972-7303.
Web site: www.redeagleranch.com/index.html.

The sport's national organization is the U.S. Polo Association, which can supply interested persons with more information. The address is: Suite 505, 771 Corporate Drive, Lexington, KY 40503. Telephone: (800) 232-8772. Web site: www.us-polo.org. Many of the following clubs belong to the USPA's Eastern Circuit:

Pennsylvania

Brandywine Polo Club. Telephone: (610) 268-8692. Web site: www.brandywinepolo.com/.

Indoor and outdoor games, usually on Sundays at 3 P.M. Admission charge. Call for information and directions.

Maryland

Potomac Polo Club, Michael Mulddon Field, Poolesville, MD. Telephone: (301) 972-7303. Web site: www.redeagleranch.com.

Field located on Jerusalem Road, Poolesville, MD. Games Sundays, usually at 1 P.M. and 3 p.m, June through October. Shows and entertainment frequently precede games. High-goal invitational tournaments played several times during season.

Maryland Polo Club, Monkton, MD. Telephone: (410) 557-6448.

Matches are played at Ladew Polo Field in Baltimore County, Maryland. Admission charge. Call for information and directions.

Virginia

Polo Great Meadow, The Plains, VA. Telephone: (540) 253-9845. Web site: www.greatmeadowpoloclub.com/.

Twilight polo matches on Friday nights from June through September. Admission charge for the benefit of local charities.

Rappahanock Polo Club, P.O. Box 989, Alexandria, VA 22312. Telephone: (703) 937-4177. Call for information.

Middleburg Polo Club, Middleburg, VA. Telephone: (703) 777-1403. Call for information.

Virginia Beach Polo Club, 2585 West Landing Road, Virginia Beach, VA 23456. Telephone: (757) 627-1980. Web site: virginiabeachpoloclub.com.

RAILROADS

Rail fans at this end of the country have a lot going for them. Because many American railroads were begun in the East, there are many opportunities locally to see restored engines, passenger cars, and other railway memorabilia displays. Some museums offer rides on restored trains. Prices vary depending on the distance traveled. Some trains go only a few miles; others travel 50 miles or more. You will also find that there are hundreds of other railfans in this area who have organized club meetings and frequent excursions on vintage trains.

Delaware

The Wilmington and Western Steam Railroad, in Greenbank at the junction of Routes 2 and 41, has regularly scheduled trips to nearby towns. 2201 Newport Gap Pike, Wilmington, DE 19808. Telephone: (302) 998-1930. Web site: www.wwrr.com.

Maryland

The Brunswick Railroad Museum in Brunswick, two miles off Route 340 southwest Frederick, is the home of the Brunswick Model Railroad Club and Sidetrack Gift Shop. The museum has an extensive collection of old trains, including a circa 1925 wooden caboose. Open Friday, 10 A.M. to 2 P.M., Saturday, 10 A.M. to 4 P.M., and Sunday, 1 to 4:00 P.M. From April to December the museum is also open on Thursdays, 10 A.M. to 2 P.M. Admission charge. Each August the museum has a Railroad Weekend, and every October it sponsors the Brunswick Railroad Days. Telephone: (301) 834-7100. Web site: www.brrm.net.

The B&O Railroad Museum in Baltimore is dedicated to bettering public awareness of the B&O Railroad. The museum provides interactive exhibits that focus on the people and machines that were responsible for the railroad. It offers adult, youth, and senior tours. B&O Railroad Museum, 901 West Pratt Street, Baltimore, MD 21223. Telephone: (410) 752-2490. Web site: www.borail.org.

The Ellicott City B&O Railroad Station Museum, at the corner of Main Street and Maryland Avenue, is America's oldest remaining station. The Patapsco Guard and Patapsco Citizens are the main attraction as this museum creates a living history of the railroad during the Civil War. The museum is open in the summer, Wednesday through Monday, 11 A.M. to 4 P.M. Times vary the rest of the year. 2711 Maryland Avenue, Ellicott City, MD 21043. Telephone: (410) 461-1945.

The Marion Station Railroad Museum and Gift Shoppe, at 28380 Crisfield-Marion Road, Marion, MD 21838, is a restored PRR

Passenger Station. It carries antiques dating to 1898. The museum is open April to December, Wednesday, Thursday, and Friday 9:00 A.M. to 5:00 P.M.; Saturday 10 A.M. to 3 P.M. Telephone: 888-838-7638. Web site: www.trainweb.com/marionstation.

The Western Maryland Railway Historical Society Museum, on North Main Street in Union Bridge, has restored trains as well as railroad memorabilia photos, and artifacts. Open Sunday, from 1 to 4 P.M., or call to make an appointment. Tours are available with 30 days' notice. Telephone: (410) 775-0150. Web site: moosevalley.org/wmrhs.

Pennsylvania

You can take a ride through the picturesque Aughwick Valley in an authentic steam train. **The East Broad Top Railroad** is a National Historic Landmark, located in Rockhill Furnace, PA. Open daily, June through October. Call for schedules and departures. Telephone: (814) 447-3011. Web site: www.ebtrr.com.

Other rides are offered by the **Gettysburg Scenic Railway** from its depot at 106 North Washington Street in Gettysburg. Seventy-five minute train rides from Gettysburg to Biglerville are offered Wednesday through Sunday from April through October. Special excursions such as the Fall Foliage Special, a Halloween Ghost Train, and a Civil War Train ride where passengers watch a battle reenactment from the train are also offered. Reservations advised. Fare charge. 106 North Washington Street, Gettysburg, PA 17325. Telephone: (717) 334-6932.

The **Strasburg Rail Road** and the state-owned **Railroad Museum of Pennsylvania,** which are located across from each other on Route 741 east of Strasburg, have such extensive collections that their coaches have been used in films and movies. You can have lunch or dinner on special train runs, or simply enjoy the scenery. Trains run daily, May through October; weekends only during the winter months. Strasburg Railroad, P.O. Box 96 Strasburg, PA 17579-0096. Telephone: (717) 687-7522. Web site: www.strasburgrailroad.com. Museum hours vary seasonally, call or check the Web site for information. Railroad Museum of Pennsylvania, P.O. Box 15, Strasburg, PA 17579. Telephone: (717) 687-8628. Web site: www.rrmuseumpa.org.

Virginia

America's Railroads on Parade is located in Williamsburg and has a collection of over 4,000 trains. 9125 Pocahontas Trail, Williamsburg, VA 23185. Telephone: (757) 220-8725.

The Virginia Museum of Transportation, in Roanoke, has seven steam engines and one of the largest model train layouts in the Southeast. Located at 303 Norfolk Avenue, Roanoke, VA 24016. Telephone: 540-342-5670. Web site: www.vmt.org.

West Virginia

The historic C&O station in Cass burned to the ground in 1975, but a replica has been faithfully executed on the same spot. The **Cass Railroad** offers excursions through the Monongahela National Forest to Whittaker, which takes about 2½ hours per outing. Also in Cass, the History Museum has displays of railroad memorabilia and old photos. Cass Scenic Railroad State Park, PO Box 107, Cass, WV 24927. Telephone: (304) 456-4300 or (800) CALL WVA. Web site: www.cassrailroad.com.

Clubs

Two national railroad clubs have chapters in the area: **National Railway Historical Society** and the **Railroad Enthusiasts, Inc.** Membership as well as participation on trips are open to the general public. If you love old trains, you will find plenty of camaraderie here, as well as opportunities to learn. There are often chances to help repair old engines and cars. Chapters located within the geographic scope of this book are listed below and on the following pages.

NATIONAL RAILWAY HISTORICAL SOCIETY

Delaware
Wilmington Chapter, NRHS, P.O. Box 1261, Wilmington, DE 19899. Telephone: (302) 239-1332. Web site: www.wilmingtonnrhs.com.

Maryland
Baltimore Chapter, NRHS, P.O. Box 100, Lutherville, MD 21094-0100. Telephone: (410) 837-1164. Web site: baltimorenrhs.org.

Western Maryland Chapter, NRHS, P.O.Box 1331, Cumberland, MD 21501-1331. Telephone: (301) 724-0442. Web site: home.comcast.net/~phstakem/rr/wmar-nrhs.htm.

Potomac Chapter, NRHS, P.O. Box 235, Kensington, MD 20895. Telephone: (301) 251-9461. Web site: www.trainweb.org/PotomacNRHS.

Hagerstown Chapter, NRHS, P.O. Box 4175, Hagerstown, MD 21741-4175. Telephone: (301) 739-4665. Web site: www.roundhouse.org.

Perryville Chapter, NRHS, P.O. Box 326, Perryville, MD 21903. No telephone or Web site.

New Jersey

West Jersey Chapter, NRHS, P.O. Box 647, Palmyra, NJ 08065-0647. Web site: www.westjersey-nrhs.org.

Tri-State Chapter, NRHS, P.O. Box 1217, Morristown, NJ 07962-1217. Telephone: (973) 656-0707. Web site: www.tristaterail.org/.

North Carolina

East Carolina Chapter, NRHS, P.O. Box 40, New Hill, NC 27562-0040. Telephone: (919) 362-5416. Web site: www.nhvry.org.

Old North State Chapter, No permanent address. Telephone: (919) 218-6513.

Pennsylvania

Lehigh Valley Chapter, NRHS802 Wedgewood Lake Drive, Stroudsburg, PA 18360.

Cumberland Valley Chapter, NRHS, P.O. Box 1317, Chambersburg, PA 17201-1317.

Lake Shore Chapter, NRHS, P.O. Box 571, North East, PA 16428-0571. Telephone: (814) 725-1911. Web site: www.grape-track.org.

Harrisburg Chapter, NRHS, 637 Walnut Street, Harrisburg, PA 17101. Telephone: (717) 232-6221. Web site: harrisburgnrhs.org.

Lancaster Chapter, NRHS, 10 Railroad Avenue, Christiana, PA 17509. Telephone: (610) 593-4968. Web site: nrhs1.org.

Delaware Valley Chapter, NRHS, P.O. Box 558, Yardley, PA 19067. Web site: www.delvalnrhs.org/.

Central Pennsylvania Chapter, NRHS, P.O. Box 145, White Deer, PA 17887.

Philadelphia Chapter, NRHS, P.O. Box 7302, Philadelphia, PA 19101-7302. Web site: www.trainweb.org/phillynrhs.

Pottstown and Reading Chapter, NRHS, P.O. Box 94, Shillington, PA 19607-0094. Web site: rrsignal.com/nrhs.

ROCK CLIMBING ━━━━━━━━━━━━━━━━━━━

Rock climbing is a such a popular sport in the mid-Atlantic area that on any given weekend, year round, you can find dozens of enthusiasts climbing mountains and cliffs throughout the area. Some belong to clubs. Others have linked up with instructors or guides through an outdoor gear store or adventure outfitter, and others will simply be out with a friend or two. University-based clubs are especially popular because they often own equipment members can borrow for an outing.

In recent years, indoor climbing gyms have sprung up in nearly every major city giving outdoor climbers a secure place to practice and refine their skills. Gym climbing has now evolved its own competitive branch of the original outdoor sport. Check the local Yellow Pages or online under "rock climbing" for nearby facilities.

Many groups and outfitters that have interest in outdoor activities sponsor organized rock climbing trips as well as lessons at all levels, including beginners. Equipment shops also have frequent on-site activities as well as films and talks by area experts. Lessons are frequently given by both individual rock climbers and schools. Make sure your instructor and his or her organization are qualified and have taken necessary liability and insurance precautions. You will usually be asked to sign a waiver.

Most clubs, schools, and shops are in metropolitan areas because that is where enthusiasts live. Members or students then carpool or bus to sites. Popular spots in this area are Great Falls, MD; Old Rag Mountain, VA; and (especially for ice climbing) Shenandoah National Park, VA; Carderock and Rocks State Park, MD; the New River Gorge and Seneca Rocks, WV. (Seneca Rocks is one of the best spots in the entire mid-Atlantic region.)

CLUBS

Appalachian Mountain Club (AMC), founded in 1876, is America's oldest conservation and recreation organization. Its 82,000 members enjoy and help preserve and maintain the rivers, mountains, and trails of the Northeastern U.S. Web site: www.outdoors.org.

The Delaware Valley Chapter of the AMC has more than 5,000 members in Pennsylvania, mid and southern New Jersey and northern Delaware. Web site: www.amcdv.org.

The D.C. Chapter is the southernmost of the AMC's 12 chapters. The 2,500 members live in Maryland and Virginia as well as in the District of Columbia. Web site: www.amc-dc.org.

The Potomac Appalachian Trail Club (PATC) has more than 7,000 members in the region. Its main purpose is the upkeep and improvement of 970 miles of hiking trails, 30 shelters, and 28 cabins in VA, MD, WV, PA and DC. Outings and activities include hiking, camping, canoeing, and kayaking and a special membership section for those interested in climbing. The Mountaineering group goes climbing nearly every weekend and works on its own and with other groups to conserve and protect climbing resources in the area. Events and outing are also open to nonmembers. PATC Offices in Vienna are open to the public Monday through Thursday evenings, 7 P.M. to 9 P.M., and on Thursdays and Friday, noon to 2 P.M. 118 Park Street, S.E., Vienna, VA 22180. Call to confirm hours. Telephone: (703) 242-0315. Web site: www.patc.net.

NATIONAL PARKS

For climbing opportunities in national parks, search the Web site: www.nps.gov.

Regional Favorites

Great Falls, MD, one of the locations of the George Washington Memorial Parkway. Telephone: (703) 285-2965. Web site: www.nps.gov/grfa/index.htm.

New River Gorge, WV, has 1400 established climbs. Its National Park Web site lists climbing routes by difficulty. Several of the outfitters in the area that arrange whitewater rafting trips also organize guided climbing and instructional outings. New River Gorge Web site: www.nps.gov/neri/planyourvisit/climbing.htm.

Blue Ridge Parkway Web site: www.nps.gov/blri/index.htm.

Harpers Ferry requires a special permit to climb the Cliffs of Maryland Heights. Inquire at the Ranger Station in the Lower Town. Web site: www.nps.gov/hafe/index.htm.

Delaware Water Gap is a 67,210 acre national recreation area stretching northeast along 40 miles of the Delaware River parallel to Route 309 from Stroudsburg, PA into New Jersey. Web site: www.nps.gov/dewa/index.htm.

SAILING

Mid-Atlantic residents are fortunate to be living near many excellent large and somewhat sheltered bays, sounds, and major rivers. The best way to enjoy them is not by gazing longingly from ashore, but by experiencing the power of the bounding main under sail. There are literally hundreds of marinas, charter companies, sailboat rental places, and schools waiting to help you set sail. Rather than list vast numbers of these organizations, this section is necessarily limited to sailing schools and other commercial establishments offering instruction. Whether you are just starting out or you want to polish your skills, you are sure to find a school or class to meet your needs. Ask a few questions before you sign on at a particular school. Find out if you will get "hands on" experience on the water, or if your learning is confined to classrooms. If you do go on the water, ask what the ratio of passengers to crew will be, and how many people will be aboard. You want to try out your new skills, but you won't get a chance if the boat is packed with other students. Make sure the instructor does not hog the helm and that he or she rotates students through each crew job so that you get a chance to be skipper, cockpit crew, and foredeck crew during the course.

In addition to the selection of commercial schools and establishments listed below, you can also take excellent courses in basic **sailing** and boating skills from your local Coast Guard Auxiliary flotilla or Red Cross chapter.

Delaware
Rehoboth Bay Sailing Association, Route One, Indian Beach, DE. Telephone: (302) 227-9008. Web site: www.rbsa.org.

Maryland
Annapolis Sailing School, 601 Sixth Street, P.O. Box 3334, Annapolis, MD 21403. Telephone: (800) 638-9192. Web site: annapolissailing.com.

Chesapeake Sailing School, 7074 Bembe Beach Road, Annapolis, MD 21403. Telephone: (410) 295-0555. Web site: www.sailingclasses.com.

Baysail on the Chesapeake, Tidewater Marina, 100 Bourbon Street, Havre de Grace, MD 21078. Telephone: (410) 939-2869, Web site: www.baysail.net.

Downtown Sailing Center, 1425 Key Highway, Baltimore, MD 21230. Telephone: (410) 727-0722. Web site: www.downtownsailing.org.

Severn Sailing Association, 311 First Street, Annapolis, MD 21403. Telephone: (410) 268-8744. Web site: www.severnsailing.org.

New Jersey
Corinthian Yacht Club, P.O. Box 260, Cape May, NJ 08204. Telephone: (609) 884-8000. Web site: www.cyccm.com.

Virginia
BOAT U.S., 880 S. Pickett Street, Alexandria, VA 22304. Telephone: (703) 461-4666. Web site: www.boatus.com.

Belle Haven Marina, 1 Belle Haven Road, Alexandria, VA 22307. Telephone: (703) 768-0018. Web site: www.saildc.com. **Washington Sailing Marina,** 1 Marina Drive, Alexandria, VA. Telephone: (703) 548-9207. Web site: www.washingtonsailingmarina.com.

VINEYARDS

(Introduction by David Pursglove)

One of the more interesting day trips in the mid-Atlantic region is a visit to a working vineyard and winery, or a "winery tour" that can take you to five or six **wineries** on a weekend.

American colonists made wine of sorts in Virginia and Maryland, and in the years before Prohibition there was a sizable "wine industry." Some statistics led to the impression that Virginia, for instance, was one of the country's largest wine-producing states. However, much of that wine was made from grapes brought by rail from California. Much was not even made in Virginia, but was California's cheapest tank-car wine bottled in Virginia. A little wine, usually rather poor, was made in Virginia from grapes grown in Virginia. Those grapes often were scuppernongs, a thick-skinned, musky fruit that is the source of several cultivated grapes.

Now, a growing and correctly termed wine industry has developed in the mid-Atlantic region, and the trained viticulturalists (grape growers) and viniculturists (wine makers) are making good wine from the right grapes. Before you begin a tour of the wineries—where you will taste the wines as part of the tour, or, in several instances, chat in the homes of the families who own the smallest wineries—you will want to understand the wines. They will usually be quite different from the wines you are accustomed to from Europe and California and even different from the ones you may have tasted from New York. The vineyard and winery owners will hope you approach their wines for what they are—wines of the mid-Atlantic made from the grapes that make the best area wines—and not compare and rate them against wines from other regions and from other grapes.

In America, wines are made primarily from two kinds of grapes, and from yet a third kind developed especially for eastern North America. California wines, because of the state's climate, soil, and freedom from certain plant diseases, are produced from the same grapes used in Europe. These are the traditional "wine grapes" such as the chardonnay that yields white Burgundy, pinot noir that produces red Burgundy, cabernet sauvignon that makes up the largest portion of fine Bordeaux reds, riesling that results in the best German wines, and many other names familiar on California bottles and common in Europe, such as gamay, barbera, sauvignon blanc, gewurztraminer, etc. Those grapes grow in the eastern U.S. only with difficulty, although some of the vineyards in Maryland and Virginia do produce small quantities of good wine from them.

The grapes that were native to eastern North America when the first settlers arrived and some that were later developed from them are basically "table grapes," or eating grapes, and do not, as a rule, produce good wine. They may be "wild" or "foxy" in flavor, a bit bubblegum-ish, perhaps acidic or too fruity or "grapey." Some people like wines from the native grapes and their eastern descendants, but most people prefer the wines from Euro-Californian (vinifera) grapes. Some eastern grapes you may encounter are the most popular table grape, concord, whose wine (usually sweet and red, although occasionally dry and white) is enjoyed by millions and disliked by other millions; ives; cataba (which is now being handled better by some wineries that are making an acceptable, yet still very much "eastern," wine from it); niagara; and scuppernong, which is an acquired taste, and most wine drinkers have not acquired it. The chief virtue of these grapes, other than their often fine table qualities, is that they grow easily in the mid-Atlantic climate and resist diseases indigenous to this part of the country, including root louse, mildew, and various rots.

One of our worst diseases, phylloxera, a root louse, was inadvertently carried to Europe around the middle of the 19th century and nearly wiped out Europe's vineyards. Grape hybridizers, especially in France, attempted crossings of European fine-wine grapes with native American grapes that were resistant to the disease. They were partly successful and many "French-American hybrids" were planted. But greater success was achieved by grafting European wine grapes to American grape rootstock, and most of the hybrids have been pulled out of European vineyards.

But, in this country, wine-grape growers pursued the art of hybridizing and crossed the already successful French-American varieties even further with more American and more French in order to develop grapes that would withstand the rigors of growing here, but which would give us the fine wines of European and California grapes.

A pioneer hybridizer was an editor of the Baltimore Sun and protégé of H. L. Mencken, Philip Wagner of Riderwood, on the northern edge of Baltimore at what is now the Beltway. To prove his efforts, Wagner and his wife Jocelyn built a small winery that they named Boordy. (Wagner, whenever asked what the name meant, said, "It's simply a great place name of the future.") The wines were different from any available here before the time of Boordy Vineyards. They were far superior to wines made from native grapes, yet not—in the opinion of longtime wine drinkers—up to the standards of Europe or California. Today, most wine enthusiasts taste them, and all the other hybrid wines now produced around here, as their own kind of wine and forego the comparison against Euro-Californian wines. But Philip and Jocelyn Wagner, with their Boordy Vineyards, put this part of the country in the business of making good table wines. Boordy was a small place and the Wagners very private people. Getting to take a tour of Boordy was a major event. In 1980, the Wagners sold Boordy to the DeFord family, who had been longtime grape suppliers and were closely associated with the winery. Young Rob DeFord had studied wine making professionally. The DeFords moved the winery, although the Wagners maintain the original experimental grape nursery.

Most of the following vineyards offer tours and winetasting. As you plan your outing, consider that:

(1) The winery may also be the proprietor's home and manners for visiting a home should be observed. (2) Most wineries in Maryland charge a small tour fee. (3) Addresses listed are mailing addresses and the vineyard or winery may not be quite at the town listed. Call ahead for directions and days and hours for visits. (4) Some wineries offer picnic and children's playground facilities. It is hoped persons using those facilities will pay a tour fee or buy some wine.

WINERY ORGANIZATIONS AND RESOURCES

The following organizations and resources offer information about vineyards and winery tours in their respective states:

The Association of Maryland Wineries, 516 North Charles Street, Suite 406, Baltimore, MD 21201.
Telephone: (800) 237-WINE.

Web site: www.marylandwine.com. **Garden State Wine Growers Association.** Web site: www.newjerseywines.com. **Pennsylvania Wine Association,** 411 Walnut Street, Harrisburg, PA 17101. Telephone: (877) 4PA-WINE. Web site: www.pennsylvaniawine.com. **Virginia Wine Marketing Office,** P.O. Box 1163, Richmond, VA 23218. Telephone: (804) 344-8200. Web site: www.virginiawine.org.

WINERIES

Delaware

Nassau Valley Vineyards, 33 Nassau Commons, Lewes, DE. Telephone: (302) 645-9463. Web site: www.nassauvalley.com.

Maryland

Basignani Winery Ltd., 15722 Falls Road, Sparks, MD 21152. Telephone: (410) 472-0703. Web site: www.basignani.com.

Berrywine Plantations Winery and Linganore Wine Cellars, 13601 Glissans Mill Road, Mount Airy MD 21771. Telephone: (410) 795-6432 or (301) 831-5889. Web site: www.linganorewines.com.

Boordy Vineyards, 12820 Long Green Pike, Hydes, MD 21082. Telephone: (410) 592-5015. Web site: www.boordy.com. (Oldest winery in Maryland.)

Byrd Vineyards, P.O. Box 215, Myersville, MD 21773. Telephone: (301) 293-1110.

Catoctin Vineyards, 805 Greenbridge Road, Brookville, MD 20833. Telephone: (301) 774-2310.

Cygnus Wine Cellars, 3130 Long Lane, Manchester, MD 21102. Telephone: (410) 374-6395. Web site: www.cygnuswinecellars.com.

Deep Creek Winery, 177 Frazee Ridge Road, Friendsville, MD 21531. Telephone: (301) 746-4349.

Elk Run Vineyards, 15113 Liberty Road, Mount Airy MD 21771. Telephone: (410) 775-2513. Web site: www.elkrun.com.

Fiore Winery, 3026 Whiteford Road, Pylesville, MD 21132. Telephone: (410) 879-4007. Web site: www.fiorewinery.com.

The Loew Vineyards, 14001 Liberty Road, Mount Airy MD 21771. Telephone: (301) 831-5464. Web site: www.loewvineyards.net.

Woodhall Vineyards and Wine Cellars, 17912 York Road, Parkton, MD 21120. Telephone: (410) 357-8644. Web site: www.woodhallwinecellars.com.

Ziem Vineyards, 16651 Spielman Road, Fair Play, MD 21733. Telephone: (301) 223-8352.

New Jersey

Balic Winery, 6623 U.S. Highway 40, Mays Landing, NJ 08330. Telephone: (609) 625-2166. Web site: www.balicwinery.com.
Cape May Winery and Vineyard, 709 Townbank Road, Cape May, NJ 08514. Telephone: (609) 884-1169.

Pennsylvania

Adams County Winery, 251 Peach Tree Road, Orrtanna, PA 17353. Telephone: (717) 334-4631. Web site: www.adamscountywinery.com.
Allegro Vineyards, 3475 Sechrist Road, Brogue, PA 17309. Telephone: (717) 927-9148. Web site: www.allegrowines.com.
Blue Mountain Vineyards, 7627 Grape Vine Drive, New Tripoli, PA 18066. Telephone: (610) 298-3068. Web site: www.bluemountainwine.com.
Brookmere Farm Vineyards, 5369 S.R. 655, Belleville, PA 17004. Telephone: (717) 935-5380. Web site: www.brookmerewine.com.
Buckinham Valley Vineyards, 1521 Route 413, P.O. Box 371, Buckingham, PA 18912. Telephone: (215) 794-7188. Web site: www.pawine.com.
Calvaresi Winery, 107 Shartlesville Road, Bernville, PA 19506. Telephone: (610) 488-7966. Web site: www.calvaresiwinery.com.
Chaddsford Winery, 632 Baltimore Pike, Chadds Ford, PA 19317. Telephone: (610) 388-6221. Web site: www.chaddsford.com.
Cherry Valley Vineyard, Lower Cherry Valley Road, Saylorsburg, PA 18353. Telephone: (570) 992-2255. Web site: www.cherryvalleyvineyards.com.
Country Creek Vineyard and Winery, 133 Cressman Road, Telford, PA 18969. Telephone: (215) 723-6516. Web site: countrycreekwinery.com.
Mount Hope Estate and Winery, 83 Mansion House Road, Manheim, PA 17545. Telephone: (717) 665-7021. Web site: www.parenfaire.com.
Naylor Wine Cellars, 4069 Vineyard Road, Stewartstown, PA 17363. Telephone: (800) 292-3370. Web site: www.naylorwine.com.
Nissley Vineyards, 140 Vintage Drive, Bainbridge, PA 17502. Telephone: (717) 426-3514. Web site: www.nissleywine.com.

Virginia
Northern Region
Farfelu Vineyard, 13058 Crest Hill Road, Flint Hill, VA 22627. Telephone: (540) 364-2930. Web site: www.farfeluawine.com.

Gray Ghost, 14706 Lee Highway, Amissville, VA 20106. Telephone: (540) 937-4869. Web site: www.grayghostvineyards.com.

Hartwood Winery, 345 Hartwood Road, Fredericksburg, VA 22406. Telephone: (540) 752-4893. Web site: www.hartwoodwinery.com.

Linden Vineyards, 3708 Harrels Corner Road, Linden, VA 22642. Telephone: (540) 364-1997. Web site: www.lindenvineyards.com.

Loudoun Valley Vineyards, 38516 Charlestown Pike, Waterford, VA 20197. Telephone: (540) 882-3375. Web site: www.loudounvalleyvineyards.com.

Naked Mountain Vineyard, P.O. Box 115, Markham, VA 22643. Telephone: (540) 364-1609. Web site: www.nakedmtnwinery.com.

Oasis Winery, 14141 Hume Road, Hume, VA 22639. Telephone: (800) 304-7656 or (540) 635-7627. Web site: www.oasiswine.com.

Piedmont Vineyards, P.O. Box 286, Middleburg,, VA 20118. Telephone: (540) 687-5528. Web site: www.piedmontwines.com.

Swedenburg Estate Winery, Valley View Farm, Middleburg, VA 20117. Telephone: (540) 687-5219. Web site: www.virginiawine.org/wineries.

Tarara Vineyards and Winery, 13648 Tarara Lane, Leesburg, VA 20176. Telephone: (703) 771-7100. Web site: www.tarara.com.

Willowcroft Farm Vineyards, 38906 Mt. Gilead Road, Leesburg, VA 20175. Telephone: (703) 777-8161. Web site: www.willowcroftwine.com.

Eastern Region
Ingleside Plantation Vineyards, 5872 Leedstown Road, Oak Grove, VA 22443. Telephone: (804) 224-8687. Web site: www.inglesidevineyards.com.

Williamsburg Winery, Ltd., 5800 Wessex Hundred, Williamsburg, VA 23185. Telephone: (757) 229-0999. Web site: www.williamsburgwinery.com.

Windy River Winery, 20268 Teman Road, Beaverdam, VA 23015. Telephone: (804) 449-6996. Web site: www.virginiawine.org/wineries.

Central Region
Afton Mountain Vineyards, 234 Vineyard Lane, Afton, VA 22920. Telephone: (540) 456-8667.

Autumn Hill Vineyards, 301 River Drive, Stanardsville, VA 22973. Telephone: (434) 985-6100. Web site: www.autumnhillwine.com.
Barboursville Vineyards, 17655 Winery Road, Barboursville, VA 22923. Telephone: (540) 832-3824. Web site: www.barboursvillewine.net/winery.
Burnley Vineyards, 4500 Winery Lane, Barboursville, VA 22923. Telephone: (540) 832-2828. Web site: www.burnleywines.com.
Dominion Wine Cellars, 1 Winery Avenue, Culpeper, VA 22701. Telephone: (757) 229-0999. Web site: www.williamsburgwinery.com.
Grayhaven Winery, 4675 East Grey Fox Circle, Gum Spring, VA 23065. Telephone: (804) 556-3917. Web site: www.grayhavenwinery.com.
Horton Cellares/Montdomaine Cellars, 6399 Spotswood Trail, Gordonsville, VA 22942, (800) 829-4633. Web site: www.hvwine.com.
Jefferson Vineyards, 1353 Thomas Jefferson Pkwy, Charlottesville, VA 22902, (434) 977-3042. Web site: www.jeffersonvineyards.com.
Lake Anna Winery, 5621 Courthouse Road, Spotsylvania, VA 22553. Telephone: (540) 895-5085. Web site: www.lawinery.com.
Mountain Cove Vineyards, 1362 Fortunes Cove Lane, Lovingston, VA 22949. Telephone: (434) 263-5392. Web site: www.mountaincovevineyards.com.
Oakencroft Vineyard and Winery, 1486 Oakencroft Lane, Charlottesvile, VA 22901. Telephone: (434) 872-0207. Web site: www.oakencroft.com.
Prince Michel Vineyards/ Rapidan River Vineyards, HCR 4, Box 77, Leon, VA 22725. Telephone: (800) 800-WINE. Web site: www.princemichel.com.
Rebec Vineyards, 2229 North Amherst Hwy., Amherst, VA 24521. Telephone: (434) 946-5168. Web site: www.rebecwinery.com.
Rose River Vineyards, Route 648, Box 186, Syria, VA 22743. Telephone: (540) 923-4050. Web site: www.roseriverwinery.com.
Stonewall Vineyard and Winery, Route 2, Box 107A, Concord, VA 24538. Telephone: (434) 993-2158. Web site: www.stonewallwine.com.
White Hall Vineyards, Sugar Ridge Road, White Hall, VA 22987. Telephone: (434) 823-8615. Web site: www.whitehallvineyards.com.
Wintergreen Winery, 462 Winery Lane, PO Box 648, Nellysford, VA 22958. Telephone: (434) 361-2519. Web site: www.wintergreenwinery.com.

Shenandoah Valley
Deer Meadow Vineyard, 199 Vintage Lane, Winchester, VA 22602. Telephone: (800) 653-6632 or (540) 877-1919.
Guilford Ridge Vineyards, 328 Running Pine Road, Luray, VA 22835. Telephone: (540) 778-3853.
North Mountain Vineyard and Winery, 4374 Swartz Road, Maurertown, VA 22644. Telephone: (540) 436-9463. Web site: www.virginiawine.org/wineries.
Shenandoah Vineyards, 3659 South Ox Road, Edinburg, VA 22824. Telephone: (540) 984-8699. Web site: www.shentel.net/shenvine.

Southwest Region
Chateau Morrisette Winery, PO Box 766, Meadows of Dan, VA 24120. Telephone: (540) 593-2865. Web site: www.thedogs.com.
Dye's Vineyard, RR 2, Box 357, Honaker, VA 24260. Telephone: (276) 686-8300. Web site: www.ruralretreatwinery.com.
Tomahawk Mill Winery, 9221 Anderson Mill Road, Chatham, VA 24531. Telephone: (434) 432-1063. Web site: www.tomahawkmill.com.
Villa Appalaccia Winery, Route 1, Box 661, Floyd, VA 24091. Telephone: (540) 358-0357. Web site: www.villaappalaccia.com.

West Virginia
Forks of Cheat Winery, 2811 Stewartstown Road, Morgantown, WV 26508. Telephone: (877) WV-WINES. Web site: www.wvwines.com.
Potomac Highland Winery, Fried Meat Ridge Road, Keyser, WV. Telephone: (304) 788-3066. Web site: www.phwinery.com.
Robert F. Pliska and Company Winery, Purgitsville, WV. Telephone: (304) 289-3493.
West-Whitehill Winery, Moorefield, WV. Telephone: (304) 538-2605.

WHITEWATER RAFTING

The call of white water has become stronger in recent years and thousands of area residents now exchange their business suits for bathing suits (or wet suits) on weekends. **Whitewater rafting** is truly a sport suitable for all ages and degrees of skill. This area is blessed with rafting opportunities ranging from mild, family outings to rapids equalizing those of the famed Colorado. All that is required to enjoy the sport is an ability to swim moderately well (you will always be wearing a life jacket) and a taste for outdoor adventure.

Spring, summer, and fall are all good times for whitewater rafting. The months of April and May usually provide the most exciting trips because the melting spring snow causes the rivers to swell and makes the rapids more challenging. Fall is also delightful with its colorful autumn foliage lining the banks, and a good trip in summer, with the hot sun beating down and the cool, clear water beckoning, is hard to beat. The price of most guided trips includes the rental of all rafting equipment (raft, paddle, life jacket), guide services, and transportation at the end of the trip back to the meeting point. Lunch is usually (but not always) included. Reservations are necessary, and should be made well in advance for large groups or for popular weekends.

Rafting is a sport in which everyone is expected to do his or her share of the paddling. On some trips, especially the more difficult ones, there will be a guide in every raft to direct the group's efforts. On easier trips, the guides may be in kayaks, or in only the first and last rafts, in which case each raft selects a leader to navigate a course down the river.

While most people drive to the various rivers where there is whitewater rafting, there are groups and organizations that sponsor trips and sometimes arrange transportation. One such organization is the American Rivers Conservation Council, which offers a variety of rafting trips on local rivers and can also provide information on outfitters as well as on trips in the West. ARCC's address is American Rivers Conservation Council, 1025 Vermont Avenue NW, Suite 720, Washington, D.C. 20005. Telephone: (202) 347-7550. Web site: www.americanrivers.org. Other groups that organize raft trips include local ski clubs and county recreation departments. (Also see groups listed in the "Canoeing and Kayaking Section of this book.)

The sports calendar in the weekend section of your local newspaper is another good source of information on such trips. Another alternative is to make individual contact with private outfitters and join a scheduled trip. A sample list of outfitters follows for each river in the area. Others can be found online, especially through www.wvrafting.com. As most rafting trips start early in the morning and are some distance from Baltimore-Washington-Richmond, consider arriving the day before.

RIVERS

Maryland

The Potomac River, through the Mather Gorge, runs wild and free for several miles below Great Falls. This spectacular wilderness area, located just minutes from downtown Washington, offers a wonderful one-day raft trip suitable for beginners. The river is enjoyable year round, but is more exciting in the early spring or after heavy rains. This river has been known to be dangerous, however, so some parts should only be attempted by experienced rafters. Web site: www.nps.gov/grfa/index.htm.

Pennsylvania

The Youghiogheny River in southwestern Pennsylvania flows through beautiful Ohiopyle State Park. The river provides an intermediate trip chockfull of exciting rapids, gorgeous scenery, and inviting places to swim. Advanced boaters can rent their own rafts. The Youghiogheny is runnable all year, and is approximately four hours from Washington or Baltimore and six hours from Richmond. Web site: www.dcnr.state.pa.us/stateparks/findapark/ohiopyle/index.htm.

The Lehigh River, in the Poconos of eastern Pennsylvania, provides a raft run through a wild, rugged mountain gorge. The best times to raft are the spring and fall, although certain portions of the river can be run all summer. Continuous, easily navigated rapids give beginners and intermediates plenty of excitement. The Lehigh is a five-hour drive from the Washington area and approximately four hours from Baltimore. Web site: www.dcnr.state.pa.us/stateparks/findapark/lehighgorge/index.htm.

Virginia

Richmond's historic **James River** offers an unusual trip that begins in a beautiful wilderness setting and ends up beneath towering buildings in the heart of the city. Although the pace is relaxed, excitement builds to a crescendo as paddlers encounter the thrilling Falls of Richmond. The trip is suitable for beginners and intermediates. For a list of outfitters, check www.virginia.org.

West Virginia

For a list and description of whitewater outfitters in West Virginia, visit www.wvwhitewater.com and click on "Outfitters."

The Shenandoah River near Harpers Ferry provides a beautiful setting for a half-day, beginner raft trip. Spectacular views of the surrounding Blue Ridge Mountains alternate with glimpses of historic churches, bridges, and other structures. The rafting season is April through October. The Shenandoah is a little more than an hour from Washington or Baltimore and approximately 2½ hours from Richmond.

The Dry Fork, near Davis, is a tiny mountain river only runnable in the early spring. The raft trip features rapid after rapid in a fairyland of cascading waterfalls, sheer rock cliffs, and lush pockets of farmland. It is suitable for beginners and intermediates. The river is approximately 4½ hours from Washington and five hours from Baltimore or Richmond.

The Cheat River, at Albright, is one of the most scenic and challenging rivers in the area. It contains more than 20 major rapids in less than 12 miles, and is a good trip for intermediate and advanced rafters. It is usually runnable in rafts until early June. In the dry summer months, it can be paddled in one-person inflatables. The drive from Washington or Baltimore is approximately four hours; about six hours from Richmond.

The Gauley River and **The New River** are probably the most challenging rafting rivers on the East Coast. It should only be attempted by rafters who have experienced such rivers as the Cheat or the New. Because of an upstream dam, paddlers can only be sure of good water levels in the Gauley in September and October, when the Army Corps of Engineers schedules releases in order to lower the level of the reservoir. The New is good for spring and summer rafting, one part for those who want calmer waters (or are under 12 years old). The other section may have up to Category V rapids, on a scale where VI is the roughest. Both rivers are six to seven hours from Washington and approximately five hours from Richmond.

WINDSURFING (BOARDSAILING) ——————

Most people's idea of boardsailing is a grueling afternoon attempting to keep a sail and board upright, spending as much time in the water as out. Truthfully, that will probably describe your first hour or two at the sport, but experts practically guarantee you will be sailing along in no time at all. "Boardsailing" or "sailboarding" are the generic name for the sports, although you will occasionally hear it referred to as "windsurfing." (Windsurfer is a brand name of a sailboard.) The only piece of equipment you'll need to join the fun is a sailboard, a contraption invented in California in the mid-1960s. The flat board has a universal joint allowing the mast and sail to turn in all directions. The idea is to stand on the board, hold onto a bar across the sail, and keep the whole thing upright while trying to catch the wind.

Sailboards sell for between $600 and $1,000, but you can rent them for about $10 an hour. Depending on local regulations, you may need to be certified to rent. The certification process entails a two-day, six-hour course during which students learn how to rig and de-rig their sailboards, plus sailing tactics and emergency procedures.

Most sailboard manufacturers such as Windsurfer and Mistral have their own national and international clubs with local "fleets" that offer lessons and sponsor races and regattas. To participate in their events (except for lessons), you must own their brand of sailboard. There are more than 160 manufacturers around the country, so the list of fleets is too numerous to mention. Any sailboard dealer, however, can direct you to fleets in your area.

Some of the best boardsailing locations on the East Coast are along North Carolina's Outer Banks. Other popular spots are Pohick Bay (Virginia) and Sandy Point State Park (Maryland).

The following is a selection of instructors in the area and some of the many outfitters who rent sailboards.

Delaware

East of Maui, 104 St. Louis Street, Dewey Beach, DE 19971. Telephone: (302) 227-4703. Web site: www.eastofmaui.com.

Maryland

Sailing, Etc., 4605 Coastal Highway, Ocean City, MD 21842. Telephone: (410) 723-1144.

East of Maui, 2303 Forest Drive, Suite E, Annapolis, MD 21401. Telephone: (410) 573-9463. Web site: www.eastofmaui.com.

North Carolina

Kitty Hawk Sports, Multiple locations in Outer Banks Area. Telephone: (877) 359-8447. Call for information and locations. Web site: www.khsurf.com.

CALENDAR OF EVENTS

This section is a small sampling of events that were selected to appeal to a wide range of interests. Many of the annual events listed here have been held for dozens of years, and in some cases hundreds of years. The actual dates may vary from year to year, so call the state, county, or city tourist office or check their Web site before you plan any trip. The "Hotlines" section of this book may be of help.

JANUARY

North Carolina
Martin Luther King, Jr. March. Elizabeth City State University. Elizabeth City. Telephone: (252) 335-3400. Web site: www.ecsu.edu.

West Virginia
Shanghai Parade. A century-old parade that brings in the New Year with a touch of humor. Lewisburg. Telephone: (304) 645-1000. Web site: www.greenbrierwv.com.

FEBRUARY

Delaware
Victorine Valentine's Day. Make Victorian Valentine crafts, see holiday cookies baked the nineteenth-century way, and learn about Victorine du Pont Bauduy, eldest daughter of the DuPont Company's Founder. Wilmington. Telephone: (302) 658-2400.
Web site: www.hagley.lib.de.us/events.html.

Maryland
Black History Month Celebration. Presentations vary each year,

and may focus on such subjects as Buffalo Soldiers, musicians, African tales. Harmony Hall Regional Center. Fort Washington. Telephone: (301) 203-6040. **Happy Birthday Mozart.** A musical extravaganza. Clarice Smith Performing Arts Center, University of Maryland. College Park. Telephone: (301) 405-7794 or (301) 405-2787. **Valentine Sweetheart Tea.** A special tea in a beautiful Belair Mansion. Bowie. Telephone: (301) 809-3089.

New Jersey
World's Largest Polar Bear Plunge. More than 1,000 participants take an icy plunge into the Atlantic to benefit the Special Olympics. Point Pleasant Beach. Telephone: (732) 213-5387.

Pennsylvania
The Great American Chocolate Festival. A celebration of all things chocolate. Usually held around Valentine's Day. Hershey. Telephone: (800) HERSHEY. Web site: www.hersheypa.com.

Virginia
George Washington Birthday Celebration. Old Town Alexandria and Fort Ward Park. Web site: www.washingtonbirthday.com.

West Virginia
Fasnacht. Combined Mardi Gras and Winterfest celebration. Date depends on when Ash Wednesday falls on the calendar. Helvetia. Telephone: (304) 924-5503 (Grandpa John's Restaurant) or (304) 924-5063 (Helvetia Public Library). Web site: www.wvculture.org/history/wvhs1311.html (or)

MARCH

Maryland
Maple Sugarin' Festival. Maple syrup demonstrations, taste testing, crafts and more. Westminster. Telephone: (410) 848-9040. **SMHSA Horse Show.** An outdoor equestrian event to open the spring season. Prince George's County Equestrian Center. Upper Marlboro. Telephone: (301) 952-7999.

New Jersey
Sherlock Holmes Weekend. Weekend of mystery for amateur sleuths in a Victorian setting. Cape May. Telephone: (800) 275-4278.

Web site: www.capemaymac.org/content/subpage_main.aspx?id=96.

North Carolina

Jazz by Candlelight. Annual fund-raiser. Elizabeth City. Web site: www.rivercitycdc.org/jazz_by_candlelight.html.
Tryon Palace Decorative Arts Symposium. Lectures by experts, receptions, concerts, and tours. New Bern. Telephone: (252) 514-4900. or (800) 767-1560.
Historic Edenton Antiques Show and Sale. Edenton. Telephone: (800) 775-0111.

West Virginia

West Virginia Maple Syrup Festival. Historical society sponsors pancake feeds, quilt and antique show and sale, a woodchopping exhibition, arts and crafts demonstrations, a muzzle loading contest, fresh maple syrup suppers, dances and more. Pickens. Telephone: (304) 924-5096. Web site: pickenswv.squarespace.com/maple-syrup-festival/.
George Washington's Bathtub Celebration. Readings from George Washington's Diaries about his visits to Berkeley Springs and his enjoyment in "taking the waters." Merchant sales, exhibitions of George Washington's bathtub, and special "kick up your heels" nightlife. Berkeley Springs. Telephone: (800) 447-8797.
Web site: www.berkeleysprings.com.

APRIL

Delaware

Delaware Contest for Young Musicians Winners' Recital. Wilmington. Web site: www.visitdelaware.com.
Great Delaware Kite Festival. Children and adults compete for kite-flying awards; crafts, food, and fun for all ages. Cape Henlopen State Park. Lewes. Telephone: (302) 645-8983.

Maryland

Fish Hawk Festival Bicycle Tour. Flat scenic routes of 25, 50, and 62 miles on Maryland's Eastern Shore. All proceeds benefit the Mount Vernon Volunteer Fire Department. Starting point is Princess Anne. Web site: www.skipjack.net/le_shore/fishhawk.
John Wilkes Booth Escape Route Tour. Surratt House Museum. Clinton. Telephone: (301) 868-1121. Web site: www.surratt.org.

New Jersey

Tulip and Garden Festival Crafts Show. Thousands of tulips, arts, crafts, entertainment and trolley and walking tours. Cape May. Telephone: (609) 884-5404. Web site: www.capemaymac.org/tours/index.html.

North Carolina

Plymouth Living History Weekend. Reenactment of the Civil War Battle of Plymouth. Encampment on the banks of the Roanoke River, with skirmishes and torchlight tour of the historic district. Telephone: (252) 793-1377. Web site: www.livinghistoryweekend.com.

Inter Tribal Powwow. Native music, story telling, demonstrations, exhibits, native food, dancing and more. Hatteras. Telephone: (252) 995-4440. Web site: nativeamericanmuseum.org.

Pennsylvania

Sheep Shearing Days. Historic Thomas Neely Farm, George Washington's headquarters. Washington Crossing Historic Park. Titusville. Telephone: (609) 737-0623.

Native American Cultural Festival. A celebration of Native American culture through song, dance, storytelling and more. Graeme Park. Horsham. Telephone: (215) 343-0965.

Eastern National Antique Show. Harrisburg. Telephone: (610) 437-5534. Web site: easternnationalshows.com.

Virginia

Anniversary of Jefferson's Birthday. Outdoor ceremony each April 13 at Thomas Jefferson's gravesite at Monticello; featured speaker, fife and drum musical tribute, laying of a wreath. Charlottesville. Telephone: (434) 984-9800. Web site: www.monticello.org.

West Virginia

Spring Dulcimer Week. Special classes in mountain and hammered dulcimer music at the Augusta Heritage Center of Davis and Elkins College. Elkins. Telephone: (304) 636-1209 or (800) 624-3157. Web site: augustaheritagecenter.org/about-augusta.

International Ramp Cook-Off. Enjoy ramps (also known as "Easter onions") in various forms and recipes and other festivities. Elkins City Park. Elkins. Telephone: (304) 636-2717.

Spring Mountain Festival. Fishing derby, jousting, and muzzeloaders are among the activities. Contact Grant County Chamber of Commerce. Petersburg. Telephone: (304) 257-2722.
Helvetia Ramp Supper. An annual event since 1934. Helvetia. Since there is no official Chamber of Commerce, try contacting the local library if you do not find the information you need on the town's Web site. Helvetia Public Library telephone: (304) 924-5063. Web site: helvetia.lib.wv.us.

MAY

Delaware
Delmarva Hot Air Balloon and Craft Festival. Features many hot air balloons and craft dealers. Sometimes held in June. Milton. Telephone: (302) 684-8404 or (302) 856-1818 (Southern Delaware Chamber of Commerce).
Web sites: www.visitsoutherndelaware.com/milton.html.
Winterthur Point-to-Point Races. This long-time annual event features an antique carriage parade, bagpipers in traditional dress, a tailgate competition, pony races, and flat and steeplechase horse races on a glorious American estate. Winterthur (near Wilmington). Telephone: (800) 448-3883.
Web site: www.winterthur.org/calendar/point_to_point.asp.

Maryland
Cape St. Claire Strawberry Festival. Annual celebration of all things related to strawberries except hives. Parade, strawberry daiquiris, sundaes, and shortcake, old fashioned games, a beer garden, live music, crafts, animals, and demonstrations. Cape St. Claire. Telephone: (410) 757-1223.
Soft Shell Spring Fair. Seafood, sides, beverages, crafts, entertainment, kids' activities in a town whose heritage is closely connected with the tides and what it harvests from the water. City Dock. Crisfield. Telephone: (401) 968-0852. Web site: www.crisfield.net.

New Jersey
Wildwood International Kite Festival. World's largest kite festival. On the beach in Wildwood. Wilwood. Telephone: (800) WW-BY-SEA.
World Series of Birding. Begun in 1984 and now billed as the nation's premier conservation event, this is a bird watching contest

that raises dollars for conservation causes of the participants' choice. Opportunities for fun, teamwork, nature observation, and a share of the glory of helping raise money and public awareness levels for bird protection. State-wide. Telephone: (609) 884-2736. Web site: www.birdcapemay.org/wsob.shtml.

Redbank Jazz and Blues Festival. Food and jazz festival featuring local restaurants. Memorial Day Weekend. Red Bank. Telephone: (732) 933-1984.

North Carolina
Emerald Isle Homes Tour and Art Show. Coordinated through the Public Library. Emerald Isle. Telephone: (252) 728-2050.

Pennsylvania
Spring Corn Festival. The Lenni Lenape (Delaware Indians) celebrate spring planting. Allentown. Telephone the Museum of Indian Culture for details and other events throughout the year: (610) 797-2121. Web site: www.lenape.org/index_files/CalendarofEvents.htm.

Gettysburg Bluegrass Festival. Four day outdoor music festival featuring top Bluegrass performers. Also held in August. Gettysburg. Telephone: (800).642-TENT. Web site: www.gettysburgbluegrass.com/.

Lehigh River Fishing Festival. Fishing contests and vendors, free seminars, great food and many more activities. Jim Thorpe. Telephone: (570) 325-5810. Web site: www.visitjimthorpe.com/.

Virginia
Blessing of the Fleet. Marks the opening of the fishing season in this charming waterfront town. On Virginia's Northern Neck. May be combined with a visit to the Reedville Fisherman's Museum. Historic Reedville. Telephone: (804) 453-6529. Web site: www.rfmuseum.com/.

Battle of Drewry's Bluff. Civil War encampment and renactment. Richmond. Telephone: (804) 226-1981. Web site: www.nps.gov/rich/historyculture/drewrys-bluff.htm.

West Virginia
Wildflower Pilgrimage. Recreational and educational events at Blackwater Falls State Park; 10 different tours available. Davis.

Telephone: (304) 558-2754. Web site: www.wvdnr.gov.
Historic Bramwell Coal Baron Mansion Tours. Step into the past as you tour coal barons' mansions. Tours are also offered in December. Bramwell.Telephone: (304) 8381. Web site: www.bramwellwv.com/bramwell2.html. **Scottish Festival & Celtic Gathering.** (Sometimes begins in April.) Celtic music, bagpiping competitions, living history presentations, dog trials and herding demonstrations, Old Church of Scotland worship service and more. Clarksburg. Telephone: (304)842-0370. Web site: www.scots-westvirginia.org/.

JUNE

Delaware
Delmarva Chicken Festival. An annual event of the Delmarva Poultry Industry, Inc. for more than 50 years. Cooking contests, demonstrations, music, arts and crafts and the world's largest frying pan. Various locations on the Delmarva Peninsula, which includes nearby parts of Delaware/Maryland/Virginia. Telephone: (302) 856-9037. **Positively Dover.** Celebrates Delaware's African-American and Ethnic cultures. Drummers and dancers, gospel and jazz, stepping and marching performances. Some 100 booths, multi-cultural selection of foods. On the Legislative Mall. Dover. Telephone: (302) 736-0101. Web site: www.icclarts.org/AFRAMFestPos_Dover.html.

Maryland
Soap Box Derby. A youth racing program run nationally since 1934. Stock, superstock and masters division racers, entertainment and food. Leonardtown. Web site: www.somd.com/leonardtown/. **Fishing Rodeo.** Awards for the largest fish and the largest amount of fish. Deep Creek Lake. (301) 895-5759.

New Jersey
United States Equestrian Team Festival of Champions. Showcases the Olympic disciplines of dressage, show jumping, endurance and combined driving. USET Olympic Training Center. Gladstone. Telephone: (908) 234-1251. Web site: www.uset.org. **Re-enactment of the Battle of Monmouth.** Commemorates the longest battle of the American Revolution and one of its turning

points. Monmouth Battlefield State Park. Monmouth. Telephone: (732) 462-9616. Web site:www.state.nj.us/dep/parksandforests/index.html.

North Carolina

Annual Bass Fishing Tournament. Edenton. Telephone: (252) 482-5343.

Annual Air Race Classic. An all-women cross country air race ends at the Dare County Regional Airport. Manteo. Telephone: (252) 473-2600. Web site: www.fly2mqi.com.

Pennsylvania

Lehigh River Dam Release Weekend. The Army Corps of Engineers open the dam to give the Lehigh River an extra boost. Live Music. Class II and III rapids. Jim Thorpe. Telephone: (800) WHITEWATER.

Kitchen Kettle Berry Festival. Old fashioned berry festival with a great variety of foods made from berries. Intercourse. Telephone: (717) 768-8261. Web site: www.kitchenkettle.com.

Virginia

Waterfront Festival. Explore the historic seaport of Old Town Alexandria and see the vitality of the Potomac today. Majestic ships, pirates, treasure hunt, Virginia Wine Court, amusement rides, parrots, delectable treats and children's craft tents. Alexandria. Telephone: (703) 549-8300. Web site: www.waterfrontfestival.org.

Juneteeth. A public festival celebrating the emancipation. Richmond. (804) 644-3900.

West Virginia

Allegheny Echoes. Celebrate Appalachian music and verse with a week of instruction and fun. Snowshoe. Telephone: (304) 799-7121. Web site: www.alleghenyechoes.com.

Ronceverte River Festival. Canoe, raft and a rubber duck race are just some of the highlights of this two-day festival. Ronceverte. Telephone: (304) 647-3825.

JULY

Delaware

Rockwood Museum's Ice Cream Festival. Re-creation of late 19th-century ice cream socials in a park surrounding a Victorian mansion. Wilmington. Telephone: (302) 761-4340. Web site: www.rockwood.org.

Maryland

Smith Island Day. Skiff races and barbeque, exhibits at museum; Crisfield and Smith Island cultural alliance. Ewell. Telephone: (410) 425-3351. Web site: www.visitsomerset.com.

New Jersey

Night in Venice. Water parade of more than 100 decorated boats and 300 decorated bay front homes. Great Egg Harbor Bay. Telephone: (609) 525-9300. Web site: www.ocnjonline.com/recreatparks/bayside.html.

North Carolina

Rogallo Kite Festival. In honor of Francis M. Rogallo, NASA scientist and inventor of the flexible wing. Jockey's Ridge State Park. Nags Head. Telephone: (877) 359-8447. Web site: www.kittyhawkkites.com.

Pennsylvania

Gettysburg Civil War Heritage Days. Battle re-enactments, living history camps, band concerts and other activities. Gettysburg. (717) 334-6274. Web site: www.gettysburg.travel/visitor/event.asp.

Hanover Dutch Festival. Celebrate Pennsylvania Dutch heritage. Crafters perform skills in blacksmithing, canning, quilting, sculpting and more. The area's German heritage is celebrated with an evening of song and story. Hanover. Telephone: (717) 637-6130. Web site: www.hanoverchamber.com.

Peddler's Village Teddy Bear's Picnic. "Beary" charming competitions and activities for teddy bear owners and buffs of all ages. Bear appraisals. Live music. Lahaska. Telephone: (215)794-4000. Web site: www.peddlersvillage.com.

Virginia

Deborah Blueberry and Craft Festival. Blueberries, homemade goods, crafts & artwork. Chincoteague. Telephone: (757) 894-2334.

Pony Swim and Auction. "Salt Water Cowboys" herd the world-famous Chincoteague ponies across the narrowest part of Assateague Channel at low tide, after which they are examined by veterinarians. After a resting period, they are herded through town to a corral at the Firemans Carnival Grounds where they stay until the next day's auction. The Pony Auction not only provides a source of revenue for the fire department, but it also serves to trim the herd's numbers. To retain the permit to graze on the Assateague National Wildlife Refuge, the herd must not exceed 150 horses. Chincoteague. Telephone: (757) 336-6161. Web site:www.virginia.org/directory/Events/

West Virginia
Mountain State Street Machines Auto Extravaganza. Car show and concessions. Elkins. Telephone: (304) 636-4335. Web site: www.erccc.com.
Pioneer Days in Pocahontas County. Old-mountain festival with bluegrass, fiddle and banjo concerts, street dances, food vendors, horse and buggy rides, and more. Marlinton. Telephone: (800) 336-7009.Web site: www.pocahontascountywv.com.
Appalachian String Band Music Festival. A five-day mountaintop gathering of musicians and friends with contests, concerts, workshops, square dances, camping and a hymn sing. Sometimes starts in August. Clifftop. Telephone: (304) 558-0220. Web site: www.wvculture.org.

AUGUST

Delaware
Delaware State News Sandcastle Contest. Teams of all ages compete for awards in three categories: castles, animals and freeform. Rehoboth Beach. Telephone: (302) 227-2233. Web site: festivalsandevents.com/festival.php?state=DE.

Maryland
Maryland Renaissance Festival. Recreation of a sixteenth century English village, Revel Grove. Jousting, pubs, food, crafts, costume rentals, and performances on eight stages. Crownsville. Telephone: (800) 296-7304. Web site: www.rennfest.com.
Allegany Multi-Cultural Festival. Music, ethnic foods, and family fun. Cumberland. Telephone: (301) 724-5700. Web site: www.alleganyfest.20m.com.

New Jersey
Country Corn Celebration. Featuring corn in many forms—corn chowder, corn bread, corn shelling, corn roasting, cornhusk-doll

making, mini-corn-wreath crafting and live music. Cold Spring Village. Cape May. Telephone: (609) 898-2300. Web site: www.hcsv.org

North Carolina

National Park Service Founder's Day. Featuring National Park Service historic aircraft and speakers honoring the founding of the National Park Service. Kill Devil Hills. Telephone: (252) 473-2111. Web site: www.nps.gov/wrbr.

Pennsylvania

Roasting Ears of Corn Food Fest. Fun and food for all ages with a special emphasis on roasting corn. Salisbury Township. Telephone: (610) 797-2121. Web site: www.museumofindianculture.org.
Pennsylvania Renaissance Faire. Visit the days of yesteryear with knights and fair maidens. Cornwall. Telephone: (717) 665-7021. Web site: www.parenaissancefaire.com.

Virginia

Down Home Family Reunion. African-American folk festival with food, storytelling music and crafts. Richmond. Telephone: (804) 644-3900.

West Virginia

Dulcimer Weekend. Gathering of dulcimer enthusiasts includes workshops, jamming sessions, and a Saturday evening concert open to beginner to advanced Mountain and hammered dulcimer players. Salem. Telephone: 740-446-9244. Web site: www.salemwv.com.
Snowshoe Mountain Bike Challenge. Competition in uphill climbs, cross-country and dual slalom biking. Snowshoe. Telephone: (800) 422-3304. Web site: www.randolphcountywv.com/.
Battle of Dry Creek Civil War Re-enactment. The August 1863 battle is brought to life with living history encampment, artillery demonstration, dress parade, refreshments. White Sulphur Springs. Web site: www.battleofdrycreek.org/dry_creek_web_wip_003.htm.

SEPTEMBER

Delaware

Winterthur's Craft Festival. Traditional and contemporary crafts, artwork, folk art, and fine furniture and demonstrations; by 180 artists; also entertainment for children. Winterthur (near Wilmington). Sometimes held in late August. Telephone: (302) 888-4600. Web site: www.winterthur.org.

Brandywine Arts Fesitival. More than 200 exhibitors from 30 states. Wilmington. Telephone: (302) 690-5555. Web site: www.brandywinearts.com.

Nanticoke Indian PowWow. Annual gathering of local Nanticoke tribe with over 50 other tribes from across the country. Millsboro. Telephone: (302) 945-7022. Web site: www.nanticokeindians.org.

Maryland

Gospel Music Crab Feast. Spiritual music and all the crab you can eat. Inner Harbor. Baltimore. Telephone: (856) 668-6796 or (856) 338-0461.

Honey Harvest Festival. Hay rides, watching bees and beekeepers in action, honey and crafters' booths, candle and decoration demonstrations, plus entertainment and food. Westminster. Telephone: (410) 887-1815. Web site: www.oregonridge.org/honeyhrvst.php.

The Maryland Wine Festival. Tasting of local wines, seminars, stage entertainment, crafts, food, and farmhouse tours. Westminster. Telephone: (800) 272-1933. Web site: www.marylandwine.com.

North Carolina

U.S. Boomerang Association Competition. Dozens of events and workshops illustrate the art of this sport. Open to novices as well as experts. Kill Devil Hills. Telephone: (877) 359-8447. Web site: www.kittyhawkkites.com.

Bald is Beautiful Convention. Annual gathering of "baldies" for hair-raising fun and hair-free frolicking on the Crystal Coast. Morehead City. Telephone: (252) 726-1855.

New Jersey

Miss America Week and Miss America Pageant. An annual competition with representatives from all 50 states. Atlantic City. Telephone: (609) 653-8700. Web site: www.missamerica.org.

Thunder on the Beach. Monster truck competition on the beach. Wildwood. Telephone: (609) 523-8051. Web site: www.thundermoto.com.

Civil War Weekend, Cold Spring Village. Among the many activities are Civil War re-enactments, regimental music, a military "wedding" and candlelight tour of the camp. Cape May. Telephone: (609) 898-2300. Web site: www.hcsv.org.

Pennsylvania
Harrisburg Gallery Walk. Enjoy the sites and sounds of 25 exhibition sites in one afternoon. Harrisburg. Telephone: (717) 236-1432.
7 Sweets and Sours Festival. Enjoy Lancaster County's biggest harvest festival. Intercourse. Telephone: (800) PADUTCH.
Peddler's Village Scarecrow Festival. Scarecrow-making workshops, ideal for families who like to work together. Pumpkin-painting workshop. Live entertainment. Lahaska.Telephone: (215) 794-4000. Web site: www.peddlersvillage.com/festivals/scarecrow_festival.aspx.

Virginia
Virginia Indian Heritage Festival and Native American Pow-wow. Martinsville. Telephone: (540) 666-8600.

West Virginia
Treasure Mountain Festival. Civil War living history and reenactment. Franklin. Telephone: (304) 358-3261. Web site: tmf.squarespace.com.
Autumn Harvest Festival and Roadkill Cook-Off. Arts, crafts, music, and wild game cooking contest, tractor and trailer pulls. Marlinton. Telephone: (800) 336-7009. Web site: www.pocahontascountywv.com.
Leaf Peepers Festival. Fall foliage tours, ghost walk, mountain biking, hiking, music, fly casting lessons, craft show, and more. Canaan and Davis/Tucker County. Telephone: (304) 259-5315. Web site: www.canaanvalley.org/leafpeepers.

OCTOBER

Delaware
Apple-Scrapple Festival. Craft, art, cat shows, 5K run, apple pie baking and scrapple carving contests. Bridgeville. Telephone: (302) 245.2038 . Web site: www.applescrapple.com.
Kent-Sussex Quilt Show. Exhibition of quilts and wall hangings, country store, vendors, demonstrations, quilt auction and more. Milford. Telephone: (302) 539-2606.

Rehoboth Beach Annual Jazz Festival. Rehoboth, Dewey and Lewes. Telephone: (302) 569-9112. Web site: www.rehobothjazz.com.
Sea Witch Halloween and Fiddlers Festival. Everything from broom tossing contest to ocean side horse show. Rehoboth Beach. Telephone: (302) 227-2233. Web site: www.beach-fun.com.

Maryland

Autumn Glory Festival. Fall foliage festival. Two parades, banjo and fiddle championships, crafts, antiques, concerts, and music. Oakland. Telephone: (301) 387-4386. Web site: www.garrettchamber.com.
Grand Militia Muster. Largest gathering of 17th-century re-enactments units in the U.S. Competitions, color, and pageantry. St. Mary's City. Telephone: (800) 726-1634 or (240) 895-4990. Web site: www.stmaryscity.org.
Fells Point Fun Festival. Largest urban festival on the East Coast in a delightful historical seaport community. Baltimore. Telephone: (410) 675-6756. Web site: www.preservationsociety.com.

New Jersey

Victorian Week. History comes to life with house tours, period fashion shows, craft workshops, and celebrations of all things Victorian. Cape May. Telephone: (609) 884-3860. Web site: www.capemaytimes.com/cape-may/victorian-week.htm.
Powhatan Renape Nation Juried American Indian Arts Festival. Over 150 Native American artists and entertainers; demonstrations, native foods, traditional woodland Indian campsite, longhouse building, and more. Rankokus Indian Reservation, Rancocas. Telephone: (609) 702-1473. Web site: www.powhatan.org/.

North Carolina

Indian Summer Days. Annual craft show, auction, town-wide sales, and food. Ahoskie. Telephone: (252) 332-2042.
Artrageous Art Extravaganza. Kill Devil Hills. Telephone: (252) 473-5558. Web site: www.darearts.org.
Scuppernong River Festival. A down-home, small town festival. Columbia. Telephone: (252) 796-1996. Web site: visittyrrellcounty.com.
Peanut Festival. Crafts, food, and more. Edenton. Telephone: (252) 562-2740. Web site: www.mainstreetedenton.com/events.html.
Elizabeth City Historic Ghost Walk. Elizabeth City. Telephone: (888) 936-7387. Web site: echna.org/HistoricGhostWalk/default.html.

Pennsylvania
Happy Hauntings. Three weekends of Halloween family fun at Dutch Wonderland. Rides, magic show, pumpkin painting and more. Lancaster. Telephone: (866) 386-2839. Web site: www.dutchwonderland.com.
Bucks County Pumpkinfest. Hayrides, museum tours, gigantic pumpkins carved by local artists, and more. Doylestown. Telephone: (215) 345-6644 or (800) 221-6333.

Virginia
Between the Waters Bike Tour. Four different routes from seaside to bayside, followed by a traditional Eastern Shore oyster roast. Cape Charles. Telephone: (757) 678-7157. Web site: www.cbes.org/events/events_biketour.asp.
Blue Ridge Folklife Festival. Traditional foods, crafts, music, games, and working animal competitions. Ferrum. Telephone: (540) 365-4412. Web site: blueridgefolklifefestival.com.
Eastern Shore Birding Festival. An annual celebration during the fall migration of the neotropical songbirds and raptors. Melfa. Telephone: (757) 581 1081. Web site: www.esvafestivals.org.

West Virginia
Old Fashioned Apple Harvest Festival. A weekend of family events. Burlington. Telephone: (304) 289-6010.
Old Time Week and Fiddlers Reunion. A week-long session of workshops in fiddle, guitar, banjo, dance, and folklore celebrates old-time music. Performances by more than 30 West Virginia master artists. Elkins. (304) 637-1209.
Lumberjackin' Blugrassin' Jamboree. A family-oriented event, the jamboree features a woodman's competition, bluegrass music and a variety of arts and crafts by area residents. Mullens. Telephone: (304) 294-4000.

NOVEMBER

Delaware
World Championship Punkin Chunkin. Machines powered by anything handy attempt to toss pumpkins further than ever before. Millsboro. Telephone: (302) 684-8196. Web site: www.punkinchunkin.com.
Winterthur Yuletide. Discover how people have visualized their

favorite holiday traditions over time. Displays recreated from paintings, sketches, and other images include creative table settings, colorful floral displays, the hustle of holiday shopping, toys and treats, and the evolution of the Christmas tree. Vignettes depicting seasonal customs from long ago allow you to experience what the holidays were like for earlier generations of Americans. Wilmington. Telephone: (800) 448-3883. Web site: www.winterthur.org/?p=529.

Maryland
Hearth and Home in Early Maryland. From everyday meals to feasts, discover the colonial table. Food preservation, preparation, and hearth cooking. St. Mary's City. Telephone: (800) 762-1634. Web site: www.stmaryscity.org.

New Jersey
The Holidays at Wheaton Village. Holiday exhibition held in the Museum of American Glass. Millville. Telephone: (856) 825-6800 or (800) 998-4552. Web site: www.wheatonvillage.org.

Christmas in Cape May. Includes decorated Victorian homes and a special Dickens Christmas Extravaganza. Cape May. Web site: www.capemaymac.org/christmas.html.

North Carolina
Arts & Crafts Show. Artists and artisans from all over North Carolina. Edenton. Telephone: (800) 775-0111.

Pennsylvania
Peddler's Village Annual Apple Festival. Traditional fall celebration featuring craftspeople, live entertainment and pie-eating contests. Enjoy a variety of apple treats including apple butter, cider, dumplings, fritters, and apples dipped in caramel and apples unadorned. Lahaska. Telephone: (215) 794-4000. Web site: www.peddlersvillage.com.

Virginia
Berkeley Plantation First Thanksgiving Festival. Celebrate the 1619 landing of the original colonists at Berkeley Plantation, the site of the first official Thanksgiving in America. A day dedicated to history, food, and fun, with tours of the 1726 manor house, Thanksgiving dinner at Berkeley's Coach House Tavern, walks in the colorful autumn gardens, and a formal living history program. Charles City.

Telephone: (804) 829-6018. Web site: www.berkeleyplantation.com.
Fall Barrel Tasting. Sample wines from American and French oak barrels. See how the wines are maturing. Live music, tours, tastings, souvenir glass, wine, and gift specials. Ingleside Vineyards. Oak Grove. Telephone: (804) 224-8687. Web site: www.inglesidevineyards.com.

West Virginia
Over the Mountain Studio Tour. Artists open their studios to the public. From Shepherdstown to Middleway, you are invited to travel from studio to studio, to gain a better understanding of the time and talent involved in handcrafting works of art. Charles Town. Telephone: (800) 624•0577. Web site: studiotourwv.org.

DECEMBER

Nearly every community sponsors a Christmas parade, and many historic homes are specially decorated and open for tours. This is also high season for musical performances with a holiday theme. Check the state or regional tourism Web sites for details.

Delaware
"The Nutcracker" Ballet. Dover. Telephone: (302) 734-9717. Web site: dancebtd.com.
Newark Winterfest. Carriage rides to ice sculptors and a Christmas tree lighting. Newark. Telephone: (302) 366-7060.
First Night Wilmington. Alcohol-free New Year's Eve party for all ages. Wilmington. Telephone: (302) 576-3095 .

Maryland
A Christmas Candlelight Tour. Candlelight walk through historic Annapolis. Reservations required. Annapolis. Telephone: (410) 268.7601. Web site: annapolistours.com/candlelight_stroll.htm.
Candlelight Tour of Historic Houses of Worship. Self-guided tours of historic churches and a synagogue. Frederick. Telephone: (800) 999-3613 or (301) 600-2888. Web site: www.fredericktourism.org.

New Jersey
Yuletide Tour of Historic Salem. A festive holiday tour of decorated private early American and Victorian homes, churches, and museums, with characters from the past. Web site: salemcitynj.com/18701.html.

North Carolina
. Water parade of yachts and sailboats adorned with Christmas cheer. New Bern. Telephone: (252) 639-2901.

Christmas at the Market. Historic Edenton heralds in the Christmas season with a storefront decorating contest, great gift box giveaway, ceremony of lights, and caroling on the courthouse green. Edenton. Telephone: (252) 482-3400.

Wright Brothers' Anniversary of Flight. A festival celebrating general aviation, future flight, the military, and more. Aircraft flybys and daily themed events. Kill Devil Hills. Telephone: (252) 441-7430.

Pennsylvania
Gettysburg Yuletide Festival. Tours of decorated historic homes, caroling, concerts, holiday dessert tasting, craft shows, farmers market, parade, fireworks, Santa Claus, and much more. Gettysburg. Telephone: (717) 334-6274. Web site: www.gettysburgcvb.com.

Virginia
The Bizarre Bazaar's Christmas Collection. A high-quality Christmas marketplace featuring seasonal Christmas decorations and holiday foods, new and unique gift lines and decorative accessories for the home and garden. Richmond. Telephone: (804) 673-7015. Web site: www.thebizarrebazaar.com.

Hampton Holly Days Parade & Lighted Boat Parade. Marching bands, floats, drill teams, beauty queens, plus Santa and the Mrs. In the nautical parade, sail and power boats light up the Hampton River. Hampton. Telephone: (800) 800-2202. Web site: visithampton.com.

West Virginia
Old Fashioned Christmas Dinners. Traditional dinners at the Graham House, one of the oldest and most historic homes in West Virginia. Lowell. Telephone: (304) 466-5502.

Bramwell Christmas Homes Tour. Candlelight tour of historic coal baron mansions. Bramwell. Telephone: (866) 248-8381.

Appalachian Coal Town Christmas. Located at New River Park at the Beckley Exhibtion Coal Mine & Youth Museum. Light display tours underground in a once-operational coal mine, tours of the Mountain Homestead, horse-drawn wagon rides, carolers, vendors, and more. Beckley. Telephone: (304) 256-1747. Web site: www.beckley.org/exhibition_coal_mine/index.html.

HOTLINES AND WEB SITES

- Audubon Naturalist Society. Telephone: (301) 652-9188. Web site: www.audubonnaturalist.org
- **National Park Service.** Telephone: (202) 208-3818. Web site: www.nps.gov

DELAWARE

- **Delaware Tourism Office.** Telephone: (866) 2-VISIT-DE. Web site: www.visitdelaware.com
- Bethany-Fenwick Area Chamber of Commerce. Telephone: (800) 962-SURF. Web site: www.bethany-fenwick.org
- Cape May-Lewes Ferry. Telephone: 800-64-FERRY. Web site: www.capemaylewesferry.com
- Kent County Convention and Visitors Bureau. Telephone: (800) 233-KENT. Web site: www.visitdover.com
- Lewes Chamber of Commerce and Visitors Bureau, Inc. Telephone: (302) 645-8073. Web site: www.leweschamber.com
- Rehoboth/Dewey Beach Chamber of Commerce. Telephone: (800) 441-1329. Web site: www.beach-fun.com
- **(State Parks) Delaware Division of Parks and Recreation.** Telephone: (302) 739-9220. Web site: www.destateparks.com
- Greater Wilmington Convention and Visitors Bureau. Telephone: (800) 489-6664. Web site: www.wilmcvb.org

MARYLAND

- **Maryland Office of Tourism.** Telephone: (866) 639-3526. Web site: visitmaryland.org

- Annapolis and Anne-Arundel County Visitors Bureau. Telephone: (410) 280-0445. Web site: www.visitannapolis.org
- Baltimore Area Convention and Visitors Association. Telephone: (877) BALTIMORE. Web site: baltimore.org
- The Baltimore County Conference and Visitors Bureau. Telephone: (401) 887-2849. Web site: www.enjoybaltimorecounty.com
- Carroll County Tourism. Telephone: (800) 272-1933. Web site: www.carrollcountytourism.org
- Charles County Tourism. Telephone: (310) 259-2500. Web site: www.meetcharlescounty.com
- Dorchester County Department of Tourism. Telephone: (800) 522-TOUR. Web site: www.tourdorchester.org
- Tourism Council of Frederick County. Telephone: (800) 999-3613. Web site: www.fredericktourism.org
- Howard County Tourism. Telephone: (800) 288-TRIP. Web site: www.visithowardcounty.com
- Kent County Office of Tourism. Telephone: (410) 778-0416. Web site: www.kentcounty.com
- Conference and Visitors Bureau of Montgomery County. Telephone: (877) 789-6904. Web site: www.visitmontgomery.com
- Ocean City Office of Tourism. Telephone: (800) OC-OCEAN. Web site: www.ococean.com
- Queen Anne's County Office of Tourism. Telephone: (410) 758-4098. Web site: qactv.wordpress.com
- Somerset County Tourism. Telephone: (800) 521-9189. Web site: www.visitsomerset.com
- **(State Parks) Maryland Department of Natural Resources.** Telephone: (877) 620-8DNR. Web site: www.dnr.state.md.us
- Wicomico County Tourism. Telephone: (800) 332-TOUR. Web site: www.wicomicotourism.org
- Worcester County Tourism. Telephone: (800) 852-0335. Web site: www.visitworcester.org

NEW JERSEY

- **New Jersey Commerce and Economic Growth Commission.** Telephone: (800) VISITNJ. Web site: www.visitnj.org
- Atlantic City Convention and Visitors Authority. Telephone: (888) AC-VISIT. Web site: www.atlanticcitynj.com
- Greater Atlantic City Golf Association. Telephone: (800) GOLF-222. Web site: www.gacga.com

- Cape May County Tourism Department. Telephone: (800) 227-2297. Web site: thejerseycape.com
- Cape May-Lewes Ferry. Telephone: (800) 64-FERRY or (800) 643-3779. Web site: www.capemaylewesferry.com
- **(State Parks) New Jersey Division of Parks and Forestry.** Web site: www.state.nj.us/dep/parksandforests/parks
- Greater Wildwood Chamber of Commerce. Telephone: (609) 729-4000. Web site: www.gwcoc.com

NORTH CAROLINA

- **North Carolina Division of Tourism.** Telephone: (800) VISIT-NC. Web site: www.visitnc.com
- Dare County Tourist Bureau. Telephone: (877) 629-4386. Web site: www.outerbanks.org
- Edenton Visitors Center. Telephone: (252) 482-2637. Web site: cupolahouse.org/visitors_center.html
- Elizabeth City Chamber of Commerce. Telephone: (252) 335-4365. Web site: www.elizabethcitychamber.org
- **(State Parks) North Carolina Division of Parks and Recreation.** Telephone: (919) 707.9300 or (877) 772-6762. Web site: www.ncparks.gov
- Outer Banks Visitor Bureau. Telephone: (252) 473-2138. Web site: www.outer-banks.com/visitor-info

PENNSYLVANIA

- **Pennsylvania Center for Travel and Tourism.** Telephone: (800) VISIT-PA. Web site: www.visitpa.com
- Bucks County Conference and Visitors Bureau, Inc. Telephone: (800) 836-BUCKS. Web site: visitbuckscounty.com
- Chester County Conference and Visitors Bureau. Telephone: (610) 719-1730. Web site: www.brandywinevalley.com
- Gettysburg Convention and Visitors Bureau. Telephone: (717) 334-6274 or (800) 337-5015. Web site: www.gettysburg.travel
- Harrisburg/Hershey/Carlisle Tourism and Convention Bureau. Telephone: (800) 995-0969. Web site: www.visithhc.com
- Historical Society of Berks County. Telephone: (610) 375-4375. Web site: www.berkshistory.org
- Lancaster County Historical Society. Telephone: (717) 392-4633. Web site: www.lancasterhistory.org

- Lebanon County Historical Society. Telephone: (717) 272-1473. Web site: lebanoncountyhistoricalsociety.org
- Pennsylvania Dutch Convention and Visitors Bureau. Telephone: (800) PA-DUTCH. Web site: www.padutchcountry.com
- Reading and Berks County Visitors Bureau. Telephone: (800) 443-6610. Web site: www.readingberkspa.com
- **(State Parks) Pennsylvania Department of Conservation and Natural Resources.** Telephone: (888) PA-PARKS. Web site: www.dcnr.state.pa.us/stateparks
- York County Convention and Visitors Bureau. Telephone: (888) 858-YORK. Web site: www.yorkpa.org

VIRGINIA

- **Virginia Tourism Corporation.** Telephone: (800) 847-4882. Web site: www.virginia.org
- Albemarle County Historical Society. Telephone: (434) 296-1492. Web site: www.albemarlehistory.org
- Arlington Convention and Visitors Service. Telephone: (800) 677-6267. Web site: www.stayarlington.com
- Alexandria's Convention and Visitors Association (Ramsay House). Telephone: (800) 388-9119. Web site: www.visitalexandriava.com
- Charlottesville/Albemarle Convention & Visitors Bureau. Telphone: (877) 386-1103. Web site: www.visitcharlottesville.org
- Charlottesville Regional Chamber of Commerce. Telephone: (434) 295-3141. Web site: www.cvillechamber.org
- Eastern Shore of Virginia Tourism Commission. Telephone: (757) 787-8268. Web site: www.esvatourism.org
- Fairfax Convention and Visitors Bureau. Telephone: (800) 732-4732. Web site: www.fxva.com
- Fredericksburg Area Tourism. Telephone: (800) 678-4748. Web site: www.visitfred.com
- Guide to Historic Central Virginia. Web site: http://www.cvco.org/tourism/histrich
- Historical Society of Western Virginia. Telephone: (540) 342-5770. Web site: www.vahistorymuseum.org
- Loudoun Convention and Visitors Association. Telephone: Telephone: (800) 752-6118. Web site: www.visitloudoun.org

- Newport News Tourism. Telephone: (888) 493-7386. Web site: www.newport-news.org
- Naval Station Norfolk. Telephone: (757) 322-2366. Web site: www.navalstationnorfolk.com
- **Northern Virginia Regional Park Authority.** Telephone: (703) 352-5900. Web site: www.nvrpa.org
- Petersburg Department of Tourism. Telephone: (804) 733-2400. Web site: www.petersburg-va.org
- Portsmouth Convention and Visitors Bureau. Telephone: (800) PORTS-VA. Web site: www.ci.portsmouth.va.us/tourism/docs/tourism.htm
- Richmond Metropolitan Convention & Visitors Bureau. Telephone: (888) RICHMOND. Web site: www.visitrichmondva.com/contact
- Shenandoah Valley Travel Association Information Center. Telephone: (800) VISIT-SV. Web site: www.visitshenandoah.org/Home.aspx
- **(State Parks) Virginia Department of Conservation and Recreation.** Telephone: (800) 933-PARK. Web site: www.dcr.virginia.gov/state_parks/index.shtml
- Virginia Beach Visitor's Center. Telephone: (800) VA-BEACH. Web site: www.visitvirginiabeach.com

WEST VIRGINIA

- **West Virginia Division of Tourism.** Telephone: (800) CALL-WVA. Web site: wvtourism.com/default.aspx
- Appalachian Trail Conference. Telephone: (304) 535-6331. Web site: www.appalachiantrail.org
- Greenbrier County Convention and Visitors Bureau. Telephone: (800) 833-2068. Web site: www.greenbrierwv.com
- West Virginia/Martinsburg- Berkley County Convention and Visitors Bureau. Telephone: (304) 264-8801. Web site: www.travelwv.com
- **(State Parks) West Virginia Natural Resources.** Telephone: (800) CALL-WVA. Web site: www.wvparks.com

INDEX